Deploying Cisco Wide Area Application Services,

Second Edition

Joel Christner, CCIE No. 15311
Zach Seils, CCIE No. 7861
Nancy Jin

Cisco Press

800 East 96th Street

Indianapolis, IN 46240

Deploying Cisco Wide Area Application Services, Second Edition

Joel Christner, Zach Seils, Nancy Jin

Copyright© 2010 Cisco Systems, Inc.

Published by:
Cisco Press
800 East 96th Street
Indianapolis, IN 46240 USA

Printed in the United States of America

First Printing January 2010

Library of Congress Cataloging-in-Publication data is on file.

ISBN-13: 978-1-58705-912-4

ISBN-10: 1-58705-912-6

Warning and Disclaimer

This book is designed to provide information about deploying Cisco Wide Area Application Services (WAAS). Every effort has been made to make this book as complete and as accurate as possible, but no warranty or fitness is implied.

The information is provided on an "as is" basis. The authors, Cisco Press, and Cisco Systems, Inc. shall have neither liability nor responsibility to any person or entity with respect to any loss or damages arising from the information contained in this book or from the use of the discs or programs that may accompany it.

The opinions expressed in this book belong to the author and are not necessarily those of Cisco Systems, Inc.

Trademark Acknowledgments

All terms mentioned in this book that are known to be trademarks or service marks have been appropriately capitalized. Cisco Press or Cisco Systems, Inc., cannot attest to the accuracy of this information. Use of a term in this book should not be regarded as affecting the validity of any trademark or service mark.

Corporate and Government Sales

The publisher offers excellent discounts on this book when ordered in quantity for bulk purchases or special sales, which may include electronic versions and/or custom covers and content particular to your business, training goals, marketing focus, and branding interests. For more information, please contact: **U.S. Corporate and Government Sales   1-800-382-3419   corpsales@pearsontechgroup.com**

For sales outside the United States please contact: **International Sales   international@pearsoned.com**

Feedback Information

At Cisco Press, our goal is to create in-depth technical books of the highest quality and value. Each book is crafted with care and precision, undergoing rigorous development that involves the unique expertise of members from the professional technical community.

Readers' feedback is a natural continuation of this process. If you have any comments regarding how we could improve the quality of this book, or otherwise alter it to better suit your needs, you can contact us through email at feedback@ciscopress.com. Please make sure to include the book title and ISBN in your message.

We greatly appreciate your assistance.

Publisher: Paul Boger

Associate Publisher: Dave Dusthimer

Executive Editor: Mary Beth Ray

Managing Editor: Patrick Kanouse

Senior Development Editor: Christopher Cleveland

Project Editor: Ginny Bess Munroe

Editorial Assistant: Vanessa Evans

Cover Designer: Sandra Schroeder

Book Designer: Louisa Adair

Composition: Mark Shirar

Cisco Representative: Erik Ullanderson

Cisco Press Program Manager: Anand Sundaram

Copy Editor/Proofreader: Deadline Driven Publishing

Technical Editors: Jim French, Jeevan Sharma

Indexer: Angie Bess

Americas Headquarters	Asia Pacific Headquarters	Europe Headquarters
Cisco Systems, Inc.	Cisco Systems (USA) Pte. Ltd.	Cisco Systems International BV
San Jose, CA	Singapore	Amsterdam, The Netherlands

Cisco has more than 200 offices worldwide. Addresses, phone numbers, and fax numbers are listed on the Cisco Website at **www.cisco.com/go/offices.**

CCDE, CCENT, Cisco Eos, Cisco HealthPresence, the Cisco logo, Cisco Lumin, Cisco Nexus, Cisco StadiumVision, Cisco TelePresence, Cisco WebEx, DCE, and Welcome to the Human Network are trademarks; Changing the Way We Work, Live, Play, and Learn and Cisco Store are service marks; and Access Registrar, Aironet, AsyncOS, Bringing the Meeting To You, Catalyst, CCDA, CCDP, CCIE, CCIP, CCNA, CCNP, CCSP, CCVP, Cisco, the Cisco Certified Internetwork Expert logo, Cisco IOS, Cisco Press, Cisco Systems, Cisco Systems Capital, the Cisco Systems logo, Cisco Unity, Collaboration Without Limitation, EtherFast, EtherSwitch, Event Center, Fast Step, Follow Me Browsing, FormShare, GigaDrive, HomeLink, Internet Quotient, IOS, iPhone, iQuick Study, IronPort, the IronPort logo, LightStream, Linksys, MediaTone, MeetingPlace, MeetingPlace Chime Sound, MGX, Networkers, Networking Academy, Network Registrar, PCNow, PIX, PowerPanels, ProConnect, ScriptShare, SenderBase, SMARTnet, Spectrum Expert, StackWise, The Fastest Way to Increase Your Internet Quotient, TransPath, WebEx, and the WebEx logo are registered trademarks of Cisco Systems, Inc. and/or its affiliates in the United States and certain other countries.

All other trademarks mentioned in this document or website are the property of their respective owners. The use of the word partner does not imply a partnership relationship between Cisco and any other company. (0812R)

About the Authors

Joel Christner, CCIE No. 15311, is a distinguished engineer at StorSimple, Inc. Before StorSimple, Joel was a technical leader in the Application Delivery Business Unit (ADBU) at Cisco Systems, Inc., driving the long-term product strategy, system architecture, and solution architecture for the Cisco Wide Area Application Services (WAAS) product and the Cisco broader application delivery solution. Previously, Joel was director of product management for Reconnex Corporation (acquired by McAfee), the industry leader in data loss prevention (DLP) solutions. Prior to joining Reconnex, Joel was the senior manager of technical marketing for ADBU at Cisco Systems, Inc, and a key contributor to the WAAS product line, helping shape the system architecture, craft the product requirements, and enable a global sales team to sell and support the product in a hyper-competitive market. Joel is co-author of the first edition of this book and also co-author of *Application Acceleration and WAN Optimization Fundamentals* (Cisco Press) with Ted Grevers, Jr, which outlines architecture and relevance for WAN optimization and application acceleration technologies in today's dynamic IT organizations.

Zach Seils, CCIE No. 7861, is a technical leader in the Application Delivery Business Unit (ADBU) at Cisco Systems, Inc. Zach is currently focused on developing the architecture and network integration aspects of next-generation WAN optimization and application acceleration platforms. In addition, Zach is frequently engaged with partners and internal Cisco engineers worldwide to advise on the design, implementation, and troubleshooting of Cisco WAAS. Previously, Zach was a technical leader in the Cisco Advanced Services Data Center Networking Practice, where he served as a subject matter expert in Application Networking Services for the largest Enterprise and Service Provider customers at Cisco. Zach is co-author of the first edition of this book and was also a technical reviewer of *Application Acceleration and WAN Optimization Fundamentals* (Cisco Press) by Joel Christner and Ted Grevers, Jr.

Nancy Jin is a senior technical marketing engineer in the Application Delivery Business Unit (ADBU) at Cisco Systems, Inc. where she helps develop requirements for product features, drive sales enablement, and manage technical training development for the Cisco WAAS product family. Before Cisco, Nancy held senior systems engineering positions with well-known network and managed service providers, including InterNAP Network Services, Telstra USA, Sigma Networks, and MCI Worldcom.

About the Technical Reviewers

Jim French resides in New Jersey. He has more than 15 years of experience in information technologies. A 12-year veteran of Cisco, Jim has been in the position of distinguished system engineer since early 2003 and holds CCIE and CISSP certifications. Since joining Cisco, he has focused on routing, switching, voice, video, security, storage, content networking, application delivery, and desktop virtualization. Primarily, Jim has helped customers decrease their upfront capital investments in application infrastructure, reduce application operational costs, speed application time to market, increase application touch points (interactions), increase application availability, and improve application performance. Working internally with Cisco marketing and engineering, Jim is instrumental in driving new features, acquisitions, and architectures into Cisco solutions to make customers successful. Prior to joining Cisco, Jim received a BSEE degree from Rutgers University College of Engineering in 1987 and later went on to obtain an MBA from Rutgers Graduate School of Management in 1994. In his spare time, Jim enjoys spending time with family, friends, running, racquetball, basketball, soccer, traveling, coaching youth recreation sports, and fathering his amazing son Brian.

Jeevan Sharma, CCIE No. 11529, is a technical marketing engineer at Cisco. He works with Application Delivery Business Unit (ADBU). Jeevan has more than 9 years of experience at Cisco and 13 years of overall Information Technology experience. Since joining Cisco, he has held various technical roles in which he has worked extensively with Cisco customers, partners, and system engineers worldwide on their network designs, and the implementation and troubleshooting of Cisco products. Working with engineering and product management at Cisco, he has been focused on systems and solutions testing, new feature development and product enhancements to improve the quality of Cisco products, and solutions for customers. Prior to Cisco, Jeevan worked at CMC Limited and HCL Technologies, where he spent time with customers on their network design and systems integration. In his spare time, Jeevan enjoys family and friends, tennis, hiking, and traveling.

Dedications

This book is dedicated to my beautiful wife Christina, our family, and to our Lord and Savior Jesus Christ; through Him all things are possible.

—Joel Christner

This book is dedicated to my love. You have opened my eyes and heart and soul to things I never knew were possible. I am honored that you have let me in your life. I can never thank you enough for these things. Your unfaltering love, caring heart, and beautiful smile are what inspires me to keep going day after day. I love you.

—Zach Seils

This book is dedicated to my most supportive family. To my husband Steve, my parents, and parents-in-law, thank you for always being there for me. To my lovely sons Max and Leo, I love you!

—Nancy Jin

Acknowledgments

From Joel Christner: To Christina, my beautiful, loving, and patient wife—thank you. I promise I won't write another book for a little while. This time, I mean it. I know you've heard THAT before.

I'd like to express my deepest appreciation to you, the reader, for taking the time to read this book. Zach, Nancy, and I are honored to have been given the opportunity to earn a spot in your personal library, and we look forward to your feedback.

To Zach and Nancy, for being such great co-authors and good friends. Your expertise and ability to clearly articulate complex technical concepts are unmatched, and I'm thankful to have been given the opportunity to collaborate with you. Many thanks to Jim French and Jeevan Sharma, our technical reviewers. Your attention to detail and focus helped keep our material accurate and concise. It was a pleasure working with you on this book—and at Cisco.

A tremendous thank you to the production team at Cisco Press—your guidance has been great, and Zach, Nancy, and I appreciate you keeping us on track and focused.

From Zach Seils: To my love, I could not have finished this project without your constant encouragement. Thank you. To Rowan, Evan, and Jeeper, I love you guys more than you will ever know.

To the technical reviewers Jim French and Jeevan Sharma, Thanks for all your hard work to make this edition of the book a top-notch technical reference. I know that the quality of this project increased significantly due to your contributions.

I'd like to give special thanks to my co-authors Joel and Nancy, thanks for making this project happen and your patience throughout the writing process.

Thanks to the Cisco Press team for your patience and support throughout this project.

From Nancy Jin: My most sincere appreciation goes to Joel Christner, who introduced me to this wonderful opportunity. It is a great honor to work with such a talented team. Thank you, Jim French and Jeevan Sharma, for doing such great a job as the technical reviewers. Thank you Cisco Press for working on this project with us.

Contents at a Glance

Contents

Icons Used in This Book

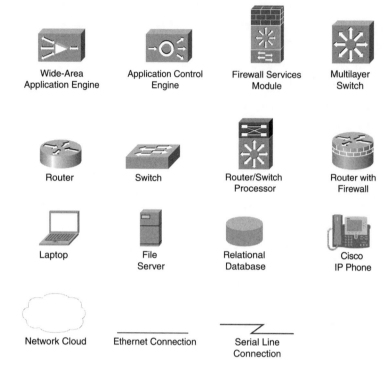

Wide-Area Application Engine

Application Control Engine

Firewall Services Module

Multilayer Switch

Router

Switch

Router/Switch Processor

Router with Firewall

Laptop

File Server

Relational Database

Cisco IP Phone

Network Cloud

Ethernet Connection

Serial Line Connection

Command Syntax Conventions

The conventions used to present command syntax in this book are the same conventions used in the IOS Command Reference. The Command Reference describes these conventions as follows:

- **Boldface** indicates commands and keywords that are entered literally as shown. In actual configuration examples and output (not general command syntax), boldface indicates commands that are manually input by the user (such as a **show** command).

- *Italic* indicates arguments for which you supply actual values.

- Vertical bars (|) separate alternative, mutually exclusive elements.

- Square brackets ([ ]) indicate an optional element.

- Braces ({ }) indicate a required choice.

- Braces within brackets ([{ }]) indicate a required choice within an optional element.

Foreword

I am pleased to write the foreword to the second edition of *Deploying Cisco Wide Area Application Services (WAAS)*. Over the past few years, WAN Optimization technology has become a standard component of enterprise networks. The benefits accruing from the use of the technology for server consolidation, simplified IT management, and improvement of the efficiency of information sharing and network utilization have earned it a place at the top of customers' buying priorities.

At Cisco, we have made several innovations to our award-winning WAAS solution that continues to expand the benefits it offers our customers. These include the use of virtualization technology—that is, Virtual Blades (VB)—to rapidly deploy a network service "anytime, anywhere," and a variety of application specific acceleration techniques that we developed in collaboration with the leading application vendors.

At Cisco, we believe that WAN optimization technology needs to be closely integrated with the routing/VPN architecture of the enterprise network so that customers can benefit from a single, optimized, shared network fabric that delivers all applications: voice, video, and data.

The authors combine experience from their work with thousands of customers who have deployed large installations of WAAS with a deep knowledge of enterprise and service provider network design, IOS, application-aware networking technologies, and WAAS to provide a comprehensive set of best practices for customer success. I strongly recommend customers who are interested in WAN optimization and particularly Cisco WAAS to read this volume. It will help you accelerate your understanding of the solution and the benefits you can accrue.

George Kurian
Vice President and General Manager, Application Networking and Switching
Cisco Systems, Inc.

Introduction

IT organizations are realizing the benefits of infrastructure consolidation and virtualization—cost savings, operational savings, better posture toward disaster recovery—and the challenges associated. Consolidating infrastructure increases the distance between the remote office worker and the tools they need to ensure productivity—applications, servers, content, and more. Application acceleration and WAN optimization solutions such as Cisco Wide Area Application Services (WAAS) bridge the divide between consolidation and performance to enable a high-performance consolidated infrastructure.

This book is the second edition of *Deploying Cisco Wide Area Application Services*, and updates the content to reflect the innovations that have been introduced in version 4.1.3 of the Cisco Wide Area Application Services (WAAS) solution, whereas the first edition was written to version 4.0.13. Along with coverage of the key components of the Cisco WAAS solution, this edition expands on the concepts introduced in the first edition to provide a more complete understanding of the solution's capabilities, how to use them effectively, and how to manage them. This edition expands upon the first edition to include coverage for new solution components including application-specific acceleration techniques, hardware form factors, virtualization, application performance management (APM), monitoring and reporting enhancements, and workflow enhancements. Additional technical reference material is provided in the appendices to help familiarize users of version 4.0 with changes that have occurred in the command-line interface (CLI) with the introduction of the 4.1 release. A quickstart guide is provided to help users quickly deploy in a lab or production pilot environment in order to quantify the benefits of the solution. A troubleshooting guide can also be found at the end which helps associate difficulties encountered with potential steps for problem resolution.

Goals and Methods

The goal of this book is to familiarize you with the concepts and fundamentals of sizing and deploying Cisco WAAS in your environment. The book provides a technical introduction to the product, followed by deployment sizing guidelines, through integration techniques, and configuration of major components and subsystems. The intent of the book is to provide you with the knowledge that you need to ensure a successful deployment of Cisco WAAS in your environment, including configuration tips, pointers, and notes that will guide you through the process.

Who Should Read This Book?

This book is written for anyone who is responsible for the design and deployment of Cisco WAAS in their network environment. The text assumes the reader has a basic knowledge of data networking, specifically TCP/IP and basic routing and switching technologies.

As the WAAS technology continues to evolve, the content in this book will provide a solid framework to build on. Mastering the topics in this book will ensure that you can approach any WAAS design project with confidence.

How This Book Is Organized

Although this book could be read cover to cover, it is designed to be flexible and allow you to easily move between chapters and sections of chapters to cover just the material that you need to work with . Although each of the chapters builds upon the foundation laid by previous chapters, enough background information is provided in each chapter to allow it to be a standalone reference work in and of itself. Chapter 1 provides a technical examination of the Cisco WAAS product and its core capabilities, along with use cases and the "why you care" about each of the solution components. Chapters 2 through 10 are the core chapters and, although they can be covered in any order, it is recommended that they be covered sequentially for continuity. Chapter 11 provides a series of use cases for the Cisco WAAS product family, which can also provide insight into how other customers use this technology to meet their business infrastructure requirements. Appendices are provided to help augment and also summarize what is discussed in the core chapters. Following is a description of each chapter:

- **Chapter 1, "Introduction to Cisco Wide Area Application Services (WAAS):"** This chapter provides a technical examination and overview of Cisco WAAS and its core components.

- **Chapter 2, "Cisco WAAS Architecture, Hardware, and Sizing:"** This chapter discusses the Cisco WAAS appliance and router-integrated network module hardware family, positioning of each of the platforms, and system specifications that impact the design of a solution relative to the performance and scalability of each component.

- **Chapter 3, "Planning, Discovery, and Analysis:"** Planning is a critical part to any successful WAAS deployment. Spending ample time at the beginning of the project to understand the requirements, including those imposed by the existing network environment, is critical for a successful deployment. Chapter 3 gives you a head start by outlining the key topic areas that should be taken into consideration as you are planning your WAAS deployment.

- **Chapter 4, "Network Integration and Interception:"** This chapter provides an in-depth review of the network integration and interception capabilities of Cisco WAAS. The topics discussed in Chapter 4 form the foundation for the design discussions in subsequent chapters.

- **Chapter 5, "Branch Office Network Integration:"** This chapter provides a detailed discussion of the different design options for deploying Cisco WAAS in the branch office environment. Several design options are discussed, including detailed configuration examples.

- **Chapter 6, "Data Center Network Integration:"** This chapter examines the key design considerations for deploying WAAS in the data center. Sample design models and configuration examples are provided throughout the chapter. Best practices recommendations for scaling to support hundreds or thousands of remote sites are also included.

- **Chapter 7, "System and Device Management:"** This chapter walks you through the initial deployment of the Central Manager and each of the accelerator WAAS devices, including the setup script, registration, federated management, and use of management techniques such as device groups. This chapter also provides a detailed understanding of integration with centralized authentication and authorization, alarm management, an introduction to the monitoring and reporting facilities of the CM, CM database maintenance (including backup and recovery), and the XML-API.

- **Chapter 8, "Configuring WAN Optimization:"** This chapter guides you through the WAN optimization framework provided by Cisco WAAS, including each of the optimization techniques and the Application Traffic Policy manager. This chapter also examines the configuration of optimization policies, verification that policies are applied correctly, and an examination of statistics and reports.

- **Chapter 9, "Configuring Application Acceleration:"** This chapter focuses on the application acceleration components of Cisco WAAS, including configuration, verification, and how the components interact. This chapter also looks closely at how these components leverage the underlying WAN optimization framework, how they are managed, and an examination of statistics and reports.

- **Chapter 10, "Branch Office Virtualization:"** This chapter examines the virtualization capabilities provided by certain Cisco WAAS appliance devices, including configuration, management, and monitoring.

- **Chapter 11, "Case Studies:"** This chapter brings together various topics discussed in the previous chapters through several case studies. The case studies presented focus on real-world deployment examples, a discussion of the key design considerations, options, and final device-level configurations.

- **Appendix A, "WAAS Quickstart Guide:"** Appendix A provides a quickstart guide to help you quickly deploy WAAS in a proof-of-concept lab or production pilot.

- **Appendix B, "Troubleshooting Guide:"** Appendix B provides a troubleshooting guide, which helps you isolate and correct commonly encountered issues.

- **Appendix C, "4.0/4.1 CLI Mapping:"** Appendix C provides a CLI mapping quick reference to help identify CLI commands that have changed between the 4.0 and 4.1 versions.

Chapter 1

Introduction to Cisco Wide Area Application Services (WAAS)

IT organizations struggle with two opposing challenges: to provide high levels of application performance for an increasingly distributed workforce and to consolidate costly infrastructure to streamline management, improve data protection, and contain costs. Separating the growing remote workforce from the location that IT desires to deploy infrastructure is the wide-area network (WAN), which introduces significant delay, packet loss, congestion, and bandwidth limitations, impeding a users' abilities to interact with applications and the data they need in a high-performance manner conducive to productivity. These opposing challenges place IT organizations in a difficult position as they must make tradeoffs between performance and cost, as shown in Figure 1-1.

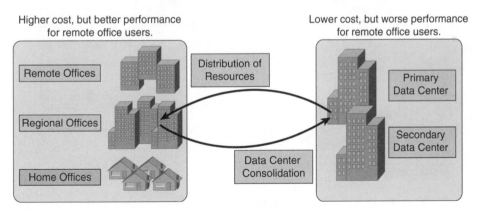

Figure 1-1 *Tradeoffs Between Performance and Cost*

Cisco Wide Area Application Services (WAAS) is a solution designed to bridge the divide between application performance and infrastructure consolidation in WAN environments. Leveraging appliances, router modules, or software deployed at both ends of a WAN connection and employing robust optimizations at multiple layers, Cisco WAAS is able to ensure high-performance access for remote workers who access distant application infrastructure and information, including file services, e-mail, the Web, intranet and portal applications, and data protection. By mitigating the performance-limiting factors of the WAN, Cisco WAAS not only improves performance, but also positions IT organizations to better consolidate distributed infrastructure to better control costs and ensure a stronger position toward data protection and compliance. Coupled with providing performance-improving techniques to enable consolidation of branch office infrastructure into the data center, Cisco WAAS provides an extensive platform for branch office virtualization, enabling IT organizations to deploy or retain applications and services in the branch office in a more cost-effective manner.

Figure 1-2 shows the deployment architecture for the Cisco WAAS solution.

The purpose of this book is to discuss the Cisco WAAS solution in depth, including a thorough examination of how to design and deploy Cisco WAAS in today's challenging enterprise networks. This chapter provides an introduction to the performance barriers that are created by the WAN and a technical introduction to Cisco WAAS and its capabilities. This chapter also examines the software architecture of Cisco WAAS and outlines how each of the fundamental optimization components overcomes those application performance barriers. Additionally, this chapter examines the virtualization capabilities provided by Cisco WAAS to enable branch infrastructure consolidation while allowing applications that must be deployed in the branch office to remain deployed in the branch office.

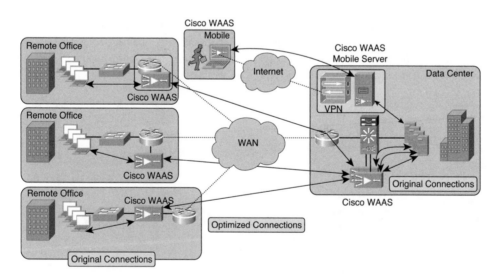

Figure 1-2   *Cisco WAAS Solution Architecture*

The chapter ends with a discussion of how Cisco WAAS fits into a network-based architecture of optimization technologies and how these technologies can be deployed in conjunction with Cisco WAAS to provide a holistic solution for improving application performance over the WAN. This book was written according to version 4.1.3 of the Cisco WAAS solution, whereas the first edition was written according to version 4.0.13. Although this book provides thorough coverage of Cisco WAAS, it does not provide thorough coverage of Cisco WAAS Mobile, which is the software client deployed on laptops and desktops that provides similar functionality. However, many of the same principles that apply to Cisco WAAS Mobile are similar to those described in this book as it relates to performance challenges and overcoming them.

Understanding Application Performance Barriers

Before examining how Cisco WAAS overcomes performance challenges created by network conditions found in the WAN, it is important to have an understanding of what conditions are found in the WAN and how they impact application performance. Applications today are becoming increasingly robust and complex compared to applications of ten years ago—making them more sensitive to network conditions—and it is certain that this trend will continue. The first performance-limiting factors to examine are those that are present in the application stack on the endpoints (sender and receiver). The second set of performance-limiting factors, which are examined later in this section, are those the network causes. Figure 1-3 shows a high-level overview of these challenges, each of which is discussed in this section.

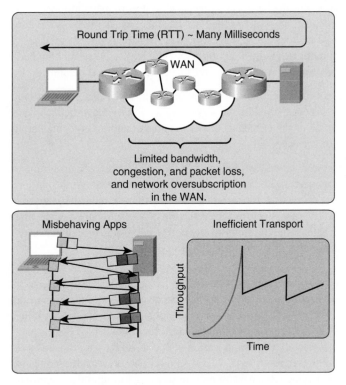

Figure 1-3 *Factors Impacting Application Performance*

Layer 4 Through Layer 7

Server application instances primarily interact with user application instances at the application layer of the Open Systems Interconnection (OSI) model. At this layer, application layer control and data messages are exchanged to perform functions based on the b process or transaction being performed. For instance, a user might 'GET' an object stored on a web server using HTTP, or perform write operations against a file stored on a file server in the data center. Interaction at this layer is complex because the number of operations that can be performed over a proprietary protocol or even a standards-based protocol can be literally in the hundreds or thousands. This is generally a direct result of the complexity of the application itself and is commonly caused by the need for end-to-end state management between the client and the server to ensure that operations complete successfully—or can be undone if the transaction or any of its steps happens to fail. This leads to a high degree of overhead in the form of *chatter*—which, as you see later, can significantly impact performance in environments with high latency. As the chatter increases, the efficiency of the protocol decreases due to the amount of data and time spent on the network devoted to nonproductive process increases. Consider the following examples:

- A user accessing his portal homepage on the company intranet might require the download of an applet to the local machine, which after it is downloaded, uses some form of middleware or web services to exchange control messages to populate the dashboard with individual objects, which are each generally fetched sequentially with metadata about each object exchanged and examined beforehand.

- A user processing transactions on an online order processing system might cause several requests against the server application to allow the browser to appropriately render all of the elements—including images and text—contained in the construction of the page.

- A user interactively working with a file on a file server causes numerous control and data requests to be exchanged with the server to manage the authenticity and authorization of the user, file metadata, and the file itself. Further, after the server has determined the user is able to access the file in a certain capacity, the interactive operations against the file are typically performed using small block sizes and have a tendency to jump around the file erratically.

Between the application layers on a given pair of nodes exists a hierarchical structure of layers between the server application instance and user application instance, which also add complexity—and performance constraints—above and beyond the overhead produced by the application layer chatter described previously. For instance, data that is to be transmitted between application instances might pass through a shared (and pre negotiated) presentation layer. This layer might be present depending on the application, because many applications have built-in semantics around data representation that enable the application to not require a distinct presentation layer. In such cases, the presentation layer is handled in the application layer directly. When a discrete presentation layer exists for an application, it becomes responsible for ensuring that the data conforms to a specific structure, such as ASCII, Extended Binary Coded Decimal Interchange Code (EBCDIC) or Extensible Markup Language (XML). If such a layer exists, data might need to be rendered prior to being handed off to the transport layer for delivery over an established session or over the network directly, or prior to being delivered to the application layer for processing. The presentation layer would also take responsibility for ensuring that application messages conform to the appropriate format. If the application messages do not conform to the appropriate format, the presentation layer would be responsible for notifying the peer that the message structure was incorrect.

From the presentation layer, the data might be delivered to a session layer, which is responsible for establishing an overlay session between two endpoints. Session layer protocols are commonly found in applications that are considered stateful, that is, transactions are performed in a nonatomic manner and in a particular sequence or order. This means that a sequence of exchanges is necessary to complete an operation, and a failure of any sequence causes the entire transaction to fail. In such scenarios, all exchanges up to the failed exchange for the same operation must be performed again. Session layer protocols commonly provide operation-layer error correction on behalf of the application, that is, should a part of an operation fail, the session layer can manage the next attempt on behalf of the application layer to offload it transparently so that the user is not impacted. This is in stark contrast with stateless applications, where each transaction or piece of a transaction is atomic and recovered directly by the application. In other words, all the details necessary to complete an operation or a portion of an operation are fully contained in a single exchange. If an exchange fails in a stateless application, it can simply be attempted again by the application without the burden of having to attempt an entire sequence of operations.

Session layer protocols provide applications with the capability to manage checkpoints and recovery of upper-layer protocol (ULP) message exchanges, which occur at a transactional or procedural layer as compared to the transport of raw segments (which are chunks of data transmitted by a transport protocol such as the Transmission Control Protocol [TCP], which is discussed later). Similar to the presentation layer, many applications might have built-in semantics around session management and might not use a discrete session layer. However, some applications—commonly those that use some form of remote procedure calls (RPC)—do require a discrete session layer. When present, the session layer manages the exchange of data through the underlying transport protocol based on the state of the checkpoints and of the current session between the two communicating nodes. When the session layer is not present, applications have direct access to the underlying connection that exists between sender and receiver and thus must own the burden of session and state management.

Whether the data to be exchanged between a user application instance and server application instance requires the use of a presentation layer or session layer, data to be transmitted across an internetwork between two endpoints is generally handled by a transport protocol.

The transport protocol is primarily responsible for data delivery and data multiplexing. It provides facilities that transmit data from a local socket (that is, an endpoint on the transmitter, generally referenced by an IP address, port number, and protocol) to a socket on a remote node over an internetwork. This is commonly called *end-to-end delivery*, as data is taken from a socket (generally handled as a file descriptor in the application) on the transmitting node and marshaled across the network to a socket on the receiving node.

Commonly used transport layer protocols include TCP, User Datagram Protocol (UDP), and Stream Control Transmission Protocol (SCTP). Along with data delivery and multiplexing, the transport protocol is commonly responsible for providing guaranteed delivery and adaptation to changing network conditions, such as bandwidth changes or congestion. Some transport protocols, such as UDP, do not provide such capabilities. Applications that leverage UDP either implement their own means of guaranteed delivery or congestion control, or these capabilities simply are not required for the application. For transport protocols that do provide guaranteed delivery, additional capabilities are almost always implemented to provide for loss recovery (retransmission when data is lost due to congestion or other reasons), sharing of the available network capacity with other communicating nodes (fairness through congestion avoidance), and opportunistically searching for additional bandwidth to improve throughput (also part of congestion avoidance).

The components mentioned previously, including transport, session, presentation, and application layers, represent a grouping of services that dictate how application data is exchanged between disparate nodes end-to-end. These components are commonly called Layer 4 through Layer 7 services, or L4–7 services, or application networking services (ANS). L4–7 services rely on the foundational packet services provided by lower layers for routing and delivery to the endpoint, which includes the network layer, data link layer, and physical layer. With the exception of network latency caused by distance and the speed of light, L4–7 services generally add the largest amount of operational latency that impacts the performance of an application. This is due to the tremendous amount of processing and overhead that must take place to accomplish the following:

- Move data into and out of local and remote socket buffers (transport layer).

- Maintain long-lived sessions through tedious exchange of state messages and transaction management between nodes (session layer).

- Ensure that message data conforms to representation requirements as data moves into and out of the application itself (presentation layer).

- Exchange application control and data messages based on the task being performed (application layer).

Figure 1-4 shows the logical flow of application data through the various layers of the OSI model as information is exchanged between two communicating nodes.

The performance challenges caused by L4–7 can generally be classified into the following categories:

- Latency

- Bandwidth inefficiencies

- Throughput limitations

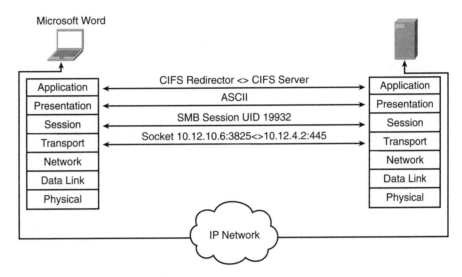

Figure 1-4   *Layer 4–7 Performance Challenges*

Many applications do not exhibit performance problems due to these conditions because they were designed for and operated in LAN environments; however, when applications are operated in a WAN environment, virtually *any application* is negatively impacted from a performance perspective, as most were not designed with the WAN in mind. These performance-limiting factors—latency, bandwidth inefficiencies, and throughput limitations—are examined in the following three sections.

Latency

L4–7 latency is a culmination of the processing delays introduced by each of the four upper layers involved in managing the exchange of application data from node to node: application, presentation, session, and transport. It should be noted that, although significant, the latency added in a single message exchange by L4–7 processing in the node itself is typically minimal compared to latency found in the WAN itself. However, the chatter found in the applications and protocols might demand that information be exchanged multiple times over that network. This means that the latency impact is multiplied and leads to a downward spiral in application performance and responsiveness.

Application (Layer 7) layer latency is defined as the processing delay of an application protocol that is generally exhibited when applications have a *send-and-wait* type of behavior, that is, a high degree of chatter, where messages must execute in sequence and are not parallelized.

Presentation layer (Layer 6) latency is defined as the amount of latency incurred by ensuring data conforms to the appropriate representation and managing data that is not correctly conformed or cannot be correctly conformed.

Session layer (Layer 5) latency is defined as the delay caused by the exchange or management of state-related messages between communicating endpoints. For applications and protocols where a session layer protocol is used, such messages may be required before any usable application data is transmitted, even in between exchanges of usable application data.

Transport layer (Layer 4) latency is defined as the delay in moving data from socket buffers (the memory allocated to a socket, for either data to transmit or received data) in one node to the other. This can be caused by delays in receiving message acknowledgements, lost segments and the retransmissions that follow, and inadequately sized buffers that lead to the inability of a sender to send or a receiver to receive.

One of many examples that highlight pieces of the aforementioned latency elements can be observed when a user accesses a file on a file server using the Common Internet File System (CIFS) protocol, which is predominant in environments with Microsoft Windows clients and Microsoft Windows servers, or network-attached storage (NAS) devices that are being accessed by Microsoft Windows clients. In such a case, the client and server must exchange a series of small *administrative* messages prior to any file data being sent to a user, and these messages continue periodically as the user works with the file being accessed to manage state. When *productive* messages (those containing actual data) are sent, small message block sizes are used, thereby limiting throughput. Every message that is exchanged utilizes a discrete session that has been established between the client and server, which in turn uses TCP as a transport protocol. In essence, every upper-layer message exchange is bounded in throughput by session management, small message sizes, inefficient protocol design, packet loss and retransmissions, and delays in receiving acknowledgements.

For instance, the client must first establish a TCP connection to the server, which involves a three-way handshake between the client and server. After the TCP connection has been established, the client must then establish an end-to-end session with the server, which involves the session layer (which also dictates the dialect of the protocol used between the two). The session layer establishes a virtual channel between the workstation and server, performing validation of user authenticity against an authority, such as a domain controller. With the session established, the client then fetches a list of available shared resources and attempts to connect to that resource, which requires that the client's authorization to access that resource be examined against security policies, such as access control entries based on the user's identity or group membership. After the user is authenticated and authorized, a series of messages are exchanged to examine and traverse the directory structure of this resource while gathering the necessary metadata of each item in the directory to display the contents to the user. After the user identifies a file of interest and chooses to open that file, a series of lock requests must be sent against various portions of the file (based on file type) in an attempt to gain access to the file. After access to the file has been granted, file input/output (I/O) requests (such as read, write, or seek) are exchanged between the user and the server to allow the user to interactively work with the file.

Each of the messages described here requires that a small amount of data be exchanged over the network and that each be acknowledged by the recipient, causing operational latency that might go unnoticed in a local-area network (LAN) environment. However, the operational latency described previously can cause a significant performance barrier in environments where the application operates over a WAN where a high amount of latency is present, as each exchange occurs over the high latency WAN, thereby creating a multiplicative latency effect.

Figure 1-5 shows an example of how application layer latency alone in a WAN environment can significantly impede the response time and overall performance perceived by a user. In this example, the one-way latency is 100 ms, leading to a situation where only 3 KB of data is exchanged in 600 ms of time, or 5 KB of data in 1 s of time (representing a maximum throughput of 40 kbps). This example assumes that the user has already established a TCP connection, established a session, authenticated, authorized, and successfully opened the file. It also assumes there is no packet loss or other form of congestion encountered, and there are no other performance-limiting situations present.

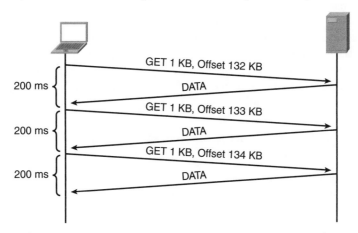

Figure 1-5   *Latency-Sensitive Application Example*

Note that although the presentation, session, and transport layers do indeed add latency, it is commonly negligible in comparison to latency caused by the application layer requiring that multiple message exchanges occur before any productive data is transmitted. It should also be noted that the transport layer performance is subject to the amount of perceived latency in the network due to the following factors, all of which can impact the capability of a node to transmit or receive at high rates of throughput:

■   Delays in receiving acknowledgements

■   Retransmission delays that are a result of packet loss

■   Undersized buffers

■   Server oversubscription or overloading

Performance limitations encountered at a lower layer impact the performance of the upper layers; for instance, a performance limitation that impacts TCP directly impacts the performance of any application operating at Layers 5–7 that uses TCP. The section, "Network Infrastructure," in this chapter examines the impact of network latency on application performance—including the transport layer.

Bandwidth Inefficiencies

The lack of available network bandwidth (discussed in the "Network Infrastructure" section in this chapter) coupled with application layer inefficiencies create an application-performance barrier. Although network bandwidth is generally not a limiting factor in a LAN environment, this is unfortunately not the case in the WAN. Bandwidth inefficiencies create performance barriers when an application is inefficient in the way information is exchanged between two communicating nodes and bandwidth is constrained. For instance, assume that ten users are in a remote office that is connected to the corporate campus network by way of a T1 line (1.544 Mbps). If these users use an e-mail server (such as Microsoft Exchange Server) in the corporate campus or data center network, and an e-mail message with a 1-MB attachment is sent to each of these users, the e-mail message is transferred over the WAN once for each user when they synchronize their Inbox, or ten times total. In this example, a simple 1-MB attachment causes 10 MB or more of WAN traffic. Such situations can massively congest enterprise WANs, and similar situations can be found frequently, including the following examples (to cite just a few):

■ Redundant e-mail attachments being downloaded over the WAN from email servers multiple times by multiple users over a period of time

■ An email with an attachment being sent by one user in a branch office to one or more users in the same branch office when the email server is in a distant part of the network

■ Multiple copies of the same file stored on distant file servers being accessed over the WAN by multiple users over a period of time from the same branch office

■ A user in a branch office accessing a file on a file server, and then emailing a copy of that same file to people throughout the organization

■ Multiple copies of the same web object stored on distant intranet portals or application servers being accessed over the WAN by multiple users over a period of time from the same branch office

Additionally, the data contained in objects being accessed across the gamut of applications used by remote office users likely contain a significant amount of redundancy when compared to other objects accessed using other applications. For instance, one user might send an e-mail attachment to another user over the corporate WAN, whereas another user accesses that same file (or a different version of that file) using a file server protocol over the WAN such as CIFS. Aside from the obvious security (firewall or intrusion detection systems and intrusion prevention systems [IDS/IPS]) and resource provisioning technologies (such as quality of service [QoS] and performance routing), the packet network itself has historically operated in a manner independent of the applications that rely on the network. This means that characteristics of the data being transferred were generally not considered, examined, or leveraged by the network while routing information throughout the corporate network from node to node.

Some applications and protocols have since added semantics that help to minimize the bandwidth inefficiencies of applications operating in WAN environments. For instance, the web browsers of today have built-in client-side object caching capabilities. Objects from Internet sites and intranet applications that are transferred over the WAN commonly have metadata associated with them (found in message headers) that provide information to the client web browser that enable it to make a determination on whether the object in question can be safely cached for later reuse should that object be requested again.

By employing a client-side cache in such applications, the repeated transmission of objects can be mitigated when the same user requests the same object using the same application when the object has not changed, which helps minimize the amount of bandwidth consumed by the application and the latency perceived by the user. Instead, this object can be fetched from the local cache in the user's browser and used for the operation in question, thereby eliminating the need to transfer that object over the network. Although this improves performance for that particular user, this information goes completely unused when a different user attempts to access that same object from the same server and same web page, as the application cache is wholly contained on each individual client and not shared across multiple users. That is, a cached object on one user's browser is not able to be used by a browser on another user's computer.

Application-level caching is isolated not only to the user that cached the object, but also to the application in that user's workstation that handled the object. This means that although the user's browser has a particular object cached, a different application has no means of leveraging that cached object, and a user on another workstation accessing the same object on the same server has no means of leveraging that cached object. Similarly, one web browser on a workstation has no way to take advantage of cached objects that were fetched using a different web browser, even if done on the same machine. The lack of information awareness in the network—coupled with inefficient and otherwise unintelligent transfer of data—can lead to performance limitations for virtually the entire WAN.

Throughput Limitations

Like bandwidth inefficiencies, throughput limitations can significantly hinder performance. A throughput limitation refers to the inability of an application to take advantage of the network that is available to it and is commonly a direct result of latency and bandwidth inefficiencies. That is, as application latency in a send-and-wait application increases, the amount of time that is spent waiting for an acknowledgement or a response from the peer directly translates into time where the application is unable to do any further useful work. Although many applications allow certain operations to be handled in a parallel or asynchronous manner—that is, not blocked by a send-and-wait message exchange—many operations that are critical to data integrity, security, and coherency must be handled in a serial manner. In such cases, these operations are not parallelized, and before subsequent messages can be handled, these critical operations must be completed in a satisfactory manner.

Similarly, bandwidth inefficiency can be directly correlated to throughput limitations associated with a given application. As the amount of data exchanged increases, the probability of encountering congestion also increases—not only in the network, but also in the presentation, session, and transport layer buffers. With congestion comes packet loss caused by buffer exhaustion due to lack of memory to store the data, which leads to retransmission of data between nodes (if encountered in the network) or repeated delivery of application data to lower layers (if encountered at or above the transport layer). Although the previous three sections focused primarily on latency, bandwidth inefficiencies, and throughput limitations as application layer performance challenges, the items discussed in the next section, "Network Infrastucture," can also have a substantial impact on application layer performance. The next section focuses primarily on the network infrastructure aspects that impact end-to-end performance and discusses how these negatively impact performance.

Network Infrastructure

The network that exists between two communicating nodes can also create a tremendous number of application-performance barriers. In many cases, the challenges found in L4–7 are exacerbated by the challenges that manifest in the network infrastructure. For instance, the impact of application layer latency is multiplied when network infrastructure latency increases. The impact of application layer bandwidth inefficiencies are compounded when the amount of available bandwidth in the network is not sufficient. Packet loss in the network has an adverse effect on application performance as transport protocols or the applications themselves react to loss events to normalize connection throughput around the available network capacity and retransmit data that was supposed to be delivered to the node on the other end of the network. Such events cause backpressure all the way up the application stack on both sender and recipient and have the capability in some cases to bring performance nearly to a halt. Serialization and queuing delays in intermediary networking devices, while typically negligible in comparison to other factors, can also introduce latency between communicating nodes.

This section focuses specifically on the issues that are present in the network infrastructure that negatively impact application performance and examines how these issues can worsen the performance limitations caused by L4–7 challenges discussed previously. These issues include bandwidth constraints, network latency, and packet loss (commonly caused by network congestion).

Bandwidth Constraints

Network bandwidth can create performance constraints related to application performance. Bandwidth found in the LAN has evolved over the years from Ethernet (10 Mbps), to Fast Ethernet (100 Mbps), to Gigabit Ethernet (1 Gbps), to 10-Gigabit Ethernet (10 Gbps), and eventually 40 or 100-Gigabit Ethernet (100 Gbps) will be deployed. In most cases, the bandwidth capacity on the LAN is not a limitation from an application-performance perspective, but in certain cases, application performance can be directly impacted by LAN bandwidth. WAN bandwidth, on the other hand, is not increasing as rapidly as LAN bandwidth, and the price of bandwidth in the WAN is significantly higher than the price of bandwidth in the LAN. This is largely because WAN bandwidth is commonly provided as a service from a carrier or service provider, and the connections must traverse a "cloud" of network locations to connect two geographically distant networks. As these connections are commonly connecting networks over long distances, the cost to deploy the infrastructure is much higher, and that cost is transferred directly to the company taking advantage of the service. Furthermore, virtually every carrier has deployed its network infrastructure in such a way that it can provide service for multiple customers concurrently to minimize costs. Most carriers have done a substantial amount of research into what levels of oversubscription in the core of their network are tolerable to their customers, with the primary exception being dedicated circuits provided by the provider to the subscriber where the bandwidth is guaranteed.

Alternatively, organizations can deploy their own infrastructure—at a significant cost. Needless to say, the cost to deploy connectivity in a geographically distributed manner is much more than the cost to deploy connectivity in a relatively well-contained geography, and the price relative to bandwidth is much higher as the distance being covered increases.

The most common WAN circuits found today are an order of magnitude smaller in bandwidth capacity than what can be deployed in today's enterprise LAN environments. The most common WAN link found in today's remote office and branch office environment is the T1 (1.544 Mbps), which is roughly 1/64 the capacity of a Fast Ethernet connection and roughly 1/664 the capacity of a Gigabit Ethernet connection, which is commonplace in today's network environments. Digital Subscriber Line (DSL), Asymmetric Digital Subscriber Line (ADSL), and Ethernet to the branch are also quickly gaining popularity, offering much higher levels of bandwidth than the traditional T1 and in many cases, at a lower price point.

When examining application performance in WAN environments, it is important to note the bandwidth disparity that exists between LAN and WAN environments, as the WAN is what connects the many geographically distributed locations. Such a bandwidth disparity makes environments where nodes are on disparate LANs and separated by a WAN susceptible to a tremendous amount of oversubscription. In these cases, the amount of bandwidth that can be used for service is tremendously smaller than the amount of bandwidth capacity found on either of the LAN segments connecting the devices that are attempting to communicate. This problem is exacerbated by the fact that there are commonly tens, hundreds, or even in some cases thousands of nodes that are trying to compete for this precious and expensive WAN bandwidth. When the amount of traffic on the LAN awaiting service over the WAN increases beyond the capacity of the WAN itself, the link is said to be oversubscribed, and the probability of packet loss increases rapidly.

Figure 1-6 provides an example of the oversubscription found in a simple WAN environment with two locations, each with multiple nodes attached to the LAN via Fast Ethernet (100 Mbps), contending for available bandwidth on a T1 (1.544 Mbps). In this example, the location with the server is also connected to the WAN via a T1, the potential for exceeding 500:1 oversubscription is realized, and the probability of encountering a substantial amount of packet loss is high.

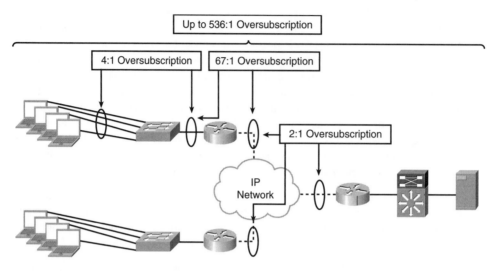

Figure 1-6   *Bandwidth Oversubscription in a WAN Environment*

When oversubscription is encountered, traffic that is competing for available WAN bandwidth must be queued to the extent allowed by the intermediary network devices, including routers. The queuing and scheduling disciplines applied on those intermediary network devices can be directly influenced by a configured policy for control and bandwidth allocation (such QoS). In any case, if queues become exhausted (full) on these intermediary network devices (cannot queue additional packets), packets must be dropped, because there is no memory available in the device to temporarily store the data while it is waiting to be serviced. Loss of packets likely impacts the application's ability to achieve higher levels of throughput and, in the case of a connection-oriented transport protocol, causes the communicating nodes to adjust their rates of transmission to a level that allows them to use only their fair share of the available bandwidth or to be within the capacity limits of the network.

As an example, consider a user transmitting a file to a distant server by way of the File Transfer Protocol (FTP). The user is attached to a Fast Ethernet LAN, as is the server, but a T1 WAN separates the two locations. The maximum achievable throughput between the two for this particular file transfer is limited by the T1, because it is the slowest link in the path of communication. Thus, the application throughput (assuming 100 percent efficiency and no packet loss) would be limited to roughly 1.544 Mbps (megabits per second), or 193 kBps (kilobytes per second). Given that packet loss is imminent, and no transport protocol is 100 percent efficient, it is likely that the user would see approximately 90 percent of line-rate in terms of application throughput, or roughly 1.39 Mbps (174 kBps).

In this example, the user's FTP application continues to send data to TCP, which attempts to transmit on behalf of the application. As the WAN connection becomes full, packets need to be queued on the WAN router until WAN capacity becomes free. As the arrival rate of packets is likely an order of magnitude higher than the service rate (based on the throughput of the WAN), the router queue becomes exhausted quickly and packets are dropped by the router. As TCP on the sender's computer detects that packets have been lost (not acknowledged by the recipient because they were dropped in the network), TCP continually adjusts its transmission rate such that it continually normalizes around the available network capacity while also managing the retransmission of lost data. This process of adjusting transmission rate according to available bandwidth capacity is called *normalization*; it is an ongoing process for most transport protocols including TCP.

Taking the example one step further, if two users performed the same test (FTP transfer over a T1), the router queues (assuming no QoS policy favoring one user over the other) become exhausted even more quickly as both connections attempt to take advantage of available bandwidth. As the router queues become exhausted and packets begin to drop, TCP on either user machine reacts to the detection of the lost packet and adjusts its throughput accordingly. The net result is that both nodes—assuming the same TCP implementation was used and other factors were consistent (same round-trip distance between the senders and recipients, CPU, memory, to name a few)—detect packet loss at an equivalent rate and adjust throughput in a similar manner. As TCP is considered a transport protocol that provides fairness to other TCP nodes attempting to consume some amount of bandwidth, both nodes would rapidly normalize—or converge—to a point where they were sharing the bandwidth fairly, and connection throughput would oscillate around this point of convergence (roughly 50 percent of 1.39 Mbps, or 695 kbps, which equals 86.8 kBps). This example is simplistic in that it assumes there is no packet loss or latency found in the WAN, that both endpoints are identical in terms of their characteristics, and that all packet loss is due to exhaustion of router queues. The impact of transport protocols is examined as part of the discussions on network latency, loss, and congestion in the following sections.

Network Latency

The example at the end of the previous section did not take into account network latency. It considered only bandwidth constraints due to network oversubscription. *Network latency*, another performance "problem child," is the amount of time taken for data to traverse a network in between two communicating devices. Network latency is considered the "silent killer" of application performance, as most network administrators have simply tried (and failed) to circumvent application-performance problems by adding bandwidth to the network. Due to the latency found in the network, additional bandwidth might never be used, and performance improvements might not be realized. Put simply, network latency can have a significant effect on the maximum amount of network capacity that can be consumed by two communicating nodes—even if there is a substantial amount of unused bandwidth available.

In a campus LAN, latency is generally under 1 millisecond (ms), meaning the amount of time for data transmitted by a node to be received by the recipient is less than 1 ms. Of course, this number might increase based on how geographically dispersed the campus LAN is and on what levels of utilization and oversubscription are encountered. As utilization and oversubscription increase, the probability of packets being queued for an extended period of time increases, thereby likely causing an increase in latency.

In a WAN, latency is generally measured in tens or hundreds of milliseconds, much higher than what is found in the LAN. Latency is caused by the fact that it takes some amount of time for light or electrons to transmit from one point and arrive at another, commonly called a *propagation delay*. This propagation delay can be measured by dividing the speed at which light or electrons are able to travel by the distance that they are traveling. For instance, light (transmitted over fiber optic networks) travels at approximately $2 * 10^8$ meters per second, or roughly 66 percent of the speed of light traveling through space. The speed at which electrons traverse a conductive medium is much slower. Although this seems extremely fast on the surface, when stretched over a great distance, the latency can be quite noticeable. For instance, in a best case yet unrealistic scenario involving a fiber optic network spanning 3000 miles (4.8 million meters) with a single fiber run, the distance between New York and San Francisco, it takes roughly 24.1 ms in one direction for light to traverse the network from one end to the other. In a perfect world, you could equate this to approximately the amount of time it takes a packet to traverse the network from one end to the other. This of course assumes that there are no serialization delays, loss, or congestion in the network, all of which can quickly increase the perceived latency. Assuming that the time to transmit a segment of data over that same link in the reverse direction was the same, it takes at least 48.2 ms for a transmitting node to receive an acknowledgment for a segment that was sent, assuming the processing time spent on the recipient to receive the data, process it, and return an acknowledgement was inconsequential. When you factor in delays associated with segmenting, packetization, serialization delay, and framing on the sender side, along with processing and response times on the recipient side, the amount of perceived latency can quickly increase.

Figure 1-7 shows how latency in its simplest form can impact the performance of a telephone conversation, which is analogous to two nodes communicating over an internetwork. In this example, there is one second of one-way latency, or two seconds of round-trip latency.

The reason network latency has an impact on application performance is two-fold. First, network latency introduces delays that impact mechanisms that control rate of transmission. For instance, connection-oriented, guaranteed-delivery transport protocols, such as TCP, use a sliding-window mechanism to track what transmitted data has been successfully received by a peer and how much additional data can be sent.

As data is received, acknowledgments are generated by the recipient and sent to the sender, which not only notifies the sender that the data is received, but also relieves window capacity on the sender so that the sender can transmit more data if there is data waiting to be transmitted. Transport protocol control messages, such as acknowledgements, are exchanged between nodes on the network, so any latency found in the network also impacts the rate at which these control messages can be exchanged.

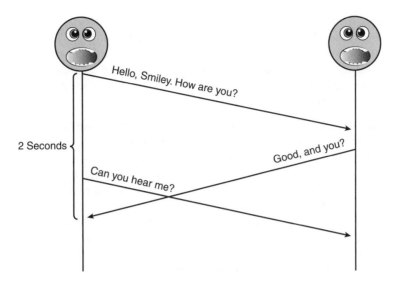

Figure 1-7   *Challenges of Network Latency*

As the length of time increases that a sender has to wait for a recipient's acknowledgement to a segment that was sent, the amount of time taken to relieve the sender's sliding window equally increases.

As the latency increases, the ability of the sender to fully utilize the available bandwidth might decrease, simply because of how long it takes to receive acknowledgements from the recipient. Overall, network latency impacts the rate at which data can be drained from a sender's transmission buffer into the network toward the recipient. This has a cascading effect in that buffers allocated to the transport protocol can become full, which causes backpressure on the upper layers (including the application itself), directly affecting the rate of delivery of application layer data into the transport protocol, which is discussed later in this section.

Latency not only delays the receipt of data and the subsequent receipt of the acknowledgment for that data, but also can be so large that it actually renders a node unable to leverage all the available bandwidth. As described earlier, some amount of time is required to transport light or electrons from one point to another. It can be said that during that period of time (in a perfect world), light or electrons propagate at a consistent rate through the medium from one point to another. Light pulses or electrons are transmitted according to a synchronized or unsynchronized clock between the two endpoints in such a way that many pulses of light or many electrons can be traversing the medium at any point in time, all in the sequence that they were initially transmitted. As a medium can contain multiple light pulses or multiple electrons (at any one point in time), network links can be said to have some amount of *capacity*—that is, the quantity of light pulses or electrons propagating through the medium at one point in time is going to be greater than one and can actually be measured to have tangible amount. When considering that these pulses of light or electrons are merely signals that when interpreted in groups comprise a frame of data, the capacity of a network medium can be measured in some number of bytes. This capacity value can be determined by multiplying the one-way latency of the network link with the maximum transmission rate in bytes and is called the *bandwidth delay product (BDP)*. Note that the transmission rate must be first converted to bytes if initially represented in bits per second (simply divide the bits per second by eight to arrive at bytes).

The problem where a sending node is unable to fully utilize the available capacity of the network can be encountered when the BDP of the network, which is the amount of data that can be in flight at any one given time, is greater than the sender's capacity to transmit data (as dictated by the window and other factors). For instance, a DS3 (45 Mbps, or roughly 5.63 MBps) with 100 ms of latency can have up to 563 KB (5.63 MBps * .1) of data in flight and traversing the link at any point in time (assuming the link is 100 percent utilized). Given that many computers today have only a small amount of memory allocated for each TCP connection (64 KB, unless window scaling is used), if the network BDP exceeds 64 KB, the transmitting node is not able to successfully "fill the pipe." This is primarily due to the sender's window not being relieved quickly enough because of the latency caused by the network impacting the speed at which acknowledgements are received, or the sender's buffer not being large enough to send data at a rate that would keep the link full (the sender is continually waiting for acknowledgements), or both.

Note   This also assumes that the recipient has large enough receive buffers on the distant end to allow the sender to continue transmission without delay. Constraints on the receiver can certainly cause similar situations.

Figure 1-8 shows an example of how latency and small buffers render the transmitter unable to fully capitalize on the available bandwidth capacity.

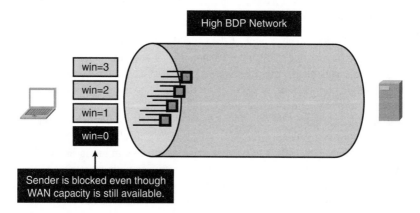

Figure 1-8   *Latency and Small Transmission Buffers*

The second impact on application performance, which was alluded to earlier, is related to application-specific messages that must be exchanged using these latency-sensitive transport protocols. Most applications today are robust and require that a series of control messages be exchanged between nodes before any real "work" is done. In many cases, these control messages are exchanged in a serial fashion, where each builds upon the last until ultimately small pieces of usable data are exchanged (described as chatter earlier and known as "application ping-pong"). In many cases, these same applications exchange only a small amount of data, and each small piece of data is followed by yet another series of control messages leading up to the next small piece of data. To compound the problem mentioned earlier where a sender is unable to fully take advantage of a network link, in this scenario, senders using a send-and-wait application protocol find themselves in an even worse condition. Not only does it take a substantial amount of time for each of the small messages to be acknowledged, but also there are several of them lined up in sequence, and only one can be sent at a time.

As this section has shown, latency has an impact on the transmitting node's transport protocol and its capability to effectively utilize available WAN capacity. Furthermore, applications that exhibit "ping-pong" behavior are impacted even further due to the latency encountered when exchanging application layer messages over the impacted transport protocol. The next section examines the impact of packet loss and congestion on throughput and application performance.

Loss and Congestion

Packet loss and congestion also have a negative impact on application throughput. Although packet loss can be caused by anything from signal degradation to faulty hardware, it is most commonly the result of either of the following two scenarios:

■ Internal oversubscription of allocated connection memory in a transmitting node (the application tries to place too much data into the transport protocol)

■ Oversubscribed intermediary network device queues (discussed earlier in this chapter, one or more nodes on the network send data at a rate faster than the intermediary device can provide service to that data)

Packet loss is not generally a scenario that can be proactively reported to a transmitter; that is, a router that drops a particular packet generally does not notify a transmitting node that a specific packet has been dropped due to a congested queue. Packet loss is generally handled reactively by a transmitting node based on the acknowledgments that are received from the recipient—or the lack of receipt of said acknowledgement. For instance, in the case of a connection-oriented transport protocol, if 5 KB of data is sent in five unique 1-KB segments, an acknowledgment of only four of the five segments would cause the transmitter to retransmit the missing segment after some period of time. This behavior varies among transport protocols and is dependent upon the extensions to the transport protocol that are being used, but the general behavior remains consistent: an unacknowledged segment is likely a segment that was contained in a packet that was lost (network oversubscription, buffer out of memory, node unreachable) or not received correctly (due to signal degradation or errors). Double and triple acknowledgments might also be used to indicate the window position of a segment that was not successfully received, to inform the transmitter as to which segment(s) should be resent.

In the case of TCP, the lack of an acknowledgment causes the transmitter not only to resend, but also to reevaluate and adjust the rate at which it was sending data. A loss of a segment causes TCP to adjust its window capacity to a lower value to cover scenarios where too much data is being sent—either too much data for the network to deliver (due to oversubscription of the network) or too much data for the recipient to receive (due to congested receive buffers). The net effect is that, upon encountering packet loss and subsequently having to retransmit data, the overall throughput of the connection might be decreased to try and find a rate that does not congest the network or the recipient. This behavior is called *congestion avoidance*, as TCP adjusts its rate in attempt to match the available capacity in the network and the recipient, and this is accomplished through constant manipulation of the *congestion window (cwnd)*.

The most common TCP implementation found today, TCP Reno, reduces the congestion window by 50 percent upon encountering packet loss. Although reducing the congestion window by 50 percent does not necessarily correlate to a 50 percent decrease in connection throughput, this reduction can certainly constrain a connection's ability to fully utilize the bandwidth available on the link. During congestion avoidance with TCP Reno, each successful transmission (signaled by the sender receiving an acknowledgment of a segment by the intended recipient) causes the congestion window to increase by one segment size. This means that if node A sends a segment to node B, node B acknowledges that segment, and node A receives that acknowledgement, node A attempts to place a larger amount of data on the network (up to the maximum window size). The purpose of the congestion window is to allow TCP to first react to packet loss, which ensures throughput is adjusted to not congest the network and provide fairness with others attempting to transmit, and to continue to try and find the maximum transmission rate as a result of continually increasing the congestion window for each successful and acknowledged transmission.

Figure 1-9 shows an example of how packet loss impacts the TCP congestion window, which can impact overall application throughput.

This "backoff" behavior not only helps TCP normalize around the available network capacity and available capacity in the recipient buffer, but also helps to ensure fairness among nodes that are competing for the available WAN bandwidth.

Now that you have looked at some of the challenges associated with application performance in WAN environments, the next section introduces Cisco Wide Area Application Services (WAAS), examining the Cisco WAAS product capabilities and its major components.

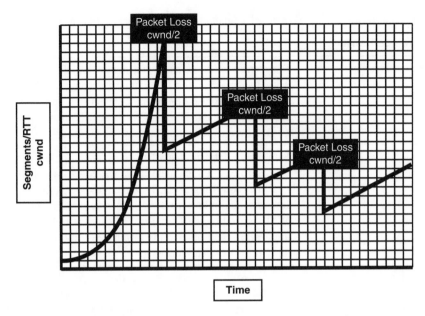

Figure 1-9   *Impact of Packet Loss on TCP's Congestion Window*

Introduction to Cisco WAAS

The previous sections examined the most common causes of application-performance challenges found in WAN environments. Although the previous sections did not cover every possible performance barrier, they summarized and briefly examined the largest of these problems. With this fundamental understanding of what contributes to application-performance challenges, one might ask "how are they solved?" Each application-performance challenge has an appropriate solution, and these solutions must be implemented in a hierarchical manner and at the appropriate point within the network, as shown in Table 1-1.

Cisco WAAS provides a solution to the performance barriers presented by the WAN by employing a series of application-agnostic optimizations, also known as WAN optimization, in conjunction with a series of application-specific optimizations, also known as application acceleration. WAN optimization refers to employing techniques at the transport protocol that apply across any application protocol using that network or transport protocol. Application acceleration refers to employing optimizations directly against an application or an application protocol that it uses. WAN optimization has broad applicability, whereas application acceleration has focused applicability. The two are complementary, that is, the performance improvements provided by WAN optimization complement those provided by application acceleration. When combined, WAN optimization and application acceleration provide a multiplier effect on application performance, where the sum of improvement is commonly a substantial amount greater than the improvement provided by using only one of the two.

Table 1-1 *Solutions to Application-Performance Barriers Found in the WAN*

Performance Barrier	Technology Solution
Application layer latency	Reordering, resequencing, or generally parallelization of serial tasks, object and metadata prefetching, read-ahead, write-behind, reuse of existing connections, and local response handling. These technologies minimize the impact of latency on application message exchanges.
Application layer bandwidth inefficiencies	Safe object data and metadata caching, and object prepositioning to enable local delivery at the edge of the network near the requesting user. These technologies improve performance and minimize bandwidth consumption on the WAN caused by inefficient use of bandwidth by specific applications and offload the origin server by reducing the amount of I/O that reaches it.
Network bandwidth consumption and congestion	Compression and network layer or transport layer data deduplication over the WAN. These technologies increase the efficiency data transmission over the WAN, improve application throughput, and minimize bandwidth consumption to increase throughput and performance.
Packet loss sensitivity and throughput	Optimized transport protocol implementation including advanced congestion avoidance algorithms, TCP extensions, and TCP proxy architectures. These technologies shield senders and receivers from conditions found in the WAN and take full advantage of available network capacity, thereby maximizing throughput.
Prioritization and resource allocation	End-to-end QoS, including classification (both basic and deep packet inspection), prequeuing operations, hierarchical queuing and scheduling, post-queuing optimization. These technologies align network resources with business priority and application requirements to ensure consistent performance and predictable behavior.

Along with providing dramatic performance improvements, Cisco WAAS is a *transparent* solution. Transparency refers to the fact that the solution does not impact operational behavior or other components that exist end-to-end. Cisco WAAS is transparent in three domains:

- **Client nodes:** No changes are needed on a client node to benefit from the optimization provided by Cisco WAAS. The only exception to this is Cisco WAAS Mobile—which requires installation of a software client—and is used to support remote users that are not in a remote office where a WAAS device is present.

- **Servers:** No changes are needed on a server node to benefit from Cisco WAAS.

- **Network:** Cisco WAAS provides the strongest levels of interoperability with technologies deployed in the network, including QoS, NetFlow, IP service-level agreements (IP SLA), access control lists (ACL), and firewall policies, which ensures seamless integration into the network. Transparency to the network and the functions deployed in the network was pioneered by Cisco with the WAAS solution.

This unique combination of three domains of transparency allows Cisco WAAS the least disruptive introduction into the enterprise IT infrastructure of any WAN optimization or application acceleration solution. This level of transparency provides compatibility with existing network capabilities, which also allows customers to create the most compelling end-to-end application-performance management solutions involving many technologies that all help achieve performance objectives.

The following sections examine the WAN optimization and application acceleration components of Cisco WAAS in detail.

WAN Optimization

Cisco WAAS implements a number of WAN optimization techniques to help overcome challenges encountered in the WAN. These optimizations include a foundational set of three key elements:

- **Data Redundancy Elimination (DRE):** DRE is an advanced bidirectional data deduplication mechanism that uses disk and memory to minimize the amount of redundant data found on the WAN. DRE takes advantage of a loosely synchronized per-peer compression history. When redundant data is identified, the WAAS device sends a signature referencing that data to the peer as opposed to sending the original data, thereby providing potentially high levels of compression. Nonredundant data is added to the compression history on both peers and is sent across the WAN to the peer with newly generated signatures.

- **Persistent LZ Compression (PLZ):** PLZ utilizes Lempel-Ziv (LZ) compression with extended memory per connection to provide higher levels of compression, which helps minimize the bandwidth consumed when data is transferred over the network. PLZ is helpful for data that is identified as nonredundant by DRE and can compress signatures that are sent by DRE on behalf of redundant chunks of data.

- **Transport Flow Optimization (TFO):** TFO is a series of TCP optimizations that helps mitigate performance barriers associated with TCP. TFO includes advertising and negotiation of large initial windows, selective acknowledgement, window scaling, large buffers, and an advanced congestion avoidance algorithm that helps "fill the pipe" while preserving fairness among optimized and unoptimized connections. TFO is implemented as a TCP proxy, which shields communicating nodes from performance-limiting WAN conditions, thereby increasing throughput

These technologies provide a compound benefit when used together. TFO enables communicating nodes to maximize the use of available bandwidth capacity. When coupled with DRE, the data that is transmitted over the WAN are small signatures referencing previously seen chunks of data (along with chunks of data that are nonredundant), and this data is compressed by PLZ. The net effect is that the pipe is filled with *compressed* and *deduplicated* data, meaning that a substantial throughput improvement can be realized.

Determining which optimization to apply is a function of the Application Traffic Policy (ATP), which can be managed discretely per WAAS device or in the Cisco WAAS Central Manager console, which provides scalable, secure, and simple management of a large network of Cisco WAAS devices. In the factory-default configuration, Cisco WAAS devices are preconfigured with policies for more than 150 applications, meaning that optimization and acceleration can be realized without additional configuration. The policy to be applied to a given connection is dependent upon a negotiation that occurs between WAAS devices during the establishment of connections between two endpoints, which is where automatic discovery is applied to determine the WAAS devices that participate in the process of optimization (automatic discovery is discussed later in this chapter in the section, "Other Features").

The data path for optimization in the Cisco WAAS device is the TCP proxy, which is used for each connection that is optimized by Cisco WAAS. The TCP proxy enables Cisco WAAS to transparently insert itself as a TCP-compliant intermediary. In this way, Cisco WAAS devices receive and temporarily buffer data sent from a host and locally acknowledge data segments. By employing a TCP proxy, Cisco WAAS can also send larger blocks of data to the optimization components, which permits higher levels of compression to be realized when compared to per-packet architectures in which the compression domain might be limited by the size of the packets being received.

Data in the TCP proxy is then passed through the associated optimization components based on the configured policy, and the optimized traffic is transmitted across the WAN using the optimized TCP implementation, which is intercepted by the distant peer WAAS device. By implementing a TCP proxy, Cisco WAAS devices can shield communicating nodes from unruly WAN conditions such as packet loss or congestion. Should the loss of a segment be encountered, Cisco WAAS devices can extract the segment from the TCP proxy retransmission queue and retransmit the optimized segment, thereby removing the need for the original transmitting node to retransmit the data that was lost in transit. Transmitting nodes enjoy the benefits of having LAN-like TCP performance, exhibiting the characteristics of minimal packet loss and rapid acknowledgment. By using a TCP proxy, Cisco WAAS allows data to be drained from the transmitting nodes more quickly and nearly eliminates the propagation and proliferation of performance-limiting challenges encountered in the WAN from impacting the endpoints that are communicating.

Figure 1-10 shows the Cisco WAAS TCP proxy architecture and how it provides a buffer that prevents WAN performance from impacting transmitting nodes.

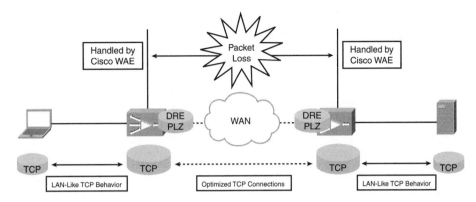

Figure 1-10   *Cisco WAAS TCP Proxy Architecture*

The following sections examine each of these optimizations in more detail.

Data Redundancy Elimination

DRE is an advanced, bidirectional, per-peer, lossless data deduplication algorithm that leverages both memory (high throughput and high I/O rates) and disk (persistent and large compression history). DRE examines data in-flight for redundant patterns (patterns that have been previously identified) and works in an application-agnostic manner, meaning that redundant patterns found in traffic for one application could be leveraged for another application. As redundant patterns are identified, they are replaced with a signature that references the redundant pattern in the peer WAAS device's compression history. As these signatures are only 5 bytes in size, and the redundant pattern identified could potentially be up to 32 kilobytes in size, DRE can provide significant levels of compression for flows containing data that has been previously identified, which helps minimize bandwidth consumption on the WAN.

DRE is bidirectional, meaning patterns identified during one direction of traffic flow can be leveraged for traffic flowing in the opposite direction. DRE is also application agnostic in that patterns identified in a flow for one application can be leveraged to optimize flows for a different application. An example of the bidirectional and application-agnostic characteristics of DRE is as follows. Assume two users are located in the same remote office, which is connected to the corporate campus by way of a T1 WAN. Both the remote office and the corporate campus have Cisco WAAS devices installed. Should the first user download an e-mail containing an attachment, the compression history on each of the WAAS devices in the connection path would be updated with the relevant data patterns contained in the flow. Should the second user have a copy of that file, or a file containing similarities, and upload that file by way of another application such as FTP, the compression history that was previously built from the e-mail transfer could be leveraged to provide tremendous levels of compression for the FTP upload.

Chunking and Pattern Matching

As data from a connection configured for DRE optimization enters the TCP proxy, it is buffered for a short period of time. After data builds up in the buffer, the large block of buffered data is passed to DRE to enter a process known as encoding. Encoding encompasses chunking (breaking the data into smaller pieces) and pattern matching (identifying previously seen, redundant patterns). Essentially, encoding is the process of taking transmitted data in from a transmitting node, eliminating redundancy, updating the compression library with any new data, and transmitting deduplicated messages.

DRE encoding calculates a message validity signature over the original block of data. This message is used by the decoding process on the peer WAAS device to ensure correctness when rebuilding the message based on the signatures contained in the encoded message. A sliding window is used over the block of data to be compressed, which employs a CPU-efficient calculation to identify breakpoints in the data based on the actual data being transferred, which is also known as *content-based chunking*. Content-based chunking utilizes the actual data itself to identify breakpoints in the data and, as such, is less sensitive to slight changes (additions, removals, changes) upon subsequent transfers of the same or similar data. With content-based chunking, if a small amount of data is inserted into a chunk during the next transmission, the chunk boundaries shift with the insertion of data, allowing DRE better isolation of the new data, which helps retain high levels of compression as the other chunks remain valid.

Each chunk that is identified is assigned a 5-byte signature. This signature is used as the point of reference on each Cisco WAAS device for that particular chunk of data. As DRE is encoding data, if any chunk of data is found in the DRE compression history, it is considered redundant, and the signature is transmitted instead of the chunk. For instance, if a 256-byte chunk is found to be redundant and is replaced with the associated signature, an effective compression ratio of more than 50:1 is realized for that particular chunk of data. If any chunk of data is not found in the DRE compression history, the chunk and its generated signature are added to the local DRE compression history for later use. In this case, both the chunk and the signature are transmitted to allow the peer to update its DRE compression history, which is typically less than a 1 percent increase in the amount of data transmitted.

Figure 1-11 illustrates the encoding and decoding process at a high level, which also serves as a reference for how DRE operates through the rest of the section.

After the encoding process is complete, the encoding WAAS device can process the encoded message with the message validity signature that was calculated for the original block of data through PLZ for additional levels of compression. Aside from the message validity signature, the encoded message contains signatures for data patterns that are recognized as redundant and signatures and data for data patterns that are identified as nonredundant. This compressed and deduplicated message is then transmitted over the network, intercepted by the peer WAAS device, and the decoding process begins, which is the same as the encoding process but in the reverse direction.

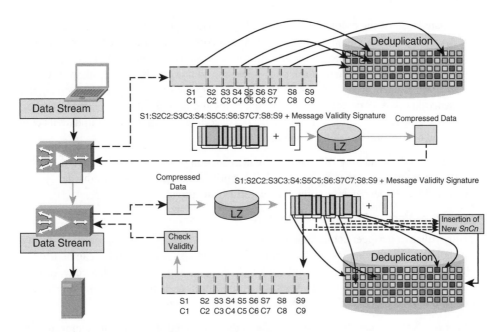

Figure 1-11   *Data Redundancy Elimination Encoding*

Message Validation

DRE uses two means of verifying that encoded messages can be properly rebuilt and match the original data being transmitted. As the decoding WAAS device (closest to the recipient) receives an encoded message, it begins to parse the encoded messages to separate signatures that were sent without an associated chunk of data (redundant data that should exist in the compression history) and signatures that were sent with an accompanying chunk of data (nonredundant data that should be added to the compression history). Should PLZ compress the message, the decoding WAAS device first decompresses the message prior to decoding that message.

As the decoding WAAS device receives an encoded message, each signature identifying redundant data is used to search the DRE compression history and is replaced with the appropriate chunk of data if found. If the signature and associated chunk of data are not found, a synchronous nonacknowledgment is sent to the encoding WAAS device to request that the signature and chunk of data both be resent. This enables the WAAS device to rebuild the message with the missing chunk while also updating its local compression history. For chunks of data that are sent with an accompanying signature (new data), the local compression history is updated on the recipient device, the signature is removed from the message so that only the data remains, and the data is transmitted to the recipient.

After the decoding WAAS device has rebuilt the original message based on the encoded data and chunks from the compression history, it then generates a new message validity signature. This message validity signature, which is calculated over the rebuilt message, is compared against the original message validity signature generated by the encoding WAAS device. If the two signatures match, the decoding WAAS device knows that the message has been rebuilt correctly, and the message is returned to the TCP proxy for transmission to the recipient. If the two signatures do not match, the decoding WAAS device sends a synchronous nonacknowledgment over the entire message, requesting that the encoding WAAS device send all the signatures and data chunks associated with the message that failed decoding. This enables the decoding WAAS device to update its compression history and transmit the message as intended.

To better understand how DRE works, the next section provides a brief overview of two different architectures that are used by WAN optimization products for redundancy elimination: per-peer architectures and shared architectures.

Per-Peer Versus Shared Architecture

DRE utilizes a per-peer compression history as opposed to a shared compression history. Although a shared compression history (one where chunks and signatures can be used across multiple peer devices) provides a longer compression history, such architectures can impose throughput limitations and synchronization challenges as storage is reallocated through the process of eviction of chunks and signatures.

Eviction is the process by which chunks and the associated signatures are removed from the compression history to make capacity available for new chunks and signatures that are detected. As disk and memory are finite, this process occurs frequently based on the arrival rate of new data. Eviction decisions can be made based on one of many different algorithms, and the three most common are as follows:

- **First-in first-out (FIFO):** A queue is maintained, whereby incoming data is added to the head of the queue, moving existing data toward the tail of the queue. As new space is required, the chunks and signatures at the tail of the queue are removed to provide capacity to store the new data.

- **Least-recently-used (LRU):** As new space is required, the chunks and signatures of data that are considered the oldest (determined by a timestamp that records the last access to the chunk and signature) are removed to provide capacity to new data.

- **Least-frequently-used (LFU):** As new space is required, the chunks and signatures that have been used the least (determined by a reference count) are removed to provide capacity to new data.

In virtually any eviction scheme, high and low watermarks are used to determine when to *start* eviction (*high watermark*, that is, a certain percentage of storage is used) and when to *stop* eviction (*low watermark*, that is, when a certain amount of capacity has become available due to the eviction process). Eviction of data is generally stateful in a per-peer architecture, and stateless in a shared compression history architecture.

With a shared compression history architecture, each device needs to map a per-peer index (referencing the signatures that have been used with a specific peer) to a global index (which maps those signatures to locations in memory or on disk where the actual chunk of data is stored). This model is considered hierarchical in that a global repository of chunk and signature data is maintained, and a signature map is maintained for each peer that references the chunks and signatures found in the global repository. Such models are I/O intensive due to the need for multiple lookups and can limit the overall throughput of compression. When deployed at the WAN boundary of a data center, such architectures can limit the overall performance of a solution, possibly even leading to the need to deploy a much larger number of devices. Furthermore, when eviction events occur, some number of chunks of data and associated signatures are removed from the global repository. As many peers reference those chunks, multiple peers might become unsynchronized, leading to additional overhead driven by resynchronization. Because this can impact a potentially large number of peers, performance across many peers can deteriorate during the resynchronization process. This behavior is commonly referred to as a *resynchronization storm* or *cascading synchronization failure.*

With a per-peer compression history architecture, each device holds the chunks of data and signatures associated with a specific peer separately. Although this leads to a shorter compression history due to potentially redundant storage of data, this architecture is less susceptible to being a throughput bottleneck as it is less I/O intensive. When eviction events occur, those events are isolated to a specific peer, thereby isolating resynchronization to a specific peer rather than to a potentially large number of devices. This architecture enables devices to opportunistically utilize storage capacity for their peer devices (storage can be reallocated dynamically across peers based on traffic load from that peer) to maximize performance based on where the performance is required. Given that WAAS devices provide hundreds of gigabytes or even terabytes of compression history, weeks of data can still be stored in locations even with large WAN links and multiple peers. This provides WAAS the same level of benefit as a shared compression history architecture (because the age of data is inversely related to the frequency at which users access it), but without the risk of resynchronization storms, cascading synchronization failures, or throughput bottlenecks caused by inefficient and wasteful I/O.

Figure 1-12 shows the difference between per-peer compression history architectures and shared compression history architectures.

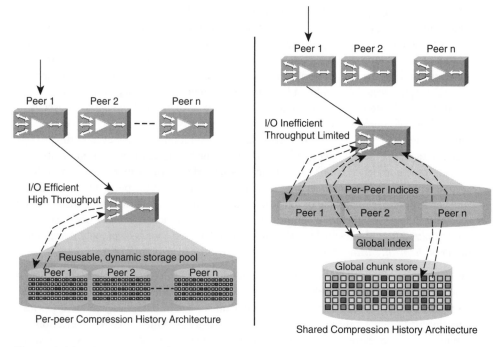

Figure 1-12 *Comparison of Compression History Architectures*

Persistent LZ Compression

Cisco WAAS can also employ PLZ compression as an optimization based on configured policy. PLZ is a lossless compression algorithm that uses an extended compression history for each TCP connection to achieve higher levels of compression than standard LZ variants can achieve. PLZ is helpful for data that has not been identified as redundant by DRE and can even provide additional compression for DRE-encoded messages, as the DRE signatures are compressible. PLZ is similar in operation to DRE in that it uses a sliding window to analyze data patterns for redundancy, but the compression history is based in memory only and is far smaller than that found in DRE.

Transport Flow Optimization

Cisco WAAS TFO is a series of optimizations that is leveraged for connections that are configured for optimization. By employing TFO, communicating nodes are shielded from performance-limiting WAN conditions such as packet loss and latency. Furthermore, TFO enables nodes to more efficiently use available network capacity and minimize the impact of retransmission. TFO provides the following suite of optimizations:

- **Large initial windows:** Large initial windows, found in RFC 3390, enables TFO to mitigate the latency associated with connection setup, as the initial congestion window is increased. This enables the connection to more quickly identify the band-width ceiling during slow-start and enter congestion avoidance at a more rapid pace.

■ **Selective acknowledgment (SACK) and extensions:** SACK, found in RFCs 2018 and 2883, enables a recipient node to explicitly notify the transmitting node which ranges of data have been received in the current window. With SACK, if a block of data goes unacknowledged, the transmitting node needs only to retransmit the block of data that was not acknowledged. SACK helps minimize the bandwidth consumed upon retransmission of a lost segment.

■ **Window scaling:** Window scaling, found in RFC 1323, allows communicating nodes to have an enlarged window. This enables larger amounts of data to be outstanding and unacknowledged in the network at any given time, which allows end nodes to better utilize available WAN bandwidth.

■ **Large buffers:** Large TCP buffers on the WAAS device provide the memory capacity necessary to keep high-BDP WAN connections full of data. This helps mitigate the negative impact of high-bandwidth networks that also have high latency. Additionally, WAAS devices employ adaptive buffering to allocate memory dynami-cally to connections that benefit from larger memory allocation, eliminating the need for tedious static buffer configuration which results in inefficient memory allocation.

■ **Advanced congestion avoidance:** Cisco WAAS employs an advanced congestion avoidance algorithm that provides bandwidth scalability (fill the pipe, used in con-junction with window scaling and large buffers) without compromising on cross-connection fairness. Unlike standard TCP implementations that use linear congestion avoidance, TFO leverages the history of packet loss for each connection to dynami-cally adjust the rate of congestion window increase when loss is not being encoun-tered. TFO also uses a less-conservative backoff algorithm should packet loss be encountered (decreasing the congestion window by 12.5 percent as opposed to 50 percent), which enables the connection to retain higher levels of throughput in the presence of packet loss. Cisco WAAS TFO is based on Binary Increase Congestion (BIC) TCP.

Figure 1-13 shows a comparison between typical TCP implementations and TFO. Notice how TFO can more quickly realize available network capacity and begin leveraging it. When congestion is encountered, TFO is able to more intelligently adjust its throughput to accommodate other connections while preserving bandwidth scalability.

Secure Sockets Layer (SSL) Optimization

SSL-encrypted applications can also be optimized by WAAS through SSL optimization. SSL optimization enables WAAS devices to become trusted intermediary devices to decrypt incoming encrypted data, apply the appropriate set of optimization, and reen-crypt data for further delivery over the WAN. Private keys are installed into the WAAS Central Manager secure store, a passphrase-protected and encrypted vault, and then deployed to data center WAAS devices. Disk encryption can be applied to all WAAS

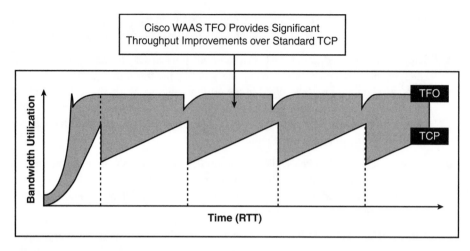

Figure 1-13   *Comparison of TCP Reno and Cisco WAAS TFO*

devices to ensure protection of stored data found in optimized TCP connections should a device or its disks be physically compromised.

SSL optimization allows the data center WAAS device to act as an SSL proxy for the origin server, enabling the WAAS device to control the SSL session. Session keys are securely distributed to the peer WAAS device participating in optimizing the SSL session, which allows both devices the capability to decrypt, optimize, and re-encrypt traffic. SSL optimization provides full support for a number of critical security-related features including Online Certificate Status Protocol (OCSP), certificate revocation checks/validation, and interoperates with web proxies. Figure 1-14 shows how WAAS becomes a trusted man-in-the-middle to intercept and optimize SSL-encrypted sessions while preserving the security model in place and the trust boundary for private key data.

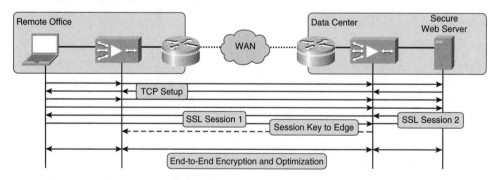

Figure 1-14   *High Level Overview of Cisco WAAS SSL Optimization*

This section focused on the WAN optimization components of Cisco WAAS, whereas the next section focuses on the application acceleration components of Cisco WAAS. As mentioned previously, WAN optimization components are applied generally and have broad applicability, whereas application acceleration components are applied specifically to an application or application protocol. The two, when combined, generally provide a greater degree of performance improvement than can be found when using only one or the other.

Application Acceleration

Application acceleration refers to employing protocol optimizations directly against applications or the application protocols that they use. WAN optimization refers to techniques employed generally against a network layer or transport layer protocol (Cisco WAAS employs them against the transport layer), whereas application acceleration is employed at a higher layer to a specific application or specific application protocol. The optimization concepts found in application acceleration are in many ways common across applications and application protocols, but must be implemented separately because they must operate within the definition of a specific application or protocol. Thus, this section starts with a high-level overview of the types of acceleration capabilities provided in WAAS and then examines each of the applications for which WAAS has explicit acceleration support.

Ensuring application correctness (do not break the application), data integrity (do not corrupt the data), data coherency (do not serve stale data), and security (do not give access to those who should not have it) are of paramount importance in any application acceleration solution. With WAN optimization components, ensuring these items is easy—the optimizations employed are done against a lower layer with well-defined semantics for operation and they do not impact the behavior of the application or protocol directly. With application acceleration, however, ensuring these items is more difficult, as applications and application protocols are more diverse, complex, and finicky with respect to how they must be handled. Any changes that are applied to application or application protocol traffic on the wire must be done in such a way that the application behavior (including its characteristics surrounding correctness, data integrity, data coherency, and security) is functionally identical to the behavior without acceleration. Cisco works directly with Independent Software Vendors (ISV) to license protocol and application specifications prior to developing acceleration techniques to ensure that these characteristics are maintained. This is in stark contrast to solutions that might rely on risky reverse engineering, which might not allow the solution visibility into application or application protocol corner cases.

Table 1-2 lists the high-level application acceleration techniques that can be found in Cisco WAAS. Note that this list is not all-inclusive and focuses only on the techniques that are commonly applied to accelerated applications.

The application of each of these optimizations is determined dynamically for each connection or user session. Because Cisco WAAS is strategically placed in between two communicating nodes, it is in a unique position not only to examine application messages being exchanged to determine what the state of the connection or session is, but also to leverage state messages being exchanged between communicating nodes to determine what level of optimization can safely be applied.

Table 1-2   *Cisco WAAS Application Acceleration Techniques*

Acceleration Technique	Functional Description and Value
Object caching	Object caching enables Cisco WAAS to, when safe, store copies of previously accessed objects (files, other content) to be reused by subsequent users. This only occurs when the application state permits caching, and cached objects are served to users only if application state requirements are met and the object has been validated against the origin server as having not changed. Object caching mitigates latency (objects served locally), saves WAN bandwidth (does not have to be transferred over the WAN), minimizes server workload (does not have to be transferred from the server), and improves application performance.
Metadata caching	Metadata caching enables Cisco WAAS to, when safe, temporarily store metadata information about objects to be reused when subsequent requests come in. This data is stored only for short periods of time, when safe to do so, to satisfy inefficient application requests. Metadata caching mitigates latency (redundant requests handled locally) and minimizes server workload (does not have to be handled by the server when appropriate), thus improving performance.
Local response handling	By employing stateful optimization, Cisco WAAS can locally respond to certain message types on behalf of the server. This occurs only when the application state permits such behavior and can help minimize the perceived latency as fewer messages are required to traverse the WAN. As with object caching and metadata caching, this helps reduce the workload encountered on the server while also improving application performance.
Prepositioning	Prepositioning is used to allow an administrator to specify what content should be proactively copied to a remote Cisco WAAS object cache. This helps improve first-user performance by better ensuring a "cache hit" and can be used to populate the DRE compression history, which is by nature able to be used by multiple applications. Population of the DRE compression history is helpful in environments where the object being prepositioned can be written back from the remote location with some changes applied, which is common in software development and CAD/CAM environments.
Read-ahead	Read-ahead enables Cisco WAAS to, when safe, increase read request sizes on behalf of users, or initiate subsequent read requests on behalf of users, to allow the origin server transmit data ahead of the user request. This enables the data to reach the edge device in a more timely fashion, which in turn means the user's requests can be handled more quickly. Read-ahead is helpful in cache-miss scenarios, in cases where the object is not fully cached, or in cases where caching cannot be used. Read-ahead minimizes the WAN latency penalty by prefetching information.

Table 1-2 *Cisco WAAS Application Acceleration Techniques*

Acceleration Technique	Functional Description and Value
Write-behind	Write-behind enables Cisco WAAS to, when safe, locally acknowledge write requests from a user application. Write-behind is effective with applications where blocks of data are written in sequence and only at breakpoints or at the end of the operation do write operations need to be firmly acknowledged by the server. This enables Cisco WAAS to streamline the transfer of data over the WAN, minimizing the impact of WAN latency.
Multiplexing	Multiplexing refers to a group of optimizations that can be applied independently of one another or in tandem. These include fast connection setup, TCP connection reuse, and message parallelization. Multiplexing helps overcome WAN latency associated with TCP connection management and application layer message handling, thereby improving performance by eliminating a portion of the latency caused by connection setup over the WAN and serialized message handling. These optimizations allow data to be transferred over the network more quickly.
Stream splitting	Stream splitting is similar to object caching in that it enables data to be transferred once over the network and reused across multiple users. With stream splitting, WAAS can identify any redundant requests for Windows Media video streams and reuse the existing stream to service the subsequent user requests. Stream splitting provides an *n:1* bandwidth multiplier in that a single stream could potentially be servicing a large number of users, thereby saving bandwidth and enabling organizations to more confidently deploy live video end-to-end. Similarly, stream splitting provides video server offload, which minimizes video server infrastructure requirements.

As of Cisco WAAS v4.1.3, Cisco WAAS employs all or a subset of these optimizations against a variety of application protocols, including:

- **Common Internet File System (CIFS):** CIFS is the predominant protocol in use between Microsoft Windows clients and servers for file sharing and printing.

- **Messaging Application Programming Interface (MAPI):** MAPI is the API used over Remote Procedure Calls (RPC) between Microsoft Exchange and compatible clients such as Microsoft Outlook, for e-mail, calendaring, and collaboration.

- **Hypertext Transfer Protocol (HTTP):** HTTP is the protocol used for Internet and intranet applications and is growing in popularity as an application-agnostic transport for other applications.

- **Network File System (NFS):** NFS is the predominant protocol in use in Linux and UNIX environments for file sharing.

- **Real Time Streaming Protocol (RTSP):** For Windows Media video streams using RTSP over TCP (RTSPT), Cisco WAAS can provide stream splitting to dramatically reduce bandwidth requirements to support live video to remote locations.

- **Replication applications:** Cisco WAAS can accelerate TCP-based replication and backup applications to minimize bandwidth consumption, maximize application-layer throughput, minimize replication and backup windows, and improve data protection posture.

The following sections provide examples of some of the application acceleration techniques provided by Cisco WAAS. It is important to note that Cisco WAAS employs application layer acceleration capabilities only when safe to do so. The determination on "safety" is made based on state information and metadata exchanged between the two communicating nodes. In any circumstance where it is not safe to perform an optimization, Cisco WAAS dynamically adjusts its level of acceleration to ensure compliance with protocol semantics, data integrity, and data coherency.

Object and Metadata Caching

Object and metadata caching are techniques employed by Cisco WAAS to allow a device to retain a history of previously accessed objects and their metadata. These techniques are leveraged in CIFS acceleration, and metadata caching is employed in NFS acceleration. Unlike DRE, which maintains a history of previously seen data on the network (with no correlation to the upper-layer application), object and metadata caching are specific to the application being used, and the cache is built with pieces of an object or the entire object, along with its associated metadata. With caching, if a user attempts to access an object, directory listing, or file attributes that are stored in the cache, such as a file previously accessed from a particular file server, the file can be safely served from the edge device. This assumes the user has successfully completed authorization and authentication and the object has been validated (verified that it has not changed). Caching requires that the origin server notify the client that caching is permitted through opportunistic locks or other state propagation mechanisms.

Note that message exchanges involving file locks (opportunistic locks or otherwise) are not handled directly by Cisco WAAS, but are rather handled between the client and the server. This ensures that there are no "locking" issues when users across sites access the same file, or "stuck locks" should a WAAS device fail.

Object caching provides numerous benefits, including:

- **LAN-like access to cached objects:** Objects that can be safely served out of cache are served at LAN speeds by the WAAS device adjacent to the requester.

■ **WAN bandwidth savings:** Object caching minimizes the transfer of redundant objects over the network, thereby minimizing overall WAN bandwidth consumption.

■ **Server offload:** Object caching minimizes the amount of workload that must be managed by the server being accessed. By safely offloading work from the server, IT organizations might be in a position to minimize the number of servers necessary to support an application.

Figure 1-15 shows an example of object caching and a cache hit as compared to a cache miss. In both examples (cache miss, cache hit), messages related to correctness, data integrity, data coherency, and security are not shown, but are handled end-to-end by the server natively.

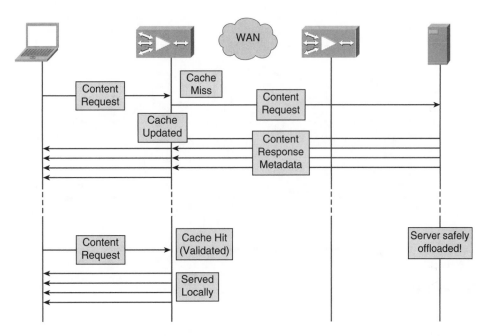

Figure 1-15   *Examining Cache Hit and Cache Miss Scenarios*

As shown in Figure 1-15, when a cache hit occurs, object transfers are done on the LAN adjacent to the requesting node, which minimizes WAN bandwidth consumption and improves performance. When a cache miss occurs, the object is fetched from the origin server in an optimized fashion and, if applicable, the data read from the origin server is used to build the cache to improve performance for subsequent users. This is often referred to as the "first-user penalty" for caching.

With object caching, substantial server utilization savings can be realized. This is an important consideration given that one of the primary use cases of deploying WAN optimization and application acceleration is to enable centralization of infrastructure from the remote offices to the data center. With Cisco WAAS, not only can file servers be *centralized*, but also *consolidated* after they are centralized. This is an important distinction, in that not only can you service a global workforce from a small number of locations, but deploy file services infrastructure more efficiently and cost-effectively, while also providing unparalleled levels of scalability in your server infrastructure.

Figure 1-16 shows server workload caused by a user working with files stored on that server. Figure 1-17 shows an example of how Cisco WAAS in that same use case can minimize the workload placed on CIFS file servers, thereby enabling consolidation after server infrastructure is consolidated.

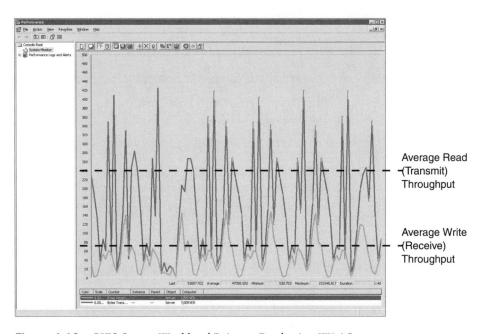

Figure 1-16   *CIFS Server Workload Prior to Deploying WAAS*

Prepositioning

Prepositioning is a function by which an administrator can specify which objects should be proactively placed in the cache of a specific edge device or group of edge devices. By using prepositioning, an administrator can ensure high-performance access to an object for the first requesting user (assuming caching is safe to be used for the user's session), eliminating the first-user penalty. Prepositioning is helpful in environments where large object transfers are necessary. For instance, CAD/CAM, medical imaging, software distribution, and software development all require the movement of large files. Prepositioning can help improve performance for remote users while also offloading the WAN and servers in the data center. Prepositioning can also be used as a means of prepopulating the DRE compression history, because the DRE compression history is refreshed each time a prepositioned object changes or is added.

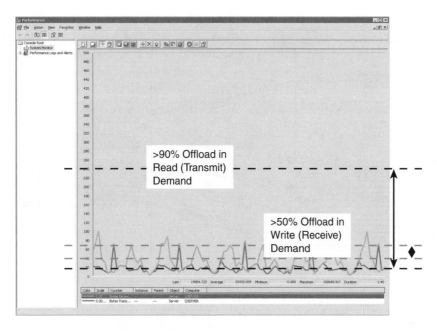

Figure 1-17   *CIFS Server Workload After Deploying WAAS*

Read-Ahead

Read-ahead is a technique that is useful both in application scenarios where caching can be applied and in scenarios where caching cannot be applied. Read-ahead is applicable to CIFS, NFS, and MAPI, and allows the Cisco WAAS device, when applicable, to either increment the size of the application layer read request on behalf of the user, or generate additional read requests on behalf of the user. The goal of read-ahead is two-fold:

- When used in a cache-miss scenario where caching is permitted, provide near-LAN response times to overcome the first-user penalty. Read-ahead, in this scenario, enables the WAAS device to begin immediate and aggressive population of the edge cache.

- When used in a cache-miss scenario or a scenario where caching is not permitted, aggressively fetch data on behalf of the user to mitigate network latency. Read-ahead, in this scenario, is not used to populate a cache with the object, but rather to proactively fetch data that a user might request. Data prefetched in this manner is only briefly cached to satisfy immediate read requests that are for blocks of data that have been read ahead.

Figure 1-18 shows an example of how read-ahead can allow data to begin transmission more quickly over the WAN, thereby minimizing the performance impact of WAN latency.

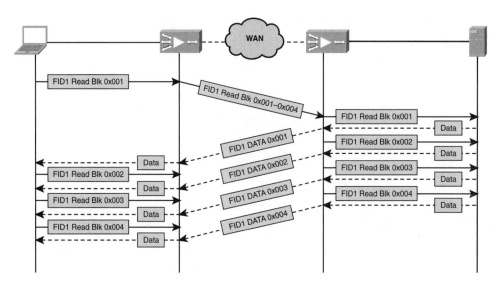

Figure 1-18 *Read-Ahead in Caching and Noncaching Scenarios*

Write-Behind

Write-behind is an optimization that is complementary to read-ahead optimization. Read-ahead focuses on getting the information to the edge more quickly, whereas write-behind focuses on getting the information to the core more quickly—at least from the perspective of the transmitting node. In reality, write-behind is a technique by which a Cisco WAAS device can positively acknowledge receipt of an application layer write request, when safe, to allow the transmitting node to continue to write data. This optimization is commonly employed against application protocols that exhibit high degrees of ping-pong, especially as data is written back to the origin server, and is supported for CIFS, NFS, and MAPI.

As an optimization that provides local acknowledgement for write requests that have not yet been received by the server being written to, write-behind is employed only against write requests that can be recovered in the event of network disconnection or device failure. Most application protocols support write requests that are asynchronous, that is, the acknowledgement of that request by the server has no impact on the way the client sending the data handles that data. Synchronous write requests, on the other hand, generally confirm to the client that the data has been received by the server successfully and provide an indication to the client that the client no longer needs to retain that information. Similarly, CIFS supports information recovery in the event of disconnection through the use of temporary files with change logs for certain applications, which can be discerned through an examination of protocol traffic on the network. Cisco WAAS only employs write-behind where safe to do so, that is, for asynchronous write requests that have no direct bearing on data integrity in and of themselves. Synchronous write requests are handled by the server and not locally handled by WAAS to ensure that data integrity is not compromised.

Figure 1-19 shows an example of how write-behind can allow write data to begin transmission more quickly over the WAN, thereby minimizing the performance impact of WAN latency. Note how the final write operation (COMMIT) is not locally acknowledged by WAAS but allowed to propagate to the origin server. Such mechanisms exist in the protocols accelerated by WAAS and are handled as described previously to ensure data integrity and that no data is lost in the event of a disconnection or device failure.

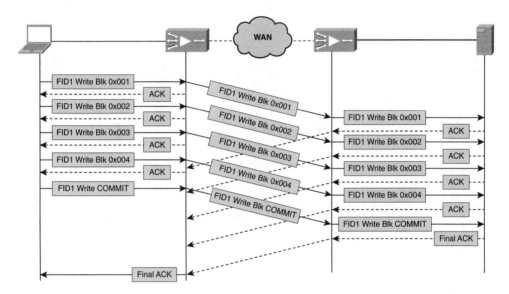

Figure 1-19   *Write-Behind Optimization in WAAS*

Local message handling is similar to write-behind in that messages that are asynchronous can be responded to locally by WAAS when safe to do. As such, a separate section is not devoted to this topic. Rather, the concepts discussed for write-behind can be examined.

Multiplexing

Multiplexing is a term that refers to any process where multiple message signals are combined into a single message signal. Multiplexing, as it relates to Cisco WAAS, refers to the following optimizations:

■ **TCP connection reuse:** By reusing existing established connections rather than creating new connections, TCP setup latency can be mitigated, thereby improving performance. TCP connection reuse is applied only on subsequent connections between the same client and server pair over the same destination port, and it is applied for HTTP and MAPI.

■ **Message parallelization:** For protocols that support batch requests, Cisco WAAS can parallelize otherwise serial tasks into batch requests. This helps minimize the latency penalty, because it is amortized across a series of batched messages as opposed to being experienced on a per-message basis. For protocols that do not support batch requests, Cisco WAAS can "predict" subsequent messages and presubmit those messages on behalf of the user in an attempt to mitigate latency. Message parallelization is supported for CIFS, NFS, and MAPI.

Figure 1-20 shows an example of how Cisco WAAS can reuse existing TCP connections to mitigate latency and performance impact caused by applications that use parallel connections.

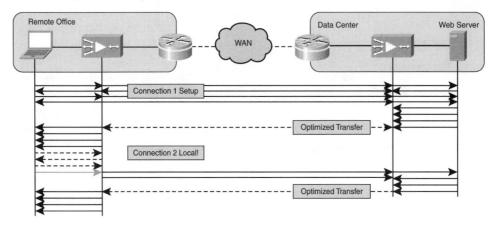

Figure 1-20   *TCP Connection Reuse*

This section focused on the application-specific acceleration components of Cisco WAAS. The next section focuses on the integration aspects of Cisco WAAS as it relates to the ecosystem that is the enterprise IT infrastructure and additional value-added features that are part of the Cisco WAAS solution.

Other Features

Cisco WAAS is a unique application acceleration and WAN optimization solution in that it is the only solution that not only provides the most seamless interoperability with existing network features, but also integrates physically into the Cisco Integrated Services Router (ISR). With the Cisco ISR, customers can deploy enterprise edge connectivity to the WAN, switching, wireless, voice, data, WAN optimization, and security in a single platform for the branch office. (The router modules and the appliance platforms are examined in the next chapter.) The following are some of the additional features that are provided with the Cisco WAAS solution:

■   **Network transparency:** Cisco WAAS is fundamentally transparent in three domains—client transparency, server transparency (no software installation or configuration changes required on clients or servers), and network transparency. Network transparency allows Cisco WAAS to interoperate with existing networking and security functions such as firewall policies, optimized routing, QoS, and end-to-end performance monitoring. Figure 1-21 illustrates network transparency.

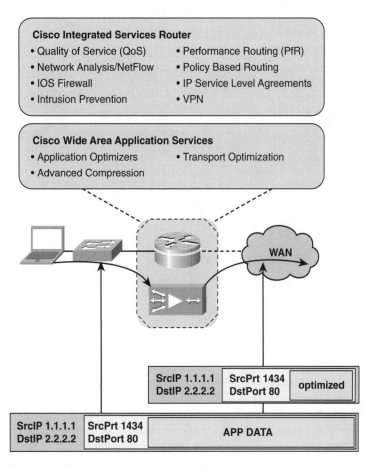

Figure 1-21 *Cisco WAAS Network Transparency*

■ **Enterprise-class scalability:** Cisco WAAS can scale to tens of gigabits of optimized throughput and tens of millions of optimized TCP connections using the Cisco Application Control Engine (ACE), which is an external load-balancer and is discussed in detail in Chapter 6, "Data Center Network Integration." Without external load balancing, Cisco WAAS can scale to tens of gigabits of optimized throughput and over one million TCP connections using the Web Cache Coordination Protocol version 2 (WCCPv2), which is discussed in both Chapter 4, "Network Integration and Interception," and Chapter 6.

■ **Trusted WAN optimization:** Cisco WAAS is a trusted WAN optimization and application acceleration solution in that it integrates seamlessly with many existing security infrastructure components such as firewalls, IDS, IPS, and virtual private network (VPN) solutions. Integration work has been done on not only Cisco WAAS but adjacent Cisco security products to ensure that security posture is not compromised when Cisco WAAS is deployed. Cisco WAAS also supports disk encryption (using AES-256 encryption) with centrally managed keys. This mitigates the risk of data loss or data leakage if a WAAS device is compromised or stolen. Figure 1-22 illustrates trusted WAN optimization.

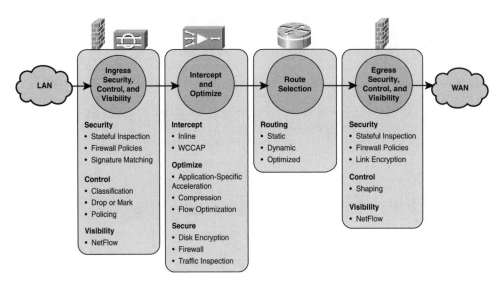

Figure 1-22   *Trusted WAN Optimization*

■ **Automatic discovery:** Cisco WAAS devices can automatically discover one another during the establishment of a TCP connection and negotiate a policy to employ. This eliminates the need to configure complex and tedious overlay networks, also known as *tunnels* or *peering rules*. By mitigating the need for overlay topologies, Cisco WAAS permits optimization without requiring that administrators manage the optimization domain and topology separate from the routing domain. Chapter 8, "Configuring WAN Optimization," covers automatic discovery in detail.

■ **Scalable, secure central management:** Cisco WAAS devices are managed and monitored by the Cisco WAAS Central Manager. The Central Manager can be deployed in a highly available fashion using two Cisco WAAS devices. The Central Manager is secure in that any exchange of data between the Central Manager and a managed Cisco WAAS device is done using SSL, and management access to the Central Manager is encrypted using HTTPS for web browser access or SSH for console access (Telnet is also available). The Central Manager provides a simplified means of configuring a system of devices through device groups and provides role-based access control (RBAC) to enable segregation of management and monitoring, along with integration into third-party management systems, such as TACACS, RADIUS, or Microsoft Active Directory. Chapter 7, "System and Device Management," covers the Central Manager in more detail.

■ **Integration with Cisco Network Analysis Module (NAM) and NetQoS Performance Center:** Cisco WAAS devices integrate with the Cisco Network Analysis Module (NAM) and NetQoS Performance Center (including NetQoS Super Agent) to enable end-to-end application performance including accurate network baselining before and after optimization, performance validation, and response time analysis. WAAS devices are able to send TCP data related to optimized flows to either the NAM or NetQoS to enable accurate depiction of response time, where other TCP proxy-based systems obfuscate response time metrics due to local TCP acknowledgements. Figure 1-23 shows an example of the response time analysis capabilities of NetQoS showing the accuracy of Cisco WAAS and the inaccuracy of other solutions. Chapter 8 covers NAM and NetQoS integration in more detail.

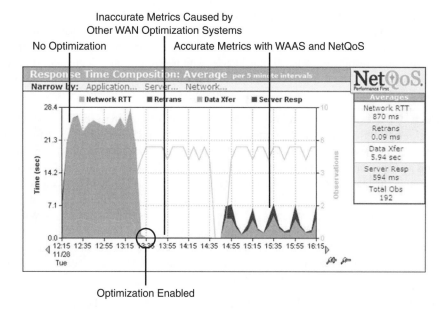

Figure 1-23   *Accurate Performance Measurement using NetQoS*

Branch Virtualization

Although the WAN optimization and application acceleration techniques provided by Cisco WAAS can certainly enable centralization and ultimately consolidation while providing users with high performance access to centralized applications and data, some applications simply cannot be removed from the branch office. Many of these applications are fundamentally required to allow users access to the network, in helping them find resources they need to interact with, or support their day-to-day tasks. Such applications include IP address assignment, user login and authentication, name resolution, and the simple ability to print. These applications are simply too vital to be removed from the branch office, as they are required to allow workers onto the network, which must occur prior to any productive work. In many cases, removing them from the branch office could be disastrous, as a network outage or device failure in that location could prevent the users from being able to do their jobs.

Techniques exist in these applications to minimize the impact of a network outage. For instance, the Dynamic Host Configuration Protocol (DHCP)—used to assign IP addresses to nodes connecting to the network—issues IP addresses based upon a lease. Should a DHCP server be unavailable, a node is free to continue using an IP address as long as the lease has not expired. Active Directory (AD), a vital component of a Microsoft infrastructure, provides authentication, profile, and policy management. AD profile information can be cached locally on the client, enabling users to login while a domain controller cannot be reached. The Domain Name Service (DNS), used to resolve network names to IP addresses, provides records with expiration, which are reused until they expire.

However, what about the roaming user who visits an office while the WAN is disconnected, who cannot access these resources because the servers have been consolidated to the data center, and who cannot rely on these techniques because the user has never interacted with these resources? What about the user who needs to print a document to review collaboratively with other local team members when the WAN is down and the print server had been consolidated to the data center?

Cisco WAAS extends the benefits of infrastructure consolidation to those services that must reside in the branch. Kernel-integrated virtualization is provided on the Cisco Wide Area Virtualization Engine (WAVE) that allows I/T organizations to deploy operating systems and applications on branch office WAAS devices. In doing so, the applications can remain in the branch while also allowing branch infrastructure to be minimized. Rather than managing one or more dedicated servers, Cisco WAAS Virtual Blades (VB) can be used on the branch WAAS device to host operating systems such as Microsoft Windows Server 2003 or Microsoft Windows Server Core 2008 (and other versions) and applications such as AD, DNS, DHCP, and print services. Figure 1-24 shows an example of branch office virtualization using Cisco WAAS VBs to host Microsoft Windows services in the branch office without the extra hardware.

Chapter 10, "Branch Office Virtualization," covers virtualization and discusses VBs in more detail.

The WAAS Effect

What is the effect of deploying WAAS? Thousands of customers have deployed Cisco WAAS to tens of thousands of locations to overcome the performance boundary presented by the WAN, enable centralization of costly remote office infrastructure, consolidate infrastructure resources in the data center to improve efficiency, minimize bandwidth consumption and mitigate bandwidth upgrades, and provide consistent performance for users regardless of where they are in the network. The performance of most TCP-based applications can be improved by 4X or more (some even beyond 100X), which enables users to have consistent performance accessing centralized applications and data over the WAN as they had when accessing those same applications and data locally. In cases where users were already accessing applications and data over a WAN, the performance

Virtual Blades
Windows Server Core 2008
Active Directory
DNS Server
DHCP Server
Print Server
VB 2
VB n
Remote Office
WAN

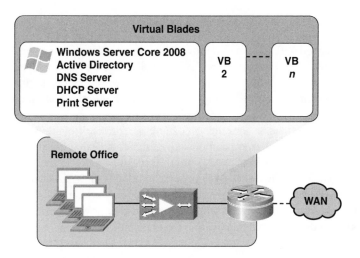

Figure 1-24 *Virtualization of Branch Office Servers Using WAAS Virtual Blades*

improvement provided can be substantial, allowing each person to complete more in a given work day. Figure 1-25 shows some common performance improvements found in today's enterprise networks with today's enterprise applications.

Category
Applications
Acceleration Factor (Average, Peak)
File Sharing
Windows (CIFS)
UNIX (NFS)
2-20X Avg
>100X Peak
Email
Microsoft Exchange
Lotus Notes
Internet Mail
2-10X Avg
50X Peak
Web and Collaboration
HTTP
WebDAV
FTP
Microsoft SharePoint
2-10X Avg
100X Peak
Software Distribution
Microsoft SMS
Altiris
HP Radia
2-20X Avg
>100X Peak
Enterprise Applications
Microsoft SQL
Oracle, SAP
Lotus Notes
2-5X Avg
20X Peak
Backup Applications
Microsoft NTBackup
Legato, Veritas
CommVault
2-10X Avg
50X Peak
Data Replication
EMC, NetApp
Data Domain
Veritas, DoubleTake
2-10X Avg
50X Peak
Video
WMT/RTSP
VoD Playback (CIFS)
2-20X Avg
>100X Peak

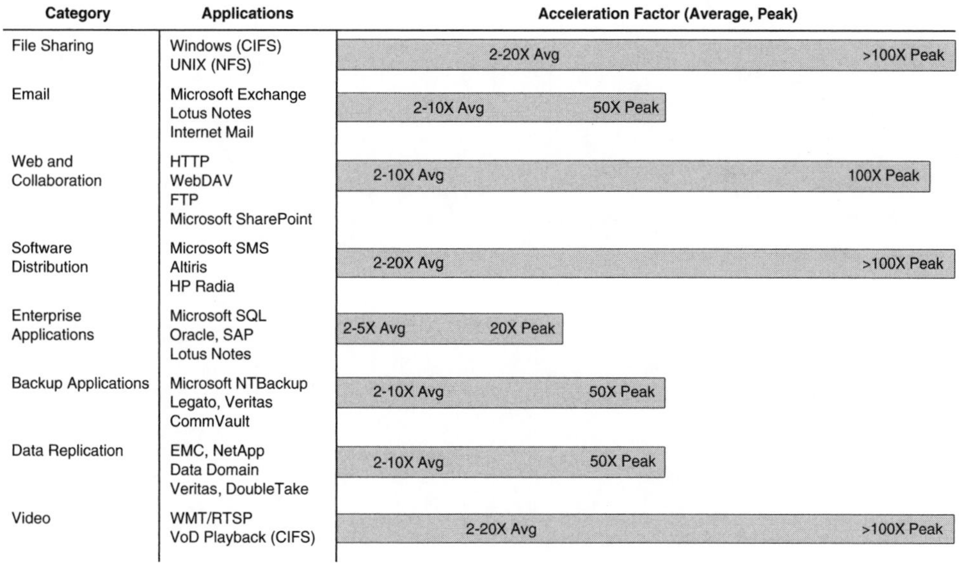

Figure 1-25 *Common Performance Improvements Provided by WAAS*

Summary

IT organizations are challenged with the need to provide high levels of application performance for an increasingly distributed workforce. Additionally, they are faced with an opposing challenge to consolidate costly infrastructure to contain capital and operational expenditures. Organizations find themselves caught between two conflicting realities: to distribute costly infrastructure to remote offices to solve performance requirements of a growingly distributed workforce, and to consolidate costly infrastructure from those same remote offices to control capital and operational costs and complexity. Cisco WAAS is a solution that employs a series of WAN optimization and application acceleration techniques to overcome the fundamental performance limitations of WAN environments to enable remote users to enjoy near-LAN performance when working with centralized application infrastructure and content, while also providing a powerful platform for consolidation both into the data center and within the branch office.

Chapter 2

Cisco WAAS Architecture, Hardware, and Sizing

Chapter 1, "Introduction to Cisco Wide Area Application Services (WAAS)," introduced the performance challenges created by the wide-area network (WAN) and how they are addressed by the Cisco WAAS solution. Cisco WAAS is a software component that is resident on a hardware device deployed at each location with users and servers. This hardware device, which can be deployed as a router-integrated network module for the Integrated Services Router (ISR) or as an appliance, is named either Cisco Wide-Area Application Engine (WAE) or Cisco Wide-Area Virtualization Engine (WAVE). The distinction between the two is that a WAVE device, available only as an appliance, can also provide branch office virtualization services in conjunction with WAN optimization and application acceleration. WAE devices provide only WAN optimization and application acceleration and do not provide virtualization.

This chapter provides an introduction to the Cisco WAAS hardware family, along with an in-depth examination of the hardware and software architecture. This chapter also looks at the licensing options for Cisco WAAS, positioning for each of the hardware platforms, and performance and scalability metrics for each of the platforms.

Cisco WAAS Product Architecture

The Cisco WAAS product family consists of a series of appliances and router-integrated network modules that are based on an Intel x86 hardware architecture. The product family scales from 512 MB of memory to 24 GB of memory, utilizing single-processor subsystems up to dual quad-core processor subsystems. Each Cisco WAAS device, regardless of form factor, is configured with some amount of hard disk storage and a compact flash card. The compact flash card is used for boot-time operation and configuration files, whereas the hard disk storage is used for optimization data (including object cache and Data Redundancy Elimination [DRE]), swap space, software image storage repository, and guest operating system storage in the case of WAVE devices. Having a compact flash card enables the device to remain accessible on the network should the device suffer hard drive subsystem failure for troubleshooting and diagnostics purposes (in such a scenario, optimization and virtualization services would not be operational). Also, by using the compact flash card in this way, a WAAS device can successfully boot and become accessible on the network if no disks are available to the device.

The foundational layer of the Cisco WAAS software is the underlying Cisco Linux platform. The Cisco Linux platform is hardened to ensure that rogue services are not installed and secured such that third-party software or other changes cannot be made. The Cisco Linux platform hosts a command-line interface (CLI) shell similar to that of Cisco IOS Software, which, along with the Central Manager and other interfaces, form the primary means of configuring, managing, and troubleshooting a device or system. All relevant configuration, management, monitoring, and troubleshooting subsystems are made accessible directly through this CLI as opposed to exposing the Linux shell.

The Cisco Linux platform hosts a variety of services for WAAS run-time operation. These include disk encryption, Central Management Subsystem (CMS), interface manager, reporting facilities, network interception and bypass, application traffic policy (ATP) engine, and kernel-integrated virtualization services, as shown in Figure 2-1.

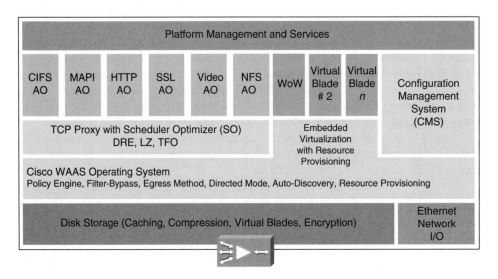

Figure 2-1   *Cisco WAAS Hardware and Software Architecture*

The following sections examine each of the Cisco WAAS architecture items. Cisco WAAS optimization components, including Data Redundancy Elimination (DRE), Persistent LZ Compression (PLZ), Transport Flow Optimization (TFO), and application accelerators, are discussed in detail in Chapter 1, and thus are not discussed in this chapter.

Disk Encryption

Cisco WAAS devices can be configured to encrypt the data, swap, and spool partitions on the hard disk drives using encryption keys that are stored on and retrieved from the Central Manager. The disk encryption feature uses AES-256 encryption, the strongest commercially available encryption, and keys are stored only in the WAAS device memory after they have been retrieved from the Central Manager during the device boot process. Should a WAAS device be physically compromised or a disk stolen, power is removed from the device, which destroys the copy of the key in memory (memory is not persistent). When the hard disks are encrypted, loss of the key renders data on the disk unusable and scrambled. Keys are stored in the Central Manager database (which can be encrypted) and synchronized among all Central Manager devices for high availability. If a WAAS device is not able to retrieve its key from the Central Manager during boot time, it remains in pass-through mode until connectivity is restored or disk encryption is administratively bypassed. Additionally, the fetching of the key from the Central Manager is done over the Secure Sockets Layer (SSL)-encrypted session that is used for message exchanges between the WAAS devices and the Central Manager devices.

Central Management Subsystem

CMS is a process that runs on each WAAS device, including accelerators and Central Managers. This process manages the configuration and monitoring components of a WAAS device and ensures that each WAAS device is synchronized with the Central Manager based on a scheduler known as the Local Central Manager (LCM) cycle. The LCM cycle is responsible for synchronizing the Central Manager CMS process with the remote WAAS device CMS process to exchange configuration data, fetch health and status information, and gather monitoring and reporting data. The CMS process is tied to a management interface configured on the WAAS device known as the primary interface, which is configured on the WAAS device CLI prior to registration to the Central Manager. Any communication that occurs between WAAS devices for CMS purposes is done using SSL-encrypted connections for security.

Interface Manager

The Cisco WAAS device interface manager manages the physical and logical interfaces that are available on the WAAS device. Each WAAS device includes two integrated Gigabit Ethernet interfaces (including the network modules, one interface is internal and shares connectivity to a peer interface in the router through the router backplane, the other is external and can be cabled to a LAN switch, similar to an appliance). Each WAAS appliance has expansion slots to support one or more additional feature cards, such as the inline bypass adapter, which has two two-port fail-to-wire pairs. The interface manager also provides management over logical interfaces that can be configured over physical interfaces. Logical interfaces include active/standby interfaces, where one physical interface is used as a primary interface and a second interface is used as a backup in the event the primary interface fails. Another logical interface is the PortChannel interface, which can be used to team WAAS device interfaces together for the purposes of high availability and load balancing. It should be noted that active/standby interfaces are used when WAAS device interfaces connect to separate switches, whereas PortChannel interfaces are used when the WAAS device interfaces connect to the same switch.

Monitoring Facilities and Alarms

Cisco Linux provides an interface for the Cisco WAAS software to use for purposes of monitoring and generating alarms. Cisco WAAS supports the Simple Network Management Protocol (SNMP) versions 1, 2c, and 3, and a host of Management Information Bases (MIB) that provide complete coverage over the health of each individual WAAS device. Cisco WAAS also supports the definition of up to four syslog servers, which can be used as alarm recipients when syslog messages are generated. The WAAS Central Manager also has an alarm dashboard, which is described in Chapter 7, "System and Device Management." The Central Manager makes an application programming interface (API) available for third-party visibility systems, which is also discussed in Chapter 7, Chapter 8, "Configuring WAN Optimization," and Chapter 9, "Configuring Application Acceleration." Transaction logs can be configured to be stored on each of the accelerator devices in the network for persistent retention of connection statistics, which might be useful for troubleshooting, debugging, or analytics purposes. Transaction logs are not covered in this book, but a full reference on their usage can be found in the Cisco WAAS documentation.

Note   The alarm book (which covers syslog messages, SNMP traps, and Central Manager dashboard alarms), error book (which covers console messages), and product documentation can be downloaded from Cisco.com at http://www.cisco.com/cgi-bin/tablebuild.pl/waas41.

Network Interception and Bypass Manager

The network interception and bypass manager is used by the Cisco WAAS device to establish relationships with intercepting devices where necessary and ensure low-latency bypass of traffic that the WAAS device is not intended to handle. The Web Cache Coordination Protocol version 2 (WCCPv2) is a protocol managed by the network interception and bypass manager to allow the WAAS device to successfully join a WCCPv2 service group with one or more adjacent routers, switches, or other WCCPv2-capable server devices. WCCPv2 is discussed in more detail in Chapter 4, "Network Integration and Interception." Other network interception options, which are also discussed in Chapter 4, include policy-based routing (PBR), physical inline interception, and Application Control Engine (ACE). As flows are intercepted by the WAAS device and determined to be candidates for optimization, those flows are handed to the Application Traffic Policy (ATP) engine to identify what level of optimization and acceleration should be applied based on the configured policies and classifier matches. The ATP is discussed in the next section, and Chapter 8 and Chapter 9 discuss the configuration and management of policies.

Application Traffic Policy Engine

Although the foundational platform component of Cisco WAAS is Cisco Linux, the foundational optimization layer of the Cisco WAAS software (which is as much a component of the Cisco Linux platform as it is the software) is the ATP engine. The ATP is responsible for examining details of each incoming flow (after being handled by the interception and bypass mechanisms) in an attempt to identify the application or protocol associated with the flow. This association is done by comparing the packet headers from each flow against a set of predefined, administratively configured, or dynamic classifiers, each with its own set of one or more match conditions. Flows that do not have a match with an existing classifier are considered "other" traffic and are handled according to the policy defined for other traffic, which indicates that there are no classifier matches and that the default policy should be used.

When a classifier match is found, the ATP examines the policy configuration for that classifier to determine how to optimize the flow. The ATP also notes the application group to which the classifier belongs to route statistics gathered to the appropriate application group for proper charting (visualization) and reporting. The configured policy dictates which optimization and acceleration components are enacted upon the flow and how the packets within the flow are handled. The list of configurable elements within a policy include the following:

- **Type of policy:** Defines whether the policy is a basic policy (optimize, accelerate, and apply a marking), Wide Area File Services Software (WAFS) transport (used for legacy mode compatibility with WAAS version 4.0 devices), and end-point mapper (EPM, used to identify universally-unique identifiers for classification and policy).

- **Application:** Defines which application group the statistics should be collected into, including byte counts, compression ratios, and others, which are then accessible via the WAAS device CLI or Central Manager.

- **Action:** Defines the WAN optimization policy that should be applied to flows that match the classifier match conditions. This includes:

  - **Passthrough:** Take no optimization action on this flow

  - **TFO Only:** Apply only TCP optimization to this flow, but no compression or data deduplication

  - **TFO with LZ Compression:** Apply TCP optimization to this flow, in conjunction with persistent LZ compression

  - **TFO with Data Redundancy Elimination:** Apply TCP optimization to this flow, in conjunction with data deduplication

  - **Full Optimization:** Apply TCP optimization, persistent LZ compression, and data duplication to this flow

- **Accelerate:** Accelerate the traffic from within this flow using one of the available application accelerators. This provides additional performance improvement above and beyond those provided by the WAN optimization components defined in Action and includes (the capabilities are described in detail in Chapter 1):

■ **MS Port Mapper:** Identify application based on its universally unique identifier, which allows WAAS to appropriately classify certain applications that use server-assigned dynamic port numbers

■ **Common Internet File System (CIFS):** Acceleration for Microsoft file-sharing environments

■ **HTTP:** Acceleration for intranet and Internet applications that use the hypertext transfer protocol

■ **NFS:** Acceleration for UNIX file-sharing environments

■ **MAPI:** Acceleration for Microsoft Exchange e-mail, calendaring, and collaboration environments

■ **Video:** Acceleration for Windows Media over RTSP streams

■ **Position:** Specify the priority order of this policy. Policies are evaluated in priority order, and the first classifier and policy match determines the action taken against the flow and where the statistics for that flow are aggregated.

■ **Differentiated Services Code Point (DSCP) Marking:** Apply a DSCP value to the packets in the flow. WAAS can either preserve the existing DSCP markings or apply a specific marking to the packets matching the flow based on the configuration of this setting.

Settings configured in the policy are employed in conjunction with one another. For instance, the CIFS policy is, by default, configured to leverage the CIFS accelerator prior to leveraging the "full optimization" (DRE, PLZ, TFO) capabilities of the underlying WAN optimization layer. This can be coupled with a configuration that applies a specific DSCP marking to the packets within the flow. This is defined in a single policy, thereby simplifying overall system policy management. Classifiers within the ATP can be defined based on source or destination IP addresses or ranges, TCP port numbers or ranges, or universally-unique identifiers (UUID). The ATP is consulted only during the establishment of a new connection, which is identified through the presence of the TCP synchronize (SYN) flag which occurs within the first packet of the connection. By making a comparison against the ATP using the SYN packet of the connection being established, the ATP does not need to be consulted for traffic flowing in the reverse direction, as the context of the flow is established by all WAAS devices in the path between the two endpoints and applied to all future packets associated with that particular flow. In this way, classification performed by the ATP is done once against the three-way handshake (SYN, SYN/ACK packets) and is applicable for both directions of traffic flow.

Figure 2-2 shows how the ATP engine interacts with a flow and a particular policy. For more information on ATP, including configuration, please see Chapter 8 and Chapter 9.

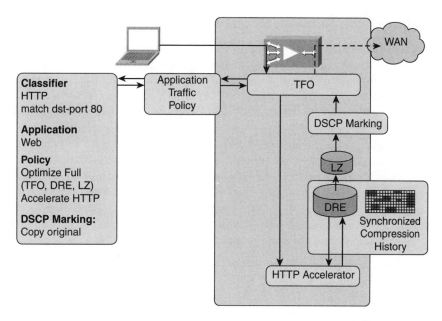

Figure 2-2 *Connection Interaction with Application Traffic Policy*

Virtual Blades

Cisco WAAS utilizes Kernel-based Virtual Machine (KVM) technology from Red Hat (via the Qumranet acquisition) to allow the WAVE appliance (and the WAE-674) to host third-party operating systems and applications. As of version 4.1.3, Microsoft Windows Server, versions 2003 and 2008, are supported for installation on the WAAS Virtual Blade (VB) architecture, and certain configurations can be bundled and packaged within the WAVE configuration with full support from the Cisco Technical Assistance Center (TAC). This configuration includes Microsoft Windows Server 2008 Core, Active Directory read-only domain controller, DNS server, DHCP server, and print server. The WAAS VB architecture helps enable customers to further consolidate infrastructure by minimizing the number of physical servers required in the branch office for those applications which are not good candidates for centralization into a data center location.

Hardware Family

The current Cisco WAAS hardware family consists of three router-integrated network modules, two desktop appliance models, and four rack-mounted appliance models. With such a diverse hardware portfolio, Cisco WAAS can be deployed in each location with the appropriate amount of optimization capacity for the needs of the users or servers in that particular location. This section examines the specifics of each of the current and legacy hardware platforms and positioning of each. Performance and scalability metrics for each are examined later in this chapter, along with best practices around accurately sizing a Cisco WAAS deployment.

Router-Integrated Network Modules

The Cisco WAAS router-integrated network modules are designed to provide optimization services for the remote branch office or enterprise edge. These modules, which are single-processor systems based on the Network Module Enhanced (NME) hardware, can occupy an empty or available NME-capable slot in a Cisco Integrated Services Router (ISR), including models 2811, 2821, 2851, 3825, and 3845. The ISR is an ideal platform for the branch office in that it provides a converged service platform for the remote office, including routing, switching, wireless, voice, security, and WAN optimization in a single chassis (platform, software version, and slot capacity dependent). In addition, the ISR provides a strong foundation for application performance management (APM) solutions in that along with WAAS, other performance-related features can be configured, including quality of service (QoS) for network provisioning, Performance Routing (PfR) for optimal path selection and network utilization, and NetFlow for visibility into traffic distribution, throughput, and other metrics.

Figure 2-3 shows a picture of the Cisco NME-WAE family of WAAS integrated network modules and the ISR family.

Cisco ISR 3845   Cisco ISR 3825   Cisco ISR 282, 2851   Cisco ISR 2811

Cisco WAAS NME-302   Cisco WAAS NME-502   Cisco WAAS NME-522

Figure 2-3   *Cisco ISR Family and WAAS Network Modules*

The Cisco NME-WAE family includes three models: the NME-WAE-302, NME-WAE-502, and NME-WAE-522. Each network module has a single hard disk with capacity ranging from 80 to 160 GB. With only a single drive, the NME-WAE is not capable of Redundant Array of Inexpensive Disks (RAID). NME-WAE devices integrate into the network using WCCPv2 as a means of interception (Policy-Based Routing [PBR] can also be used, but WCCPv2 is preferred). Both methods of integration and interception are discussed in Chapter 4. The NME-WAE family does not provide support for virtualization in the branch office; a WAVE appliance model or WAE-674 is required for virtualization support. Each NME-WAE has two network interfaces:

- **One internal:** Connected to the ISR backplane, which communicates with an internal network interface on the ISR

■ **One external:** Accessible through the front of the module, which can be attached to a LAN switch

Figure 2-4 shows the architecture of the NME, internal and external interfaces, and intersection points between the NME and the ISR.

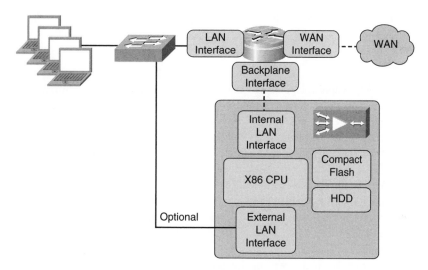

Figure 2-4   *Cisco WAAS Network Module Architecture*

NME-WAE Model 302

The Cisco NME-WAE model 302 (NME-WAE-302) is designed for customers who want to employ only basic WAN optimization capabilities, which are permitted through the use of the Transport license (licensing is discussed later in this chapter). These capabilities include the ATP engine, DRE, PLZ, and TFO. This module is not capable of running the advanced services enabled by the Enterprise license (discussed later in the chapter), including application layer acceleration or disk encryption. The NME-WAE-302 is a single-processor system with 512 MB of RAM and a single 80-GB hard disk.

NME-WAE Model 502

The Cisco NME-WAE model 502 (NME-WAE-502) is designed for customers who want to employ WAN optimization capabilities and application acceleration features for an enterprise edge location. The NME-WAE-502 can be configured with the Enterprise license, providing full WAN optimization functionality, application acceleration functionality, and other features enabled by the Enterprise license including disk encryption and NetQoS integration. The NME-WAE-502 is a single-processor system with 1 GB of RAM and a single 120-GB hard disk. The NME-WAE-502 is capable of supporting a larger number of users than the NME-WAE-302, as discussed in the "Performance and Scalability Metrics" section later in this chapter.

NME-WAE Model 522

The Cisco NME-WAE model 522 (NME-WAE-522) is designed for customers who want to employ appliance-equivalent functionality to an enterprise edge location in the ISR. The NME-WAE-522 supports the full suite of Enterprise license features, including all WAN optimization and application acceleration capabilities. The NME-WAE-522 is a single-processor system with 2 GB of RAM and a 160-GB hard disk, serving as the most powerful network module available as of this writing.

Appliances

The Cisco WAAS appliance family is designed to be deployed in a location of any size, including the small branch office, campus networks, or the largest of enterprise data center networks. The Cisco WAAS appliance family includes the WAE and the newer WAVE devices. Cisco WAVE appliances are current-generation and provide support for branch office virtualization, whereas WAE appliances (with the exception of the WAE-674) do not. The Cisco WAE family includes models 512, 612, 674, 7341, and 7371, and the Cisco WAVE family includes models 274, 474, and 574. WAE appliance models 512 and 674, along with WAVE appliance models 274, 474, and 574, are targeted toward branch office deployments, whereas the WAE appliance models 674, 7341, 7371 are targeted toward regional office and data center deployments. The WAE-674 is a hybrid device that is commonly used for larger branch offices (and those where virtualization is required), but works equally well as a data center device where virtualization is not used. This should not imply that the device characterization presented is fixed; devices should be placed in locations according to performance and scalability sizing and feature requirements.

The WAE appliance models 512, 612, 674, 7341, and 7371, along with WAVE appliance model 574, each have externally accessible hard disk drives and RAID support (some models support hot-swappable disk drives). WAVE appliance models 274 and 474 do not have externally accessible hard disk drives, and with a single hard disk drive, do not support RAID.

Each WAE and WAVE appliance has two built-in Gigabit Ethernet interfaces, which can be deployed independently of one another or as a pair in either an active/standby configuration or PortChannel configuration. Such interface configurations are discussed in Chapter 5, "Branch Office Network Integration," and Chapter 6, "Data Center Network Integration." The WAE and WAVE appliance families both have one or more Peripheral Component Interconnect (PCI) expansion slots that support installation of additional feature cards, such as the physical in-path interception card. Each WAE or WAVE appliance can be deployed using a variety of network interception techniques, including physical inline interception, WCCPv2, PBR, and ACE (all are described in Chapter 4). Any appliance model can be used as a core (data center) or edge (branch office) device, although performance and scalability recommendations presented in this chapter must be followed. Figure 2-5 shows an image of the Cisco WAE appliance family, and Figure 2-6 shows an image of the Cisco WAVE appliance family.

Figure 2-5 *Cisco WAAS WAE Appliance Family*

Figure 2-6 *Cisco WAAS WAVE Appliance Family*

Note The WAE model 7326 is end-of-life and is not covered in this section; however, its performance and scalability metrics are covered in this chapter to support those who have already deployed these devices in their networks and wish to continue using them with WAAS v4.1.

WAVE Model 274

The Cisco WAVE model 274 (WAVE-274) is a single-processor desktop model that is designed for deployment in small and medium-sized branch office locations or small data center locations. The WAVE-274 is configured with 3 GB of RAM. The WAVE-274 provides full WAN optimization and application acceleration capabilities and supports virtualization with up to two VBs. The WAVE-274 can be configured with any license available for WAAS. The WAVE-274 includes a single 250-GB SATA2 hard disk drive, and therefore does not support RAID. The WAVE-274 includes an inline card (with support for one WAN link) and the Enterprise license (discussed in the "Licensing" section of this chapter).

WAVE Model 474

The Cisco WAVE model 474 (WAVE-474) is a single-processor desktop model that is designed for deployment in small- and medium-sized branch office locations or small data center locations. Like the WAVE-274, the WAVE-474 is configured with 3 GB of

RAM. The WAVE-474 provides full WAN optimization and application acceleration capabilities and supports virtualization with up to two VBs. The WAVE-474 can be configured with any license available for WAAS. The WAVE-474 includes a single 250-GB SATA2 hard disk drive, and with a single drive, it does not support RAID. The WAVE-474 is similar to the WAVE-274, but supports a larger number of optimized TCP connections and higher levels of WAN bandwidth. The WAVE-474 includes an inline card (with support for two WAN links) and the Enterprise license (discussed in the "Licensing" section of this chapter).

WAE Model 512

The Cisco WAE model 512 (WAE-512) is a single-processor rack-mount system that is designed for deployment in small- and medium-sized branch office locations or small data center locations. The WAE-512 can be configured with 1 or 2 GB of RAM. In either configuration, the WAE-512 can provide full WAN optimization and application acceleration capabilities, but does not support virtualization. With an increase in memory configuration, the WAE-512 supports a larger number of optimized TCP connections and a greater amount of WAN bandwidth. Regardless of memory configuration, the WAE-512 can be configured with the Transport, Enterprise, or Video license. The WAE-512 supports two 250-GB SATA2 hard disk drives, which are configured automatically for software RAID-1.

WAVE Model 574

The Cisco WAVE model 574 (WAVE-574) is a quad-core rack-mount system that is designed for deployment in large branch office locations or small data center locations. The WAVE-574 can be configured with either 3 GB or 6 GB of RAM and either one or two 500 GB SATA hard disk drives. With two drives, the system is configured automatically for software RAID-1. The 6 GB RAM configuration affords the WAVE-574 support for increased WAN bandwidth and optimized TCP connections and enables the 574 to increase its VB support from two to six (assuming 512MB of RAM is allocated for each VB). The WAVE-574 supports the full breadth of features and capabilities offered by any available Cisco WAAS license.

WAE Model 612

The Cisco WAE model 612 (WAE-612) is a dual-core processor rack-mount system that is designed for deployment in medium-sized branch office locations or medium-sized data center locations. The WAE-612 can be configured with 2 GB or 4 GB of RAM (4 GB of RAM provides greater WAN bandwidth support and higher optimized TCP connection counts) and, in any configuration, supports the full breadth of features and capabilities offered by the Transport, Enterprise, and Video licenses. The WAE-612 supports two 300-GB SAS hard disk drives, which are configured automatically for software RAID-1 and are hot-swap capable.

WAE Model 674

The Cisco WAE model 674 (WAE-674) is a quad-core rack-mount system that is designed for deployment in large branch office locations or medium to large data center locations. The WAE-674 can be configured with either 4 GB or 8 GB of RAM and three 300 GB SAS hard disk drives, which are capable of hot-swap. The 4 GB RAM configuration affords the WAE-674 support for up to two VBs, and the 8 GB RAM configuration affords the WAE-674 support for up to six VBs. Additionally, the increased memory configuration provides support for a greater amount of WAN bandwidth and optimized TCP connections. The WAE-674 is unique in that it can be configured with or without VB support (the only device in the hardware family that can), and when configured without VB support, the WAE-674 can support an even higher level of WAN bandwidth and optimized TCP connections. The reason for this level of configurability is the unique position of the WAE-674, which can be used for branch offices and data centers of virtually any size. The WAE-674 supports the full breadth of features and capabilities offered by any available Cisco WAAS license.

WAE Model 7341

The Cisco Cisco WAE model 7341 (WAE-7341) is a single quad-core rack-mount system (four processors) that is designed for deployment in large enterprise data centers. The WAE-7341 includes 12 GB of RAM and four 300-GB Serial-Attached SCSI (SAS) hard disk drives, which are configured automatically for hardware RAID-5 and support hot-swap. The WAE-7341 supports the full breadth of features and capabilities offered by the Transport, Enterprise, and Video Cisco WAAS licenses, but not virtualization.

WAE Model 7371

The Cisco WAE model 7371 (WAE-7371) is a dual quad-core rack-mount system (eight processors) that is designed for deployment in the largest of enterprise data centers and under the most demanding conditions. The WAE-7371 includes 24 GB of RAM and six 300-GB SAS hard disk drives, which are configured automatically for hardware RAID-5 and support hot-swap. The WAE-7371 supports the full breadth of features and capabilities offered by the Transport, Enterprise, and Video Cisco WAAS licenses, but not virtualization.

Licensing

Each Cisco WAAS device, whether it is an appliance (WAE or WAVE) or a router-integrated network module, must be configured with one or more licenses. This license dictates what features are permitted to be configured on the device. Licenses are not enforced in WAAS; however, licenses can only be applied to platforms that support the particular license in question. Four licenses exist for Cisco WAAS and configuration of licenses are discussed in Chapter 7:

- **Transport license:** Enables a WAAS device to apply only basic WAN optimization capabilities. It supports use of TFO, DRE, and PLZ. WAAS devices configured with the Transport license cannot provide Enterprise license features including application-acceleration capabilities, disk encryption, or any other features provided by other licenses. WAAS devices configured with the Transport license can, however, register with and be managed and monitored by a WAAS device configured as a Central Manager. The Transport license is supported by all Cisco WAAS hardware platforms.

- **Enterprise license:** Allows a WAAS device to apply all the WAN optimization provided by the Transport license and all the application acceleration functionality with the exception of Video (which is licensed separately). Additionally, the Enterprise license enables support for disk encryption and NetQoS integration. Like the Transport license, WAAS devices configured with the Enterprise license can register with and be managed and monitored by a WAAS device configured as a Central Manager. Configuration of a WAAS device as a Central Manager requires the Enterprise license. The Enterprise license is supported by all Cisco WAAS hardware platforms with the exception of the network module model 302 (NME-302).

- **Video:** Allows a WAAS device to apply stream splitting to Windows Media over Real-Time Streaming Protocol (RTSP) traffic. The Video license is commonly applied in conjunction with the Enterprise license. The Video license is supported by all Cisco WAAS hardware platforms with the exception of the network module model 302 (NME-302).

- **Virtual-Blade:** Allows a WAAS device to host third-party operating systems and applications in one or more VBs in the branch office, including Microsoft Windows Server. The Virtual-Blade license is supported on all Cisco WAVE appliances in addition to the WAE model 674.

Performance and Scalability Metrics

Design of a Cisco WAAS solution involves many factors, but the cornerstone of the solution design is based on the performance and scalability metrics required for the solution as a whole and for each individual location where WAAS is deployed. Every component in an end-to-end system has a series of static and dynamic system limits. For instance, a typical application server might be limited in terms of the number of connections it can support, disk I/O throughput, network throughput, CPU speed, or number of transactions per second. Likewise, each Cisco WAAS device has static and dynamic system limits that dictate how and when a particular WAAS device is selected for a location within an end-to-end design. This section examines the performance and scalability metrics of the Cisco WAAS hardware family, and provides a definition of what each item is and how it is relevant to a localized (per location) design and an end-to-end system design.

The static and dynamic limits referred to are used as a means of identifying which device is best suited to provide services to a particular location in the network. The device might be deployed as an edge device, where it connects to potentially many peer devices in one or more data center locations, or as a core device, where it serves as an aggregation point for many connected edges. WAAS devices can also be deployed as devices to optimize links between data center locations, where devices on each side are realistically core devices. A fundamental understanding of the performance and scalability metrics is paramount in ensuring a sound design. Although WAAS devices have no concept of "core" or "edge," the deployment position within the network has an effect on the type of workload handled by a device and should be considered—primarily as it relates to TCP connection count and peer fan-out (how many peers can connect to a device for the purposes of optimization). This section examines each of the performance and scalability system limits, both static and dynamic, that should be considered. These include device memory, disk capacity, the number of optimized TCP connections, WAN bandwidth and LAN throughput, the number of peers and fan-out, and the number of devices managed.

Device Memory

The amount of memory installed in a device dictates the level of performance and scalability the device can provide. As the memory capacity increases, the ability of a WAAS device to handle a larger number of connections, a larger addressable index space for compression, or a longer history of compression data also increases. Having larger amounts of memory also enables the WAAS device to run additional services, such as application acceleration, disk encryption, or virtualization, and positions the device to accept additional features that might be introduced in future software releases.

The NME-WAE family members have fixed memory capacity and cannot be upgraded. Thus, the system limits for the NME-WAE family are static. From the WAE appliance family, the 7341 and 7371 have fixed memory configurations. However, the WAE-512, WAE-612, and WAE-674 have configurable memory options, in that:

- The WAE-512 can be configured with 1 GB or 2 GB of memory.

- The WAE-612 can be configured with 2 GB or 4 GB of memory.

- The WAE-674 can be configured with 4 GB or 8 GB of memory.

For devices that support flexible memory configuration (such as the WAE-512, WAE-612, and WAE-674), higher levels of WAN bandwidth can be realized, along with an increase in the number of optimized TCP connections that can be handled concurrently by that device. For virtualization-capable platforms, a larger number of VBs can be supported. The WAVE appliance family models 274 and 474, like the network modules, are fixed configuration and do not support a memory upgrade, whereas the 574 model—like the WAE 512, 612, and 674—does support memory configuration (either 3 GB or 6 GB).

The amount of installed memory directly impacts what license is supported on each of the device models. The Transport license can be configured on any WAAS hardware model. WAAS hardware models that have 1 GB of memory or more (all do except the NME-WAE-302) can be configured with the Enterprise license, which allows the WAAS device to operate all of the Enterprise license features.

Previous versions of Cisco WAAS (version 4.0.x and version 4.1.x when using legacy mode compatibility) had distinct *core* and *edge* CIFS acceleration services. With legacy mode, a device with 1 GB of RAM can support only edge services for CIFS, whereas a device with 2 GB of RAM or more can support edge or core services, or both together. As of Cisco WAAS version 4.1.1, this deployment mode is no longer required unless interoperability with version 4.0.x is required. Generally speaking, most customers upgrade the entire network in a short and well-defined period of time and can take advantage of the simplified deployment model provided in 4.1.x, which does not have such restrictions.

Disk Capacity

Optimization services in the Cisco WAAS hardware family leverage both memory and disk. From a disk perspective, the larger the amount of available capacity, the larger the amount of optimization history that can be leveraged by the WAAS device during runtime operation. For instance, an NME-WAE-502 has 120 GB of physical disk capacity, of which 35 GB is available for use by DRE for compression history. With 35 GB of compression history, one can estimate the length of the compression history given WAN conditions, expected network utilization, and assumed redundancy levels.

Table 2-1 shows how the length of the compression history can be calculated for a particular WAAS device, along with an example. This example assumes a T1 WAN that is

Table 2-1   *Calculating Compression History*

Step	Action	Example Result
1	Convert WAN capacity to bytes (divide the number of bits per second by 8)	(T1 = 1.544 Mbps) / 8 = 193 KBps
2	Identify maximum WAN throughput for a given day (convert from seconds to minutes, to hours, to a single day)	193 KB/sec * 60 sec/min 11.58 MB/min * 60 min/hr 694.8 MB/hr * 24 hr/day Total 16.68 GB/day
3	Identify WAN throughput given utilization (multiply by the number of hours and utilization per hour)	(694.8 MB/hr * 8 hours) * 75% utilization = 4.168 GB (694.8 MB/hr * 16 hours) * 50% utilization = 5.56 GB Total = 9.72 GB/day
4	Identify WAN throughput given utilization and expected redundancy (multiply daily throughput by expected redundancy or compressibility)	9.72 GB/day * .25 (as .75 is 75% redundancy) = 2.43 GB/day
5	Calculate compression history (divide capacity by daily throughput)	Storage capacity of unit divided by daily throughput 35 GB / 2.43 GB/day = 14.4 days of history

75 percent utilized during business hours (75 percent utilization over 8 hours per day) and 50 percent utilized during nonbusiness hours (16 hours per day), and assumes that data traversing the network is 75 percent redundant (highly compressible by DRE). This table also assumes an NME-WAE-502 with 35 GB of allocated capacity for DRE compression history.

It is generally recommended that, at minimum, five days of compression history be available in a WAAS device to better ensure that substantial performance improvements are possible. In the example in Table 2-1, the NME-WAE-502 contains enough storage capacity to provide an effective compression history of two weeks. In most cases, users tend to access data that is newer more frequently, whereas older data is accessed less frequently. Because of this, having five days worth of compression history could even be considered overkill.

The disk capacity available to a WAAS device is split among five major components:

- **DRE compression history:** This capacity is used for storing DRE chunk data and signatures.

- **CIFS cache:** This capacity is preallocated on all devices using the Enterprise license.

- **Print services:** This capacity is preallocated for print spool capacity. Print services require that the Enterprise license be configured and that CIFS edge services be configured, which implies that legacy mode is being used. In cases where print services are configured, the 1 GB of disk capacity is allocated. Given that 1 GB is a fraction of the total storage capacity of a device, it is not accounted for in Table 2-2.

- **Platform services:** This capacity is preallocated for operating system image storage, log files, and swap space.

- **Virtual Blades:** This capacity is preallocated for any guest operating systems and applications that are installed to run in a WAAS VB.

Table 2-2 shows the storage allocation for each WAAS device for each of these components.

Number of Optimized TCP Connections

Each WAAS device has a static number of TCP connections that can be optimized concurrently. Each TCP connection is allocated memory and other resources within the system, and if the concurrently optimized TCP connection static limit is met, additional connections are handled in a pass-through fashion. Adaptive buffering (memory allocation) is used to ensure that more active connections are allocated additional memory, and less active connections are only allocated the memory they require.

The TCP connection limit of each WAAS device can be roughly correlated to the number of users supported by a given WAAS device model, but note that the number of TCP connections open on a particular node can vary based on user productivity, application behavior, time of day, and other factors. It is commonly assumed that a user will have 5 to

Table 2-2 *Disk Capacity Allocation per Platform*

Platform	Total Usable Capacity	DRE	CIFS	VBs
NME-WAE-302	80 GB	30 GB	0 GB	0 GB
NME-WAE-502	120 GB	35 GB	49 GB	0 GB
NME-WAE-522	160 GB	67 GB	67 GB	0 GB
WAVE-274	250 GB	40 GB	120 GB	35 GB
WAVE-474	250 GB	60 GB	120 GB	35 GB
WAE-512-1GB	250 GB RAID-1	60 GB	120 GB	0 GB
WAE-512-2GB	250 GB RAID-1	80 GB	100 GB	0 GB
WAVE-574-3GB	500 GB RAID-1	80 GB	120 GB	60 GB
WAVE-574-6GB	500 GB RAID-1	120 GB	120 GB	180 GB
WAE-612-2GB	300 GB RAID-1	100 GB	120 GB	0 GB
WAE-612-4GB	300 GB RAID-1	120 GB	120 GB	0 GB
WAE-674-4GB	600 GB RAID-5	120 GB	120 GB	120 GB
WAE-674-8GB	600 GB RAID-5	150 GB (with VB) 320 GB (without VB)	120 GB	200 GB (with VB) 0 GB (without VB)
WAE-7326	900 GB RAID-1	320 GB	230 GB	0 GB
WAE-7341	900 GB RAID-5	500 GB	230 GB	0 GB
WAE-7371	1500 GB RAID-5	1 TB	230 GB	0 GB

15 connections open at any given time, with roughly 6 to 10 of those connections requiring optimization. If necessary, policies can be adjusted on the WAAS Central Manager to pass through certain applications that might realize only a small amount of benefit from WAAS. This type of change could potentially help increase the number of users that can be supported by a particular WAAS device.

Table 2-3 shows the optimized TCP connection capacity per device model.

Table 2-3   *Optimized TCP Connection Capacity per Platform*

Network Module	Connection Capacity	Appliance	Connection Capacity
NME-WAE-302	250	WAVE-274	200
NME-WAE-502	500	WAVE-474	400
NME-WAE-522	800	WAE-512-1GB	600
		WAE-512-2GB	1200
		WAVE-574-3GB	750
		WAVE-574-6GB	1300
		WAE-612-2GB	1600
		WAE-612-4GB	4800
		WAE-674-4GB	2000
		WAE-674-8GB (with VB)	4000
		WAE-674-8GB (without VB)	6000
		WAE-7326	5000
		WAE-7341	12,000
		WAE-7371	50,000

The number of connections a typical user has in a location can be determined by using tools that exist in the operating system of the user's workstation. Although the estimate of six to ten optimized TCP connections is accurate for the broad majority of customers, those that wish to more accurately determine exactly how many connections a typical user has open at any given time can do so.

Microsoft provides two methods for determining the number of connections that are open on a given computer. The first is through the Command Prompt program **netstat**. By opening a Command Prompt window (click **Start > Run**, then type **cmd** and click **Ok**) and typing the command **netstat**, you can see a list of the open connections from the computer to all of the other endpoints to which that computer is connected. Notice the connections that are in the state of ESTABLISHED. These connections are currently open and in use and have not yet been closed. In many cases, the protocol associated with the connection is listed next to the foreign address, but some might not be. From here, you can identify the servers to which the user is connected and determine which should and should not be optimized. Figure 2-7 shows an example of the output of this command.

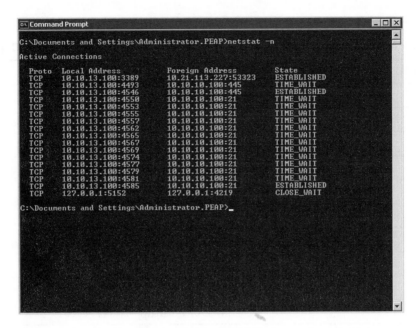

Figure 2-7   *Determining the Number of TCP Connections In Use Using netstat*

Another tool provided by Microsoft that (along with many other things) provides visibility into the number of TCP connections in use on a particular computer is Performance Monitor. Performance Monitor can be accessed by clicking **Start > Run** and typing **perfmon,** followed by clicking **Ok.** From within the Performance Monitor window, click the **+** sign, select the TCP performance object, and then add the **Connections Established** counter. Doing so shows you the number of connections established over time, and this data can even be exported for offline use. Figure 2-8 illustrates an example output from Performance Monitor showing the number of established TCP connections.

Linux, UNIX, and Macintosh provide similar tools to understand the number of connections that are open on a given computer. The **netstat** command is available on virtually any Linux distribution and is available in most UNIX platforms and versions of Apple's Macintosh OS/X operating system.

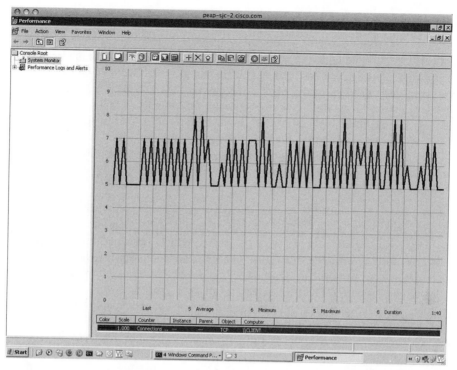

Figure 2-8   *Determining the Number of TCP Connections in Use Using Performance Monitor*

For the data center, the sum of all remote office TCP connections should be considered one of the key benchmarks by which the data center sizing should be done. Note that the largest Cisco WAAS device supports up to 50,000 optimized TCP connections—which is approximately 5,000 users (assuming ten TCP connections per user). For organizations that need to support a larger number of users or want to deploy the data center devices in a high-availability manner, multiple devices can be used. The type of network interception used (discussed in Chapter 4) determines the aggregate number of optimized TCP connections that can be supported by a group of Cisco WAAS devices deployed at a common place within the data center. Recommended practice dictates that sites that require high availability be designed with *N+1* availability in consideration relative to the number of maximum optimized TCP connections—that is, if 100,000 optimized TCP connections must be supported, the location should have a minimum of two WAE-7371 devices to support the workload, a third WAE-7371 device to handle failure of one of the devices, and use an interception mechanism such as WCCP or ACE that supports load-balancing of workload across the entire set of three devices. Other considerations apply, as discussed in Chapter 4.

WAN Bandwidth and LAN Throughput

WAAS devices are not restricted in software or hardware in terms of the amount of WAN bandwidth or LAN throughput supported. However, recommendations are in place to specify which WAAS device should be considered for a specific WAN environment. WAN bandwidth is defined as the amount of WAN capacity that the WAAS device can fully use when employing the full suite of optimization capabilities (this includes DRE, PLZ, TFO, and the other application acceleration capabilities). LAN throughput is defined as the maximum amount of application layer throughput (throughput as perceived by the users and servers) that can be achieved with the particular WAAS hardware model and an equivalent or more-powerful peer deployed at the opposite end of the network.

For some deployment scenarios, it is desired to use the Cisco WAAS devices only for TCP optimization. Cisco WAAS TFO provides a powerful suite of optimizations to better allow communicating nodes to "fill the pipe" (that is, fully leverage the available WAN bandwidth capacity) when the application protocol is not restricting throughput due to application-induced latency. Each Cisco WAAS device has a TFO-only throughput capacity that can be considered when WAAS devices are deployed strictly for TCP optimization only. This is recommended only for situations where compression, redundancy elimination, and application acceleration are not required, and the application throughput has been validated to be hindered only by the performance of the TCP implementation in use. This is common in some data center to data center applications—such as data replication or data protection—where the traffic that is sent is previously compressed, redundancy eliminated, or encrypted. TFO attempts to fully utilize the available bandwidth capacity, but might be hindered by congestion in the network (not enough available bandwidth) or performance impedance caused by application protocol chatter.

Table 2-4 shows the WAN bandwidth supported by each WAAS device model and the maximum LAN-side throughput and TFO-only throughput capacity. Note that other factors can influence these values and throughput levels can be achieved only when the link capacity available supports such a throughput level. For instance, a LAN throughput maximum of 150 Mbps is not possible on a Fast Ethernet connection; rather, a Gigabit Ethernet connection is required. Similarly for throughput speeds more than 1 Gbps, multiple 1-Gbps interfaces must be used.

The amount of bandwidth required per site is the sum of available WAN capacity that can be used at that site and not the sum of all WAN bandwidth for every connected peer. For instance, if a branch office has four bundled T1 links (totaling 6 Mbps of aggregate WAN throughput) but only two are used at any given time (high availability configuration), a device that supports 3 Mbps or more is sufficient to support the location.

Table 2-4 *WAN Bandwidth and LAN Throughput Capacity per WAAS Device*

WAAS Device Model	WAN Supported	LAN Throughput Maximum	TFO-Only Throughput Maximum
NME-WAE-302	4 Mbps	90 Mbps	100 Mbps
NME-WAE-502	4 Mbps	150 Mbps	150 Mbps
NME-WAE-522	8 Mbps	2000 Mbps	250 Mbps
WAVE-274	2 Mbps	90 Mbps	150 Mbps
WAVE-474	4 Mbps	90 Mbps	250 Mbps
WAE-512-1GB	8 Mbps	100 Mbps	350 Mbps
WAE-512-2GB	20 Mbps	150 Mbps	400 Mbps
WAVE-574-3GB	8 Mbps	100 Mbps	350 Mbps
WAVE-574-6GB	20 Mbps	150 Mbps	400 Mbps
WAE-612-2GB	45 Mbps	250 Mbps	450 Mbps
WAE-612-4GB	90 Mbps	350 Mbps	500 Mbps
WAVE-674-4GB	45 Mbps	250 Mbps	450 Mbps
WAVE-674-8GB (with or without VB)	90 Mbps	350 Mbps	500 Mbps
WAE-7326	155 Mbps	450 Mbps	600 Mbps
WAE-7341	310 Mbps	800 Mbps	800 Mbps
WAE-7371	1 Gbps	1.5 Gbps	1.8 Gbps

Similarly, if a data center has four DS-3 links (totaling 180 Mbps of aggregate WAN throughput) but uses only three at a time (*N+1* configuration), a device that supports 135 Mbps of WAN bandwidth or more is sufficient to support that location. The WAN throughput figures mentioned in the preceding table are (as discussed previously) not limited in hardware or software. In some cases, the WAN throughput that a device achieves might be higher than the values specified here. Those interested in using a smaller device to support a larger WAN link (for instance, qualifying a WAVE-274 for an 8-Mbps ADSL connection) are encouraged to test the system under those conditions and validate the performance prior to making a decision to use that specific platform.

Number of Peers and Fan-Out

Each Cisco WAAS device has a static system limit in terms of the number of concurrent peers it can actively communicate with at any one given time. When designing for a particular location where the number of peers exceeds the maximum capacity of an individual device, multiple devices can be deployed, assuming an interception mechanism that uses load balancing is employed (such as WCCPv2 or ACE; these are discussed in

Chapter 4). In cases where load balancing is used, TCP connections are distributed according to the interception configuration, thereby allowing for near-linear scalability increases in connection count, peer count, and WAN bandwidth, as devices are added to the pool. Load-balancing interception techniques are recommended when multiple devices are used in a location, and in general, an *N+1* design is recommended.

Peer relationships are established between Cisco WAAS devices during the automatic discovery process on the first connection optimized between the two devices. These peer relationships time out after ten minutes of inactivity (that is, no active connections are established and optimized between two peers for ten minutes). Each WAAS device supports a finite number of active peers, and when the peer relationship is timed out, that frees up peering capacity that can be reused by another peer. Data stored in the DRE compression history remains intact even if a peer becomes disconnected due to inactivity, unless the DRE compression history becomes full. In cases where the DRE compression history becomes full, an eviction process is initiated to remove the oldest set of data in the DRE compression history to make room for new data.

Table 2-5 shows the maximum number of concurrent peers supported per WAAS platform. If peers are connected beyond the allocated limit, the WAE permits the connections to be

Table 2-5   *Maximum Supported Peers per WAAS Device*

Network Module	Concurrent Peers	Appliance	Recommended Concurrent Peers
302	5	WAVE-274	35
502	15	WAVE-474	35
522	40	512-1GB	35
		512-2GB	70
		WAVE-574-3GB	35
		WAVE-574-6GB	70
		612-2GB	210
		612-4GB	350
		WAVE-674-4GB	100
		WAVE-674-8GB (no VB)	200
		WAVE-674-8GB (with VB)	200
		7326	600
		7341	1400
		7371	2800

established and gracefully degrades performance as needed. Connections associated with peers in excess of the maximum fan-out ratio are able to use the existing compression history but are not able to add new chunks of data to it. The end result is lower effective compression ratios for the connections using peers that are in excess of the specified fan-out ratio.

The number of peers supported by a device is typically the last factor that should be considered when sizing a solution for a particular location. The primary reason being that the WAN capacity or number of connections supported at the maximum concurrent peers specification is generally an order of magnitude higher than what the device can support. For instance, although a WAE-7371 can support up to 2800 peers, even if those peers were the NME-302 (each supporting 250 optimized TCP connections), it is not able to handle the 700,000 possible optimized TCP connections that all 2,800 NME-302s were attempting to optimize with it. It is best to size a location first based on WAN bandwidth capacity and TCP connections, and in most cases, only a simple validation that the number of peers supported is actually required.

Number of Devices Managed

Each Cisco WAAS deployment must have at least one Cisco WAAS device deployed as a Central Manager. The Central Manager is responsible for system-wide policy definition, synchronization of configuration, device monitoring, alarming, and reporting. The Central Manager can be deployed only on appliances and can be deployed in an active/standby fashion. When a certain WAAS device is configured as a Central Manager, it is able to, based on the hardware platform selected for the Central Manager, manage a maximum number of WAAS devices within the topology. Only WAAS appliances can be configured as Central Manager devices, and in high-availability configurations, each Central Manager WAE should be of the same hardware configuration. Although hardware disparity between Central Manager WAEs works, it is not a recommended practice given the difference in the number of devices that can be managed among the WAE hardware models. It should be noted that standby Central Managers (such a configuration is examined in Chapter 7) receive information in a synchronized manner identical to how accelerator WAAS devices do. Table 2-6 shows the maximum number of managed nodes that can be supported by each WAAS appliance when configured as a Central Manager.

Use of multiple WAAS devices configured as Central Manager devices do not increase the overall scalability in terms of the number of devices that can be managed. To manage a number of devices greater than the capacities mentioned in the preceding table, multiple autonomous Central Managers are needed. For instance, in an environment with 3000 devices, two separate instances of Central Manager are required, and each instance can be comprised of a single device or multiple devices deployed in a high availability primary/standby configuration.

Table 2-6 *Central Manager Scalability*

Appliance	Managed Nodes
WAVE-274	125
WAVE-474	250
WAE-512-1GB	500
WAE-512-2GB	750
WAVE-574-3GB	500
WAVE-574-6GB	1000
WAE-612-2GB	750
WAE-612-4GB	1500
WAE-674-4GB	1500
WAE-674-8GB	2000

Replication Acceleration

The WAE-7341 and WAE-7371 devices support a deployment mode called *Replication Accelerator*, which requires Cisco WAAS version 4.0.19, or a version newer than that from the 4.0 train. This mode of acceleration is used for data center to data center deployments where replication and backup acceleration is required, and when configured, adjusts the behavior of the WAAS device to allocate larger blocks of memory to a smaller number of connections, and minimizes the processing latency of DRE by using only memory for deduplication. Although only memory is used for DRE, the DRE data is persistent in that it is written to disk, but the disk is used only to reload the previous compression history. This enables WAAS to provide high levels of throughput necessary to accelerate replication and backup traffic between data centers.

The network typically found in these cases is high-bandwidth and relatively low latency (above 10–20 ms), where a significant amount of data needs to be moved from one location to another location in a short period of time. The performance and scalability metrics of replication accelerator mode are different than the performance and scalability metrics that would normally be considered for these devices when not deployed in replication accelerator mode and are documented in Table 2-7.

Table 2-7 *Replication Accelerator Performance and Scalability Metrics*

Appliance	WAN Bandwidth	LAN Throughput	Optimized TCP Connections	Concurrent Peers	DRE Capacity
WAE-7341	310 Mbps	800 Mbps	2500	4	12 GB
WAE-7371	1 Gbps	1.5 Gbps	5000	9	24 GB

Although all WAAS devices in a given network can be managed by a common Central Manager, WAAS devices configured in replication accelerator mode can only peer with other WAAS devices that are configured as replicator accelerator devices. Should intermediary application accelerator devices exist in the network path between two replication accelerator devices (this is generally rare, as replication accelerator devices are deployed between backend networks as opposed to the enterprise WAN), the application accelerator devices are not able to peer with replication accelerator devices.

Replication accelerator devices are commonly deployed on backend data center to data center networks and not the enterprise WAN due to the high bandwidth requirements. WAAS devices configured as replication accelerators are commonly found deployed as follows:

- **Directly attached to one or more storage array IP/Ethernet interfaces:** Such a deployment model dedicates the devices to optimize replication for that particular array and that particular interface.

- **Directly attached to one or more storage fabric switch or director IP/Ethernet interfaces:** Including the Cisco MDS 9000 family, such a deployment model enables the devices to optimize replication or backup traffic traversing fabrics in distant sites over IP.

- **Directly behind the data center interconnect device:** Such a deployment model enables optimization of any traffic between data centers. In this deployment model, replication accelerator should be carefully considered against the standard application accelerator mode which may be more applicable in cases where a large body of non-replication and nonbackup traffic exists.

Virtual Blades

The Cisco WAVE appliance family and the WAE-674 provide branch office virtualization capabilities that enable consolidation of remote branch office servers onto the WAAS device as a shared platform. Sizing for VBs should be done in conjunction with sizing for WAN optimization and application acceleration because the available disk capacity to support VBs and the number of VBs supported varies per platform based on the hardware configuration as shown in Table 2-8.

To accurately size a virtualization solution for a branch office, it is necessary to understand the minimum and recommended memory requirements to support the operating system and applications you plan to install on top of that operating system. Many vendors support installation of their server operating system onto systems with only 512 MB of memory, which increases the maximum number of VBs that can be installed on a WAAS device; however, many have requirements for larger amounts of memory.

Additionally, consider the disk capacity requirements necessary for each VB, and reconcile that amount with the total VB storage capacity of the platform selected for that given location. Even the smallest virtualization-capable WAAS device (the WAVE-274) supports 35 GB of disk capacity for VBs—meaning that with two VBs, configured, you have

Table 2-8 *VB Capacity*

Appliance	VB Disk Capacity	VB Memory Capacity	Maximum Number of VBs (512 MB RAM each)
WAVE-274	35 GB	1 GB	2
WAVE-474	35 GB	1 GB	2
WAVE-574-3GB	60 GB	1 GB	2
WAVE-574-6GB	180 GB	3 GB	6
WAE-674-4GB	120 GB	1 GB	2
WAE-674-8GB	200 GB	3 GB	6

approximately 17.5 GB of disk space for each. Storage capacity allocation is flexible in that you can allocate as much space as is available from the pool to any particular VB. However, you should ensure that you size the system for the location with enough capacity to support the current application and operating system requirements as well as future requirements. More information on configuration and deployment of VBs can be found in Chapter 10, "Branch Office Virtualization."

Summary

The Cisco Wide-Area Application Engine family includes three network modules for the Integrated Services Router and six appliance models spanning two desktop models and four rack-mount appliance models. This breadth of portfolio provides customers with the flexibility necessary to allocate the right platform for each network location where WAN optimization, application acceleration, and virtualization capabilities are needed. Four licenses are available for Cisco WAAS, including the Transport license (WAN optimization capabilities only), Enterprise license (all application accelerators except video, and certain other features), Video (Windows Media over RTSP stream splitting), and Virtual-Blades (branch office virtualization platform). Sizing of a Cisco WAAS solution requires consideration of a number of factors, including network conditions (WAN bandwidth and LAN throughput), number of users and concurrent optimized TCP connections, disk capacity and compression history, memory, concurrently connected peers, and virtualization requirements. By following the recommended guidelines for performance and scalability, a robust Cisco WAAS design can be realized, thereby allowing administrators to deploy the solution confidently to improve application performance over the WAN while enabling centralization and consolidation of costly infrastructure.

Chapter 3

Planning, Discovery, and Analysis

Proper planning is a critical step to any successful Wide Area Application Services (WAAS) deployment. Understanding the business goals, project goals, expected results, and technical requirements when deploying WAAS helps to ensure that the proposed solution and design can meet those goals. Most problems encountered during the deployment of a WAAS solution stem from not having a complete understanding of the environment in which the solution is deployed. Treating the existing infrastructure and its characteristics as part of the requirements for the solution helps prevent issues during the deployment phase of the project.

This chapter outlines the project content and critical requirements that you should collect as part of the WAAS design discovery and analysis process. The following sections cover the various different types of requirements—from user communities to IT infrastructure—that will help you define a final WAAS solution design.

Planning Overview

When planning a Cisco WAAS deployment, you need to take into consideration the different aspects of an infrastructure. Oftentimes, the planning process involves resources from multiple technology teams. Although Cisco WAAS is a network-integrated technology, it is not uncommon for the application, server, and storage teams to become involved in the project as stakeholders. In some cases, these teams drive the project and deployment of the WAAS solution.

The level of involvement from the various teams depends on the business or project purpose for deploying the solution. For example, if the primary (initial) driver behind deploying Cisco WAAS is to enable the consolidation of remote branch office file servers, storage, and data, then the file server and storage teams might be heavily involved in the project. In contrast, if the primary driver for the project is reducing wide-area network (WAN) bandwidth consumption in an effort to delay or prevent upgrading circuits, then the solution might involve only the network engineering teams and it might leverage only the application-agnostic features of the WAAS solution. The key point is that the first thing you should understand is what drives the need for the solution.

In addition to understanding the reason(s) for deploying the WAAS solution, you should have a keen understanding of the project timelines. The amount of time allocated for the project impacts how detailed you can be in your requirements collection and analysis activities. The complexity of the infrastructure is directly related to the amount of time that should be allocated for the planning stages of the project. It also helps to have an understanding of the change control processes that are affected by your design recommendations. For example, if you know that the Cisco IOS version on all of the branch office routers needs to be upgraded to support Web Cache Communication Protocol (WCCP) for off-path interception, you might want to make that recommendation as soon as possible to allow adequate time for scheduling and change control.

The remaining sections of this chapter discuss the specific types of requirements that you should collect prior to a deployment of WAAS, why it is important to collect each of those requirements, and which aspects of the WAAS design they directly or indirectly influence.

Planning Overview Checklist

The planning overview checklist includes a list of items that helps you understand what business reasons drive the project and which groups within the organization have a vested interest.

- Understand the business drivers that influence the need for a WAAS solution.

- Understand the project scope, timelines, and goals.

- Identify the resources and teams that need to be involved to ensure success.

- Identify the processes and procedures you need to follow or update during and after deployment of WAAS.

Requirements Collection and Analysis

There are many different types of requirements that range from business requirements to specific technical requirements, such as the WAN characteristics of the existing network infrastructure. Requirements can be collected using a variety of interactive techniques, including interviews and workshops, and noninteractive techniques, such as questionnaires and requests for static forms to be completed. Static information such as WAN characteristics (bandwidth and latency), device models, and software versions can be collected using standard templates, which typically do not require much interaction. However, interactive discussion is beneficial for collecting other types of requirements, such as network topology, traffic flows, and application use cases. Basically, an interactive requirements collection session should be used for any type of requirement for which the answer to a question generates more questions from you. Do not underestimate the value of involving the end user early in the process. A significant part of your design validation testing should include user- and application-specific use cases.

Wherever possible, you should develop requirements based on templates or "models." For example, instead of collecting requirements from every single site where you plan to deploy WAAS, you should identify a handful of representative sites, where each has characteristics similar to a larger grouping of sites. This might include some sites that are not the most obvious choice for deploying WAAS. The key is to make sure that your sample represents all of the significant variations inn your environment. This type of categorization greatly speeds the design process and enables the solution to be deployed in a consistent, standard manner. Figure 3-1 shows an example of collecting similar sites into a small number of groups.

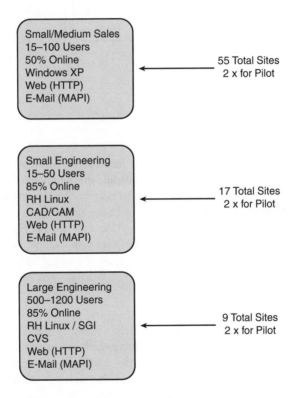

Figure 3-1 *Grouping Similar Sites into Representative Groups*

This technique can also carry over into your design development process. You can create different deployment models based on the specific requirements of the sites. For example, you might have one deployment model for all of your small- and medium-sized sales offices, and you might use another model for all of your large engineering facilities. Figure 3-2 shows an example of scaling your design using standardized deployment models.

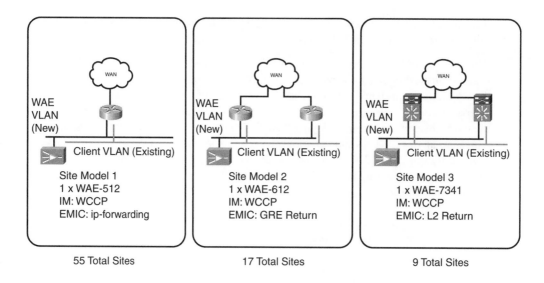

Figure 3-2 *Scalable Design Deployment Models*

Site Information

First and foremost, you need to understand the details of the locations where WAAS is deployed. Start by composing a list of sites, including the geographic location, site type, hours of operation, and number of users. This list becomes the foundation on which you build deployment models for your design. You should also note sites that do not fall into a standard configuration or deployment model. These sites need to be addressed on a case-by-case basis as part of the design. You can start with a simple list of sites, such as the example in Table 3-1.

Site Types

The site type refers to the primary business function performed at the site. For example, your site list might include sales offices, manufacturing locations, engineering facilities, and multipurpose campuses. Identifying the type of site is useful because it enables you to classify the types of users and other characteristics about the site. You might have an

Table 3-1 *Key Site Information*

Site Name	Site Type	Hours	Users/Concurrent
Austin, TX	Remote Sales	8–5, M–F	25/15

existing standard for the types of networking equipment that are deployed to a given type of site. Also, users at different types of sites usually require different sets of applications, which place different loads on the network infrastructure. Identifying these attributes can help you understand the sizing requirements for a site, which helps you to size the overall WAAS solution and develop different models for deployment.

User Population

There are different types of users, or populations, in every customer environment. Understanding the users that are affected by deploying Cisco WAAS helps with solution sizing and test use case development. The types of information that you should collect about the user community include:

- Location of users

- Location(s) of resources accessed by users

- Types of users (administrative, engineering, and so on)

- Client systems (traditional desktops or laptops, handheld devices, and so on)

- Common and critical applications and software versions

You should also try to determine the percentage of users concurrently online at any given point in time. You typically see that anywhere from 60 to 80 percent of the total number of users at a site are online and actively working. This helps you understand the total load that is placed on the WAAS infrastructure and provides better visibility into how the location should be sized.

Document each unique community of users for easy reference. These user community profiles help you when determining which sites should be considered for pilot testing and deployment.

Physical Environment

The WAAS solution has a physical footprint at each location where it is deployed. It is important not to overlook the physical requirements of the solution, particularly cabling. In some cases, it might be necessary to perform a physical site assessment as part of the planning and design process. The site assessment checklist should address the following areas:

- Determine whether the site has adequate power and cooling for the required number and type of WAAS devices. This should include appliances and available network module slots in routers when deploying the Network Module Enhanced–Wide-Area Application Engine (NME-WAE).

- Determine whether the site has available rack space for the number and type of WAAS appliances. Note that the 73xx series appliances require a four-post rack for installation.

- Identify a physically secure location for installation of the WAAS hardware.

- Determine whether there are available interfaces and cabling for the local-area network (LAN) and console interfaces of each WAAS device.

The physical requirements for each WAAS appliance can be found on cisco.com at the following location:

http://cisco.com/en/US/products/ps6474/products_data_sheets_list.html

Site Information Checklist

Before moving on to collect network infrastructure requirements, use the following site information checklist to ensure that all necessary site requirements have been collected.

- Create a list of basic site information including site type, hours of operation, and number of users.

- Develop user community profiles consisting of user types, applications used, and device types.

- Validate physical infrastructure through site surveys and assessments.

Network Infrastructure

The network infrastructure is one of the most important areas to focus on when designing a Cisco WAAS solution. This is where you spend the majority of your time from a requirements collection, analysis, and design perspective. Because WAAS is a network-integrated WAN optimization and application acceleration solution, having an in-depth understanding of the network infrastructure is required for a successful deployment. For example, the differences in the WAN characteristics of a low-bandwidth, high-latency satellite network and a high-speed, low-latency MPLS-based WAN are significant. These differences impact not only how the solution is sized and the configuration is tuned, but also the expectations that should be set for the amount of performance gain to be expected.

WAN Topology

You should develop a high-level WAN topology, specifically focusing on the portions of the WAN where WAAS is deployed. The topology should show all major network nodes and identify critical routing and switching devices, service providers, and network link types. This information gives you a "big picture" view of the network infrastructure, which helps you understand how the users and resources identified in the previous section are tied together. Figure 3-3 shows a sample high-level topology diagram.

If you are dealing with a large WAN infrastructure, you need to represent the different site types in your topology diagram. In Figure 3-3, the different site types are represented with an indication of how many actual sites of that type exist.

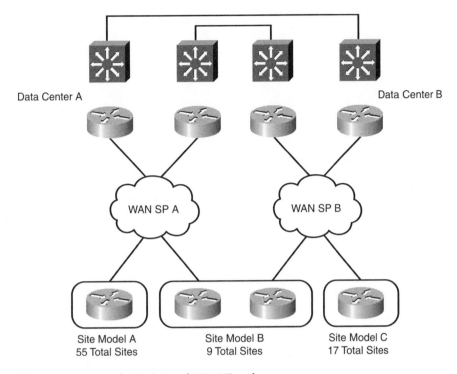

Figure 3-3   *Sample High-Level WAN Topology*

An important aspect of understanding the WAN infrastructure is collecting information about the bandwidth, latency, and loss characteristics. This information is used for sizing the hardware for each location and for tuning the configuration after the solution is deployed. For each site type, you should document the following:

■   Number and type of WAN links and any high-availability or load-balancing configurations including Hot Standby Router Protocol (HSRP), Virtual Router Redundancy Protocol (VRRP), Gateway Load Balancing Protocol (GLBP), or equal-cost multipath routing

■   WAN bandwidth, expected utilization, and committed rates

■   Round-trip time (RTT) latency

■   Packet loss (as a percentage)

You should also collect existing WAN utilization statistics so that you can compare a before and after picture of deploying Cisco WAAS. There are a number of methods for collecting WAN utilization and application performance statistics. Per-application statistics can be collected using NetFlow from the existing routers and switches in the network infrastructure. NetFlow statistics show WAN utilization on a per-application basis, which enables you to see which types of applications can potentially benefit the most from deploying Cisco WAAS. Figure 3-4 shows an example WAN utilization graph generated by NetQoS ReporterAnalyzer from NetFlow data.

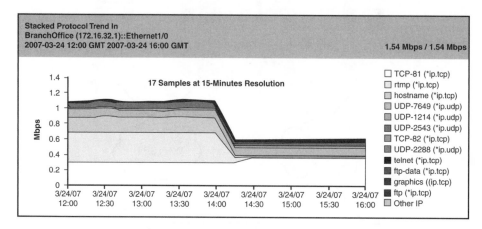

Figure 3-4   *Per-Application Link Utilization Using NetQoS ReporterAnalyzer*

Per-application response time statistics can also be useful when assessing the need for Cisco WAAS. Version 4.0.13 of Cisco WAAS added a feature called FlowAgent, which enables each WAAS device to export application response time statistics to a NetQoS SuperAgent device. The SuperAgent Aggregator is then able to compile the end-to-end response time characteristics of each application by comparing the measured response time from the data center with the measured response time from the branch, providing a more complete view of how the application performs. When SuperAgent is deployed prior to Cisco WAAS, existing application response time statistics are available to show the benefit of application performance for Cisco WAAS. Figure 3-5 shows an example NetQoS SuperAgent application response time report.

Note   More information on using Cisco WAAS with NetQoS SuperAgent is available on cisco.com at http://tinyurl.com/nv7uww and is also discussed in chapter 8, "Configuring WAN Optimization."

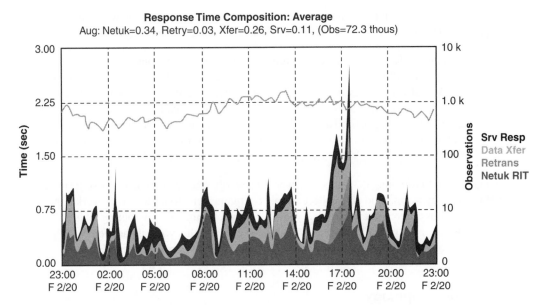

Figure 3-5   *NetQoS SuperAgent Application Response Time Report*

Remote Office Topology

After you establish a high-level overview of the WAN network topology, you can dive into the site-level network infrastructure details. For each type of site identified, a site-level analysis should include the physical and logical network topology, the make and model of networking equipment, and the associated software versions. It is also important to remember the LAN infrastructure because the WAAS devices physically integrate with the LAN environment.

As with the site information requirements, you should generate a set of remote office models. It is not necessary to generate a topology diagram for every remote office, but instead create a template based on your site information templates. The network topology and equipment information should provide another level of detail for the site topology templates. Make sure to inquire about the use of firewalls or other deep-packet inspection technologies, because you need to consider integration with these types of technologies in your design.

A short description for each remote office type should be provided. The following example provides a brief description of the key characteristics of the topology:

> For Site Model 2, the WAN access router terminates multiple physical circuits, each with a single PVC back to a different headend data center. The WAN bandwidth for Site Model 2 is 1.536 Mbps. For LAN connectivity, the WAN access router has a FastEthernet connection to a LAN switch. The LAN switch functions purely at Layer 2. 802.1Q trunking is used across the FastEthernet connection to carry multiple virtual local area networks (VLAN). The default gateway for devices on any VLAN is the IP address of the WAN access router for that particular VLAN.

In addition to topology diagrams, equipment lists, software versions, and a description of the topology, you should also collect sample configurations from the key network components. It is also recommended that you collect the output from the routing table on each device. The configuration and routing table output helps you validate your understanding of the site and any additional features or configuration items of interest.

Data Center Topology

After you collect the requirements for the various types of remote offices, you can address each data center. In recent years there has been a push for standardization in the data center, but it is still common for organizations to have multiple data centers deployed using different topologies and different types of networking equipment. It is also normal for data centers in different geographical locations to leverage different WAN transport providers, each one with varying service levels and capabilities. Finally, data centers can be designed for different purposes altogether. For example, some data centers might host internal applications and services, whereas other data centers might be built to support external Internet applications such as e-commerce. It is recommended that you address WAAS data center integration one data center at a time.

As with the remote offices, you need a detailed topology diagram for each data center, including equipment models, software versions, sample configuration, and so on. Figure 3-6 shows a sample data center topology diagram.

Another area to pay close attention to in the data center is the use and placement of other intelligent network technologies. This includes items such as firewalls, Intrusion Detection System (IDS) Intrusion Prevention System (IPS), content switches, Network-Based Application Recognition (NBAR), content-caching devices, and any other device that interacts with Layer 4 through Layer 7 or can directly manipulate the flow of traffic. Any other technology that validates, manipulates, examines, or otherwise relies on information in the transport and application layers contained within packets should be well documented. Because WAAS also interprets and manipulates TCP traffic for optimization purposes, you need to address integration with these technologies as part of your WAAS design. Chapter 5, "Branch Office Network Integration," and Chapter 6, "Data Center Network Integration," provide a detailed discussion of placement considerations and integration with other intelligent network technologies.

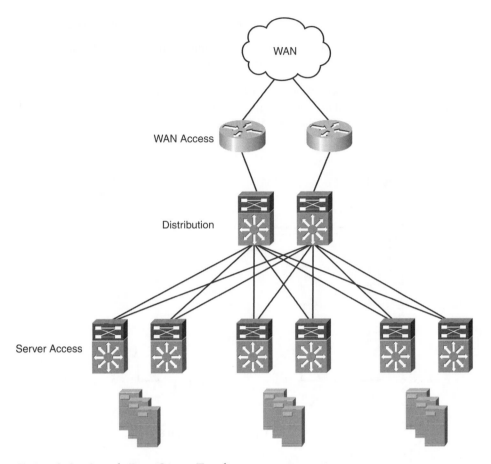

Figure 3-6   *Sample Data Center Topology*

Traffic Flows

Understanding traffic flows, both in a single site and between multiple sites, is important. WAAS relies on in-path and off-path interception techniques to receive traffic for optimization. Regardless of the interception mechanisms chosen for the design, the underlying assumption is that WAAS must be inserted into the data path between the client and server on both sides of a network link and for both directions of traffic flow. This means that you have to understand how traffic flows between clients and servers over the existing network infrastructure. For each site profile that is created, you should map the various different traffic flow patterns over the network topology. Be sure to explicitly call out the following characteristics:

■   Default gateway selection: How do host systems at each location select a default gateway? Are default gateway redundancy techniques such as HSRP, VRRP, or GLBP used? Is equal-cost multipath routing used?

■   Which paths are preferred when multiple entry and exit points exist for a site?

■   How do traffic flows change when there is a failure in the network? What is the expectation of the WAAS solution during each type of failure?

You should document each major type of flow with a source and destination site, the capacity of the flow, and the performance requirements of the flow. Figure 3-7 shows the sample WAN topology with the major flow types.

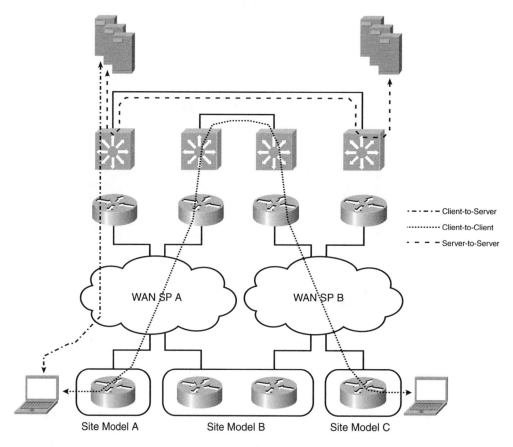

Figure 3-7   *WAN Topology with Flow Types*

Figure 3-7 shows three different flow types:

■   Client-to-server

■   Client-to-client

■   Server-to-server

Each type of flow likely has different capacity and performance requirements. Table 3-2 shows some common characteristics for different types of flow.

Table 3-2 *Flow Type Characteristics*

Flow Type	Characteristics
Client-to-server	Many-to-few relationship. Upload capacity requirements are generally low for most use cases. Download capacity requirements are relatively high for most use cases. Example: Remote file access or web browsing.
Client-to-client	Many-to-many relationship. Upload and download capacity requirements are usually equal. Example: Peer-to-peer file sharing or Voice over IP (VoIP).
Server-to-server	Few-to-few relationship. Asynchronous or synchronous flows. Generally high-capacity requirements. Example: Server replication or N-tier application architectures.

In addition to the source and destination of the flows, you should also have an understanding of the number of concurrent flows. This is most commonly derived from the number of users at a site and the percentage of concurrently online users. In general, most enterprise users have between 5 and 10 concurrent established TCP connections that require or can benefit from optimization. This is only a general observation and should be validated in your environment. This number can also vary by the type of user. For example, an engineer who frequently works on collaborative projects with many colleagues around the world might have more concurrent connections than does a graphic designer who works mostly with local files.

The importance of understanding how traffic flows over the network infrastructure cannot be overstated. Understanding the various flows helps you determine where in the network infrastructure WAAS devices should be placed and which interception options are available. Each identified flow pattern should be tested to ensure that the proposed design performs as expected.

Network Infrastructure Checklist

Before moving on to collect application-specific requirements, use the following network infrastructure checklist to ensure that all necessary network infrastructure requirements have been collected.

- Identify the physical and logical network topologies.
- Identify the existing and planned IP addressing schemes.
- Identify the hardware models of all relevant network equipment (routers and switches).
- Identify the standard IOS versions in use.

- Identify the WAN characteristics for all sites where WAAS will be deployed.

- Identify the transport technologies in use.

- Identify the WAN and LAN bandwidth for all sites where WAAS will be deployed.

- Identify the RTT latency for all sites where WAAS will be deployed.

- Identify the packet loss percentage (if any) for all links that optimized traffic will traverse.

- Collect sample device configurations for all relevant network devices.

- Identify the existing routing policy.

- Document traffic flows across the existing network topology.

Application Characteristics

It is common for enterprises to have hundreds or even thousands of different applications running across the network. Your requirements gathering should focus on the key applications used by the business. Consider collecting information for the top *n* applications, where *n* is some reasonable number such as 5 or 10. In many cases, the WAAS solution might be targeted at improving the performance of a specific application or it might be targeted to improve the performance for a broad set of applications. Understanding these applications in depth is important, because they have the biggest impact on the design and might be the driving force behind the funding of the project. You need to understand the network characteristics of the critical applications in your environment. This might require involving the specific application team who supports the application to understand how it was deployed. This can include information such as whether or not the application is performing compression or encryption. You should collect the following key pieces of information about each application:

- Application name

- Vendor

- Version, including patches and service packs

- Locations deployed

- Protocols and ports used

- Network capacity and performance requirements

- Number of concurrent connections used by the application

- Whether or not native application compression is enabled

- Whether or not native application encryption is enabled

The network capacity and performance requirements are from the perspective of the application. For example, what are the throughput and response-time requirements for a given application? Understanding the performance requirements of the applications helps you identify which WAAS optimizations (such as compression) provide the most benefit.

Additional requirements are also collected for applications for which WAAS provides application-specific acceleration, such as Common Internet File System (CIFS) acceleration; these are discussed in Chapter 9, "Configuring Application Acceleration."

Application Requirements Checklist

Before moving on to collect WAAS application optimizer requirements, use the following application requirements checklist to ensure that all necessary application requirements have been collected.

- Identify the top *n* applications that are critical to the success of the project.

- Evaluate the network characteristics of critical applications.

- Develop application-specific use cases for lab validation and pilot testing.

- Define minimum network capacity and performance requirements.

- Review existing baseline performance statistics.

Application Optimizer Requirements

WAAS provides both application-agnostic WAN optimization and application-specific acceleration (through the use of application optimizers [AO]). When using AOs, it is important to understand how applications are configured or how they behave to provide the highest degree of performance improvement. This section examines each of the AOs provided by WAAS and the additional pieces of information that should be collected for each. Each of the AOs listed here are covered in detail in Chapter 9.

CIFS Accelerator

The CIFS Application Optimizer (CIFS AO) in Cisco WAAS requires the collection and analysis of additional information by the team designing the solution. This additional information is used for configuring advanced features and functionality such as content prepositioning. Because the CIFS AO provides application-specific acceleration, it is also important to understand which vendor implementations you are dealing with both from the perspective of the client and from the server. The level of acceleration the CIFS AO is capable of providing depends on the behavior of the specific CIFS implementation used. Areas that you should address as part of the file services requirements include the following:

- The client operating system versions being used, including the service pack level

- The types of file servers that are accelerated using the CIFS AO

- The type of content that is served from the file servers

- The CIFS TCP ports that are allowed and supported

- The namespace used for the file services environment (This should include not only global namespace technologies such as Distributed File System (DFS), but also whether a file server name maps to multiple IP addresses/interfaces.)

- The role or function (general file services, software distribution, and so on) of the file server that is accelerated

The amount of data hosted by the origin file servers also has an impact on the sizing of the WAAS device for each location. WAAS devices deployed near clients provide a separate CIFS object cache used by the CIFS AO for serving local copies of previously cached content. The CIFS object cache is typically sized to hold what is considered the active working set for a site. The active working set of data is the amount of data that is currently accessed and updated by users at a site. The active working set is typically up to 5 percent of the total data footprint for a site, as only the most frequently and recently used content needs to be cached. Objects that are not cached are fetched in an accelerated manner, which still yields LAN-like performance.

The CIFS AO preposition functions enable you to prepopulate the CIFS AO object cache in remote office WAAS devices with frequently accessed content. This feature is commonly used in cases where remote clients access software distribution packages or updates located on centralized file servers. If you anticipate using the file server preposition function of WAAS, the following additional requirements should be collected:

- The total size of the content to be prepositioned

- The number of objects (directories and files) to be prepositioned

- The frequency that preposition content is scheduled to change or the frequency that it should be refreshed in the branch office WAAS devices

Advanced Features

Several advanced features are used in file service environments today, some of which you need to take into consideration when deploying Cisco WAAS. You should document the use and implementation details of the following advanced features as part of your requirements collection:

- **Microsoft Volume Shadow Copy Services (VSS):** Provides a mechanism for creating point-in-time copies of data

- **Microsoft Access-Based Enumeration (ABE):** Filters the folders visible to a user based on the user's access rights

- **Dynamic shares:** Dynamically associate users with a specific share based on the user's credentials

■ **SMB Signing (also known as digital signatures):** Cryptographic integrity mechanism used to sign messages between clients and servers for the purpose of authentication and message integrity validation

File Services Utilization

For each file server that is accelerated using the CIFS AO, you need to know the peak number of concurrent CIFS sessions terminated on that file server. This information is used for solution sizing. On a Microsoft Windows file server, this information can be collected using the Microsoft Performance Monitor (Perfmon) utility shown in Figure 3-8.

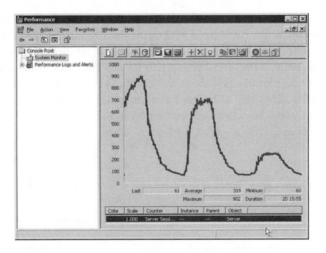

Figure 3-8   *Microsoft Performance Monitor*

File Services Requirements Checklist

The following checklist consolidates the file services requirements recommended for planning a successful Cisco WAAS deployment:

■ Identify the client OS versions being used.

■ Identify the type of file servers and OS versions used.

■ Identify the size of the active data set for cache sizing.

■ Understand the namespace and client use cases.

■ Baseline the existing file server performance for concurrent sessions and open files.

■ Identify the types of applications used by clients when accessing data stored on CIFS file servers.

■ Identify sets of commonly used data (such as software image files, video-on-demand files, home directories, or frequently-accessed documents) that might be good candidates for prepositioning.

MAPI Accelerator

The Messaging Application Programming Interface Application Optimizer (MAPI AO) provides several performance improvements for Microsoft Exchange email traffic, including:

- Reduced send and receive time for e-mail messages and improved response time for interactive control operations

- Faster downloads of Outlook Address Book (OAB) while significantly reducing bandwidth consumption

The MAPI AO works in conjunction with the EndPoint Mapper (EPM) AO to identify and accelerate Microsoft Exchange e-mail traffic. By default, the MAPI protocol negotiates the TCP ports used between the client and server. The client first opens a Microsoft Remote Procedure Call (MS-RPC) connection on TCP port 135, after which the client and server exchange information about the specific application requested using a unique identifier (UUID). After the TCP ports are negotiated, subsequent connections from the client are made using the negotiated port. Figure 3-9 shows an example of the MS-RPC negotiation process.

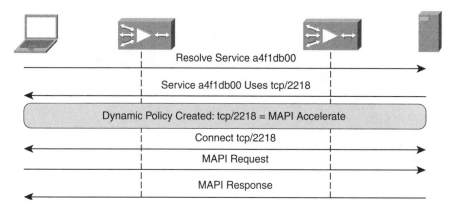

Figure 3-9 *MS-RPC Transport Negotiation*

The EPM AO monitors MS-RPC connections and creates dynamic policy entries based on the UUID negotiated between the client and server. The following MS-RPC applications are identified as part of the default Application Traffic Policy (ATP) in WAAS:

- Microsoft Exchange Directory Referral (RFR) Interface

- Microsoft SQL Server

- Microsoft Exchange Server STORE Electronic Messaging System Microsoft Data Base (EMSMDB) Interface (MAPI)

- Microsoft NT Directory Replication Service (DRS) Interface

- Microsoft NT File Replication Service (FRS)

- Microsoft Exchange Directory Name Service Provider Interface (NSPI) Proxy

As with the CIFS AO, it is important to understand the client Microsoft Outlook and server Microsoft Exchange versions used in your environment. In addition, it is important to understand whether features such as encryption or nonstandard transport protocols are configured.

MAPI Requirements Checklist

The following checklist includes the MAPI requirements recommended for planning a successful Cisco WAAS deployment:

- Identify the Microsoft Outlook client version(s) used.

- Identify the Microsoft Exchange server version(s) used.

- Identify the protocol (MAPI, RPC-over-HTTP, RPC-over-HTTPS, and so on) used to communicate between the client and server.

- Identify whether native MAPI encryption is used.

- Identify whether Exchange was deployed using a static TCP port in lieu of the default dynamic port.

HTTP Accelerator

The HTTP Application Optimizer (HTTP AO) accelerates web-based applications using the following functions:

- Decouples the WAN-side and LAN-side segments of the client to server TCP connection through connection reuse

- Provides "hints" to the compression process resulting in better compression and improved overall compression efficiency

- Identifies HTTP proxy connections to HTTPS servers and disables compression on encrypted traffic that follows

The HTTP AO does not require any changes to the web client or server applications to work. By default, TCP ports 80, 8080, 8000, 8001, and 3128 are classified as HTTP traffic.

HTTP Requirements Checklist

The ports used by HTTP-based applications and other application information should be collected as part of the HTTP AO requirement checklist:

- Identify the HTTP version(s) used.

- Identify any hosts using nonstandard TCP ports for HTTP-based applications.

- Identify the presence of any proxy servers or web caches in the environment.

NFS Accelerator

The Network File System (NFS) Application Optimizer (NFS AO) provides acceleration for environments where NFS over TCP is used. NFSv3, which is the most commonly implemented version of NFS, is optimized with protocol specific optimizations in addition to TCP transport optimizations. The NFS AO is best suited for bulk transfer applications, as opposed to transactional applications.

NFS Requirements Checklist

To aid in determining the fit for the NFS AO in your environment, use the following checklist:

- Identify the version(s) of NFS used.

- Identify the transport protocol(s) used (TCP or User Datagram Protocol [UDP]).

- Identify the NFS server operating system type(s) and version(s) used.

- Identify which applications use NFS.

- Identify the typical traffic patterns and use cases (transactional versus bulk transfer, and so on).

Video Accelerator

The Video Application Optimizer (Video AO) performs local "splitting" of live video streams sourced from a Microsoft Windows Media Server or compatible Content Delivery Network (CDN). When multiple users at a location are watching the same live stream, WAAS ingests a single live stream across the WAN and splits into as many local streams on the LAN as there are users watching the video. The obvious benefit to this approach is an N times reduction in the WAN bandwidth requirements for live streaming, where N is equal to the number of simultaneous users requesting the same live stream. In addition, by only pulling a single live stream across the WAN, the load is reduced on the origin Windows Media Server.

Video Requirements Checklist

The following checklist helps you identify key information about the video deployment in your environment.

- Identify the type(s) of video protocols used.

- Identify the Windows Media Server version.

- Identify the number of users in a site and expected number of concurrent live streams.

- Identify the number of video on demand (VoD) files, their average size, and typical lifespan.

- Identify the access method(s) for VoD files.

- Identify the access method(s) for live video streams.

- Identify the video encoding rate for live streams.

- Identify whether the WAN has multicast enabled.

SSL Accelerator

The SSL Application Optimizer (SSL AO) provides the capability to decrypt and re-encrypt Secure Sockets Layer (SSL) traffic, which enables the full benefit of WAAS compression on SSL traffic between a client and server. The SSL AO can accelerate SSL Version 3 (SSLv3) and Transport Layer Security Version 1 (TLSv1) protocols. It bypasses requests that use SSLv2 and TLSv1.1/1.2. The Cisco WAAS optimizations are transparent and automatic, and do not require any configuration changes to either the client or server environments. The SSL AO fully preserves the existing enterprise security architecture.

Implementing the WAAS SSL AO requires specific information from the existing client and server SSL environments.

SSL Requirements Checklist

The following checklist assists you with collecting the SSL information necessary to successfully deploy the SSL AO in your environment.

- Identify the SSL and TLS versions used.

- Identify the hostnames, IP addresses, and ports of the servers you want to accelerate.

- Identify the cipher suites used by the SSL servers you want to accelerate.

- Identify which Certificate Authority (CA)—internal or external—is used for site identify verification.

- Identify which CAs are trusted by the client web browsers.

- Identify and collect the certificates and private keys for servers you want to accelerate.

- Identify whether Online Certificate Status Protocol (OCSP) is used for certificate revocation, and if so, identify the OCSP responders.

- Identify if wildcard certificates or keys can be used.

- Identify whether client certificate authentication, authorization, or both are required.

- Identify whether encryption of data at rest (that is, cached data on disk) is required.

Replication Accelerator

The Replication Accelerator feature in WAAS is not a specific Application Optimizer (AO), but a device mode used for optimizing data center to data center storage replication and backup traffic. Because the Replication Accelerator device mode is limited to optimizing storage replication and backup traffic, the following custom requirements should be collected:

■ Identify the types of storage arrays used in for replication.

■ Identify whether replication traffic is Fibre Channel over IP (FCIP) versus native (array-based).

■ Identify the number of data centers used for storage replication.

■ Identify the amount of bandwidth dedicated for storage replication traffic.

■ Identify the type of storage replication traffic (SRDF/A, SnapMirror, FCIP, and so on).

■ Identify whether or not replication traffic is natively compressed, encrypted, or both.

■ Identify whether the storage replication traffic is TCP- or UDP-based.

■ Identify the number of concurrent TCP connections established between replication devices.

■ Identify the recovery point objective (RPO) and recovery time objective (RTO) requirements for storage.

■ Identify link bandwidth and latency.

Platform Requirements

Platform requirements address the basic information required for configuration of WAAS devices. This includes information such as hostname standards, DNS domain membership, NTP server IP addresses, IP addressing schemes, and so on. This type of information can be collected using standard request forms and templates.

Platform Requirements Checklist

The following platform requirements checklist helps identify the basic information needed to get each WAAS activated and communication on the network.

■ Identify the IP address and subnet mask that will be used for each WAAS device.

■ Identify the IP address of the default gateway that will be used for each WAAS device.

■ Identify the DNS domain name(s) that will be configured on the WAAS devices (up to three).

■ Identify the DNS server IP addresses that will be configured on the WAAS devices.

- Identify the NTP server IP addresses that will be configured on the WAAS devices. Alternatively, for deployments where NTP is not used (not recommended), identify the time zone for each WAAS device.

Scalability Requirements

The overall scalability of your WAAS design is determined by the hardware you deploy and the network interception mechanisms you choose. Chapter 2, "Cisco WAAS Architecture, Hardware, and Sizing," provides the capabilities of each WAAS device model. It is important to understand the scalability boundaries of your design. The scalability requirements you identify help define which choices you make as part of the design development process. As you size the WAAS solution, make sure you allow some room for organic growth of the solution, which can come in many forms including simple hiring and corporate acquisition.

Scalability Requirements Checklist

The following scalability requirements checklist assists you with collecting key scalability requirements for the Cisco WAAS design. Be sure to document not only the current scalability requirements, but future scalability requirements as well.

- Determine how many concurrent users the design should scale to handle, and how many concurrent TCP connections the design should scale to handle.

- Determine how many sites the design should scale to handle.

- Determine how many additional users per site the design should scale to handle to accommodate future growth.

- Determine how many new sites the design should scale to handle.

Availability Requirements

Availability requirements influence the design and configuration by determining how much redundancy is built into the individual components and the design as a whole. Availability requirements can also influence the hardware selection and solution sizing decisions. Availability requirements should address the following areas:

- Acceptable levels of service loss

- Acceptable levels of capacity loss

- Expected failure detection and response times

- Automatic or manual recovery expectations

Availability requirements are also a good place to document various failure test cases. These test cases can be used to validate the resiliency of the proposed design through lab validation and testing.

Availability Checklist

The Availability Checklist that follows includes requirements that you use to determine the amount of redundancy needed in the Cisco WAAS design.

■ Identify any capacity requirements that should be upheld even when a failure occurs.

■ Identify the failure detection and response time requirements.

■ Identify the device component availability requirements.

■ Identify the device availability requirements.

Management Requirements

The requirements for management of the WAAS solution are sometimes overlooked. "Management" is a somewhat general term that can be interpreted in many different ways. WAAS includes a robust central management platform (discussed in Chapter 7, "System and Device Man"); however, any "good network citizen" must integrate cleanly into the broader IT infrastructure management elements that are present, along with operational processes and procedures. What you are mostly interested in determining here is which NMS platform(s) the WAAS solution needs to integrate with and which protocol interfaces are used. WAAS 4.1 supports the following management protocols:

■ WAAS Central Manager and XML-API (discussed in Chapters 7 through 9)

■ SNMP v1/2c/3 (discussed in Chapter 7)

■ Syslog (discussed in Chapter 7)

■ FlowAgent (limited to NetQoS SuperAgent, discussed in Chapter 8)

After you understand the systems and protocol interfaces required, you can collect more practical information for the device-specific configurations.

Cisco WAAS Central Manager and XML-API

WAAS devices naturally integrate with the WAAS Central Manager (CM) through the CMS service. This and a robust overview of the CM are covered in Chapter 7. The XML-API is also covered in detail in Chapter 7, and WAN optimization and application acceleration-specific elements are covered in Chapters 8 and 9, respectively. In terms of the XML-API, it is recommended that you identify any independent software vendor (ISV) systems that might integrate through this API. From there, it is important to validate that the software version of the system is capable of supporting WAAS integration through the XML-API.

SNMP Trap/Inform Routing

SNMP traps/informs generated by Cisco WAAS can be routed to various NMS devices. Up to four trap/inform destinations can be specified. Table 3-3 can be used for collecting SNMP trap/inform types and destinations. It is best to collect this information prior to deployment, and configuration can be synchronized either through standard CLI configuration templates or through the use of device groups as described in Chapter 7.

Table 3-3 *SNMP Trap/Inform Routing*

Device Name	IP Address	Community String
zas01.cisco.com	10.88.88.88	notsopublic

SNMP Community Strings

Cisco WAAS supports read-only SNMP objects for querying the status of each WAAS device and collecting utilization statistics. The following SNMP Management Information Bases (MIB) are supported by Cisco WAAS (this list is also covered in more detail in Chapter 7):

- ACTONA-ACTASTOR-MIB

- CISCO-CDP-MIB

- CISCO-CONFIG-MAN-MIB

- CISCO-CONTENT-ENGINE-MIB

- CISCO-ENTITY-ASSET-MIB

- CISCO-SMI

- CISCO-TC

- ENTITY-MIB

- EVENT-MIB

- HOST-RESOURCES-MIB

- MIB-II

- SNMP-COMMUNITY-MIB

- SNMP-FRAMEWORK-MIB

- SNMP-NOTIFICATION-MIB

- SNMP-TARGET-MIB

- SNMP-USM-MIB

- SNMPV2-MIB

- SNMP-VCAM-MIB

One of the important pieces of information exposed through SNMP is the WAAS Alarm Book, which provides an explanation for all types of alarms generated by WAAS and is accessed using SNMP using the CISCO-CONTENT-ENGINE-MIB. The WAAS Alarm Book is available on Cisco.com at the following location:

http://www.cisco.com/cgi-bin/tablebuild.pl/waas41

Table 3-4 can be used for collecting SNMP community string information.

Table 3-4   *SNMP Community Strings*

Community	Notes
notsopublic	Traps only

Syslog Servers

Syslog messages generated by Cisco WAAS can be routed to various NMS devices. Up to four syslog destinations can be specified. The WAAS Error Message Book contains an explanation and proposed action for the syslog messages generated by WAAS. The Error Message Book is available on Cisco.com at the following location:

http://www.cisco.com/cgi-bin/tablebuild.pl/waas41

Table 3-5 can be used for collecting syslog server information. Similar to SNMP, it is helpful to have this information available prior to the deployment, and configuration of Syslog servers can be synchronized through CLI configuration templates or CM device group settings.

Table 3-5   *Syslog Routing*

Log Level	Server Name	IP Address
7 (debug)	sys01.cisco.com	10.44.72.189

Management Requirements Checklist

The management requirements checklist assists you with the collection of network management requirements needed to successfully monitor and manage the Cisco WAAS deployment.

■ Understand which management systems you are required to integrate WAAS into.

■ Identify the specific management protocols you need to configure.

■ Collect the information required to configure support for the various management protocols.

Security Requirements

There are two primary aspects to the security of the WAAS solution: data encryption and management access control.

WAAS 4.1 includes encryption for the cached content on a WAAS device configured with the Enterprise license. The disk encryption feature is configurable on a device-by-device basis and can be configured on a large number of devices simultaneously using device groups in the CM. From a requirements perspective, all you need to do is identify the sites where disk encryption should be enabled, which is usually in remote offices only. In most cases, WAAS devices deployed in campus or data center locations are physically secured, thus removing the need to encrypt the disk drives; however, in environments where the information is sensitive, or previously encrypted (and accelerated through the SSL AO), it might be beneficial to employ disk encryption on all devices.

Cisco WAAS supports multiple methods for authenticating administrative users, including Terminal Access Controller Access-Control System (TACACS), Remote Authentication Dial In User Service (RADIUS), and Windows Authentication. AAA Accounting is also supported using TACACS. WAAS also supports Role-Based Access Control (RBAC), which allows you to further limit what administrative functions a user can perform, and which WAAS devices (or groups of devices) they can be performed on. RBAC is based on the following two concepts:

■ **Roles:** Defines a set of objects (configuration pages) in the Central Manager GUI that a user can access

■ **Domains:** Defines a set of WAAS devices or device groups that a user can access

A user account can be assigned to one or more roles and domains. When no roles or domains are assigned to a user account, the built-in "default" role is applied, which provides the user with no access to any of the Central Manager objects. Figure 3-10 shows the Central Manager roles configuration page.

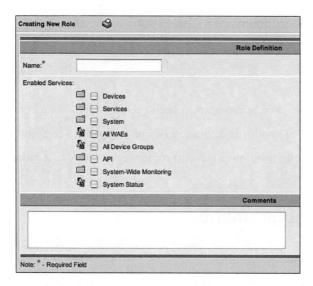

Figure 3-10   *Configuring Central Manager Roles*

The requirements you need to collect/define fall into three primary areas are:

■   Security server information

■   Role definitions

■   Domain definitions

■   User groups

The security server information includes information such as IP addresses and shared encryption keys. For example, you can define up to three TACACS servers or up to five RADIUS servers for authentication.

For roles definitions, you need to define different classes of users, and which portions of the Central Manager GUI they should have access to. Table 3-6 provides a format for defining this information.

Similar to the role definitions, you also need to define the domain a user belongs to. By default, a user has access to all of the WAAS devices registered to the Central Manager. If you have a requirement to limit which devices a user (or group of users) can access, you need to create one or more domain. Table 3-7 provides a format for defining this information.

Table 3-6 *Central Manager Role Definitions*

Role Name	Description	CM Pages Required
NA-Admins	North America Admins	My WAN > Report My WAN > Monitor > *<all>* Device Groups > AllDevicesGroup > Configure Device Groups > AllDevicesGroup > Monitor

Table 3-7 *Central Manager Domain Definitions*

Domain Name	Entry Type	Description	Devices/DeviceGroups
NorthAmerica	Device Groups	All devices in NA	NAEastCoast NACentral NAWestCoast

Security Requirements Checklist

The Security Requirements Checklist ensures that you understand the security requirements of the environment you are deploying WAAS in. These requirements give you an indication of which advanced security features are required in your deployment.

- Determine which devices should be configured with disk encryption.

- Identify the authentication, authorization, and accounting method you use.

- Collect the AAA server information (IP addresses, encryption keys, and so on).

- Determine which users need access to the WAAS infrastructure.

- Develop roles and domains based on the type and scope of administrative access required.

Virtualization Requirements

The Virtual Blade Technology feature provides the capability to host guest operating systems, applications, and services on Cisco Wide Area Virtualization Engine (WAVE) hardware. This architecture enables Cisco WAAS to provide the best mix of distributed and centralized IT services. As of the WAAS 4.1.x software release, the following applications are certified to run as a virtual blade on Cisco WAAS:

- Windows on WAAS (WoW)

- Active Directory (AD), DNS, DHCP and Print services on Windows Server 2003 and 2008

- Cisco Application and Content Networking Services (ACNS)

- Cisco Network Analysis Module (NAM)

Implementing the WAAS Virtual Blades Technology requires specific information from the existing IT environment.

Virtualization Requirements Checklist

The following checklist assists you with collecting the requirements necessary to successfully deploy the Virtual Blades Technology feature in your environment.

- Identify the services (AD, DNS, DHCP, web acceleration, network analysis, and so on) that need to be hosted locally in the remote office environment.

- Identify the Microsoft Windows Server version required, if applicable.

- Identify the CPU, memory, and storage requirements for each virtual blade.

Additional information on the Windows on WAAS (WoW) is available at the following location:

http://windowsserveronwaas.com/

Additional information on running Cisco ACNS as a virtual blade is available here:

http://tinyurl.com/yhzsaom

Additional information on running Cisco NAM as a virtual blade is available here:

http://tinyurl.com/yf7g7ph

Summary

This chapter reviewed the key requirements that you should collect and analyze as part of developing a Cisco WAAS solution design. The approach outlined in this chapter treats everything as a requirement, whether it is a new requirement for a specific feature in the WAAS solution, or a requirement imposed by the existing network infrastructure. Although it is important to define as many of the requirements up front, you should not let the collection of requirements impede the overall progress of the project. You have to find a balance between the level of detail you need to move forward and the amount of time allocated for the discovery and analysis process. Requirements will likely change over the course of the project, and you are almost always certain to discover new requirements during lab validation and pilot deployment.

Chapter 4

Network Integration and Interception

This chapter provides an in-depth review of the network integration and interception capabilities of Cisco Wide Area Application Services (WAAS). The chapter begins by describing the options for basic network connectivity, including link aggregation and network interface card (NIC) teaming. This is followed by a discussion of the interception methods available for redirecting traffic to a WAAS device for optimization. The techniques and methods discussed in this chapter form the foundation of the design and deployment solutions presented in subsequent chapters of the book.

Interface Connectivity

Each Cisco Wide-Area Application Engine (WAE) has two 10/100/1000BASE-T Ethernet interfaces. In a typical deployment, each WAE is connected using a single interface to a local area network (LAN) switch or router. By default, WAE interfaces auto-negotiate their speed and duplex. You can optionally configure the interface speed to 10 or 100 Mbps. For the interface speed to run at 1000 Mbps, it must be configured for auto-negotiation. The duplex of the interface is also configurable.

Caution   Do not configure WAE interfaces for half-duplex operation. The collision and retransmission behavior of half-duplex Ethernet has a negative impact on WAE performance.

The router-integrated network module (NME-WAE) is also equipped with two Ethernet interfaces, but only one interface is accessible externally. The other interface connects directly to the internal router PCI bus at 1 Gbps and is configured in a similar manner as an external interface would be configured on a WAE appliance. Unlike a WAE appliance configuration, the WAE interface IP address and default gateway are configured as part of the Cisco IOS interface configuration where the NME-WAE is installed. Figure 4-1 shows the physical interface layout on the router-integrated NME-WAE.

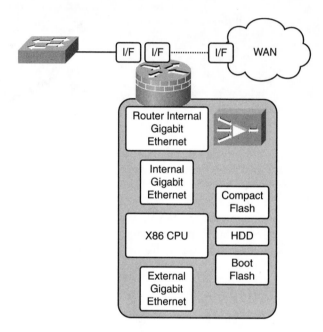

Figure 4-1 *NME-WAE Physical Interface Connectivity*

The WAE interface configuration options are similar to the Cisco IOS configuration options, both in terms of function and command line interface (CLI) commands. Example 4-1 shows the interface configuration options available on a WAE.

Example 4-1 *WAE Interface Configuration Options*

```
WAE-612(config)# interface gigabitEthernet 1/0
WAE-612(config-if)# ?
  autosense       Interface autosense
  bandwidth       Interface bandwidth
  cdp             Cisco Discovery Protocol Interface Config commands
  channel-group   Configure PortChannel group
  description     Interface specific description
  exit            Exit from this submode
```

```
   full-duplex      Interface fullduplex
   half-duplex      Interface halfduplex
   ip               Interface Internet Protocol Config commands
   mtu              Set the interface Maximum Transmission Unit (MTU)
   no               Negate a command or set its defaults
   shutdown         Shutdown the specific interface
   standby          Standby interface config commands
WAE-612(config-if)#
```

One of the interface configuration commands that behaves differently in WAAS versus IOS is the **bandwidth** command. The **bandwidth** interface configuration command in WAAS is used to specify the speed of the interface when auto-negotiation is disabled. The way in which the **standby** interface command is used is another important difference between WAAS and IOS. In IOS, the **standby** interface command is used for configuring the Hot Standby Router Protocol (HSRP) feature, whereas in WAAS, it is used to configure the standby interface feature, described in the next section. You can see from the output in Example 4-1 that the remaining WAAS interface configuration commands are similar to the corresponding IOS interface configuration commands.

You can explicitly configure the interface with an IP address and subnet mask, or the WAE can acquire an IP address using Dynamic Host Configuration Protocol (DHCP). Each WAE interface can also be configured with multiple secondary IP addresses. It is also possible for the same interface to acquire an IP address through DHCP and have multiple secondary IP addresses statically configured. By default, the interfaces on a WAE are administratively disabled and are automatically enabled when a valid IP address is configured.

Each WAE interface is primarily referenced using the standard Cisco IOS interface-naming scheme:

> *interface-name slot/port*

Note   Cisco WAAS uses a space between the interface-name and slot/port designation.

This is how WAE interfaces are referred to during configuration through the CLI or GUI. The interfaces also have an internal name by which the Linux operating system knows them. Table 4-1 shows the mapping between the internal and external interface names.

Table 4-1 *WAE External and Internal Interface Names*

IOS Name	Internal Name
gigabitEthernet 1/0	eth0
gigabitEthernet 2/0	eth1

Understanding the internal name of an interface is useful for understanding system log messages and using internal operating system tools, such as Ethereal or Tcpdump, which are useful for capturing traffic for offline analysis.

Just like the interface configuration, the outputs of interface **show** commands in WAAS are similar to Cisco IOS. Example 4-2 shows the output from the **show interface** command in WAAS.

Example 4-2 *WAE show interface Command Output*

```
AST6-CCO-02# show interface gigabitEthernet 1/0
Type:Ethernet
Ethernet address:00:11:25:AB:43:28
Internet address:10.88.81.2
Broadcast address:10.88.81.15
Netmask:255.255.255.240
Maximum Transfer Unit Size:1500
Metric:1
Packets Received: 966044
Input Errors: 0
Input Packets Dropped: 0
Input Packets Overruns: 0
Input Packets Frames: 0
Packet Sent: 1046794
Output Errors: 0
Output Packets Dropped: 0
Output Packets Overruns: 0
Output Packets Carrier: 0
Output Queue Length:1000
Collisions: 0
Interrupts:17
Flags:UP BROADCAST RUNNING MULTICAST
Link State: Interface is up,line protocol up
Mode: autoselect, full-duplex, 1000baseTX
AST6-CCO-02#
```

Note The Link State output in the **show interface** command output shown in Example 4-2 has been added in WAAS version 4.1 to show the administrative and line protocol status of the interface.

Link Aggregation Using PortChannel

To increase the available interface bandwidth for a WAE, Cisco WAAS supports PortChannel. PortChannel allows for the grouping of multiple physical interfaces to create a single "virtual" interface. The virtual interface, which functions as a single interface, has the aggregate bandwidth of the available physical interfaces in the channel group. PortChannel is useful when the output from a single WAE exceeds the physical limitations of a single interface. For example, some remote sites might have only 100-Mbps LAN connections available, whereas the traffic from a single WAE can easily exceed 100 Mbps. In these situations, using PortChannel to group both physical WAE interfaces together provides 200 Mbps of usable interface bandwidth.

In addition to increasing the available interface bandwidth, the PortChannel has automatic failure and recovery detection based on the link state of each individual interface. In the event of a single interface failure, traffic continues to pass over the remaining interface in the channel group. The PortChannel interface uses the MAC address from one of the physical interfaces in the group. The same MAC address is used persistently for the PortChannel interface, even if the physical interface associated with that MAC address goes down. The formation of a PortChannel in WAAS is based purely on device configuration. WAAS does not support Cisco Port Aggregation Protocol (PAgP) or 802.3ad Link Aggregation Control Protocol (LACP). When configuring PortChannel between a WAE and a LAN switch, the channel mode on the LAN switch should be set to On for the WAE PortChannel.

By default, the WAE load balances packets across all available interfaces in the channel group using a round-robin algorithm. By distributing packets across both physical links in a round-robin fashion, a single TCP connection can leverage the bandwidth of the entire PortChannel. WAAS also supports load balancing using a hash of the source/destination IP addresses and TCP ports. When load balancing traffic across the PortChannel using a hash of the source/destination IP addresses and TCP ports, each TCP connection is bound to a single physical link in the PortChannel. This limits the maximum throughput for a single TCP connection to the bandwidth of a single physical interface in the PortChannel. Figure 4-2 shows a WAE connected to a single LAN switch using PortChannel.

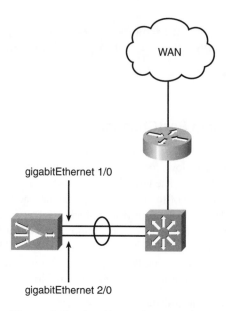

Figure 4-2 *Appliance Connected Using PortChannel Feature*

PortChannel Configuration

Configuring PortChannel in WAAS involves the following steps:

Step 1. Create a virtual PortChannel interface.

Step 2. Configure an IP address and subnet mask for the PortChannel interface.

Step 3. Assign the physical interfaces to the PortChannel.

Example 4-3 shows a basic PortChannel configuration.

Example 4-3 *WAE PortChannel Configuration*

```
!
interface PortChannel 1
 description ** PortChannel Link to Switch ABC ***
 ip address 10.10.10.5 255.255.255.0
 exit
!
interface GigabitEthernet 1/0
 channel-group 1
 exit
interface GigabitEthernet 2/0
 channel-group 1
 exit
!
```

You should observe the following limitations when configuring PortChannel in WAAS:

■   Only a single virtual PortChannel interface is supported.

■   DHCP is not supported on PortChannel interfaces.

■   Both interfaces in the channel group must run at the same speed and duplex.

■   Access control lists (ACL) are still applied to each physical interface.

The load-balancing algorithm used for distributing traffic across the PortChannel is configured using the following global configuration command:

port-channel load-balance *src-dst-ip-port* ¦ **round-robin**

To check the status of the PortChannel interface, use the **show interface PortChannel** *channel-number* command. Example 4-4 demonstrates the output of this command.

Example 4-4   *WAAS show interface PortChannel Output*

```
AST6-CCO-01# show interface PortChannel 1
Interface PortChannel 1 (2 physical interface(s)):
        GigabitEthernet 1/0 (active)
        GigabitEthernet 2/0 (active)
— — — — — — — — — — .
Type:Ethernet
Ethernet address:00:11:25:AB:43:32
Internet address:10.88.80.130
Broadcast address:10.88.80.255
Netmask:255.255.255.128
Maximum Transfer Unit Size:1500
Metric:1
Packets Received: 815996
Input Errors: 0
Input Packets Dropped: 0
Input Packets Overruns: 0
Input Packets Frames: 0
Packet Sent: 321842
Output Errors: 0
Output Packets Dropped: 0
Output Packets Overruns: 0
Output Packets Carrier: 0
Output Queue Length:0
Collisions: 0
Flags:UP BROADCAST RUNNING MASTER MULTICAST
Link State: Interface is up,line protocol up
AST6-CCO-01#
```

Each member of the channel group, along with the status of the interface, is shown at the beginning of the output. The MASTER flag in the example output indicates that this is the virtual PortChannel interface. Also, notice the Ethernet address, which is taken from one of the physical interfaces in the channel group. Example 4-5 demonstrates the same command for each physical interface in the channel group.

Example 4-5   *Channel Group Member Interface Output*

```
AST6-CCO-01# show interface gigabitEthernet 1/0
Type:Ethernet
Ethernet address:00:11:25:AB:43:32
Internet address:10.88.80.130
Broadcast address:10.88.80.255
Netmask:255.255.255.128
Maximum Transfer Unit Size:1500
Metric:1
Packets Received: 816176
Input Errors: 0
Input Packets Dropped: 0
Input Packets Overruns: 0
Input Packets Frames: 0
Packet Sent: 321880
Output Errors: 0
Output Packets Dropped: 0
Output Packets Overruns: 0
Output Packets Carrier: 0
Output Queue Length:1000
Collisions: 0
Base address:0x2000
Flags:UP BROADCAST RUNNING SLAVE MULTICAST
Link State: Interface is up,line protocol up
Mode: full-duplex, 100baseTX
AST6-CCO-01#
AST6-CCO-01# show interface gigabitEthernet 2/0
Type:Ethernet
Ethernet address:00:11:25:AB:43:32
Internet address:10.88.80.130
Broadcast address:10.88.80.255
Netmask:255.255.255.128
Maximum Transfer Unit Size:1500
Metric:1
Packets Received: 0
Input Errors: 0
Input Packets Dropped: 0
Input Packets Overruns: 0
Input Packets Frames: 0
```

```
Packet Sent: 0
Output Errors: 0
Output Packets Dropped: 0
Output Packets Overruns: 0
Output Packets Carrier: 0
Output Queue Length:1000
Collisions: 0
Base address:0x3400
Flags:UP BROADCAST SLAVE MULTICAST
Link State: Interface is up,line protocol up
Mode: autoselect
AST6-CCO-01#
```

The command output for each physical interface is the same as it is without PortChannel configured, with the following exceptions:

■ The SLAVE flag is set, indicating that the interface is part of a PortChannel group.

■ The Ethernet address for each interface is the same and matches the MAC address used by the virtual PortChannel interface.

Using the Standby Interface Feature

When you do not require increased interface bandwidth but desire interface redundancy, you can use the standby interface feature. The standby interface feature configures both physical interfaces on the WAE in an active/standby failover pair. At any point in time, only one of the interfaces is active and passing traffic. The second interface, or standby interface, is passively waiting to take over in the event that the active interface fails. When the active interface fails, the standby interface takes over the active role. When the previously active interface recovers, it assumes the standby role. The interface configured as the primary is preferred as the active interface.

The standby interface feature has become a popular choice for deployments because the WAE can be physically connected to two different LAN switches. This prevents the failure of a single LAN switch or switchport from disrupting the operation of the WAE. Figure 4-3 shows an example of an appliance connected using the standby interface feature.

The failure of the active interface in the standby group is detected by monitoring the link state of the active interface. Line protocol is up when the RUNNING flag is present on the Ethernet interface. If line protocol fails on the active interface, the interface is marked as down.

The interface state is checked once every 100 milliseconds. If the active link fails, the next available interface is activated. When the primary interface recovers, it becomes the active interface for the group. When a new interface is activated, the WAAS device generates a gratuitous ARP to update the MAC address for the shared IP on all other devices on the same subnet. This prevents devices from sending traffic to the shared IP address on the WAAS device to the MAC address of the failed WAAS device interface.

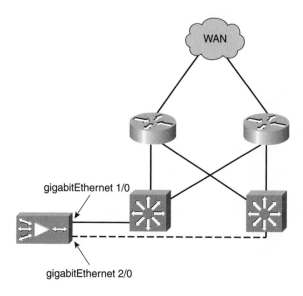

Figure 4-3   *Appliance Connected Using Standby Interface Feature*

Standby Interface Configuration

Configuring the standby interface feature in WAAS involves the following steps:

Step 1.   Create a virtual standby interface.

Step 2.   Configure an IP address and subnet mask for the standby interface.

Step 3.   Assign the physical interfaces to the standby group.

Example 4-6 shows a basic standby interface configuration.

Example 4-6   *WAE Standby Interface Configuration*

```
!
interface Standby 1
 ip address 10.88.80.130 255.255.255.128
 exit
!
interface GigabitEthernet 1/0
 standby 1 primary
 no autosense
 bandwidth 100
 full-duplex
 exit
```

```
interface GigabitEthernet 2/0
 standby 1
 exit
!
```

You should observe the following guidelines when configuring the standby interface feature within WAAS:

■ The physical interfaces in the standby group do not require IP addresses.

■ The interface configured as **primary** is always preferred and active when it is available.

■ The standby interface feature is not supported as an interface type with the WAAS Virtual Blades (VB) feature.

■ Only a single standby interface is supported.

The virtual standby interface uses the MAC address of the active interface. When the active interface fails and the standby interface takes over, the WAE generates a gratuitous ARP request to update the adjacent devices with the new MAC address associated with the standby interface IP address.

To check the status of the standby interface, use the **show interface Standby** *standby-interface-number* command. Example 4-7 shows the output of this command.

Example 4-7   *WAAS show interface Standby Interface Output*

```
AST6-CCO-01# show interface Standby 1
Interface Standby 1 (2 physical interface(s)):
    GigabitEthernet 1/0 (active) (primary) (in use)
    GigabitEthernet 2/0 (inactive)
— — — — — — — — —.
Type:Ethernet
Ethernet address:00:14:5E:67:13:2A
Internet address:10.88.80.133
Broadcast address:10.88.80.255
Netmask:255.255.255.128
Maximum Transfer Unit Size:1500
Metric:1
Packets Received: 3657482
Input Errors: 0
Input Packets Dropped: 0
Input Packets Overruns: 0
Input Packets Frames: 0
Packet Sent: 3225787
Output Errors: 0
```

```
Output Packets Dropped: 0
Output Packets Overruns: 0
Output Packets Carrier: 0
Output Queue Length:0
Collisions: 0
Flags:UP BROADCAST RUNNING MASTER MULTICAST
Link State: Interface is up,line protocol up
AST6-CCO-01#
```

Each member of the standby group and the status of the interface are shown in the output. The current active interface is also displayed. The output for each physical interface is shown in Example 4-8.

Example 4-8   *Standby Group Member Interface Output*

```
AST6-CCO-01# show interface gigabitEthernet 1/0
Type:Ethernet
Ethernet address:00:11:25:AB:43:32
Internet address (secondary): 10.88.80.130 Netmask: 255.255.255.128
Maximum Transfer Unit Size:1500
Metric:1
Packets Received: 819025
Input Errors: 0
Input Packets Dropped: 0
Input Packets Overruns: 0
Input Packets Frames: 0
Packet Sent: 322492
Output Errors: 0
Output Packets Dropped: 0
Output Packets Overruns: 0
Output Packets Carrier: 0
Output Queue Length:1000
Collisions: 0
Base address:0x2000
Flags:UP BROADCAST RUNNING MULTICAST
Mode: full-duplex, 100baseTX
AST6-CCO-01#
AST6-CCO-01# show interface gigabitEthernet 2/0
Type:Ethernet
Ethernet address:00:11:25:AB:43:33
Maximum Transfer Unit Size:1500
Metric:1
Packets Received: 0
Input Errors: 0
```

```
Input Packets Dropped: 0
Input Packets Overruns: 0
Input Packets Frames: 0
Packet Sent: 0
Output Errors: 0
Output Packets Dropped: 0
Output Packets Overruns: 0
Output Packets Carrier: 0
Output Queue Length:1000
Collisions: 0
Base address:0x3400
Flags:UP BROADCAST MULTICAST
Mode: autoselect
AST6-CCO-01#
```

In this output, the only indication that the interface is a member of a standby group is the SLAVE flag.

Interception Techniques and Protocols

There are two approaches for leveraging the network infrastructure to intercept and redirect traffic to WAAS for optimization. The first method relies on interception protocols or routing configuration used by the networking components (routers and switches) to selectively intercept traffic and redirect it to the WAAS infrastructure. This method is referred to as off-path interception. The most common method for off-path network interception is the Web Cache Communication Protocol (WCCPv2).

The second method places the WAE physically inline between two network elements, most commonly a router and LAN switch. All traffic between the two network elements is passed through the WAE, which can then selectively intercept traffic for optimization. This method is referred to as *in-path interception*, because the WAE is physically placed in the data path between the clients and servers.

This section discusses both off-path (WCCPv2) and in-path interception in detail. It also discusses other interception options for specific use cases, such as policy-based routing (PBR) and content switching. These additional interception options add to the flexibility with which WAAS can be integrated into existing network infrastructures of all sizes.

Web Cache Communication Protocol

This section does not provide an exhaustive reference for the WCCPv2 protocol. Rather, it provides enough information about the protocol background and concepts to enable you to understand the WCCPv2 implementation in Cisco WAAS. For an in-depth understanding of the WCCPv2 protocol, you are encouraged to read the

WCCPv2 protocol draft. The full WCCPv2 IETF draft is available online at http://www.wrec.org/Drafts/draft-wilson-wrec-wccp-v2-00.txt.

WCCP Overview

WCCP is a transparent interception protocol first developed by Cisco Systems, Inc. in 1997. WCCP is a control plane protocol that runs between devices running Cisco IOS and WCCP "clients" such as WAAS. The protocol enables the network infrastructure to selectively intercept traffic based on IP protocol and transport protocol port numbers, and redirect that traffic to a WCCP client. WCCP is considered transparent, because it allows for local interception and redirection of traffic without any configuration changes to the clients or servers. WCCP has built-in load-balancing, scalability, fault-tolerance, and service assurance (fail open) mechanisms. Figure 4-4 shows the basic functions of WCCP.

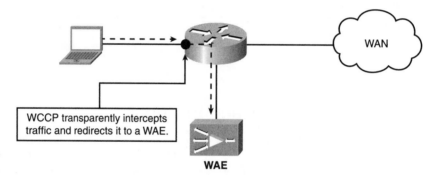

Figure 4-4 *Basic WCCP Functionality*

The current version, WCCPv2, is used by Cisco WAAS to transparently intercept and redirect all TCP traffic, regardless of port. The following section describes the basic WCCPv2 concepts and how they are specifically used by Cisco WAAS.

Service Groups

The routers and WAEs participating in the same service constitute a service group. A service group defines a set of characteristics about what types of traffic should be intercepted, as well as how the intercepted traffic should be handled. There are two types of service groups:

■ Well-known services

■ Dynamic services

Well-known services, also referred to as static services, have a fixed set of characteristics that are known by both IOS and WCCPv2 client devices. There is currently a single well-known service called web-cache. This service redirects all TCP traffic with a destination port of 80. The characteristics of a dynamic service are initially only known to the

WCCPv2 clients within the service group. The characteristics of the service group are communicated to the IOS devices by the first WCCPv2 client device to join the service group.

A unique service ID, which is a number from 0 to 255, identifies service groups. Service IDs 0 to 50 are reserved for well-known services.

The WCCPv2 implementation in WAAS supports a single dynamic WCCPv2 service, the tcp-promiscuous service. Although referred to in WAAS as a single service, the tcp-promiscuous service is in fact two different services. The two service IDs enabled with the tcp-promiscuous service are 61 and 62. These are the two service group IDs that are configured in IOS when using WCCPv2 with WAAS. Two different service groups are used because by default both directions (client-to-server and server-to-client) of a TCP connection must be transparently intercepted. To optimize a connection, WAAS must see both directions of the connection on the same WAE. Not only does WAAS intercept the connection in both directions, but it also intercepts the connection on both sides of the WAN link. Because the packet Layer 3 and Layer 4 headers are preserved, transparent interception is used on both sides of the WAN in both directions to redirect connections to the WAAS infrastructure for optimization. Figure 4-5 shows a basic topology with WCCPv2 interception configured for WAAS.

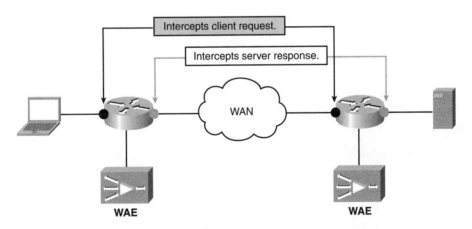

Figure 4-5   *Basic Network Topology with WCCP*

What is the difference between services 61 and 62? You can view the service attributes using CLI commands in both WAAS and IOS. Example 4-9 shows the attributes of services 61 and 62 using the IOS CLI.

Example 4-9   *WCCP Service Group Attributes*

```
AST6-RTR-02# show ip wccp 61 service
WCCP service information definition:
        Type:          Dynamic
```

```
            Id:              61
            Priority:        34
            Protocol:        6
            Options:         0x00000501
            — — — —
                Hash:        SrcIP
                Alt Hash:    SrcIP SrcPort
                Ports:       -none-

AST6-RTR-02#
AST6-RTR-02# show ip wccp 62 service
WCCP service information definition:
            Type:            Dynamic
            Id:              62
            Priority:        34
            Protocol:        6
            Options:         0x00000502
            — — — —
                Hash:        DstIP
                Alt Hash:    SrcIP SrcPort
                Ports:       -none-

AST6-RTR-02#
```

A description of each value is provided in Table 4-2.

Table 4-2   *WCCP Service Group Attributes*

Value	Description
Type	Well-known or dynamic service.
Id	The numeric service ID for the group.
Priority	The priority for the service group. When multiple service groups are configured on the same interface in the same direction, they are evaluated in descending priority order.
Protocol	The IP protocol number defined by the service group.
Options	Flags field indicating further service characteristics.
Hash	The value(s) in the redirected packet used as the hash key.
Alternate Hash	The value(s) in the redirected packet used as the alternate hash key.
Ports	The Layer 4 port numbers defined by the service group.

The command output shows that the only difference between services 61 and 62 is the value from the packet used as the hash key. By default, service group 61 hashes on the source IP address and service group 62 hashes on the destination IP address. Later, this chapter discusses the significance of the hash key used in each service group. By default, the **spoof-client-ip** feature is enabled for both services. This is the WCCPv2 feature that allows WAAS to handle optimized traffic transparently. Traffic forwarded to the WAE uses the same source and destination IP addresses and TCP ports as when it entered the WAE.

The tcp-promiscuous services define TCP as the protocol and do not define any ports. By not defining any ports as part of the service groups, this causes interception and redirection of all TCP traffic. When traffic passes through an interface in the IOS device with WCCPv2 redirection configured, it is evaluated against the protocol and port combination defined by the service to determine whether or not the packet should be redirected. By default this is the only criteria that is used to determine whether or not a packet is redirected. It is important to note that the IOS WCCPv2 implementation is not stateful. This means that IOS WCCPv2 is only dealing with redirected traffic on a packet-by-packet basis. It does not keep track of the TCP connection state for redirected traffic. On the other hand, the WCCPv2 implementation in WAAS is stateful. WAAS tracks each connection as a flow throughout the life of the connection.

Forwarding and Return Methods

WCCPv2 supports different methods for forwarding redirected traffic from IOS router or switch to a WAE, and for the WAE to return traffic to the IOS router/switch for forwarding. These methods are referred to as the *forwarding* and *return* methods and are negotiated between IOS and the WAE when a WAE joins the service group.

The forwarding method defines how traffic that is being redirected from IOS to the WAE is transmitted across the network. The first forwarding method, GRE forwarding, encapsulates the original packet in a WCCP GRE header with the destination IP address set to the target WAE and the source IP address set to the WCCPv2 router ID of the redirecting router. When the WAE receives the GRE-encapsulated packet, the GRE header is removed, and the packet is processed. Figure 4-6 shows an example of GRE forwarding.

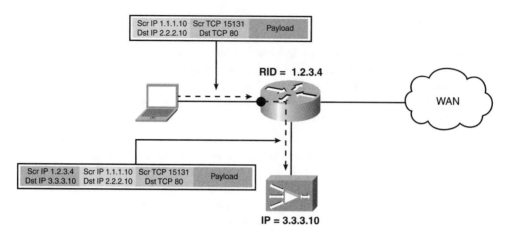

Figure 4-6   *WCCP Redirection Using GRE Forwarding*

The second forwarding method, L2 forwarding, simply rewrites the destination MAC address of the packet being redirected to equal the MAC address of the target WAE. This forwarding method assumes that the WAE is Layer 2 adjacent to the redirecting router. L2 forwarding was originally developed for the WCCPv2 implementation on hardware-based platforms, such as the Catalyst 6500. Figure 4-7 shows an example of L2 forwarding.

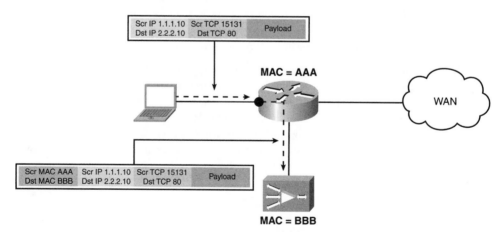

Figure 4-7   *WCCP Redirection Using L2 Forwarding*

One of the benefits of L2 forwarding is that it allows for the WCCPv2 redirection to occur in hardware on Cisco Catalyst Series switches, the Cisco Nexus 7000 Series switches, and the Cisco ASR 1000 Series routers. In fact, on the Catalyst 3560/3750 and 4500/4948 series switches, the only forwarding method supported by WCCPv2 is L2 forwarding.

Additional information about the configuration requirements for deploying WCCPv2 on Cisco hardware-based platforms is provided in the "WCCP Configuration" section.

The return method defines how traffic should be returned from the WAE to the redirecting router/switch for normal forwarding. Like the forwarding method, there are two different return methods:

■ **GRE return:** Egress traffic from the WAE using GRE return is encapsulated using WCCP GRE, with a destination IP address of the WCCPv2 router ID and a source IP address of the WAE itself. When the WCCPv2-enabled router receives the returned packet, the IP GRE header is removed and the packet is forwarded normally. WCCPv2 in IOS knows not to re-intercept traffic returned to it using GRE return.

■ **L2 return:** The L2 return method returns traffic to the WCCPv2-enabled router by rewriting the destination MAC address of the packet to equal the MAC address of the WCCPv2-enabled router.

Whether the negotiated return method is used by WAAS to inject traffic back into the network infrastructure is determined by the configured egress method, which is discussed later in this chapter.

Load Distribution

When multiple WAEs exist in a service group, WCCPv2 automatically distributes redirected traffic across all WAEs in the service group. When traffic passes through an IOS device with WCCPv2 redirection configured, the IOS device assigns traffic for that connection to a bucket. Each bucket is assigned to a specific WAE. The method that determines to which bucket traffic is assigned, which determines how traffic is distributed across multiple WAEs within a service group, is called the assignment method. The bucket assignments are communicated from the lead WAE to all of the IOS devices in the service group. The assignment method can use either a hashing or masking scheme and is negotiated between IOS and WAE during the formation of the service group.

Hash assignment, which is the default assignment method, performs a bitwise hash on a key identified as part of the service group. In WAAS, the hash key used for service group 61 is the source IP address, whereas the hash key used for service group 62 is the destination IP address. The hash is not configurable and is deterministic in nature. This means that all of the routers within the same service group makes the same load-balancing decision given the same hash key. This deterministic behavior is what allows WCCPv2 to support asymmetric traffic flows, so long as both directions of the flow pass through WCCPv2-enabled IOS devices in the same service group. Hash assignment uses 256 buckets. Figure 4-8 shows an example of the hash assignment method and bucket-based distribution model used by WCCPv2.

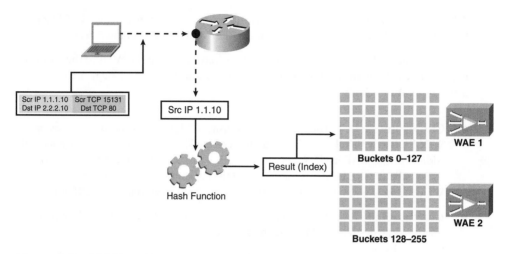

Figure 4-8   *WCCP Redirection Using Hash Assignment*

The second assignment method is called mask assignment. With mask assignment, the source IP address, destination IP address, source port, and destination port are concatenated and ANDed with a 96-bit mask to yield a value. The resulting 96-bit value is compared to a list of mask/value pairs. Each mask/value pair is associated with a bucket, and each bucket is in turn assigned to a WAE. Unlike hash assignment, the number of buckets used with mask assignment depends on the number of bits used in the mask. By default, WAAS uses a mask of 0x1741. This results in 2^6 buckets that can be assigned across the WAEs in a service group. With current Catalyst WCCPv2 implementations, up to 7 bits can be defined for the mask. Figure 4-9 shows an example of the mask assignment method and bucket-based distribution model used by WCCPv2.

Failure Detection

After a WAE has successfully joined a service group, a periodic keepalive packet is sent every 10 seconds (by default) from the WAE to each router in the service group. The keepalive mechanism occurs independently for each configured service group. If a router in the service group has not received a keepalive packet from the WAE in 2.5 times the keepalive interval, the router unicasts a Removal Query (RQ) message to that WAE requesting that it immediately respond. If no response is received within 5 seconds, for a total of 30 seconds (by default) since the last keepalive message from the WAE, the WAE is considered offline and is removed from the service group. Figure 4-10 illustrates this behavior.

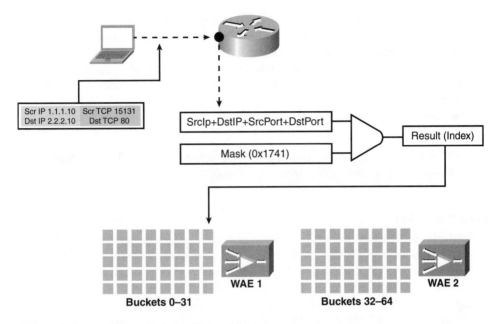

Figure 4-9   *WCCP Redirection Using Mask Assignment*

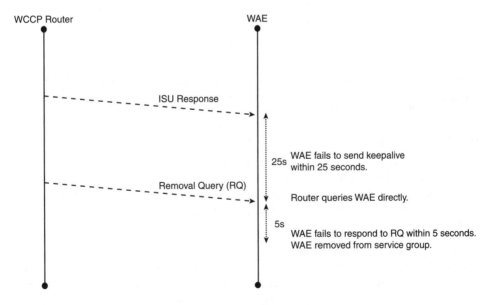

Figure 4-10   *WCCP Keepalive Timeout*

When the WAE is removed from the service group, it is reflected in the Router View advertised from each router in the service group. When the lead WAE determines that a

WAE has been removed from the service group, it generates a Redirect Assignment (RA) message to each router in the service group. The RA message instructs the routers how to reallocate the buckets across the remaining WAEs in the service group. The length of time required to calculate the new assignments might vary depending upon when the group of WAEs becomes stable. The WAE waits a minimum of 1.5 times the keepalive interval. The maximum length of time depends on when the IOS device sends an update message without any changes indicated, typically between 25 and 45 seconds.

Note   On hardware-based platforms, such as the Catalyst 6500, it might take additional time to reprogram the updated redirected instructions in hardware.

Flow Protection

When a WAE (re)joins the service group, a new RA message is generated by the lead WAE. When the new WAE begins receiving redirected traffic from the routers in the service group, it does one of two things, depending on whether or not the redirected traffic is associated with a new TCP connection or part of an existing connection. Traffic associated with newly established connections is evaluated against the Application Traffic Policy (ATP) and processed normally by the WAE. Traffic associated with existing connections is forwarded directly to the WAE that previously owned the bucket for that connection. This WCCPv2 mechanism is called flow protection and is enabled by default. Flow protection allows for existing connections to continue to be optimized even when the traffic assignments for the WAEs in a service group change.

Note   The flow protection feature is the only case where the WCCP process on a WAAS device communicates directly with another WAAS device.

Graceful Shutdown

After the **no wccp ver 2** command is issued, WCCPv2 checks whether any connections are being served by the WAE. If zero connections are being served, the shutdown is immediately carried out. If there are more than zero connections being served, WCCPv2 waits for the user-configured **wccp shutdown max-wait** *XX* time (120 seconds by default).

During this time, if the connection count goes down to zero, shutdown is immediately done. At the end of the max-wait time, if the connection count has decreased but is still non-zero, the shutdown count waits another 60 seconds, in the hope that if the connection count has decreased other connections might complete too. At the end of the max-wait time, if the connection count has not decreased, shutdown is immediately done. During the 60-second incremental wait, if the connection count becomes zero, shutdown is done. At the end of the 60-second incremental wait, if the connection count has not reduced, the shutdown is done. At the end of the 60-second incremental wait, if the count has further reduced but is still non-zero, another 60-second incremental wait is done.

Scalability

With WCCPv2, each service group can support up to 32 routers and 32 WAEs. This means that a single service group can support $N \times 32$ concurrent optimized TCP connections, where N is the number of concurrent optimized TCP connections supported by the largest WAE model. Each WAE in the service group is manually configured with the IP address of each router in the service group. The WAE then uses unicast packets to exchange WCCPv2 messages with each router. It is not required that the routers in the service are manually configured with the IP address of each WAE in the service group. Each router listens passively for WCCPv2 messages from the WAEs in the service group and responds only as a result of receiving those messages.

The WAE in the service group with the lowest IP address is elected as the "lead" WAE. The lead WAE is responsible for communicating the list, or view, of the routers in the service group to the service group routers. The lead WAE is also responsible for informing the routers how traffic should be distributed across WAEs in the service group through the use of RA messages. Upon receiving the view of the routers in the service group from the lead WAE, each router responds individually with a Router View. The Router View contains a list of each WAE that the router is currently communicating with. What is implied is that the routers in the service group do not communicate directly with each other; they learn about each other through the Router View advertised by the WAE. Likewise, the WAEs in a service group do not communicate directly with each; they learn about each other from the WAE View advertised by the routers.

Redirect Lists

For deployments where you might want to limit redirection to specific types of traffic, you can use a WCCPv2 redirect list. WCCP redirect lists are also useful for restricting transparent interception during proof of concept or pilot testing to a limited set of hosts and/or applications. A WCCPv2 redirect list is a standard or extended IOS access list that is associated with a WCCPv2 service. Traffic passing through an interface on the router with WCCPv2 redirection configured must match not only the protocol/port specified as part of the service group, but also a permit entry in the redirect list. Packets that match the service group protocol/port criteria but do not match a permit entry in the redirect list are forwarded normally. Example 4-10 demonstrates the use of a WCCPv2 redirect list.

Example 4-10   *WCCP Redirection Using a Redirect List*

```
!
access-list 100 permit ip 10.10.10.0 0.0.0.255 any
access-list 100 permit ip any 10.0.0.0 0.0.0.255
access-list 100 deny ip any any
!
ip wccp 61 redirect-list 100
ip wccp 62 redirect-list 100
!
```

In this example, TCP traffic sourced from or destined to subnet 10.10.10.0/24 are intercepted and redirected by WCCPv2. All other traffic that matches the **deny** entry in the access list are not redirected to WAAS. An alternative to this approach is to deny specific types of traffic from redirection, such as management traffic, and permit all other traffic. Example 4-11 shows how this could be done.

Example 4-11   *WCCP Redirect List Denying Management Traffic*

```
!
ip access-list extended waas
 remark WAAS WCCP Mgmt Redirect List
 deny    tcp any any eq telnet
 deny    tcp any any eq 22
 deny    tcp any any eq 161
 deny    tcp any any eq 162
 deny    tcp any any eq 123
 deny    tcp any any eq bgp
 deny    tcp any any eq tacacs
 deny    tcp any eq telnet any
 deny    tcp any eq 22 any
 deny    tcp any eq 161 any
 deny    tcp any eq 162 any
 deny    tcp any eq 123 any
 deny    tcp any eq bgp any
 deny    tcp any eq tacacs any
 permit tcp any any
!
ip wccp 61 redirect-list waas
ip wccp 62 redirect-list waas
!
```

Service Group Placement

The placement of service groups 61 and 62 should not be overlooked in your deployment. The placement refers to which IOS interfaces are configured with service group 61 and which interfaces are configured with service group 62. In addition, the direction that interception occurs on the interfaces is important. Interception is configured in either the inbound or outbound direction. Inbound redirection evaluates traffic against the service group criteria as it enters the interface of a router, while outbound redirection evaluates traffic after it has already been switched through the router and is exiting the egress (based on routing table lookup) interface. In general, inbound redirection is more efficient on hardware-based platforms and is the only interception direction supported on some hardware-based platforms such as the Catalyst 3560/3750 and Catalyst 4500 switches. In most deployments, service group 61 should be configured on the client-facing interfaces. The client-facing interfaces might differ depending on whether you are configuring WCCP in a remote branch office or in the Data Center. For example, when deploying WCCPv2 on a remote-office WAN router, service group 61 is configured to intercept a client request. Configuring group 61 inbound on the router's LAN interface or outbound on the router's WAN interface accomplishes this. By using service group 61 to intercept traffic in the client-to-server direction, WCCP performs load balancing in the service group based on the client IP address. Figure 4-11 shows an example of configuring service group 61 inbound on the router's LAN interface.

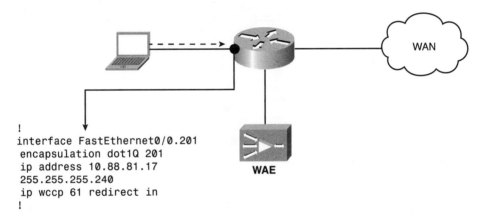

```
!
interface FastEthernet0/0.201
encapsulation dot1Q 201
ip address 10.88.81.17
255.255.255.240
ip wccp 61 redirect in
!
```

Figure 4-11   *WCCP Service Group 61 Placement*

For the reverse direction of the connection, service group 62 is used. Service group 62 is configured in the opposite direction of service group 61. Because traffic is flowing in the reverse direction (server-to-client), the load balancing is also occurring on the client IP address. Using the same example shown in Figure 4-11, Figure 4-12 shows service group 62 configured inbound on the router's WAN interface. It also shows the complete placement and configuration using both service groups.

WCCP Configuration

This section provides a basic overview of configuring WCCPv2 within both IOS and WAAS. Detailed WCCPv2 configurations specific to various design options are presented in Chapter 5, "Branch Office Network Integration," and Chapter 6, "Data Center Network Integration."

There are three primary steps involved when configuring WCCPv2 in WAAS:

Step 1.   Define WCCPv2 router list

Step 2.   Enable WCCPv2 tcp-promiscuous services

Step 3.   Enable WCCPv2

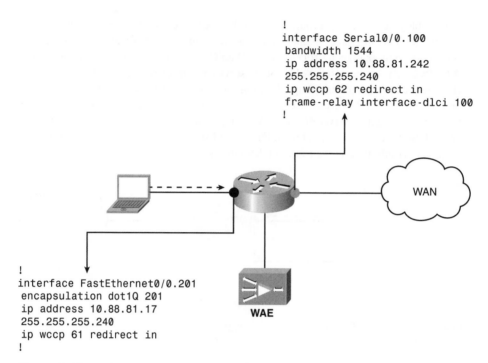

```
!
interface Serial0/0.100
bandwidth 1544
ip address 10.88.81.242
255.255.255.240
ip wccp 62 redirect in
frame-relay interface-dlci 100
!
```

WAN

```
!
interface FastEthernet0/0.201
encapsulation dot1Q 201
ip address 10.88.81.17
255.255.255.240
ip wccp 61 redirect in
!
```

WAE

Figure 4-12 *WCCP Service Group 61 and 62 Placement*

Each of these steps is described next. First, you must define which routers the WAE establishes WCCPv2 communication with. WCCPv2 can be configured to use either unicast or multicast for communication. Unicast is the most commonly deployed configuration and is available on all IOS platforms. For unicast communication, you must define the IP address of each router in the service group that the WAE communicates with. This is done using a router list. A router list is configured using the following syntax:

wccp router-list *1-8 ip_addr...*

Example 4-12 shows a basic WCCP router list configuration.

Example 4-12 *WAAS WCCP Router List Configuration*

```
wccp router-list 1 10.10.10.1
```

Up to six IP addresses can be defined per line. For deployments where there are more than six routers in the service group, additional router IP addresses can be defined by configuring a second line using the same router list number. Example 4-13 shows a WCCPv2 router list configured with ten IP addresses.

Example 4-13 *WCCP Router List Using Multiple IP Addresses*

```
wccp router-list 1 10.10.10.1 10.10.10.2 10.10.10.3 10.10.10.4 10.10.10.5
10.10.10.10.6
wccp router-list 1 10.10.10.7 10.10.10.8 10.10.10.9 10.10.10.10
```

Caution   Do not use virtual IP addresses, such as an HSRP virtual IP (VIP) address, in the WCCPv2 router list. The router list should contain only interface IP addresses. When the WAE is L2 adjacent to the WCCP-enabled router(s), the IP address(es) used in the WCCP router list should be the directly connected interface IP addresses. In cases where the WAE is not L2 adjacent to the WCCP-enabled router(s) (that is, the WAE is one or more L3 hops away from the WCCP-enabled router or routers), a loopback interface IP address should be used in the router list configuration. Using a loopback interface IP address improves the reliability of the WCCP service group, because the loopback interface IP address is not tied to the availability of any single physical interface.

For the second step, the WCCPv2 tcp-promiscuous service is enabled and associated with the router list created in the first step. The following command syntax is used:

```
wccp tcp-promiscuous router-list-num 1
```

The final configuration step is to enable WCCPv2 using the command **wccp version 2**. This command starts the WCCPv2 negotiation with any IOS devices configured in the router list. Example 4-14 shows a complete WCCPv2 configuration in Cisco WAAS.

Example 4-14   *Complete WAAS WCCP Configuration*

```
!
wccp router-list 1 10.10.20.1
wccp tcp-promiscuous router-list-num 1
wccp version 2
!
```

The IOS WCCPv2 configuration involves two steps. First, the WCCPv2 services are enabled in global configuration mode. The WCCPv2 services in IOS are configured using the numeric service ID, as opposed to the service name used on the WAAS configuration. Example 4-15 shows the tcp-promiscuous services configured in IOS.

Example 4-15   *Cisco IOS WCCP Global Configuration*

```
!
ip wccp 61
ip wccp 62
!
```

The second step involves configuring WCCPv2 redirection on each interface through which client and server data passes. Unless you are using the WCCPv2 negotiated return egress method discussed later in this chapter, WCCPv2 redirection should never be configured on the interface connecting to the WAE. Interception is configured in either the inbound or outbound direction. When using outbound redirection, the **ip wccp redirect exclude in** command must be configured on the interface connecting to the WAE. This prevents traffic coming into the WCCPv2 server (router) from being re-intercepted, which would cause a redirection loop. Example 4-16 demonstrates a complete IOS WCCPv2 configuration, including the use of the **ip wccp redirect exclude in** command.

Example 4-16   *Complete Cisco IOS WCCP Configuration*

```
!
ip wccp 61
ip wccp 62
!
ip cef
!
interface Serial0/0
 bandwidth 1536
 no ip address
 encapsulation frame-relay
!
interface Serial0/0.100
 ip add 10.88.80.18 255.255.255.252
 ip wccp 61 redirect out
 ip wccp 62 redirect in
 frame-relay interface-dlci 100
!
interface GigabitEthernet0/0
 no ip address
 duplex auto
 speed auto
!
interface GigabitEthernet0/0.1
 description ** Branch Client VLAN **
 encapsulation dot1q 10
 ip address 10.10.10.1 255.255.255.0
!
interface GigabitEthernet0/0.20
 description ** Branch WAE VLAN **
 ip address 10.10.20.1 255.255.255.0
 ip wccp redirect exclude in
!
end
```

Note that the **ip wccp redirect exclude in** command is configured on the subinterface connecting to the WAE. This is required because outbound redirection is used on the

serial interface connecting to the WAN. An alternative configuration is shown in
Example 4-17.

Example 4-17   *Cisco IOS WCCP Configuration Using Inbound Redirection*

```
!
ip wccp 61
ip wccp 62
!
ip cef
!
interface Serial0/0
 bandwidth 1536
 no ip address
 encapsulation frame-relay
!
interface Serial0/0.100
 ip add 10.88.80.18 255.255.255.252
 ip wccp 62 redirect in
 frame-relay interface-dlci 100
!
interface GigabitEthernet0/0
 no ip address
 duplex auto
 speed auto
!
interface GigabitEthernet0/0.1
 description ** Branch Client VLAN **
 encapsulation dot1q 10
 ip address 10.10.10.1 255.255.255.0
 ip wccp 61 redirect in
!
interface GigabitEthernet0/0.20
 description ** Branch WAE VLAN **
 ip address 10.10.20.1 255.255.255.0
!
end
```

This example uses inbound redirection on the interface connecting to the client subnet
and the serial interface connecting to the WAN. Because outbound redirection is not
used, the **ip wccp redirect exclude in** command is not required on the interface connecting to the WAE.

Hardware-Based Platforms

In addition to running WCCPv2 on software-based IOS platforms such as the Cisco Integrated Services Router (ISR), WCCPv2 is supported on several Cisco hardware-based platforms. At the time of this writing, the following Cisco hardware-based platforms support WCCPv2 for use with Cisco and other WCCP clients.

- Catalyst 3560/3750

- Catalyst 4500/4900

- Catalyst 6500, Sup2

- Catalyst 6500, Sup32

- Catalyst 6500, Sup720

- Nexus 7000 Series Switches

- ASR 1000 Series Aggregation Services Routers

With the exception of the Catalyst 6500/Sup720, Nexus 7000, and ASR 1000, the hardware-based platforms require L2 forwarding and mask assignment for all of the redirection to happen in hardware. The 6500/Sup720, Nexus 7000, and ASR 1000 are capable of performing GRE forwarding in hardware, but still require mask assignment for hardware acceleration. In addition to the requirements for forwarding and assignment methods, only inbound WCCPv2 redirection should be used on hardware-based platforms. In fact, the Catalyst 3560/3750, Catalyst 4500/4900, Nexus 7000, and ASR 1000 only support inbound redirection. Although it is possible to configure outbound redirection on the Catalyst 6500 platform, it is not recommended because it causes the first packet for every redirected connection to be processed in software by the Supervisor. Likewise, using the **ip wccp redirect exclude in** command on a Catalyst 6500 causes the first packet for every flow entering the interface to be processed by the MSFC and switched in software. However, because inbound redirection is the recommendation for hardware-based platforms, this command is not required.

The following configuration guidelines should be followed to ensure WCCPv2 redirection on hardware-based platforms is handled completely in hardware:

- Use L2 forwarding instead of GRE forwarding.

- Always use mask assignment.

- Only use inbound redirection.

- Do not use the **ip wccp redirect exclude in** command.

The L2 forwarding and mask assignment options are configured as part of the service definition in WAAS. These capabilities are advertised to the WCCPv2-enabled IOS devices when a WAE first joins the service group. Example 4-18 demonstrates the WAAS WCCPv2 configuration with the L2 forwarding and mask assignment options.

Example 4-18   *WCCP Configuration Using L2 Forwarding and Mask Assignment*

```
!
wccp router-list 1 10.10.20.1
wccp tcp-promiscuous router-list-num 1 l2-redirect mask-assign
wccp version 2
!
```

Unlike the hash algorithm used with hash assignment, the mask used for mask assignment is configurable. If there are between one and two WAAS devices in the WCCP service group, a mask of 0x1 should be used. If there are three or more WAAS devices in the service group, the recommended mask depends on the WAAS design. A more detailed discussion of the WCCP mask is provided in Chapter 6. The mask is applied to the source IP address for service group 61 and is applied to the destination IP address for service group 62. Depending on the IP addressing used in your environment, you might want to change the default mask to provide for better load distribution among the WAEs in a service group. The default mask is changed on the WAE using the following command syntax:

```
wccp tcp-promiscuous mask src-ip-mask 0-4261412864
```

The configured mask is applied to service group 61. Service group 62 mirrors the configuration and cannot be configured separately. Example 4-19 shows using a non-default mask with WCCPv2.

Example 4-19   *Custom WCCP Mask*

```
!
wccp router-list 1 10.10.20.1
wccp tcp-promiscuous mask src-ip-mask 0x1
wccp tcp-promiscuous router-list-num 1 l2-redirect mask-assign
wccp version 2
!
```

Policy-Based Routing

PBR provides another alternative for transparent interception with WAAS, although it is less commonly deployed than WCCPv2 and inline interception. PBR can be used in situations where customers are unable to run WCCPv2 or inline interception. PBR can also be used in conjunction with a content switch, such as the Cisco Application Control Engine (ACE), to provide transparent interception and load balancing for large-scale data center deployments. Deployment examples using PBR for transparent interception are provided in Chapters 5 and 6.

PBR functions in a similar manner to WCCPv2, in that a router/switch running Cisco IOS is configured to intercept interesting traffic and redirect it to a WAE. Unlike WCCPv2, no configuration is required on the WAE to support interception using PBR. The following configuration steps are required for a basic PBR configuration:

Step 1.   Create an access list to define interesting traffic for redirection.

Step 2.   Create a route map that matches the ACL created in Step 1 and sets an IP next-hop address of the target WAE.

Step 3.   Apply the route map to interfaces through which client and server traffic traverses.

Example 4-20 demonstrates a basic PBR configuration used for redirecting all TCP traffic to a single WAE.

Example 4-20   *Policy-Based Routing Configuration*

```
!
ip cef
!
access-list 199 permit tcp any any
!
route-map WAAS-INTERCEPT 10
 match ip address 199
 set ip next-hop 10.10.20.5
!
interface Serial0/0
 bandwidth 1536
 no ip address
 encapsulation frame-relay
!
interface Serial0/0.100
 ip add 10.88.80.18 255.255.255.252
 ip policy route-map WAAS-INTERCEPT
 frame-relay interface-dlci 100
!
interface GigabitEthernet0/0
 no ip address
 duplex auto
 speed auto
!
interface GigabitEthernet0/0.1
 description ** Branch Client VLAN **
 encapsulation dot1q 10
 ip address 10.10.10.1 255.255.255.0
 ip policy route-map WAAS-INTERCEPT
!
interface GigabitEthernet0/0.20
```

```
description ** Branch WAE VLAN **
ip address 10.10.20.1 255.255.255.0
!
end
```

Because PBR evaluates only traffic entering an interface, the route map entries are configured on both the client and server-facing interfaces. This is the equivalent of using only inbound redirection with WCCPv2. The **set ip next-hop** command in the route map is configured with the IP address of the WAE. By default, PBR does not validate to availability of the IP address specified as the next-hop address. As long as the next-hop address exists in the routing table, the route map entry is applied. On some platforms and software versions, Cisco Service Assurance Agent (SAA) can be used to track the availability of the next-hop IP address. If the next-hop address becomes unreachable, traffic matching the route map entry is forwarded normally using the routing table.

Other difference between WCCPv2 and PBR is that PBR does not perform automatic load distribution and failover when multiple WAEs exist. The first next hop IP address configured in the route map is used until it becomes unavailable. Only at that point is traffic redirected to a secondary next hop IP address in the route map. Chapters 5 and 6 provide examples of PBR deployments that include next hop availability tracking using SAA and load distribution among multiple WAEs.

Note   The Nexus 7000 Series switches provide the capability to distribute traffic among multiple PBR next-hop IP addresses. An example of this configuration is provided in Chapter 6.

Inline Interception

An alternative to the various off-path interception mechanisms is to place the WAE physically inline between two network elements, such as a WAN access router and LAN switch. Figure 4-13 shows a basic topology with the WAE deployed physically inline.

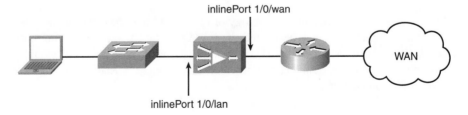

Figure 4-13   *WAE Physical In-Path Deployment*

Physical inline interception is an attractive option for situations where it is not possible or ideal to run WCCPv2. It is also possible that the networking equipment at a site is provided and managed by a managed service provider (MSP). The MSP might not be able to configure or support a WCCPv2 solution on the managed devices.

To support physical inline interception, the WAE requires a separate inline module. The inline module is a 2- or 4-port, fail-to-wire NIC with each pair of ports in a unique inline group. Each inline group has a synchronous pair of inline ports that interconnect two network elements. Traffic entering one inline port is optimized by WAAS (when applicable) and switched out the opposite inline port in the same group. The inline group functions like a transparent Layer 2 bridge.

On platforms that support a 4-port inline module, the WAE can support designs where multiple paths out of a site exist for redundancy and load sharing. Each unique path is connected to the WAE through a separate inline group. Figure 4-14 shows a sample remote site topology with multiple WAN routers and a single WAE deployed with inline interception.

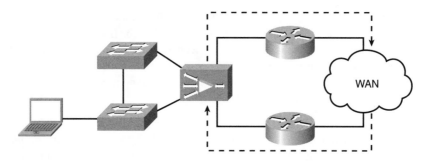

Figure 4-14 *Physical In-Path Deployment Using Multiple Routers*

As the arrows in Figure 4-14 indicate, traffic can enter or leave the site through either router. Even though the same flow enters the site through one inline group and exits the site through another inline group, the connection is still optimized. The optimized connection state is not tied to a physical interface, but is tracked for the WAE as a whole independent of the interfaces traversed by the traffic.

Note There is an assumption in the topology of Figure 4-14 that the client subnet does not function as a transit network between the two WAN routers (that is, there is no routing protocol running between the routers across the LAN). Otherwise this topology would require an inter-router link, disabling routing on the host subnet and enabling routing on the inter-router link/subnet.

Each inline group functions in one of two operating modes:

■ **Intercept operating mode:** Traffic entering the inline group is evaluated against the ATP for optimization.

- **Bypass operating mode:** All traffic entering the inline group is bridged without any optimization.

The bypass operating mode is designed to enable the WAE to continue passing traffic if the WAE loses power. A keepalive mechanism between the network drivers and the inline module is used to determine if the WAE is functioning properly and can optimize connections.

The keepalive frequency is configurable between 1 and 10 seconds. The default failover timer is set to 3 seconds. The transition between intercept operating mode and bypass operating mode does cause a momentary loss of line protocol. If one or more of the inline ports are connected to a LAN switch, this transition in interface state can cause the Spanning Tree Protocol (STP) recalculation. To prevent the STP calculation from interrupting traffic forwarding, the switchport connected to the inline module on the WAE should have the STP PortFast feature enabled. Failure of a single inline port in the group is propagated to the other port in the group. For example, if the LAN0 port in InlineGroup 1/0 goes down, the WAE takes down line protocol on the WAN0 port in the same inline group. This propagation of interface state between the ports in the same inline group prevents situations where adjacent devices connected to an operational InlinePort believe the network path to be online and usable, when in reality the connection on the other side of the WAE is unavailable.

When a WAE is deployed physically inline, all traffic between the two network elements is seen by the WAE. Non-TCP traffic is bridged through the inline module without modification. In addition, packets associated with a connection that was first seen on the opposite inline port in a group are bridged. This type of traffic flow is common when a WAE is deployed inline on a trunk between a router and LAN switch. If the router is providing routing for traffic going between Virtual Local Area Networks (VLAN) locally, it is possible for traffic to traverse the inline module twice. Figure4-15 shows an example of this type of traffic flow.

The inline module also supports 802.1Q trunk connections between the two network elements. An added benefit to using the inline module is the ability to define which VLANs are evaluated for interception. Traffic that is received by the inline module tagged with a VLAN ID that is excluded from interception is bridged without any optimization. This capability is supported only for tagged VLANs. Traffic received by the inline module on untagged VLANs is intercepted and evaluated against the ATP for optimization and acceleration. By default, TCP traffic received on all VLANs is intercepted and evaluated against the ATP. VLANs can be excluded or included for interception using the following commands:

```
no inline vlan all
inline vlan 100
```

Example 4-21 shows the resulting InlineGroup configuration.

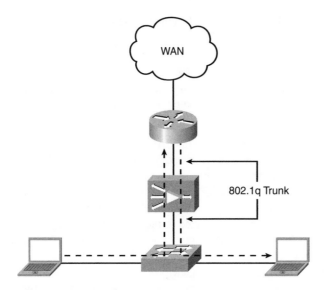

Figure 4-15   *Physical In-Path Deployment with One-Armed Routing*

Example 4-21   *WAE InlineGroup Configuration*

```
!
interface InlineGroup 1/0
 inline vlan all
 no inline vlan native,0-99,101-4095
 exit
!
```

There are different sequences of the inline CLI command that result in the same VLAN filter being applied. For example, the following results in all VLANs except for 100 being intercepted.

```
inline vlan all
no inline vlan 100
```

However, so does the following:

```
inline vlan native
inline vlan 0-4095
no inline vlan 100-110
inline vlan 101-200
```

In terms of VLAN assignment, the most permissive command takes precedence. If the inline group is already configured with **inline vlan all**, you need to selectively remove VLANs from interception or remove all VLANs and selectively add individual VLANs back for interception.

When an inline group is in bypass operating mode, a physical cross-connect is enabled between the two ports in the inline group. This behavior essentially creates a crossover cable between the two network elements. In cases where the two network elements are unable to communicate using a crossover cable, line protocol is not restored when the inline group is in bypass operating mode. This is generally a nonissue when the switchport that the LAN InlinePort is connected to supports automatic medium-dependent interface crossover (MDIX). MDIX enables the switchport to automatically detect the pinouts of the cables used to connect two devices. In cases where the switchport does not support this capability, the cabling guidelines outlined in Table 4-3 should be followed.

Table 4-3   *WAE Inline Module Cabling Guidelines*

Connection	Required Cable
Switch to switch (no WAE)	Crossover
Switch to router (no WAE)	Straight-through
Router to router (no WAE)	Crossover
Switch to WAE	Straight-through
WAE to switch	Crossover
Switch to WAE	Straight-through
WAE to switch	Straight-through
Router to WAE	Straight-through
WAE to router	Straight-through
WAE to WAE	Crossover

Content Switching

Content switching is the final interception mechanism discussed in this chapter. Content switches have traditionally provided load-balancing services for servers, firewalls, and content caches. Within the context of WAAS, content switching provides dedicated hardware for intercepting and load balancing connections across a farm of WAEs. Using content switches for transparent interception with WAAS is useful for large data center deployments, complex topologies, and integration with other advanced features such as application protocol optimization and SSL-offload. In addition, customers with existing content switching deployments can leverage their experience and investments in content switches for transparent interception with WAAS. The ACE is the Cisco content switch that is discussed in this section. Deployment and configuration examples for integrating ACE with Cisco WAAS are provided in Chapter 6.

Application Control Engine

The Cisco ACE module is a service module for the Cisco Catalyst 6500 series switches and Catalyst 7600 series routers. ACE provides intelligent load balancing and security services for enterprise applications and network devices. ACE can be used in a large-scale data center environment to transparently intercept and load balance connections for WAAS. The following are some of the key performance characteristics of Cisco ACE:

■ Up to 16 Gbps of throughput and 345,000 connections per second per module

■ Up to 4 million concurrent connections

■ Support for up to 250 virtual partitions, allowing customers to create virtual ACE modules using a single hardware module

■ Up to 16,000 real servers, which when used with Cisco WAAS provides nearly infinite scalability

■ High availability and scalability by using up to four ACE modules in the same Catalyst 6500 chassis or across multiple chassis

There are two common deployment models for integrating ACE into the network infra-structure: bridge mode and routed mode.

In bridge mode, ACE is used to merge two VLANs together. In order for traffic to pass between the two VLANs, it must pass through the ACE module. As traffic passes through the ACE module, it is evaluated against the configured service policies to deter-mine whether or not it should be acted upon. The IP subnet used on the bridged VLAN is the same. Figure 4-16 shows an ACE module deployed using bridge mode.

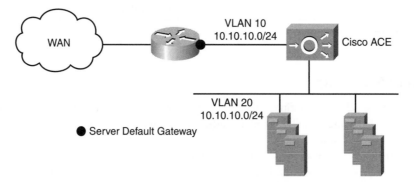

Figure 4-16 *ACE Deployed Using Bridge Mode*

The WAN-facing VLAN in Figure 4-16 is referred to as the client-side VLAN. The VLAN facing the data center resources is referred to as the server-side VLAN. As traffic enters the client-side VLAN, it is evaluated against the configured service policy. Traffic match-ing the service policy is redirected to a WAE, which has a dedicated VLAN interface configured on the ACE module. Traffic egressing the WAE comes back into the ACE module, where it is switched out the server-side VLAN toward the origin server.

In contrast to bridge mode, deploying ACE in routed mode allows for traffic to be routed between two different IP subnets. Using this deployment model, the client and server-side VLANs are on different IP subnets. Because the ACE module is a Layer 3 hop, traffic must be directed to the ACE module through the routing configuration of the hosts or network infrastructure. Figure 4-17 shows an ACE module deployed using routed mode.

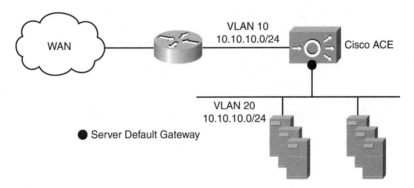

Figure 4-17 *ACE Deployed Using Routed Mode*

ACE is typically deployed in conjunction with WAAS using transparent, or directed, mode. This means that the ACE module does not perform any Network Address Translation (NAT) of traffic passing through it.

Egress Methods

Cisco WAAS provides several options for handling egress traffic received on intercepted connections. These options allow for flexibility when determining where to integrate WAAS into the existing network infrastructure, and help preserve the original path selection for traffic flows. These deployment options, referred to as the egress, are discussed in detail in this section.

The first egress method available in Cisco WAAS is IP forwarding. Egress traffic received on intercepted connections is forwarded based on the configuration of the local WAE routing table, which typically means that traffic is forwarded to the configured default gateway. In addition to supporting a single default gateway, WAAS supports up to 1024 static routes. Static routes are configured with a next hop IP address of a directly connected interface; recursive next hop IP addresses are not supported. Although it is possible to configure multiple static routes for the same destination, there is no support for equal-cost multipath (ECMP). Only a single route is installed in the routing table at a time. Note that traffic originating from the WAE itself also uses IP forwarding, regardless of the egress method configuration. The IP forwarding egress method is suited for basic topologies where only a single egress path for traffic exists, or in situations where other egress methods are not supported.

For more complex topologies, the IP forwarding egress method can lead to undesirable forwarding of traffic for intercepted connections. Take for example the topology shown in Figure 4-18. This example shows a remote office with multiple WAN routers connecting to diverse circuits. Traffic can enter or leave the site through either router. When multiple paths exist for traffic leaving a site, it is common for either HSRP or the Gateway Load Balancing Protocol (GLBP) to be used for default gateway redundancy. HSRP provides an active/standby configuration based on a virtual IP (VIP) address. At any given point in time, a single VIP address is "active" on one of the routers. Hosts are configured with the HSRP VIP address as their default gateway, causing all traffic from those hosts to be forwarded to one of the two routers. In the case of GLBP, either router can be selected as the outbound path for a host, depending on the specific GLBP configuration. Because GLBP operates based on MAC addresses, a WAE running Cisco WAAS appears as a single host. This means that traffic egressing a WAE also selects one of the two routers to forward outbound traffic to. For deployments that use GLBP for default-gateway redundancy, the issue with IP forwarding is the most pronounced.

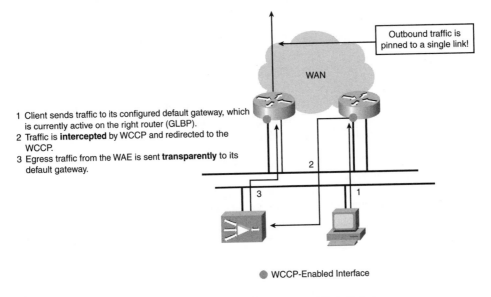

Figure 4-18 *Branch Topology with Multiple Entry and Exit Points*

You can see in Figure 4-18 how all egress traffic from the WAE is "pinned" to a single router. This can defeat the purpose of deploying GLBP in the first place, which is to distribute outbound traffic across both routers.

There are several options with WAAS for preserving the network path affinity originally chosen by the host system or network elements. The first option leverages the WCCPv2 return mechanism. Recall from earlier in this chapter that the WCCPv2 return mechanism is used by WCCPv2 clients to handle bypass traffic by sending it back to the WCCPv2-enabled router that redirected it. Cisco WAAS has the ability to leverage the WCCP GRE return method negotiated between the router and WAE for forwarding egress traffic from the WAE. The following CLI command changes the egress method to negotiated return:

```
egress-method negotiated-return intercept-method wccp
```

If GRE is the return method negotiated between the WAE and IOS, traffic received on optimized connections is encapsulated in a GRE header with a destination IP address of the WCCPv2 router ID and a source IP address of the WAE. When the WCCPv2-enabled IOS device receives the GRE-encapsulated packet, it removes the GRE header and forwards the packet normally. Because the GRE header uses a source IP address of the WAE, the IOS WCCPv2 process knows not to re-intercept the packet. This capability to return traffic to the IOS device that redirected it allows for the preservation of the original path selection made by the host or network infrastructure.

Another benefit of the GRE return method is that the WAE can reside on the same IP subnet with clients or servers that it optimizes connections for. This greatly simplifies branch deployments by removing the requirement for a separate subnet dedicated to the WAE. Figure 4-19 shows the same topology as Figure 4-18, except using the negotiated return egress method instead of IP forwarding.

The second option available is called Generic Generic Routing Encapsulation (GGRE). GGRE functions in a similar manner to WCCP GRE Return, but leverages a traditional GRE tunnel interface in IOS to receive egress traffic from one or more WAEs in the service group. GGRE was developed for two primary purposes:

■ Substituting for WCCP GRE on hardware-based platforms (such as the Catalyst 6500) that process WCCP GRE Return traffic in software (causing high CPU utilization).

■ Providing a configurable interface in IOS for handling traffic returning from one or more WAEs in a service group. Because traffic is received on an interface, policies such as access control and Optimized Edge Routing (OER) can be applied to the egress traffic.

With Generic GRE Return, a tunnel interface is configured in IOS on all of the WCCP-enabled routers in the service group. The tunnel interface is configured as either a point-to-point or a point-to-multipoint interface.

Note For the Catalyst 6500 platform to process GRE traffic in hardware, the tunnel source IP address for point-to-point tunnels must use a different interface for each WAE in the service. For this reason, a single point-to-multipoint tunnel should be used on each Catalyst 6500 in the service group when multiple WAEs exist in the service group.

The key parts of the IOS tunnel interface configuration include the following:

■ **Tunnel Source Address:** A Layer 3 interface used as the source IP address of GRE encapsulated packets. The tunnel source address must match the IP address configured in the WAE WCCP router-list.

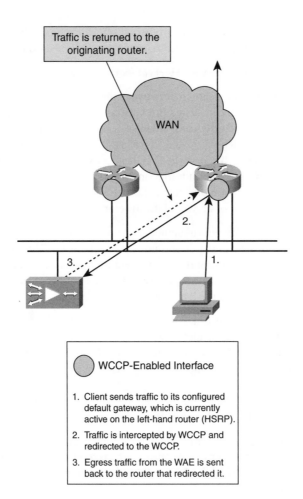

Figure 4-19 *Branch Topology Using GRE Return Egress Method*

- **Tunnel Destination Address:** For a point-to-point tunnel, this is the IP address of the target WAE. For a point-to-multipoint tunnel (recommended), no tunnel destination address is configured.

- **Tunnel IP Address:** An IP address configured on the IOS tunnel interface.

Example 4-22 shows an example point-to-multipoint tunnel interface configuration in IOS.

Example 4-22 *IOS Point-to-Multipoint Configuration Example*

```
!
interface Vlan105
 ip address 10.88.80.130 255.255.255.128
```

```
  standby 105 ip 10.88.80.129
end
!
interface Tunnel52
 ip address 10.10.10.1 255.255.255.0
 no ip redirects
 tunnel source Vlan105
 tunnel mode gre multipoint
end
```

In WAAS, the WCCP and egress method configurations are used to automatically create the tunnel interface and associate the tunnel interface with the correct intercepting router. Example 4-23 shows the WAE WCCP and egress method configurations.

Example 4-23 *WAE WCCP and Egress Method Configuration*

```
!
wccp router-list 1 10.88.80.130
wccp tcp-promiscuous router-list-num 1 mask-assign
wccp version 2
!
egress-method generic-gre intercept-method wccp
!
```

In the previous example, note that the IP address configured in the WCCP router list (10.88.80.130) matches the interface IP address on Vlan105 in IOS. This is required in order for the tunnel interface to come up on the WAE.

Note The tunnel interface in WAAS is automatically created internally and does not show up in the running configuration or **show interface** command output.

Directed Mode

By default, WAAS handles traffic transparently by preserving the source/destination IP addresses and TCP ports, even for optimized connections. The transparent mode of operation allows for end-to-end traffic visibility, which eases interoperability with existing network-based Quality of Service (QoS), access control, and performance management/reporting capabilities. The WAAS 4.1 release added an alternative mode of operation called *Directed Mode*. Directed Mode transports optimized connections using a non-transparent mechanism between two WAAS devices.

Directed Mode uses User Datagram Protocol (UDP) encapsulation to send optimized traffic between two WAAS devices. The source and destination IP addresses of the UDP header are the IP addresses of the WAE themselves.

Directed Mode still relies on the auto-discovery process to establish the peer relationship between two WAEs. This implies that all intermediate firewalls must permit TCP connections for the desired applications between clients and servers whose traffic is optimized by WAAS. After the auto-discovery process succeeds, the server-side WAE sends a TCP reset (RST) packet toward the client-side WAE to clear out the connection state on any intermediate devices between the WAEs. Future traffic for the connection is then encapsulated in a UDP header with a configurable source and destination port of 4050. Figure 4-20 shows the connection setup process for Directed Mode connections.

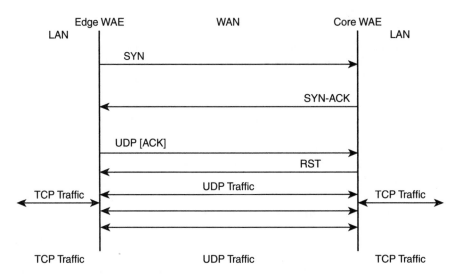

Figure 4-20   *Connection Setup for Directed Mode Connections*

Network Integration Best Practices

The following network integration best practices are recommended for the majority of WAAS deployments.

- **Leave the physical WAE interfaces set to auto-sense:** Because it is possible that some of your WAEs are able to run at 1Gbps speed, leaving all the WAEs deployed set to auto-sense simplifies the configuration and deployment. In addition, an alarm is raised in the Central Manager if an interface negotiates to half duplex.

- **Use PortChannel for interface redundancy when both physical WAE interfaces connect to the same LAN switch:** Improve performance by providing 2X the available LAN bandwidth.

- **Use a standby interface for interface redundancy when both physical WAE interfaces connect to different LAN switches:** Increase WAE availability in the event of a problem with the primary interface or connected LAN switch.

■ **Always configure a MD5 password for WCCP service groups:** Protect the integrity of the service group members by making sure that only authorized devices can join the service group.

■ **Stick to inbound WCCP redirection:** Even on software-based platforms, inbound redirection is more efficient.

■ **On hardware-based platforms, configure WCCP** using the following guidelines:

   ■ Use L2 forwarding instead of GRE forwarding.

   ■ Always use mask assignment.

   ■ Only use inbound redirection.

   ■ Do not use the **ip wccp redirect exclude in** command.

■ **Only use the WCCP GRE return egress method on software-based platforms (that is, ISR routers):** Hardware-based platforms process WCCP GRE return traffic completely in software, which causes serious performance issues.

■ **Run a recommended version of IOS for WCCP:** Tables 4-4 and 4-5 list the minimum recommended IOS versions when running WCCP with Cisco WAAS.

Table 4-4   *Minimum IOS Recommendations: Software-Based Platforms*

Major Version	M Train	T Train
12.2	12.2(26)	12.2(14)T
12.3	12.3(13)	12.3(14)T5
12.4	12.4(10)	12.4(20)T

Table 4-5   *Minimum IOS Recommendations: Hardware-Based Platforms*

Platform	Version
Catalyst 3560/3750	12.2(46)SE
Catalyst 4500/4900	12.2(40)SG
Catalyst 6500, Sup2	12.2(18)SXF13
Catalyst 6500, Sup32	CatOS 8.5/12.2(18)SXF13
Catalyst 6500, Sup720 (Native)	12.2(18)SXF13
Catalyst 6500, Sup720 (Hybrid)	CatOS 8.5/12.2(18)SXF13
Nexus 7000 Series Switch	NX-OS 4.2
ASR 1000 Series Aggregation Services Router	IOS XE 2.1

Summary

This chapter provided a detailed examination of the various methods for integrating WAAS into the network infrastructure. The chapter reviewed the various techniques for physical connectivity, including options for increased interface bandwidth and high availability. The chapter also previewed the network interception techniques that are used to transparently redirect traffic to the WAAS infrastructure for optimization. Particular focus was given to WCCPv2 and inline interception, which are the two most common interception methods. The interception method you choose is a site-local decision. For example, you can use WCCPv2 at some locations and inline at other locations. Finally, the chapter discussed the different egress methods available in WAAS, which provide control over how traffic on intercepted connections is reinserted into the network after redirection to a WAE. You should now have a good feel for the flexibility of the WAAS solution when it comes to network integration. The techniques available enable Cisco WAAS to integrate into network infrastructures of any size and complexity. The next chapter begins to put these various techniques to use, as you look at specific deployment models for the branch office environment.

Chapter 5

Branch Office Network Integration

This chapter provides a detailed discussion of the different methods for integrating Cisco Wide Area Application Services (WAAS) into the branch office network infrastructure. It examines both in-path and off-path integration options, applying them to small, medium-sized, and large branch office topologies of various configurations. In-path deployments leverage the inline module available for the Wide Area Application Engine (WAE) appliance models. Off-path deployments in the branch can use Web Cache Communications Protocol (WCCP) or Policy Based Routing (PBR). The preferred interception methods in the branch office environment are WCCP or inline interception. Detailed device configurations are provided for each scenario, leveraging current Cisco best practices. This chapter also discusses different deployment scenarios when integrating with Cisco IOS Firewall (IOS FW).

In-Path Deployment

Deploying WAAS in-path means that the WAE is physically placed between two network components, typically a WAN router and LAN switch. Inline deployments are intended primarily for branch office environments, as opposed to the data center. Each WAE supports one two- or four-port inline network interface card, which allows a single WAE to support interception on one or two physical paths. The in-path deployment model is typically used in branch office environments where the network topology is less complex than the data center infrastructure. In-path deployments are attractive for branch offices in the following cases:

- The WAN access router (or other WCCP-enabled router) is unable to sustain the increased traffic throughput enabled by Cisco WAAS. For example, 1 Mbps of compressed traffic from the WAN can decode into tens or hundreds of megabits-per-second worth of uncompressed traffic between the local WAE and clients. Some branch office routers are not suitable for such high levels of throughput. As a general rule, if the branch WAN bandwidth throughput is greater than or equal to 10 Mbps, an in-path deployment model should be considered.

- The IOS routers or switches do not support WCCP or it is not feasible to upgrade the IOS version to a release that is recommended with WCCP. In these cases, an in-path deployment might provide an alternate method for interception that does not require software or configuration changes to the existing branch office network infrastructure.

- The IOS router or switches are not under the administrative control of the group deploying WAAS. This is sometimes the case when the network equipment in a branch office is provided and managed by a service provider. In other cases, the team responsible for deploying WAAS might not have administrative access to the network devices, and therefore might not be comfortable, depending on another team for operational support of the solution.

In all these cases, deploying WAAS in-path provides an alternative to off-path deployment models. The following sections describe the in-path integration options for various reference topologies.

Nonredundant Branch Office

A basic branch office topology includes a single WAN router and LAN switch. The router is used for connecting the branch office to the WAN and routing traffic between local users and remote resources across the WAN. The site might have multiple Virtual Local Area Network (VLAN), with the WAN router responsible for routing traffic locally between the VLANs. The reference topology has two existing VLANs, one for data traffic and one for VoIP traffic. This topology enables demonstration of the per-VLAN interception capabilities of the inline module. Figure 5-1 shows a logical representation of the nonredundant reference branch office topology discussed in this section.

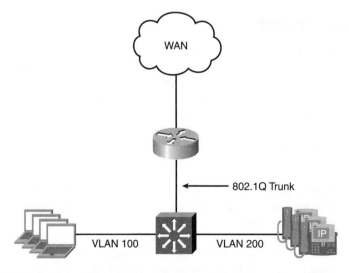

Figure 5-1   *Nonredundant Reference Topology*

In this scenario, the goal is to optimize traffic from clients on the data VLAN accessing resources at other locations across the WAN. Traffic from the VoIP VLAN should be passed through without optimization. Because an in-path deployment model is being used, a WAE with an inline module installed is physically placed in the network path between the WAN router and the LAN switch. Figure 5-2 shows the branch office topology with a WAE deployed in-path between the WAN router and LAN switch.

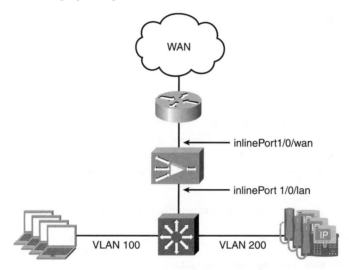

Figure 5-2 *Nonredundant In-Path Branch Office Topology*

The WAN0 port of inlineGroup 1/0 is connected to the LAN interface of the WAN router using a crossover cable, and the LAN0 port of inlineGroup 1/0 is connected to a switchport on the LAN switch using a straight-through cable. Other than ensuring that the bandwidth and duplex match between the WAN router and LAN switch, no configuration changes are required on the WAN router or LAN switch to accommodate an in-path deployment.

The switchport connecting to the LAN0 port of the WAE inline module should have the **PortFast** feature enabled. Because there is a brief loss of line protocol, this enables faster recovery of traffic forwarding when the inlineGroup transitions between intercept and bypass operating mode.

Because VLAN 200 is carrying the VoIP traffic, any packets with this VLAN ID are excluded from optimization. Packets tagged with VLAN ID 200 are bridged through the inline module without any optimization. Transmission Control Protocol (TCP) traffic on all other VLANs, including any untagged VLANs, is intercepted and optimized (based on policy configuration). Example 5-1 shows the inlineGroup configuration of the WAE.

Example 5-1 *WAE inlineGroup Configuration*

```
!
interface InlineGroup 1/0
```

```
        inline vlan all
        no inline vlan 200
        no autosense
        bandwidth 100
        full-duplex
        exit
interface InlineGroup 1/1
        inline vlan all
        shutdown
        exit
!
```

In Example 5-1, the speed and duplex of the inlineGroup are manually set to 100 Mbps, full-duplex. Note that the speed and duplex configuration settings are applied to the inlineGroup. This ensures that the same interface settings are applied consistently to both ports in the inlineGroup, which is required for proper operation during bypass operating mode.

Example 5-2 shows the full WAE configuration that is used for this deployment scenario.

Example 5-2   *Small to Medium-Sized Branch Office In-Path WAE Configuration*

```
WAE512# show running-config no-policy
! WAAS version 4.1.3b (build b9 Jul 30 2009)
!
device mode application-accelerator
!
hostname WAE512
!
primary-interface GigabitEthernet 1/0
!
interface GigabitEthernet 1/0
 ip address 10.88.80.155 255.255.255.128
 exit
interface GigabitEthernet 2/0
shutdown
exit
interface InlineGroup 1/0
inline vlan all
no inline vlan 200
no autosense
bandwidth 100
full-duplex
exit
```

```
     interface InlineGroup 1/1
      inline vlan all
      shutdown
      exit
     !
     ip default-gateway 10.88.80.130
     !
     no auto-register enable
     !
     ! ip path-mtu-discovery is disabled in WAAS by default
     !
     ntp server 10.88.80.142
     !
     username admin password 1 $1$gfYExN4R$WlJ9i/.C34QsNRpuPgpz.1
     username admin privilege 15
     username admin print-admin-password 1
CEC32C13191F9B56AAD3B435B51404EE 6E73ED22
     DDAFAA4FACD2513341E6B7C
   !
   authentication login local enable primary
   authentication configuration local enable primary
   !
   central-manager address 10.88.80.142
   cms enable
   !
   ! End of WAAS configuration
   WAE512#
```

Note that interface GigabitEthernet 1/0 is configured with an IP address and specified as
the primary interface. In this example, one of the built-in Ethernet interfaces is used for
management traffic to and from the WAE. The default gateway specified in the configuration is used only for traffic sourced from the WAE itself. Alternatively, you can configure an IP address on the inlineGroup interface, which allows you to deploy the WAE
without using one of the built-in Ethernet interfaces for management. Example 5-3 shows
the inlineGroup configured with a management IP address.

Example 5-3 *Management IP Address on inlineGroup*

```
     !
     primary-interface InlineGroup 1/0
     !
     interface GigabitEthernet 1/0
      shutdown
      exit
```

```
        interface GigabitEthernet 2/0
         shutdown
         exit
        !
        interface InlineGroup 1/0
         ip address 10.88.80.137 255.255.255.128
         inline vlan all
         no inline vlan 200
         no autosense
         bandwidth 100
         full-duplex
         exit
    interface InlineGroup 1/1
     inline vlan all
     shutdown
     exit
    !
    ip default-gateway 10.88.80.129
     !
```

The IP address associated with the inlineGroup is applied to the WAN0 interface. Also note that the primary interface has been configured as inlineGroup 1/0.

Note   The IP address configured on the InlineGroup is reachable only when the InlineGroup is in intercept operating mode. Because of this dependency, Cisco recommends configuring one of the native Ethernet interfaces (that is GigabitEthernet 1/0) as the dedicated management interface for in-path deployments.

Redundant Branch Office

Medium to large branch offices typically have multiple WAN routers and LAN switches for increased capacity and improved availability of the WAN resources. The links between the WAN routers and LAN switches can be configured either as Layer 2 trunks, as in the previous scenario, or as point-to-point routed links. The reference topology is configured with routed links between the WAN routers and LAN switches. The LAN switches handle local routing between VLANs. Figure 5-3 shows the redundant reference branch office topology discussed in this section.

In this scenario, the goal is to optimize traffic from clients accessing resources at other locations across the WAN. Because the links between the WAN routers and LAN switches do not carry all the VLANs for the site, all TCP traffic is intercepted and optimized (based on policy configuration).

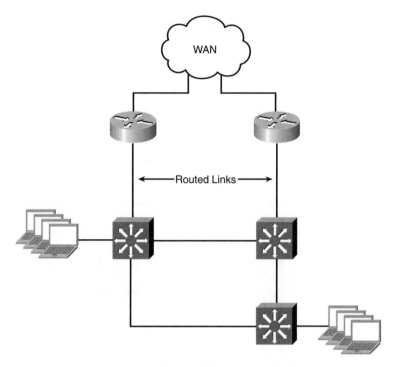

Figure 5-3 *Redundant Branch Office Reference Topology*

Traffic can be excluded from optimization by creating a policy in the Application Traffic Policy (ATP) that instructs the WAE to handle certain IP addresses or ranges of IP addresses as pass-through. See Chapter 8, "Configuring WAN Optimization," for more information on configuring custom traffic policies.

A WAE with an inline module installed is physically placed in the network path between the WAN router and the LAN switch. The in-path deployment model for the redundant reference topology leverages both inline groups in a single 4-port inline module to intercept traffic on two physical paths. Traffic can traverse either inlineGroup when entering or existing the site, which supports environments with asymmetric traffic flows. Figure 5-4 shows the large redundant branch office topology with a WAE deployed in-path between the WAN routers and LAN switches.

The WAN0 port of each inlineGroup is connected to the LAN interface of one of the WAN routers using a crossover cable. The LAN0 port of each inlineGroup is connected to a switchport in the LAN infrastructure using a straight-through cable. In this reference topology, the LAN port for each inlineGroup is connected to separate switches, but these could just as well be connected to the same switch. Again, there is no special configuration required on the WAN router LAN interfaces or LAN switchports to support the in-path deployment model (other than ensuring the bandwidth and duplex match between the WAN routers and LAN switches).

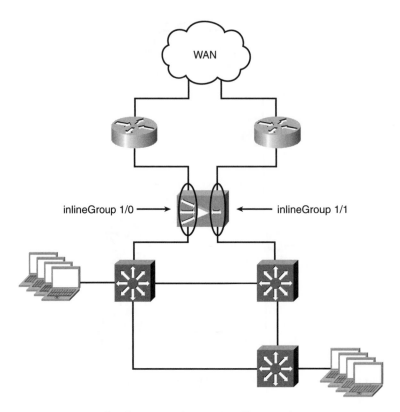

Figure 5-4   *Redundant In-Path Branch Office Deployment*

> **Tip**   The switchport connecting to the LAN0 ports of the WAE inline module should have the **PortFast** feature enabled. This enables faster recovery of traffic forwarding when the inlineGroup transitions between intercept and bypass operating mode.

Example 5-4 shows the inlineGroup configuration of the WAE.

Example 5-4   *Redundant Branch Office inlineGroup Configuration*

```
!
interface InlineGroup 1/0
 inline vlan all
 exit
interface InlineGroup 1/1
 inline vlan all
 exit
 !
```

Because this reference topology represents a medium or large branch office, both inline groups are configured with the default setting to autosense the speed and duplex of the individual ports, which allows them to negotiate to 1 Gbps. Example 5-4 also specifies the **inline vlan all** command, which instructs the WAE to intercept all TCP-based traffic, regardless of the VLAN it is associated with.

Example 5-5 shows the full WAE configuration that is used for this deployment model.

Example 5-5 *Redundant Branch Office In-Path WAE Configuration*

```
WAE512# show running-config no-policy
! WAAS version 4.1.3b (build b9 Jul 30 2009)
!
device mode application-accelerator
!
hostname WAE512
!
primary-interface GigabitEthernet 1/0
!
interface GigabitEthernet 1/0
 ip address 10.88.80.155 255.255.255.128
 exit
interface GigabitEthernet 2/0
shutdown
exit
interface InlineGroup 1/0
 inline vlan all
 exit
interface InlineGroup 1/1
 inline vlan all
 exit
!
ip default-gateway 10.88.80.130
!
no auto-register enable
!
! ip path-mtu-discovery is disabled in WAAS by default
!
ntp server 10.88.80.142
!
username admin password 1 $1$gfYExN4R$WlJ9i/.C34QsNRpuPgpz.1
username admin privilege 15
username admin print-admin-password 1 CEC32C13191F9B56AAD3B435B51404EE
6E73ED22ADDAFAA4FACD2513341E6B7C
!
authentication login local enable primary
```

```
authentication configuration local enable primary
!
central-manager address 10.88.80.142
cms enable
                  !
                  ! End of WAAS configuration
WAE512#
```

Serial Inline Clustering

In both the nonredundant and redundant topologies, you can serially connect multiple WAEs in a back-to-back configuration for high availability and overload scalability. Cisco supports clustering up to two WAEs in this fashion. Figure 5-5 shows two WAEs serially clustered for high availability.

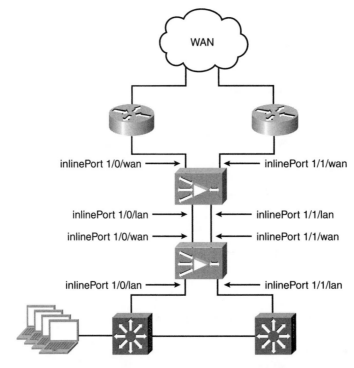

Figure 5-5   *Clustering Multiple WAEs for High Availability*

Unlike the off-path integration models discussed later in this chapter, serial clustering does not provide any active/active load sharing across the clustered WAEs. The first WAE in the cluster to receive the TCP SYN packet initiates optimization for that connection. When a peer WAE is discovered across the WAN, the second WAE in the cluster determines through the TFO auto-discovery process that it is in the middle of two other

WAEs. This causes the intermediate WAE to handle the connections as passthrough. If one of the WAEs in the cluster becomes overloaded or unavailable, the remaining WAE in the cluster begins optimizing new connections. Existing connections are seen as *In Progress* and handled as passthrough. Figure 5-6 shows the behavior of the clustered WAEs when the first WAE exceeds its maximum optimized connection limit.

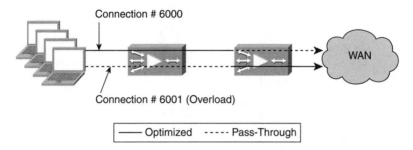

Figure 5-6 *Serial Clustering Overload Connection Handling*

Off-Path Deployment

Off-path deployments involve leveraging intelligence within the network infrastructure to intercept and redirect traffic to WAAS. With off-path deployments, the WAE is logically inline, as opposed to physically inline as with in-path deployments. Common off-path deployment techniques include WCCP, PBR, and server load balancing (SLB). This chapter focuses on deployments using WCCP and PBR in the branch office. WCCP is the preferred transparent interception mechanism for off-path WAAS deployments. Server load balancing is discussed as one of the data center network integration options in Chapter 6, "Data Center Network Integration."

Small to Medium-Sized Nonredundant Branch Office

The branch office topology discussed in this section includes a single WAN router and one or more LAN switches. The WAN router can be either a software- or hardware-based platform and is used for connecting the branch office to the WAN and routing traffic between local users and remote resources across the WAN. The site has one or more VLANs upon which clients are located. In addition, local resources such as servers and printers might be present on a dedicated VLAN. Figure 5-7 shows the nonredundant reference branch office topology discussed in this section.

In this scenario, the goal is to optimize traffic to and from local VLANs accessing resources at other locations across the WAN. Traffic between local VLANs should be excluded from interception. For an off-path deployment, the WAE is connected to the network through one of the built-in Ethernet interfaces. WCCP is configured on the WAN router to intercept all TCP traffic and redirect it to the WAE.

If the site uses a software-based platform for WCCP interception, the WAE can be deployed on one of the existing VLANs. This minimizes the amount of configuration change at the site required to deploy WAAS, because a separate VLAN doesn't need to be dedicated to the WAE. WCCP is configured to intercept traffic both inbound and out-bound on the router WAN interface. This approach allows for traffic between local VLANs to pass without interception and without the need for a WCCP redirect list.

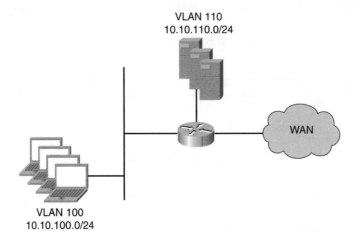

Figure 5-7   *Small to Medium-Sized Nonredundant
Reference Topology*

Figure 5-8 shows the branch office topology for this scenario.

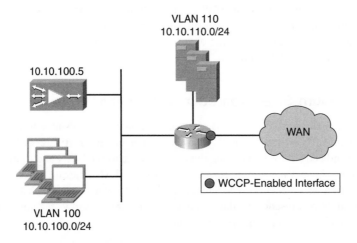

Figure 5-8   *Off-Path Nonredundant Branch Office
Deployment*

When the WAE is located on the same VLAN with hosts it is optimizing connections for, the router needs some way to differentiate between traffic sourced from a host and traf-fic coming from the WAE. To accomplish this, the WAE is configured to use WCCP Generic Routing Encapsulation (GRE) return as the egress method. This causes the WAE to return egress traffic to the intercepting router encapsulated in a WCCP GRE header. The WCCP GRE header uses the WAE IP address as the source IP address and the intercepting router as the destination IP address. By definition of the protocol, WCCP does not intercept GRE-encapsulated traffic sourced from the WAE registered in a service group defined on the router. Figure 5-9 shows the traffic flow between the WAE and intercepting router when WCCP GRE return is configured as the egress method.

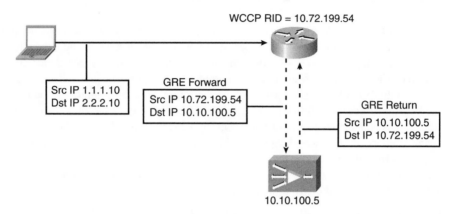

Figure 5-9 *WCCP GRE Return Traffic Flow*

Example 5-6 shows the WCCP configuration of the WAN router.

Example 5-6 *Off-Path Nonredundant Branch Office WCCP Configuration*

```
!
hostname WR-01
!
ip wccp 61 password cisco
ip wccp 62 password cisco
!
interface FastEthernet0/0
 no ip address
 duplex auto
 speed auto
!
interface FastEthernet0/0.100
 encapsulation dot1q 100
 ip address 10.10.100.1 255.255.255.0
!
interface FastEthernet0/0.110
 encapsulation dot1q 110
 ip address 10.10.110.1 255.255.255.0
!
```

```
interface Serial0/0
      description ** Link to WAN **
      ip address 10.72.199.54 255.255.255.252
      ip wccp 61 redirect out
ip wccp 62 redirect in
!
```

Remember that Cisco WAAS uses two WCCP service groups, 61 and 62, for interception on the WAN router. It is important to pay attention to which interfaces and in which direction you apply each service group. In a branch office, where you have a high concentration of clients, service group 61 is configured to intercept traffic in the client-to-server direction. In Example 5-6, this means that service group 61 is configured outbound on the WAN interface (Serial0/0). Service group 61 intercepts requests leaving the router from clients on interface Serial0/0. Service group 62 is configured inbound on the server-facing interface, in this example Serial0/0. This ensures that service group 62 intercepts responses from the remote servers coming in from the WAN. When there are multiple WAEs deployed at a branch office, this placement of the two service groups causes WCCP to perform load distribution based on the client IP addresses.

Example 5-7 shows the configuration of the WAE in this deployment scenario.

Example 5-7 *Off-Path Nonredundant Branch Office WAE Configuration*

```
WAE512# show running-config no-policy
! WAAS version 4.1.3b (build b9 Jul 30 2009)
!
device mode application-accelerator
!
hostname WAE512
!
primary-interface GigabitEthernet 1/0
!
interface GigabitEthernet 1/0
 ip address 10.10.100.5 255.255.255.0
 exit
interface GigabitEthernet 2/0
 shutdown
 exit
!
ip default-gateway 10.10.100.1
!
no auto-register enable
!
! ip path-mtu-discovery is disabled in WAAS by default
!
```

```
      ntp server 10.88.80.142
      !
      wccp router-list 1 10.10.100.1
      wccp tcp-promiscuous router-list-num 1 password ****
   wccp version 2
   !
   egress-method negotiated-return intercept-method wccp
   !
   username admin password 1 $1$8RHM7A.5$o9.5RCkltxTxMfruk.8EN1
   username admin privilege 15
   username admin print-admin-password 1
CEC32C13191F9B56AAD3B435B51404EE 6E73ED22
   DDAFAA4FACD2513341E6B7C
   !
   authentication login local enable primary
   authentication configuration local enable primary
   !
   central-manager address 10.88.80.142
   cms enable
   !
   ! End of WAAS configuration
   WAE512#
```

Note the **egress-method** command in Example 5-7. This tells the WAE to use the return
method negotiated via WCCP to handle traffic for connections received using WCCP.

Caution   At the time of this writing, Cisco WAAS supports WCCP GRE Return, Generic
GRE Return, and IP forwarding as egress methods. Both the WCCP and Generic GRE
return methods require WCCP GRE as the forwarding method. If the egress method is configured for Generic GRE or negotiated return and the WAE has negotiated WCCP L2 return
with the intercepting router, the WAE falls back to IP forwarding as the egress method.

Also note that a default gateway is still configured. The default gateway is used for forwarding traffic sourced from the WAE itself, regardless of the egress method configured.

An alternate deployment model for this scenario uses a hardware-based WAN router,
such as the ASR 1000 series router. When the WAN router in this scenario is a hardware-
based platform, the WAE needs to be deployed on a new, dedicated VLAN. The dedicated VLAN is required because current hardware-based platforms support only inbound
WCCP interception and generally don't support decapsulating WCCP GRE return traffic
in hardware. WCCP is configured to intercept traffic inbound on the router client and
server facing interfaces. To prevent traffic between local VLANs from being intercepted, a
WCCP redirect list is used.

Figure 5-10 shows the topology for this scenario.

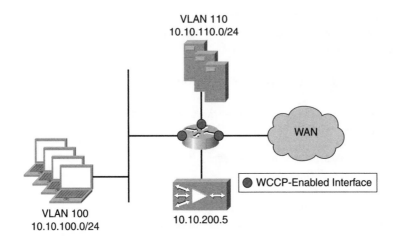

Figure 5-10 *Off-Path Nonredundant Branch Office Deployment*

Example 5-8 shows the WCCP configuration of the WAN router for this scenario.

Example 5-8 *Off-Path Nonredundant Branch Office WCCP Configuration*

```
!
hostname WR-01
!
ip wccp 61 password cisco redirect-list LOCAL-SUBNETS
ip wccp 62 password cisco
!
interface GigabitEthernet1/2/2
 no ip address
 duplex auto
 speed auto
!
interface GigabitEthernet1/2/2.100
 encapsulation dot1q 100
 ip address 10.10.100.1 255.255.255.0
 ip wccp 61 redirect in
!
interface GigabitEthernet1/2/2.110
 encapsulation dot1q 110
 ip address 10.10.110.1 255.255.255.0
 ip wccp 61 redirect in
!
interface GigabitEthernet1/2/2.200
```

```
              description ** Dedicated WAE VLAN **
              encapsulation dot1q 200
              ip address 10.10.200.1 255.255.255.0
              !
             interface GigabitEthernet1/2/3
              description ** Link to WAN **
              ip address 10.72.199.54 255.255.255.252
              ip wccp 62 redirect in
 !
ip access-list extended LOCAL-SUBNETS
 deny ip any 10.10.100.0 0.0.0.255
 deny ip any 10.10.110.0 0.0.0.255
 permit ip any any
 !
```

Note that the WCCP redirect list is applied only to service group 61. The access list
LOCAL-SUBNETS prevents interception of traffic from any source destined to the local
subnets. Because service group 61 is applied only inbound on the LAN interfaces, it is
the only service group that requires the redirect list.

Example 5-9 shows the configuration of the WAE in this deployment scenario.

Example 5-9   *Off-Path Nonredundant Branch Office WAE Configuration*

```
          WAE512# show running-config no-policy
          ! WAAS version 4.1.3b (build b9 Jul 30 2009)
          !
          device mode application-accelerator
          !
          hostname WAE512
       !
       primary-interface GigabitEthernet 1/0
       !
       interface GigabitEthernet 1/0
        ip address 10.10.200.5 255.255.255.0
        exit
       !
       ip default-gateway 10.10.200.1
       !
       no auto-register enable
       !
       ! ip path-mtu-discovery is disabled in WAAS by default
       !
       ntp server 10.88.80.142
       !
```

```
          wccp router-list 1 10.10.200.1
          wccp tcp-promiscuous router-list-num 1 password **** l2-redirect mask-
assign
          wccp version 2
          !
          username admin password 1 $1$gfYExN4R$WlJ9i/.C34QsNRpuPgpz.1
          username admin privilege 15
          username admin print-admin-password 1 CEC32C13191F9B56AAD3B435B51404EE
6E73ED22
          DDAFAA4FACD2513341E6B7C
          !
          authentication login local enable primary
          authentication configuration local enable primary
     !
     central-manager address 10.88.80.142
     cms enable
     !
     ! End of WAAS configuration
     WAE512#
```

Note the following configuration differences on the WAE when running WCCP on a hardware-based platform:

■ Layer 2 WCCP forwarding is configured with the **l2-redirect** option on the **wccp tcp-promiscuous** service group command.

■ WCCP mask assignment is configured with the **mask-assign** option on the service group command.

■ There is no explicit egress method configuration, which means that the default egress method **ip forwarding** is used.

Enhanced Network Module (NME-WAE)

The Network Module Enhanced WAE (NME-WAE) provides a router-integrated network module capable of running Cisco WAAS. When deploying the NME-WAE, WCCP is required as the interception mechanism. Traffic entering the router is intercepted by WCCP and redirected over an internal GigabitEthernet interface to the NME-WAE. Figure 5-11 shows a remote branch topology using a router-integrated NME-WAE.

The internal GigabitEthernet interface available on the NME-WAE is exposed in the router IOS configuration as an interface named **IntegratedServicesEngine***slot/port*. This interface is configured in a similar manner to any other IOS interface, with the following exceptions:

■ The IP address of the WAE is configured on the IntegratedServicesEngine interface using the command **service-module ip address** *addr mask*.

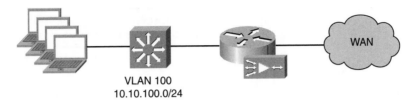

Figure 5-11 *Branch Deployment Model Using NME-WAE*

■   The default gateway of the WAE is configured on the IntegratedServicesEngine inter-
    face using the command **service-module ip default-gateway** *addr*.

Example 5-10 shows the full configuration of the IntegratedServicesEngine interface in IOS.

Example 5-10   *NME-WAE IOS Interface Configuration*

```
!
interface Integrated-Service-Engine1/0
 ip address 10.88.81.17 255.255.255.240
 ip wccp redirect exclude in
 service-module ip address 10.88.81.18 255.255.255.240
 service-module ip default-gateway 10.88.81.17
 no keepalive
!
```

Note that the **ip wccp redirect exclude in** command is configured on the
IntegratedServicesEngine interface. This ensures that the WCCP process running on the
router does not re-intercept any traffic coming into the router from the NME-WAE.
After the required interface configuration is complete in the router, the WAE can be
accessed and managed just like an external WAE appliance. Because the NME-WAE
does not have an external console interface for out-of-band management, additional command-line interface (CLI) commands are available in IOS for managing the NME-WAE.

Two-Arm Deployment

At small to medium-sized sites where an off-path deployment is used with a low-end
router, the WAE can be deployed in a two-arm mode to help offload decoded traffic
directly to the local client subnet. The two-arm deployment model is intended for small
to medium-sized branch offices that have a single host subnet. The two-arm deployment
model still leverages WCCP to transparently intercept and redirect traffic to the primary
interface of the WAE. The primary interface of the WAE resides on a dedicated subnet,
separate from the hosts it is optimizing connections for. The difference with this deployment model is that the second built-in Ethernet interface on the WAE is directly connected to the same subnet as the local hosts. Figure 5-12 shows an example of this topology.

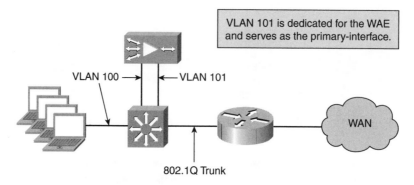

Figure 5-12   *Two-Arm WAE Deployment*

The primary interface of the WAE is used for receiving traffic intercepted using WCCP and serves as the interface through which the default gateway is configured. The egress method used in this deployment model is IP forwarding. The second WAE interface is configured with an IP address in the local host subnet. This allows optimized traffic that is received across the WAN to be decoded in the WAE and then sent directly to the local destination host systems, bypassing the need to return through the WAN access router. Bypassing the WAN access router reduces the increased levels of throughput that can cause performance problems for legacy routers when WAAS is deployed. Figure 5-13 shows the traffic flow in a two-arm deployment model.

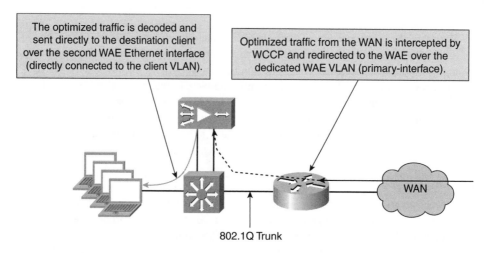

Figure 5-13   *Two-Arm Deployment Traffic Flow*

Example 5-11 shows the WCCP configuration of the WAN router.

Example 5-11 *Two-Arm Deployment WAN Router Configuration*

```
!
hostname WR-01
 !
 ip wccp 61 password cisco
 ip wccp 62 password cisco
 !
 interface FastEthernet0/0
  no ip address
  duplex full
  speed 100
 !
 interface FastEthernet0/0.201
  description ** Branch Client Subnet **
  encapsulation dot1Q 201
ip address 10.10.101.1 255.255.255.240
ip wccp 61 redirect in
!
interface FastEthernet0/0.202
 description ** Branch WAE Subnet **
 encapsulation dot1Q 202
 ip address 10.10.100.1 255.255.255.240
 ip wccp redirect exclude in
!
interface Serial0/0
 description ** Link to WAN **
 ip address 10.88.81.254 255.255.255.252
 ip wccp 62 redirect in
 !
```

Example 5-12 shows the WAE configuration that is used for this deployment model.

Example 5-12 *Two-Arm Deployment WAE Configuration*

```
WAE512# show running-config no-policy
! WAAS version 4.1.3b (build b9 Jul 30 2009)
!
device mode application-accelerator
!
!
hostname WAE512
!
primary-interface GigabitEthernet 1/0
!
interface GigabitEthernet 1/0
 ip address 10.10.100.5 255.255.255.0
```

```
        exit
                            interface GigabitEthernet 2/0
                             ip address 10.10.101.5 255.255.255.0
                             exit
                            !
                            ip default-gateway 10.10.100.1
                            !
                            no auto-register enable
                            !
                            ! ip path-mtu-discovery is disabled in WAAS by default
                            !
                            ntp server 10.88.80.142
                            !
                            wccp router-list 1 10.10.100.1
                            wccp tcp-promiscuous router-list-num 1 password ****
                            wccp version 2
                            !
                            username admin password 1
$1$gfYExN4R$WlJ9i/.C34QsNRpuPgpz.1
                            username admin privilege 15
                            username admin print-admin-password 1
CEC32C13191F9B56AAD3B435B51404EE 6E73ED22
                            DDAFAA4FACD2513341E6B7C
                            !
                            authentication login local enable primary
                            authentication configuration local enable primary
                            !
                            central-manager address 10.88.80.142
                            cms enable
        !
        ! End of WAAS configuration
        WAE512#
```

Large Nonredundant Branch Office

The large nonredundant branch office topology has a similar topology as the small to medium-sized branch. The primary differences are the number of LAN switches and the routing configuration. At larger branch locations, it is also possible for the WAN router to be a hardware-based platform, such as a Cisco 7600 Series router or a Catalyst 6500 Series switch with a FlexWAN module. Large branch offices have clients on multiple VLANs, which not only access resources across the WAN, but also communicate between each other locally. In these cases, it is most common for the LAN switches to provide IP routing capabilities. Figure 5-14 shows the large nonredundant reference branch office topology discussed in this section.

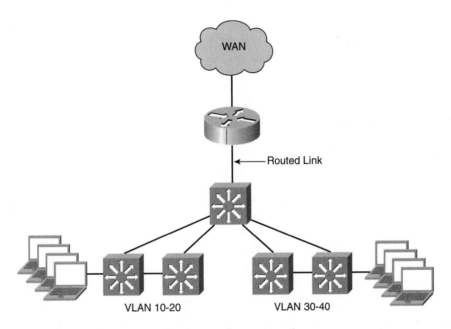

Figure 5-14 *Large Nonredundant Reference Topology*

Here the link between the WAN access router and the LAN switch is a point-to-point routed link. The goal is to optimize traffic from clients going across the WAN. Because there are multiple existing VLANs and maintaining the proximity of the WAE to the WAN access layer is desired, it makes sense to create a new VLAN on the top-level LAN switch dedicated for the WAEs that are deployed in this branch. WCCP is still configured on the WAN router to intercept all TCP traffic and redirect it to the WAE. Figure 5-15 shows the branch office topology for this deployment model.

Unlike the small to medium-sized topology, the LAN switch performs routing for the subnet the WAE resides on. Because WCCP interception is still configured on the WAN access router, the WAE is multiple Layer 3 hops away from the intercepting router. This scenario requires that WCCP be configured to use both GRE forwarding and GRE return, because the intercepted traffic must traverse an intermediate Layer 3 hop between the intercepting router and the WAE.

Example 5-13 shows the WCCP configuration of the WAN router.

Example 5-13 *Large Nonredundant Deployment WAN Router Configuration*

```
!
hostname WR-01
```

```
!
ip wccp 61 password cisco
ip wccp 62 password cisco
!
interface Loopback0
 ip address 10.32.77.66 255.255.255.255
!
interface FastEthernet0/0
 ip address 10.88.80.1 255.255.255.252
 ip wccp 61 redirect in
 duplex full
 speed 100
!
interface Serial0/0
 description ** Link to WAN **
 ip address 10.88.81.254 255.255.255.252
 ip wccp 62 redirect in
!
```

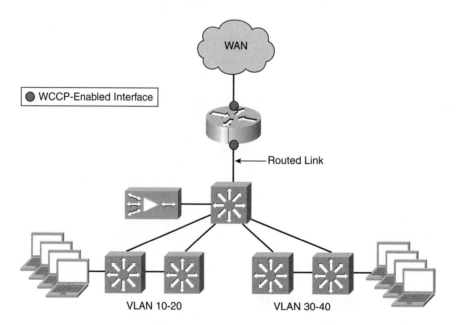

Figure 5-15 *Large Nonredundant Deployment*

Example 5-14 shows the configuration of the LAN switch in this deployment scenario.

Example 5-14   *Large Nonredundant Deployment LAN Switch Configuration*

```
            !
            interface GigabitEthernet1/0/1
             ip address 10.88.80.2 255.255.255.252
            !
            <removed for brevity>
!
interface Vlan196
 ip address 10.88.81.17 255.255.255.240
!
ip route 0.0.0.0 0.0.0.0 10.88.80.1
ip classless
!
end
```

Example 5-15 shows the configuration of the WAE in this deployment scenario.

Example 5-15   *Large Nonredundant Deployment WAE Configuration*

```
    WAE512# show running-config no-policy
    ! WAAS version 4.1.3b (build b9 Jul 30 2009)
    !
    device mode application-accelerator
    !
    hostname WAE512
    !
    primary-interface GigabitEthernet 1/0
    !
    interface GigabitEthernet 1/0
     ip address 10.88.80.137 255.255.255.128
     exit
    interface GigabitEthernet 2/0
     shutdown
     exit
    !
    ip default-gateway 10.88.80.129
    !
    no auto-register enable
!
! ip path-mtu-discovery is disabled in WAAS by default
!
ntp server 10.88.80.142
!
wccp router-list 1 10.32.77.66
wccp tcp-promiscuous router-list-num 1 password ****
```

```
wccp version 2
!
egress-method negotiated-return intercept-method wccp
!
username admin password 1 $1$gfYExN4R$WlJ9i/.C34QsNRpuPgpz.1
username admin privilege 15
username admin print-admin-password 1
CEC32C13191F9B56AAD3B435B51404EE 6E73ED22ADDAFAA4FACD2513341E6B7C
!
authentication login local enable primary
authentication configuration local enable primary
!
central-manager address 10.88.80.142
cms enable
!
! End of WAAS configuration
WAE512#
```

The default gateway of the WAE is configured as the switched virtual interface (SVI) on the LAN switch where the WAE subnet is located. However, because the WAE is multiple Layer 3 hops away from the intercepting router, the IP address configured in the WCCP router list is the Loopback0 interface address on the intercepting router. This is recommended to provide stability to the WCCP process on the intercepting router and allow for WCCP to continue operating if there are multiple paths available between the WAE and the intercepting router. Another example of this configuration is provided for the redundant branch office topology.

Another option in this scenario is to move the WCCP interception functionality to the LAN switch. This is useful in cases where you might not have administrative access to the WAN access router or you want to leverage the performance of the LAN switch to perform WCCP interception in hardware. Figure 5-16 shows the branch office topology for this deployment model.

This topology configures WCCP interception on the Cisco Catalyst LAN switch. The LAN switch in this case handles routing for the subnet the WAE resides on. No configuration changes are required on the WAN access router.

Example 5-16 shows the IOS configuration of the LAN switch in this deployment scenario.

Example 5-16   *WCCP on LAN Switch Configuration*

```
!
ip wccp 61 password cisco
```

```
     ip wccp 62 password cisco
     !
interface GigabitEthernet1/0/1
 ip address 10.88.80.2 255.255.255.252
 ip wccp 62 redirect in
!
<removed for brevity>
!
interface Vlan100
 ip address 10.88.81.1 255.255.255.240
 ip wccp 61 redirect in
!
interface Vlan196
 ip address 10.88.81.17 255.255.255.240
!
ip route 0.0.0.0 0.0.0.0 10.88.80.1
ip classless
!
end
```

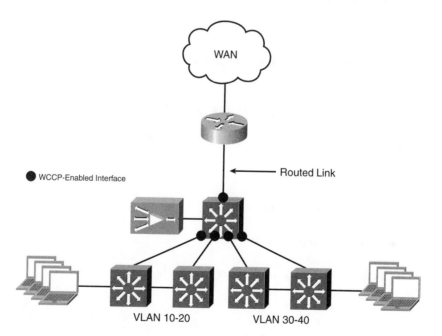

Figure 5-16 *WCCP Interception on LAN Switch*

WCCP is configured on interface GigabitEthernet1/0/1, which is the physical routed interface connecting to the WAN router at the site. WCCP interception is also enabled on all the client-facing SVI interfaces.

Caution   Do not use the command **ip wccp redirect exclude in** on hardware-based platforms. This command is not handled in the hardware forwarding path and can cause traffic to be handled in software.

Tip   When configuring WCCP on a hardware-based platform, always use inbound redirection to ensure full hardware acceleration.

Example 5-17 shows the configuration of the WAE in this deployment scenario.

Example 5-17   *WCCP on LAN Switch Deployment WAE Configuration*

```
WAE512# show running-config no-policy
! WAAS version 4.1.3b (build b9 Jul 30 2009)
!
device mode application-accelerator
!
hostname WAE512
!
primary-interface GigabitEthernet 1/0
!
interface GigabitEthernet 1/0
ip address 10.88.80.137 255.255.255.128
exit
interface GigabitEthernet 2/0
shutdown
exit
!
ip default-gateway 10.88.80.129
!
no auto-register enable
!
! ip path-mtu-discovery is disabled in WAAS by default
!
ntp server 10.88.80.142
!
wccp router-list 1 10.32.77.66
wccp tcp-promiscuous router-list-num 1 password **** 12-redirect mask-
assign
wccp version 2
```

```
       !
       username admin password 1 $1$gfYExN4R$WlJ9i/.C34QsNRpuPgpz.1
       username admin privilege 15
       username admin print-admin-password 1  CEC32C13191F9B56AAD3B435B51404EE
6E73ED22ADDAFAA4FACD2513341E6B7C
       !
       authentication login local enable primary
       authentication configuration local enable primary
       !
       central-manager address 10.88.80.142
  cms enable
  !
  ! End of WAAS configuration
  WAE512#
```

Because WCCP is running on a hardware-based platform in this configuration, there are two additional WCCP options configured on the WAE:

- **l2-redirect:** The **l2-redirect** option tells the Catalyst 3750 to redirect traffic to the WAE by rewriting the destination MAC address of redirected traffic to equal the MAC address of the target WAE (as opposed to encapsulating the packet in a WCCP GRE header).

- **mask-assign:** The **mask-assign** option is an alternative to the default hash assignment, which is optimized for use in hardware-based platforms. Both of these options are required to ensure that WCCP redirection is handled completely in hardware.

Off-Path Redundant Topology

Redundant branch office network topologies present additional challenges in that there are multiple paths traffic can traverse within the site and when entering and existing the WAN. It is common for the traffic load from the site to be distributed across multiple WAN links for increased capacity/performance and to minimize the impact of a single WAN link outage. When deploying WAAS in redundant branch office topologies, one of the design goals is to preserve the original path selection, or outbound load distribution, of traffic across multiple WAN links. The following sections explore various placement and interception configuration options for off-path integration in redundant branch office topologies.

Small to Medium-Sized Redundant Branch Office

Small/medium redundant branch offices have multiple WAN routers and one or more LAN switches. The site might have multiple VLANs, with the WAN router responsible for routing traffic locally between the VLANs. The reference topology has a single existing VLAN. Figure 5-17 shows the redundant reference branch office topology discussed in this section.

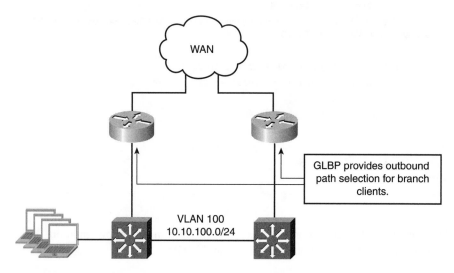

Figure 5-17   *Small to Medium-Sized Redundant Reference Topology*

In this scenario, all IP routing for the branch is handled by the WAN routers (that is, the LAN switches function only at Layer 2). The WAN access routers are configured with Global Load Balancing Protocol (GLBP) on the LAN interfaces to provide default gateway redundancy for the local host systems. Traffic can enter or exit the site through either WAN router. Because there is only a single existing VLAN, and the links between the WAN access routers and the LAN switches are not configured as trunks, adding a dedicated VLAN for the WAE is not desirable. In these cases, the WAE is deployed on the existing VLAN with the hosts it is optimizing connections for. Figure 5-18 shows the branch office topology for this deployment model.

Both WAN access routers are configured with WCCP for transparent interception. Because both WAN access routers are members of the same WCCP service group, traffic can enter or exit the remote office through either router. The deterministic behavior of WCCP ensures that traffic is redirected to the correct WAE in both directions. Egress traffic from the WAEs is returned directly to the intercepting routers' real interface IP addresses (as opposed to the GLBP virtual IP addresses) using WCCP GRE return as the egress method. In addition to allowing the WAE to reside on the same VLAN with client systems, this configuration preserves the original WAN router selection for intercepted traffic.

Tip   The use of WCCP GRE return as an egress method is only intended for software-based platforms (ISR, 7200, and so on). If a hardware-based platform is used as the WAN access routers (in other words, Cisco Catalyst switch), IP forwarding or Generic GRE should be used as the egress method.

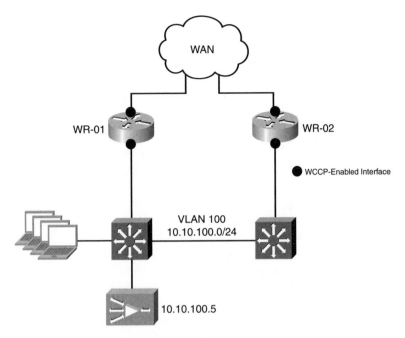

Figure 5-18   *Small to Medium-Sized Branch Office Redundant Deployment*

As traffic is redirected to the WAE, the WAE records the source IP address (from the WCCP GRE header) of the intercepting router that redirected the traffic to it. This enables the WAE to return the traffic to the intercepting router it came from once processing is complete. This behavior is performed on a connection-by-connection basis and is a key feature that enables the existing WAN router selection to be preserved. Example 5-18 shows the configuration of the WAN routers.

Example 5-18   *Small to Medium-Sized Redundant Deployment WAN Router Configuration*

```
!
hostname WR-01
!
ip wccp 61 password cisco
ip wccp 62 password cisco
!
interface FastEthernet0/0
 ip address 10.10.100.2 255.255.255.0
 ip wccp 61 redirect in
 speed 100
 full-duplex
 glbp 1 ip 10.10.100.1
```

```
   glbp 1 priority 105
   glbp 1 preempt delay minimum 60
   glbp 1 load-balancing host-dependent
   glbp 1 authentication text cisco
  !
 interface Serial0/0
  description ** Link to WAN **
  ip address 10.88.81.254 255.255.255.252
  ip wccp 62 redirect in
  !


                           !
                           hostname WR-02
                           !
                           ip wccp 61 password cisco
                           ip wccp 62 password cisco
                           !
                           interface FastEthernet0/0
                            ip address 10.10.100.3 255.255.255.0
                            ip wccp 61 redirect in
                            speed 100
                            full-duplex
                            glbp 1 ip 10.10.100.1
                            glbp 1 priority 100
                            glbp 1 preempt delay minimum 60
                            glbp 1 load-balancing host-dependent
                            glbp 1 authentication text cisco
                           !
                           interface Serial0/0
                            description ** Link to WAN **
                            ip address 10.88.81.250 255.255.255.252
                            ip wccp 62 redirect in
                            !
```

Example 5-19 shows the WAE configuration that is used for this deployment model.

Example 5-19 *Small to Medium-Sized Redundant Deployment WAE Configuration*

```
                    WAE512# show running-config no-policy
                     ! WAAS version 4.1.3b (build b9 Jul 30 2009)
                     !
                    device mode application-accelerator
                     !
```

```
                        hostname WAE512
                        !
                        primary-interface GigabitEthernet 1/0
                        !
                        interface GigabitEthernet 1/0
                         ip address 10.10.100.5 255.255.255.0
                         exit
                        interface GigabitEthernet 2/0
                         shutdown
                         exit
                        !
                        ip default-gateway 10.10.100.1
                        !
                        no auto-register enable
                        !
                        ! ip path-mtu-discovery is disabled in WAAS by default
                        !
                        ntp server 10.88.80.142
                        !
                        wccp router-list 1 10.10.100.2 10.10.100.3
                        wccp tcp-promiscuous router-list-num 1 password ****
                        wccp version 2
                        !
                        egress-method negotiated-return intercept-method wccp
                        !
                        username admin password 1 $1$gfYExN4R$WlJ9i/.C34QsNRpuPgpz.1
                   username admin privilege 15
                   username admin print-admin-password 1
CEC32C13191F9B56AAD3B435B51404EE 6E73ED22ADDAFAA4FACD2513341E6B7C
                        !
                   authentication login local enable primary
                   authentication configuration local enable primary
                        !
                   central-manager address 10.88.80.142
                   cms enable
                        !
                   ! End of WAAS configuration
                   WAE512#
```

It is important to analyze the current routing configuration and traffic flows at sites with redundant topologies. It is possible even when deploying the WAEs on a dedicated subnet to experience a redirection loop for traffic that transits between routers on host subnets. Figure 5-19 shows an example of how a redirection loop can be created when traffic passes between WAN access routers on host VLANs.

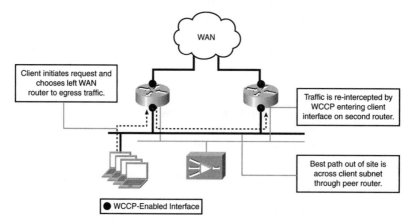

Figure 5-19   *Redirection Loop with WCCP Interception on Transit Paths*

The solution is to prevent traffic from transiting between routers over the existing host subnets and make the newly created WAE subnet the transit path between the WAN access routers. If the host subnets are not a transit path between the WAN access routers, it is possible to deploy the WAEs on an existing host subnet. If any of the current host subnets are serving as transit paths between the WAN access routers, the WAEs should be deployed on a dedicated subnet that can also serve as the new transit path. Figure 5-20 shows the modified traffic flow with the WAE subnet serving as the transit path between the WAN access routers.

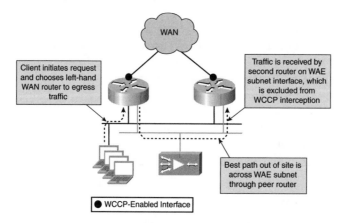

Figure 5-20   *Dedicated WAE Subnet as Transit Path*

Example 5-20 shows the configuration of the WAN routers.

Example 5-20 *Small to Medium-Sized Redundant Deployment WAN Router Configuration*

```
!
hostname WR-01
!
ip wccp 61 password cisco
ip wccp 62 password cisco
!
interface FastEthernet0/0
 no ip address
 duplex full
 speed 100
!
interface FastEthernet0/0.201
 ip address 10.10.100.2 255.255.255.0
 ip wccp 61 redirect in
 speed 100
 full-duplex
glbp 1 ip 10.10.100.1
glbp 1 priority 105
glbp 1 preempt delay minimum 60
glbp 1 load-balancing host-dependent
glbp 1 authentication text cisco
!
interface FastEthernet0/0.202
 ip address 10.88.81.2 255.255.255.240
 ip wccp redirect exclude in
 speed 100
 full-duplex
 glbp 2 ip 10.88.81.1
 glbp 2 priority 105
 glbp 2 preempt delay minimum 60
 glbp 2 load-balancing host-dependent
 glbp 2 authentication text cisco

!
interface Serial0/0
 description ** Link to WAN **
 ip address 10.88.81.254 255.255.255.252
 ip wccp 62 redirect in
!
router ospf 100
 passive-interface FastEthernet0/0.201
 network 10.10.100.0 0.0.0.255 area 0
network 10.88.81.0 0.0.0.15 area 0
```

```
      network 10.88.81.252 0.0.0.3 area 0
      !
      !
      hostname WR-02
      !
      ip wccp 61 password cisco
      ip wccp 62 password cisco
      !
      interface FastEthernet0/0
       no ip address
       duplex full
       speed 100
      !
      interface FastEthernet0/0.201
       ip address 10.10.100.3 255.255.255.0
       ip wccp 61 redirect in
       speed 100
       full-duplex
       glbp 1 ip 10.10.100.1
       glbp 1 priority 100
       glbp 1 preempt delay minimum 60
       glbp 1 load-balancing host-dependent
       glbp 1 authentication text cisco
      !
      interface FastEthernet0/0.202
   ip address 10.88.81.3 255.255.255.240
   ip wccp redirect exclude in
   speed 100
   full-duplex
   glbp 2 ip 10.88.81.1
   glbp 2 priority 100
   glbp 2 preempt delay minimum 60
   glbp 2 load-balancing host-dependent
   glbp 2 authentication text cisco

 !
 interface Serial0/0
  description ** Link to WAN **
  ip address 10.88.81.250 255.255.255.252
  ip wccp 62 redirect in
 !
```

```
router ospf 100
 passive-interface FastEthernet0/0.201
 network 10.10.100.0 0.0.0.255 area 0
 network 10.88.81.0 0.0.0.15 area 0
 network 10.88.81.248 0.0.0.3 area 0
 !
```

In Example 5-20, the interface connecting to the client subnet is set as passive under the OSPF process. This prevents a routing protocol adjacency from forming across the client subnet, which prevents it from becoming a transit path.

Note Make sure that any static routes that are configured with a next-hop address across a client subnet are changed to use the WAE subnet as the transit path. Using the client subnet as a transit path between routers can create the potential for a redirection loop.

Example 5-21 shows the WAE configuration that is used for this deployment model.

Example 5-21 *Dedicated WAE Subnet WAE Configuration*

```
WAE512# show running-config no-policy
! WAAS version 4.1.3b (build b9 Jul 30 2009)
!
device mode application-accelerator
!
hostname WAE512
!
primary-interface GigabitEthernet 1/0
!
interface GigabitEthernet 1/0
 ip address 10.88.81.5 255.255.255.240
 exit
interface GigabitEthernet 2/0
 shutdown
 exit
!
ip default-gateway 10.88.81.1
!
```

```
no auto-register enable
!
! ip path-mtu-discovery is disabled in WAAS by default
!
ntp server 10.88.80.142
!
wccp router-list 1 10.88.81.2 10.88.81.3
wccp tcp-promiscuous router-list-num 1 password ****
wccp version 2
!
egress-method negotiated-return intercept-method wccp
!
username admin password 1 $1$gfYExN4R$WlJ9i/.C34QsNRpuPgpz.1
                        username admin privilege 15
                        username admin print-admin-password 1
CEC32C13191F9B56AAD3B435B51404EE 6E73ED22ADDAFAA4FACD2513341E6B7C
                        !
                        authentication login local enable primary
                        authentication configuration local enable primary
                        !
                        central-manager address 10.88.80.142
                        cms enable
                        !
                        ! End of WAAS configuration
                        WAE512#
```

Large Redundant Branch Office

Large branch offices are much more likely to implement a multilayer Core, Distribution, and Access topology. It is also common for the WAN routers at large branch offices to be hardware-based platforms, such as Catalyst 6500 Series switches or 7600 Series routers. With a more extensive network infrastructure in large branch offices comes more options for where to configure interception. Figure 5-21 shows the large redundant reference branch office topology discussed in this section.

All the switch-to-switch links in the reference topology are routed links. Traffic load is distributed across both WAN routers as it leaves the site. You want to preserve this routing behavior after WAAS is deployed. Because this topology uses hardware-based WAN routers, using WCCP GRE return as the egress method is not recommended. Instead, use Generic Generic Routing Encapsulation (GGRE) as the egress method. Using GGRE as the egress method accomplishes the same stateful return of traffic to the intercepting router as WCCP GRE Return. Because GGRE requires WCCP GRE as the forwarding method, the WAEs can be placed multiple Layer 3 hops away from the intercepting routers. In this particular scenario, the WAEs are attached to a VLAN created on the LAN distribution switches. Figure 5-22 shows the branch office topology for this deployment model.

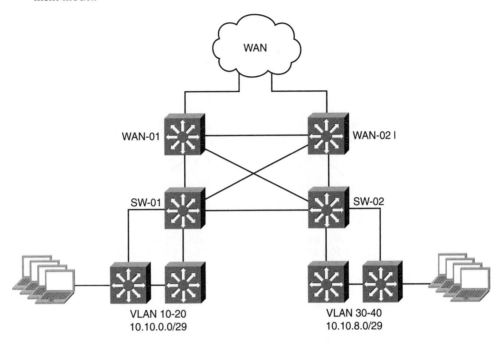

Figure 5-21 *Large Redundant Reference Topology*

A dedicated VLAN is created for the WAEs on the LAN distribution switches. To facilitate WCCP L2 forwarding, the WAE VLAN is trunked between the two LAN distribution switches. This enables traffic to be intercepted on either LAN distribution switch and get redirected to the correct WAE. Hot Standby Routing Protocol (HSRP) is configured on the WAE VLAN to provide default gateway redundancy.

Example 5-22 shows the IOS configuration of both WAN routers.

Example 5-22 *Large Redundant Off-Path Deployment WAN Router Configuration*

```
!
hostname WAN-01
!
ip wccp 61 redirect-list NO-LOCAL-TRAFFIC password cisco
ip wccp 62 redirect-list NO-LOCAL-TRAFFIC password cisco
!
interface Loopback0
 ip address 44.77.22.3 255.255.255.0
```

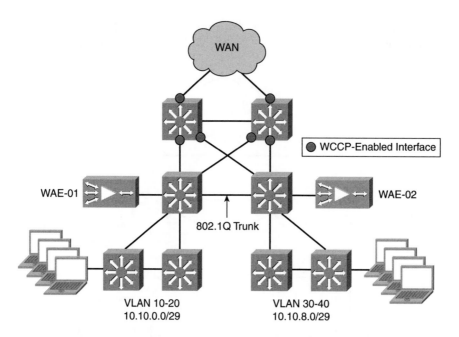

Figure 5-22   *Large Redundant Off-Path Deployment*

```
                            !
                            interface Tunnel52
                             description ** Multipoint Tunnel for WAAS Egress
Traffic **
                             ip address 10.10.10.3 255.255.255.0
                             no ip redirects
                             tunnel source Loopback0
                             tunnel mode gre multipoint
                             !
                            interface GigabitEthernet1/0
                             description ** Link to WAN **
                             ip address 10.88.81.250 255.255.255.252
                             ip wccp 61 redirect in
                             !
                            interface GigabitEthernet1/1
                             description ** Link to WAN-02 Router **
```

```
      ip address 10.88.81.246 255.255.255.252
     !
     interface GigabitEthernet2/0
      description ** Link to SW-01 Switch **
      ip address 10.88.81.254 255.255.255.252
      ip wccp 62 redirect in
     !
     interface GigabitEthernet2/1
      description ** Link to SW-02 Switch **
      ip address 10.88.81.242 255.255.255.252
      ip wccp 62 redirect in
     !
     ! Output removed for brevity>
     !
     ip access-list extended NO-LOCAL-TRAFFIC
      deny ip 10.10.0.0 0.0.15.255 10.10.0.0 0.0.15.255
      permit ip any any
     !
     end
!
hostname WAN-02
!
ip wccp 61 redirect-list NO-LOCAL-TRAFFIC password cisco
ip wccp 62 redirect-list NO-LOCAL-TRAFFIC password cisco
!
interface Loopback0
 ip address 44.77.22.4 255.255.255.0
!
interface Tunnel52
 description ** Multipoint Tunnel for WAAS Egress Traffic **
 ip address 10.10.10.4 255.255.255.0
 no ip redirects
 tunnel source Loopback0
 tunnel mode gre multipoint
!
interface GigabitEthernet1/0
 description ** Link to WAN **
 ip address 10.88.81.238 255.255.255.252
```

```
      ip wccp 61 redirect in
    !
    interface GigabitEthernet1/1
     description ** Link to WAN-01 Router **
     ip address 10.88.81.234 255.255.255.252
    !
    interface GigabitEthernet2/0
 description ** Link to SW-02 Switch **
 ip address 10.88.81.230 255.255.255.252
 ip wccp 62 redirect in
!
interface GigabitEthernet2/1
 description ** Link to SW-01 Switch **
 ip address 10.88.81.226 255.255.255.252
 ip wccp 62 redirect in
!
! Output removed for brevity>
!
ip access-list extended NO-LOCAL-TRAFFIC
 deny ip 10.10.0.0 0.0.15.255 10.10.0.0 0.0.15.255
 permit ip any any
!
end
```

Example 5-23 shows the configuration of the WAEs in this deployment scenario.

Example 5-23   *Large Redundant Off-Path Deployment WAE Configuration*

```
WAE7326TEST# show running-config no-policy
! WAAS version 4.1.3 (build b23 Mar 14 2009)
!
device mode application-accelerator
!
hostname WAE-01
!
ip domain-name asdcnp-waas.cisco.com
!
primary-interface GigabitEthernet 1/0
!
     interface GigabitEthernet 1/0
        ip address 10.88.81.5 255.255.255.240
```

```
                exit
              interface GigabitEthernet 2/0
               shutdown
               exit
               !
              ip default-gateway 10.88.81.1
               !
              no auto-register enable
               !
              ! ip path-mtu-discovery is disabled in WAAS by default
               !
              ip name-server 10.88.80.53
               !
              logging console priority debug
               !
              ntp server 10.88.80.132
               !
              wccp router-list 1 44.77.22.3 44.77.22.4
              wccp tcp-promiscuous router-list-num 1 password **** mask-
assign
              wccp version 2
               !
              egress-method generic-gre intercept-method wccp
               !
              username admin password 1 $1$9sUrMTLk$HgJmIK/fggJ5RxktX6Bos.
           username admin privilege 15
           username admin print-admin-password 1
CEC32C13191F9B56AAD3B435B51404EE 6E73ED22ADDAFAA4FACD2513341E6B7C
               !
           authentication login local enable primary
           authentication configuration local enable primary
               !
           tfo tcp optimized-send-buffer 2048
           tfo tcp optimized-receive-buffer 2048
               !
           central-manager address 10.88.80.142
           cms enable
               !
           ! End of WAAS configuration
           WAE-01#
```

Both WAE configurations are the same, except for the WAE IP address itself. Because
WCCP is running on a hardware-based platform in this configuration, mask assignment is

included as part of the WCCP options configured on the WAE. The **mask-assign** option is an alternative to the default hash assignment, which is optimized for use in hardware-based platforms. Mask assignment is required to ensure that WCCP redirection is handled completely in hardware. The default gateway of the WAE is configured as the HSRP VIP. In the WCCP router list, the IP address of the loopback interface on each WAN router is used.

Inbound WCCP interception is configured on the interfaces connecting to the WAN routers and the interfaces connecting to the LAN access switches.

> **Tip** When configuring WCCP on a hardware-based platform, always use inbound redirection to ensure full hardware acceleration.

Policy-Based Routing Interception

PBR is another transparent interception option for off-path deployments. PBR is configured on the same routers and switches where you would normally configure WCCP. You should take into account the following items when considering PBR for transparent interception:

- PBR requires more configuration steps in IOS than does WCCP.

- The only egress method supported with PBR is IP forwarding. This means that the WAEs cannot be deployed multiple L3 hops away from the intercepting routers.

- By default, PBR does not provide load distribution among multiple WAEs at a site.

- By default, PBR does not track the availability of the WAE to receive traffic (requires the IOS IP SLA feature).

Based on these limitations, PBR is recommended over WCCP only as a last resort. The remainder of this section provides sample configurations for using PBR for transparent interception with WAAS.

The following example shows the configuration steps required to use PBR for WAAS interception:

Step 1. Configure an access list to match the traffic you want to redirect to WAAS:

```
!
access-list 100 permit tcp any any
access-list 100 deny ip any any
!
```

Step 2. Create a route map that references the access list and sets a next-hop IP address of the WAE:

```
!
route-map WAAS permit 10
```

```
            match ip address 100
            set ip next-hop 10.88.81.2
     !
```

Step 3.   Apply PBR to the individual interfaces:

```
     !
     interface FastEthernet0/0
      no ip address
      duplex full
      speed 100
     !
     interface FastEthernet0/0.201
      description ** Branch Client Subnet **
      encapsulation dot1Q 201
      ip address 10.88.81.17 255.255.255.240
      ip policy route-map WAAS
     !
     interface FastEthernet0/0.202
      description ** Branch WAE Subnet **
      encapsulation dot1Q 202
      ip address 10.88.81.1 255.255.255.240
     !
     interface Serial0/0
      description ** Link to WAN **
      ip address 10.88.81.254 255.255.255.252
      ip policy route-map WAAS
```

By default, PBR does not verify that the IP next-hop address specified in the route map is reachable. This can lead to a situation where traffic is being redirected to a WAE that is down. You can configure IOS devices to check the availability of IP next-hop address(es) using a combination of IP SLA features and the **set ip next-hop verify-availability** route map command.

Example 5-24 shows how to configure the WAN router to verify that the **IP next-hop** address specified in the route map is up and reachable.

Example 5-24   *Verifying IP Next Hop Address Using IP SLA*

```
!
hostname WR-01
!
ip sla monitor 10
 type echo protocol ipIcmpEcho 10.88.81.2
 frequency 10
ip sla monitor schedule 10 life forever start-time now
!
```

```
track 10 rtr 10 reachability
!
route-map WAAS permit 10
 match ip address 100
 set ip next-hop verify-availability 10.88.81.2 10 track 10
 !
```

If the IP next-hop address becomes unavailable, the WAN router starts forwarding traffic natively across the WAN using the entries in the routing table as opposed to the policy route.

Another limitation of PBR is scenarios where multiple WAEs are deployed at a single site. Multiple WAEs can be deployed at a single site for scalability, redundancy, or both. The route map command **set ip next-hop** allows you to define multiple IP addresses. Example 5-25 shows a route map with multiple next-hop addresses configured.

Example 5-25 *Multiple IP Next Hop Addresses*

```
!
route-map WAAS permit 10
        match ip address 100
        set ip next-hop 10.88.81.2 10.88.81.3
!
```

In Example 5-25, the IP addresses of both WAEs are configured as IP next-hop addresses. The problem with this configuration is that the second IP address, 10.88.81.3, is used only if the first IP address becomes unavailable. When the failover occurs to the second WAE, all traffic associated with existing TCP connections are forwarded unoptimized. As new TCP connections are established, they are optimized. So at any given time, only a single WAE receives traffic. A potential workaround for this is to use multiple route map entries to manually distribute traffic to each WAE. In Example 5-26, the LAN subnet at the location is using IP subnet 10.10.10.0/24. PBR is configured to send even-numbered hosts to the first WAE and odd-numbered hosts to the second WAE. Each route map entry would be configured with the IP addresses of both WAEs, so if one fails, traffic is rerouted to the other WAE.

Example 5-26 *Traffic Distribution with PBR*

```
        !
        hostname WR-01
        !
        ip sla monitor 10
         type echo protocol ipIcmpEcho 10.88.81.2
         frequency 10
        ip sla monitor schedule 10 life forever start-time now
```

```
     ip sla monitor 20
      type echo protocol ipIcmpEcho 10.88.81.3
      frequency 10
     ip sla monitor schedule 20 life forever start-time now
     !
     track 10 rtr 10 reachability
     !
     track 20 rtr 20 reachability
     !
     access-list 100 permit tcp 10.10.10.1 0.0.0.254 any
     access-list 100 permit tcp any 10.10.10.1 0.0.0.254
     access-list 101 permit tcp 10.10.10.0 0.0.0.254 any
     access-list 101 permit tcp any 10.10.10.1 0.0.0.254
     !
     route-map WAAS permit 10
   match ip address 100
   set ip next-hop verify-availability 10.88.81.2 10 track 10
   set ip next-hop verify-availability 10.88.81.3 20 track 20
 !
 route-map WAAS permit 20
  match ip address 101
  set ip next-hop verify-availability 10.88.81.3 10 track 20
  set ip next-hop verify-availability 10.88.81.2 20 track 10
  !
```

Cisco IOS Firewall Integration

Cisco IOS Firewall (IOS FW) is a fundamental part of the integrated threat-control
solution available on Cisco low- and midrange routing platforms. An enhancement in
Cisco IOS Release 12.4(11)T2 allows Cisco IOS FW and Cisco IOS IPS to recognize
traffic being optimized by Cisco WAAS. With this enhancement, Cisco IOS FW observes
the TCP options used in WAAS automatic discovery. If Cisco IOS FW notices that a
connection has successfully completed WAAS automatic discovery, it permits the initial
sequence number shift for the connection and maintains the Layer 4 state on the
optimized connection.

Note   The capability of Cisco WAAS to interoperate with Cisco IOS FW and Cisco IOS
IPS applies only to the Cisco IOS Zone-Based Policy Firewall starting from Release
12.4(11)T2. Cisco IOS Classic Firewall does not incorporate the Cisco WAAS interoperability enhancement.

In a branch office deployment, it is common to have security features such as Cisco IOS FW, Cisco IOS IPS, or IPsec VPN deployed on an ISR router. Cisco WAAS has three different deployment options:

■ **Cisco WAAS deployed with an NME-WAE on the same router as Cisco IOS FW and IOS IPS, using WCCP redirect for traffic interception:** This scenario supports IPsec VPN, IOS FW, and IOS IPS features.

■ **Cisco WAAS deployed as an off-path, standalone appliance, using WCCP redirection for traffic interception:** This scenario also supports IPsec VPN, IOS FW, and IOS IPS features. The configuration for this option is the same as for the previous option.

■ **Cisco WAAS deployed as an inline appliance, in front of the ISR router:** This scenario supports IPsec VPN and IOS FW. In this case, because IOS FW and IOS IPS receive WAAS optimized packets, Layer 7 inspection on the client side is not supported. The IOS IPS feature is partially supported because traffic is uncompressed during the first few round trip times (RTT), and IOS IPS works if a signature is matched at the beginning of a connection.

An edge Cisco WAAS with Cisco IOS FW or Cisco IOS IPS is applied at branch office sites that must inspect traffic moving to and from a WAN connection and might use VPN connectivity. Cisco IOS Firewall monitors traffic for optimization indicators (TCP options and subsequent TCP sequence number changes) and allows optimized traffic to pass while still applying Layer 4 stateful inspection and deep packet inspection to all traffic, maintaining security while accommodating Cisco WAAS optimization advantages.

Example 5-27 shows a configuration with IOS FW and WCCP interception configured on the same router.

Example 5-27   *IOS Firewall and WCCP Interception*

```
!
ip wccp 61
ip wccp 62
!
ip inspect WAAS enable
class-map type inspect match-any most-traffic
 match protocol icmp
 match protocol ftp
 match protocol tcp
 match protocol udp
!
policy-map type inspect p1
 class type inspect most-traffic
  inspect
 class class-default
```

```
    zone security inside
    zone security outside
    zone-pair security in-out source inside destination outside
  service-policy type inspect p1
zone-pair security out-in source outside destination inside
  service-policy type inspect p1
!
interface GigabitEthernet0/0
  description Trusted interface
  ip address 10.70.0.1 255.255.255.0
  ip wccp 61 redirect in
  zone-member security inside
!
interface GigabitEthernet0/1
  description Untrusted interface
  ip address 10.72.2.3 255.255.255.0
  ip wccp 62 redirect in
  zone-member security outside
!
interface Integrated-Service-Engine1/0
  ip address 10.70.100.1 255.255.255.252
  ip wccp redirect exclude in
  zone-member security inside
  service-module ip address 10.70.100.2 255.255.255.252
  service-module ip default-gateway 10.70.100.1
  !
```

Summary

This chapter explored various options for integrating Cisco WAAS into the branch office network infrastructure. Different topology and configuration scenarios were discussed, including both in-path and off-path interception options. As a point of reference, configuration examples for using policy-based routing for transparent interception were provided. Finally, integration with Cisco IOS Firewall was reviewed, including deployment options and the associated device configurations. The material in this chapter provides you with a solid set of options for integrating WAAS into a common branch office network topologies.

Chapter 6

Data Center Network Integration

Data center network integration is a key component to a successful Cisco Wide Area Application Services (WAAS) deployment. This chapter examines the key design considerations for deploying WAAS in the data center environment, including considerations for environments with multiple data centers. Sample design models and configurations are provided throughout this chapter, including the latest recommendations for integrating with Cisco firewall solutions commonly found in data center environments. This chapter also provides best-practice recommendations for data center deployments that can scale to support hundreds or thousands of remote sites.

Data Center Placement

Determining where to deploy WAAS within the data center infrastructure requires careful consideration and planning. Data center environments are generally made up of complex network infrastructures, multiple layers of devices, diverse paths over which traffic can flow, and numerous types of systems performing various functions. This section focuses on how to determine where WAAS should be deployed within the data center, irrespective of the interception method used. Subsequent sections in this chapter provide design recommendations and sample configurations for network interception in the data center. Figure 6-1 shows the sample data center topology that is used as a reference for discussing where within a data center WAAS should be deployed.

Starting from the top of the topology shown in Figure 6-1, traffic enters the data center through any of several Cisco routers located at the WAN edge. All the WAN edge routers are aggregated into a pair of Cisco Catalyst 6500 Series switches. From there, traffic passes through another pair of Cisco Catalyst 6500 Series switches, which act as the core of the data center network infrastructure. Connecting to the core switches are multiple pairs of distribution switches, each providing connectivity for a different block of resources within the data center. For example, one resource block hosts multiple server farms, while another block provides connectivity to multiple Internet service providers

(ISP) for corporate Internet connectivity, and yet another block could be present, connecting to downstream access layer infrastructure to support campus users.

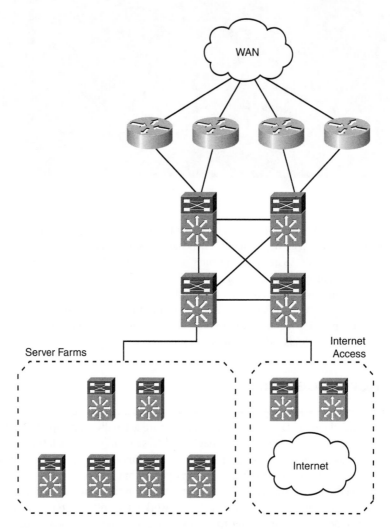

Figure 6-1 *Reference Data Center Topology*

The first logical location within the data center to consider deploying WAAS is at the WAN edge, or the point where traffic from remote branch offices first enters the data center from the WAN. The benefits to deploying WAAS at this location include:

- The WAN edge is a natural aggregation point for traffic destined to or sourced from a remote branch office, and that is a good candidate for optimization. This is an important point, because passing intra-data center traffic through WAAS unnecessarily consumes resources and can potentially constrain throughput.

- The WAN edge layer in the data center is less likely to contain other application-aware components, such as firewalls, Intrusion Detection System/Intrusion Prevention System (IDS/IPS), and server load balancers that require visibility into multiple layers of the traffic flows.

- The configuration required to support this deployment model is kept simple, because transparent interception needs to be configured and maintained only in a single location.

Deploying WAAS at a single aggregation point also provides the best hardware resource utilization, because a single cluster of WAAS devices can handle optimization and acceleration services for all WAN traffic. Figure 6-2 shows the reference data center topology with WAEs deployed at the WAN edge.

There are, however, reasons that can lead you to deploy WAAS deeper in the data center, that is, farther away from the WAN edge and closer to the server farms or host systems. Take for example the topology in Figure 6-3, which shows a sample topology with multiple interconnected data centers.

In this example, each remote branch office has WAN connectivity to both data centers. Users in the branch offices access resources in both data centers simultaneously. If the routing policy is such that users always take the most direct path to and from each data center, then deploying WAAS at the WAN edge in each data center enables traffic to either data center to be optimized. Figure 6-4 shows this scenario with sample traffic flows to each data center with WAAS deployed at the WAN edge.

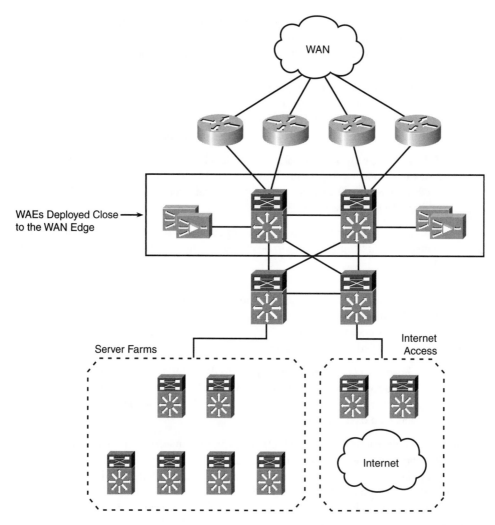

Figure 6-2   *WAN Edge WAAS Placement*

Figure 6-4 shows that, in a steady state, traffic from the remote branch office to either data center is optimized. However, in cases where traffic flows asymmetrically between the remote branch office and the data centers, the WAN edge might not be the best location to deploy WAAS in the data center. Asymmetric traffic flows can be the result of a WAN failure, for example, if the WAN link between the remote branch office and Data Center A in Figure 6-4 were to fail. Asymmetric traffic flows can also be caused by deliberate design; for example, if the routing policy dictates that both WAN links in the branch office are equal cost paths (that is, traffic can enter or leave over either WAN link, regardless of the final destination), all traffic from the branch office to Data Center A flows across the WAN link to Data Center B, and then across the link between Data

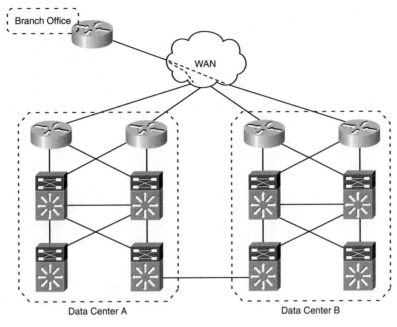

Figure 6-3 *Multi-Data Center Reference Topology*

Center B and Data Center A. Figure 6-5 shows the traffic flow during a WAN link failure between the branch office and Data Center A.

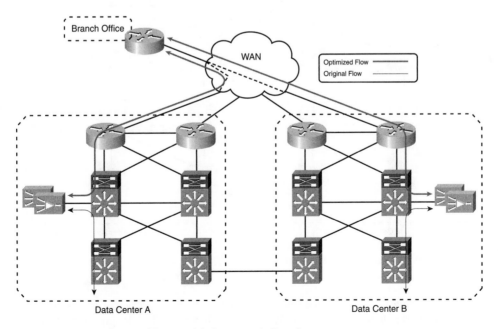

Figure 6-4 *Dual Data Center with Symmetric Routing*

At the time of the failure, connections that were optimized between the branch office WAE and the WAEs at the WAN edge in Data Center A are reset, because the WAEs in Data Center A no longer sees the traffic. Connections between the branch office and Data Center B continues to be optimized. As users reconnect to resources in Data Center A, the WAEs located in Data Center B intercept the connections and begin optimization. This same behavior happens again when the WAN link between the branch office and Data Center A is restored. Connections between hosts in the branch office and Data Center A begin flowing over the direct connection between the two sites. Because the connections are no longer seen by the WAEs in Data Center B, those connections are reset. As the connections are re-established, they are optimized between the branch office WAE and the WAEs in Data Center A.

Tip As a general recommendation, when the network topology provides multiple paths over which traffic can flow, the WAAS design should assume that traffic flows asymmetrically over both paths, even if the current design intends for traffic to flow symmetrically.

There are two design approaches to handle cases where traffic flows asymmetrically between multiple sites and the WAN edge is not the ideal location to deploy WAAS. The first approach stretches the transparent interception logic across the WAN edge layers in

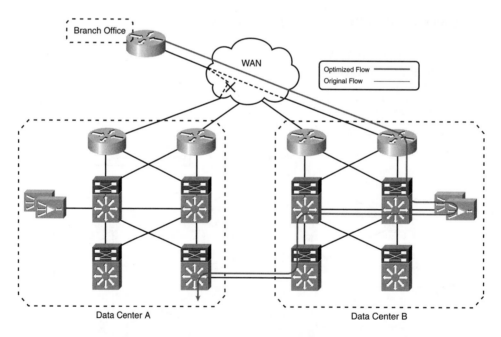

Figure 6-5 *WAN Failure Causes Asymmetric Traffic Flows*

both data centers. This approach ensures that traffic entering or leaving either data center WAN edge is redirected to the same WAE in both directions. The design approach is easily accomplished with Web Cache Communication Protocol (WCCP), by configuring a single WCCP service group that spans the WAN edge layer of both data centers. Figure 6-6 shows the use of a single WCCP service group to encompass the WAN edge layer of both data centers.

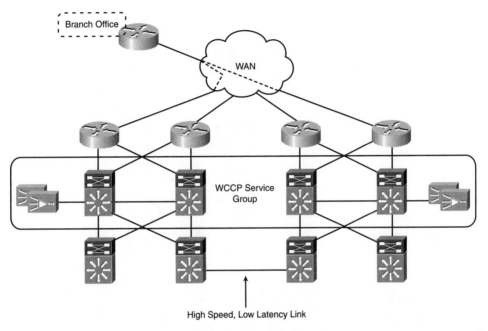

Figure 6-6   *Single WCCP Service Group Spanning Multiple Data Centers*

This design approach assumes that the data centers are "well connected"—that is, the connectivity between data centers is high bandwidth (>100 Mbps) and low latency (<10 msec). In essence, the WAEs in both data centers act as a single logical cluster. This design and the associated configurations are discussed in more detail later in this chapter.

The second design approach involves moving the location where WAAS is deployed closer toward the host resources and away from the WAN edge. In this topology, WAAS should be deployed behind the point in the data center topology where the two data centers are interconnected. Moving the WAEs and interception configuration behind the point of connectivity between the data centers eliminates the potential for traffic to only be seen in a single direction by the data center WAEs. Figure 6-7 shows the reference topology with WAAS deployed behind the point of asymmetric traffic flows.

As you consider moving WAAS away from the WAN edge and deeper into the data center, you need to take into consideration other components in the data center that rely on access to various pieces of information in the traffic flow. These other components can include firewalls, IDS/IPS, and server load balancers, just to name a few. Understanding the traffic visibility requirements of these devices is required as part of the design process.

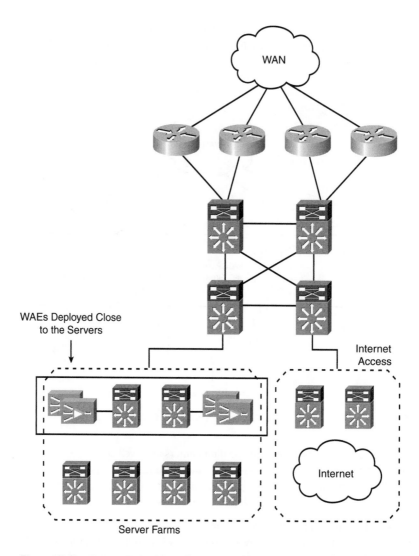

Figure 6-7   *Server Farm Distribution WAAS Placement*

Consider the example of a server load balancer, such as the Cisco Application Control Engine (ACE). If ACE intercepts traffic for load balancing before it is intercepted by WAAS, there is the potential that information within the packet that ACE relies on to make a load-balancing decision is obscured. Because this example is dealing with HTTP traffic, the default policy action in WAAS is Full Optimization (TFO+DRE+LZ) plus HTTP specific acceleration. This means that the payload of the TCP segment is compressed and is not readable by the load-balancing functions in ACE. If ACE is configured to make a load-balancing decision based on content in the Layer 7 HTTP header, it does not have access to that information. In this case, the WAEs need to be deployed in front of ACE, so that the optimized connections are terminated prior to being intercepted by ACE for load balancing. This is just one example of how other application-aware components in the data center can potentially conflict with the optimizations provided by WAAS. Understanding the capabilities of these components and their placement within the data center is a key design consideration.

Another key consideration as you look at deploying WAAS closer to the server farm is the impact on sizing—that is, the number of WAEs required in the data center to support the solution deployment. When WAAS devices are deployed at a common aggregation point for all traffic, a single cluster of WAEs can be used. If you move WAAS closer to the server farm infrastructure, and, due to the network topology, end up configuring interception at multiple locations in the data center, the number of WAEs required to support the design could increase. Figure 6-8 shows an example topology where WAAS has been deployed in multiple server farm distribution blocks.

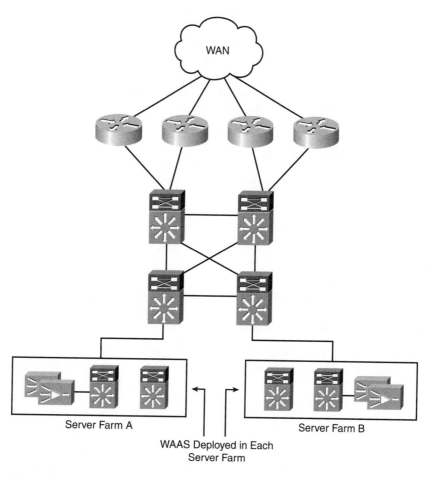

Figure 6-8 *Multiple WAAS Clusters*

The impact on sizing of splitting the design into multiple clusters within the data center is two-fold:

- Redundancy for each cluster must be accounted for separately. Data center deployments generally use $n+1$ sizing, where n is the number of WAEs required to support the expected load. The "+1" provides an additional WAE, which allows for the failure of a single WAE in the cluster without losing any cluster resource capacity. When you have multiple WAE clusters in the data center, having the same redundancy requirements means that each cluster is sized for $n+1$. This increases the number of WAEs required in the data center by the number separate WAE clusters that are deployed.

- Depending on what is driving the number of WAEs required in the data center, you might end up having to replicate the same number of WAEs in each separate cluster. For example, in a large deployment with 1000 remote branch offices, it is possible that the number of peer WAEs (also known as the *fan-out ratio*) is the determining factor in how many WAEs are deployed in the data center. If the data center design calls for two separate clusters of WAEs, one for each server farm, and all the remote branches are talking to resources in both server farms concurrently, then each cluster needs the same number of WAEs to support the fan-out ratio.

The following section discusses the specific network interception design options and associated configurations for the data center environment.

Deployment Solutions

This section provides the design and configuration details for deploying WAAS with transparent interception in the data center. The two transparent interception methods discussed are Web Cache Communication Protocol (WCCP) and server load balancing. The sever load balancing design includes the ACE from Cisco.

WCCP

WCCP provides a scalable and transparent interception method suitable for both the remote branch office and data center environments. Figure 6-9 shows the reference data center topology with WCCP enabled on the WAN edge routers.

This case assumes that traffic flows symmetrically through the WAN edge in a single data center. Note that the placement of service groups 61 and 62 in the configuration is reversed from the branch office configuration. In the data center, service group 61 is configured on the client-facing interfaces, whereas service group 62 is configured on the server-facing interfaces. This ensures that the WCCP load-distribution decision is based on the client IP address end-to-end. This is discussed in more detail in the section "Scaling Transparent Interception" later in this chapter.

In Figure 6-9, WCCP is enabled on the Cisco WAN edge routers. The WAEs are connected to the WAN distribution switches on their own VLAN. WCCP is configured for

WCCP GRE forwarding and WCCP GRE return. The assignment method used depends on the WAN router platform (software or hardware based) used. To preserve the original path selection and prevent the possibility of a redirection loop, the egress method is configured for WCCP negotiated return or Generic Generic Routing Encapsulation (GGRE) return. This ensures that egress traffic from the WAEs is returned to the original intercepting router after processing. Example 6-1 shows the relevant portions of each WAN edge router configuration for this deployment model.

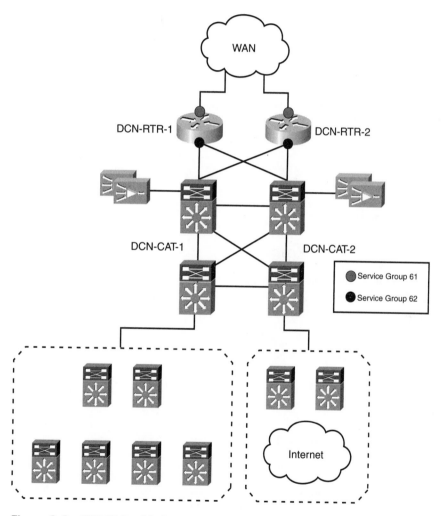

Figure 6-9   *WCCP Enabled on WAN Edge Routers*

Example 6-1 *WAN Edge Router WCCP Configuration*

```
!
hostname DCN-RTR-1
!
ip wccp 61 password cisco
ip wccp 62 password cisco
!
ip cef
!
interface Loopback0
 ip address 10.88.81.1 255.255.255.255
 no ip unreachables
!
interface GigabitEthernet0/1
 ** Link to DCN-CAT-1 **
 ip address 10.88.80.1 255.255.255.252
 ip wccp 62 redirect in
 duplex auto
 speed auto
 media-type gbic
 negotiation auto
!
interface GigabitEthernet0/2
 ** Link to DCN-CAT-2 **
 ip address 10.88.80.5 255.255.255.252
 ip wccp 62 redirect in
 duplex auto
 speed auto
 media-type gbic
 negotiation auto
!
interface ATM1/0
 no ip address
 load-interval 30
 no atm scrambling sts-stream
 no atm ilmi-keepalive
!
interface ATM1/0.55 point-to-point
 description ** 45 Mbps PVC to MPLS Service **
 bandwidth 45000
 ip address 10.19.176.5 255.255.255.252
 ip wccp 61 redirect in
 no snmp trap link-status
 pvc 1/55
```

```
   vbr-nrt 44209 44209
   broadcast
   encapsulation aal5snap
  !
 !
 !
hostname DCN-RTR-2
 !
ip wccp 61 password cisco
ip wccp 62 password cisco
 !
ip cef
 !
interface Loopback0
 ip address 10.88.81.2 255.255.255.255
 no ip unreachables
 !
interface GigabitEthernet0/1
  ** Link to DCN-CAT-2 **
  ip address 10.88.80.9 255.255.255.252
  ip wccp 62 redirect in
  duplex auto
  speed auto
  media-type gbic
  negotiation auto
 !
interface GigabitEthernet0/2
  ** Link to DCN-CAT-1 **
  ip address 10.88.80.13 255.255.255.252
  ip wccp 62 redirect in
  duplex auto
  speed auto
  media-type gbic
  negotiation auto
 !
interface ATM1/0
 no ip address
 load-interval 30
 no atm scrambling sts-stream
 no atm ilmi-keepalive
 !
interface ATM1/0.55 point-to-point
 description ** 45 Mbps PVC to MPLS Service **
 bandwidth 45000
```

```
ip address 10.19.176.9 255.255.255.252
ip wccp 61 redirect in
no snmp trap link-status
pvc 1/55
 vbr-nrt 44209 44209
 broadcast
 encapsulation aal5snap
 !
!
```

Example 6-2 shows a sample configuration for a WAE in this deployment model.

Example 6-2 *WCCP in WAN Edge Routers WAE Configuration*

```
WAE7326TEST# show running-config no-policy
! WAAS version 4.1.3 (build b23 Mar 14 2009)
!
device mode application-accelerator
!
hostname DC-WAE-01
!
ip domain-name asdcnp-waas.cisco.com
!
primary-interface GigabitEthernet 1/0
!
interface GigabitEthernet 1/0
 ip address 10.74.155.11 255.255.255.0
 exit
interface GigabitEthernet 2/0
 shutdown
 exit
!
ip default-gateway 10.74.155.1
!
no auto-register enable
!
! ip path-mtu-discovery is disabled in WAAS by default
!
ip name-server 10.88.80.53
!
!
ntp server 10.88.80.132
!
wccp router-list 1 10.88.81.1 10.88.81.2
```

```
wccp tcp-promiscuous router-list-num 1 password ****
wccp version 2
!
egress-method negotiated-return intercept-method wccp
!
username admin password 1 $1$vP9JXLqC$ApP5jqoOsIzPSpZl87vmI1
username admin privilege 15
username admin print-admin-password 1 CEC32C13191F9B56AAD3B435B51404EE
6E73ED22ADDAFAA4FACD2513341E6B7C
!
authentication login local enable primary
authentication configuration local enable primary
!
!
central-manager address 10.88.80.142
cms enable
!
! End of WAAS configuration
WAE7326TEST#
```

If the WAN edge routers are a software-based platform and you want to take advantage of hardware-accelerated interception, WCCP can be configured on the WAN distribution switches instead of the WAN edge routers. Figure 6-10 shows the reference data center topology with WCCP enabled on the WAN distribution switches.

In this example, WCCP is enabled on the Cisco WAN distribution switches. Using WCCP GRE forwarding provides some flexibility with the actual placement of the WAEs (the WAEs can reside one or more Layer 3 hops away from the intercepting switches in this topology). In this particular topology, the Wide-Area Application Engines (WAE) are placed on a dedicated VLAN. To preserve the original path selection and prevent the possibility of a redirection loop, the egress method is configured for GGRE. This ensures that egress traffic from the WAEs is returned to the intercepting router after processing. Example 6-3 shows the relevant portions of each WAN distribution switch configuration for this deployment model.

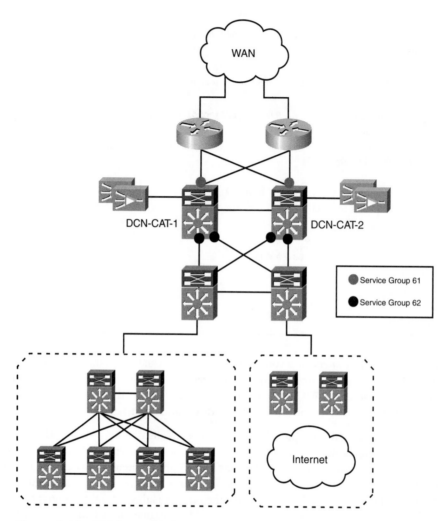

Figure 6-10   *WCCP Enabled on WAN Distribution Switches*

Example 6-3   *WAN Distribution Switch WCCP Configuration*

```
!
hostname DCN-CAT-1
!
ip wccp 61 password cisco accelerated
ip wccp 62 password cisco accelerated
!
vlan 65
!
!
interface Tunnel52
 description ** Multipoint Tunnel for WAAS Egress Traffic **
 ip address 10.10.10.1 255.255.255.0
```

```
 no ip redirects
 tunnel source Loopback0
 tunnel mode gre multipoint
!
!
interface Loopback0
 ip address 44.77.22.3 255.255.255.255
!
interface Port-channel50
 description ** PC between CAT-1 to CAT-2 **
 switchport
 switchport trunk encapsulation dot1q
 switchport trunk allowed vlan 1,65
 switchport mode trunk
 no ip address
!
interface GigabitEthernet1/1
 description ** Link to DCN-RTR-1 **
 ip address 10.88.80.2 255.255.255.252
 ip wccp 61 redirect in
!
interface GigabitEthernet1/2
 description ** Link to DCN-RTR-2 **
 ip address 10.88.80.6 255.255.255.252
 ip wccp 61 redirect in
!
interface GigabitEthernet1/3
 switchport
 switchport access vlan 65
 switchport mode access
 no ip address
 spanning-tree portfast
!
interface GigabitEthernet1/4
 switchport
 switchport access vlan 65
 switchport mode access
 no ip address
 spanning-tree portfast
!
interface GigabitEthernet1/5
 switchport
 switchport access vlan 65
 switchport mode access
 no ip address
 spanning-tree portfast
```

```
!
interface GigabitEthernet1/6
 switchport
 switchport access vlan 65
 switchport mode access
 no ip address
 spanning-tree portfast
!
interface GigabitEthernet1/41
 description ** Link to DCN-CORE-1 **
 ip address 10.88.80.17 255.255.255.252
 ip wccp 62 redirect in
!
interface GigabitEthernet1/42
 description ** Link to DCN-CORE-2 **
 ip address 10.88.80.21 255.255.255.252
 ip wccp 62 redirect in
!
interface GigabitEthernet1/47
 description CAT-1 to CAT-2 LINKS
 switchport
 switchport trunk encapsulation dot1q
 switchport trunk allowed vlan 1,65
 switchport mode trunk
 no ip address
 channel-group 50 mode desirable
!
interface GigabitEthernet1/48
 description CAT-1 to CAT-2 LINKS
 switchport
 switchport trunk encapsulation dot1q
 switchport trunk allowed vlan 1,65
 switchport mode trunk
 no ip address
 channel-group 50 mode desirable
!
interface Vlan1
 no ip address
 shutdown
!
interface Vlan65
 description ** WAAS WAE Vlan **
 ip address 10.74.155.3 255.255.255.0
 standby 1 ip 10.74.155.1
 standby 1 priority 105
 standby 1 preempt
```

```
 standby 2 ip 10.74.155.2
!
!
hostname DCN-CAT-2
!
ip wccp 61 password cisco accelerated
ip wccp 62 password cisco accelerated
!
vlan 65
!
!
interface Tunnel52
 description ** Multipoint Tunnel for WAAS Egress Traffic **
 ip address 10.10.10.2 255.255.255.0
 no ip redirects
 tunnel source Loopback0
 tunnel mode gre multipoint
!
!
interface Loopback0
 ip address 44.77.22.4 255.255.255.255
!
interface Port-channel50
 description ** PC between CAT-2 to CAT-1 **
 switchport
 switchport trunk encapsulation dot1q
 switchport trunk allowed vlan 1,65
 switchport mode trunk
 no ip address
!
interface GigabitEthernet1/1
 description ** Link to DCN-RTR-2 **
 ip address 10.88.80.10 255.255.255.252
 ip wccp 61 redirect in
!
interface GigabitEthernet1/2
 description ** Link to DCN-RTR-1 **
 ip address 10.88.80.14 255.255.255.252
 ip wccp 61 redirect in
!
interface GigabitEthernet1/3
 switchport
 switchport access vlan 65
 switchport mode access
 no ip address
 spanning-tree portfast
```

```
!
interface GigabitEthernet1/4
 switchport
 switchport access vlan 65
 switchport mode access
 no ip address
 spanning-tree portfast
!
interface GigabitEthernet1/5
 switchport
 switchport access vlan 65
 switchport mode access
 no ip address
 spanning-tree portfast
!
interface GigabitEthernet1/6
 switchport
 switchport access vlan 65
 switchport mode access
 no ip address
 spanning-tree portfast
!
interface GigabitEthernet1/41
 description ** Link to DCN-CORE-2 **
 ip address 10.88.80.25 255.255.255.252
 ip wccp 62 redirect in
!
interface GigabitEthernet1/42
 description ** Link to DCN-CORE-1 **
 ip address 10.88.80.29 255.255.255.252
 ip wccp 62 redirect in
!
interface GigabitEthernet1/47
 description CAT-2 to CAT-1 LINKS
 switchport
 switchport trunk encapsulation dot1q
 switchport trunk allowed vlan 1,65
 switchport mode trunk
 no ip address
 channel-group 50 mode desirable
!
interface GigabitEthernet1/48
 description CAT-1 to CAT-2 LINKS
 switchport
 switchport trunk encapsulation dot1q
```

```
 switchport trunk allowed vlan 1,65
 switchport mode trunk
 no ip address
 channel-group 50 mode desirable
!
interface Vlan1
 no ip address
 shutdown
!
interface Vlan65
 description ** WAAS WAE Vlan **
 ip address 10.74.155.4 255.255.255.0
 standby 1 ip 10.74.155.1
 standby 1 preempt
 standby 2 ip 10.74.155.2
 standby 2 priority 105
!
```

Example 6-4 shows a sample configuration for a WAE in this deployment model.

Example 6-4   *WCCP on WAN Distribution Switches WAE Configuration*

```
WAE7326TEST# show running-config no-policy
! WAAS version 4.1.3 (build b23 Mar 14 2009)
!
device mode application-accelerator
!
hostname WAE7326TEST
!
ip domain-name asdcnp-waas.cisco.com
!
primary-interface GigabitEthernet 1/0
!
interface GigabitEthernet 1/0
 ip address 10.88.80.133 255.255.255.128
 exit
interface GigabitEthernet 2/0
 shutdown
 exit
!
ip default-gateway 10.74.155.2
!
no auto-register enable
!
```

```
! ip path-mtu-discovery is disabled in WAAS by default
!
ip name-server 10.88.80.53
!
logging console priority debug
!
ntp server 10.88.80.132
!
wccp router-list 1 44.77.22.3 44.77.22.4
wccp tcp-promiscuous router-list-num 1 password **** mask-assign
wccp version 2
!
egress-method generic-gre intercept-method wccp
!
username admin password 1 $1$vP9JXLqC$ApP5jqoOsIzPSpZl87vmI1
username admin privilege 15
username admin print-admin-password 1 CEC32C13191F9B56AAD3B435B51404EE
6E73ED22ADDAFAA4FACD2513341E6B7C
!
windows-domain netbios-name "WAE7326TEST"
!
authentication login local enable primary
authentication configuration local enable primary
!
central-manager address 10.88.80.142
cms enable
!
! End of WAAS configuration
WAE7326TEST#
```

This same configuration can be used when deploying WAAS deeper in the data center toward the server farms.

As discussed in the previous section, deploying WAAS in the WAN distribution layer when multiple data centers and asymmetric routing are involved requires that the WCCP service group span the WAN edge routers or switches in both data centers. Figure 6-11 shows a sample data center topology with a single WCCP service group that includes the WAN distribution switches in both data centers.

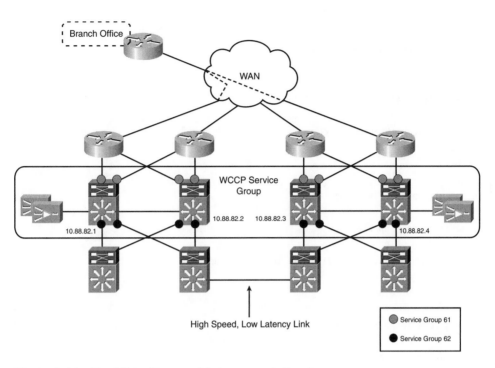

Figure 6-11 *Dual Data Center with Asymmetric Routing*

In Figure 6-11, WCCP is enabled on the Cisco WAN distribution switches. The WAEs are directly connected to the WAN distribution switches on a dedicated VLAN, which is trunked between the two switches in the local data center. All the WAEs in both data centers register with each pair of WAN distribution switches in both data centers. WCCP is configured for WCCP GRE forwarding and mask assignment. To preserve the original path selection and prevent the possibility of a redirection loop, the egress method is configured for GGRE. This ensures that egress traffic from the WAEs is returned to the original intercepting router after processing. Example 6-5 shows a sample configuration for a WAE in this deployment model.

Example 6-5 *Dual Data Center WAE Configuration*

```
WAE7326TEST# show running-config no-policy
! WAAS version 4.1.3 (build b23 Mar 14 2009)
!
device mode application-accelerator
!
hostname WAE7326TEST
!
ip domain-name asdcnp-waas.cisco.com
```

```
!
primary-interface GigabitEthernet 1/0
!
interface GigabitEthernet 1/0
 ip address 10.88.80.133 255.255.255.128
 exit
interface GigabitEthernet 2/0
 shutdown
 exit
!
ip default-gateway 10.88.80.130
!
no auto-register enable
!
! ip path-mtu-discovery is disabled in WAAS by default
!
ip name-server 10.88.80.53
!
logging console priority debug
!
ntp server 10.88.80.132
!
wccp router-list 1 44.77.22.2 44.77.22.3
wccp tcp-promiscuous router-list-num 1 password **** mask-assign
wccp version 2
!
egress-method generic-gre intercept-method wccp
!
username admin password 1 $1$vP9JXLqC$ApP5jqoOsIzPSpZl87vmI1
username admin privilege 15
username admin print-admin-password 1 CEC32C13191F9B56AAD3B435B51404EE
6E73ED22ADDAFAA4FACD2513341E6B7C
!
windows-domain netbios-name "WAE7326TEST"
!
authentication login local enable primary
authentication configuration local enable primary
!
central-manager address 10.88.80.142
cms enable
!
! End of WAAS configuration
WAE7326TEST#
```

Server Load Balancing

Using a server load balancer, such as the Cisco ACE, provides an alternative to WCCP for transparent interception in the data center. ACE is best suited for designs where WCCP is unable to meet the scalability requirements of the deployment or in data center designs where virtualization is used to provide logically separate infrastructures for different types of traffic. ACE can be deployed in either bridged mode or routed mode. Bridged mode is the equivalent of having ACE inline, because it bridges all traffic between VLANs. Routed mode requires that traffic be forwarded to ACE as a Layer 3 next hop. This is done by having traffic destined to a virtual IP address hosted on ACE, or using policy-based routing (PBR) to redirect traffic to ACE. Design and configuration examples of deploying ACE in bridged and routed mode for WAAS interception are provided in this section.

Figure 6-12 shows a topology where ACE is deployed in bridged mode at the server farm distribution layer.

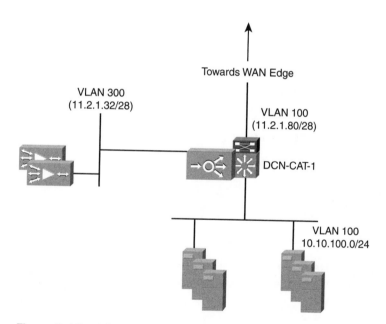

Figure 6-12 *ACE Bridged Mode Deployment*

In this deployment model, ACE bridges all traffic between VLAN 100 and VLAN 200. All traffic flows through ACE, regardless of whether or not the traffic is intercepted and redirected to a WAE for optimization. When the packet arrives on VLAN 100 in the Catalyst 6500 switch, it is passed through to the ACE module. A service policy configured to intercept all TCP traffic redirects the packet to one of the WAEs in the WAAS cluster. The WAE selected by the ACE load-balancing algorithm records the packet TCP options and returns the packet to its configured default gateway, which is the IP address configured on the WAAS VLAN in ACE. ACE forwards the packet based on the destination IP address and its routing configuration.

When a SYN-ACK response from the origin server arrives on VLAN 200, it is matched against the original flow created when the SYN packet was intercepted by ACE. Because the WAAS VLAN is configured with **mac-sticky**, the ACE returns the packet back to the WAE that handled the original SYN packet. The WAE matches the SYN-ACK with the original SYN packet and continues the TFO auto-discovery process. The packet is then returned to the ACE and routed back toward the WAN edge.

Example 6-6 shows the Catalyst 6500 and ACE configuration for this deployment model.

Example 6-6 *Catalyst 6500 and ACE Bridged Mode Configuration*

```
!
hostname DCN-CAT-1
!
svclc multiple-vlan-interfaces
svclc module 1 vlan-group 10
svclc vlan-group 10  100,200,300
!
interface Vlan100
 description ** Client-Side VLAN **
 ip address 11.2.1.81 255.255.255.240
!
!
hostname DCN-ACE-1
!
arp interval 15
!
access-list PERMIT-ALL line 10 extended permit ip any any
access-list PERMIT-ALL line 20 extended permit icmp any any
!
rserver host DCN-WAE-2
  ip address 11.2.1.34
  inservice
rserver host DCN-WAE-2
  ip address 11.2.1.35
  inservice
!
serverfarm host WAAS
  transparent
  predictor hash address source
```

```
    rserver DCN-WAE-1
      inservice
    rserver DCN-WAE-2
      inservice
!
class-map match-any ALL-TCP
  description ** Match all TCP traffic **
  10 match virtual-address 0.0.0.0 0.0.0.0 tcp any
!
class-map type management match-any ACE-MANAGEMENT
  2 match protocol telnet any
  3 match protocol ssh any
  4 match protocol icmp any
class-map match-any TCP-ALL
  2 match virtual-address 0.0.0.0 0.0.0.0 tcp any
!
policy-map type management first-match ACE-MANAGEMENT
  class ACE-MANAGEMENT
    permit
policy-map type loadbalance first-match TCP-ALL
  class class-default
    serverfarm WAAS
policy-map multi-match WAAS-INTERCEPTION
  class TCP-ALL
    loadbalance vip inservice
    loadbalance policy TCP-ALL
!
service-policy input ACE-MANAGEMENT
!
interface vlan 300
  description ** WAAS WAE VLAN **
  ip address 11.2.1.40 255.255.255.240
  no normalization
  mac-sticky enable
  access-group input PERMIT-ALL
  access-group output PERMIT-ALL
  no shutdown
interface vlan 100
  description ** Client-Side VLAN **
  bridge-group 100
  no normalization
  access-group input PERMIT-ALL
  access-group output PERMIT-ALL
  service-policy input WAAS-INTERCEPT
```

```
   no shutdown
interface vlan 200
   description ** Server-Side VLAN **
   bridge-group 100
   no normalization
   access-group input PERMIT-ALL
   access-group output PERMIT-ALL
   service-policy input WAAS-INTERCEPT
   no shutdown
!
interface bvi 100
   ip address 11.2.1.83 255.255.255.240
   no shutdown
!
ip route 0.0.0.0 0.0.0.0 11.2.1.81
!
```

IP normalization is also disabled on the ACE VLAN interfaces with the command **no normalization**. This is required to allow the WAAS TFO auto-discovery process to function properly.

No special configuration is required on the WAE when ACE is used for interception. The default gateway configured on the WAE is the alias IP address of the WAE VLAN configured in ACE.

When ACE is deployed in routed mode, ACE must become a Layer 3 next hop for traffic in order for interception to take place. Because WAAS is transparent at Layer 3, traffic is not destined to a VIP configured on ACE. For this deployment model, ACE is used in combination with PBR to intercept interesting traffic for optimization. PBR is configured in the network infrastructure devices, with a next-hop IP address of a VLAN interface on ACE.

The routed mode topology is similar to bridged mode, the primary difference being how traffic is intercepted by ACE. In the routed mode deployment, PBR is configured on the Catalyst 6500 switch to intercept TCP traffic that is optimized by WAAS. The PBR configuration sets a next-hop address of an IP address configured on the ACE module. The WAEs are placed on a dedicated VLAN that is routed by the ACE module. Example 6-7 shows the ACE configuration for this deployment model.

Example 6-7 *Catalyst 6500 and ACE Routed Mode Configuration*

```
!
hostname DCN-CAT-1
!
vlan 500
!
```

```
interface Vlan100
 description ** Link to Data Center WAN Edge **
 ip address 10.88.81.6 255.255.255.252
 ip policy route-map PBR-TO-ACE
!
interface Vlan200
 ip address 172.16.0.1 255.255.254.0
 ip policy route-map PBR-TO-ACE
!
interface Vlan500
 description ** Link to DCN-ACE-1 **
 ip address 30.30.5.4 255.255.255.0
!
ip access-list extended PBR-TO-ACE
 permit tcp any any
!
route-map PBR-TO-ACE permit 10
 match ip address PBR-TO-ACE
 set ip next-hop 30.30.5.1
!
!
hostname DCN-ACE-1
!
arp interval 15
!
access-list PERMIT-ALL line 10 extended permit ip any any
access-list PERMIT-ALL line 20 extended permit icmp any any
!
rserver host DCN-WAE-1
  ip address 30.30.51.10
  inservice
rserver host DCN-WAE-2
  ip address 30.30.51.11
  inservice
!
serverfarm host WAAS
  transparent
  rserver DCN-WAE-1
    inservice
  rserver DCN-WAE-2
    inservice
!
class-map type management match-any ACE-MANAGEMENT
  2 match protocol telnet any
```

```
  3 match protocol ssh any
  4 match protocol icmp any
class-map match-any TCP-ALL
  2 match virtual-address 0.0.0.0 0.0.0.0 tcp any
!
policy-map type management first-match ACE-MANAGEMENT
  class ACE-MANAGEMENT
    permit
policy-map type loadbalance first-match TCP-ALL
  class class-default
    serverfarm WAAS
policy-map multi-match WAAS-INTERCEPTION
  class TCP-ALL
    loadbalance vip inservice
    loadbalance policy TCP-ALL
!
service-policy input ACE-MANAGEMENT
!
interface vlan 500
  description ** Client-Side VLAN **
  ip address 30.30.5.1 255.255.255.0
  no normalization
  access-group input PERMIT-ALL
  access-group output PERMIT-ALL
  service-policy input WAAS-INTERCEPTION
  no shutdown
interface vlan 501
  description ** WAAS WAE VLAN **
  ip address 30.30.51.1 255.255.255.0
  no normalization
  mac-sticky enable
  access-group input PERMIT-ALL
  access-group output PERMIT-ALL
  no shutdown
!
ip route 0.0.0.0 0.0.0.0 30.30.5.4
!
```

Again, no special configuration is required on the WAE when ACE is used for interception. The default gateway configured on the WAE is the IP address of the WAE VLAN configured in ACE.

Scaling Transparent Interception

As organizations continue to consolidate more IT resources into the data center, the data center becomes a natural aggregation point for traffic from the remote branch offices. Due to the high traffic volumes, diverse routing paths, and increasing number of data center resources accessed from remote branch offices, in-path deployment models are not considered a scalable solution for data center environments. The preferred transparent interception method in data center environments is either WCCP or ACE. Both of these interception methods provide the availability and scalability features required to support large-scale WAAS deployments. Each interception method, along with best-practice recommendations and configuration examples, is discussed in turn in the following sections.

WCCP Scalability

The placement of services 61 and 62 in the router configuration plays an important role in the scalability of the WAAS solution. When multiple WAEs are deployed in the branch, the goal is to distribute load across the WAEs in the service group as evenly as possible. The TCP promiscuous services perform load distribution at IP address–level granularity. In most environments, the number of clients is far greater than the number of servers; therefore, performing load distribution based on the client IP address makes it statistically more likely that clients are distributed more evenly across multiple WAEs. In contrast, if load is distributed based on server IP address, the effectiveness of DRE could potentially increase, because all content for a single server IP address resides in a single WAE. However, using the server IP address does not allow for linear scalability of the solution. In addition, there is a potential for "hot spots," where in a cluster of WAEs only one or two WAEs are used for the majority of traffic. This can happen due to the limited number of server IP addresses, and the potential for virtual IP addresses, proxy addresses, and other heavily used destination IP addresses being pinned to a single WAE.

The hash function used by WCCP hash assignment is designed to distribute client load across all of the WAEs in a service group. Although this is appropriate for branch office deployments, load distribution in the data center must also take into consideration the fan-out ratio. Take for example a branch office with hosts using IP addresses in the 10.48.136.0/23 network. In the data center, there are three WAEs deployed in a cluster. Example 6-8 shows the hash bucket distribution for each of the three WAEs.

Example 6-8   *Data Center WAE Hash Bucket Distribution*

```
AST6-RTR-02# show ip wccp 61 detail
WCCP Client information:
        WCCP Client ID:         10.88.81.2
        Protocol Version:       2.0
        State:                  Usable
        Initial Hash Info:      00000000000000000000000000000000
                                00000000000000000000000000000000
```

```
        Assigned Hash Info:      FFFFFFFFFFFFFFFFFFFFFFFC0000000000
                                 0000000000000000000000000000000000
        Hash Allotment:          86 (33.59%)
        Packets s/w Redirected:  0
        Connect Time:            1d22h
        Bypassed Packets
          Process:               0
          Fast:                  0
          CEF:                   0
        WCCP Client ID:          10.88.80.138
        Protocol Version:        2.0
        State:                   Usable
        Initial Hash Info:       0000000000000000000000000000000000
                                 0000000000000000000000000000000000
        Assigned Hash Info:      0000000000000000000000000000000000
                                 FFFFFFFFFFFFFFFFFFFFFF80000000000
        Hash Allotment:          85 (33.20%)
        Packets s/w Redirected:  0
        Connect Time:            00:01:55
        Bypassed Packets
          Process:               0
          Fast:                  0
          CEF:                   0
        WCCP Client ID:          10.88.80.137
        Protocol Version:        2.0
        State:                   Usable
        Initial Hash Info:       0000000000000000000000000000000000
                                 0000000000000000000000000000000000
        Assigned Hash Info:      000000000000000000003FFFFFFFFFF
                                 000000000000000000007FFFFFFFFFF
        Hash Allotment:          85 (33.20%)
        Packets s/w Redirected:  0
        Connect Time:            00:00:50
        Bypassed Packets
          Process:               0
          Fast:                  0
          CEF:                   0
AST6-RTR-02#
```

In the preceding output, each WAE has received roughly 33 percent of the hash buckets in the table. Which data center WAE they are redirected to can be determined by looking at a small sample of client IP addresses from the branch network. Example 6-9 shows the results of this test.

Example 6-9   *Client Distribution Across Data Center WAEs*

```
AST6-RTR-02# show ip wccp 61 hash 0.0.0.0 10.48.136.10 0 0
WCCP hash information for:
    Primary Hash:    Src IP: 10.48.136.10
        Bucket: 184
    WCCP Client: 10.88.81.2
AST6-RTR-02#
AST6-RTR-02# show ip wccp 61 hash 0.0.0.0 10.48.136.50 0 0
WCCP hash information for:
    Primary Hash:    Src IP: 10.48.136.50
        Bucket: 128
    WCCP Client: 10.88.80.137
AST6-RTR-02# show ip wccp 61 hash 0.0.0.0 10.48.136.200 0 0
WCCP hash information for:
    Primary Hash:    Src IP: 10.48.136.200
        Bucket: 122
    WCCP Client: 10.88.80.138
AST6-RTR-02# show ip wccp 61 hash 0.0.0.0 10.48.137.20 0 0
WCCP hash information for:
    Primary Hash:    Src IP: 10.48.137.20
        Bucket: 167
    WCCP Client: 10.88.80.137
AST6-RTR-02# show ip wccp 61 hash 0.0.0.0 10.48.137.70 0 0
WCCP hash information for:
    Primary Hash:    Src IP: 10.48.137.70
        Bucket: 245
    WCCP Client: 10.88.81.2
AST6-RTR-02# show ip wccp 61 hash 0.0.0.0 10.48.137.222 0 0
WCCP hash information for:
    Primary Hash:    Src IP: 10.48.137.222
        Bucket: 109
    WCCP Client: 10.88.80.138
AST6-RTR-02#
```

You can see from the output that clients from a single branch are redirected to all three WAEs in the data center cluster. This results in a DRE context for the branch office WAE in every data center WAE. Although this might not pose a problem for small and medium-sized WAAS deployments, as you start to scale to hundreds or thousands of WAEs, keeping a DRE context for every remote WAE in every data center WAE does not scale. For example, if you have a WAAS deployment made up of 350 remote branch offices, you might choose to deploy three WAE-7341s in the data center to support the fan-out ratio. However, when hash assignment is used, each of the three WAE-7341s likely has a peer relationship with all 350 remote branch WAEs. Therefore, when the number of remote WAEs in a deployment exceeds the fan-out ratio supported by a single WAE in the data center, hash assignment is not recommended.

With WCCP mask assignment, you can influence the load distribution by adjusting the position of the bit in the mask to take only the network portion of the IP address into consideration. Example 6-10 shows the mask/value set distribution across the three WAEs in the data center.

Example 6-10   *Data Center WAE Mask/Value Distribution*

```
DCN-CAT-8# show ip wccp 61 detail
WCCP Cache-Engine information:
        Web Cache ID:           10.88.81.2
        Protocol Version:       2.0
        State:                  Usable
        Redirection:            GRE
        Packet Return:          GRE
        Packets Redirected:     0
        Connect Time:           00:02:53
        Assignment:             MASK
        Mask    SrcAddr     DstAddr     SrcPort DstPort
        --      ----.       ----.       ----. ----.
        0000: 0x00001741 0x00000000 0x0000   0x0000
        Value SrcAddr     DstAddr       SrcPort DstPort CE-IP
        ---.  ----.       ----.         ----. ----. --.
        0042: 0x00001240 0x00000000 0x0000   0x0000   0x0A585102 (10.88.81.2)
        0043: 0x00001241 0x00000000 0x0000   0x0000   0x0A585102 (10.88.81.2)
        0044: 0x00001300 0x00000000 0x0000   0x0000   0x0A585102 (10.88.81.2)
        0045: 0x00001301 0x00000000 0x0000   0x0000   0x0A585102 (10.88.81.2)
        0046: 0x00001340 0x00000000 0x0000   0x0000   0x0A585102 (10.88.81.2)
        0047: 0x00001341 0x00000000 0x0000   0x0000   0x0A585102 (10.88.81.2)
        0048: 0x00001400 0x00000000 0x0000   0x0000   0x0A585102 (10.88.81.2)
        0049: 0x00001401 0x00000000 0x0000   0x0000   0x0A585102 (10.88.81.2)
        0050: 0x00001440 0x00000000 0x0000   0x0000   0x0A585102 (10.88.81.2)
        0051: 0x00001441 0x00000000 0x0000   0x0000   0x0A585102 (10.88.81.2)
        0052: 0x00001500 0x00000000 0x0000   0x0000   0x0A585102 (10.88.81.2)
        0053: 0x00001501 0x00000000 0x0000   0x0000   0x0A585102 (10.88.81.2)
        0054: 0x00001540 0x00000000 0x0000   0x0000   0x0A585102 (10.88.81.2)
        0055: 0x00001541 0x00000000 0x0000   0x0000   0x0A585102 (10.88.81.2)
        0056: 0x00001600 0x00000000 0x0000   0x0000   0x0A585102 (10.88.81.2)
        0057: 0x00001601 0x00000000 0x0000   0x0000   0x0A585102 (10.88.81.2)
        0058: 0x00001640 0x00000000 0x0000   0x0000   0x0A585102 (10.88.81.2)
        0059: 0x00001641 0x00000000 0x0000   0x0000   0x0A585102 (10.88.81.2)
        0060: 0x00001700 0x00000000 0x0000   0x0000   0x0A585102 (10.88.81.2)
        0061: 0x00001701 0x00000000 0x0000   0x0000   0x0A585102 (10.88.81.2)
        0062: 0x00001740 0x00000000 0x0000   0x0000   0x0A585102 (10.88.81.2)
```

```
0063: 0x00001741 0x00000000 0x0000   0x0000   0x0A585102 (10.88.81.2)


Web Cache ID:              10.88.80.137
Protocol Version:          2.0
State:                     Usable
Redirection:               GRE
Packet Return:             GRE
Packets Redirected:        0
Connect Time:              00:01:44
Assignment:                MASK
Mask   SrcAddr    DstAddr      SrcPort DstPort
——   ———·     ———·       ———· ———·
0000: 0x00001741 0x00000000 0x0000   0x0000
Value SrcAddr    DstAddr      SrcPort DstPort CE-IP
——· ———·      ———·       ———· ———· ——·
0011: 0x00000241 0x00000000 0x0000   0x0000   0x0A585089 (10.88.80.137)
0012: 0x00000300 0x00000000 0x0000   0x0000   0x0A585089 (10.88.80.137)
0013: 0x00000301 0x00000000 0x0000   0x0000   0x0A585089 (10.88.80.137)
0014: 0x00000340 0x00000000 0x0000   0x0000   0x0A585089 (10.88.80.137)
0015: 0x00000341 0x00000000 0x0000   0x0000   0x0A585089 (10.88.80.137)
0016: 0x00000400 0x00000000 0x0000   0x0000   0x0A585089 (10.88.80.137)
0017: 0x00000401 0x00000000 0x0000   0x0000   0x0A585089 (10.88.80.137)
0018: 0x00000440 0x00000000 0x0000   0x0000   0x0A585089 (10.88.80.137)
0019: 0x00000441 0x00000000 0x0000   0x0000   0x0A585089 (10.88.80.137)
0020: 0x00000500 0x00000000 0x0000   0x0000   0x0A585089 (10.88.80.137)
0021: 0x00000501 0x00000000 0x0000   0x0000   0x0A585089 (10.88.80.137)
0022: 0x00000540 0x00000000 0x0000   0x0000   0x0A585089 (10.88.80.137)
0023: 0x00000541 0x00000000 0x0000   0x0000   0x0A585089 (10.88.80.137)
0024: 0x00000600 0x00000000 0x0000   0x0000   0x0A585089 (10.88.80.137)
0025: 0x00000601 0x00000000 0x0000   0x0000   0x0A585089 (10.88.80.137)
0026: 0x00000640 0x00000000 0x0000   0x0000   0x0A585089 (10.88.80.137)
0027: 0x00000641 0x00000000 0x0000   0x0000   0x0A585089 (10.88.80.137)
0028: 0x00000700 0x00000000 0x0000   0x0000   0x0A585089 (10.88.80.137)
0029: 0x00000701 0x00000000 0x0000   0x0000   0x0A585089 (10.88.80.137)
0030: 0x00000740 0x00000000 0x0000   0x0000   0x0A585089 (10.88.80.137)
0031: 0x00000741 0x00000000 0x0000   0x0000   0x0A585089 (10.88.80.137)
Web Cache ID:              10.88.80.138
Protocol Version:          2.0
State:                     Usable
Redirection:               GRE
Packet Return:             GRE
Packets Redirected:        0
Connect Time:              00:00:44
Assignment:                MASK
```

```
     Mask  SrcAddr    DstAddr    SrcPort DstPort
     — —   — — —.      — — —.     — — —. — — —.
     0000: 0x00001741 0x00000000 0x0000  0x0000
     Value SrcAddr    DstAddr    SrcPort DstPort CE-IP
     — —.  — — —.      — — —.     — — —. — — —. — —.
     0000: 0x00000000 0x00000000 0x0000  0x0000  0x0A58508A (10.88.80.138)
     0001: 0x00000001 0x00000000 0x0000  0x0000  0x0A58508A (10.88.80.138)
     0002: 0x00000040 0x00000000 0x0000  0x0000  0x0A58508A (10.88.80.138)
     0003: 0x00000041 0x00000000 0x0000  0x0000  0x0A58508A (10.88.80.138)
     0004: 0x00000100 0x00000000 0x0000  0x0000  0x0A58508A (10.88.80.138)
     0005: 0x00000101 0x00000000 0x0000  0x0000  0x0A58508A (10.88.80.138)
     0006: 0x00000140 0x00000000 0x0000  0x0000  0x0A58508A (10.88.80.138)
     0007: 0x00000141 0x00000000 0x0000  0x0000  0x0A58508A (10.88.80.138)
     0008: 0x00000200 0x00000000 0x0000  0x0000  0x0A58508A (10.88.80.138)
     0009: 0x00000201 0x00000000 0x0000  0x0000  0x0A58508A (10.88.80.138)
     0010: 0x00000240 0x00000000 0x0000  0x0000  0x0A58508A (10.88.80.138)
     0032: 0x00001000 0x00000000 0x0000  0x0000  0x0A58508A (10.88.80.138)
     0033: 0x00001001 0x00000000 0x0000  0x0000  0x0A58508A (10.88.80.138)
     0034: 0x00001040 0x00000000 0x0000  0x0000  0x0A58508A (10.88.80.138)
     0035: 0x00001041 0x00000000 0x0000  0x0000  0x0A58508A (10.88.80.138)
     0036: 0x00001100 0x00000000 0x0000  0x0000  0x0A58508A (10.88.80.138)
     0037: 0x00001101 0x00000000 0x0000  0x0000  0x0A58508A (10.88.80.138)
     0038: 0x00001140 0x00000000 0x0000  0x0000  0x0A58508A (10.88.80.138)
     0039: 0x00001141 0x00000000 0x0000  0x0000  0x0A58508A (10.88.80.138)
     0040: 0x00001200 0x00000000 0x0000  0x0000  0x0A58508A (10.88.80.138)
     0041: 0x00001201 0x00000000 0x0000  0x0000  0x0A58508A (10.88.80.138)
DCN-CAT-8#
```

The default mask used for mask assignment is 0x1741. Looking at the same six IP addresses from the branch office, the mask function results in the redirection outlined in Table 6-1.

In this case, the default mask is sufficient to redirect all traffic from the remote branch office to a single WAE in the data center cluster. However, if the number of WAEs in the cluster increases to 9, traffic sourced from the 10.48.136.0/23 address space begins getting distributed across multiple WAEs in the cluster. Determining when to change the default mask in data center deployments depends on the number of subnet mask bits used on the IP addressing scheme of the remote branch offices.

Table 6-1   *Client Distribution Across Data Center WAEs*

IP Address	Mask	Result	WAE
0xa30880a (10.48.136.10)	0x1741	0x0	10.88.80.138
0xa308832 (10.48.136.50)	0x1741	0x0	10.88.80.138
0xa3088c8 (10.48.136.200)	0x1741	0x40	10.88.80.138
0xa308914 (10.48.138.20)	0x1741	0x100	10.88.80.138
0xa308946 (10.48.137.70)	0x1741	0x140	10.88.80.138
0xa3089de (10.48.137.222)	0x1741	0x140	10.88.80.138

For large deployments, the default WCCP mask used in the data center should be changed by shifting to the left by the number of host bits in the IP addressing scheme for the remote branch office. By shifting the default mask to the left by the number of host bits in the addressing scheme, the variations in the host addressing are taken out of the load-distribution calculation. In Table 6-1, there are nine host bits in a /23 addressing scheme. This results in the following change to the default mask:

```
0x1741 << 9 = 0x2e8200
```

Using a mask of 0x2e8200 in this example pins all traffic from 10.48.136.0/23 to a single data center WAE, regardless of the number of WAEs in the cluster. This provides the optimal balance of load distribution and fan-out control.

ACE Scalability

Similar logic applies when using ACE for transparent interception with WAAS. The mechanism in ACE that controls the distribution of traffic among WAEs is called the predictor method. When intercepting traffic flowing from clients to servers, a predictor method that hashes on the source IP address is applied.

The predictor method is configured in ACE as part of the server farm configuration. The syntax for the CLI command is

```
predictor hash address [source ¦ destination] [netmask]
```

Other predictor methods are available, but this discussion focuses on the address hashing method. Example 6-11 shows the predictor method CLI configuration within ACE.

Example 6-11 *ACE Predictor Method CLI Command*

```
!
serverfarm
 predictor hash address source 255.255.255.0
 !
```

This configuration tells ACE to distribute load across the WAEs based on a hash of the first three octets of the source IP address. As with the WCCP mask, the netmask configured as part of the ACE predictor hash address method should focus on the network portion of the IP address. This has the desired effect of redirecting all traffic from the same source network to the same WAE in the data center.

Firewall Integration

Firewalls are a common component deployed within the data center environment. Cisco provides unique integration capabilities between WAAS and Cisco firewall solutions, specifically IOS FW, PIX/ASA appliances, and the Firewall Switch Module (FWSM). Beginning with FWSM software release 3.2.1, FWSM can recognize WAAS-optimized connections and employ security capabilities against these optimized flows. These capabilities include identifying optimized connections by their auto-discovery TCP option and adjusting to the TCP sequence number space used by the optimized connection. In addition, deep packet inspection capabilities are dynamically disabled, avoiding unnecessary inspection of packet payloads compressed by WAAS. Example 6-12 shows the output of the command **show conn long** *x*, which displays how the FWSM recognized a WAAS-optimized connection, and the connection flag "W" (indicating a WAAS-optimized flow).

Example 6-12 *FWSM Connection Display Output*

```
FWSM# sh conn long 5
0 in use, 3 most used
Flags: A - awaiting inside ACK to SYN, a - awaiting outside ACK to SYN,
       B - initial SYN from outside, b - State bypass, C - CTIQBE media,
       D - DNS, d - dump, E - outside back connection, F - outside FIN,
       f - inside FIN, G - group, g - MGCP, H - H.323, h - H.225.0,
       I - inbound data, i - incomplete, J - GTP, j - GTP data, k - Skinny media,
       M - SMTP data, m - SIP media, n - GUP, O - outbound data,
       P - inside back connection, q - SQL*Net data, R - outside acknowledged FIN,
       R - UDP SUNRPC, r - inside acknowledged FIN, S - awaiting inside SYN,
       s - awaiting outside SYN, T - SIP, t - SIP transient, U - up
       X - xlate creation bypassed, W - WAAS Session
Network Processor 1 connections
Network Processor 2 connections
TCP out 10.1.1.1:2671 in 150.1.1.3:20 idle 0:00:00 Bytes 460698 FLAGS - UOIW

  Flags1: 0xd040 Flags2: 0x0071 Pr_tmout: 0x0002 address: 0x024000e0
```

```
 Session ID: 0x0d0e0f5d Xlate ID: 0x0205891f DeltaSeq: 0xf845d440 VCID: 0x0000
 Root:    Send Unack: 0x8005fec8 Next: 0x8005fec8 Scale: 0x07
          Win Size: 0xfff0 TCP Delta: 0x45fe
 NonRoot:Send Unack: 0xd3c0d99e Next: 0xd3c0d9bc Scale: 0x07
          Win Size: 0x2000 TCP Delta: 0xba01
 Ch Ptr (Data): 0x00000000 (Ctrl): 0x024000d6 Fn ID: 0x07 TLV List: 0x00
         AAA Delta: 0x00000000 Lu Last Sync: 0x240b571d
 L7:     Fxup Ctr: 0x0000  Flags: 0xcd3412ab
      Send Next (root): 0x00000000 (non root): 0x00000000
 Mac (root): 0x000ccf6cce80 (non root): 0x00c04f0435fd
 Vlan (root): 0150 (non root): 0080 Ifc (root): 0003 (non root): 0001
 MPC_connTimeout: 0000 mins       MPC_embConnTimeout: 0120 secs
 MPC_halfOpenTimeout: 0000 secs  MPC_halfClosedTimeout: 0000 secs
 MPC_leaf_ext_ptr: 0x0
 PC_Inspect_ptr: 0x0
 Appln Extension: 0x0
 System timestamp: 0x240b5cf6 Connection timestamp: 0x240b5cf5
```

Figure 6-13 shows a sample data center topology with an FWSM deployed in the server farm aggregation layer.

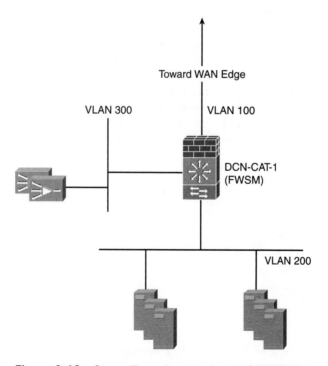

Figure 6-13 *Server Farm Aggregation with FWSM*

Example 6-13 shows the FWSM configuration for this deployment model.

Example 6-13   *FWSM Configuration with WAAS Interoperability*

```
!
hostname FWSM
enable password 8Ry2YjIyt7RRXU24 encrypted
names
!
interface Vlan200
 nameif server
 security-level 99
 ip address 160.1.1.2 255.255.255.0
!
interface Vlan100
 nameif client
 security-level 10
 ip address 80.1.1.1 255.255.255.0
!
passwd 2KFQnbNIdI.2KYOU encrypted
ftp mode passive
access-list out2 extended permit tcp any any
access-list out1 extended permit icmp any any echo
access-list out1 extended permit tcp any any eq https
access-list out1 extended permit tcp any any eq 8443
access-list out1 extended permit tcp any any eq www
access-list out1 extended permit tcp any any eq ftp
access-list out1 extended permit tcp any any eq telnet
access-list out1 extended permit tcp any any eq 4050
access-list out1 extended permit tcp any any eq 445
access-list ftp-cap extended permit tcp any any eq ftp
!
<output omitted>
!
icmp permit any server
icmp permit any echo server
icmp permit any client
icmp permit any inside
icmp permit any echo inside
no asdm history enable
arp timeout 14400
nat (inside) 1 0.0.0.0 0.0.0.0
!
static (server,client) 80.1.1.5 150.1.1.3 netmask 255.255.255.255
access-group out1 in interface server
```

```
access-group out1 in interface client
access-group out1 in interface inside
route server 170.1.1.0 255.255.255.0 160.1.1.1 1
route server 150.1.1.0 255.255.255.0 160.1.1.1 1
route server 190.1.1.0 255.255.255.0 160.1.1.1 1
route server 80.1.1.5 255.255.255.255 160.1.1.1 1
route client 0.0.0.0 0.0.0.0 70.1.1.2 1
!
<output omitted>
!
class-map inspection_default
 match default-inspection-traffic
!
policy-map global_policy
 class inspection_default
  inspect dns maximum-length 512
  inspect ftp
  inspect h323 h225
  inspect h323 ras
  inspect rsh
  inspect smtp
  inspect sqlnet
  inspect skinny
  inspect sunrpc
  inspect xdmcp
  inspect sip
  inspect netbios
  inspect tftp
  inspect waas
  inspect icmp
  inspect http
!
service-policy global_policy global
prompt hostname context
!
```

Example 6-13 shows the use of the CLI command **inspect waas**, which enables interoperability between FWSM and WAAS. This command is available in all modes and can be enabled per context.

Cisco PIX/ASA is also commonly used in data center environments. Like FWSM, PIX/ASA provides interoperability with WAAS beginning in software version 7.2.3. Example 6-14 shows a sample ASA configuration for providing interoperability with WAAS.

Example 6-14 *PIX/ASA Configuration with WAAS Interoperability*

```
!
hostname ASA
domain-name default.domain.invalid
enable password 8Ry2YjIyt7RRXU24 encrypted
names
!
interface GigabitEthernet0/0
 nameif inside
 security-level 100
 ip address 10.30.3.2 255.255.255.0
!
interface GigabitEthernet0/1
 nameif outside
 security-level 0
 ip address 10.30.2.3 255.255.255.0
!
interface GigabitEthernet0/2
 shutdown
 no nameif
 no security-level
 no ip address
!
interface GigabitEthernet0/3
 shutdown
 no nameif
 no security-level
 no ip address
!
interface Management0/0
 nameif management
 security-level 100
 ip address 171.68.96.120 255.255.255.0
 management-only
!
passwd 2KFQnbNIdI.2KYOU encrypted
boot system disk0:/asa722-33-k8.bin
ftp mode passive
dns server-group DefaultDNS
 domain-name default.domain.invalid
same-security-traffic permit intra-interface
access-list outside_access_in extended permit tcp 10.3.0.0 255.255.255.0 any eq
https
```

```
access-list outside_access_in extended permit tcp 10.3.0.0 255.255.255.0 any eq 8443
access-list outside_access_in extended permit tcp 10.3.0.0 255.255.255.0 any eq 4050
access-list outside_access_in extended permit tcp 10.3.0.0 255.255.255.0 any eq www
access-list outside_access_in extended permit tcp host 10.0.2.4 any eq 8443
access-list inside_access_in extended permit ip any any
pager lines 24
logging enable
logging console debugging
logging asdm informational
mtu inside 1500
mtu outside 1500
mtu management 1500
no failover
icmp unreachable rate-limit 1 burst-size 1
icmp permit any inside
icmp permit any outside
asdm image disk0:/asdm-522.bin
no asdm history enable
arp timeout 14400
access-group inside_access_in in interface inside
access-group outside_access_in in interface outside
route inside 10.30.0.0 255.255.255.0 10.30.3.1 1
route inside 10.30.1.0 255.255.255.0 10.30.3.1 1
route outside 10.0.2.0 255.255.254.0 10.30.2.1 1
route outside 10.0.254.0 255.255.254.0 10.30.2.1 1
route outside 10.3.0.0 255.255.255.0 10.30.2.1 1
route outside 10.30.4.0 255.255.255.0 10.30.2.1 1
route management 0.0.0.0 0.0.0.0 171.68.96.1 1
timeout xlate 3:00:00
timeout conn 1:00:00 half-closed 0:10:00 udp 0:02:00 icmp 0:00:02
timeout sunrpc 0:10:00 h323 0:05:00 h225 1:00:00 mgcp 0:05:00 mgcp-pat 0:05:00
timeout sip 0:30:00 sip_media 0:02:00 sip-invite 0:03:00 sip-disconnect 0:02:00
timeout uauth 0:05:00 absolute
http server enable
http 0.0.0.0 0.0.0.0 management
no snmp-server location
no snmp-server contact
snmp-server enable traps snmp authentication linkup linkdown coldstart
telnet 0.0.0.0 0.0.0.0 management
telnet timeout 180
ssh scopy enable
ssh 0.0.0.0 0.0.0.0 management
```

```
ssh timeout 5
console timeout 0
!
class-map inspection_default
 match default-inspection-traffic
!
!
policy-map type inspect dns preset_dns_map

 parameters
  message-length maximum 512
policy-map global_policy
  class inspection_default
  inspect dns preset_dns_map
  inspect ftp
  inspect h323 h225
  inspect h323 ras
  inspect netbios
  inspect rsh
  inspect rtsp
  inspect skinny
  inspect esmtp
  inspect sqlnet
  inspect sunrpc
  inspect tftp
  inspect sip
  inspect xdmcp
  inspect waas
 !
service-policy global_policy global
prompt hostname context
Cryptochecksum:c11b71317b49a3b461a8a3d7c19e47d1
 : end
```

Summary

This chapter looked at the design considerations that are key to a successful WAAS deployment in the data center environment. It looked at different placement and configuration options for transparent interception and discussed methods to scale transparent interception in the data center to hundreds or thousands of locations. Finally, this chapter looked at the configuration options available for integration between WAAS and popular Cisco firewall solutions such as PIX/ASA and FWSM. At this point, you should have a solid understanding of the design and network integration options available with Cisco WAAS. Subsequent chapters dive into the deployment and configuration details for the different WAAS components and features.

Chapter 7

System and Device Management

The previous chapters have introduced the capabilities of the Cisco Wide Area Application Services (WAAS) solution and described how the WAAS appliances and network modules are integrated into the network. This chapter focuses on how the Cisco WAAS devices are initially deployed in the network and then managed centrally by the Cisco WAAS Central Manager (CM).

This chapter provides an overview of Cisco WAAS device-level management and system-level management, including the capabilities of each. The chapter then focuses on installation and configuration of the devices, groups, and the system as a whole. Device groups, which help minimize ongoing configuration and management overhead, are discussed and examined. Provisioned management capabilities, enabled through role-based access control (RBAC), are discussed, and a focus is provided on integrating with external authentication systems. The chapter concludes with a discussion focusing on the remaining aspects of system and device management, including customizing charts, creating reports, and integration of Cisco WAAS into third-party management and monitoring systems using the Simple Network Management Protocol (SNMP), syslog, and the eXtensible Markup Language Application Programming Interface (XML-API).

It should be noted that this chapter does not provide an exhaustive review of everything that can be configured within Cisco WAAS via the command-line interface (CLI) or CM. Rather, it examines the items necessary to get a system of devices functionally available and ready for central management, including the majority of items that most I/T organizations find relevant. Other chapters in this book focus on the details of configuring specific components on a device or within the system and the monitoring and reporting aspects for each of those components. Thus, this chapter lays the management framework foundation that other chapters build upon.

System and Device Management Overview

Each Cisco WAAS device can be managed through one of two primary interfaces:

- **CLI:** Accessible on each Cisco WAAS device directly via console, Telnet, or Secure Shell (SSH)

- **The CM GUI:** Accessible via a web browser

In the factory-default configuration, Cisco WAAS devices do not come preconfigured with an IP address. Deploying a Cisco WAAS device initially requires that you configure a Dynamic Host Configuration Protocol (DHCP) option that informs a WAAS device of the CM IP address or Domain Name System (DNS) name (not discussed in this book), or connect to the device through a serial connection to run a CLI initial setup script, which is able to apply the appropriate configuration to the device to make it reachable on the network. This serial connection is available physically for Cisco WAAS appliances and virtually through the router CLI for Cisco WAAS network modules. After the WAAS device is reachable on the network, you can then connect it to the CM for centralized management, which uses the Centralized Management System (CMS) service discussed later in this section, or configure it further from the CLI of that particular device. Use of the CM is recommended, because it is designed to simplify management of each device and the system as a whole, while also providing individual device and system-level aggregate monitoring and reporting.

This section examines the Cisco WAAS device setup script and CLI and provides an overview of the CM and CMS service that runs on each Cisco WAAS device. This section provides a foundation for future sections in the chapter.

Initial Setup Wizard

Cisco WAAS devices are configured to automatically run the setup script when the device boots for the first time and the administrator is connected to the WAAS device via a serial connection. Many organizations find it helpful to use the built-in setup wizard to apply the initial configuration to the device. However, other organizations use scripts (or simple copy/paste operations) as an alternative when the required default configuration is more complex.

In the case of a WAAS appliance, the serial connection is physical, and the terminal emulation software should be set to use 9600 baud, 8 data bits, 1 stop bit, and no parity bits. In the case of a WAAS network module, the serial connection is virtual and accessed through the CLI of the Integrated Services Router (ISR). To access the console of the WAAS module from the ISR CLI, you need to verify that the network module is recognized and then access the virtual console session as demonstrated in Example 7-1.

Example 7-1 *Accessing the WAAS Network Module Console from the ISR CLI*

```
hostname$ telnet 172.23.143.14
```

```
Trying 172.23.143.14...
Connected to router.cisco.com.
Escape character is '^]'.


User Access Verification


Username: admin
Password:
R2821-edge#
R2821-edge# show hardware
Cisco IOS Software, 2800 Software (C2800NM-ADVENTERPRISEK9-M), Version 12.4(24)T,
RELEASE SOFTWARE (fc1)
Technical Support: http://www.cisco.com/techsupport
Copyright (c) 1986-2009 by Cisco Systems, Inc.
Compiled Wed 25-Feb-09 17:54 by prod_rel_team
!
!
!  portions removed
!
!
Cisco 2851 (revision 53.51) with 241664K/20480K bytes of memory.
Processor board ID FTX1029A114
2 Gigabit Ethernet interfaces
1 terminal line
1 Virtual Private Network (VPN) Module
1 cisco Integrated Service Engine(s)
   Cisco Wide Area Application Services Software 4.1.3 (b24 Mar 16 2009 23:24:21)
in slot 1
DRAM configuration is 64 bits wide with parity enabled.
239K bytes of non-volatile configuration memory.
62720K bytes of ATA CompactFlash (Read/Write)


Configuration register is 0x2102


R2821-edge# show interfaces
!
!
! portions removed
!
!
Integrated-Service-Engine1/0 is up, line protocol is up
  Hardware is BCM5703, address is 000a.b82e.21a0 (bia 000a.b82e.21a0)
  Internet address is 10.10.100.1/24
  MTU 1500 bytes, BW 1000000 Kbit/sec, DLY 10 usec,
```

```
     reliability 255/255, txload 2/255, rxload 5/255
  Encapsulation ARPA, loopback not set
  Keepalive not set
  Full-duplex, 1000Mb/s, link type is force-up, media type is internal
  output flow-control is XON, input flow-control is XON
  ARP type: ARPA, ARP Timeout 04:00:00
  Last input 00:00:00, output 00:00:00, output hang never
  Last clearing of "show interface" counters never
  Input queue: 0/75/0/0 (size/max/drops/flushes); Total output drops: 0
  Queueing strategy: fifo
  Output queue: 0/512 (size/max)
  5 minute input rate 20015000 bits/sec, 2065 packets/sec
  5 minute output rate 8329000 bits/sec, 1885 packets/sec
     326735821 packets input, 3850373758 bytes, 0 no buffer
     Received 398168 broadcasts, 0 runts, 0 giants, 0 throttles
     0 input errors, 0 CRC, 0 frame, 0 overrun, 0 ignored
     0 watchdog, 11219 multicast, 0 pause input
     0 input packets with dribble condition detected
     290454976 packets output, 2642016730 bytes, 0 underruns
     0 output errors, 0 collisions, 0 interface resets
     0 unknown protocol drops
     0 unknown protocol drops
     0 babbles, 0 late collision, 0 deferred
     0 lost carrier, 0 no carrier, 1 pause output
     0 output buffer failures, 0 output buffers swapped out

R2821-edge# service-module integrated-Service-Engine 1/0 session
Trying 10.10.100.1, 2066 ... Open


Cisco Wide Area Application Engine Console

Username: admin
Password:
System Initialization Finished.

pod1-nm-wae#
```

The setup script walks you through a series of questions to define the initial configuration of key device settings, including:

■ Network interface speed and duplex (or auto-negotiate)

■ Network layer configuration (DHCP or static configuration with IP address, subnet mask, default gateway, DNS server, and domain name)

At the end of the initial setup script, you are prompted to save the configuration defined by the responses provided to the script. Example 7-2 demonstrates the initial setup script for the Cisco WAAS network module family, and Example 7-3 demonstrates the initial setup script for the Cisco WAAS appliance family. If you need to return to the setup script at a later time, simply type the command **setup** from the WAAS device CLI.

Note   Cisco WAAS devices have the concept of a startup configuration and running configuration like Cisco IOS devices. The setup script ultimately populates these files with the relevant configuration components based on the responses supplied by you. When you execute **write memory** or **copy running-config startup-config**, this performs the same function as found in Cisco IOS devices.

Example 7-2   *Initial Setup Script for Cisco WAAS Network Module*

```
WARNING: Changing any of the network settings from a
telnet session may render the device inaccessible on
the network. Therefore it is suggested that you have
access to the console before modifying the network settings.

Step 1: The following defaults can be configured:
Device mode: Application-accelerator
Interception Method: WCCP
Management Interface: GigabitEthernet 1/0
Timezone: UTC 0 0
To keep above defaults and continue configuration, press 'y'
To change above defaults and continue configuration, press 'n' [y]:
Step 2: Enter Central Manager address [10.10.10.10] :
Step 3:  Enter the space separated list of routers(maximum 4) for WCCPv2
[10.10.100.1]:
Step 4: Enter hostname [pod1-nm-wae]:
Step 5: Configure NTP [none]:
Step 6:
The product supports the following licenses:
1. Transport
2. Enterprise
3. Enterprise & Video
Enter the license(s) you purchased [3]:

Based on the input, the following configurations will be done:
        primary-interface GigabitEthernet 1/0
        clock timezone UTC 0 0
        central-manager address 10.10.10.10
        cms enable
        wccp version 2
```

```
            wccp router-list 8 10.10.100.1
            wccp tcp-promiscuous router-list 8
            hostname pod1-nm-wae


Do you accept these configurations (y/n) [y]:


Would you like to apply the configurations (y/n) [y]:


This may take few moments. Please wait..
Please wait. Running 'cms enable'..All CLI configurations were applied successful-
ly.


For your reference, configuration generated during this setup session is available
at /local1/setup_gen_config.txt. You can view this file with the command, "type
/local1/setup_gen_config.txt".


Press any key to continue..


pod1-nm-wae#
```

Example 7-3 *Initial Setup Script for Cisco WAAS Appliance*

```
!
!
! Note: this device is configured for inline interception, but also has
! a management interface using one of the onboard Gigabit Ethernet ports
!
!


WARNING: Changing any of the network settings from a
telnet session may render the device inaccessible on
the network. Therefore it is suggested that you have
access to the console before modifying the network settings.


Step 1: The following defaults can be configured:
Device mode: Application-accelerator
Interception Method: Inline
Management Interface: InlineGroup 1/0
Autosense: yes
Timezone: UTC 0 0


To keep above defaults and continue configuration, press 'y'
To change above defaults and continue configuration, press 'n' [y]: n
Step 2:
Configure WAAS Settings
```

```
— — — — — — — — — — — —
Select device mode :
1.application-accelerator
2.central-manager
Enter your choice [1]:
Step 3: Enter Central Manager address [10.10.10.10] :
Step 4: Select interception method (inline|wccp|other) [inline]:
Step 5: Select the interface that should be used for management:
  1:      InlineGroup 1/0        UP        unassigned       unassigned
  2:      InlineGroup 1/1        UP        unassigned       unassigned
  3:  GigabitEthernet 1/0        UP        10.10.10.240     255.255.255.0
  4:  GigabitEthernet 2/0        DOWN      unassigned       unassigned
Enter choice [1]: 3
Step 6: Configure autosense for duplex and speed on this interface(y/n)[y]:
Step 7: Enable DHCP on this interface (y/n) [n]:
Step 8: IP address of interface [10.10.10.240]:
Step 9: Netmask of this interface [255.255.255.0]:
Step 10: Default gateway [10.10.10.1]:
Step 11: Domain name server IP [10.10.10.100]:
Step 12: Domain name [peap.local]:
Step 13: Enter hostname [pod1-dc-wae]:
Step 14: Configure NTP [none]:
Step 15: Enter timezone [PST8PDT -7 0] :
Step 16: Select interface for inline interception:
1) InlineGroup 1/0
2) InlineGroup 1/1
Enter choice : 1
Configure autosense for duplex and speed on this interface(y/n)[y]:
Step 17:
The product supports the following licenses:
1. Transport
2. Enterprise
3. Enterprise & Video
Enter the license(s) you purchased [3]:

Based on the input, the following configurations will be done:
        central-manager address 10.10.10.10
        ip default-gateway 10.10.10.1
        ip name-server 10.10.10.100
        ip domain-name  peap.local
        primary-interface GigabitEthernet 1/0
        hostname pod1-dc-wae
        clock timezone PST8PDT -7 0
        interface InlineGroup 1/0
```

```
        no shutdown
        autosense
        exit
        cms enable
        interface GigabitEthernet 1/0
        ip address 10.10.10.240 255.255.255.0
        autosense
        exit
        interface InlineGroup 1/0
        no shutdown
        autosense
        exit

Do you accept these configurations (y/n) [y]:

Would you like to apply the configurations (y/n) [y]:

For your reference, configuration generated during this setup session is available
at /local1/setup_gen_config.txt. You can view this file with the command, "type
/local1/setup_gen_config.txt".

Press any key to continue..

pod1-dc-wae#
```

Note   When using auto-negotiate on a WAAS device interface, ensure that the adjacent device's port (for instance, on the switch) is configured as auto-negotiate or full duplex. Always verify that the connection between the WAAS device and the adjacent device uses full-duplex operation by using the **show interface** command on both the switch and the WAAS device (or the appropriate command if using a nonCisco device). Use of half duplex results in lower performance than what is possible when using full duplex.

It is recommended that duplex be hard coded when working with interface speeds other than Gigabit Ethernet. Gigabit Ethernet configurations are automatically full duplex, even when set to autosense.

This setup script is available upon subsequent boot operations by interrupting the boot sequence by pressing Enter when prompted by the CLI and setting boot flags. Alternatively, you can execute the command **setup** to run the setup script again in the future. Example 7-4 shows where the boot sequence is interrupted and what prompts are provided.

Example 7-4   *Interrupting the WAAS Device Boot Sequence*

```
Cisco WAAS boot:hit RETURN to set boot flags:0009
Available boot flags (enter the sum of the desired flags):
0x4000 - bypass nvram config
0x8000 - disable login security
[CE boot - enter bootflags]:0x8000
You have entered boot flags = 0x8000
Boot with these flags? [yes]:yes
Setting the configuration flags to 0x8000 lets you into the system, bypassing all
security. Setting the configuration flags field to 0x4000 lets you bypass the NVRAM
configuration.
```

The setup script allows you to bring the Cisco WAAS device onto the network by applying a default configuration that enables it to begin optimizing traffic immediately. It is recommended that you manage the WAAS device from the CM after that device has been registered to the CM, which occurs at the end of the setup script.

The primary interface setting of the WAAS device (refer to the configuration output in the preceding examples) is used to determine which interface is used for CM registration along with all associated CM management, monitoring, and configuration traffic. The primary interface must be assigned prior to enabling CMS and is configured through the setup script. Should you need to change the primary interface in the future, you can use the configuration demonstrated in Example 7-5.

Example 7-5   *Manually Configuring the WAAS Device Primary Interface*

```
pod1-dc-wae# config t
pod1-dc-wae(config)# primary-interface gigabitEthernet 1/0
```

It is important to ensure that the WAAS device is able to reach any management-related peers (CM, syslog servers, SNMP servers). Should the CM not be reachable during the setup script, a console message indicating this condition is raised. Always ensure that the primary interface defined is either on the same subnet as the default gateway or that the appropriate static routes are defined in the device CLI. In most deployments, the primary interface is adjacent to the default gateway, but in situations where multiple addressable WAAS device interfaces are configured, there might be situations where the default gateway is adjacent to an interface that is not the primary interface. In such deployments, static routes must be defined that point to the next-hop router for the interface that is not the primary interface.

The setup script also guides you through configuring a setting on the WAAS device called the *device mode*. The device mode dictates the "personality" of the WAAS device. For WAAS device that are being deployed as a CM (whether it is primary or standby), the "central-manager" device mode is applied, whereas for WAAS devices that are being deployed in the network for the purposes of acceleration, the "application-accelerator" device mode is used (a detailed examination of CM is provided later in the chapter). A

Cisco WAAS device can run only one device mode at a time and cannot run both device modes concurrently. Example 7-6 shows how to configure the device mode for a Cisco WAAS device outside of the setup script.

Example 7-6   *Configuring the Device Mode*

```
pod1-dc-wae(config)# device mode application-accelerator
pod1-cm1-wae(config)# device mode central-manager
```

Note   Cisco WAAS devices default to the "application-accelerator" device mode. When configuring a Cisco WAAS device with the "central-manager" device mode for the first time, you need to reboot the WAAS device. The console session notifies you of this requirement. Be sure to save your configuration prior to rebooting the WAAS device. This step can be skipped when deploying devices that participate in acceleration services (device mode set to "application-accelerator"), because the configuration defaults to this device mode.

When configuring a Cisco WAAS device as a CM, it is important to also specify the role (either a primary or standby CM). Configuring a Cisco WAAS device as a "primary" makes it the active CM in the deployment. Configuring a Cisco WAAS device as a "standby" makes it a backup for the primary. Standby CM devices, like WAAS devices configured as accelerators, continually synchronize with the primary CM, including all configuration, monitoring, and reporting data for the entire WAAS network. WAAS devices configured as standby CMs might be configured *before* the primary CM has been configured; however, the CMS service cannot be enabled on a standby CM until the primary CM is configured, operational, and reachable on the network. The CMS service (examined in detail later in this chapter in the section, "Centralized Management System Service") is responsible for establishing the session between a WAAS device in question and the CM for purposes of registration and ongoing management. Example 7-7 shows the command syntax for specifying a CM role.

Example 7-7   *Configuring CM Role*

```
pod1-cm1-wae(config)# central-manager role ?
  primary  Set Central Manager role to primary
  standby  Set Central Manager role to standby
pod1-cm1-wae(config)# central-manager role primary
```

Note   Cisco WAAS devices that have been configured as CMs through the device mode command default to a CM role of primary. To configure a CM as a standby, be sure to use the command shown in Example 7-7.

Another configuration step found in the setup wizard for each Cisco WAAS device *other* than the primary CM is to specify who the CM is (WAAS devices that are defined as a primary CM use themselves as the primary CM). This step tells the WAAS device either the IP address or the hostname of the primary CM WAAS device. If you use a hostname for the CM address definition, ensure that DNS entries for the CM are configured and working properly and that the appropriate DNS configuration has been applied to the device you are attempting to register. Use of a hostname for the CM address definition is recommended, because it provides IP address portability for the CM WAAS device. Should you need to change the IP address of the CM, and each managed WAAS device uses the DNS name of the CM WAAS device in its configuration, no change is needed to all of the WAAS devices in the network. If managed WAAS devices in the network use the IP address of the CM in their configuration and you need to change the IP of the CM, you need to change the definition on *each* managed WAAS device in the network. Example 7-8 shows how to point a WAAS device to the CM using its hostname as opposed to IP address.

Example 7-8 *Specifying the CM Using Hostname*

```
pod1-dc-wae(config)# central-manager address cm1.cisco.com
```

After the CM is defined, the setup wizard verifies that the CM is reachable through the network and attempts to register the device to the CM. This can also be done manually at a later time as demonstrated in Example 7-9. CMS is a service that runs locally on each WAAS device that enables it to remain loosely synchronized with the current primary CM based on a series of scheduling intervals defined within the CM (these intervals are discussed later in the chapter in the section titled "Centralized Management System Service"). The CMS service enables you to employ configuration changes from the CM GUI and have those changes propagate to the relevant WAAS devices managed by that CM. Additionally, the CM continuously collects health, monitoring, and reporting data from each of the managed WAAS devices and provides facilities for visualization and reporting. You must enable CMS not only on the CM WAAS devices but also on all accelerator WAAS devices in the network. Example 7-9 shows how to manually enable CMS services on a WAAS device.

Example 7-9 *Enabling CM Services Manually*

```
pod1-cm-wae(config)# cms enable
Generating new RPC certificate/key pair
Restarting RPC services
Registering WAAS Central Manager...
Please wait, initializing CMS tables
Successfully initialized CMS tables
Registration complete.
Please preserve running configuration using 'copy running-config startup-config'.
Otherwise management service will not be started on reload and node will be shown
'offline' in WAAS Central Manager UI.
```

> **Note**   The **cms enable** command can be executed only after the definition of the primary interface, device mode, role, and the IP or hostname of the CM. Always use the IP or hostname of the primary CM and not the standby. CMS must be enabled on every WAAS device in the network to allow for centralized management, monitoring, and reporting.

Finally, it is best practice to save your configuration after making changes. As with other Cisco devices, using the trusted **write mem** or **copy running-config startup-config** commands suffice. The setup wizard prompts you at the end to determine if you want to save and apply the configurations specified. Should you forget to execute this command after registering with the CM and the device reboots, the association is lost, and the process of establishing communication between the WAAS device and the CM needs to be performed again.

CLI

As demonstrated in the previous section, each WAAS device is equipped with a fully functional Cisco IOS-like CLI. CLI is available through a physical serial connection (in the case of appliances), virtual console session (in the case of network modules), and Telnet and SSH (for both network modules and appliances). By default, Telnet is enabled and SSH is disabled. Example 7-10 shows how to disable Telnet and enable SSH if so desired. Although this can be performed against an individual device, it is recommended that this function be performed against the AllDevicesGroup using the CM.

Example 7-10   *Disabling Telnet and Enabling SSH*

```
pod1-dc-wae(config)# no telnet enable
pod1-dc-wae(config)# ssh-key-generate key-length 1024
Ssh host key generated successfully
Saving the host key to box ...
Host key was saved successfully and will take effect in new ssh sessions.
pod1-dc-wae(config)# sshd version 2
pod1-dc-wae(config)# sshd enable
```

> **Note**   The **ssh-key-generate** command supports key lengths between 512 and 1024 bytes. The key length should not be less than 768 bytes due to compatibility problems with most modern SSH clients.

The WAAS device CLI enables you to adjust every aspect of the configuration that is isolated to that particular WAAS device. This includes network integration, network interception, and local optimization policies. Functions that are implemented at a system level that are desirable to have synchronized across multiple WAAS devices should be configured from the CM GUI, because the CM is capable of distributing configuration elements to multiple devices through the use of device groups. Recommended practice dictates that you use the CM for all aspects of device configuration when possible, due to its simplicity. This also helps ensure configuration and policy consistency across a global network of devices, which minimizes ongoing administration and troubleshooting.

The WAAS device CLI also provides you with insight into detailed statistics about the device. Such statistics include network statistics, optimization statistics (including compression ratios, connections optimized, and details about the applied optimization), and hardware utilization (CPU, disk, and memory). This data is also captured during the CMS synchronization process and is sent to the CM for monitoring and reporting. Chapter 8, "Configuring WAN Optimization," and Chapter 9, "Configuring Application Acceleration," provide an examination of key statistics and reports related to WAN optimization and application acceleration.

CM Overview

The Cisco WAAS CM is a secure, scalable, and simple management system built on a distributed computing architecture that is designed to simplify the deployment, management, monitoring, and reporting of a large-scale Cisco WAAS network. When a WAAS device is configured as a CM and services have been initialized and activated, this device then provides a secure web GUI for management users, while also communicating directly with each WAAS device in the network for the purposes of:

■ Synchronizing device configuration bidirectionally

■ Gathering health and liveliness information

■ Retrieving monitoring and statistics data

CM is *secure* in that it uses HTTP over Secure Sockets Layer (HTTPS using TCP port 8443) for management GUI access. Users must authenticate to the CM either using a preconfigured local user account or through integration with a back-end authentication provider, such as RADIUS, TACACS+, or Active Directory. Additionally, the CM communicates with managed accelerators using HTTPS over TCP port 443. Key management is simplified with Cisco WAAS in that keys are self-signed and generated by the CM and the managed nodes.

Note   If firewalls exist in your environment between the CM WAAS devices and accelerator devices, be sure to allow TCP ports 443 and 8443 to pass through. These ports are used for management and CMS services. It is also recommended that ports for Telnet (TCP 23), SSH (TCP 22), SNMP (UDP 161, 162) and syslog (UDP 514) be permitted. NetBIOS (TCP 135, 137, 138, 139) should be enabled if registering a WAAS device into a domain when a firewall is deployed between the WAAS device and the domain controller. DNS ports should be enabled when performing name resolution on a WAAS device through a firewall (UDP 53). When deploying WAAS using directed mode, the directed mode port used between WAAS devices should be allowed to pass through the firewall (UDP 4050). If fast offline detection is configured in the CM, UDP 2000 should be allowed to pass through the firewall.

For legacy mode services including Wide Area File Services (WAFS) and print services (discussed in Chapter 9), WAFS connection ports should be allowed to pass (TCP 4050) and Common Internet File System (CIFS) ports should be enabled (TCP 139, 445, 50139).

CM is *scalable* in that up to 2500 nodes can be managed under a single CM. The number of nodes that can be managed by a single CM is based on which hardware platform is selected. Sizing for CM was discussed in detail in Chapter 2, "Cisco WAAS Architecture, Hardware, and Sizing." Additionally, a standby CM can be deployed to ensure high availability. Because the standby CM device synchronizes its local CMS database with the primary CM (including configuration, monitoring data, reporting data, and more) the same way an accelerator device would, should the primary CM device fail, the standby can be configured to take over operation as the primary. Deploying a standby CM provides only high availability and does nothing to increase the number of nodes that can be managed. For deployments larger than 2000 nodes, multiple autonomous (independent) CMs are necessary. WAAS devices can register only with a single CM, and in such cases where the size of the network exceeds 2000 nodes, not all WAAS devices are registered to the same CMs.

CM is *simple* in that it provides a powerful yet easy-to-use interface for managing a large WAAS deployment and similarly provides powerful monitoring and reporting capabilities. CM has the ability to logically group WAAS devices into device groups, which enables you to apply a configuration change once but ensure that the change is automatically propagated to the managed WAAS devices within that device group. With device groups, you can apply a configuration change across the entire WAAS network with a few clicks, and the CM handles the distribution of the configuration change automatically to all WAAS devices in the device group.

Figure 7-1 shows the CM GUI login page, which is accessible by browsing to the IP address or DNS name of the CM WAAS device using HTTPS and specifying port 8443 (that is, https://ip_address_of_cm_device:8443). The default credentials can be used to access the WAAS CM, which are the username of **admin** and the default password of **default**.

After you log into the WAAS CM, you are presented with a dashboard for the My WAN context. The CM GUI is contextual, that is, the menu structure and contents of the workspace are directly related to the context in which you reside. For example, switching to the context of a particular device or a device group alters the menu structure and contents of the workspace. Figure 7-2 shows the CM My WAN context homepage that is displayed after login.

Figure 7-1 *CM Login Page*

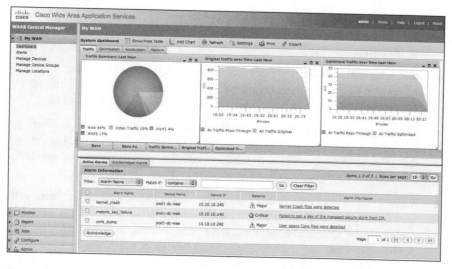

Figure 7-2 *CM My WAN Context Homepage*

Notice that the top-left drawer is called My WAN, which is used to indicate the current context. In this context, the homepage provides the following information and functions:

- **Context-driven drawers:** The drawers on the left-hand side of the workspace (My WAN, Monitor, Report, Jobs, Configure, and Admin) provide access to specific functions for management, configuration, monitoring, reporting, and other purposes. These drawers change based on the context you are currently in, and include:

  - **Top-level context:** The top-level context can be My WAN (representing the entire system), a device within the system (representing the elements related to an individual device), a device group within the system (representing the elements related to a device group), or a location name (representing the elements related to a location that has been defined in the system). This context provides high-level information for the context, and where appropriate, alarms, activation-related information, assignment to a device group, and other settings.

- **Monitor:** This drawer provides access to monitoring charts and supporting data tables for WAN optimization functions, application acceleration functions, and platform-related data. When in the device context, this drawer also provides access to each of the current connections being handled by that device.

- **Report:** This drawer provides access to pre-configured and user-defined reports, which are comprised of monitoring data and schedules that specify frequency of delivery via e-mail.

- **Jobs:** This drawer allows you to manage files associated with various versions of WAAS software, and the distribution of those software files to the appropriate devices for purposes of WAAS software version upgrade and downgrade.

- **Configure:** This drawer provides facilities to configure elements of the system that range from device settings, network settings, optimization settings, and services.

- **Admin:** This drawer provides access into managing the administrative functions related to the system including authentication and access control, the secure store (for encryption key storage on the CM, discussed later), and logs.

- **System Dashboard Charts:** Configurable charts are displayed in the workspace that summarize traffic, optimization, acceleration, and platform statistics. The configuration of these charts (including timeframes, components visualized, and which charts are shown) is fully customizable and is described later in this chapter.

- **Alarms:** Alarms that have been raised by devices in the system are presented in the workspace, along with the details of each alarm (including severity), device details (including device name and IP address), and troubleshooting hyperlinks. These alarms can be acknowledged (which removes them from the Active Alarms tab and moves them into the Acknowledged Alarms tab) after the outstanding issue has been resolved. Additionally, clicking the alarm information provides you quick access to the device's homepage, telnet access, device logs, or show commands.

The context that is currently visible can easily be identified by looking at the name of the top drawer on the left-hand side of the screen. Changing contexts can be done in a number of ways:

- **From My WAN:** From the My WAN context, you can change to a device context by clicking **Manage Devices** and selecting a device, to a device group context by clicking **Manage Device Groups** and selecting a device group, or to a location context by clicking **Manage Locations** and selecting a location. All these links are found in the My WAN drawer found in the left side of the screen.

- **From a device:** From the device context, you can change to the My WAN context by clicking the **My WAN** hyperlink in the breadcrumbs section above the workspace, to another device using the **View All Devices** link in the device drawer or the **Devices** link in the breadcrumbs section, or to a device group or location context by first going back to the My WAN context.

- **From a device group:** From the device group context, you can change to the My WAN context by clicking the **My WAN** hyperlink in the breadcrumbs section above the workspace, to another device group using the **View All Device Groups** link in the device group drawer or the **Device Groups** link in the breadcrumbs section, or to a device or location context by first going back to the My WAN context.

- **From a location:** From the location context, you can change to the My WAN context by clicking the **My WAN** hyperlink in the breadcrumbs section above the workspace, to another location using the **View All Locations** link in the location drawer or the **Locations** link in the breadcrumbs section, or to a device or device group context by first going back to the My WAN context.

Having the ability to quickly context shift within the CM GUI provides you with rapid movement among various areas and aspects of the system and minimizes the need for having a discrete GUI for every device. Figure 7-3 shows the location of the context-switching links found in the CM.

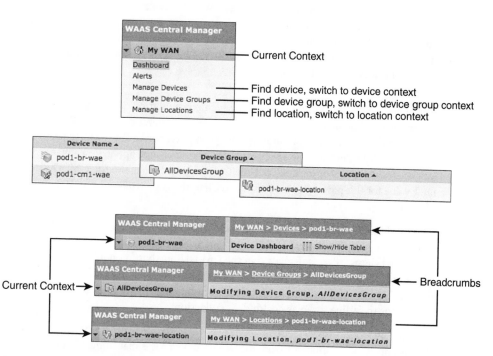

Figure 7-3 *Context Switching in the WAAS CM*

The CM enables you to configure virtually every aspect of the Cisco WAAS network, including device configuration, network configuration, network interception, domain integration, optimization policies, and more. Using the CM enables simplistic management of a large number of devices from a single console, eliminating the need to manage each device in a discrete manner. Rather than providing an exhaustive examination of each aspect that can be configured here, details about each are provided in the appropriate sections for each of these topic areas in this chapter and later chapters.

Centralized Management System Service

The CMS service is the heart of the management and monitoring framework for Cisco WAAS. CMS is the process that runs on each WAAS device in the network—whether it is a CM device or an accelerator—and ensures that configuration and statistical information remain synchronized between the CM WAAS device and each managed WAAS device. CMS uses self-signed and self-generated certificates to encrypt communications between the CM WAAS device and each managed WAAS device, and all data transmitted between the CM and the managed WAAS devices occurs over TCP port 443 (as described in the previous section, access to the CM GUI uses TCP port 8443). The certificates that are used by CMS are generated when CMS is initialized for the first time, which can be either during the execution of the setup wizard or when the **cms enable** command issued.

The CMS processes on the CM and on managed WAAS devices synchronize on a schedule known as the Local Central Management (LCM) cycle. The LCM cycle triggers the synchronization of the CMS processes on a schedule that is configured within the CM GUI itself. A series of variables and their associated parameters dictate the rate of synchronization between the CM and managed WAAS devices:

- **Data Feed Poll Rate:** Defines the rate at which configuration data is synchronized between the CM and managed WAAS devices. The configuration synchronization is bidirectional, meaning a configuration change applied on the CM propagates to a managed WAAS device. Conversely, a configuration change applied on a managed WAAS device itself (for instance, via the CLI) propagates back to the CM. The default value for this parameter is 300 seconds, and the supported range is 30 to 1800 seconds.

- **Health Monitor Collect Rate:** Defines the rate at which the CM examines the health of each managed WAAS device. This includes service status, load conditions, and subsystem status. Alarms displayed in the CM GUI are based on information gathered during the collection of health monitoring information. The default value for this parameter is 120 seconds, and the supported range is 1 to 3600 seconds (configuring 0 for this value disables health data collection).

- **Monitoring Collect Rate:** Defines the rate at which the CM gathers statistics about the optimization components from the WAAS devices it is managing. This includes information about optimized connections, compression ratios, byte count, traffic mix, and other acceleration data. Graphs displayed in the CM GUI that visualize how the system or an individual WAAS device is optimizing are based on data collected on this interval. The default value for this parameter is 60 seconds and the supported range is 60–1800 seconds.

Note   The preceding variables are configurable within the CM GUI under the My WAN context in the Configure drawer by clicking the **System Properties** link. Along with these variables, this page enables you to configure other system-wide parameters, including CM GUI session timeout, device recovery key, data retention monitoring, default time granularity for monitoring charts, and whether overlapping device groups are permitted. Additionally, this page enables you to globally enable or disable monitoring from the CM.

The default settings for the variables in the preceding list ensure support for large deployments. The granularity of the timeframes represented by these variables can be decreased for smaller deployments, which increases the frequency of health checking, configuration synchronization, and the granularity of monitoring data. For deployments larger than 100 devices, it is recommended that the default values be preserved.

Figure 7-4 shows the CM GUI page where the timers can be found. To manipulate these values, simply click the **Edit** icon found next to the property, make the changes as appropriate, and click **Submit** on the Property Configuration page. Figure 7-4 does not show all properties that are available for configuration on this page.

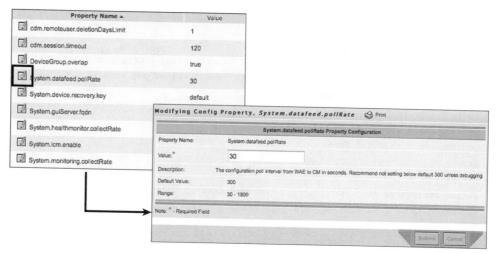

Figure 7-4   *CM System Timers*

The state of the CMS service can be verified from the CLI of the WAAS device and appears in the device list page in the CM (which can be reached from the **My WAN > Manage Devices** link). The **show cms info** command can be executed on a CM device or a managed WAAS device. This command shows the following:

■ Device registration information, including device mode and role. Role is displayed only if the WAAS device is configured as a CM.

■   CMS service information, including the state of the CMS service (shown as cms_cdm in the command output) and management GUI service (shown as cms_httpd in the command output).

Example 7-11 demonstrates the output of this command. In this example, the service is not running, as evidenced in the output of the first execution of **show cms info**. The example then shows the service being enabled, and then the output of **show cms info** with the services running correctly.

Example 7-11   *Viewing CMS Registration and Service Status*

```
pod1-cm-wae# show cms info
Device registration information :
Device Id                          = 166
Device registered as               = WAAS Central Manager
Current WAAS Central Manager role   = Primary


CMS services information :
Service cms_httpd is not running
Service cms_cdm is not running
pod1-cm-wae # config
pod1-cm-wae (config)# cms enable
Please preserve running configuration using 'copy running-config startup-config'.
Otherwise management service will not be started on reload and node will be shown
'offline' in WAAS Central Manager UI.
pod1-cm-wae (config)# exit
pod1-cm-wae # copy running-config startup-config
pod1-cm-wae # show cms info
Device registration information :
Device Id                          = 166
Device registered as               = WAAS Central Manager
Current WAAS Central Manager role   = Primary
CMS services information :
Service cms_httpd is running
Service cms_cdm is running
```

Note   If the cms_cdm service is not running, the device cannot be managed centrally (if configured as an accelerator) or cannot manage WAAS devices (if configured as a CM). If the cms_httpd service is not running, the management GUI is not accessible. In situations where the CMS service is disabled on a WAAS device, it reports as Offline in the CM GUI.

Device Registration and Groups

The previous sections provided details on the WAAS setup wizard, establishing basic network connectivity to each WAAS device in the network, defining the CM, and enabling CMS services. During the process of enabling CMS services, a WAAS device "registers" with the CM WAAS device. That is, the WAAS device contacts the CM and announces that it is interested in associating itself with the CM. In doing so, the WAAS device can then be managed by the CM and report monitoring and statistical information back to the CM for visualization. Because the exchange of information between the CM and its managed WAAS devices is encrypted, the first step of the process is for the WAAS device that is attempting to register to generate a self-signed certificate and encryption key material. This material, along with the material generated by the CM WAAS device, is used to encrypt information exchanged between the CM and the managed WAAS devices.

When a WAAS device registers with the CM, the CM creates an entry in the CMS database for the registering device and assigns a device ID to that device (the device ID can be determined through the **show cms info** command as demonstrated in Example 7-11). This entry is linked to the registering WAAS device hostname to provide a simplified means of recovering device identity and configuration if a WAAS device needs to be replaced. If an entry with that name already exists, the registration of the new WAAS device fails. In such cases, the existing entry needs to be deleted from the CM GUI, or in the case of device replacement, the identity should be recovered onto the new WAAS device from the entry that exists in the CM database.

To recover a device identity from the CM database onto a new WAAS device that is replacing a failed WAAS device, use the **cms recover identity** command. This command takes an additional argument—the global device identity recovery password—which is set in the CM GUI on the same page as the system timers. For instance, if the global device identity recovery password is **default**, the command shown in Example 7-12 could be used to recover the identity from the CM.

Example 7-12   *Recovering Device Identity*

```
pod1-br-wae# cms recover identity default
This device is already registered with Central Manager. Continuing with identity
recovery will result in loss  of current registration information. Do you want to
continue identity recovery (yes¦no) [no]? yes
Is device identity recovery used for WAFS 3.x device migration to WAAS (yes¦no)
[no]? no
Registering WAAS Application Engine...
Sending device identity recovery request to Central Manager with address
10.10.10.10
Please wait, initializing CMS tables
Successfully initialized CMS tables
Registration complete.
```

The global device identity recovery property can be found at **My WAN > Configure > System Properties** under the System.device.recovery.key property. Note that for a device identity recovery to succeed, you must first deactivate the device and then mark the device as replaceable. This can be accomplished in the device context at **Device > Activation**. Figure 7-5 shows the activation configuration page for a device. If the device is running legacy CIFS services and the core or edge service is enabled on the device you are replacing, this device is reloaded upon successful activation.

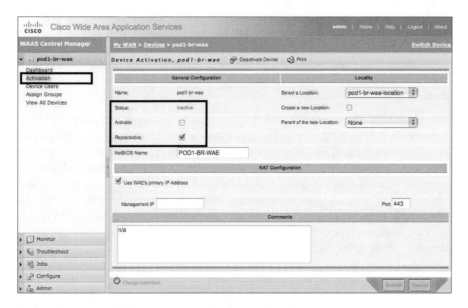

Figure 7-5   *Controlling Device Activation and Replacement*

After executing the device identity recovery process shown in Example 7-12, the WAAS device, in terms of its relationship with the CM, automatically is activated and the flag that identifies the device as replaceable is removed. A WAAS device in the state of Active is able to synchronize configuration, health, and monitoring data with the WAAS CM, whereas a WAAS device in the state of inactive can not. In this way, a WAAS device that is inactive is *registered* with the CM but not *manageable*.

Device Activation

Device activation is a function performed on the CM that can take one or all inactive WAAS devices and enable them for active participation within the Cisco WAAS network. Activation is a process that can be done only through the CM GUI and cannot be done through the device CLI. Activation takes a few simple clicks within the CM GUI, and then up to three iterations of the LCM cycle before the activation is complete. Therefore, device activation can take up to three times the time interval configured for the CM system data feed poll rate shown previously in Figure7-4. Device activation is done automatically when using the CLI setup wizard or when manually executing CMS enable. Should you need to deactivate or activate a device, this action can be performed from the device context under **Device > Activation** as shown in Figure 7-5. If you have multiple deactivated devices in your network and wish to activate them all simultaneously, this can be done at **My WAN > Manage Devices** as shown in Figure 7-6.

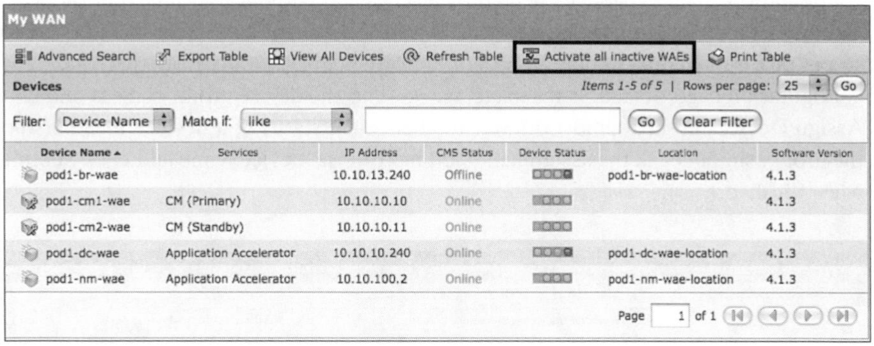

Figure 7-6   *Activating All Inactive WAAS Devices*

After a device has been activated, it transitions to a state called *Pending* where the initial configuration is propagated to the device and synchronization is performed between the device and the CM. As mentioned earlier, it generally takes up to three LCM iterations for the activation to finalize, and the WAAS device remains in the *Pending* state until activation is complete. After activation is completed, the WAAS device has generated keys and established a secure session to the CM, synchronized its configuration, and had its state changed to *Online*. When a device transitions to the state of *Online*, it can be managed, configured, and monitored from the CM.

Note   Another property of each device in the network is its configured *location*. Locations provide a means of logically grouping WAAS devices into similar sites. Locations are not yet used by functional components of WAAS; however, they are used in future releases to support features that require location awareness. At press time, location groups do not merit coverage.

Device Groups

One of the most powerful usability features of the WAAS CM is the ability to logically group devices into configuration containers. These containers, called *device groups*, allow you to rapidly apply a configuration change across multiple WAAS devices simultaneously by simply applying a change to the group. With device groups, the daunting task of implementing a seemingly simple configuration change across a large number of devices becomes a painless click of the mouse button.

The CM provides support for up to 256 device groups. The device group list—which allows you to create and manage device groups—can be found in **My WAN > Manage**

Device Groups. Devices are added to device groups either during the creation of the device group or by going directly to the device homepage and assigning the WAAS device to a series of groups. After a device group has one or more members, configuration changes applied to the device group in the CM GUI are automatically distributed to each of the WAAS devices that are assigned to that device group. This distribution of configuration changes happens behind the scenes and without user intervention, which can significantly streamline management of deployments of any size. Figure 7-7 demonstrates an example of assigning WAAS devices to a device group, from the device group configuration page. To access this page, navigate to the device group context and click **Assign Devices** in the topmost drawer. To change the status of a device's membership to the group, simply click the assignment icon next to the device name and click **Submit** when finished.

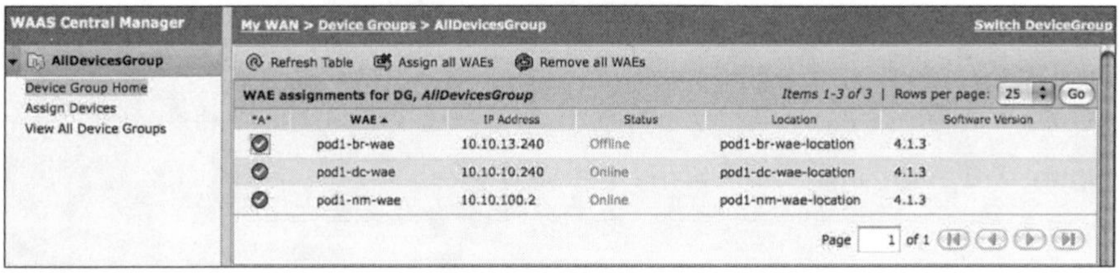

Figure 7-7 *Assigning WAAS Devices to a Device Group*

The CM provides a default device group, called *AllDevicesGroup*, which all Cisco WAAS devices are automatically joined to upon creation within the CM database. Although the *AllDevicesGroup* device group is commonly the only device group used for smaller deployments, it is recommended that you take some time to think through which device groups are relevant to your organization and use the *AllDevicesGroup* device group for any configuration items that must be identical across the entire infrastructure and not vary from device to device. Any configuration items that might vary from device to device should be applied to smaller device groups, or be applied directly to the device as a last resort. Some functional uses of the device grouping capabilities of Cisco WAAS CM include the following:

■ **Device group by time zone:** Enables you to employ a common time, date, time zone, and Network Time Protocol (NTP) configuration for each device within the same time zone. Also, this enables you to isolate configuration changes to all devices within a specific timezone when necessary. Creating and using a device group for this purpose is only necessary for customers that configure devices into specific time zones and are not using GMT.

■ **Device group by location type:** Enables you to group devices by classification of the type of location they are deployed in. For instance, you might choose to create a group for all devices that are deployed in data center locations or create a device group for all devices deployed as router modules. This enables you to apply common configuration settings across all devices in similar location types or form factors.

- **Device group by WAN link capacity:** Enables you to group devices by the WAN link type that the device supports. For instance, you might define a T1 device group, or an LFN device group for WAAS devices that are supporting high-BDP networks. This enables you to apply a common configuration across all devices that are supporting similar link speeds, distances, or other similar characteristics. This is generally only necessary when directly manipulating TCP buffer sizes or when using legacy WAFS features, which include bandwidth parameters.

- **Device group by services configured:** Enables you to group devices by the types of services configured. For instance, you might have specific devices that perform full optimization and acceleration and some that perform only TCP optimization. Alternatively, you might have devices that support virtual blades (VB) and others that do not, or, devices that are running certain application accelerators and others that are using a different set of application accelerators.

As outlined in the preceding list, there are countless uses for device groups. Device groups can be created to serve just about any configuration purpose. Keep in mind that a device group enables administrators to configure nearly anything that can be configured directly against an individual WAAS device, thereby enabling administrators to "scale themselves," that is, minimize their administrative burden. Also note that changes made to a device group are synchronized with managed WAAS devices within that device group on the same schedule that configuration changes applied directly to a managed WAAS devices are made—this is based on the same LCM cycle described earlier. If a WAAS device is a member of two or more device groups and configuration conflicts exist, the configuration contained in the last modified device group is applied. Therefore, try to define your device groups and assign devices in such a way that there is little, if any, overlap.

Note CM WAAS devices cannot belong to a device group.

Provisioned Management

The CM is designed to allow multiple departments within the same organization to have provisioned management authority. In many environments, it is necessary to allow different teams with different responsibilities—potentially even in different parts of the company—to have some level of administrative privilege over a portion of the infrastructure. Furthermore, many organizations prefer to leverage a centralized platform for authenticating and authorizing users that attempt to access enterprise infrastructure resources. The CM integrates cleanly into environments that have requirements such as these by providing:

- **Role-based access control (RBAC):** Enables the definition of users, roles, and domains to segregate management responsibility and user privilege across devices in the Cisco WAAS network

- **Integration with authentication providers:** Enables delegation of authentication functions for users accessing a WAAS device or the CM to a trusted third party such as TACACS+, RADIUS, or Microsoft Active Directory

By providing these two capabilities, the Cisco WAAS CM enables IT organizations with disparate management teams and centralized authentication providers to streamline integration of Cisco WAAS management into their existing business processes by enabling granular control of management responsibility and assignment of permissions. The following sections examine each of these systems in detail, along with their configuration.

Role-Based Access Control

RBAC is a feature within the Cisco WAAS CM that provides a flexible means of assigning management and administrative responsibility with granularity levels required by today's demanding organizations. With RBAC, the network team can have the appropriate permissions within the CM to adjust the networking parameters on all or specific devices (or groups of devices) within the Cisco WAAS network, while the Network Operations Center (NOC) team is provided read-only access to monitoring data, and the system administrators have full control.

RBAC is built upon three fundamental components:

- **User:** The entity that is attempting to authenticate with the CM for the purpose of managing the system.

- **Role:** A template that identifies which pages and functions within the CM that an associated user is able to access and in what capacity (no access, read-only access, and read-write access).

- **Domain:** A template that identifies either a specific set of devices or a specific set of device groups that an associated user is able to access.

With the combination of users, roles, and domains, the system-wide administrator for WAAS can allocate, in a granular manner, a specific set of configuration pages and permissions for those pages to all users associated with a particular role. The administrator can then filter the area within the WAAS network from which those configuration pages can be used by applying a domain, which limits the devices upon which the user is allowed to execute those functions. In this way, a user, once authenticated, is associated with one or more roles, which determine the pages within the CM the user is allowed to access, the functions that the user is able to perform, and the permission level the user is assigned for those functions (no access, read-only, read-write). The user is then associated with a domain, which identifies which devices or device groups a user is able to perform those functions against.

Note   Domains can be defined only as a collection of unique devices or as a collection of device groups. You cannot configure a single domain that contains a list of unique devices along with a list of specific device groups. In such cases, two domains would be necessary—one containing the devices and the other containing the device groups.

Users can have association with multiple roles and to multiple domains. Permissions provided to a user in the CM are additive; that is, the sum of all permissions provided to the user by all associated roles is the net effective set of operations the user is allowed to perform. Similarly with domains, the sum of all devices and device groups listed in all domains assigned to the user become the net effective domain of control the user is allowed to access.

Figure 7-8 shows the tabular listing and configuration page for roles, which can be found in the My WAN context at **Admin > Roles**. Notice from this page you can either create a new role or click the **Edit** icon next to an existing role. After you have either clicked **Create New Role** or the **Edit** icon next to an existing role, you see either an empty configuration page if you chose to create a new role, or, the existing configuration for a role you chose to edit.

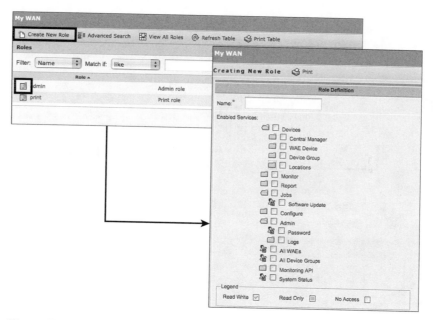

Figure 7-8 *Configuring a Role*

In the role configuration page, notice that the workspace shows a listing of entities that are similar to the drawers on the left of the workspace, and the contents of each folder align with the contents of the drawers and pages within each drawer. When configuring a role, you essentially define which pages in the GUI the user assigned to that role is able to visit—and in what capacity. The legend underneath the directory of entities shows that a user's access to a specific page or hierarchy of pages can either be no access (empty selection square), read-only (filled selection square), or read-write (checkmark in selection square). When assigning permissions to an item displayed as a folder in the directory tree, note that the permission propagates to all children contained within that folder.

Figure 7-9 shows the configuration page for a domain, which can be accessed in the My WAN context at **Admin > Domains**. Like the configuration of a role, from this page you can either create a new domain or edit an existing domain. In the domain configuration page, notice that only three properties exist:

- **Comments:** Free-form text for you to use to later recall why the domain is present

- **Entity type:** Specify where the domain refers to one or more individual WAAS devices, or one or more WAAS device groups

- **One or more entities:** According to the entity type configured

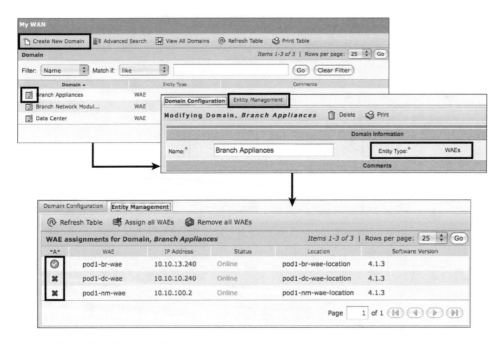

Figure 7-9 *Configuring a Domain*

Unlike roles, which enable you to configure no access, read-only access, and read-write access to specific GUI pages, domains are binary—either a user associated with a domain has access to a device or the user does not. If the user is not assigned to a domain that contains a specific device as an entity, that user does not have access to that device. If the user is assigned to a domain that contains a specific device as an entity, that user has access to that device, but in accordance with the permissions that are defined in the roles that are assigned to that user.

Consider the following example. Zach is a Cisco WAAS administrator and hires Joel to manage his U.S. Cisco WAAS network. Zach also hires Baruch to manage his Cisco WAAS network in Israel. Zach does not want Joel to be able to apply any configuration changes to Baruch's devices in Israel, and he does not want Baruch to be able to change any of Joel's devices in the United States. Zach also has a location in Switzerland where there are two WAAS devices deployed. Rather than hire an administrator in Switzerland, Zach decides to assign one WAAS device each to Joel and Baruch, thus dividing management responsibilities for Switzerland between the two.

Using a combination of device groups, users, roles, and domains, Zach's job provisioning Cisco WAAS management is simplified. A single device group for all WAAS devices in the United States is created, and all WAAS devices in the United States are assigned to this device group, which is assigned to Joel. Similarly, a device group is created for all WAAS devices in Israel, which is assigned to Baruch. One domain is created for each of the two devices in Switzerland, with one of the domains assigned to Joel and the other to Baruch. To summarize, Joel and Baruch are each assigned to two domains:

- Joel is assigned to a U.S. domain, which calls out the device group for the WAAS devices in the United States and another domain that identifies one of the WAAS devices in Switzerland.

- Baruch is assigned to the domain that represents the Israel WAAS devices and another domain that identifies the other WAAS device in Switzerland.

With domains, the system administrator is able to control what devices are accessible to system users.

Figure 7-10 shows the configuration page for assigning roles and domains to a particular user. Note that this page can be accessed in the CM GUI by going to **My WAN context > Admin > Users**. Assigning roles and domains to a user is similar to specifying devices or device groups referenced by a domain.

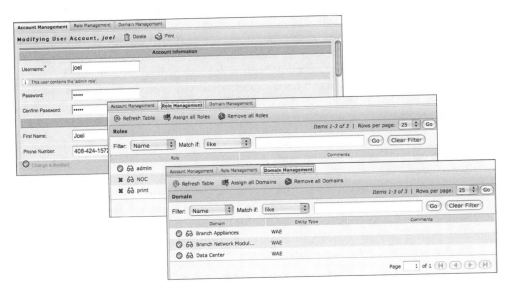

Figure 7-10   *Assigning Roles and Domains to a User*

As evidenced in this section, the available permissions and devices against which a user is able to employ change is the sum of the available permissions provided by the assigned roles and domains. Configuration of users, roles, and domains can all be found under the **My WAN context > Admin.**

Integration with Centralized Authentication

Authentication for users attempting to access the CM is, by default, performed against a local database stored in the CM WAAS device itself, which contains the credentials of authorized system users. Users that are created in the CM are automatically synchronized to each of the WAAS devices that are managed by that CM. In some deployments, it might be desirable to allow the CM to leverage a third-party centralized authentication provider, such as TACACS+, RADIUS, or Active Directory, to manage user accounts and passwords. Cisco WAAS can leverage these third-party providers to authenticate users, which enables you to avoid having to manage user credentials on yet another system deployed within the infrastructure.

In previous versions of WAAS (before 4.1.x), it was required that users be explicitly defined within the CM and then associated with roles and domains—whether authenticated locally or remotely. This process was cumbersome in that the WAAS administrators needed to know (in advance) which users would require system access and configure accounts specifically for those users. With 4.1.x, this is no longer the case. Local users, (those that are authenticated without use of a third-party authentication provider) must still be defined within the CM, and the roles and domains must be assigned. For users authenticated by a third-party authentication provider, the configuration is much different. WAAS allows nonlocal users to be authenticated in one of two ways:

■ **Remotely authenticated, but with local user definition and local mapping to roles and domains:** In this scenario, user authentication involves a third-party authentication provider, but the assignment of permissions (roles) and devices or groups the user can manage (domains) is defined on the CM. Users must be defined on the CM in this model, which is fundamentally identical to the behavior in 4.0.x.

■ **Remotely authenticated, relying on user groups from the authentication provider:** In this scenario, user authentication involves a third-party authentication provider, and the assignment of permissions (roles) and devices or groups the user can manage (domains) are applied to *user groups*, which must be defined on the CM and represent the group membership of the user as it pertains to the third-party authentication provider.

In the case where a user is locally defined, a successful login allows the user the permissions directly assigned to the user account through the assigned roles and domains. Local authentication is enabled by default. To configure the type of authentication to be used by the CM, navigate to the CM context, and then to **Configure > Security > Authentication Methods.** It should be noted that this configuration should be applied to each CM (including standby CMs) in the network to ensure consistency. Additionally, if you want to ensure consistent authentication methods to other accelerators in the network when using the CLI, perform the same steps on each accelerator or on the necessary device groups. Such a configuration is a good candidate to use on the AllDevicesGroup, which is present by default and cannot be deleted.

After you navigate to the **Configure > Security > Authentication Methods** page, you see the screen as shown in Figure 7-11.

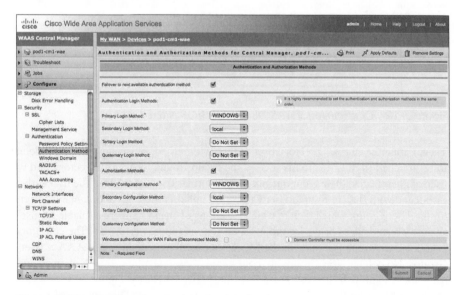

Figure 7-11 *Configuring Authentication Settings*

On this page, notice a number of key settings. By default, each device is configured for *local* authentication, which requires that credential management be done within the CM and within each device. This is also the behavior when the **Authentication Login Methods** and **Authorization Methods** are unchecked. It is recommended that **Failover to the next available authentication method** be selected when using authentication or authorization other than local and have one of each of the login and authorization methods be set to **local** to ensure that users can still login to the system should the configured authentication or authorization provider(s) be unavailable. The next sections examine integration into Windows Authentication, TACACS+, and RADIUS.

Windows Authentication

If you are configuring Windows authentication, that is, you are using Active Directory or NT domain authentication, you must configure the NetBIOS name of the WAAS devices and register them with the domain. Be sure that the NetBIOS names chosen for the WAAS device(s) do not overlap with any existing computer names in the network or with one another; otherwise, the devices with the overlapping names are not able to register. Additionally, the WAAS device clocks should be synchronized to be within 5 minutes of the domain to enable the secure session to establish (otherwise, the process fails). To configure the NetBIOS name of a device, switch to the device context and go to the Activation page under the device's top drawer as shown in Figure 7-12. From this page, specify the NetBIOS name for the WAAS device and click **Submit**. Note that this step should be performed on each WAAS device that you desire to register to the Windows domain.

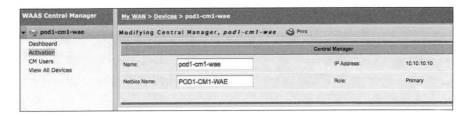

Figure 7-12 *Configuring WAAS Device NetBIOS Name*

Then, define the Active Directory user groups within the CM to allow roles and domains to be attached to it. User groups specify the groups found in Active Directory, and when users authenticates, their group membership information is examined. The user is then associated with the configured User Group, and inherits the roles and domains assigned to that User Group, which dictate which functions of the system are available for use and against which devices or device groups such actions can be performed. The configuration page for User Groups is found in the My WAN context under **Admin > AAA > User Groups**. No default User Groups are configured; these must be manually defined and the name must align with the group names within Active Directory. Figure 7-13 shows an example of two configured User Groups, which map to Active Directory group names. Notice that the Users User Group is only assigned to the NOC role and has access only to branch devices (through the associated domains), whereas the Domain Administrators User Group is assigned to the admin role and has access to all domains.

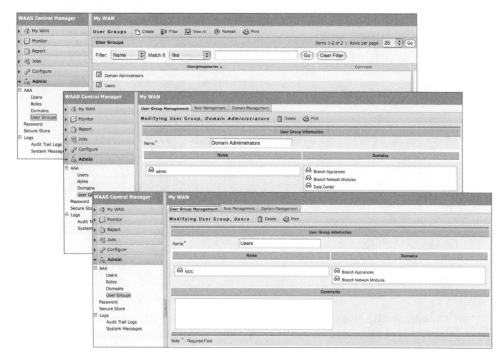

Figure 7-13   *Configuring User Groups*

The next step is to define the workgroup and domain name, which can be done in the device context under **Configure > Network > WINS** as shown in Figure 7-14. If you join the device into a Windows NT domain, check the **NT** box found on the right. If a WINS server is available in your network (not required), supply the IP address of the WINS server in the **WINS Server** box, and click **Submit**.

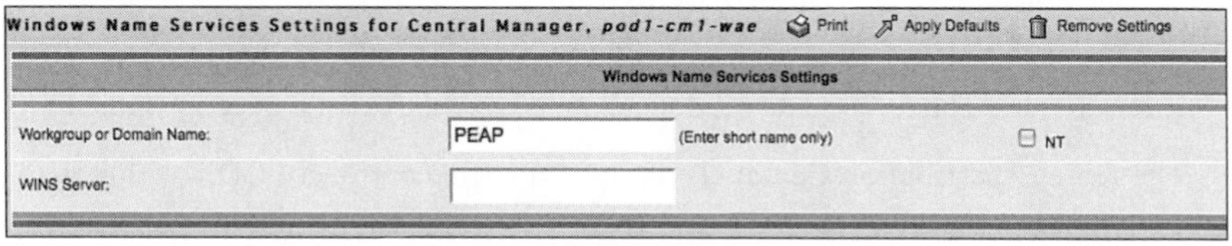

Figure 7-14   *Specifying the Workgroup or Domain Name*

Next, you need to configure the parameters for the domain, which can be done in the device context under **Configure > Security > Authentication > Windows Domain**, as shown in Figure 7-15.

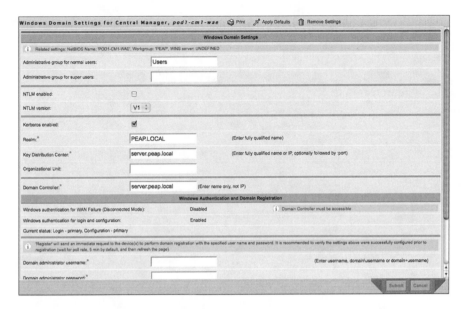

Figure 7-15   *Specifying the Windows Domain Parameters*

On this page, specify the following parameters:

- **Administrative group for normal users:** Specifies which domain user group has normal CLI privileges, that is, a user in this group cannot make configuration changes in the CLI.

- **Administrative group for super users:** Specifies which domain user group has super user CLI privileges, that is, a user in this group can make configuration changes in the CLI.

- **NTLM authentication:** Enable NTLM and specify the version of NTLM to use, if you wish to use NTLM authentication. This is common in Windows NT domains, but can also be used in newer Windows domains.

- **Kerberos authentication:** Enable Kerberos authentication and specify its parameters. This is commonly used in Active Directory domains (starting with Windows 2000 and higher). The parameters for Kerberos authentication include:

  - **Realm:** The fully-qualified domain name of the Active Directory domain

  - **Key Distribution Center:** Typically a domain controller FQDN within the Active Directory domain

  - **Organizational Unit:** The organizational unit (OU) to which the device should be added

- **Domain and Domain Controller settings:** Specify the FQDN of a domain controller within the domain, along with the credentials of a user that has privileges to add the machine into the domain.

When you have supplied these parameters, click **Submit** to save them. Before proceeding to the step of joining the device to the domain, be sure to verify the following. Note that it is preferred that these configuration changes and verification be performed using the CM and the AllDevicesGroup when possible:

- **Domain name configuration:** Verify that the domain name configured on the device is set to be the same as the domain you are joining.

    - Via the CLI, use the **ip domain-name** command under global configuration mode.

    - Via the CM, check the configuration found on the device context at **Configure > Network > DNS**.

- **Domain name server configuration:** Verify that the DNS server address has been specified on the device that you are attempting to join to the Windows domain.

    - Via the CLI, use the **ip name-server** command under global configuration mode.

    - Via the CM, check the configuration found on the device context at **Configure > Network > DNS**.

- Verify that the time configuration on the device is within 5 minutes from the time on the domain controller that you are attempting to register with. This can be examined by using the **show clock** command in the CLI. The devices should be within the supported time window if NTP is used and the same server is used on the WAAS devices and the domain controller.

After you verify the preceding items, return to the Windows Domain parameters page found on the device context under **Configure > Security > Authentication > Windows Domain**. If the domain credentials are empty, reenter them and click the **Register** button. A pop-up tells you to check the status of the registration using the **Show Authentication Status** button, which is similar to that found in Figure 7-16. Should the registration succeed, the pop-up window presented after clicking **Show Authentication Status** has green checkmarks on the right-hand side in the Status column, and the configuration page window shows SUCCESS Join is OK under Windows Authentication and Domain Registration. Both are shown together in Figure 7-16.

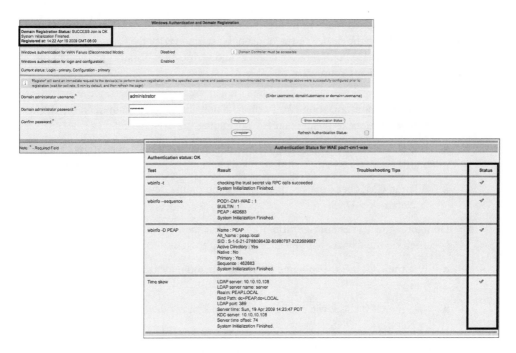

Figure 7-16 *Authentication Status Window*

Example 7-13 shows the resultant configuration in the device CLI, along with the commands necessary to verify from the CLI that the device has successfully joined the domain. Portions of output have been removed for readability.

Example 7-13 *Windows Domain CLI Configuration and Verification Output*

```
pod1-cm1-wae# show running-config
!
hostname pod1-cm1-wae
clock timezone PDT -8 0
ip domain-name peap.local
ip name-server 10.10.10.100
!
kerberos local-realm PEAP.LOCAL
kerberos realm peap.local PEAP.LOCAL
kerberos server PEAP.LOCAL server.peap.local port 88
!
windows-domain workgroup "PEAP"
windows-domain netbios-name "POD1-CM1-WAE"
windows-domain realm "PEAP.LOCAL"
windows-domain password-server "server.peap.local"
windows-domain security ADS
```

```
windows-domain administrative group normal-user "Users"
!
authentication login local enable primary
authentication login windows-domain enable secondary
authentication configuration local enable primary
authentication configuration windows-domain enable secondary
authentication fail-over server-unreachable
!
pod1-cm1-wae# show windows-domain
  Login Authentication for Console/Telnet Session: enabled (secondary)
  Configuration Authentication for Console/Telnet Session: enabled (secondary)
    Authentication scheme fail-over reason: server unreachable

  Windows domain Configuration:
  — — — — — — — — — — — — — — — —.
    Workgroup: PEAP
    Comment:
    Net BIOS: POD1-CM1-WAE
    Realm: PEAP.LOCAL
    WINS Server: 0.0.0.0
    Password Server: "server.peap.local"
    Security: ADS
```

Should the attempt to join the domain be unsuccessful, the pop-up presented when clicking **Show Authentication Status** has a red X next to the item that failed, along with information helpful in diagnosing why the join failed. In general, the items in the preceding bulleted list of Windows domain parameters, prior to clicking the **Register** button, cover the primary reasons that a device is unable to join to the domain. Should you ever need to unregister the device from the domain, click **Unregister**, and check in the domain management tools for your domain to verify that the device is no longer listed.

As a best practice, you should adhere to the following guidelines to ensure successful integration and security when using third-party integration providers:

- Create a series of new roles based on the permissions that authenticated users should have per user type.

- Define all administrative users and assign them to the appropriate groups, or, define the administrative User Groups and assign them the appropriate roles and domains.

- Minimize the permissions available in the default roles such that any undefined user has little or no privileges on the system.

- Specify secondary and tertiary servers as needed, with a failover to the local user database. This ensures availability of management access if third-party authentication providers are unavailable.

Example 7-14 shows how to manually configure primary and secondary authentication servers as needed, with failover to the local user database. Note that the CLI also allows for the definition of tertiary and quaternary servers. Be sure to use the **authentication fail-over server-unreachable** command shown in Example 7-14 to only allow login authentication to fail over to the next service in the configuration should the current login server service be unavailable or unreachable. It is best practice to have **local** authentication at the end of the list as an authentication provider of last resort.

Example 7-14 *Configuring Primary and Secondary Servers and Authentication Failover*

```
pod1-cm1-wae# # config
pod1-cm1-wae# (config)# authentication login tacacs enable primary
pod1-cm1-wae# (config)# authentication configuration tacacs enable primary
pod1-cm1-wae# (config)# authentication login local enable secondary
pod1-cm1-wae# (config)# authentication configuration local enable secondary
pod1-cm1-wae# (config)# authentication fail-over server-unreachable
```

Note **authentication login** commands determine what authentication provider to consult to see if the user has permission to log into the WAAS device. **authentication configuration** commands determine what authentication provider to consult to see what configuration access privileges users have on the WAAS device should they authenticate successfully.

TACACS+ Authentication

Cisco WAAS also supports TACACS+ as a means of authenticating and authorizing users. TACACS+ is configured in the device context (or in the device group context) at **Configure > Security > Authentication > TACACS+**. Similar to Windows Authentication, if you desire to use TACACS+, it must be listed as a configured authentication or authorization provider as shown previously in Figure 7-11. Figure 7-17 shows the configuration for TACACS+.

The configurable elements on this page include:

■ **Use ASCII Password Authentication:** Enable this setting when the ASCII password type is used for authentication with TACACS+.

■ **Time to Wait:** Specify the length of time the device should wait for a response before considering TACACS+ unreachable, which triggers the system to use the next available server. By default, this value is set to 5 seconds.

■ **Number of Retransmits:** Specify the number of times the device attempts to reach the TACACS+ server before considering it unavailable. By default, this value is set to two attempts.

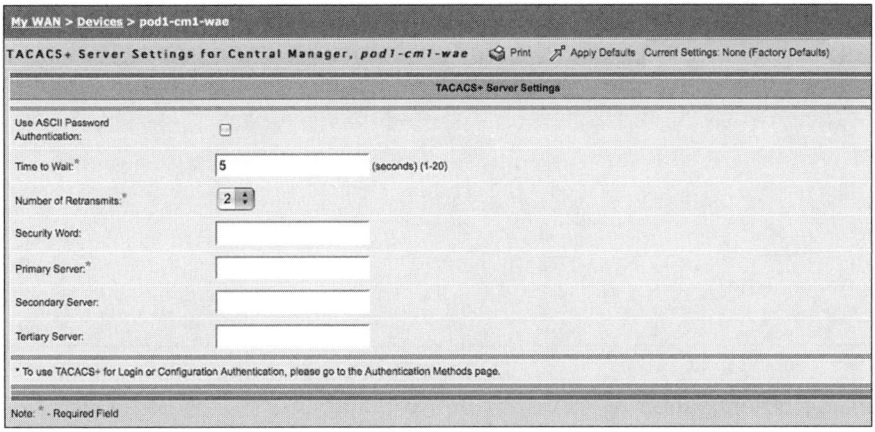

Figure 7-17   *TACACS+ Configuration*

■ **Security Word:** Specify the secret key that is to be used between WAAS and the TACACS+ server. If a key is specified (this field is not required), an identical key must be configured on the TACACS+ server, otherwise the service is unavailable.

■ **TACACS+ Servers:** Specify up to three TACACS+ servers, that are used in order (Primary, Secondary, Tertiary).

With these configurations applied, click the **Submit** button, which saves the settings. The resultant CLI commands are applied to the device as shown in Example 7-15, which also demonstrates the commands required to display the status of TACACS+. Portions have been removed for readability.

Example 7-15   *TACACS+ CLI Configuration Output and Verification*

```
pod1-cm1-wae# show running-config
!
tacacs key ****
tacacs password ascii
tacacs host 10.10.10.100 primary
tacacs host 10.10.10.101
tacacs host 10.10.10.102
!
pod1-cm1-wae# show tacacs
    Login Authentication for Console/Telnet Session: disabled
    Configuration Authentication for Console/Telnet Session: disabled
    Authentication scheme fail-over reason: server unreachable

    TACACS+ Configuration:
    — — — — — — — — — —·
```

```
Key         = *****
Timeout     = 5
Retransmit  = 2
Password type: ascii


Server                          Status
_ _ _ _ _ _ _ _ _ _ _ _ _ _     _ _ _
10.10.10.100                    primary
10.10.10.101
10.10.10.102
```

RADIUS Authentication

Similarly, Cisco WAAS also supports RADIUS as a means of authenticating and authorizing users. Like TACACS+, RADIUS is configured in the device context (or in the device group context) at **Configure > Security > Authentication > RADIUS**. Similar to Windows Authentication, if you desire to use RADIUS, it must be listed as a configured authentication or authorization provider as shown previously in Figure 7-11. Figure 7-18 shows the configuration for RADIUS.

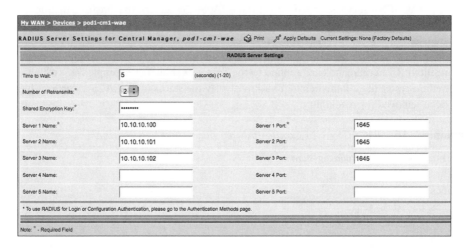

Figure 7-18 *RADIUS Configuration*

The configurable elements on this page include the following:

- **Time to Wait:** Specify the length of time the device should wait for a response before considering RADIUS unreachable, which triggers the system to use the next available server. By default, this value is set to 5 seconds.

- **Number of Retransmits:** Specify the number of times the device attempts to reach the RADIUS server before considering it unavailable. By default, this value is set to two attempts.

- **Shared Encryption Key:** Specify the secret key that is to be used between WAAS and the RADIUS server for encrypting communications. This key is required, and an identical key must be configured on the RADIUS server, otherwise user authentication fails.

- **RADIUS Servers and Ports:** Specify up to five RADIUS servers and the port numbers that should be used, which are used in order.

With these configurations applied, click the **Submit** button, which saves the settings. The resultant CLI commands are applied to the device as shown in Example 7-16, which also demonstrates the commands required to display the status of RADIUS. Portions have been removed for readability.

Example 7-16   *RADIUS CLI Configuration Output and Verification*

```
pod1-cm1-wae# show running-config
!
radius-server key ****
radius-server host 10.10.10.100 auth-port 1645
radius-server host 10.10.10.101 auth-port 1645
radius-server host 10.10.10.102 auth-port 1645
!
pod1-cm1-wae# show radius
Login Authentication for Console/Telnet Session: disabled
Configuration Authentication for Console/Telnet Session: disabled
Authentication scheme fail-over reason: server unreachable

Radius Configuration:
— — — — — — — — — —.
Timeout       = 5
Retransmit    = 2
Key           = ****
Servers
— — —.
IP  10.10.10.100    Port =   1645
IP  10.10.10.101    Port =   1645
IP  10.10.10.102    Port =   1645
```

With the completion of how to configure authentication, the next section focuses on configuration, monitoring, and management of the Cisco WAAS Network.

Device Configuration, Monitoring, and Management

This section focuses on the device-specific configuration and management capabilities of the CM, particularly from a device perspective and not from a WAN optimization, application acceleration, or virtualization service perspective. Chapters 8 and 9 include an examination of using the CM to configure and monitor WAN optimization and application acceleration services, and Chapter 10, "Branch Office Virtualization," provides an examination of using the CM to configure and manage VBs. This chapter focuses on configuration, monitoring, and reporting aspects that are not related to the optimization capabilities of Cisco WAAS. This section examines the device homepage, monitoring charts, reporting facilities, configurable items, status and health monitoring, and software upgrade and rollback. The section concludes with an introduction to the XML-API available in the WAAS CM, which provides simple integration into numerous third-party visibility systems—or into your own management platforms.

Alarms, Monitoring, and Reporting

Upon login, the CM provides you with a system-wide dashboard that shows a tabular view of all configured monitoring charts (in four groups—traffic, optimization, acceleration, and system) and the active alarms that have been generated by devices in the system. An alarm can be generated when a condition that requires administrator attention is encountered. For instance, an interface might be operating in half-duplex mode, or, a service might have stopped. Additionally, a tab is present that allows you to examine the acknowledged alarms, that is, those that have been viewed by the administrator and are considered to be resolved or are otherwise not of interest. Figure 7-2, earlier in the chapter, provides a snapshot of the system-level dashboard.

Managing Alarms

Any login alarms generated by devices in the network appear in the lower section of the dashboard. Information is provided with each alarm, and links are provided by hovering over the alarm information that allows you to remediate the alarm. Alarm information includes:

- **Alarm name:** The name of the alarm that was generated, which can be cross-referenced in the alarm book to understand what the alarm means

- **Device name:** The name of the device where the condition that generated the alarm was encountered

- **Device IP:** The IP address of the device where the condition that generated the alarm was encountered

- **Alarm severity:** The severity or criticality of the alarm

- **Alarm information:** A helpful description of the alarm

Note   The Cisco WAAS alarm book and error message book for each version of WAAS is available at cisco.com at http://www.cisco.com/cgi-bin/tablebuild.pl/waas41.

Additional help for CM alarms can be found in the Cisco WAAS product documentation at http://www.cisco.com/en/US/products/ps6870/tsd_products_support_series_home.html.

By hovering over the alarm information, a pop-up window as shown in Figure 7-19 appears, allowing you to take action against the alarm. The list of remediation actions includes:

- **Edit/Monitor Device:** Clicking this link takes you to the device context homepage, so you can visit the appropriate configuration or monitoring sections to diagnose and correct the problem.

- **Telnet to Device:** Opens a Telnet window to the device so you can access the CLI and diagnose and correct the problem.

- **View Device Log:** Jumps to the device context, **Admin > Logs** so you can view the system message log to understand the conditions that may have caused the problem.

- **Run Show Commands:** Jumps to the device context, **Troubleshoot > CLI Commands > Show commands** so you can execute CLI commands from the CM GUI that enable you to understand, diagnose, and correct the issue.

Figure 7-19 *Alarm Information Diagnostics Popup*

After you remediate the issue, you can select the checkbox next to the alarm and click the **Acknowledge** button. This provides a pop-up enabling you to type in any comments associated with the alarm or the resolution of that alarm, and the alarm is then moved into the Acknowledged Alarms tab. Acknowledged alarms can also be unacknowledged, which places them back in the Active Alarms tab.

Monitoring Charts

Monitoring charts for network baselining, measuring optimization, measuring acceleration, and platform statistics are available in two places in the CM dashboard:

- On the Dashboard link for the My WAN context or in the context of a specific device

- Under the Monitor drawer for the My WAN context or in the context of a specific device

The monitoring capabilities of the Cisco WAAS CM are rich and enable you to directly control what charts are displayed on any given page. On the dashboard page (in this section, dashboard refers to either the dashboard link on the My WAN context or the device context), monitoring charts are separated into four tabs, each of which provide a different and unique purpose. The content displayed in the charts is based on the current context. For example, in the My WAN context, the charts present system-wide statistics, whereas in the device context, the charts present statistics from an individual device:

- **Traffic:** By default, this tab provides the traffic summary (pie chart showing distribution by configured application groups), original traffic over time (byte counts for original traffic versus pass-through traffic), and optimized traffic over time (byte counts for optimized traffic versus pass-through traffic). These charts are useful for baselining your network, that is, determining what applications are on the network and the throughput of each before and after WAAS optimization.

- **Optimization:** By default, this tab provides the compression summary (top ten applications by percent compression applied), bandwidth optimization for all traffic (the effective capacity, also known as X-Factor), and traffic volume and reduction (showing byte counts of traffic original versus optimized and the percentage of traffic reduction). These charts are useful for understanding how well WAAS is optimizing your network.

- **Acceleration:** By default, this tab provides estimated time savings for HTTP, Messaging Application Programming Interface (MAPI), and NFS, based on the levels of application acceleration applied to these protocols. These charts are helpful for understanding how much performance improvement and timesavings are provided by WAAS for these applications.

- **Platform:** On the My WAN context, provides a summary of the devices being managed (number of devices by status, number of alarms by severity, and software versions), which is helpful for identifying problems in the network or device irregularities. In the device context, provides the CPU utilization for the device, which is helpful to understand the CPU load on the device from the functions it is performing.

By default, each chart is filtered to show only the last hour of data. This can be changed on each chart directly by using the **Settings** button, or globally through the System Properties link found in the My WAN context under the Configure drawer by adjusting the **System.monitoring.timeFrameSettings** property. From this property, you can set the timeframe for all monitoring charts to **Last Hour, Last Day, Last Week**, or **Last Month**. When using the **Settings** button to manipulate a chart directly, you can also specify a custom date range.

The properties of a chart that can be manipulated vary from chart to chart when using the **Settings** button. All charts support manipulation of the time frame being visualized. Certain charts enable you to adjust the series of data that is shown, which enables you to filter by application groups if so desired. To make more room for charts in the workspace, click the **Show/Hide Table** button, which maximizes the chart space by eliminating the table beneath it. Additionally, any chart can be "grabbed" by the corner to dynamically resize it, or you can "grab" the chart title to move the chart around the workspace. Similarly, you can maximize or minimize charts by clicking either the **Maximize** or **Minimize** button found in the chart title, or simply clicking the chart name in the chart legend. Additionally, a minimize button appears in the vertical separator between the charting workspace and the table of contents that enables you to collapse the table of contents for more charting area. Figure 7-20 shows an example of how to manipulate chart dimensions. In this figure, notice that the data table has been hidden to maximize the room for visualizing the charts.

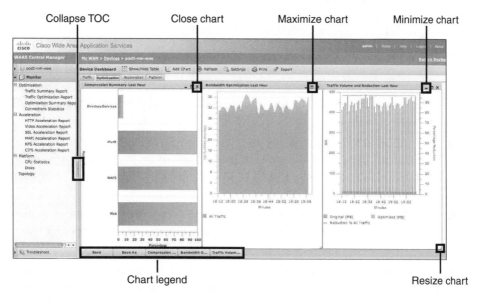

Figure 7-20 *Manipulating Chart Layout and Dimensions*

Charts can be added or removed from any of these tabs—up to a maximum of six charts per tab—by using the **Add Chart** button. This allows you to select which charts are available on the tab (and which are not). Should you manipulate the charting dashboard and wish to make the current layout the default, you can click the **Save** button in the chart legend, which ensures that the view you select is retained for the next time you visit this tab. The **Save As** button in the chart legend enables you to save the view as a report template (which is accessible in the Report drawer in the system context, discussed later), which can be scheduled for regular delivery as a PDF.

The Monitor drawer (found in both the My WAN and device context) provides another level of monitoring for the system and individual devices. Charts are organized in the Monitor drawer in three groups (optimization, acceleration, and platform), and like the charts in the Dashboard, can be manipulated, views can be saved as the default for the page, and charts can be saved to reports (again, discussed later in the chapter). The Monitor drawer provides more detailed charts than those provided by default on the

Dashboard, but due to the ability to manipulate virtually any view, Dashboard tabs can be configured to change which charts are viewed, and that includes those charts that are (by default) available only under the Monitor drawer.

The Monitor drawer default charts include:

- **Optimization > Traffic Summary Report:** Shows the traffic summary, original traffic over time, and optimized traffic over time. This is similar to the Traffic tab in the dashboard as described previously.

- **Optimization > Traffic Optimization Report:** Shows the traffic volume and reduction, bandwidth optimization, and compression over time. This is similar to the Optimization tab in the dashboard as described previously.

- **Optimization > Optimization Summary Report:** Shows the top ten applications by compression and compression by application over time. This is similar to the Optimization tab in the dashboard as described previously, but also Shows the levels of compression achieved by specific applications should the chart settings be configured accordingly.

- **Optimization > Connection Statistics:** Available only in the device context, shows the current connections that are being handled by that device, along with the optimization policy and other statistics. From here, individual connections can be examined for more detail.

- **Acceleration > HTTP Acceleration Report:** Shows the estimated time savings, bandwidth optimization, and number of optimized and bypassed connections for the HTTP application optimizer (AO).

- **Acceleration > Video Acceleration Report:** Shows the number of incoming versus outgoing bytes, bandwidth optimization, and number of optimized versus bypassed connections for the Video AO. Additionally, the Details tab provides reasons why video connections might have been bypassed from optimization.

- **Acceleration > SSL Acceleration Report:** Shows the number of optimized SSL connections, bandwidth optimization, and reasons for acceleration bypass for SSL traffic.

- **Acceleration > MAPI Acceleration Report:** Shows the estimated time savings, bandwidth optimization, and number of optimized versus bypassed connections for MAPI (Microsoft Outlook and Exchange) traffic. Additionally, the Details tab provides specific details on the percentage of local versus remote requests (request optimization), local versus remote response time (response time optimization), versions of Outlook detected on the network, and reasons why MAPI connections were bypassed from acceleration.

- **Acceleration > NFS Acceleration Report:** Shows the estimated time savings, bandwidth optimization, and number of optimized versus bypassed connections for NFS (UNIX file sharing). Additionally, the Details tab provides specific details on the percentage of local versus remote responses (request optimization), local versus remote response time (response time optimization), versions of NFS detected on the network, and reasons why NFS connections were bypassed from acceleration.

■ **Acceleration > CIFS Acceleration Report (only available in the device context):**
Shows the number of accelerated CIFS sessions, number of open (and accelerated) files, request hit rate percentage for the CIFS cache, and cache disk space and resource utilization percentage. Additionally, the Details tab provides the number of objects in the CIFS cache and the average client throughput for optimized connections.

Chapters 8 and 9 provide more details on the specifics of each optimization chart. Any charts in the Dashboard page or in the Monitor drawer can be customized to your liking, and views can be saved as defaults by using the **Save** button. Any view can be saved as a report by using the **Save As** button, which can then be scheduled for later delivery. Any view that you encounter can quickly be printed to a PDF by using the **Print** button in the page heading, and the raw statistics from the supporting data table can be fetched in CSV format by using the **Export** button in the page heading as shown in Figure 7-21.

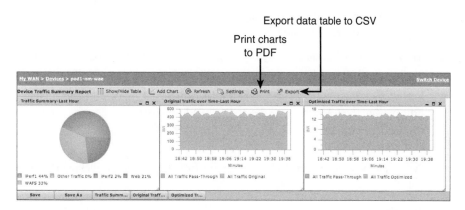

Figure 7-21   *Printing Charts to PDF and Downloading Raw Table Data*

Managing Reports

Along with providing powerful monitoring capabilities and customization, the WAAS CM also provides a series equally powerful and flexible reporting capabilities. Reports are available only in the My WAN context under the Report drawer, which encompasses all factory-default reports as well as those that were saved by system users using the **Save As** button described in the previous section. Under the Report drawer in the My WAN context, there are two links. The first is Manage Reports, which is shown in Figure 7-22.

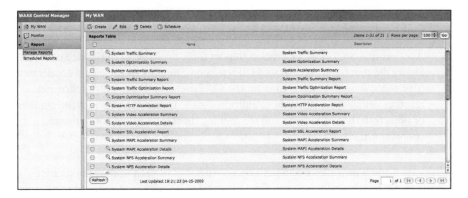

Figure 7-22   *Managing Reports*

This page shows you the factory-default and user-defined reports and gives you the ability to:

■ **Create a new report:** Clicking the **Create** button creates a blank workspace from which you can add charts (using the **Add Chart** button) and the data table you want to present in the report (in the lower part of the workspace).

■ **View a report:** Clicking the magnifying glass next to any report takes you to the view of that report so you can adjust chart settings, add or remove charts, or change views.

■ **Edit an existing report:** By selecting the checkbox next to a report and clicking the **Edit** button, the CM gives you the ability to adjust chart settings, add or remove charts, or change views. This is functionally equivalent to clicking the magnifying glass next to the report.

■ **Delete an existing report:** Delete the report from the listing by clicking the **Delete** button.

■ **Schedule a report:** By clicking the **Schedule** button, you can schedule the e-mail delivery of the PDF version of the report. Configurable parameters include the date of delivery, time of delivery, frequency (how many times the report should be delivered), e-mail recipients, and the devices from which statistics should be evaluated in generating the report.

Reports must be scheduled to run at some point in the future. Should you want to have a report run immediately, you can schedule the report to run in a few moments from the present time for one-time execution.

SNMP, Syslog, and System Logs

Cisco WAAS supports internal and external logging mechanisms to enable integration into existing monitoring systems. As mentioned earlier in the chapter, alarms that are generated on a particular WAAS device are driven by events that require administrator attention and cause an alarm to be generated in the alarm section of the My WAN dashboard.

The CM also provides robust audit logging for any configuration changes that were made while a user was logged into the CM and facilities to view system logs from each and every device in the network. These audit trails are enabled automatically and require no additional user configuration. Figure 7-23 shows an example audit trail that can be found in the My WAN context at **Admin > Logs > Audit Trail Logs.**

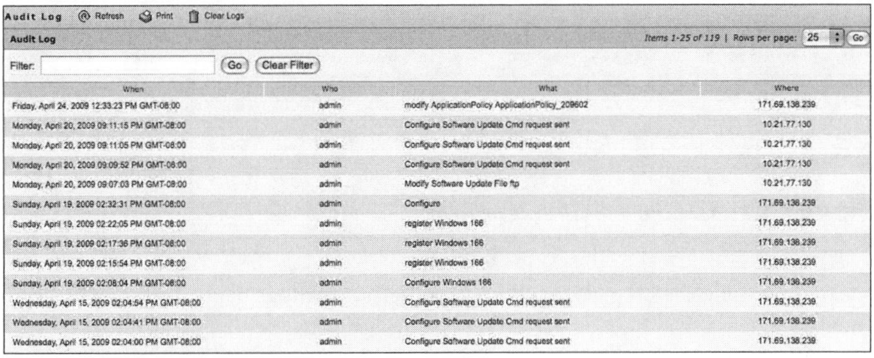

Figure 7-23   *CM Audit Trail Logs*

The logs found on this page contain the following information:

- **When:** When the action was taken.
- **Who:** Which user performed an action on the system.
- **What:** What action the user performed on the system.
- **Where:** What IP address the action came from.

Logs can be filtered by using the Filter shown in the page heading, which filters on the who, what, or where column automatically. For instance, if you supply an IP address and click **Go**, the log messages are filtered based on the presence of that IP address.

Similarly, system messages, which include alarm data, can be viewed from the My WAN context at **Admin > Logs > System Messages.** The system message repository contains all the system messages that have been sent to the CM from the managed WAAS devices and those that were generated locally on the CM itself. Figure 7-24 shows an example of the CM system messages table.

Whereas the audit trail shows what function was performed by a particular user, the system messages table contains information about alarms and events that have been generated on the CM or managed nodes. The system messages table also includes a Severity column to identify how critical the message is and an icon that allows you to export the table for offline viewing and analysis. Logs can be truncated using the **Truncate** button to minimize the number of entries that are retained. The logs can also be exported in CSV format using the **Export** button. Additionally, the logs that are displayed can be

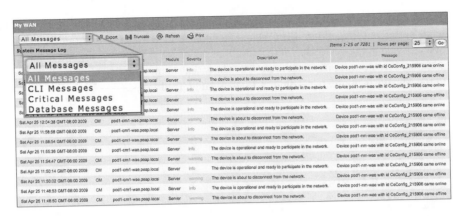

Figure 7-24 *CM System Messages Table*

filtered by using the drop-down in the upper-left of the logs page to select whether you want to see:

- **All Messages:** Display all system messages that have been generated by any WAAS device in the network.

- **CLI Messages:** Display only those messages that are related to the application of a CLI to a WAAS device in the network.

- **Critical Messages:** Display only those messages that are critical in nature.

- **Database Messages:** Display only those messages that are related to the databases managed by the CM and WAAS devices, including the CMS database and secure store.

As noted previously, detailed descriptions for each of the log messages can be found in the product documentation and the alarm book and error message book (http://www.cisco.com/cgi-bin/tablebuild.pl/waas41). The CM, as well as any WAAS device, supports definition of up to four external syslog servers and robust SNMP configuration. Syslog is configured from the device or device group homepage under **Configure > Monitoring > Log Settings > System Log.** It is recommended that a common pool of syslog servers be used across all devices in the network for coherent logging; configuration of syslog settings is a good candidate for configuration within the *AllDevicesGroup* device group. On this page, the following items can be configured:

- **Global enable/disable of system logging and facility:** Enable or disable system logging, and specify the syslog facility that should be used for syslog messages.

- **Console logging:** Enable or disable console logging, along with the minimum priority level of messages that should be displayed on the console. Note that this type of logging should be used sparingly, because it can increase CPU utilization and the console can become flooded and difficult to interact with.

■ **Disk logging:** Enable or disable logging to disk, including the name of the file that should be used, the minimum priority level for messages that should be logged, and the maximum size of an individual log file (recycle size) before another file is used.

■ **Host settings:** Enable or disable logging to an external syslog server, including the hostname of each server, minimum priority required before a message is sent, port number to use, and maximum number of messages that can be sent per second to each server.

Figure 7-25 shows the syslog configuration for a specific device, and Example 7-17 shows the resultant CLIs that are produced on the WAAS device because of this configuration. In the example, portions were removed to improve readability and focus.

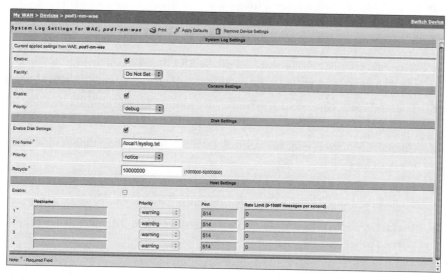

Figure 7-25 *Configuring Internal and External Logging*

Example 7-17 *Internal and External Logging CLI Configuration*

```
pod1-nm-wae# show running-config
!
logging facility syslog
logging host 10.10.10.100 priority alert rate-limit 500
logging console enable
logging console priority emergency
logging disk priority alert
!
```

Note   The /local1 directory in the device filesystem is the default location where syslog messages are stored. You can create new directories if desired from the CLI using the **mkdir** command and remove directories using the **rmdir** command. To list the contents of a directory, use either the **dir** command (detailed listing) or **ls** command (less detailed). To view the contents of a file, use the **type** command followed by the filename or the **type-tail** command followed by the filename to view the last page of a file.

Files stored in the device filesystem can be copied off to an external location using the **copy disk ftp** command, which requires you to supply the hostname or IP address of the destination, remote file directory, remote filename, local filename, and credentials. This is helpful for manually copying log files off the system for offline viewing or analysis.

Similarly, SNMP can be configured from within the device or device group homepage under **Configure > Monitoring > SNMP**. A number of subitems exist under SNMP, each of which provides a separate configuration area. These include:

- **General settings:** Globally enable or disable SNMP and specify which facilities should have traps generated when conditions dictate that a message should be sent.

- **Trigger:** Create, edit, and delete triggers for specific Management Information Bases (MIB) and customize the conditions that must be met before a trap is generated.

- **Community:** Create, edit, and delete SNMP communities, including read/write permissions for each.

- **Groups:** Create, edit, and delete SNMP groups, define the security model (version) for each, and specify the read, write, and notify view for each.

- **Users:** Define SNMP users, associate the users to SNMP groups, and define authentication parameters for each.

- **Views:** Create, edit, and delete SNMP views, for the purposes of restricting a group of users to viewing only a specific MIB tree. This includes definition of a name which represents a subtree and the MIB (defined as a family).

- **Hosts:** Create, edit, and delete SNMP hosts, which defines where traps should be sent, including the hostname, community or user, type of authentication that should be used to this host, and timer values such as retry (the number of times the device should attempt to send a message) and timeout (the amount of time to wait before determining that an attempt to send a message has expired).

- **Asset tag:** Defines an asset tag (as used by CISCO-ENTITY-ASSET-MIB) for the device.

- **Contact information:** Defines the contact information for the device, including the name and location.

Although these settings can be configured from the device CLI using the global configuration mode command **snmp-server**, it is recommended that these parameters be configured from the *AllDevicesGroup* device group to be applied uniformly across all devices in the network. Certain parameters, however, such as the asset tag, should be configured individually on each device.

> **Note** For a full list of the numerous MIBs supported by Cisco WAAS and additional details about each MIB, including the download location, please visit http://tinyurl.com/n8mzk4
>
> Integration of WAAS into an SNMP management system might require that MIBs be compiled by the management system. Please refer to your SNMP management system documentation for details on how such steps are performed.

Example 7-18 demonstrates a CLI configuration from a WAAS device that shows how these elements are configured. Given the vast array of CLI configuration options for SNMP, it is recommended that such configuration be performed from the WAAS CM for simplicity. Portions of the CLI output have been removed for readability and clarity.

Example 7-18 *CLI Configuration of WAAS SNMP Monitoring*

```
pod1-nm-wae#show run
!
snmp-server enable traps config
snmp-server enable traps content-engine disk-read
snmp-server enable traps content-engine disk-write
snmp-server enable traps content-engine disk-fail
snmp-server enable traps content-engine overload-bypass
snmp-server enable traps content-engine transaction-log
snmp-server enable traps alarm raise-critical
snmp-server enable traps alarm clear-critical
snmp-server enable traps alarm raise-major
snmp-server enable traps alarm clear-major
snmp-server enable traps alarm raise-minor
snmp-server enable traps alarm clear-minor
snmp-server enable traps wafs cslog
snmp-server enable traps wafs eslog
snmp-server enable traps wafs mgrlog
snmp-server enable traps entity
snmp-server enable traps snmp authentication
snmp-server enable traps snmp cold-start
snmp-server enable traps event
snmp-server mib persist event
snmp-server host 10.10.10.100 public
snmp-server group public v2c
snmp-server community public rw
```

```
snmp-server notify inform
!
```

Upgrading and Downgrading Software

The CM provides facilities that enable you to upgrade or downgrade the software version installed on one or many WAAS devices within the network with ease. From within the CM itself, you can define a software image and all related parameters associated with that image. This entry, called a *software file entry*, is a link to the actual binary file used by the WAAS device to download and then install the software. When a software file entry is applied to a WAAS device or a device group, the details of the entry are sent to that WAAS device, which causes the device to initiate a connection to the download location to begin downloading. If the WAAS device is successful in its connection attempt, it downloads the file referenced in the link provided to it by the CM. If the download succeeds, the WAAS device attempts to install the software. The software file entry can be configured to cause the WAAS device to automatically reboot, which causes the software to be installed immediately after download. When a WAAS device attempts to download a software image, it attempts to optimize the TCP connection with a given peer should one exist in the network. As such, the reload flag should be used only in cases where intermediary devices or optimization peers are not also trying to install the software. Otherwise, you might have a situation where an edge device is in the middle of a download of the image that is optimized with a peer, where that peer fetches the image more quickly and reboots in the middle of the other device's download. When this happens, devices retry their download, but it can extend the amount of time necessary for devices at the fray of the network to download and install their images.

The configuration page for defining a software file entry can be found in the My WAN context at **Jobs > Software Update**. Figure 7-26 shows this page, along with the configuration page for a software file entry.

The parameters associated with a software file entry include:

- **Software File URL:** Specify the download protocol (HTTP or FTP) and the remainder of the URL necessary for a device to directly download the image

- **Username:** The username that should be supplied by the device (if prompted) to the HTTP or FTP server to properly authenticate and download the software file.

- **Password:** The password that should be supplied by the device (if prompted) to the HTTP or FTP server to properly authenticate and download the software file.

- **Software Version:** The version of the software that the file contains, in the format X.Y.Z, where X is the major version, Y is the minor version, and Z is the maintenance version.

- **File Size:** Enables you to specify the size of the file. This is an optional parameter, and can be used in conjunction with the Validate Software File Settings to verify that the connectivity to the file is correct and that the size of the file is correct.

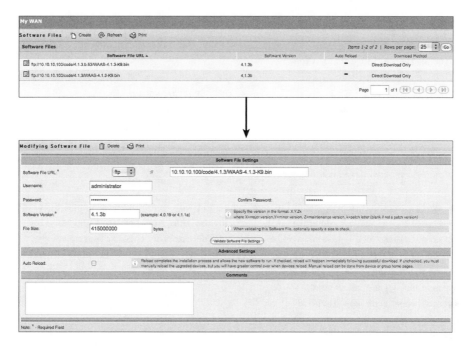

Figure 7-26 *Software File Entry Definition Page*

■ **Auto Reload:** Checking this checkbox causes the WAAS device to automatically reboot if it successfully downloads the software file. This box is not checked by default, meaning the device does not automatically reload.

The Validate Software File Settings causes the CM to connect to the repository directly,
attempting to authenticate using the supplied credentials, in effort to validate the presence of the file in the path supplied and the file size.

Any time a software upgrade or downgrade is applied to a WAAS device, that WAAS
device must be rebooted for the new version to be installed. It is important to note that
when applying a software image to a CM WAAS device, if the software image contains
an earlier version than the previously installed image, it might be necessary to downgrade
the CMS database to support the schema used by the newly installed version.

Example 7-19 shows the output of **show cms info** and **cms database downgrade**, which
are used, respectively, to verify that a database downgrade is required and to perform a
downgrade of the database. Be sure to disable CMS services prior to the downgrade and
enable CMS services after the downgrade.

Example 7-19 *Downgrading the CMS Database*

```
pod1-cm1-wae# show cms info
DOWNGRADE REQUIRED
--------
```

```
A database downgrade is required to enable CMS services. Please use
the 'cms database downgrade' command to perform the database downgrade.
Device registration information :
Device Id                           = 142
Device registered as                = WAAS Central Manager
Current WAAS Central Manager role    = Primary
CMS services information :
Service cms_httpd is not running
Service cms_cdm is not running
pod1-cm1-wae# cms database downgrade

The system will perform a database downgrade without applying a downgrade script.
Please refer to product documentation to confirm that the previously-installed
software release does not require a downgrade script for this release.
Proceed with database downgrade [no]? yes
Creating database backup file cms-db-04-05-2009-03-32.dump
Database downgrade succeeded.
pod1-cm1-wae# show cms info
Device registration information :
Device Id                           = 142
Device registered as                = WAAS Central Manager
Current WAAS Central Manager role    = Primary
CMS services information :
Service cms_httpd is not running
Service cms_cdm is not running
pod1-cm1-wae# config term
pod1-cm1-wae(config)# cms enable
```

When upgrading a CM to a newer software version, the software installation automatically adjusts the schema of the CMS database if necessary during the reboot and installation of the software. All the information necessary about prior version database schemas is retained in the CM; thus, when performing an upgrade, the system can automatically identify what version was installed prior and make the appropriate changes to the database to support the new version's schema. However, older versions have no way of knowing what schema a future version uses. As such, a database downgrade might be necessary if downgrading software versions on the CM itself to adjust the schema appropriately to the older version.

An issue related to software upgrade is the recommended order of upgrade. The CM is capable of managing any device that has an equivalent or older version of software installed upon it. That is, the CM can determine which configuration items are configurable on any WAAS device managed by that CM. Thus, if the CM is of a newer version than the WAAS devices that it is managing, it determines which configuration elements can be applied to the lower-version devices. This is a change from previous versions of WAAS where the CM needed to be the lowest version in the network.

Note   The 4.1 CM can manage any WAAS device that is the same version, or any WAAS device that has a previous 4.1 version installed. That means, for example, that a CM running v4.1.3 can manage devices running v4.1.1d. The 4.1 CM can also manage 4.0 WAAS devices, assuming the 4.0 WAAS devices are running a minimum of version 4.0.19.

Software upgrades can be applied directly to a device or to an entire device group. Software upgrades can be done from one of three places:

- **Device context:** In the device context **Dashboard** link, click the **Update Software** button in the Device Info pane.

- **Device group context:** In the device group context, click the **Software Update** link found in the Jobs drawer.

- **Device CLI:** Use the **copy** command as demonstrated here (installs a software version from an FTP server):

  pod1-nm-wae# copy ftp install 10.10.10.100 /sw-install WAAS-4.1.3-K9.bin

It is important to reiterate that if the Auto Reload checkbox is not checked during the definition of the software image (refer back to Figure 7-26), the WAAS device must be rebooted to apply the new software version. Also, the CM GUI homepage provides details on what software versions are installed within the WAAS network and on how many WAAS devices. This provides you with a quick glimpse of any software version conflicts that might be present.

Backup and Restore of CM Database

Although some level of high availability can be provided by deploying a primary and a standby CM, it is a best practice to keep up-to-date backups of the CM database on hand in case of a system-wide outage or other disastrous scenario.

The CMS database can be backed up and restored in a manner similar to performing a configuration file backup or restore on any other Cisco device. The only caveats associated with these procedures are the following:

- A CMS database restore must be performed on a WAAS device running the *same* version of the WAAS software from which the backup was taken.

- Prior to restoring a CMS database, the CMS service must *first* be disabled.

When creating a backup of the CMS database, the WAAS software automatically drops the backup file into the directory /local1 on the CM filesystem. The way in which you navigate a filesystem on a WAAS device is identical to how you navigate a Linux server.

Example 7-20 shows how to make a backup of the CMS database, navigate the directory structure and verify the presence of the file, and finally copy the backup to an FTP server.

Example 7-20   *Backup of the CMS Database*

```
pod1-cm1-wae# cms database backup
Creating database backup file cms-db-04-25-2009-21-23_4.1.3.0.55.dump
Backup file cms-db-04-25-2009-21-23_4.1.3.0.55 is ready.
Please use `copy' commands to move the backup file to a remote host.
pod1-cm1-wae# pwd
/local1
pod1-cm1-wae# ls
!
! portions removed
!
cms-db-04-25-2009-21-23_4.1.3.0.55.dump
!
pod1-cm1-wae# copy disk ftp 10.10.10.100 / cms-db-04-25-2009-21-23_4.1.3.0.55.dump
cms-db-04-25-2009-21-23_4.1.3.0.55.dump
Enter username for remote ftp server: administrator
Enter password for remote ftp server:
Initiating FTP upload...
Sending: USER administrator
Microsoft FTP Service
Password required for administrator.
Sending: PASS *********
User administrator logged in.
Sending: TYPE I
Type set to I.
Sending: PASV
Entering Passive Mode (10,10,10,100,39,21).
Sending: CWD /
CWD command successful.
Sending PASV
Entering Passive Mode (10,10,10,100,39,22).
Sending: STOR cms-db-04-25-2009-21-23_4.1.3.0.55.dump
Data connection already open; Transfer starting.
Transfer complete.
Sent 342166 bytes
pod1-cm1-wae#
```

The process of restoring a CMS database is similar to the process of backing up the CMS database. To restore the CMS database, you must first copy the CMS database files to the local filesystem. Then, you must disable CMS services. You should then issue the **cms database restore** command and, upon successful restore, re-enable CMS services.

Example 7-21 shows how to perform a CMS database restore.

Example 7-21   *Restore of the CMS Database*

```
pod1-cm1-wae# copy ftp disk 10.10.10.100 / cms-db-04-25-2009-21-23_4.1.3.0.55.dump
/local1/ cms-db-04-25-2009-21-23_4.1.3.0.55.dump
Enter username for remote ftp server: administrator
Enter password for remote ftp server:
Initiating FTP upload...
Sending: USER administrator
Microsoft FTP Service
Password required for administrator.
Sending: PASS ***********
User administrator logged in.
Sending: TYPE I
Type set to I.
Sending: PASV
Entering Passive Mode (10,10,10,100,128,149).
Sending: CWD /
CWD command successful.
Sending PASV
Entering Passive Mode (10,10,10,100,128,150).
Receiving: STOR cms-db-09-13-2007-05-07.dump
Data connection already open; Transfer starting.
Transfer complete.
Received 146747 bytes
pod1-cm1-wae# pwd
/local1
waas-cm# ls
!
! portions removed
!
! cms-db-04-25-2009-21-23_4.1.3.0.55.dump
!
pod1-cm1-wae# config term
pod1-cm1-wae(config)# no cms enable
pod1-cm1-wae(config)# exit
pod1-cm1-wae# cms database restore /local1/ cms-db-04-25-2009-21-
23_4.1.3.0.55.dump
```

Programmatic Interfaces and the XML-API

Along with providing holistic management, monitoring, and reporting for a network of Cisco WAAS devices, the CM can also integrate into existing end-to-end visibility systems directly. Such integration allows customers to use fewer dashboards to glean greater levels of understanding of how their network is performing and what devices in the network are seeing. As described earlier, WAAS can integrate using SNMP—which provides platform statistics that can be useful from a capacity planning and troubleshooting perspective. In addition to SNMP, the WAAS CM also provides a programmatic interface—application programming interface (API)—that uses the Simple Object Access Protocol (SOAP) to exchange eXtensible Markup Language (XML) messages that contain either requests or responses for system health monitoring or performance information. As the XML-API is accessed via the CM, communications are secured using SSL and authentication must occur before data can be extracted. Additionally, access to the XML-API contents can be controlled via the RBAC facilities provided in the CM, as shown in Figure 7-27.

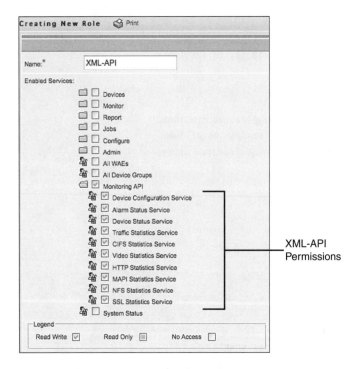

Figure 7-27 *Permissions for the XML-API*

As shown in Figure 7-27, Read Only, Read Write, and No Access permissions can be applied to any of the services made accessible via the XML-API. As of version 4.1.3, the XML-API provides only monitoring and does not provide facilities for configuration. As such, read or read-write permissions are required to be able to extract data from the XML-API. Configuration facilities are likely to be made available in future releases.

The remainder of this section examines the vendors and products that use the XML-API today, the data provided by the XML-API, and simple methods for accessing the data made available in the XML-API. An in-depth examination of the software development processes needed to integrate WAAS statistics fully into your own dashboards is outside of the scope of this book. However, numerous authoritative web services development books are available, and when equipped with an understanding of how to develop applications built on such a framework, the primary information the developer needs are the objects and interfaces, which are provided in this book. Additionally, the XML-API specification for WAAS can be downloaded from: http://tinyurl.com/ox5smg.

Note   Log files that contain entries for the XML-API can be found on the WAAS device filesystem at:

- /local1/service_logs/cms_cdm_start_log_latest
- /local1/errorlog/monapi.log
- /local1/errorlog/cms_log.current

Vendors Supporting the XML-API

The XML-API was released with Cisco WAAS v4.1.1, which became generally available in the summer of 2008. Prior to the release of 4.1.1, many vendors began investigation into and development of integration with the XML-API provided by the WAAS CM. The primary motivation behind the integration with this API was to help managed service providers (MSP) provide a broader view of end-to-end application performance from several separate data sources throughout the network, including SNMP, NetFlow, and raw data captured via SPAN ports. As of this writing, three vendors have either made software generally available or are approaching general availability of a software suite, which provides integration with the XML-API on the WAAS CM. These vendors and their products include:

- **NetQoS Performance Center:** http://www.netqos.com/
- **InfoVista Application Optimization Manager:** http://www.infovista.com/
- **Fluke Networks Visual Performance Manager:** http://www.flukenetworks.com

Although the initial focus of integration was centered around managed WAN and managed WAAS environments, enterprise and commercial organizations are finding substantial value in deploying performance management systems internally. Two key benefits that are provided by such systems are as follows:

- The ability to correlate data from multiple data sources, that is, leverage information from many different places in the network to fully understand application performance and application behavior.

■ The ability to drill-down from information measured and visualized from any data source to identify correlation in behavior across information collected from different data sources.

In a nutshell, these systems help measure application performance in many different ways, which positions organizations to better understand how their applications should be performing and why they might or might not perform in a specific way.

Data Accessible via the XML-API

The XML-API provides four classes of service today:

■ **Device configuration service:** Provides device statistics for WAAS devices and CM devices, as well as device groups

■ **Alarm status service and device status service:** Provides alarm information, device status, service status, and disk status

■ **Traffic acceleration service:** Provides traffic and application statistics for individual devices, groups, or the entire network and CPU utilization

■ **Per-accelerator statistics services:** Provides acceleration-related statistics for each of the AOs that are running on each of the WAAS devices in the network

This section looks at the full list of information provided by the device configuration service, alarm status service, device status service, and part of the traffic acceleration service related to device health. Chapter 8 examines other parts of the traffic acceleration service, and Chapter 9 examines the per-accelerator statistics services.

Device Configuration Service

The device configuration service is used to make data accessible about the WAAS devices deployed throughout the network, the CM devices, and the device groups that have been configured. This service is typically the first that is used by anyone exploring development using the XML-API, because it provides a birds-eye view of the entire network of WAAS devices and the organization (device groups) of those devices. The device configuration service is accessible through the following URL:

https://*<hostname or ip>*:8443/ws/DeviceConf

The Web Services Definition Language (WSDL) for the service is accessible at:

https://*<hostname or ip>*:8443/ws/DeviceConf?wsdl

Accessing the WSDL directly provides the XML schema of the service, but does not provide useful information. Accessing the WSDL directly is helpful in verifying that the web service is accessible, but to actually use the interfaces made accessible via web services, you need to use a tool as described later in the chapter in the section titled "Simple Method of Accessing XML-API Data." Additionally, if you are interested in integrating

WAAS health, alarms, and monitoring data into your existing dashboards, you can use the web services development tools provided in your integrated development environment (IDE) for the programming language you wish to use. In either case, the previous service URL is required.

Nine interfaces are accessible via the device configuration service, and the description of each is as follows:

- **getWANInfo:** Retrieves a listing of all WAAS devices in the network, including accelerators and CM devices. This includes device status, MAC address, device name, IP address, software version, role (device mode), location, hardware model, and numerical identifier.

- **getDeviceGroups:** Retrieves a listing of all device groups that have been configured in the network. This includes the type of each group, the numerical identifier of each group, description applied to each group, and the name of each device group.

- **getWAE:** Retrieves the same information provided by the getWANInfo call, but for a specific device based on its numerical identifier as an input parameter.

- **getWAEByName:** Retrieves the same information provided by the getWANInfo call, but for a specific device based on its device name as an input parameter.

- **getCM:** Identical to getWAE, but for fetching information about a CM device using its numerical identifier as an input parameter.

- **getCMByName:** Identical to getWAEByName, but for fetching information about a CM device using its device name as an input parameter.

- **getWAEs:** Identical to getWAE, but takes a series of numerical identifiers as input and returns the information for each device.

- **getWAEsInGroup:** Identical to getWANInfo, but only the devices that are members of the device group referenced by the supplied numerical identifier (as an input parameter) are returned.

- **getWAEsInGroupByName:** Identical to getWAEsInGroup, but uses the name of the device group as an input parameter.

Alarm Status Service

The alarm status service is used to make data accessible about the alarms that are active on WAAS devices deployed throughout the network. Using this service enables an IT organization to centralize alarm management by integrating CM GUI alarms into existing alarm dashboards. The alarm status service is accessible through the following URL:

> https://*<hostname or ip>*:8443/ws/AlarmStatus

The web services definition language (WSDL) for the service is accessible at:

> https://*<hostname or ip>*:8443/ws/AlarmStatus?wsdl

Three interfaces are accessible via the alarm statu.s service:

■ **retrieveAllAlarms:** Retrieves a listing of all alarms on all WAAS devices in the network. The output includes device name, alarm description, an alarm identifier, device status, name of the alarm, device identifier, device IP address, and alarm severity.

■ **retrieveAlarmByName:** Retrieves the same information as retrieveAllAlarms, but input parameters must be supplied to filter the list by the name of a WAE or device group, the type of object to filter by (wae or waegroup), and the name of the alarm (or an empty string).

■ **retrieveAlarmBySeverity:** Retrieves the same information provided by the retrieveAlarmByName call, filters for alarms based on severity (minor, major, critical, all).

It should be noted that alarms displayed on the CM GUI that are accessed via the XML-API can be cross-referenced using the alarm and error books which are discussed earlier in this chapter.

Device Status Service

The device status service is used to retrieve status information about a specific device in the network. Using this service enables an IT organization to monitor the health of devices, including disk and disk encryption. The device status service is accessible through the following URL:

https://*<hostname or ip>*:8443/ws/DeviceStatus

The web services definition language (WSDL) for the service is accessible at:

https://*<hostname or ip>*:8443/ws/DeviceStatus?wsdl

Four interfaces are accessible via the device status service:

■ **getDeviceStatus:** Retrieves the CM status (online, offline, pending, inactive) of a specific device based on the device name supplied as an input parameter.

■ **getDiskStatus:** Retrieves the RAID level in use on a specific device based on the device name supplied as an input parameter, along with the number of disks that are in use in the device.

■ **getDiskInformation:** Provides details on the disks in use on a specific WAAS device (based on the device name supplied as an input parameter) including disk status, disk name and presence, disk serial number, and size of the disk.

■ **getDiskEncryptStatus:** Provides the current and future disk encryption status for a specific WAAS device based on the device name supplied as an input parameter.

Traffic Acceleration Service

The traffic acceleration service is used to retrieve statistical information about traffic handled by devices in the network along with CPU utilization. The traffic statistics aspects of this service is examined in Chapter 8 after a discussion on the WAN optimization capabilities of Cisco WAAS. Using this service enables an IT organization to monitor the

CPU utilization of devices along with traffic load and how traffic is being handled. The traffic acceleration service is accessible through the following URL:

https://<*hostname or ip*>:8443/ws/TrafficStats

The web services definition language (WSDL) for the service is accessible at:

https://<*hostname or ip*>:8443/ws/TrafficStats?wsdl

Multiple interfaces are accessible via the traffic acceleration service, but only one is examined here (the remainder are examined in Chapter 8):

■ **retrieveCPUUtilization:** Displays the CPU utilization for a specific device name supplied as an input parameter and over a specific timeframe which is supplied as a second input parameter.

Note   Timeframe filters are objects applied to XML-API calls that include several parameters, including:

■ **start time:** yyyy-mm-ddThh:mm:ss, where yyyy is the year, mm is the month, dd is the day, hh is the hour, mm is the minute, ss is the second.

■ **end time:** yyyy-mm-ddThh:mm:ss, using the same convention as start time.

■ **frequency:** Either lasthour, lastweek, lastday, lastmonth, last year, or custom.

■ **timezone:** The CLI time-zone identifier, or utc (utc stands for Coordinated Universal Time).

Simple Method of Accessing XML-API Data

Numerous free open source tools are available to access SOAP and XML-API data that work well with the WAAS CM. This section makes reference to a tool called soapUI from Eviware, which can be downloaded at http://www.soapui.org/. These examples are written to soapUI v2.5.1.

After you download and install soapUI, open the application and right-click **Projects** in the navigation bar and select **New soapUI Project**. Provide a project name (any arbitrary name is fine, but using the name of the call you wish to make is recommended), and supply the WSDL link in the **Initial WSDL/WADL** field. Make sure that the **Create Requests** checkbox is selected, and then click **Ok**. soapUI then loads the definition from the WSDL URL supplied, and the Projects navigation bar updates to show the available interfaces. Figure 7-28 shows the steps necessary to access the available interfaces for a particular service.

After the navigation tab is updated, you need to configure authentication. This can be accomplished by right-clicking the Project name and clicking **Show Project View**. Then, click the **Security Configurations** tab. The screen shown in Figure 7-29 shows the page where authentication is configured.

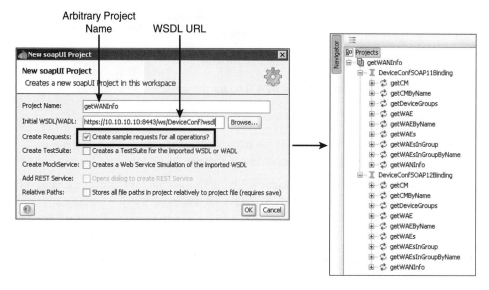

Figure 7-28 *Accessing the XML-API Using soapUI*

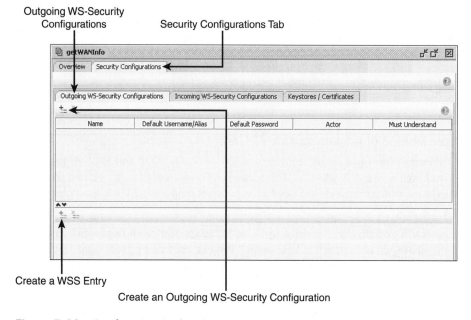

Figure 7-29 *Configuring Authentication in soapUI*

From within this window, click the upper **+**, which is shown in Figure 7-29 and labeled as **Create an Outgoing WS-Security Configuration**. As shown in Figure 7-30, supply a unique name for the configuration, click **OK**, and then add the username and password into the tabular list that appears.

Figure 7-30   *Creating Outgoing WS-Security Configuration in soapUI*

Then, click the lower **+**, which is shown in Figure 7-29 and labeled as **Create a WSS Entry.** As shown in Figure 7-31, change the type of entry to **Username**, and then supply the username and password in the Username tab that appears. Change the Password Type to **PasswordText.**

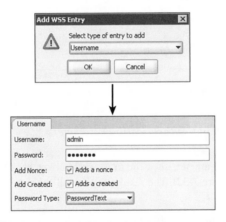

Figure 7-31   *Creating a WSS Entry in soapUI*

With the WS-Security configuration and WSS entry supplied, return to the navigation bar and expand to the interface you wish to use. Expand the interface, and notice that a **Request 1** is contained within the interface (this is an artifact of selecting **Create Requests** checkbox when creating the new soapUI project). Double-click the **Request 1** entry to cause the request to appear in the workspace. Then, click the **Aut** button in the bottom left of the request workspace window. Change the **Outgoing WSS** to the credential set created earlier (in this case, it was called **admin**). Ensure that the request URL is correct at the top of the workspace as shown in Figure 7-32.

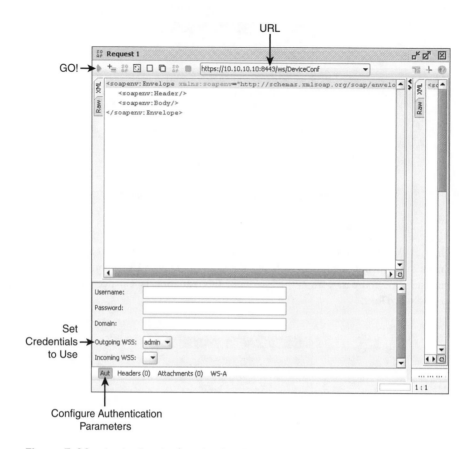

Figure 7-32 *Assigning Authentication Parameters*

After these parameters are set, click the green right-arrow at the top of the window (labeled as GO! in Figure 7-32). The results of the call are displayed in the workspace, as shown in Figure 7-33.

As described previously, this method is a simple way of accessing the XML-API and viewing the data that is made available. Customers that are interested in integrating WAAS into existing management, monitoring, and performance visibility dashboards should consider using a solution from a vendor (three recommendations are provided previously) that already supports the XML-API, or take advantage of the published XML-API specifications to integrate WAAS into a customer-owned management system.

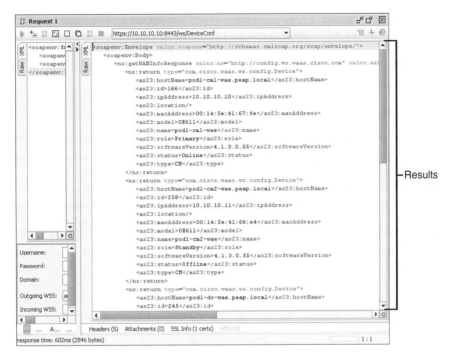

Figure 7-33 *Viewing XML-API Call Results*

Summary

This chapter provided a detailed examination of how to move from unconfigured WAAS devices to registered, grouped, monitored, upgraded devices that are integrated into the enterprise management and monitoring framework provided by the Cisco WAAS CM. An intuitive and easy-to-use setup script is provided that walks you through basic network configuration. From there, you can register devices within the CM, which provides a scalable, secure, and simple means of centralized system administration and monitoring. The CM and the managed WAAS devices remain in constant communication through the CMS service and the frequent synchronization of configuration, monitoring, and reporting data based on the configured LCM cycle. The CM provides powerful and flexible capabilities for centralized system management, including device groups, which help automate the distribution of configuration to its managed devices. The CM also provides facilities for centralized software upgrade and rollback using a scalable architecture that enables the managed nodes to directly download software images, thereby eliminating the CM as a bottleneck in the download and upgrade. Flexible monitoring and reporting enable administrators to quickly organize data that is important to them and ensure that views are preserved across administrative sessions. Useful reports can be scheduled for e-mail delivery, or chart data can be quickly fetched in PDF or CSV format directly from the CM GUI.

The CM provides intuitive alarm visualization and management mechanisms that alert you when a threshold has been exceeded. You can act upon an alarm or, if you do not want to be notified of that particular alarm again in the future, acknowledge the alarm. The CM and each of the managed WAAS devices can be integrated into existing monitoring architectures that leverage syslog and SNMP. Protection of the CM database is simple and straightforward, similar to protecting the running-configuration and startup-configuration files on a router.

With the power to configure virtually any aspect of a WAAS device and in a scalable manner, most enterprise organizations find that their day-to-day administration, management, and monitoring tasks are performed through the CM's easy-to-use interface. Having a scalable, secure, and simple architecture for centralized management of a large fabric of distributed nodes is essential for controlling operational costs associated with IT systems, which is exactly what the CM affords organizations that have deployed Cisco WAAS. Having a powerful XML-API interface for retrieving numerous pieces of monitoring information, WAAS can also integrate cleanly into existing customer management, monitoring, and performance visibility solutions, and several vendors have pre-packaged systems that include integration with the WAAS CM XML-API.

Chapter 8

Configuring WAN Optimization

The capabilities of Cisco Wide Area Application Services (WAAS) are commonly associated with the terms wide-area network (WAN) optimization and application acceleration. On the surface, these two terms seem similar, but in fact, they are fundamentally different. WAN optimization refers to a set of capabilities that operate in an application-agnostic manner, either at the transport or network layer, making the transfer of information over the WAN more efficient. In the case of Cisco WAAS, WAN optimization is implemented in the transport layer. Application acceleration, on the other hand, refers to a set of capabilities that operate in an application-specific manner, and interacts at the application protocol layer to improve performance. This chapter briefly revisits the WAN optimization capabilities of Cisco WAAS and provides an in-depth examination of WAN optimization configuration and monitoring. Chapter 9, "Configuring Application Acceleration," examines application acceleration capabilities of Cisco WAAS and their configuration and monitoring.

Cisco WAAS WAN Optimization Capabilities

Cisco WAAS provides transparent, network-integrated WAN optimization capabilities that improve efficiency and performance for almost any Transmission Control Protocol (TCP) application operating over the WAN or between data center locations. The primary Cisco WAAS WAN optimization components include:

- Transport Flow Optimization (TFO)

- Data Redundancy Elimination (DRE)

- Persistent LZ Compression (PLZ)

In addition, several features are provided by WAAS that help minimize complexity, improve integration, and enable interoperability in environments that include devices that might be problematic to WAN optimization. All these features and capabilities are configurable from either the command-line interface (CLI) or from the Central Manager (CM) graphical user interface (GUI). As a refresher, this section provides a review of the WAN optimization components and the configuration of each.

Transport Flow Optimization

TFO is the foundational optimization layer of Cisco WAAS. TFO in itself applies optimizations to TCP to improve efficiency and mitigate performance limitations, as discussed in Chapter 1, "Introduction to Cisco Wide Area Application Services (WAAS)," caused by transport latency and packet loss and maximize application throughput over the network. Along with providing these optimizations, TFO acts as the data path for all the other optimizations for Cisco WAAS. That is, other optimizations that are being employed are called after being handled by TFO.

At its lowest layer, TFO provides a TCP proxy for connections that are being optimized by the WAAS devices in the network. That is, connections from the source to the adjacent WAAS device are terminated locally by the WAAS device, new connections are managed over the WAN between WAAS devices, and new connections are generated on the remote local-area network (LAN) between the remote WAAS device and the destination. Connections between the source and the adjacent WAAS device, or between the destination and the adjacent WAAS device, are called *original connections*. Connections between the WAAS devices are called *optimized connections*. It is important to note that the TCP proxy provided by Cisco WAAS is transparent, and the original and optimized connections are dispersed physical segments of the same logical end-to-end TCP connection. Directed mode, which is discussed later in the chapter, is an alternative implementation that uses the same TCP proxy and architecture, but takes advantage of User Datagram Protocol (UDP) encapsulation which may be beneficial in certain environments.

The WAAS device, and more specifically its TCP proxy, manages the exchange of information from an original connection to an optimized connection and visa versa. For example, assume a user has a connection that is being optimized by WAAS. This user is downloading an object via HTTP from a web server. As the server is sending data in response to the user's HTTP GET request, the data is received by the WAAS device adjacent to the server as part of the original connection. The data is then buffered in the TCP receive buffer on the WAAS device optimized connection. Based on the configured policy, discussed later in the chapter, the WAAS device may pass this buffered data to other optimization services, such as DRE, PLZ, or an application accelerator for encoding or other acceleration services. TFO, which acts as a data stream processor (as opposed to a packet-processing architecture that works at Layer 3), then manages the drainage of the original data through the optimization service(s) and ultimately to the optimized connection TCP transmit buffer, and the data is subsequently transmitted. The optimized data is then received by the WAAS device adjacent to the user (through network interception or physical inline deployment) and is placed in the TCP receive buffer for the optimized connection. TFO then drains the data to the appropriate optimization or acceleration services (or both) for decoding. These services then write the original data into the original connection TCP transmit buffer, and the data is subsequently transmitted to the recipient.

Figure 8-1 shows an example of how the TCP proxy interacts with data from optimized and original connections. This assumes that automatic discovery, which is discussed later in the chapter, has already completed.

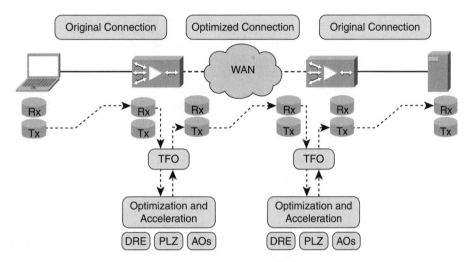

Figure 8-1   *TCP Proxy Interacting with Original and Optimized Connections*

The optimization capabilities that are enacted by TFO are determined by the policy applied to the connection. The policy that is applied to the connection, and how this is determined, is discussed later in the chapter. TFO, on its own, provides a series of optimizations, which help improve performance for TCP-based applications:

■   **Loss mitigation:** With a TCP proxy, packet loss encountered in the WAN is managed by the sending WAAS device. Thus, the TCP stack for the original sender (for instance, the user or the server) notices fewer instances of lost packets, and therefore, the TCP stack on the original sender is less impacted. In short, a TCP proxy shields the communicating nodes from the vast majority of packet loss encountered in the WAN. Furthermore, the WAAS devices employ selective acknowledgment (SACK) and extensions to minimize the amount of data that must be retransmitted when a segment has been lost in the WAN.

■   **Latency mitigation:** With a TCP proxy, impact from latency encountered in the WAN is minimized, as the adjacent WAAS devices manage TCP for each original connection. That is, the WAAS devices locally acknowledge TCP segments for the original senders as long as capacity is available in TFO for that connection, which provides the sender a LAN-like TCP experience. This enables the sending nodes to transmit more data over the network more quickly, because they do not have to wait for acknowledgments from nodes that are across the high-latency WAN before their transmit buffers can be relieved and allowed to send more data.

■   **Slow-start mitigation:** TFO employs large initial windows (see RFC 3390), which double the original segment size for new connections. By increasing the original segment size, connections exit slow-start more quickly, allowing them to more rapidly enter congestion avoidance where bandwidth scalability techniques are employed that can improve throughput. This enables short-lived connections to transmit data more rapidly from the start of the connection, resulting in fewer round-trips required to transmit the same amount of data.

■ **Bandwidth scalability:** TFO uses window scaling, large static buffers (or dynamic buffers, as discussed later in this chapter), and Binary Increase Congestion avoidance to enable certain applications to better use available bandwidth capacity. This is particularly important for high-bandwidth, high-delay, and high bandwidth-delay networks, which are generally difficult for a sender to fully capitalize on with a legacy TCP implementation, including data protection applications, replication applications, and others such as the File Transfer Protocol (FTP).

■ **Fairness:** WAAS TFO ensures performance fairness across optimized and unoptimized connections. That is, optimized connections, which are inherently more aggressive on the network, still compete fairly with unoptimized connections for available WAN bandwidth regardless of the round-trip time of any segment of any connection or the connection's characteristics including window size or congestion avoidance algorithm. In this way, optimized connections do not starve unoptimized connections of available network bandwidth, thus ensuring performance consistency across connections.

Data Redundancy Elimination

DRE is another optimization component provided by Cisco WAAS, which provides protocol-agnostic, bidirectional deduplication of data traversing the WAN. DRE leverages both disk and memory as a compression history from which data from an original connection can be compared to identify and remove redundancy from the transmission. If redundant data patterns are identified, DRE can replace the redundant pattern with signatures that the peer WAAS device understands, which are much smaller in size, and identify the original chunk of data to be used when rebuilding the message. This enables the WAAS device to provide potentially high levels of compression, particularly when managing the transmission of content that has been transmitted previously in its entirety or partially.

DRE can be thought of as a database containing chunks of data from previous exchanges on optimized connections with an index designed for fast lookup and retrieval of a chunk of data based on its signature. The DRE index is managed in memory and stored persistently on disk, which ensures that the WAAS device retains its compression history even if it is rebooted. The WAAS device memory is provisioned to allow the index to remain fully in memory to minimize swapping, ensuring high performance and low latency during run-time operation. Additionally, WAAS device memory is optimized using an extended buffer cache to minimize the impact of flushing of DRE chunk data from main memory to disk. These system adjustments help minimize the amount of operational latency incurred when leveraging DRE against an optimized connection. By optimizing access to the DRE database index and data, encode and decode operations can be performed against optimized connections without adding substantial latency to the connection or the operations it carries.

To quantify this point, WAAS devices generally add less than 1 millisecond (ms) of latency during encode or decode, meaning that when a pair of devices are optimizing traffic, typically less than 2 ms of total latency is added. Under full load conditions, this number is generally less than 5 ms of latency, and even in such scenarios, the latency added is miniscule when considering the performance improvements provided by those same optimization components. In addition, DRE itself also provides latency mitigation, which mitigates any latency it might add. By potentially replacing a large amount of data with a few small signatures, the WAAS devices can send a smaller number of packets over the optimized connections over the WAN to complete an operation than are necessary on the original connections. Thus, the amount of latency perceived by the application is often reduced.

DRE stores signature and chunk information per-peer as described in Chapter 1, meaning that entries in the DRE index and chunk repository are specific to a particular peer. This means that if a WAAS device peers with 10 other WAAS devices that are identified during automatic discovery, the DRE compression history on that WAAS device has entries specific to each of the 10 peers. Although the use of a per-peer context architecture is less efficient in terms of storage utilization (a chunk of data may be stored once for each peer that it is transferred to), it provides tremendous advantages in terms of the following:

- **Operational latency:** Connections can be quickly associated with the appropriate DRE chunk repository and index. Lookup operations are performed against a smaller, isolated database, and fewer I/O operations are required to extract data or write data.

- **Compression scalability:** By using a per-peer architecture with higher efficiency and lower latency, more data can be processed by the system with less overhead. This enables the WAAS devices to reach higher levels of throughput than a device with a shared compression architecture. Compression scalability refers to the maximum application layer throughput that the system can sustain with heavily compressed content. A system with a high degree of compression scalability is one in which the compression itself does not impede the performance of the applications being compressed.

- **Isolated eviction:** By using a per-peer architecture, eviction (removal of old data to make room for new data) is contained to a specific peer, which isolates the performance impact caused by compression peers being out of synchronization. With a shared architecture, eviction impacts all peers that have previously used any of the data that has been evicted, meaning that the performance of a substantial portion of the network could be impacted.

For a more complete examination comparing per-peer compression architectures against shared architectures, please refer to Chapter 1, which highlights the strengths and weaknesses of each.

Persistent LZ Compression

PLZ is another WAN optimization component provided by WAAS. Similar to DRE, PLZ leverages a history of previously seen information to reduce redundancy. Whereas DRE provides a peer-to-peer compression history, PLZ provides a connection-oriented compression history; that is, PLZ leverages information found within a single connection to employ compression. PLZ is applied in memory only and thus provides high levels of throughput and minimal operational latency. PLZ is effective at compressing not only content that has never been seen by DRE before, but also DRE signature information. Unlike other compression technologies, PLZ implements a persistent connection history; that is, a larger amount of memory (a larger compression window) is allocated for compression per connection than a standard LZ or DEFLATE algorithm would provide. With a larger history and compression window, PLZ is capable of generally providing higher levels of compression.

PLZ is also applied adaptively. In certain circumstances and with certain data types (such as encrypted data), PLZ might not be effective. The WAAS device analyzes connection data in real time using entropy and other calculations to determine if the data is compressible and if PLZ will have a positive effect on that data. If the WAAS device determines that the data is not compressible or that PLZ would not provide any benefit, PLZ is not employed for that portion of the data. Furthermore, if DRE compression achieves high compression ratios (above 90 percent), PLZ is not employed as aggressively for that portion of the data.

Automatic Discovery

Cisco WAAS uses an automatic discovery mechanism to intelligently determine which two WAAS devices are closest to the two nodes involved in a connection. The automatic discovery process, which is a component of TFO, is commonly referred to as TFO automatic discovery (TFO AD). TFO AD operates by adding a small 12-byte data unit to the options field of TCP connection setup packets received by a WAAS device through interception when an optimization policy is configured for that connection or connection type. This 12-byte option, which is listed as TCP option 33 (or as hex 0x21 in packet capture applications), contains the following information:

- Administrative information, including TCP option size, version, and subversion that allows for forward and backward compatibility and interoperability among WAAS devices of different versions.

- A command that informs other WAAS devices that this particular WAAS device would like to optimize this connection and a device identifier of the local device (which is the Media Access Control [MAC] address of the first GigabitEthernet interface).

- Optimization capabilities that define optimizations the WAAS device would like to apply to this connection based on the configured policy for this connection type and load conditions of the device.

The TFO AD option is applied only to TCP synchronize (SYN), synchronize and acknowledge (SYN/ACK) when the original SYN was marked, and acknowledge (ACK) messages when the SYN and SYN/ACK were marked, used for the connection setup, and is not applied to TCP data segments. The full exchange of data occurs over all three of these messages, and as such, WAAS devices must see the full three-way handshake of the TCP connection to discover one another. In situations where WAAS devices do not see the full three-way handshake, they cannot automatically discover one another and cannot apply optimization to that particular connection. Such connections are handled as pass-through.

Upon receipt of an unmarked TCP SYN packet, the first WAAS device adds the TFO AD option to the packet, containing the information in the preceding list, and forwards the packet onto the network, assuming a peer WAAS device sees the marked packet. If any additional WAAS devices along the path see the marked TCP SYN packet, those additional devices make a note of the device ID found in the marked TCP SYN packet, its version, and the level of optimization the device would like to apply. In this way, each WAAS device keeps a record of the original WAAS device that saw and marked the SYN packet, which is used later should optimization be employed.

When the destination node receives the TCP SYN packet, it generally responds with a TCP SYN/ACK packet to begin the second part of the three-way handshake (to establish the TCP connection). If the destination node does not handle TCP options, these packets are dropped, which are handled by the TFO blacklist functionality described later in the chapter. Similar to the manner in which WAAS devices react to the TCP SYN packet, the first WAAS device to see the SYN/ACK packet applies the data unit to the TCP option (using option 33), which is generally at the other end of the network from the WAAS device that originally marked the SYN packet. At this point, the WAAS device marking the SYN/ACK packet knows information about the WAAS device that marked the SYN packet, including its device ID and optimization policy. The marked SYN/ACK packet is then sent through the network toward the connection requestor. Any intermediary WAAS devices between the WAAS device sending the marked SYN/ACK packet and the original WAAS device that marked the SYN packet now know that they are not the outermost WAAS devices for this connection (that is, closest to the two endpoints of the TCP connection), because the SYN/ACK packet is marked with another device's markings, and thus does not participate in optimization. These devices consider themselves intermediary for the connection (not an outermost endpoint) and simply handle the connection traffic as pass-through, leaving the optimization of the connection to the outermost WAAS devices.

When the WAAS device closest to the connection requestor receives the marked TCP SYN/ACK packet, containing information about the WAAS device closest to the connection recipient, it examines the contents of the TFO AD option. The option, similar to the TFO AD option used on the TCP SYN packet, contains the device ID, intention to optimize, and optimization capabilities. An ACK packet containing a TFO AD option that acknowledges successful completion of automatic discovery is then generated by the WAAS device that marked the SYN packet, which notifies the WAAS device that marked the SYN/ACK packet that optimization can commence.

At this time, the connection is intercepted by the TCP proxy service of both WAAS devices, and connection data is routed through the appropriate optimization components based on the least common denominator of the optimization components advertised by both WAAS devices. The WAAS device closest to the connection destination then generates and sends a TCP ACK to the connection destination to complete the three-way handshake. The connection requestor, which just received the SYN/ACK (after it was received by the WAAS device that marked the SYN), sends an ACK to complete the establishment of the connection. As discussed earlier in the chapter, the connection between the TCP endpoint and the WAAS device is considered an *original connection*, and the connection between the two WAAS devices is considered an *optimized connection*. Figure 8-2 illustrates the full automatic discovery process. Notice that the TCP connection setup behavior remains unchanged from the perspective of the TCP endpoints (client and server in this example).

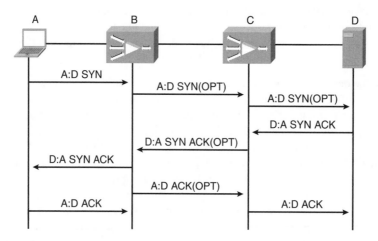

Figure 8-2   *TFO Automatic Discovery, Two WAAS Devices*

TFO AD natively supports hierarchical networks where multiple WAAS devices may exist in the path between two TCP endpoints. The operation of TFO AD automatically identifies the outermost WAAS devices for optimization—that is, the WAAS devices closest to the TCP endpoints. Any intermediary WAAS devices—that is, the WAAS devices in between the outermost WAAS devices—simply treat the connection as pass-through and allow the outermost WAAS devices to apply optimization. Pass-through connections on intermediary WAAS devices do not impact the number of connections that can be optimized by an intermediary WAAS device. Figure 8-3 shows how TFO Automatic Discovery works in a hierarchical network, that is, a network where intermediary WAAS devices exist. Notice that WAAS device C treats the connection as pass-through after the SYN/ACK with the marking from D is received.

Note   When a WAAS device has reached its connection limit or has gone into overload due to system load conditions, it does not participate in automatic discovery and, as such, cannot accept new connections to optimize. Connections encountered during this time are handled pass-through, which allows the communication between TCP endpoints to continue. If the network design, traffic flow, and placement of the WAAS devices permit, another pair of WAAS devices may be deployed in the network in such a way that enables them to optimize the connection, even if one or more intermediary WAAS devices is in an overload state or unavailable.

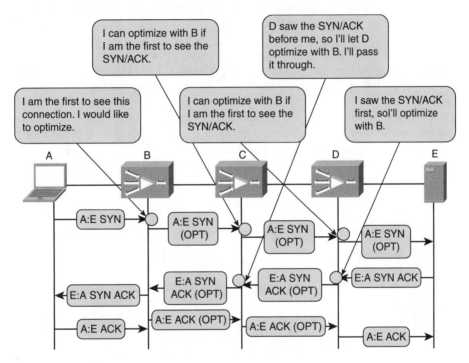

Figure 8-3 *TFO Automatic Discovery, Three or More WAAS Devices*

Directed Mode

By default, Cisco WAAS is fully network transparent in its operation and optimization. In certain environments, it is desirable to either ensure a persistent network path between accelerators or provide support in environments where devices exist that do not behave well with optimization devices. For instance, certain firewall devices and other device types do not permit connections where TCP sequence numbers deviate from the sequence numbers set in during the connection establishment. Cisco security devices provide native support for WAAS optimization, meaning they permit such traffic without impacting optimization. Devices from other vendors might not have the same level of intelligence as it relates to accepting optimized traffic.

Directed mode is a configurable option provided in Cisco WAAS that allows optimized TCP segments to be encapsulated into UDP datagrams prior to transmission over the network. This is drastically different than the tunneling approach provided in packet-processing optimization devices in a number of ways, the two most important include:

- **Automatic discovery:** Tunnels do not have to be configured between endpoints. Rather, WAAS devices still automatically discover one another. Directed mode is advertised through automatic discovery, along with tunnel establishment parameters.

- **Encapsulation of proxied traffic:** The WAAS TCP proxy is still used, and optimized segments are merely encapsulated into a UDP datagram. The benefits of the WAAS TCP proxy—including shielding TCP endpoints from loss—are still fully employed.

With directed mode, automatic discovery operates in an identical manner to how it operates when directed mode is not used. The key difference is that after peers have identified one another, UDP encapsulation is employed for all future segments for the connection, and the TCP connection over the WAN is reset to remove state between intermediary devices that perform connection state management, such as firewalls. Figure 8-4 shows the automatic discovery process when directed mode is used, and Figure 8-5 shows the encapsulation process used by directed mode as an augmentation to Figure 8-1. Figure 8-5 shows only one side of the network; assume the other side of the network is identical.

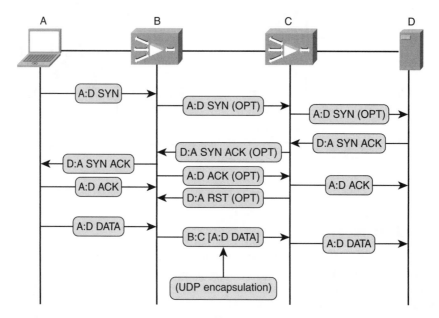

Figure 8-4 *TFO Automatic Discovery with Directed Mode*

When directed mode is employed, the TCP maximum segment size (MSS) is automatically reduced to account for the UDP encapsulation used by directed mode. Directed mode uses UDP port 4050 (IANA registered) by default, and this port number is configurable as shown later in the chapter in the section, "Directed Mode." The port number used for directed mode should be consistent on all WAAS devices that are communicating in a

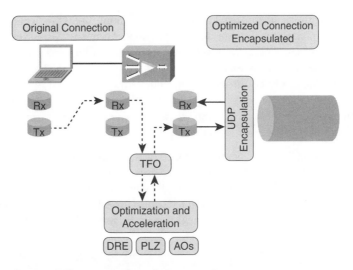

Figure 8-5 *Directed Mode Encapsulation*

directed mode deployment, and any intermediary firewalls should be configured to allow this UDP port to pass. Directed mode is a feature introduced in Cisco WAAS v4.1.1 and is not backward compatible with Cisco WAAS v4.0.

Directed mode is automatically used between two WAAS devices if one of them is configured to use directed mode. Therefore, when you configure directed mode on any device, all of its optimized connections to any v4.1.x peer automatically convert to directed mode. Any connections between a v4.1.x device configured for directed mode and a legacy (v4.0.x) peer do not use directed mode and instead use transparent mode of operation.

Configuring WAN Optimization

While the previous section provided an introduction to the WAN optimization capabilities provided by Cisco WAAS, this section examines how to configure these features. In the default configuration, all the WAN optimization facilities are automatically enabled, minimizing complexity associated with initially deploying systems. Although licenses must be configured on the system to enable these features to operate (which is discussed in this section), the configuration of these components is provided for completeness in understanding rather than as a requirement for deploying a device.

Configuring Licenses

WAN optimization features in Cisco WAAS require that the Transport license be installed on each WAAS device. Application acceleration features, discussed in Chapter 9, require that the Enterprise license be installed on each device. Additionally, certain other features rely on the Enterprise license, such as disk encryption (discussed in Chapter 9 with Secure Sockets Layer [SSL] acceleration) and FlowAgent for accurate application response time monitoring (NetQoS SuperAgent and Cisco Network Analysis Module integration). Video stream splitting, discussed in Chapter 9, requires that the video license be installed on each WAAS device. Virtual blades (VB), discussed in Chapter 10, "Branch Office Virtualization," require that the Virtual-Blade license be installed. Licenses are not enforced on each WAAS device, but they must be configured before the respective services or components can be used. Licenses can be configured from the CLI of the device, or from the CM GUI.

When configuring licenses from the CM GUI, it is important to note that they can be configured only from the device context. Licenses cannot be configured from the device group context. To configure the licenses applied on a device from the CM, as demonstrated in Figure 8-6, navigate to the *device context* > **Admin** > **License Management**, and click the appropriate checkboxes next to each license, followed by **Submit**.

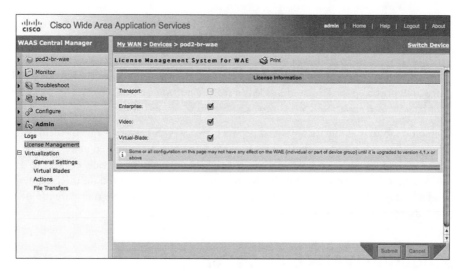

Figure 8-6   *Configuring Licenses in the CM*

Alternatively, licenses can be configured from the device CLI. Example 8-1 shows the commands used to enable a license and show the status of a license.

Example 8-1   *Adding License From CLI*

```
pod1-br-wae# license add ?
  LINE  Enter a license name ('show license' displays the list of valid names)
pod1-br-wae# license add Video ?
LINE  <cr>
pod1-br-wae# license add Video
WARNING: There is an enabled accelerator in the system, but accelerator
doesn't optimize the traffic yet. It takes about 2 minutes to start
```

```
the traffic optimization after the license is activated.
pod1-br-wae# show license ?
  ¦     Output Modifiers
  <cr>
pod1-br-wae# show license
License Name    Status        Activation Date Activated By
- - - - - - -   - - - - - -.  - - - - - - -.  - - - - - -

Transport       not active
Enterprise      active        05/05/2009      CMS
Video           active        05/06/2009      admin
Virtual-Blade   active        05/05/2009      CMS
```

Note   The Transport and Enterprise license are mutually exclusive. The Enterprise license includes the Transport license functionality. The Video and Virtual-Blade license are dependent upon the Enterprise license. Do not be alarmed if the Transport license is not active, as long as the Enterprise license is active.

Enabling and Disabling Features

All the WAN optimization features of the WAAS device can be enabled or disabled via the CLI or from the CM GUI. Additionally, these features can be enabled or disabled against multiple devices using device groups. Because TFO acts as the data path for all optimization services of Cisco WAAS, it must be enabled for any other optimization capabilities to be employed. That is, you cannot leverage DRE, PLZ, or any application accelerator, also known as an application optimizer (AO), without using TFO. If TFO is disabled, no optimization is applied. All WAN optimization and application acceleration features of the WAAS device are enabled by default. Generally, it is not necessary to disable any of these features unless you are operating in an environment where only TCP optimization is required, or, when deploying application acceleration features in a controlled manner over a period of time. The former is common in cases where bandwidth is not a performance-limiting factor, but latency or loss might be impacting application throughput. For instance, in an implementation where multiple gigabit links between data centers are in place, DRE and PLZ can be disabled, and Cisco WAAS leverage TFO to help applications "fill-the-pipe." In these scenarios, the WAAS devices help the applications better use available link capacity by overcoming latency and loss limitations. Similarly, a replication accelerator mode is provided, discussed later in this chapter in the section, "Replication Acceleration," to also provide similar optimization while also employing DRE and PLZ in addition to TFO. This mode should be used only in data center to data center scenarios where there is measurable latency (more than 20 ms) and high bandwidth.

Example 8-2 shows how to enable and disable each optimization service, including application optimizers. Note that only those features that are not enabled appear in the device running configuration.

Example 8-2   *Globally Enabling and Disabling Optimization and Acceleration Features in the Device CLI*

```
WAAS1# config
WAAS1(config)# no tfo optimize
! disables all optimization
WAAS1(config)# tfo optimize DRE yes compression none
! disables LZ only)
WAAS1(config)# tfo optimize DRE no compression LZ
! disables DRE only
WAAS1(config)# tfo optimize full
! enables all optimization
WAAS1(config)# end
WAAS1# show tfo detail


   Policy Engine Config Item           Value
   — — — — — — — — — — — —·            — —·
   State                               Registered
   Default Action                      Use Policy
   Connection Limit                    750
   Effective Limit                     740
   Keepalive timeout                   3.0 seconds


WAAS1# config
WAAS1(config)# accelerator ?
  cifs           CIFS accelerator configuration
  epm            EPM accelerator configuration
  http           HTTP accelerator configuration
  mapi           MAPI accelerator configuration
  nfs            NFS accelerator configuration
  ssl            SSL accelerator configuration
  video          VIDEO accelerator configuration
  windows-print  Windows-Print Accelerator configuration

WAAS1(config)# accelerator nfs ?
  enable     Enable accelerator
  exception  Exception handling for AO
pod1-br-wae(config)#accelerator nfs enable
Enabled nfs accelerator
```

As shown in Figure 8-7, these same features can be enabled or disabled in the CM GUI. In most cases, these features are enabled or disabled on a device group containing multiple devices throughout the network that require only a specific set of services. As an example, WAAS devices that need to perform only TCP optimization can be added to a device group, and the appropriate configuration can be applied against the device group.

For reference, these features can be enabled or disabled from the CM GUI by visiting either the *device context* or *device group context* > **Configure** > **Acceleration** > **Enabled Features.**

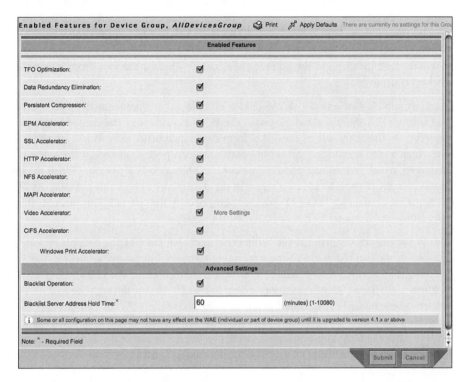

Figure 8-7   *Enabling and Disabling Optimization and Acceleration Features in the CM GUI*

Note   EndPoint Mapper (EPM) Classification, one of the features listed in Figure 8-7, is discussed later in the chapter. EPM is discussed in the context of classification, which is necessary to determine which policy and optimization/acceleration features to apply. EPM is most commonly used with MAPI (Microsoft Exchange and Outlook) acceleration, as discussed in Chapter 9.

Automatic discovery is a core component of the Cisco WAAS architecture and cannot be enabled or disabled.

TFO Blacklist Operation

Another component of TFO AD is *blacklist operation*. TFO AD leverages TCP options during connection establishment to identify the outermost WAAS devices in the traffic path between two TCP endpoints. After the WAAS devices have automatically discovered one another, they can begin optimizing the connection. In some situations, network components along the path might be configured to drop packets that contain unknown TCP options. TFO blacklist operation addresses this behavior. Should a TCP SYN drop be detected—specifically a drop of a SYN packet containing the WAAS TCP option—the WAAS device closest to the point of loss remembers that the SYN should be sent without the TCP option when going to this particular destination. Upon the next TCP SYN sent by the connection originator, the WAAS device that detected the drop strips the TCP option after processing its contents. This enables the WAAS devices to automatically discover one another up to the point in the network where the device dropping marked packets is deployed.

As an example, assume that a WAAS device is deployed in a branch office with a user, and another WAAS device is deployed at the WAN boundary of the corporate campus network, on the other side of the WAN from the branch office user. Within the data center, which is well behind the WAN boundary of the corporate network, a firewall is deployed, which is dropping packets that contain unknown TCP options. When the user in the branch attempts to access a server in the data center behind this firewall, the TCP SYN packet containing TFO AD options is dropped by the firewall. This prevents the user from establishing a TCP connection with the server.

The WAAS device deployed in the campus network—in front of the data center—detects the loss of the marked TCP SYN packet, and adds the destination IP address to the TFO blacklist for a period of 60 minutes (or the value configured for the Blacklist Server Address Hold Time). Any connections going to that IP passing through the pair of WAAS devices going toward the destination server do not have the TFO AD options appended to them. However, if a SYN/ACK packet from the server, sent in response to an unmarked SYN (with no TFO AD options), is received, the WAAS device at the WAN boundary learns that the destination server cannot receive marked packets but can receive unmarked packets.

To notify the peer WAAS device that the connection can be optimized, the campus WAAS device appends the TFO AD options to the SYN/ACK packet, which was originally sent by the server. The branch WAAS device, when in receipt of the SYN/ACK packet with the TFO AD option set, then learns that the destination server cannot receive options but can be optimized. This allows the two WAAS devices to continue to discover one another and apply optimization to the connections going to that server (or any server behind that firewall).

Figure 8-8 shows an example of the TFO blacklist operation.

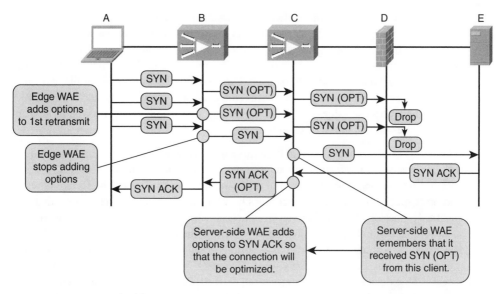

Figure 8-8 *TFO Blacklist Operation*

TFO blacklist operation is helpful in environments where a device that drops marked packets is not deployed between WAAS devices. In environments where firewalls are deployed between WAAS devices, one of the following conditions must be met to ensure interoperability with Cisco WAAS. If these conditions are not met, optimization does not happen, as devices are not able to automatically discover one another or optimized packets are not allowed to pass:

■ **Cisco firewalls:** All Cisco firewall products, including the Cisco Private Internet eXchange (PIX), Cisco Adaptive Security Appliance (ASA), IOS Firewall, and Firewall Services Module (FWSM), have software versions and configurations that provide full transparent interoperability with Cisco WAAS. A host of whitepapers and configuration guides for Cisco firewalls, including references that outline software version requirements, is available on Cisco.com.

■ **Non-Cisco firewalls:** TCP option 33 (hex 0x21) must be permitted and stateful inspection of TCP packets needs to be disabled. WAAS devices initially shift the sequence number of optimized connections by 2 GB to ensure that optimized packets are discarded if they are received by a TCP endpoint. WAAS devices perform verification of sequence numbers for optimized connections to ensure that sequence numbers are within the expected range. This provides protection against attacks that use out-of-sequence segments and is similar to the sequence number protection provided by firewalls.

In addition to use of TCP options, WAAS shifts the sequence number used at the start of the optimized connection by 2 GB. Thus, the sequence numbers between the original and optimized connections are not identical after automatic discovery has occurred. Cisco firewalls and other security devices are WAAS-aware and do not have issues with this sequence number shift, but other non-Cisco security devices might have issues with this shift. In such cases, either the device behavior that monitors TCP sequence numbers must be disabled, or, directed mode can be used. Directed mode remains compatible with certain network services, specifically those that are interested in only IP addresses or TCP port numbers, as these values are preserved during connection setup. Directed mode configuration is examined in the next section.

TFO blacklist operation is configured on the same page where WAN optimization and application acceleration features are configured, as shown in Figure 8-7. This includes operational state (enable or disable) and the server address hold time. The server address hold time, specified in minutes, determines how long a WAAS device remembers that a specific destination was unable to receive packets with TCP options applied to them. Should a connection to this destination arrive within the period specified, the WAAS device knows to automatically strip TCP options going to that server. TFO blacklist operation is enabled by default. It is only when TFO blacklist operation is disabled that it appears in the device running-configuration, or, if the hold-down timer has been changed from the default value of 60 minutes. Example 8-3 shows how to enable or disable TFO blacklist operation from the device CLI and adjust the default hold-down timer.

Example 8-3 *Configuring TFO Blacklist Operation*

```
pod1-dc-wae# config term
pod1-dc-wae(config)# no auto-discovery blacklist enable
pod1-dc-wae(config)# auto-discovery blacklist enable
pod1-dc-wae(config)# auto-discovery blacklist hold-time ?
  <1-10080>  Black-list server entry cache hold-time (default 60 minutes)
pod1-dc-wae(config)# auto-discovery blacklist hold-time 30
pod1-dc-wae(config)# end
pod1-dc-wae# show running-config ¦ include auto-disc
auto-discovery blacklist hold-time 30
pod1-dc-wae#
```

Note Notice the use of the pipe character | in the **show running-config** command in Example 8-3. The pipe character allows you to tell the WAAS device to start the output at a specific place in the output as denoted by a supplied regular expression. Additionally, you can tell the WAAS device to include only output that matches or does not match a regular expression. The following syntax example demonstrates use of the pipe character.

pod1-dc-wae# **show run | ?**

begin Begin with the line that matches

exclude Exclude lines that match

include Include lines that match

```
pod1-dc-wae# show run | begin ?
 LINE  Regular Expression
pod1-dc-wae# show run | exclude ?
 LINE  Regular Expression
pod1-dc-wae# show run | include ?
 LINE  Regular Expression
pod1-dc-wae# show run | include
```

The list of servers that have been recorded by TFO AD blacklist operation can be examined from the CLI. Additionally the CLI can be used to examine the list of connections that are currently in the automatic-discovery state. Both of these are shown in Example 8-4. It should be noted that automatic discovery typically completes in a matter of 1.5 network round trips from the perspective of the WAAS device near the connection originator, or 1 network round trip from the perspective of the WAAS device near the connection recipient. Thus, it might be difficult to track connections that are in the automatic discovery phase, because they tend to exit this phase rather rapidly.

Example 8-4   *Blacklist Servers and Connections in Automatic Discovery*

```
pod1-dc-wae# show auto-discovery ?
  blacklist  Display all entries in the Auto-Discovery blacklist server table
  list       List the connections in auto-discovery state
pod1-dc-wae# show auto-discovery blacklist ?
  netmask  Network mask to filter table output
  |        Output Modifiers
  <cr>
pod1-dc-wae# show auto-discovery blacklist netmask ?
  WORD  Display addresses matching network mask [A.B.C.D/E] (eg. 10.15.12.0/24)
pod1-dc-wae# show auto-discovery blacklist
There are no entries in the blacklist
pod1-dc-wae# show auto-discovery ?
  blacklist  Display all entries in the Auto-Discovery blacklist server table
  list       List the connections in auto-discovery state
pod1-dc-wae# show auto-discovery list ?
  |     Output Modifiers
  <cr>
pod1-dc-wae# show auto-discovery list
E: Established, S: Syn, A: Ack, F: Fin, R: Reset
s: sent, r: received, O: Options, P: Passthrough


Src-IP:Port          Dst-IP:Port     Orig-St  Term-St
pod1-dc-wae#
```

Directed Mode

As mentioned earlier in the chapter, directed mode is a feature that allows WAAS devices to encapsulate optimized connection segments into UDP datagrams for transmission over the WAN in environments where path persistence is desired or intermediary devices that do not support optimization devices exist. Directed mode configuration in the CM GUI can be done against an individual device, or an entire device group, and only two parameters exist: enable/disable and UDP port number. The default UDP port number is 4050 (this number is registered with IANA), and enabling directed mode on any WAAS device causes that device to automatically use directed mode with any other 4.1 or newer WAAS device that it peers with. A WAAS device configured with directed mode that peers with a 4.0 device still uses transparent mode to ensure backward compatibility. Figure 8-9 shows the configuration screen for directed mode.

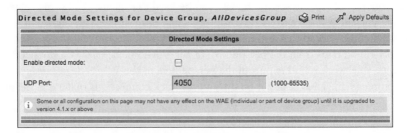

Figure 8-9 *Configuring Directed Mode in CM*

Similarly, directed mode can be configured in the device CLI. Directed mode is not enabled by default and does not appear in the running configuration until it is enabled. The command for the default port number does not appear in the running configuration unless it is changed from UDP/4050. Example 8-5 shows how to configure directed mode from the device CLI and provides relevant **show** commands that provide insight into directed mode operation.

Example 8-5 *Configuring and Monitoring Directed Mode via Device CLI*

```
pod1-dc-wae# config term
pod1-dc-wae(config)# directed-mode ?
  enable  Enable directed mode
pod1-dc-wae(config)# directed-mode enable ?
  port  Configure the directed mode UDP port
  <cr>
pod1-dc-wae(config)# directed-mode enable port ?
  <1000-65535>  Configure the Directed Mode UDP port
pod1-dc-wae(config)# directed-mode enable port 3000
```

```
pod1-dc-wae(config)# end
pod1-dc-wae# show run ¦ include directed
directed-mode enable port 3000
pod1-dc-wae# show directed-mode


Configuration Status:   Enabled
Config Item                          Mode          Value
— — — — —.                            — —           — — —
UDP port                             User          3000
```

Adaptive and Static TCP Buffering

TCP provides connection-oriented, guaranteed delivery of information between two end-points. To ensure guaranteed delivery, TCP employs end-to-end acknowledgments of delivered segments and timers to detect when segments are lost. When an acknowledgment is received from a peer, TCP understands that it no longer needs to retain a copy of that particular segment and can free that portion of its memory to accept and transmit new data. When an acknowledgment is not received, it is up to TCP to retrieve a copy of that segment from memory and retransmit the segment. In short, TCP makes extensive use of memory to ensure guaranteed delivery.

Similarly, TCP uses memory to pipeline the transmission of data. By leveraging a sliding window protocol and memory, TCP can continue to "flush" data, that is, transmit data, while also receiving an equal amount of data from an application process that is attempting to provide it with more data to transmit. In this way, TCP acts as an intermediary between the application and the network, acting as a "traffic cop" and making sure that there are no "accidents" (or that when an accident happens, an exact replica of the accident victims are created to make it look as though the accident never happened).

One of the most significant challenges associated with TCP is its inherent inability to fill a network link that is *long* in terms of distance (latency) and *fat* in terms of capacity (bandwidth). Hence, the term *long fat network* (LFN) came into existence. The challenge with filling LFNs is that a network has some amount of capacity, that is, the amount of data that can be traversing the network at any given point in time. To keep that network full, the sender and receiver must have memory allocated to the connection that matches or exceeds the amount of network capacity. Otherwise, the amount of data that is sent at any given point in time is less than the amount of data that could be carried over the network at a given point in time.

In many cases, the amount of memory allocated to TCP is generally less than the capacity of a modest network multiplied by some measurable distance. In such cases, TCP cannot receive enough data from the application to adequately saturate the network with data because the memory capacity might be inadequate given the amount of data that could be outstanding and unacknowledged on the network while waiting for acknowledgements from the other endpoint. Figure 8-10 shows an example of the performance challenges associated with having limited memory for TCP, especially when dealing with LFNs. In this example, notice the percentage of the cylinder representing the network that is occupied by the squares, which represent packets. (Hint: It's not that full!)

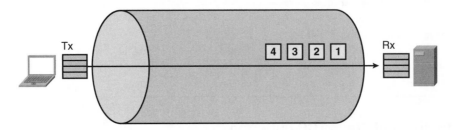

Figure 8-10   *TCP Challenges with LFNs*

TFO, which uses an optimized implementation of TCP based on Binary Increase Congestion TCP (BIC-TCP), also uses memory for the purposes of guaranteed delivery and pipelining like standard TCP. TFO also leverages other TCP optimizations, including window scaling, selective acknowledgment, and large initial windows, to improve TCP performance by allowing connections to exit slow-start more quickly and minimize the performance penalties associated with packet loss. Additionally, WAAS provides substantial amounts of memory to TFO for connection management, which enables bandwidth scalability (fill-the-pipe).

Figure 8-11 shows how throughput can be improved for LFNs when doing nothing more than allocating a larger amount of memory to TCP (assuming the application is not latency-bound). In this example, notice that WAAS devices are deployed at either end of the WAN link. WAAS devices, by default, use adaptive buffering for TCP, which enables memory allocated per connection to grow and shrink with the sender's demands. As an alternative, TCP send and receive memory capacity can be configured manually on the WAAS devices, but this is not recommended.

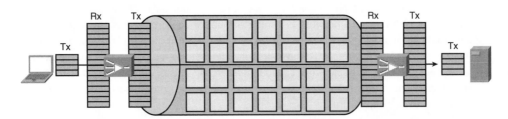

Figure 8-11   *Adding Memory to Improve TCP Performance over LFNs*

The example in Figure 8-11 shows only the benefit of providing increased memory capacity and does not show the benefit of coupling the increased memory capacity with other optimizations, including compression. Increasing the memory allocated to TCP connections, which in the case of WAAS devices is done either via adaptive TFO buffering (memory allocation adjusts as demands adjust) or static TFO buffer configuration (configured by the administrator), allows more data to be in flight between the two TCP endpoints at any given time. This is referred to as "keeping the pipe full," because it can allow the communicating TCP endpoints to fully leverage the available bandwidth of the network. When coupling other optimizations, such as DRE or PLZ, the performance improvement can be exponentially higher as "keeping the pipe full" becomes "keeping the pipe full of compressed data," or "keeping the pipe full of accelerated and compressed data." Consider a scenario where a T3 link connects a campus to a remote data center over very long distance. Although an increase to TCP memory (adjusting TFO buffers) might allow for near line-speed utilization of this link, how much more throughput could be realized if the T3 link was full of data that was compressed at a ratio of 5:1? With a 45-Mbps link carrying streams of 5:1 compressed data while operating at 90 percent of line rate, the application throughput over that network is roughly 200 Mbps. Figure 8-12 illustrates an example of how combining these optimizations impacts throughput.

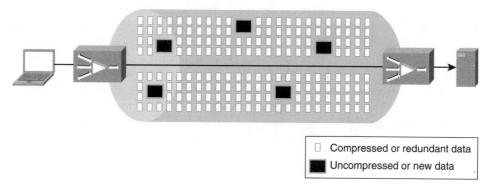

Compressed or redundant data
Uncompressed or new data

Figure 8-12   *Combining TCP Optimization with DRE and PLZ*

By default, WAAS devices monitor the memory requirements of each original and optimized TCP connection handled by the system. As the memory demands for a connection increase, the amount of allocated memory increases with it. Statically increasing the memory allocated to TCP is generally not necessary, even in situations where LFNs are encountered. By default, the WAAS devices are preconfigured with TFO buffer settings that enable the WAAS device to fill a link of capacity equal to the device's rated WAN capacity at a fair distance.

Should you need to disable adaptive buffering and configure static buffering to support a high bandwidth delay product (BDP) network (for reference, high-BDP and LFN are used interchangeably), it is recommended that you adhere to the guidelines in the list that follows. It should be noted that such a change is generally not recommended and the instructions on how to do so should be used only when guided to do so.

- Original connections should not be adjusted unless the LAN throughput has become a bottleneck for WAN throughput (which is rare) due to buffers being undersized. This is typically only common in scenarios where WAN bandwidth is in excess of 45

Mbps or the network latency is in excess of 200 ms. The buffer capacity for original connections must be large enough to accommodate the BDP of the LAN, which is equal to the bandwidth of the network (in bits) multiplied by the latency of the network (in seconds) and divided by eight (to end at a result in bytes). Given that LAN latency is nearly immeasurable, BDP on the LAN is generally small.

■ Optimized connections should be set to four times the BDP of the WAN.

For example, consider a LAN that is 100 Mbps and 1 ms in latency. This equates to 12.5 MBps * 1ms of latency, which results in a BDP of 12.5 KB. Consider a WAN link that is an OC3 in capacity (155 Mbps) with 100 ms of latency. This equates to a BDP of 19.375 MBps * 100 ms (as BDP is the product of bandwidth times delay), which results in a BDP of 1.94 MB. Given the preceding guidelines, the optimized side TFO buffers would need to be adjusted to at least 4 × 1.94 MB, or roughly 8192 KB, and the original side buffers could remain at the default configuration of 32 KB (the default value varies by platform, and 32 KB is the smallest default value).

Like other configuration aspects of the system, TFO buffer settings can be configured from either the CLI or the GUI. Adaptive buffering is enabled by the default and does not appear in the device running configuration; however, the default static buffer settings appears in the device running configuration, whether adaptive buffering is enabled or disabled. If adaptive buffering is disabled, the command used to disable it appears in the running configuration. Changes made from the CM GUI are applied based on the frequency defined by the CM system properties, and it is recommended that these changes be applied against device groups rather than against devices directly if such changes are required. In any case, the configuration change is required on both ends of the WAN link to be effective, so it makes sense to use a device group as opposed to making the configuration changes discretely on each device.

Example 8-6 shows how to configure TFO buffer settings from the CLI.

Example 8-6 *Configuring TFO Buffer Settings*

```
574-3G-DC1-2#sh run
!
! ... portions removed ...
!
tfo tcp optimized-send-buffer 2048
tfo tcp optimized-receive-buffer 2048
no tfo tcp adaptive-buffer-sizing enable
!
! ... portions removed ...
!
574-3G-DC1-2# config term
574-3G-DC1-2(config)# tfo tcp adaptive-buffer-sizing enable
574-3G-DC1-2(config)# end
574-3G-DC1-2(config)# tfo tcp ?
```

```
adaptive-buffer-sizing     TFO TCP adaptive buffer sizing
keepalive                  TCP keepalive, default enabled
optimized-mss              Optimized side TCP max segment size, default 1432
                           bytes
optimized-receive-buffer   Optimized side receive buffer size in KByte, default
                           32KB
optimized-send-buffer      Optimized side send buffer size in KByte, default
                           32KB
original-mss               Original side TCP max segment size,
                           default 1432 bytes
original-receive-buffer    Original side receive buffer size in KByte, default
                           32KB
original-send-buffer       Original side send buffer size in KByte, default 32KB
```

Additionally, a **show** command exists that enables you to see the entirety of the TFO configuration, as demonstrated in Example 8-7.

Example 8-7   *Displaying TFO Configuration*

```
574-3G-DC1-2#sh tfo tcp
Buffer Sizing Status:
   Configured:
      Adaptive buffer sizing               : enabled
         Maximum receive buffer size       : 4096 KB
         Maximum orig side receive buf size : 128 KB (capped)
         Maximum send buffer size          : 4096 KB
      Fixed buffer sizing                  : disabled
         Optimized side receive buffer size : 2048 KB
         Optimized side send buffer size   : 2048 KB
         Original side receive buffer size : 32 KB
         Original side send buffer size    : 32 KB
   Default:
      Adaptive buffer sizes                :
         Maximum receive buffer size       : 4096 KB
         Maximum send buffer size          : 4096 KB
      Fixed buffer sizes:
         Optimized side receive buffer size : 32 KB
         Optimized side send buffer size   : 32 KB
         Original side receive buffer size : 32 KB
         Original side send buffer size    : 32 KB

TFO Status:
   Adaptive buffer sizing is enabled
```

You can also configure TFO buffer settings from the CM GUI by going to either the device or device group context, then going to **Configure > Acceleration > TCP Settings**. From this page, the optimized and original side static buffer sizes can be configured. **From Configure > Acceleration > TCP Adaptive Buffering Settings**, adaptive buffering can be enabled or disabled, and the maximum send and receive buffer sizes can be configured. Both of these pages are shown in Figure 8-13. Changes to the buffer settings of a WAAS device take effect only for new connections that are established after the configuration change. Connections that were established prior to the configuration change are not impacted.

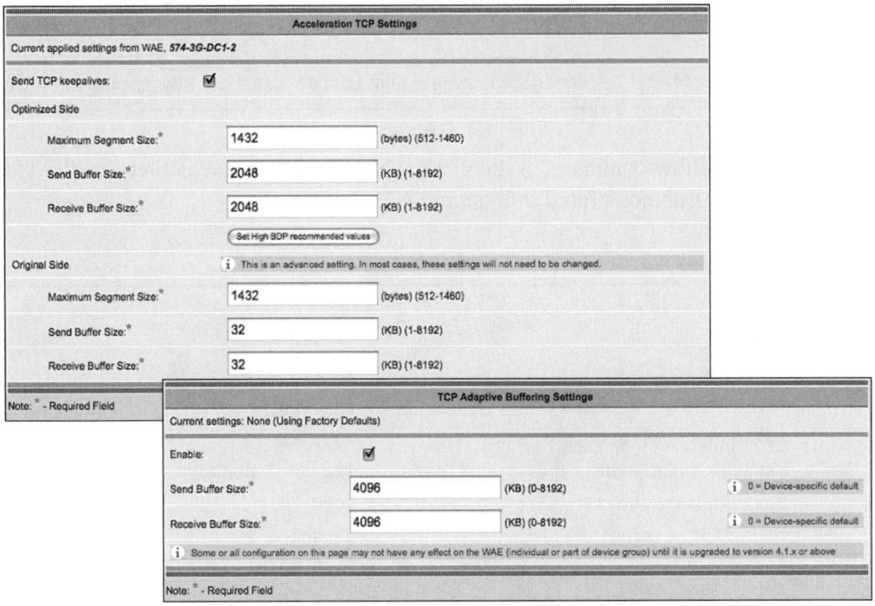

Figure 8-13 *Configuring TFO Buffer Settings from the CM GUI*

If a WAAS device encounters a situation where the system memory is oversubscribed based on the TFO buffer configuration and the number of connections to optimize, it begins reassigning memory from existing connections to support new connections. In this way, the WAAS device can adapt to changes in load, even if it is configured to allocate large amounts of memory to connections and static buffering configurations are used. With adaptive buffering, each device continually reallocates memory based on demand dynamically.

Note Additional TFO settings include TFO keepalives and MSS values. TFO keepalives, enabled by default, help the WAAS devices track connection status. If a keepalive fails after three attempts, the TCP connection the keepalive is associated with is automatically torn down. MSS settings are used to adjust the MSS used on the original and optimized connections. It might be necessary to shrink the MSS values on the optimized connection (optimized-mss) if encapsulation or Virtual Private Network (VPN) infrastructure is present in the network between the WAAS devices to ensure that fragmentation is not encountered because it can significantly impact performance. Both of these settings can be configured from the CLI or CM GUI.

Replication Acceleration

The WAN optimization capabilities presented earlier in this chapter are applicable to virtually any TCP-based application. Use of DRE and PLZ provide the benefit of making transfer of data over the WAN more efficient, allowing for potentially massive throughput increases while saving bandwidth. TFO provides an optimized transport for TCP segment data between endpoints, overcoming many of the throughput limitations caused by the WAN, including latency and packet loss. Certain applications require special attention, which is the primary intent of the application optimizers, which are discussed at length in Chapter 9. Other applications require such high degrees of throughput that use of disk-based techniques such as DRE could impact maximum application performance or limited buffer sizes could compromise maximum throughput.

Data center to data center applications are an example of the latter and have become of paramount importance over the last few years in particular. Given the challenges that face businesses of today's Internet-centric model (always on, continuous operation), including natural disaster, terrorist threats, and regulation from government or industry entities, today's companies are more concerned than ever about data protection, high availability, disaster recovery, and infrastructure mobility. The need to have access to data at all times from a mobile application instance that can be geographically moved rapidly allows these organizations the flexibility they need to keep business moving even in the event of serious disaster. Data must be secured and access to that data controlled, and data loss is becoming less acceptable.

Given that these data center to data center applications help organizations meet these objectives, and that these applications require consistent high performance operation with tremendous data sets over increasing distances, a special device mode targeted for improving the performance of these applications was introduced called *replication accelerator* mode. This mode allows the data center class WAAS devices (as of this writing, the WAE-7341 and WAE-7371) to provide lower latency processing to support higher data rates across a smaller number of TCP connections. When deployed in this mode, customers generally deploy these devices on the back-end network where IP interconnect between distant data centers exists. Figure 8-14 shows an example of a network topology including WAAS for both branch and data center applications. Note that this topology is not exhaustive, serves only as an over-simplified representation, and lists only the more common applications.

Replication accelerator is a device mode that must be configured from the CLI of each WAAS device that is operating in this mode. Only WAAS devices running 4.0.19, or any newer 4.0 version, can be configured as replication accelerator devices. These devices can

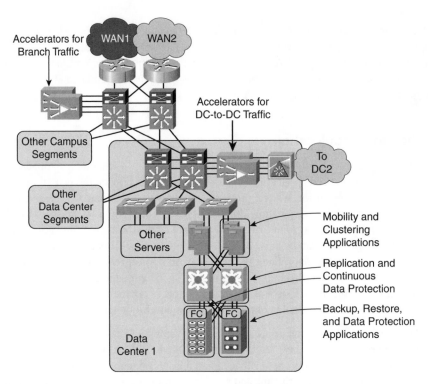

Figure 8-14 *Data Center Topology Supporting Branch and DC-to-DC Optimization*

be managed by the 4.1.x WAAS CM and from a CM that is running 4.0.19 or any newer 4.0 version. It is recommended that replication accelerator devices be placed in a device group separate from the standard application accelerator devices, as the policy configuration for replication accelerator devices is different by default (only policies related to data center to data center applications are present for replication accelerator devices, whereas a full policy set is configured by default on application accelerator devices). Policy configuration and construction is examined later in this chapter.

Example 8-8 shows the CLI configuration and verification for replication accelerator mode on a WAAS device. Note that only WAE-7341 and WAE-7371 can be configured with this device mode.

Example 8-8 *Configuring and Verifying Replication Accelerator Device Mode*

```
DC2-DC1-WAE# config term
DC2-DC1-WAE(config)# device mode ?
  application-accelerator  Configure device to function as a WAAS Engine.
  central-manager          Configure device to function as a WAAS Central
                           Manager.
  replication-accelerator  Configure device to function as a WAAS Engine for
```

```
                          replication applications.
DC2-DC1-WAE(config)# device mode replication-accelerator ?
  <cr>
DC2-DC1-WAE(config)# device mode replication-accelerator
DC2-DC1-WAE(config)# end
DC2-DC1-WAE# show device-mode ?
  configured  Display configured device mode
  current     Display current device mode
DC2-DC1-WAE# show device-mode configured ?
  |      Output Modifiers
  <cr>
DC2-DC1-WAE# show device-mode configured
Configured device mode: replication-accelerator
DC2-DC1-WAE# show device-mode current ?
  |      Output Modifiers
  <cr>
DC2-DC1-WAE# show device-mode current
Current device mode: replication-accelerator
```

When a device is configured as a replication accelerator, its performance and scalability metrics are changed as discussed in Chapter 2, "CISCO WAAS Architecture, Hardware, and Sizing." Fewer connections and fewer peers are supported and high-speed DRE (which functions in memory) is used to mitigate the latency impact of using disk. This allows the device to allocate larger amounts of memory to each connection to maximize throughput (fill-the-pipe) with rapidly compressed segments (in-memory DRE and PLZ). Replication accelerator devices support the same interception and integration techniques as application accelerator devices (Web Cache Coordination Protocol version 2 [WCCPv2], inline, Policy Based Routing [PBR], and Application Control Engine [ACE]). It is recommended that replication accelerator devices be deployed deep in the data center network, or even directly connected to the storage arrays or multiprotocol fabric switches or directors, to eliminate interception complexity at other points in the network where application accelerator devices are integrated.

Application Traffic Policy

When a WAAS device receives a packet, it first examines the IP Protocol to identify if it should be sent "up the stack" to the policy engine which acts as the mediator between the network connection and the internals of the optimization components. Any packets that are non-TCP, such as UDP, Internet Control Message Protocol (ICMP), or other packets, are bypassed quickly and not sent to the any of the optimization components. For WAAS devices deployed inline, any non-TCP packets are sent to the inlinegroup interface that is paired with the interface that the packet was initially received on. For instance, if a UDP datagram is received on InlinePort 1/0/LAN, it is forwarded directly to InlinePort 1/0/WAN with no additional processing. This is done to ensure that the packet is routed appropriately to its destination. Packets that contain TCP segments are routed to the

WAAS device policy engine, which is controlled by Application Traffic Policy (ATP), to determine how that particular flow should be handled based on policy configuration.

The ATP is the lowest layer of the optimization system itself, and acts as the "traffic director" that controls the enactment of optimization components against a flow. The ATP effectively determines whether a WAAS device applies some optimization to a flow and, if so, what level of optimization is applied. The ATP is built from three key components:

- Application groups
- Traffic classifiers
- Policy maps

Although the ATP can be configured directly on the WAAS device CLI, it is highly recommended that the ATP be configured from the CM GUI. Using the CM GUI for ATP configuration ensures consistent configuration across multiple WAAS devices in the network (via use of device groups), which can effectively eliminate policy configuration overlap or underlap as a component that requires troubleshooting when something is not working correctly. Don't worry though, if policies are mismatched between devices, they are able to negotiate to the least common denominator (common optimization features) automatically. This is discussed in the section, "Negotiating Policies," found later in this chapter.

Figure 8-15 illustrates the placement of the ATP in the WAAS device architecture.

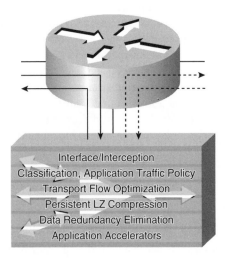

Figure 8-15   *WAAS Architecture and the Application Traffic Policy*

Application Groups

Application groups are containers for the statistics collected from traffic matched by an associated classifier and the statistics collected by the optimization components that are applied against that classifier. Application groups contain multiple policies, which match an action to a traffic classifier. All statistics for traffic rolls up to the application group based on the application group the policy is assigned to. Applications can be defined on the WAAS device directly through the CLI, or configured through the CM GUI. The application group itself has only two parameters:

- A Comments field (allowing an administrator to supply a free text definition or their own notes). Comments can be supplied only via the CM GUI.

- A checkbox that enables statistics collection for all traffic matching the classifiers defined in policies that are associated with the application group. The Enable Statistics check-box in the CM GUI has no effect on the behavior of the WAAS device, as all statistics for all applications are recorded on the WAAS device. Rather, the Enable Statistics check-box is used to indicate which application groups the CM requests from each of the managed WAAS devices.

Example 8-9 demonstrates how to configure an application group from the WAAS device CLI.

Example 8-9   *Defining and Removing an Application Group from the Device CLI*

```
pod1-br-wae# config term
pod1-br-wae(config)# policy-engine ?
  application  Application related policy engine
  config       Configuration change using factory definitions
pod1-br-wae(config)# policy-engine application ?
  classifier  Define an Application classifier
  map         Policy map list
  name        Define Application name
  set-dscp    Define default DSCP marking
  <cr>
pod1-br-wae(config)# policy-engine application name ?
  WORD  Application name (30 characters max)
pod1-br-wae(config)# policy-engine application name TestApplication ?
  set-dscp  Define name's DSCP marking
  <cr>
pod1-br-wae(config)# policy-engine application name TestApplication set-dscp ?
  <0-63>  Differentiated services codepoint value
  af11    Mark packets with AF11 dscp (001010)
  af12    Mark packets with AF12 dscp (001100)
  af13    Mark packets with AF13 dscp (001110)
  af21    Mark packets with AF21 dscp (010010)
  af22    Mark packets with AF22 dscp (010100)
  af23    Mark packets with AF23 dscp (010110)
  af31    Mark packets with AF31 dscp (011010)
```

```
  af32      Mark packets with AF32 dscp (011100)
  af33      Mark packets with AF33 dscp (011110)
  af41      Mark packets with AF41 dscp (100010)
  af42      Mark packets with AF42 dscp (100100)
  af43      Mark packets with AF43 dscp (100110)
  copy      Mark packets with dscp from ingress flow
  cs1       Mark packets with CS1 (precedence 1) dscp (001000)
  cs2       Mark packets with CS2 (precedence 2) dscp (010000)
  cs3       Mark packets with CS3 (precedence 3) dscp (011000)
  cs4       Mark packets with CS4 (precedence 4) dscp (100000)
  cs5       Mark packets with CS5 (precedence 5) dscp (101000)
  cs6       Mark packets with CS6 (precedence 6) dscp (110000)
  cs7       Mark packets with CS7 (precedence 7) dscp (111000)
  default   Mark packets with default dscp (000000)
pod1-br-wae(config)#$ame TestApplication set-dscp copy ?
  <cr>
pod1-br-wae(config)# policy-engine application name TestApplication set-dscp copy
pod1-br-wae(config)# policy-engine application
pod1-br-wae(config-pol-eng-app)# ?
  classifier  Define an Application classifier
  exit        Exit from this submode
  map         Policy map list
  name        Define Application name
  no          Negate a command or set its defaults
  set-dscp    Define default DSCP marking
pod1-br-wae(config-pol-eng-app)# name TestApplication2
pod1-br-wae(config-pol-eng-app)# name TestApplication2 ?
  set-dscp  Define name's DSCP marking
  <cr>
pod1-br-wae(config-pol-eng-app)# name TestApplication2 set-dscp ?
  <0-63>    Differentiated services codepoint value
  af11      Mark packets with AF11 dscp (001010)
  af12      Mark packets with AF12 dscp (001100)
  af13      Mark packets with AF13 dscp (001110)
  af21      Mark packets with AF21 dscp (010010)
  af22      Mark packets with AF22 dscp (010100)
  af23      Mark packets with AF23 dscp (010110)
```

```
    af31     Mark packets with AF31 dscp (011010)
    af32     Mark packets with AF32 dscp (011100)
    af33     Mark packets with AF33 dscp (011110)
    af41     Mark packets with AF41 dscp (100010)
    af42     Mark packets with AF42 dscp (100100)
    af43     Mark packets with AF43 dscp (100110)
    copy     Mark packets with dscp from ingress flow
    cs1      Mark packets with CS1 (precedence 1) dscp (001000)
    cs2      Mark packets with CS2 (precedence 2) dscp (010000)
    cs3      Mark packets with CS3 (precedence 3) dscp (011000)
    cs4      Mark packets with CS4 (precedence 4) dscp (100000)
    cs5      Mark packets with CS5 (precedence 5) dscp (101000)
    cs6      Mark packets with CS6 (precedence 6) dscp (110000)
    cs7      Mark packets with CS7 (precedence 7) dscp (111000)
    default  Mark packets with default dscp (000000)
pod1-br-wae(config-pol-eng-app)# name TestApplication2 set-dscp af11 ?
  <cr>
pod1-br-wae(config-pol-eng-app)# name TestApplication2 set-dscp af11
pod1-br-wae(config-pol-eng-app)# end
pod1-br-wae# show run ¦ include Application
!
! ... portions removed...
!
   name TestApplication set-dscp copy
   name TestApplication2 set-dscp af11
pod1-br-wae# config term
pod1-br-wae(config)# no policy-engine application name TestApplication
pod1-br-wae(config)# no policy-engine application name TestApplication2
pod1-br-wae(config)#
```

Figure 8-16 shows how to configure an application group from the CM GUI. Application groups can be found in the My WAN context by going to **Configure > Applications**. Cisco WAAS provides more than 20 application groups by default, and monitoring is enabled by default on the most commonly used application groups.

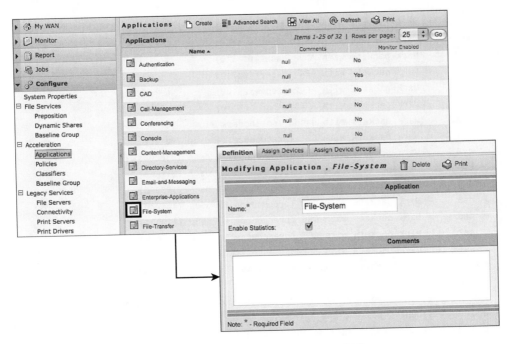

Figure 8-16 *Configuring an Application Group in the CM GUI*

After you configure an application group in the CM GUI, you must then assign it to WAAS devices managed by the CM or device groups that have been configured in the CM. By default, applications are automatically assigned to the AllDevicesGroup, which encompasses all devices registered to the CM. Should custom application groups be created, they must be associated to the appropriate devices or device groups. Association of an application group to one or more devices or device groups can be done from the application group edit page (shown in Figure 8-16) by clicking the **Assign Devices** or **Assign Device Groups** as shown in Figure 8-17. By assigning an application group to devices or device groups, the configuration on the respective devices is updated through the LCM cycle. The top screenshot in Figure 8-17 shows assignment to devices, whereas the bottom screenshot in Figure 8-17 shows assignment to device groups.

Traffic Classifiers

A traffic classifier is the component of the ATP that is responsible for defining the criteria that a flow is evaluated against to determine if it is a match for the policy. That is, the traffic classifier defines the flow characteristics that, when matched with a flow in question, would engage the configured optimization policy action. Traffic classifiers can be configured from the CM GUI or from the WAAS device CLI. Much like other configuration items, it is recommended that the CM GUI be used for classifier configuration to ensure consistency throughout the network. Match conditions within traffic classifiers can be defined using any of the following parameters:

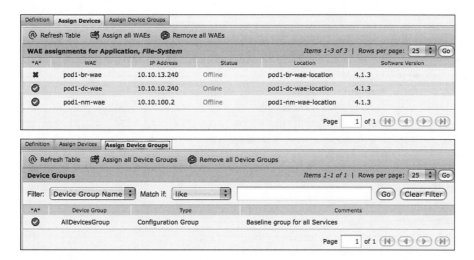

Figure 8-17   *Assigning an Application Group to a Device or Device Group*

- Source IP Address

- Source IP Wildcard

- Source TCP Port

- Source TCP Port Range

- Destination IP Address

- Destination IP Wildcard

- Destination TCP Port

- Destination TCP Port Range

Example 8-10 shows how to configure a traffic classifier from within the WAAS device CLI.

Example 8-10   *Defining, Viewing, and Removing a Traffic Classifier from the Device CLI*

```
pod1-br-wae(config)# policy-engine application ?
  classifier  Define an Application classifier
  map         Policy map list
  name        Define Application name
  set-dscp    Define default DSCP marking
  <cr>
pod1-br-wae(config)# policy-engine application classifier ?
  WORD  Classifier name (30 characters max)
pod1-br-wae(config)# policy-engine application classifier TestClassifier ?
  list   List classifier's conditions
```

```
  match  Add/Modify match condition of the classifier
  <cr>
pod1-br-wae(config)# policy-engine application classifier TestClassifier
pod1-br-wae(config-app-cls)# ?
  exit   Exit from this submode
  list   List classifier's conditions
  match  Add/Modify match condition of the classifier
  no     Negate a command or set its defaults
pod1-br-wae(config-app-cls)# list ?
  <cr>
pod1-br-wae(config-app-cls)# list
Empty
pod1-br-wae(config-app-cls)# match ?
  all  All traffic will be matched
  dst  Condition on the destination side
  src  Condition on the source side
pod1-br-wae(config-app-cls)# match src ?
  host  Specific host name
  ip    IP address and wildcard mask
  port  Condition on the port
pod1-br-wae(config-app-cls)# match src ip ?
  A.B.C.D  IP address
pod1-br-wae(config-app-cls)# match src ip 10.10.10.100 ?
  A.B.C.D  wildcard mask
pod1-br-wae(config-app-cls)# match src ip 10.10.10.100 0.0.0.255 ?
  dst   Condition on the destination side
  port  Condition on the port
  <cr>
pod1-br-wae(config-app-cls)# match src ip 10.10.10.100 0.0.0.255 dst ?
  host  Specific host name
  ip    IP address and wildcard mask
  port  Condition on the port
pod1-br-wae(config-app-cls)# match src ip 10.10.10.100 0.0.0.255 dst ip
10.10.13.100 ?
  A.B.C.D  wildcard mask
pod1-br-wae(config-app-cls)# match src ip 10.10.10.100 0.0.0.255 dst ip
10.10.13.100 0.0.0.255?
  port  Condition on the port
  <cr>
pod1-br-wae(config-app-cls)# match src ip 10.10.10.100 0.0.0.255 dst ip
10.10.13.100 0.0.0.255 port ?
  eq     Port Equal
  range  Port Range
pod1-br-wae(config-app-cls)# match src ip 10.10.10.100 0.0.0.255 dst ip
10.10.13.100 0.0.0.255 port eq ?
```

```
   <1-65535>   Port number
pod1-br-wae(config-app-cls)# match src ip 10.10.10.100 0.0.0.255 dst ip
10.10.13.100 0.0.0.255 port eq 100 ?
   <cr>
pod1-br-wae(config-app-cls)# match src ip 10.10.10.100 0.0.0.255 dst ip
10.10.13.100 0.0.0.255 port eq 100
pod1-br-wae(config-app-cls)# ?
   exit    Exit from this submode
   list    List classifier's conditions
   match   Add/Modify match condition of the classifier
   no      Negate a command or set its defaults
pod1-br-wae(config-app-cls)#  list
match src ip 10.10.10.100 0.0.0.255 dst ip 10.10.13.100 0.0.0.255 port eq 100
pod1-br-wae(config-app-cls)# end
pod1-br-wae#sh run ¦ begin Test
!
! ... portions removed ...
!
...skipping
   classifier TestClassifier
       match src ip 10.10.10.100 0.0.0.255 dst ip 10.10.13.100 0.0.0.255 port eq 100
pod1-br-wae# config term
pod1-br-wae(config)# no policy-engine application classifier TestClassifier
pod1-br-wae(config)# end
pod1-br-wae#
```

Note   Use of **match all** in the CM GUI or WAAS device CLI automatically disables all other options for that particular classifier, and all traffic is matched.

When **match all** is not specified, all items defined within the classifier must be matched for the policy to be invoked against the flow.

Alternatively, all of the match conditions can be defined on a single line with the definition of the classifier, as shown in Example 8-11. Example 8-11 shows the same classifier definition as shown in Example 8-10, but using a single command.

Example 8-11   *Single Command Defines Classifier and Match Conditions*

```
pod1-br-wae(config)# policy-engine application classifier TestClassifier match ?
   all  All traffic will be matched
   dst  Condition on the destination side
   src  Condition on the source side
pod1-br-wae(config)# policy-engine application classifier TestClassifier match src ?
   host   Specific host name
```

```
  ip    IP address and wildcard mask
  port  Condition on the port
pod1-br-wae(config)# policy-engine application classifier TestClassifier match src
ip ?
  A.B.C.D  IP address
pod1-br-wae(config)# policy-engine application classifier TestClassifier match src
ip 10.10.10.100 ?
  A.B.C.D  wildcard mask
pod1-br-wae(config)# policy-engine application classifier TestClassifier match src
ip 10.10.10.100 0.0.0.255 ?
  dst   Condition on the destination side
  port  Condition on the port
  <cr>
pod1-br-wae(config)# policy-engine application classifier TestClassifier match src
ip 10.10.10.100 0.0.0.255 dst ip 10.10.13.100 0.0.0.255 ?
  port  Condition on the port
  <cr>
pod1-br-wae(config)# policy-engine application classifier TestClassifier match src
ip 10.10.10.100 0.0.0.255 dst ip 10.10.13.100 0.0.0.255 port ?
  eq     Port Equal
  range  Port Range
pod1-br-wae(config)# policy-engine application classifier TestClassifier match src
ip 10.10.10.100 0.0.0.255 dst ip 10.10.13.100 0.0.0.255 port eq ?
  <1-65535>  Port number
pod1-br-wae(config)# policy-engine application classifier TestClassifier match src
ip 10.10.10.100 0.0.0.255 dst ip 10.10.13.100 0.0.0.255 port eq 100 ?
  <cr>
pod1-br-wae(config)# policy-engine application classifier TestClassifier match src
ip 10.10.10.100 0.0.0.255 dst ip 10.10.13.100 0.0.0.255 port eq 100
pod1-br-wae(config)#exit
pod1-br-wae#config t
pod1-br-wae(config)#no policy-engine application classifier TestClassifier
```

Note   The masks expected by the syntax in Examples 8-10 and 8-11 are identical to the masks that you would use in an IOS access list. A zero bit indicates that a match is required, whereas a one bit indicates that a match is not required. Therefore, an IP address of 10.10.10.100 with a mask of 0.0.0.255 would match anything in the 10.10.10.x subnet.

Traffic classifiers are configured in the context of a policy definition. Policy definitions can be configured in either the device or device group context (device groups are recommended) at **Configure > Acceleration > Policy Definitions.** Then, either open the policy associated with the classifier to edit and click **Edit Classifier** or create a new policy and click **Edit Classifier.** Alternatively, a new classifier can be defined by clicking **New Classifier.** Figure 8-18 shows the policy list and policy configuration page, where the **Edit Classifier** and **New Classifier** buttons are present.

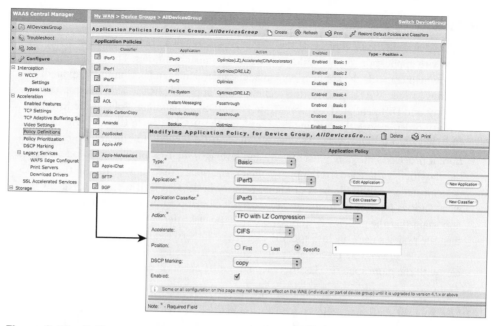

Figure 8-18   *Policy List and Classifier Management from CM GUI*

You can then edit match conditions by clicking the **Create** button, or the **Edit** icon next to existing match conditions. Figure 8-19 shows the classifier definition page, along with the match conditions configuration page. Note that a classifier can have multiple associated match conditions.

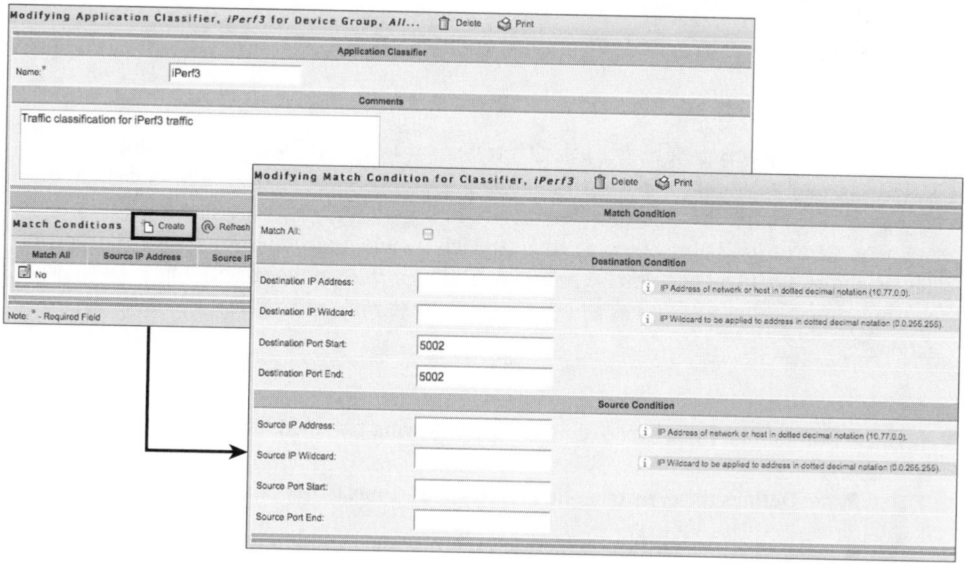

Figure 8-19   *Classifier Configuration and Match Conditions in CM GUI*

Policy Maps

Policy maps are the final piece of the ATP and perform two critical tasks: associate classifiers with application groups and assign actions to matched flows. The definition of a policy map contains the application name, classifier name, and action to be applied. Actions include WAN optimization techniques to apply, application accelerator to employ, and Differentiated Services Code Point (DSCP) handling. Policies are listed in priority order in both the running-config file of the WAAS device CLI and within the CM GUI. That is, when a WAAS device is making a determination on how to optimize a flow, it processes the policy list serially and leverages the first policy based on a match of the classifier. If there are overlapping policies, the policy that appears first in the WAAS device running-config file or is of higher priority in the CM GUI is applied. Therefore, when various policies with similar and partially overlapping policies are required, it is important that the policies with the more specific classifiers be placed at a higher priority than the policies with the less specific classifiers. Otherwise, if the policies with the more specific classifiers were placed after the policies with the less specific classifiers, the policies with the more specific classifiers would not be used.

Note   You can configure policy prioritization in the CM GUI by going to the device or device group context and then into **Configure > Acceleration > Policy Prioritization**. Policy prioritization can also be configured from the CLI, as discussed later in this section.

An example of a pair of policies with higher or lower granularity classification would be as follows:

- Policy A with classifier A and action "Full optimization"

- Policy B with classifier B and action "TFO only"

- Classifier A matches only destination port 80

- Classifier B matches destination port 80 and server IP address 10.10.10.10

If policy A were placed at a higher priority, traffic on TCP port 80 destined to address 10.10.10.10 (and any other traffic on TCP port 80) would be handled by WAAS using the action specified in policy A, rather than policy B. If policy B were placed at a higher priority, only traffic on TCP port 80 going to 10.10.10.10 would be handled by policy B, whereas the remainder would be handled by policy A. To summarize, policies with more granular classification should be placed at a higher priority than policies with less granular classification.

The definition of a policy map includes the following parameters:

- **Type:** Defines the type of policy map. The settings for Type include:

  - **Basic:** A standard optimization policy, tying an action to a classifier, and associating the statistics with an application group.

- **WAFS Transport:** Used for legacy mode CIFS acceleration compatibility. This type is discussed in Chapter 9.

- **EPM:** Identical to a Basic policy, but relies on EPM classification, which is discussed in the next section. This type of policy is used for applications that are assigned dynamic port numbers on a dispatch port based on the universally unique identifier (UUID) supplied by the requesting application.

- **Application:** Defines the application group that the policy is associated with. Any statistics gathered against flows optimized by this policy are collected into the application group statistics. From here, a new application can be defined, an existing application can be edited, or an existing application can be selected.

- **Application Classifier:** Defines the traffic classifier that defines match conditions that activate the policy actions against the flow.

- **Action:** Specifies what type of WAN optimization action to take on the flow. Actions include:

  - **Passthrough:** The flow is not optimized by the WAAS devices. Rather, it is simply passed through. Automatic discovery does not happen on a flow handled as passthrough.

  - **TFO Only:** The WAAS devices attempts to apply only TFO to this flow (pending load conditions, peer policy, and peer load conditions). Automatic discovery occurs to identify a peer WAAS device.

  - **TFO with Data Redundancy Elimination:** The WAAS devices attempts to apply TFO and DRE to this flow. Automatic discovery occurs to identify a peer WAAS device.

  - **TFO with LZ Compression:** The WAAS devices attempt to apply TFO and PLZ to this flow. Automatic discovery occurs to identify a peer WAAS device.

  - **Full Optimization (TFO with DRE and LZ):** The WAAS devices attempt to apply TFO, DRE, and PLZ to this flow. Automatic discovery occurs to identify a peer WAAS device.

- **Accelerate:** Specifies which application accelerator the flow should be accelerated by, including:

  - **Do not set:** No application accelerator is used.

  - **MS Port Mapper:** This setting instructs the WAAS device to pass the flow to the EPM subsystem for UUID-based classification. This setting is generally only used with the MS-EndPointMapper policy. Policies for applications identified by EPM classification each have their own policy, which is of type EPM as discussed previously.

  - **CIFS:** This setting instructs the WAAS device to pass the flow to the CIFS accelerator for optimizing Windows file services applications.

- **HTTP:** This setting instructs the WAAS device to pass the flow to the HTTP accelerator for optimizing Intranet and Internet applications.

- **NFS:** This setting instructs the WAAS device to pass the flow to the Network File System (NFS) accelerator for optimizing UNIX file services applications.

- **MAPI:** This setting instructs the WAAS device to pass the flow to the MAPI accelerator for optimizing Microsoft Exchange and Outlook traffic. MAPI is configured to use EPM classification by default, but simplified policies can be created based on the server IP address if use of EPM is not desired. While this is possible, it is not necessary.

- **Video:** This setting instructs the WAAS device to pass the flow to the Video accelerator for optimizing Microsoft Windows Media over Real Time Streaming Protocol (RTSP) video streams.

Note   SSL is considered an application accelerator, but its configuration is more advanced than the configuration of the other accelerators. It is covered separately in Chapter 9. SSL accelerated traffic does not require definition of SSL as a policy action; instead, other items must be configured as described in Chapter 9.

Chapter 9 provides a full examination of application acceleration capabilities. The details around policy creation are applicable to both WAN optimization and application acceleration features and is discussed at length in this chapter, but full coverage of the operation of the application accelerators is not discussed until Chapter 9.

- **Position:** Indicates the priority order of the policy. The priority can be set to First, Last, or a specific value. In situations where policies overlap, policies with higher priority are used. It is recommended that policies with more granular classification be placed higher in the priority order to ensure that they are used ahead of lower-priority policies that contain less granular classification.

- **DSCP Marking:** Indicates the DSCP value that should be applied to packets within this flow. A specific DSCP value can be applied, or, WAAS can be instructed to **copy** the incoming DSCP value to the outgoing packets, or **inherit-from-name** causes WAAS to use the DSCP value configured in the CLI against the name of the application group. By default, **inherit-from-name** is identical to **copy**, unless an explicit DSCP value has been configured against the application group in the CLI, or configured against the application group in the Edit Application, which is accessible next to the application selection drop-down box.

- **Enabled:** If this checkbox is checked, the policy is enacted on the WAAS device and added to the running-config file via the LCM cycle. If not enabled, the policy is enacted on the WAAS device and appears in the running-config file as a disabled policy.

You configure policies in the CM GUI under the *device context* or *device group context* at **Configure > Acceleration > Policy Definitions.** Figure 8-18 illustrated the policy list page and the policy definition page.

You can also define policies on the WAAS device CLI, as shown in Example 8-12. While this is possible, it is typically not recommended, as configuration of policies from the CM is much simpler and more intuitive.

Example 8-12   *Configuring Policies from Device CLI*

```
pod1-br-wae# config term
pod1-br-wae(config)# policy-engine application ?
  classifier  Define an Application classifier
  map         Policy map list
  name        Define Application name
  set-dscp    Define default DSCP marking
  <cr>
pod1-br-wae(config)# policy-engine application
pod1-br-wae(config-pol-eng-app)# map ?
  adaptor  Advanced policy map lists - separate for every adaptor
  basic    Basic policy map list - based on L3/L4 parameters only
  other    Define the action on non-classified traffic
pod1-br-wae(config-pol-eng-app)# map basic ?
  delete   Delete specific Application Policy Map from the list
  disable  Disable specific Application Policy Map from the list
  insert   Add new Application Policy Map into specific position
  list     List Application Policy Map
  move     Move specific Application Policy Map from one position to a new one
           in the list
  name     Application Name
  <cr>
pod1-br-wae(config-pol-eng-app)# map basic name ?
  WORD  the Application Name - has to be already defined
pod1-br-wae(config-pol-eng-app)# map basic name Backup ?
  classifier  Application traffic classifier
pod1-br-wae(config-pol-eng-app)# map basic name Backup classifier ?
  WORD  the Application Traffic Classifier Name - has to be already defined
pod1-br-wae(config-pol-eng-app)# map basic name Backup classifier BackupExpress ?
  action   the Action that should be taken
  disable  Add this policy disabled
pod1-br-wae(config-pol-eng-app)# map basic name Backup classifier BackupExpress
action ?
  optimize      Apply Generic Optimization
  pass-through  Don't touch the traffic, pass-through without any modification
pod1-br-wae(config-pol-eng-app)# map basic name Backup classifier BackupExpress
action optimize ?
  DRE   To Apply Generic Redundancy Optimization or not?
  full  Apply Full Generic Optimization
pod1-br-wae(config-pol-eng-app)# map basic name Backup classifier BackupExpress
action optimize DRE ?
```

```
  no   No Apply
  yes  Apply
pod1-br-wae(config-pol-eng-app)# map basic name Backup classifier BackupExpress
action optimize DRE yes ?
  compression  To Apply Generic Compression or not?
pod1-br-wae(config-pol-eng-app)# map basic name Backup classifier BackupExpress
action optimize DRE yes compression ?
  LZ    Apply LZ compression
  none  Do not do any compression
pod1-br-wae(config-pol-eng-app)# map basic name Backup classifier BackupExpress
action optimize DRE yes compression LZ ?
  accelerate  Accelerate Traffic using special adapter
  set-dscp    Define mapping's DSCP marking
  <cr>
pod1-br-wae(config-pol-eng-app)# map basic name Backup classifier BackupExpress
action optimize DRE yes compression LZ accelerate ?
  cifs           CIFS Accelerator
  http           HTTP Accelerator
  mapi           MAPI Accelerator
  MS-port-mapper Microsoft Endpoint Port Mapper
  nfs            NFS Accelerator
  video          VIDEO Accelerator
pod1-br-wae(config-pol-eng-app)# map basic name Backup classifier BackupExpress
action optimize DRE yes compression LZ
```

Additionally, you can combine the **map** command with the **policy-engine application** command to allow for definition of a policy map on a single line. Additional commands found under **policy-engine application** include the following, which are shown in Example 8-13:

- **map basic list:** Displays the list of all policies and the optimization associated with the policy. Policies are displayed in priority order, and the number to the left of the policy definition is the priority order of the policy.

- **map basic disable (#):** Specifies a policy to disable based on its number in the priority list as shown by 'map basic list.'

- **map basic insert (first|last|pos):** Allows you to insert a policy at the beginning, end, or in a specific location within the policy list. This command must be appended by the policy definition as outlined in Example 8-12.

- **map basic move from (#) to (#):** Allows you to move a policy at a specific position to another position.

Example 8-13 *Additional Policy Map Commands in Device CLI*

```
pod1-br-wae(config-pol-eng-app)# map basic list
```

```
1) name iPerf3 classifier iPerf3 action optimize DRE no compression LZ set-dscp
copy
2) name iPerf1 classifier iPerf1 action optimize full set-dscp copy
3) name iPerf2 classifier iPerf2 action optimize DRE no compression none set-
dscp copy
4) name File-System classifier AFS action optimize full
5) name Instant-Messaging classifier AOL action pass-through
!
! ... portions removed ...
!
pod1-br-wae(config-pol-eng-app)# map basic disable ?
  <1-1023>  the exact position to be disabled
pod1-br-wae(config-pol-eng-app)# map basic disable 1 ?
  <cr>
pod1-br-wae(config-pol-eng-app)# map basic insert ?
  first  begining of the list
  last   end of the list
  pos    specific position in the list
pod1-br-wae(config-pol-eng-app)# map basic insert pos ?
  <1-1023>  (1-first and 1023-last)
pod1-br-wae(config-pol-eng-app)# map basic insert pos 5 ?
  name  Application Name
pod1-br-wae(config-pol-eng-app)# map basic insert pos 5 name ?
  WORD  the Application Name - has to be already defined
pod1-br-wae(config-pol-eng-app)# map basic insert pos 5 name Backup ?
  classifier  Application traffic classifier
pod1-br-wae(config-pol-eng-app)# map basic insert pos 5 name Backup
pod1-br-wae(config-pol-eng-app)# map basic move ?
  from  from current position
pod1-br-wae(config-pol-eng-app)# map basic move from ?
  <1-1023>  the exact source position
pod1-br-wae(config-pol-eng-app)# map basic move from  1 ?
  to  to new position
pod1-br-wae(config-pol-eng-app)# map basic move from  1 to ?
  <1-1023>  the exact destination position
pod1-br-wae(config-pol-eng-app)# map basic move from  1 to 2 ?
  <cr>
pod1-br-wae(config-pol-eng-app)# map basic move from  1 to 2
```

Note   Policy engine commands are hierarchical and can be simplified by first using **policy-engine application map basic**. This takes you to a section of the CLI where you can enter commands such as **list, disable, insert**, and so on individually rather than having to enter the entire string of items such as **policy-engine application map basic** command.

Each Cisco WAAS device ships with a default policy set enabled, which includes approximately 25 application groups, 150 policy maps, and the necessary classifiers to support them. If it becomes necessary to restore the original application traffic policy settings, you can click the **Restore Default Policies and Classifiers** icon found in the device or device group context at **Configure > Acceleration > Policy Definitions**. Figure 8-20 shows the button that allows the default policy set to be restored.

Figure 8-20   *Restoring Default Policies from CM*

You can also completely remove the policy configuration from a device, or, restore the default policy set from the WAAS device using the CLI as demonstrated in Example 8-14. Note that these commands do not ask for confirmation before executing, so use these commands only when you are certain that you want to remove the current policies or restore the factory default policies.

Example 8-14   *Removing All Policies and Restoring Default Policies from Device CLI*

```
pod1-br-wae(config)# policy-engine ?
  application  Application related policy engine
  config       Configuration change using factory definitions
pod1-br-wae(config)# policy-engine config ?
  remove-all         Remove all policy engine configuration
  restore-predefined Replace all policy engine configuration with factory defaults
pod1-br-wae(config)# policy-engine config remove-all ?
  <cr>
pod1-br-wae(config)# policy-engine config restore-predefined ?
  <cr>
```

A special policy, called the *other* policy, is found at the bottom of the policy priority list. This is a required policy that acts as a catch-all and defines what the behavior of the WAAS device should be in situations where no configured classifiers (and thus, no configured policies and actions) are matched. If a flow cannot be classified, it is caught by the *other* policy, and the actions configured in this policy are applied to the flow. The *other* policy, like normal policies, can be configured from the CM GUI or the WAAS device CLI in an identical manner as shown in the figures and examples presented earlier. Two primary schools of thought exist with regard to the *other* policy:

- **Optimize full (default):** The default option is to optimize everything full if it cannot be classified. The benefit of this option is that all traffic is optimized if it cannot be classified. The downside to this option is that all unclassified traffic is optimized, which consumes connection resources in the system. Many organizations choose this option instead of identifying applications on the network that WAAS isn't classifying by default and creating the appropriate classifiers and policy maps. This option yields less efficient and controlled use of optimization resources, but requires less planning and configuration.

■ **Pass-through:** Configuring the *other* policy with pass-through causes the WAAS device to not optimize traffic that it cannot classify. The benefit of this option is that traffic that cannot be classified does not consume optimized TCP connection resources. The downside to this option is that traffic that cannot be classified is not optimized unless a specific classifier and policy map are created. This option yields more efficient and controlled use of optimization resources, but requires more planning and configuration.

Additionally, access control lists can be used to limit the types of traffic seen by a WAAS device when using off-path interception (including WCCPv2 and PBR). This is orthogonal to the policy configuration applied to the WAAS device, but can serve as another layer of filtering what traffic is seen by the WAAS device, which, as a side effect, limits the amount of traffic evaluated by the policy engine.

Negotiating Policies

Although it is certainly possible that WAAS devices deployed in the same network might have different policy configurations, it is recommended that variations in policy configurations be minimized throughout the network to ensure consistency, ease of management, and simplified troubleshooting. Even in instances where a consistent policy is employed throughout the entire network, situations exist that might cause the configured policy to not be used. Policy configurations are enforced in a best-effort manner; that is, if the WAAS device has adequate resources to perform the configured optimization, it attempts to do so. Similarly, a peer's capability to perform optimization according to the request of the initiating WAAS device are subject to the peer's current load conditions and configuration.

This behavior is especially important when examining the TFO AD process. During this process, WAAS devices announce themselves to identify a peer and advertise what optimization policy they would like to employ for the connection. In situations where the WAAS device is heavily loaded and has exhausted its optimized connection pool, it stops participation in TFO AD altogether for new connections. Thus, these connections go into pass-through, and this behavior continues until the number of optimized connections falls to a number lower than the maximum capacity of the WAAS device.

Additionally, if optimization services are unable to perform the action specified in the policy, WAAS devices might not advertise those optimization services in the TFO AD process. The result of the TFO AD process is that WAAS devices—when two or more are identified in the path between the TCP endpoints—negotiate to a set of optimization services that both WAAS devices can accommodate, effectively the *least common denominator* of the services that each device can perform at that time given configuration and load conditions. This enables the WAAS device to perform some level of optimization even if certain services are impaired or unable to be used. Naturally, the intent is to minimize such situations, and the WAAS device has numerous software watchdogs and other facilities in place that can self-repair degraded services or even restart them when they cannot be repaired. With a fully modular architecture—which is dramatically different than other approaches to WAN optimization—certain services can be restarted without disrupting the remainder of the system.

When the configured policies do not match, the least common denominator is selected. For instance, if the configured policy on two WAAS devices is Full Optimization, yet one of them advertises TFO only, the applied policy between the two WAAS devices is TFO only. Additionally, the optimization policies are consulted on each new connection encountered by a WAAS device, allowing policy changes to be implemented immediately for new connections. Changes made to policy configuration do not impact the level of optimization applied to connections that are already established and optimized; they are consulted only upon the next new connection that enters the TFO AD process. That is, a change to a policy's optimization actions does not change the optimization actions performed on connections that are already established because of the original policy.

EndPoint Mapper Classification

The purpose of the EPM classification system is to allow WAAS to accurately classify MS-RPC traffic flows that use dynamic ports assigned by a *port mapper*, also known as a *dispatcher*, which is an application that provides a port number for the originating TCP endpoint to use for its application upon receipt of application-specific information received from the originating TCP endpoint.

In the case of EPM, the application-specific information that is shared from one node to another is a UUID. In essence, when a client connects to a server for a particular application that uses UUIDs to request a dynamic port number from the server, it establishes a TCP connection on the dispatcher port and provides the UUID. The server then examines the UUID and provides a response with the TCP port number that should be used for the message exchange for that application. The client application then establishes a new TCP connection on the port returned by the server. With WAAS, this exchange is monitored by EPM and state is built allowing WAAS devices to understand what dynamic port is in use for message exchange by an application that uses UUIDs for determining the dynamic port number to use. The EPM classification system in WAAS provides classification support for common Microsoft applications including Active Directory (MS-AD) Replication, Remote-Procedure-Call applications (MS-RPC), Exchange (MS-Exchange), and File Replication Service (MS-FRS). For Microsoft applications, this service runs on TCP 135 on the server. Clients connecting to this port that supply a UUID are assigned a dynamic destination port to connect to for their particular application. The server, after this port is assigned, then opens the port locally and associates the port with the upper layer application. WAAS retains this information to apply the appropriate optimization to the connection that is established after the dynamic port number is learned.

Figure 8-21 shows the interaction between the client and server in an environment where port mappers are used.

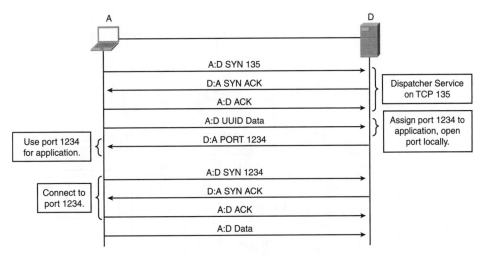

Figure 8-21 *Port Mappers and Dynamic Port Assignment*

WAAS relies on the EPM classification system to learn which dynamic ports are used by certain Microsoft applications. As a WAAS device is either physically or virtually inline to all communication entering or leaving an interception point, connections established to port mapper ports and exchanges of UUID information to receive a dynamic port assignment are also intercepted. With the EPM service, WAAS can listen to this conversation and learn what application the user is trying to use and on what port the server instructs the user to connect. Then, the appropriate action can be applied to the connection according to the policy definition.

Figure 8-22 shows the same interaction between the client and the server in a WAAS environment and how WAAS uses this information to understand what applications and ports are used.

EPM classification can be enabled or disabled through the Enabled Features page, as shown earlier in Figure 8-7. Policies exist in the default policy set to account for applications that use EPM and can be found at the bottom of the policy list (see Figure 8-16 for the location of the policy list).

Figure 8-23 shows the construction of an EPM policy for MAPI (the protocol Microsoft Exchange and Outlook use), which is similar to basic policies. The primary difference is the presence of the UUID field, which includes a default set of UUIDs including MAPI (MS-Exchange), MS-SQL-RPC, MS-AD-Replication, MS-FRS, and Custom. Choosing **Custom UUID** allows text entry into the Custom UUID text box, which enables you to specify UUIDs unique to your particular application. Also, note that for an EPM policy, the Application Classifier drop-down list box should be set to **Match All Traffic** because the EPM classifier is used rather than the regular Layer 3 (IP) and Layer 4 (TCP) classification fields provided by the traffic classification system.

Example 8-15 shows how to enable or disable EPM classification on a WAAS device using the CLI.

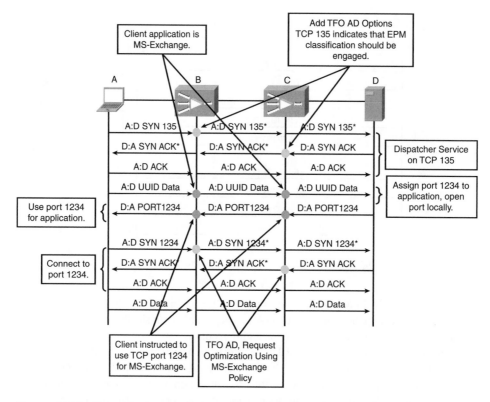

Figure 8-22   *Port Mappers and Dynamic Port Assignment with WAAS*

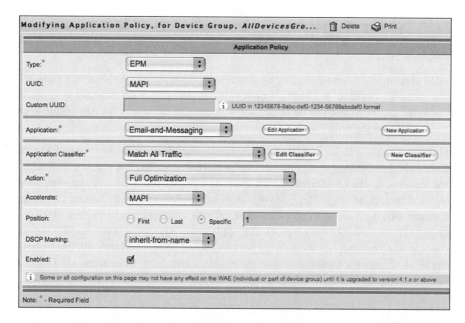

Figure 8-23   *EPM Policy Configuration in CM GUI*

Example 8-15 *Enabling or Disabling EPM Classification from Device CLI*

```
pod1-br-wae(config)# no accelerator ?
  cifs            CIFS accelerator configuration
  epm             EPM accelerator configuration
  http            HTTP accelerator configuration
  mapi            MAPI accelerator configuration
  nfs             NFS accelerator configuration
  ssl             SSL accelerator configuration
  video           VIDEO accelerator configuration
  windows-print   Windows-Print Accelerator configuration
pod1-br-wae(config)# no accelerator epm ?
  enable      Enable accelerator
  exception   Exception handling for AO
pod1-br-wae(config)# no accelerator epm enable ?
  <cr>
pod1-br-wae(config)# no accelerator epm enable
Disabled epm accelerator.
pod1-br-wae(config)# accelerator epm enable
Enabled epm accelerator
```

EPM policies can also be configured from the WAAS device CLI in a similar manner to how basic policies are configured. Example 8-16 shows the configuration of an EPM policy from the WAAS device CLI.

Example 8-16 *Configuring an EPM Policy from Device CLI*

```
pod1-br-wae(config)# policy-engine application
pod1-br-wae(config-pol-eng-app)# map ?
  adaptor  Advanced policy map lists - separate for every adaptor
  basic    Basic policy map list - based on L3/L4 parameters only
  other    Define the action on non-classified traffic
pod1-br-wae(config-pol-eng-app)# map adaptor ?
  EPM   Policy map for EPM with specific UUID
  WAFS  WAFS policy map
pod1-br-wae(config-pol-eng-app)# map adaptor EPM ?
  WORD  MAPI or UUID in 12345678-9abc-def0-1234-56789abcdef0 format
pod1-br-wae(config-pol-eng-app)# map adaptor EPM MAPI ?
  delete   Delete specific Application Policy Map from the list
  disable  Disable specific Application Policy Map from the list
```

```
   insert    Add new Application Policy Map into specific position
   list      List Application Policy Map
   move      Move specific Application Policy Map from one position to a new one
in the list
   name      Application Name
   <cr>
pod1-br-wae(config-pol-eng-app)# map adaptor EPM MAPI name ?
   WORD  the Application Name - has to be already defined
```

Note   The CLI syntax for configuring an EPM policy is no different than the CLI syntax for configuring a basic policy, after the **map adaptor EPM** *UUID* has been specified. Please refer to Example 8-12 for the syntax for configuring basic policies.

Monitoring and Reporting

The previous sections in this chapter focused on the configuration of WAAS devices for WAN optimization and policies. This section builds upon that foundation, in addition to the monitoring and reporting introduction provided in the previous chapter, and examines the monitoring and reporting facilities provided by Cisco WAAS as it relates to WAN optimization, both from the CM GUI and the CLI. This section provides an examination of automatic discovery statistics, connection statistics and details, statistics for the WAN optimization features, and monitoring charts available in the CM GUI. The section wraps up by examining how to integrate monitoring of WAN optimization statistics into third-party visibility systems, which can enable customers to achieve complete end-to-end performance visibility and more useful diagnostics and troubleshooting.

Automatic Discovery Statistics

TFO AD statistics provide useful insight into how connections are being seen by WAAS devices in the network. The WAAS device CLI exposes a great deal of information about the TFO AD process, situations encountered, and how connections were handled. These commands are useful when executed on devices at either end of a WAN link to fully understand how automatic discovery is working (or not) and in what capacity. The **show statistics auto-discovery** command from the exec mode of the WAAS device CLI provides details about the following:

- **Automatic discovery success:** How many connections have successfully completed automatic discovery

- **Automatic discovery failure:** How many connections have failed automatic discovery, and what were the reasons for failure

- **Automatic discovery infrastructure:** Success and failure conditions within automatic discovery as it relates to allocation, deallocation, and resources

Example 8-17 shows sample output from this command. Key areas are highlighted, and comments are inserted where appropriate. Some text has been removed from the command output to eliminate less commonly used information and to allow you to focus on the most important pieces of output data from this command.

Example 8-17   *CLI Automatic Discovery Statistics*

```
pod1-br-wae#show stat auto
Auto discovery structure:
        Allocation Failure:                     0
        Allocation Success:                     11934
        Deallocations:                          11934
        Timed Out:                              24
Auto discovery table:
        Bucket Overflows:                       0
        Table Overflows:                        0
        Entry Adds:                             11934
        Entry Drops:                            11934
        Entry Count:                            0
        Lookups:                                21608
!
! the above shows additions and removals from the auto
! discovery table. Maligned numbers could be indicative of
! device load problems or that half-open
! connections exist.
!
Auto discovery failure:
        No peer or asymmetric route:            1
        Insufficient option space:              0
        Invalid option content:                 0
        Invalid connection state:               0
        Missing Ack conf:                       0
        Intermediate device:                    0
        Version mismatch:                       0
!
! Asymmetric routing can be detected per the above. Additionally,
! a counter is present that shows you the number of connections that
! the device has determined itself to be intermediate, i.e. not one
! of the outermost endpoints.
```

Additional automatic discovery statistics can be gathered through the following commands, which are shown in Example 8-18:

■   **show statistics auto-discovery blacklist:** Displays the operational status and statistics for TFO AD blacklist operation, including entries and eviction, hold-down timer configuration, age of oldest entry in the blacklist table, and number of entries used as compared to number of entries available.

- **show auto-discovery blacklist:** Displays a table containing a list of the TCP endpoints that have been added to the TFO AD blacklist due to options propagation failure. This command can also be filtered by a network mask to limit the results to specific TCP endpoints.

- **show auto-discovery list:** Displays a table containing a list of the TCP connections that are presently in the automatic-discovery state and what their status is. As connections are generally built quickly, execution of this command provides an immediate point-in-time snapshot, and the command output is likely to change frequently.

Example 8-18 *Additional CLI Automatic Discovery Commands*

```
pod1-br-wae# show statistics auto-disc blacklist
Auto-Discovery Blacklist Server Table Statistics
Operation Status:                        ENABLED
Total Lookups                            11969
  Hits                                       0
  Miss (Stale Entry)                         0
  Miss (Grey Entry)                          1
  Miss (No Entry)                        11968


Table Insertions                             1
Stale Lookup Evictions                       0
Stale LRU Evictions                          0
Forced LRU Evictions                         0
Removed Due to False Insert                  1


Configured Entry Hold Time(sec)           3600
Oldest Entry Hold Time(sec)                  0


Total Entries (Free & Used)               8192
Current Free Entries                      8192
Current Used Entries                         0
Peak Used Entries                            1
pod1-br-wae# show auto-discovery ?
  blacklist  Display all entries in the Auto-Discovery blacklist server table
  list       List the connections in auto-discovery state
pod1-br-wae# show auto-discovery blacklist
There are no entries in the blacklist
pod1-br-wae# show auto-discovery ?
  blacklist  Display all entries in the Auto-Discovery blacklist server table
  list       List the connections in auto-discovery state
pod1-br-wae#sh auto-disc blacklist ?
```

```
   netmask   Network mask to filter table output
   |          Output Modifiers
  <cr>
pod1-br-wae# show auto-discovery blacklist
There are no entries in the blacklist
pod1-br-wae#show auto-discovery list
E: Established, S: Syn, A: Ack, F: Fin, R: Reset
s: sent, r: received, O: Options, P: Passthrough


     Src-IP:Port              Dst-IP:Port        Orig-St   Term-St
  10.104.140.38:40890     10.10.13.240:8443      SAsO      Unk
  10.104.140.38:40096     10.10.13.240:8443      SAsO      Unk
  10.104.140.38:41123     10.10.13.240:443       SAsO      Unk
```

Connection Statistics and Details

Along with providing visibility into the automatic discovery statistics, the WAAS device CLI provides details about the connections that are being optimized by the WAAS device. The CM GUI also provides these details in an easy-to-use connection table, which also enables you to zoom into a specific connection to watch its behavior in near real time.

Two ways exist to examine the list of optimized and pass-through connections on the WAAS device: using the CLI, or using the CM GUI. The first is from the WAAS device CLI through the use of the **show statistics connection** command. This command provides a wealth of information including counts of optimized flows, per-flow peer information with a list of optimization components applied, and a table showing connections in the automatic discovery state. Example 8-19 shows sample output from the **show statistics connection** command.

Example 8-19   *show statistics connection Command Output*

```
pod1-br-wae# show statistics connection


Current Active Optimized Flows:                      11
   Current Active Optimized TCP Plus Flows:           5
   Current Active Optimized TCP Only Flows:           1
   Current Active Optimized TCP Preposition Flows:    0
Current Active Auto-Discovery Flows:                  1
Current Active Pass-Through Flows:                    0
Historical Flows:                                   100



D:DRE,L:LZ,T:TCP Optimization,
A:AOIM,C:CIFS,E:EPM,G:GENERIC,H:HTTP,M:MAPI,N:NFS,S:SSL,V:VIDEO
```

```
ConnID   Source IP:Port          Dest IP:Port           PeerID                 Accel
88       10.10.13.100:3341       10.10.10.100:445       00:14:5e:41:eb:78      TCDL
4458     10.10.13.100:2378       10.10.10.100:5000      00:14:5e:41:eb:78      TDL
4537     10.10.13.100:2386       10.10.10.100:5001      00:14:5e:41:eb:78      T
5031     10.10.13.100:2611       10.10.10.100:80        00:14:5e:41:eb:78      THDL
5046     171.71.180.208:22223    10.10.13.240:8443      00:14:5e:41:eb:78      T
5048     171.71.180.208:22225    10.10.13.240:8443      00:14:5e:41:eb:78      T
5061     171.71.180.208:22238    10.10.13.240:8443      00:14:5e:41:eb:78      T
5067     171.71.180.208:22244    10.10.13.240:8443      00:14:5e:41:eb:78      T
5077     171.71.180.208:48822    10.10.13.240:8443      00:14:5e:41:eb:78      T
5080     10.10.13.100:2614       10.10.10.100:21        00:14:5e:41:eb:78      TDL
5081     10.10.13.100:2615       10.10.10.100:10006     00:14:5e:41:eb:78      TDL


O-ST: Origin State, T-ST: Terminal State
E: Established, S: Syn, A: Ack, F: Fin, R: Reset
s: sent, r: received, O: Options, P: Passthrough


Local IP:Port        Remote IP:Port        Peer ID              O-ST T-ST ConnType
10.10.13.240:443     171.71.180.208:2656800:14:5e:41:eb:78 SAsO Unk  INTERNAL SERVER
```

As shown in the output, the peer ID (MAC address of the primary interface of the peer WAAS device), the acceleration components that have been acted, the unique connection ID, and the tuple for the flow are listed. The connection ID can be used in other commands (some are examined in other sections in this chapter) to focus the command output to the statistics of a particular connection. Similarly, command output can be filtered on other parameters including any element in the tuple as shown in Example 8-20.

Example 8-20   *Filtering Options for show statistics connection Command*

```
pod1-br-wae# show statistics connection ?
  auto-discovery   Display currently active auto-discovery connections
  client-ip        Display active connection statistics for client ip address
  client-port      Display active connection statistics for client port number
  closed           Display closed connections
  conn-id          Display active connection statistics for connection identifier
  detail           Display detailed connection view
  egress-methods   detailed information on the egress methods
  optimized        Display currently active optimised connection
  pass-through     Display currently active passthrough connections
  peer-id          Display active connection statistics for peer idenitifier
  server-ip        Display active connection statistics for server-ip
  server-port      Display active connection statistics for server-port
  |                Output Modifiers
  <cr>
```

This same level of filtering is available for other commands within the system. A wealth of detailed data can be retrieved by filtering this command's output to a specific connection, as shown in the annotated output in Example 8-21. This output includes information about the connection, classification, policy actions, and individual optimization components that are applied to a connection. Portions of the CLI output have been removed for clarity and to allow focus on the key statistics.

Example 8-21   *Detailed Per-Connection Statistics in CLI*

```
pod1-br-wae# show statistics connection conn-id 5417
!
! ... portions removed ...
!
Connection Id:              5417
    Peer Id:                00:14:5e:41:eb:78
    Connection Type:        EXTERNAL CLIENT
    Start Time:             Thu May 21 22:21:47 2009
    Source IP Address:      10.10.13.100
    Source Port Number:     3073
    Destination IP Address: 10.10.10.100
    Destination Port Number: 80
!
! the tuple of the flow, the peer identified, and timestamps
! are all shown above.
!
    Application Name:       Web
    Classifier Name:        HTTP
    Map Name:               basic
    Directed Mode:          FALSE
    Preposition Flow:       FALSE
!
! the section above shows the application and classifier name,
! along with the type of policy map. If directed mode is used,
! or if the flow is from a preposition job (discussed in chapter
! 9), these values will be set to true.
!
    Policy Details:
            Configured:     TCP_OPTIMIZE + DRE + LZ
            Derived:        TCP_OPTIMIZE + DRE + LZ
            Peer:           TCP_OPTIMIZE + DRE + LZ
            Negotiated:     TCP_OPTIMIZE + DRE + LZ
            Applied:        TCP_OPTIMIZE + DRE + LZ
```

```
!
! notice that multiple policy items are displayed. This section is
! helpful in troubleshooting policy mismatch scenarios and identifying
! overload condition scenarios. The policy configured on the local
! device is listed, followed by the derived policy, which is based on
! local device load conditions. The peer policy as configured is
! shown, followed by the policy negotiated (based on least common
! denominator of derived and peer), and the applied policy is also
! shown. Note that load conditions and other factors may cause the
! derived policy to deviate from the configured policy and the applied
! policy from the negotiated policy.
!

     Accelerator Details:
                 Configured:   HTTP
                   Derived:    HTTP
                   Applied:    HTTP
                      Hist:    None
!
! similar to the policy details, the accelerator details are also
! provided.
!

                                    Original          Optimized
                                  _____       _____

     Bytes Read:                      113               8039
     Bytes Written:                 5430056             1040
!
! byte counts are provided to show the number of bytes read from the
! original connection (incoming data from a TCP endpoint), bytes written
! to the original connection (outgoing data to a TCP endpoint), bytes read
! from the optimized connection (incoming data from a WAAS peer), and bytes
! written to the optimized connection (outgoing data to a WAAS peer).
! In almost every circumstance, the original-side byte counts are larger
! than the optimized-side byte counts, unless the traffic is pre-compressed
! or pre-encrypted by the application or endpoints.
!


HTTP : 5417

     Time Statistics were Last Reset/Cleared:          Thu May 21
22:21:47 2009
     Total Bytes Read:                            1017     35218540
     Total Bytes Written:                         1017     35218540
     Total Bytes Buffered:                         0          0
     Total Internal Bytes Read:                    68
```

```
    Total Internal Bytes Written:                    100
    Bit Flags for I/O state:                         80
    Internal object pointer:                         134940536
    Fast connections:                                8
!
! if an accelerator is configured (discussed in chapter 9), its statistics
! will be displayed above.
!

————————- Flow 5417 dre stats —————————-

Conn-ID: 5417 10.10.13.100:3049 — 10.10.10.100:80  Peer No:  0 Status: Active
———————————————————————————————————————
Open at 05/21/2009 22:21:47, Still active
Encode:
    Overall: msg:         25, in:   1117 B, out:    439 B, ratio:  60.70%
        DRE: msg:          9, in:   1017 B, out:   1111 B, ratio:   0.00%
DRE Bypass: msg:          25, in:    100 B
         LZ: msg:          9, in:   1201 B, out:    263 B, ratio:  78.10%
 LZ Bypass: msg:          16, in:     10 B
    Avg latency:      0.229 ms    Delayed msg:               0
    Encode th-put:    190 KB/s
    Message size distribution:
    0-1K=0%  1K-5K=0%  5K-15K=0%  15K-25K=0%  25K-40K=0%  >40K=0%
Decode:
    Overall: msg:        444, in:  51490 B, out:  34393 KB, ratio:  99.85%
        DRE: msg:        436, in:  84115 B, out:  34393 KB, ratio:  99.76%
DRE Bypass: msg:          25, in:     68 B
         LZ: msg:          38, in:   5804 B, out:  38607 B, ratio:  84.97%
 LZ Bypass: msg:         406, in:  45686 B
    Avg latency:      1.443 ms
    Decode th-put:  53672 KB/s
    Message size distribution:
    0-1K=0%  1K-5K=3%  5K-15K=2%  15K-25K=3%  25K-40K=10%  >40K=81%
!
! the above provides a summary of DRE statistics for the connection up to
! the point when the CLI was executed. Notice there are sections for both
! encode (taking original data and optimizing it) and decode (taking
! optimized data and reverting it back to original), including byte counts,
! compression ratios (for both DRE and PLZ), average latency penalty
! incurred by use of PLZ and DRE, encode throughput, decode throughput,
! and the message size distribution for both encode and decode. Message
! size distribution provides insight into the size of the messages that
! are received on the original and optimized connections. Smaller message
```

```
! sizes typically indicate a transactional application, whereas larger
! message sizes typically indicate an application that is transferring
! bulk data, such as a large HTTP download (exactly what this example is
! showing), FTP, and so on.
!
! ... portions removed ...
```

The second way of accessing this information is through the CM GUI by accessing the device context and visiting **Monitor > Optimization > Connections Statistics**. This page provides you with visibility into all the optimized connections being handled by the device. The table can be filtered based on any of the tuple information (source or destination IP, source or destination port), and the table shows the tuple, the peer WAAS device ID, the applied policy (using icons, hovering over the icon displays what it means), the length of time that the connection has been open, original and optimized byte counts, compression ratio, and the classifier name in use. Connections that cannot be classified have a New Classifier button next to them, which enables you to quickly create a classifier. Doing so minimizes the use of the "Other" traffic class and allows charts to provide more useful information. Figure 8-24 shows the Connection Statistics page.

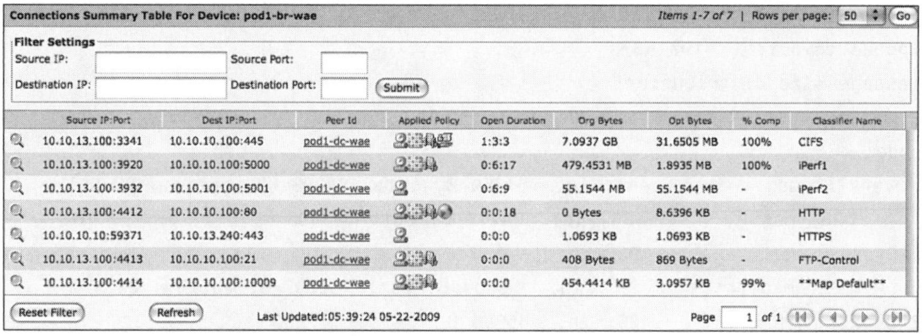

Figure 8-24   *Connection Statistics Page in CM GUI*

The magnifying glass icon next to each of the connection entries provides a simplified means of drilling into the details for a specific connection. By clicking this icon, a pop-up window displays that is automatically refreshed every three seconds to provide a near real-time view. As the connection-specific data is fetched from the WAAS device directly (based on which device's context you happen to be in at the time), it is recommended that opening connection details be performed against devices that are close in proximity to the CM device. Figure 8-25 shows an example of the pop-up window that appears when clicking the magnifying glass next to the connection entry in the tabular list.

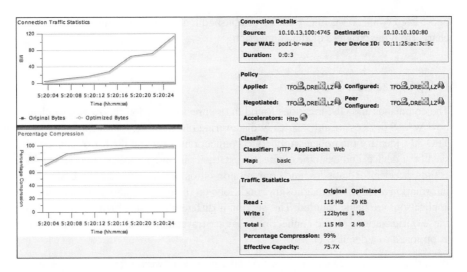

Figure 8-25 *Detailed Connection Statistics from CM GUI*

As demonstrated in Figure 8-25, you can determine the following details about the connection:

■ **Connection Details:** Includes details about four-tuple, duration (length of the connection), peer device name, and device ID of the peer WAAS device used to optimize the connection.

■ **Policy:** Includes details about the locally configured policy, configured policy on the peer, negotiated policy, and applied policy. This is identical to the **show statistics connection conn-id** output as shown previously.

■ **Classifier:** Includes details about the name of the classifier that the traffic matched, the application group that the statistics are associated with, and the type of policy map (based on configuration).

■ **Traffic Statistics:** Includes details about the original connection and optimized connection statistics, including bytes read, bytes written, total bytes, percentage compression, and effective capacity gain through optimization (represented as an X-Factor).

■ **Connection Traffic Statistics:** Provides a graphical representation of the original and optimized byte counts over time.

■ **Percentage Compression:** Provides a graphical representation of the amount of compression applied to the connection graphed over time.

The information found in the Connection Details pane continues to refresh throughout the life of the connection. Graphs and statistics are continually updated. This information is especially helpful to track the progress and performance of long-lived connections.

Short-lived connections might not be established long enough to capture meaningful charts from the progress of the connection.

WAN Optimization Statistics

The commands and GUI locations found in the previous sections allow you to identify how WAAS devices are automatically discovering one another, issues encountered during TFO AD, identify the policies applied to connections, examine the list of connections seen by a device, and examine connection statistics including policy negotiation, byte counts, accelerator statistics, and compression ratios on a per-connection basis. This information is helpful in diagnosing conditions on the network and understanding how applications are being handled. This section is different in that it focuses on the impact of these optimizations on the connections that are traversing the network at a broader level as opposed to a detail level.

Both the WAAS device CLI and the CM GUI provide powerful reporting tools that provide visibility to help administrators with four key use cases, including:

- Profiling the network to understand the types of traffic and applications that are present

- Understanding the performance improvement provided by WAAS

- Understanding device and system performance and scalability metrics

- Presenting reports to an executive team

Each of these use cases is examined in this section.

> **Note**   Creation of PDF reports and CSV export are discussed in Chapter 7, "System and Device Management." Any of the CM GUI charts that are discussed in this section can be included into the PDF reporting workflow, and CSV exporting is available from these charts.

Network Profiling

Many customers find it important to first understand their network and the application profiles on the network prior to deploying WAN optimization and application acceleration. Numerous tools exist today that provide visibility into application performance prior to deployment of Cisco WAAS to identify locations that are the best candidates for optimization. These tools include:

- **NetFlow:** NetFlow is included on many Cisco routing and switching products and is helpful in that it provides visibility data necessary to identify which applications are on the network and metrics for each, including who the top talkers are. NetFlow is comprised of two key elements—a probe with export functionality (monitoring the network and sending information about the network), and a collector (which receives the export packets from the probe. Numerous options are available for NetFlow collection, including:

- Cisco Network Analysis Module (NAM), which is available as an appliance, integrated module for the Cisco ISR and Catalyst 6500 family, or WAAS VB

- NetQoS Performance Center

- Fluke NetFlow Tracker

- Solarwinds Orion Family

- Paessler Router Traffic Grapher (PRTG)

- Plixer Scrutinizer

- **Application Response Time (ART):** ART measurement provides a more granular view of the performance of an application in that it can be used to identify the cause of performance degradation. While NetFlow can help you deduce throughput of an application, ART measurements give you visibility into *why* an application is performing the way it is performing by highlighting the interaction between client and server and showing the delay metrics for each step in processing. For instance, ART metrics can highlight delays caused by the client, the network, and the server. Network delays can be partially or wholly overcome in some cases by application acceleration and WAN optimization, whereas server delays could be caused by an overloaded system or incorrect configuration. Numerous options are available for monitoring ART, including:

- Cisco Network Analysis Module (NAM)

- NetQoS Performance Center

- Fluke Visual Performance Manager

- **SNMP MIBs:** Cisco IOS devices host a number of Management Informations Bases (MIB) that can be integrated into SNMP monitoring systems to better understand network conditions and application characteristics. These include the class-based QoS (CBQOS) MIB along with the Network Based Application Recognition (NBAR) MIB. CBQOS MIB is helpful in understanding how QoS in the network is adapting traffic to configured policy, providing visibility into application behavior, and NBAR MIB is helpful in identifying key applications that are on the network and statistics for each. SNMP is one of the most widely used monitoring protocols available today and a list of candidates would be too lengthy and too competitive to present here.

Figure 8-26 and 8-27 show examples of how the network can be profiled using NetFlow and application response time measurements using NetQoS.

WAAS devices also collect statistics about traffic traversing the network. The traffic that is examined by WAAS is influenced by the type of network interception that is in place. For instance, with WCCPv2, only TCP traffic is diverted to WAAS, and this traffic might be filtered further by redirect lists (through use of access control lists [ACL]). With inline interception, WAAS devices see all traffic, but compute only statistics against TCP traffic.

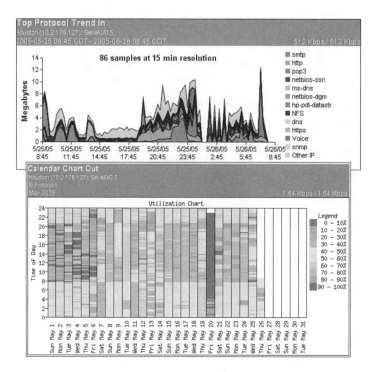

Figure 8-26 *Network Throughput and Utilization Baselining Using NetQoS*

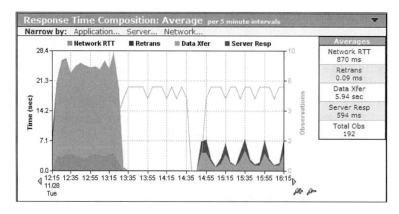

Figure 8-27 *Application Response Time Measurement Using NetQoS*

The easiest way within the WAAS CM to identify what traffic types are found on the network in a given location is to use the Traffic Summary chart, which is available in the device context and the My WAN context, using the Dashboard link under the Traffic tab. Additionally, this chart is available in the Monitor drawer at **Monitor > Traffic Summary Report**. Figure 8-28 provides an example of the Traffic Summary chart, which is helpful in understanding what applications—based on WAAS classification—have been detected on the network. As described in Chapter 7, and applicable to other charts discussed in this chapter and Chapter 9, these charts can be filtered on a variety of parameters through the Settings button. Hovering over any section of the pie shows you the name of the application group (comprised of associated classifiers) and the byte counts over the sample period for that application group.

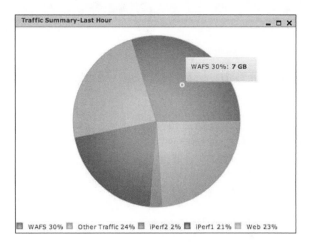

Figure 8-28 *Traffic Summary Chart in CM GUI*

Similarly, the CM GUI provides visibility into the original traffic load supplied by clients and servers in the network over the sample period configured in the settings page. This chart, called the Original Traffic over Time chart, can also be filtered to show specific application groups, whereas by default, the chart shows All Traffic, both original, and pass-through traffic. This chart, like the Traffic Summary chart, is available in the device or My WAN context using the dashboard link, or via the Traffic Summary Report found in the Monitor drawer. Figure 8-29 shows an example of the Original Traffic over Time chart. Note that the chart shows byte counts over time, which can be used to provide a reasonable estimation of throughput. In this example, the chart is filtered to show Web and All Traffic.

The CLI provides access to the raw data that is mediated and summarized by the CM prior to visualization. Rather than providing values according to the sample intervals that are defined in the CM charts, the CLI provides access to a complete sum of all counts of data since the previous system restart, service restart, or the last clearing of the statistics. The command **show statistics application** provides per-application group statistics for both inbound and outbound traffic flows and is organized by how the traffic was handled by the system. When you execute this command on its own, it returns statistics for all applications (and the output is rather long). It is best to filter the command using the name of the application group you would like to retrieve the statistics for, as shown in the annotated output in Example 8-22.

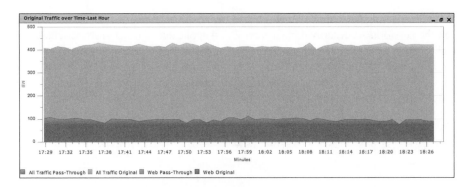

Figure 8-29 *Original Traffic over Time Chart in CM GUI*

Example 8-22 *Per-Application Group Statistics in CLI*

```
pod1-br-wae# show statistics application ?
  savings  Display application savings statistics
  WORD     Application name
  |        Output Modifiers
  <cr>
pod1-br-wae# show statistics application Web ?
  |      Output Modifiers
  <cr>
pod1-br-wae# show statistics application Web
Application              Inbound              Outbound
                         _____      _____


Web
  Opt TCP Plus:
    Bytes                      237271965             102950125
    Packets                      1503740               1565115
!
! Opt TCP Plus shows the byte counts and packet counts for traffic on
! optimized connections that have been optimized by capabilities beyond
! basic TFO, including DRE, PLZ, or an AO
!
  Orig TCP Plus:
    Bytes                     1621668256           90745719665
    Packets                     40461579              61735134
!
! Orig TCP Plus shows the byte counts and packet counts for traffic on
! original connections that have been optimized by capabilities beyond
! basic TFO, including DRE, PLZ, or an AO
!
```

```
  Opt Preposition:
    Bytes                              0                          0
    Packets                            0                          0
  Orig Preposition:
    Bytes                              0                          0
    Packets                            0                          0
  Opt TCP Only:
    Bytes                              0                          0
    Packets                            0                          0
!
! Opt TCP Only shows the byte counts and packet counts for traffic on
! optimized connections that have been optimized only by TFO
!
  Orig TCP Only:
    Bytes                              0                          0
    Packets                            0                          0
!
! Orig TCP Only shows the byte counts and packet counts for traffic on
! original connections that have been optimized only by TFO
!
! ... portions removed ...
!


                       Active              Completed
                  ————————————    ————————————
  Opt TCP Plus        1                      23349
  Preposition         0                         0
  Opt TCP Only        0                         0
  Internal Client     0                         0
  Internal Server     0                       139
  PT No Peer          0                       174
  PT Config           0                         0
  PT Intermediate     0                         0
  PT_Other            0                         1
!
! The section above shows connection counts based on the type of
! connection and how the connection was handled. This includes Opt
! TCP Plus and Opt TCP only (as described above), internal client and
! internal server (meaning the connection was initiated or terminated
! by a local WAAS process), and pass-through conditions.
!
```

Understanding WAAS Performance Improvement

In addition to being filtered by an application group name (demonstrated in Example 8-22), you can extend the **show statistics application** command to include the savings that were received for the application group by appending the keyword **savings** to the command, as demonstrated in Example 8-23. Similarly, this command can be filtered by application group, as shown in the example.

Example 8-23   *Savings Per-Application in CLI*

```
pod1-br-wae# show statistics application savings ?
  WORD   Application name
  |      Output Modifiers
  <cr>
pod1-br-wae# show statistics application savings Web
Application                  Inbound              Outbound
                             _____ _____

Web
  TCP Plus:
     Bytes                   91111823911          1528891717
     Packets                 60633781             39156677
     Compression Ratio       382.74:1             15.76:1
  Preposition:
     Bytes                   0                    0
     Packets                 0                    0
     Compression Ratio       1.00:1               1.00:1
  TCP Only:
     Bytes                   0                    0
     Packets                 0                    0
     Compression Ratio       1.00:1               1.00:1
  Overall:
     Bytes                   91111823911          1528891717
     Packets                 60633781             39156677
     Compression Ratio       382.74:1             15.76:1
```

Notice in the example how the byte counts, packet counts, and compression ratios are shown for both the inbound and outbound direction for TCP Plus traffic (optimized by an optimization component beyond TFO), preposition traffic (if preposition is applicable to the application), TCP Only (optimized only by TFO), and overall. Although this information is useful, it is often more useful to see the data plotted over time, which the CM provides from an original versus optimized throughput perspective and also from a compression-ratio perspective. A number of charts are available that provide better visibility into this data.

The first is found in the Traffic tab of the dashboard page under the device or My WAN context and is called Optimized Traffic over Time. This chart is also available under the Monitor drawer in the Traffic Summary Report. An example of this chart is shown in Figure 8-30, and like Figure 8-29, this chart is filtered. In addition to showing All Traffic, this chart is filtered to show three other application groups. Like the chart shown in Figure 8-29, this chart shows both the optimized traffic and pass-through traffic for All Traffic and each of the application groups that are selected under the Settings button. It is helpful to examine this chart while examining the Original Traffic over Time chart to see a comparison of the traffic load prior to optimization and the traffic load after optimization. Additionally, it is important to compare the amount of traffic in either case to the amount of traffic that has been passed through, that is, not optimized. Like any chart, you can hover over any of the data points in the chart, and a pop-up provides you with additional data about the sample that is hovered over.

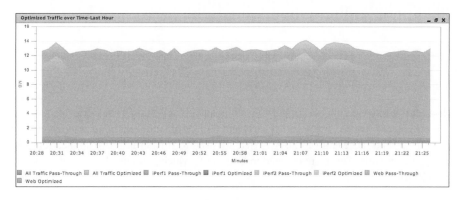

Figure 8-30   *Optimized Traffic over Time Chart in CM GUI*

Should you be interested in seeing the top applications based on compression ratios achieved, you can use the Compression Summary chart. You can find the Compression Summary chart on the Optimization tab of the Dashboard link or in the Monitor drawer under Traffic Optimization Report. This chart shows a bar graph with up to ten applications listed in order based on the compression ratio that has been achieved for the application over the sample period. A more granular compression chart called Bandwidth Optimization is also available at these same locations, which shows the effective capacity of the WAN link based on the compression ratio achieved. This chart is also filterable by application, allowing you to see per-application the "X-Factor," or multipler for the WAN capacity, provided through the use of PLZ and DRE. A third chart called Traffic Volume and Reduction combines the total traffic load applied to the device (original traffic) with the optimized traffic load and highlights the compression ratio that has been achieved. Traffic Volume and Reduction shows data from all traffic and is not filterable to a specific application group. Figure 8-31 shows an example of all three of these charts.

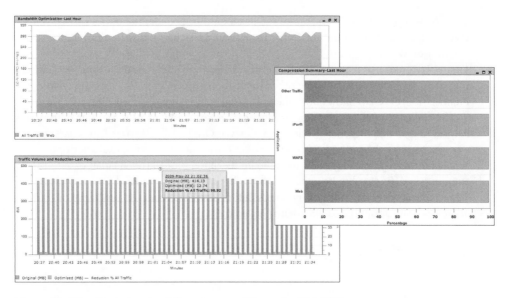

Figure 8-31   *Optimization Measurement Charts in CM GUI*

In addition to providing charts and CLI commands that quantify the performance improvement provided by WAAS, charts and CLI commands exist that provide visibility into the level of acceleration the AOs that are used to further improve application performance provide. These are covered in Chapter 9, which is focused solely on application acceleration.

Understanding Device and System Performance and Scalability Metrics

The WAAS device CLI and CM GUI provide visibility into the device and system performance and scalability metrics, which helps to answer questions such as:

- Is my device or location sized correctly?

- Do I need to add or remove devices from this location?

- Am I seeing adequate compression history on this device?

WAAS devices are like other devices on the network; they have CPUs, memory, and disk. The WAAS software is designed to make maximum use of available memory with or without load applied to ensure rapid processing of traffic; thus, monitoring memory is not a fruitful exercise. The devices are designed to operate at high levels of CPU utilization, so monitoring CPU utilization provides little value unless the utilization remains consistently high over a long period of time, indicating a possible overload condition. The device CLI and CM GUI provide visibility into the CPU utilization to identify scenarios where utilization remains consistently high. Example 8-24 shows how to monitor the CPU utilization using the device CLI.

Example 8-24 *CPU Utilization Monitoring in CLI*

```
pod1-br-wae# show processes ?
  cpu      Display CPU utilization
  debug    Display process progress. (Warning: very intrusive)
  memory   Display memory allocation of processes
  system   Display system load information.
  ¦        Output Modifiers
  <cr>
pod1-br-wae# show processes cpu ?
  ¦      Output Modifiers
  <cr>
pod1-br-wae# show processes cpu
CPU average usage since last reboot:
  cpu: 0.72% User,  19.82% System,  39.84% User(nice),  39.62% Idle
- - - - - - - - - - - - - - - - - - - - - - - - - - - - - - -
 PID  STATE PRI User T  SYS T       COMMAND
- -.  - -.  - -  - - -  - - -  - - - - - - - - - -
    1   S    0  135047  68762       (init)
    2   S   -5      0       0       (kthreadd)
    3   S   -5      0       0       (migration/0)
    4   S   -5      0       0       (ksoftirqd/0)
!
! ... portions removed ...
!
```

The CM GUI provides a chart dedicated to this task. Unlike the CLI command, which shows the average since the last reboot, the CM GUI chart shows the utilization of the CPU over the time period specified. This chart can be found in the device context only, either on the Dashboard Platform tab, or in the Monitor drawer under **Platform > CPU Statistics**. Figure 8-32 shows an example of this chart. Should you identify a device with a consistently high CPU utilization, it might be indicative of a load condition that is greater than the device's capacity. It should be noted that WAAS devices can (and should) spike to high levels of CPU utilization. This is normal; however, sustained high CPU utilization (>90 percent) is not.

Along with monitoring CPU utilization, it is helpful to monitor the state of the disk subsystem and its capacity. The **show disk** command provides insight into the physical disks, file systems, Self-Monitoring, Analysis, and Reporting Technology (SMART) status, and failure conditions, as shown in Example 8-25, which is annotated for clarity.

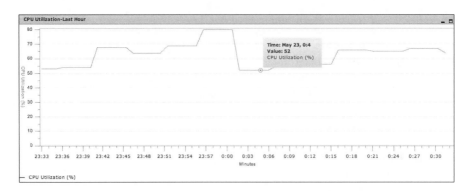

Figure 8-32 *Monitoring CPU Utilization in CM GUI*

Example 8-25 *Disk Monitoring in CLI*

```
pod1-br-wae# show disks ?
  details          Show current configurations with more details
  failed-disk-id   Show the list of disk serial numbers identified as failed
  failed-sectors   Show the list of failed sectors on the disks
  tech-support     Show hard drive diagnostic and failure prediction info (SMART)
pod1-br-wae# show disks details ?
  |       Output Modifiers
  <cr>
pod1-br-wae# show disks details

Physical disk information:
  disk00: Present    Y66E58PE   (h02 c00 i00 l00 - Int DAS-SATA)
          238472MB(232.9GB)
!
! The physical disks installed in the system are shown above, along with their
! capacity, serial number, connectivity type, and status. This system has only
! one drive, a 250GB SATA drive.
!
Mounted file systems:
  MOUNT POINT       TYPE        DEVICE        SIZE     INUSE        FREE   USE%
  /sw               internal    /dev/sdb1     991MB    912MB        79MB    92%
  /swstore          internal    /dev/sdb2     991MB    879MB       112MB    88%
  /state            internal    /dev/sdb3    3967MB    135MB      3832MB     3%
  /local/local1     SYSFS       /dev/sdb7   11903MB   1261MB     10642MB    10%
  /disk00-04        CONTENT     /dev/sdb6  211161MB   7825MB    203336MB     3%
  .../local1/spool  PRINTSPOOL  /dev/sdb8     991MB     16MB       975MB     1%

No RAID devices present.

Disk encryption feature is disabled.
!
! The above shows the file systems available on the system, the amount of
! allocated capacity, the amount of capacity consumed, the free capacity, and
```

```
! the percentage of the capacity that is available. If RAID is configured, it
! will be shown as present with a summary of the RAID device, and disk encryption
! status will be displayed.
!
pod1-br-wae# show disks ?
  details         Show current configurations with more details
  failed-disk-id  Show the list of disk serial number that has been identified
as failed
  failed-sectors  Show the list of failed sectors on the disks
  tech-support    Show hard drive diagnostic and failure prediction info (provid-
ed by SMART disk monitor)
pod1-br-wae# show disks failed-sectors

disk00
=========
(none)
!
! Any failed sectors on the disk will be indicated in the output above. Should
! a disk have failed sectors it is recommended that you have them replaced by
! contacting Cisco TAC.
!
pod1-br-wae# show disks tech-support ?
  details  Show disk monitoring info with more details
  |        Output Modifiers
  <cr>
pod1-br-wae# show disks tech-support
=== disk00 ===
=== START OF INFORMATION SECTION ===
Device Model:     Maxtor 7Y250M0
Serial Number:    Y66E58PE
Firmware Version: YAR51HW0
Device is:        In smartctl database [for details use: -P show]
ATA Version is:   7
ATA Standard is:  ATA/ATAPI-7 T13 1532D revision 0
Local Time is:    Fri May 22 17:39:39 2009 PDT
SMART support is: Available - device has SMART capability.
SMART support is: Enabled

=== START OF READ SMART DATA SECTION ===
SMART overall-health self-assessment test result: PASSED

!
! The output above shows detailed data about the device, including model,
! serial number, firmware version, and SMART status. The result of an
! overall health-assessment by SMART on the disk is shown (PASSED or FAILED).
! Detailed SMART information is shown in the next command output. For more
! detailed SMART test information and results, including the thresholds
! used by SMART on the disk, use the 'show disks tech-support details' command.
```

Aside from monitoring disk status and utilization, an important metric to monitor is the age of the oldest object in DRE. Monitoring the age of the oldest object in DRE provides a quick snapshot of how much compression history is available on a system. It is recommended that the system be sized appropriately to provide a minimum of three days worth of compression history, whereas seven days is the recommended compression history for optimum performance. As DRE is effectively a cache of TCP stream data and storage capacity is finite, it is expected that it becomes full over time. The device self-manages the eviction of old data to make room for new data automatically and does not require administrator intervention. Nor does the system require upfront planning in terms of capacity allocation within DRE across any peers that might be discovered.

To examine the age of the oldest data in DRE, use the CLI command **show statistics dre**, the output for which is annotated in Example 8-26.

Example 8-26 *DRE Monitoring in CLI*

```
pod1-br-wae#show statistics dre

Cache:
    Status: Usable, Oldest Data (age): 18h
    Total usable disk size:  26398 MB,  Used: 0.31%
      Hash table RAM  size:     99 MB,  Used: 0.00%
!
! The above shows the state of DRE (usable) and the oldest data in DRE.
! In this case (a freshly minted device) the DRE history is 18 hours long.
!


Connections:   Total (cumulative): 65773    Active: 6


Encode:
    Overall: msg:     6305101, in: 146594 MB, out:    449 MB, ratio:  99.69%
        DRE: msg:     6230398, in: 146483 MB, out:   1897 MB, ratio:  98.70%
DRE Bypass: msg:      870479, in:    111 MB
         LZ: msg:     4355231, in:   1847 MB, out:    282 MB, ratio:  84.72%
 LZ Bypass: msg:     1949870, in:    161 MB
    Avg latency:      2.068 ms     Delayed msg:    24244176
  Encode th-put:  11513 KB/s
  Message size distribution:
    0-1K=7%  1K-5K=2%  5K-15K=14%  15K-25K=31%  25K-40K=30%  >40K=13%
Decode:
    Overall: msg:     4348367, in:    430 MB, out: 195949 MB, ratio:  99.78%
        DRE: msg:     3529569, in:    596 MB, out: 195862 MB, ratio:  99.70%
DRE Bypass: msg:     1665561, in:  89431 KB
```

```
          LZ: msg:       1325711, in:      152 MB, out:      411 MB, ratio:  62.99%
    LZ Bypass: msg:       3022656, in:      277 MB
        Avg latency:        1.009 ms
     Decode th-put:    45724 KB/s
     Message size distribution:
        0-1K=9%   1K-5K=2%   5K-15K=2%   15K-25K=2%   25K-40K=11%   >40K=72%
     !
     ! Overall statistics for DRE in terms of encode and decode byte counts,
     ! compression ratios (for both DRE and PLZ), latency, throughput, and
     ! message size distribution are shown above.
     !
```

Should you have devices deployed in a location for a week or more and notice that the oldest object in your DRE history is less than a few days, it might be of value to add additional devices to increase the compression history for the site, or, move to a device with larger disk and DRE storage capacity. Similarly, interception configuration can impact the load distribution across devices and might also need to be considered.

Executive Reports

All the charts in the CM GUI are able to be added into existing or new reports as described in Chapter 7. A wealth of default reports are provided in the system and are accessible in the My WAN context under the Report drawer and by clicking on the **Manage Reports** link. On this page, notice a host of reports for WAN optimization and reports for application acceleration (discussed in Chapter 9). It is recommended that you revisit Chapter 7 for a full discussion on reporting in the CM GUI and the workflow used to create reports.

Integration with Third-Party Visibility Systems

Chapter 7 introduced the WAAS Central Manager eXtensible Markup Language-Application Programming Interface (XML-API) and a few of the interfaces that are available to integrate monitoring data into third-party systems. WAN optimization performance data can also be integrated into such systems, which enables customers better visibility into how application performance is being improved per-site and globally. Commonly called Application Performance Management (APM), such integration allows customers to take advantage of a single performance management system that utilizes multiple data sources (NetFlow SNMP, SPAN ports, WAAS CM XML-API, and WAAS FlowAgent) to correlate application performance and network condition measurements to understand how to improve application performance and ultimately uphold performance service level agreements (SLA).

WAN Optimization Monitoring with XML-API

The CM XML-API provides a number of interfaces that a third-party ISV solution can use to gather WAN optimization statistics from WAAS devices or the system as a whole. This XML-API also provides interfaces for the application optimizers, which is discussed in Chapter 9. The Traffic Acceleration service, also known as Traffic Stats and introduced in Chapter 7, provides four key interfaces:

- **getMonitoredApplications:** Takes no input, returns a list of the application groups that are defined on the CM that have been configured for monitoring.

- **retrieveAppTrafficStats:** Takes a device name, device group name or system as an input parameter along with a time frame object, and returns an array of traffic statistics that includes compressed bytes in and out, uncompressed bytes in and out pass-through bytes in and out (by pass-through reason, including peer, policy, overload, and intermediate device), the name of the application group, and the start and end times of the samples.

- **retrieveConnection:** Takes a device name and optional tuple information (source/destination IP/port) as input, and returns a list of the connections handled by that particular device, including key statistics such as tuple, peer name, applied policy, device name, connection duration, original and optimized bytes, and compression ratio.

- **retrieveCPUUtilization:** This interface is described in Chapter 7; the CPU utilization statistics over a period of time for a device are provided using this interface.

Figure 8-33 shows the output of the retrieveConnection call. This was generated using soapUI as per the instructions found in Chapter 7.

Most customers find it easier to take advantage of products from third-party independent software vendors (ISV), such as those listed in Chapter 7, to use the XML-API. This is primarily due to the fact that these systems are packaged as an integrated solution, requiring no custom development work by the customer. However, some customers that have custom-built applications for their network operations center (NOC) find that integration using the XML-API is simple (web services) and useful in terms of providing visibility into application performance and optimization metrics.

Application Response Time Monitoring

ART monitoring provides visibility into the response time elements that comprise the transfer of data to support the use of an application. ART monitoring is typically employed by using a system that collects packets promiscuously from the data center LAN and monitors the transmission of data and TCP signaling (such as acknowledgements) to determine metrics such as:

■ **Network round trip time (NRTT):** The amount of time it takes for data to reach an endpoint and for an acknowledgement to be received. This value is primarily impacted by the amount of distance between the nodes, but can also be impacted by serialization, queuing, and processing delays found in intermediary devices.

■ **Connection setup times:** The amount of time it takes for a connection to be established between TCP endpoints, along with the time delay caused by each endpoint.

■ **Server response time:** The amount of time taken by a server to process a request and send a response to that request.

■ **Retransmission delay:** The amount of time taken by an endpoint to retransmit a segment that has been determined to have been lost in the network and not delivered to the other endpoint.

■ **Data transfer time:** The amount of time it takes to fully transmit a response to a request.

■ **Total transaction time:** The amount of time it takes from the start of the request to the end of the response.

```
<soapenv:Envelope xmlns:soapenv="http://sc
   <soapenv:Header/>
   <soapenv:Body>
      <ser:retrieveConnection>
         <!--Optional:-->
         <ser:name>pod1-br-wae</ser:name>
         <!--Optional:-->
         <ser:objType>wae</ser:objType>
         <!--Optional:-->
         <ser:srcip>?</ser:srcip>
         <!--Optional:-->
         <ser:srcport>?</ser:srcport>
         <!--Optional:-->
         <ser:dstip>?</ser:dstip>
         <!--Optional:-->
         <ser:dstport>?</ser:dstport>
      </ser:retrieveConnection>
   </soapenv:Body>
</soapenv:Envelope>
```

```
<soapenv:Envelope xmlns:soapenv="http://schemas.xmlsoap.org/soap/envelope/">
   <soapenv:Body>
      <ns:retrieveConnectionResponse xmlns:ns="http://service.stats.ws.waas.cisco.com"
         <ns:return type="com.cisco.waas.ws.stats.ConnectionStats">
            <ax27:appliedpolicy>TFO,DRE,LZ,</ax27:appliedpolicy>
            <ax27:compressratio>0.9965755349485602</ax27:compressratio>
            <ax27:devicename>pod1-br-wae</ax27:devicename>
            <ax27:dstip>10.10.10.100</ax27:dstip>
            <ax27:dstport>5000</ax27:dstport>
            <ax27:duration>Sat May 23 01:20:41 GMT 2009</ax27:duration>
            <ax27:optimizedbytes>3578188</ax27:optimizedbytes>
            <ax27:originalbytes>1044889624</ax27:originalbytes>
            <ax27:peername>pod1-dc-wae</ax27:peername>
            <ax27:srcip>10.10.13.100</ax27:srcip>
            <ax27:srcport>1952</ax27:srcport>
         </ns:return>
         <ns:return type="com.cisco.waas.ws.stats.ConnectionStats">
            <ax27:appliedpolicy>TFO,DRE,LZ,CIFS</ax27:appliedpolicy>
            <ax27:compressratio>0.9981395793130258</ax27:compressratio>
            <ax27:devicename>pod1-br-wae</ax27:devicename>
            <ax27:dstip>10.10.10.100</ax27:dstip>
            <ax27:dstport>445</ax27:dstport>
            <ax27:duration>Fri May 22 06:15:29 GMT 2009</ax27:duration>
            <ax27:optimizedbytes>271134657</ax27:optimizedbytes>
            <ax27:originalbytes>145738358479</ax27:originalbytes>
            <ax27:peername>pod1-dc-wae</ax27:peername>
            <ax27:srcip>10.10.13.100</ax27:srcip>
            <ax27:srcport>4762</ax27:srcport>
         </ns:return>
```

Figure 8-33 *SoapUI Query Showing Statistics from retrieveConnection*

Gathering ART metrics is an important component in understanding end-to-end application performance. With ART, the various delay components that impact the overall performance of the application can be quickly identified, which can guide you toward the area where efforts should be focused. For instance, high connection setup times might be indicative of an overloaded server, as would server response time. Network round trip time can be indicative of suboptimal routing, or a site where WAN optimization might prove beneficial. Figure 8-34 illustrates the various elements that make up application response time.

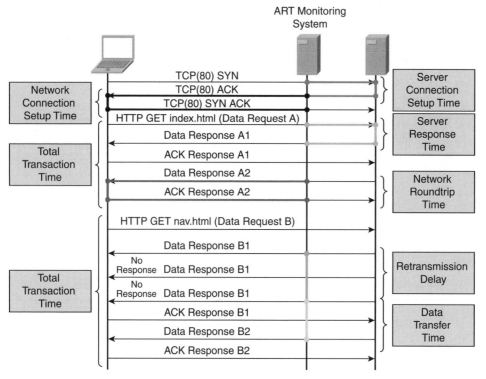

Figure 8-34 *Application Response Time Components*

ART measurement and WAN optimization are fundamentally at odds with one another. The primary reason being that most WAN optimization devices—Cisco WAAS included—act as proxies to TCP, providing local acknowledgement and taking ownership of the transmission (and retransmission) of data on behalf of the TCP endpoint. Local acknowledgements from a TCP proxy can skew the measurement of any ART metric that involves a comparison of time between two elements. For instance, network round trip time (NRTT) can be skewed and appear to be near zero, even in the highest latency WAN conditions, if an acceleration device that provides TCP proxy functionality is sitting between the ART monitoring system and the WAN router. This is commonly called *distortion* of the ART measurement, or *WOC Distortion* (WOC stands for WAN Optimization Controller), a term coined by Cathy Fulton, the CTO of NetQoS. The effects of WOC distortion can be clearly seen in Figure 8-35.

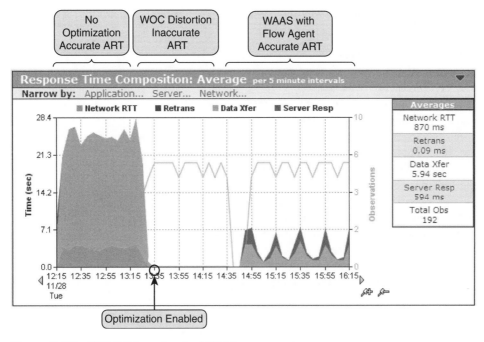

Figure 8-35 *WOC Distortion in ART Measurements*

Notice in the figure that when optimization is enabled, ART measurement becomes so skewed by the presence of the TCP proxy that it appears as though there is no delay in the network. This is primarily due to the behavior of the TCP proxy—TCP segments are locally acknowledged, and in certain cases, application-layer messages can even be locally acknowledged. Such behavior dramatically improves the performance of the application but blocks the accurate measurement of ART. To compensate for this condition, Cisco WAAS includes a feature called FlowAgent, which was developed in conjunction with NetQoS to be interoperable with the NetQoS Performance Center solution. FlowAgent is an interface that runs on WAAS devices and sends TCP ACK information for monitored servers to NetQoS Super Agent (a component of Performance Center), which can then accurately calculate ART. Notice in Figure 8-35 that with FlowAgent enabled, the ART metrics are accurate given the presence of optimization.

Note The Cisco Network Analysis Module (NAM) (which can be deployed as an appliance, integrated module for the Catalyst 6500 series or ISR, or WAAS VB) also supports FlowAgent to provide accurate ART metrics in a "WAASified" network.

FlowAgent can be configured using the device CLI or from the CM GUI. The only parameter required is the IP address of the recipient. Example 8-27 provides an annotated configuration of FlowAgent and examination of FlowAgent statistics.

Example 8-27   *Configuring FlowAgent and Viewing Statistics Using CLI*

```
pod1-br-wae# config term
pod1-br-wae(config)# flow ?
  monitor   Monitor flow performance configuration
pod1-br-wae(config)# flow monitor ?
  tcpstat-v1   tcpstat-v1 Collector configuration
pod1-br-wae(config)# flow monitor tcpstat-v1 ?
  enable   Enable flow monitoring
  host      Specify the collection control agent
pod1-br-wae(config)# flow monitor tcpstat-v1 enable
The host must be configured prior to enabling.

pod1-br-wae(config)# flow monitor tcpstat-v1 host 10.10.10.10
pod1-br-wae(config)# flow monitor tcpstat-v1 enable
pod1-br-wae(config)# end
pod1-br-wae# show stat flow ?
  filters   Display flow filters statistics
  monitor   Display monitor flow performance statistics
pod1-br-wae# show stat flow monitor ?
  tcpstat-v1   Display tcpstat-v1 Collector statistics
pod1-br-wae# show stat flow monitor tcpstat-v1 ?
  ¦       Output Modifiers
  <cr>
pod1-br-wae# show stat flow monitor tcpstat-v1

Host Connection:
  Configured host address:          10.10.10.10
  Connection State:                 Trying to Connect
  Connection Attempts:              2
  Connection Failures:              2
  Last connection failure:          Fri May 22 19:29:48 2009
  Last configuration check sent:    -Never-
  Last registration occurred:       -Never-
  Host Version:                     0.0.0
!
! The host connection shows the IP address and state of the connection
! from the WAAS device to this host, along with number of connection attempts
! and failures.
!

Collector Connection:
  Collector host address:port:      0.0.0.0:0
  Connection State:                 Not Connected
  Connection Attempts:              0
```

```
   Connection Failures:                   0
   Last connection failure:               -Never-
   Last configuration check sent:         -Never-
   Last update sent:                       -Never-
   Updates sent:                          0
   Summaries discarded:                   0
   Last registration occurred:            -Never-
   Host Version:                          0.0.0
!
! The collector host is provided to the WAAS device by the tcpstat-v1 host
! defined in the CLI. This is the host that the WAAS device will send TCP
! ACK and other data to for purposes of collection and data correlation.
!
! ... portions removed ...
```

FlowAgent can be configured in the CM GUI in either the device or device group context. The configuration page is found at **Configure > Monitoring > Flow Monitor** and is
shown in Figure 8-36. The remainder of the configuration should be done either from the
NetQoS Performance Center (or Cisco NAM), which includes configuration of specific
hosts to monitor the ART of.

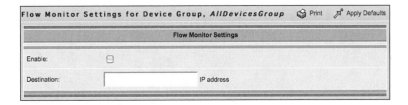

Figure 8-36   *Configuring FlowAgent Using CM GUI*

Summary

Cisco WAAS provides powerful WAN optimization capabilities, including TFO, DRE,
and PLZ, to minimize bandwidth consumption, minimize the impact of latency, and
improve overall application performance. WAAS devices automatically discover one
another during the establishment of TCP connections and advertise their availability to
optimize and the policy that they would like to employ. Devices negotiate policy based
on configured policy, load conditions, and other factors, and device groups can be used
in the CM to minimize the possibility of policy overlap or underlap across devices.

The ATP is the component of the WAAS device in which policies are configured (either
through the CLI or CM GUI) that dictate what actions a WAAS device attempts to apply
to a specific type of connection based on its classification. After a policy to apply has
been negotiated between the two peers, WAAS devices begin applying one or many opti-

mizations to the connection based on the negotiated policy and collecting statistics against the connection and the optimization components employed. These statistics are made available to the user both in the WAAS device CLI and in a number of charts in the CM GUI, which provide helpful insight into how the system is performing and what conditions are being encountered by the WAAS devices.

The XML-API provides integration into third-party visibility systems and contains interfaces that allow for detailed statistics about optimization components to be shared with these systems. FlowAgent can be used on WAAS in conjunction with Cisco NAM or NetQoS Performance Center for accurate visibility into application response time components within the network, even in the presence of WAN optimization.

While this chapter focused on the WAN optimization capabilities of WAAS, the next chapter focuses on the application acceleration capabilities of WAAS. Chapter 9 is structured in a similar manner as Chapter 8 and provides similar content but for application-specific optimization components.

Configuring Application Acceleration

Previous chapters have examined a number of aspects of Cisco Wide Area Application Services (WAAS), ranging from network integration to management to configuring WAN optimization policies. This chapter focuses on the application acceleration components of Cisco WAAS, which help enable IT organizations to

- Improve performance of accessing servers, storage, and application over the WAN to maintain LAN-like performance expectations and bolster employee productivity for centralized applications

- Improve posture toward data protection and compliance through secure acceleration and centralization of distributed infrastructure

- Consolidate servers, storage, and applications to minimize costs and operational complexity while confidently deploying applications and video globally

This chapter provides a technical overview and architectural examination of the application acceleration capabilities provided by Cisco WAAS, implemented through acceleration components called *application optimizers (AO)*. *Application optimizers* and *application accelerators* are terms that are used interchangeably throughout this section. This chapter also provides a detailed explanation of how to configure and integrate Cisco WAAS application acceleration into a network. Along with providing an examination of how Cisco WAAS accelerates many different application layer protocols, this chapter explores the use cases that are enabled through this powerful technology.

Application Acceleration Overview

As discussed earlier in the book, WAN optimization refers to techniques that are employed to overcome WAN conditions, making the WAN more tolerable from an application performance perspective and more conducive to higher performance. Whereas WAN optimization focuses specifically on application-agnostic techniques to accomplish this lofty goal, application acceleration focuses on specific applications and protocols to improve performance. To compare and contrast, WAN optimization helps improve transport characteristics, efficiency, and performance, whereas application acceleration interacts with the application protocols themselves to overcome performance-limiting factors. Employing both of these techniques to flows traversing the WAN provides the powerful framework for ensuring that distributed users can interact with applications and collaborate with other users at performance levels similar to those enjoyed by users in the corporate campus, near the application servers themselves. This level of performance might also exist due to the many years of having deployed distributed infrastructure as well.

Application acceleration, especially when deployed in conjunction with WAN optimization, bridges the divide between two opposing forces. The first force is the drive to consolidate costly infrastructure for the obvious operational and capital savings (management, utilization, efficiency, data protection, recovery, hardware, and more). The challenge with consolidation is that a large portion of enterprise users would then be separated by the WAN from the resources they need to be productive, which significantly impedes performance (as discussed earlier in the book). The second force is the drive to empower remote users to increase productivity and efficiency. This force is in stark contrast to consolidation, because a foundational concept of empowering users to increase efficiency and performance is that they have application infrastructure readily available with high performance access without limitation. This force tends to dictate the need to distribute application infrastructure.

Application acceleration helps bridge this divide by providing the best of both worlds—infrastructure consolidation and application acceleration—and provides the user with near-LAN response time in an environment where infrastructure is consolidated. Application acceleration, like WAN optimization, generally relies on a device deployed on both sides of a WAN link (such as a Cisco WAAS appliance or network module). These devices interact with application protocols to minimize the impact of latency, loss, and bandwidth limitations by acting as a transparent or nontransparent application layer proxy. The device closest to the user acts like the server to the user, whereas the device closest to the server acts like the user to the server. This architecture is similar to the TCP proxy architecture presented in Chapter 8, "Configuring WAN Optimization," but rather than interacting at the transport layer, application acceleration operates at the session layer or above.

It should be noted that some forms of application acceleration can be implemented in a single-ended manner, typically in the data center, but these capabilities are generally less powerful than those that can be provided by a symmetric solution such as Cisco WAAS. Single-ended acceleration solutions are commonly found coupled with application delivery controller (ADC) devices that provide server load balancing (SLB) functionality. Although these are effective, the broad consensus is that dual-ended solutions are able to provide orders of magnitude improvement beyond what a single-ended solution can provide. It should be noted, however, that these technologies are generally not mutually exclusive. That is, many customers have chosen to deploy both together and find the two approaches to be complementary.

Figure 9-1 shows an example of how application acceleration operates logically from a transaction flow perspective. This example looks at Common Internet File System (CIFS), which is commonly used for file sharing in Microsoft environments.

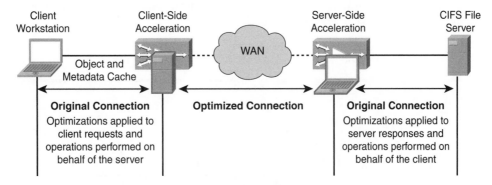

Figure 9-1 *Integration of Application Acceleration in a CIFS Environment*

As mentioned in Chapter 1, "Introduction to Cisco Wide Area Application Services (WAAS)," the application acceleration architecture of Cisco WAAS uses a number of acceleration techniques, including data and metadata caching, read-ahead, write-behind, pipelining, and multiplexing, to improve performance while enabling centralization. WAAS today supports application acceleration for CIFS (Microsoft Windows file sharing), Windows print, NFS (UNIX file sharing), Messaging Application Programming Interface (MAPI) (Microsoft Exchange/Outlook), HTTP (Intranet and Internet applications), SSL (encrypted traffic), and Windows Media over RTSP (video). The next sections provide an overview of each, including their use cases and high-level functional components. All of these acceleration capabilities take advantage of the underlying WAN optimization features provided by WAAS as discussed in Chapter 8. Cisco has taken a unique approach to developing acceleration capabilities for the protocols we are about to discuss. Rather than reverse engineering the behavior of applications using these protocols (or the protocols themselves), Cisco has chosen to license the technology and protocols directly from application vendors to ensure correctness. This is in stark contrast to other approaches that involve risky reverse-engineering, which cannot cover all permutations of protocol and application behavior.

CIFS Acceleration

CIFS acceleration is provided to help improve the performance of accessing file servers over the WAN. Through acceleration, WAAS is able to provide near-LAN performance for remote office users, which provides consistency for the user when file servers are centralized from the branch offices into the data center. Additionally, for scenarios where users are already accessing centralized file servers, performance is dramatically improved, which helps foster productivity and collaboration. Alongside improving the performance of file server access over the WAN, WAAS employs acceleration in such a way that the majority of the workload is offloaded from the file server and handled by the WAAS-enabled network. This enables organizations to not just *centralize* file servers, but also *consolidate* file servers into a smaller number of more scalable servers. Figure 9-2 provides a visualization of the actual server offload provided by Cisco WAAS through CIFS acceleration. Through WAAS CIFS server offload, many organizations have realized more than a 50% reduction in server workload.

Before WAAS   After WAAS

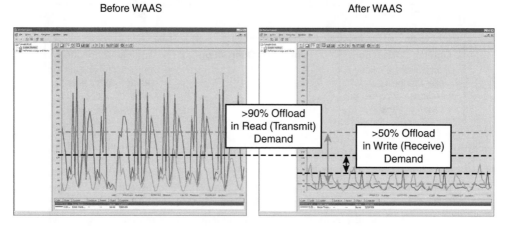

Figure 9-2   *CIFS Acceleration Offloads File Servers*

In addition to file server consolidation, CIFS acceleration is helpful in environments where software packages need to be distributed to remote offices, as well as video on demand files for training (when accessed via a file share). The reason that the CIFS acceleration in WAAS is able to address such a diverse set of use cases is due to the set of capabilities that are employed when optimizing CIFS traffic, which are described as follows:

■ **Safe data and metadata caching:** WAAS edges that are deployed close to the workstations are able to retain copies of files and their metadata to be reused when safe. This minimizes the amount of data that must be transferred from the server when the cached data is determined to still be valid (not changed). This not only offloads the file server, but also provides LAN-like performance while sending the data to the requesting user when the file is cached and has not changed.

■ **Prepositioning:** Objects and their metadata can be distributed throughout the network from the origin server in order to pre-populate the data and metadata cache in the client-side WAAS devices. This is helpful for improving first-time access performance as well as offloading the WAN from redundant object transfers for large files.

■ **Read-ahead and write-behind:** Read requests submitted by users can be augmented to increase the amount of data transferred at any given time to minimize transfer times (and rapidly populate the object cache), and write requests can be locally acknowledged (for write requests that don't require immediate commitment or guarantee) to enable the user to write data more quickly, thereby reducing transfer times.

■ **Local response handling:** Asynchronous and noncritical messages can be locally acknowledged and handled in an optimized manner to minimize the number of roundtrips across the network, which helps increase efficiency and improves response times for the users.

Figure 9-3 provides an overview of the techniques used by WAAS CIFS acceleration. Additionally, please refer back to Chapter 1 for a more detailed examination of each of these techniques.

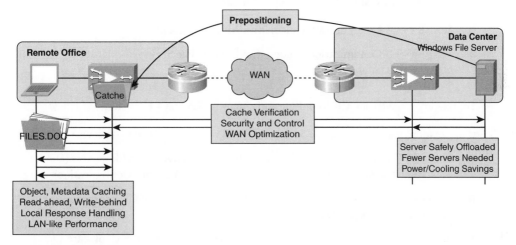

Figure 9-3   *CIFS Acceleration Techniques*

It should be noted that the CIFS acceleration capabilities of WAAS can be deployed in one of two ways: either using the CIFS AO or legacy CIFS. The CIFS AO is the newer model of accelerating CIFS traffic, whereas legacy CIFS is (you guessed it) the legacy model of accelerating CIFS traffic. Before we describe the CIFS AO (and why one would use it), we first discuss the legacy model of accelerating CIFS traffic.

Legacy CIFS acceleration is based on the capabilities found in version 4.0 of the WAAS software. These capabilities are provided in version 4.1 of the software, but it is only recommended that they be used during a migration scenario from 4.0 to 4.1. After the network has been fully upgraded to 4.1, it is recommended that legacy CIFS be removed in favor of the CIFS AO. Legacy CIFS relied on a tunnel connection between devices configured as *edge* or *core* that was established upon configuration of a *connectivity directive*. With legacy CIFS, not only was CIFS acceleration not transparent to the network, but it was also difficult to configure for hub-and-spoke networks, let alone partial or full mesh networks. Legacy CIFS also provided features such as read-only disconnected mode (access cached data in read-only mode when the WAN was down, assuming a domain controller was reachable), as well as print services. Given the introduction of virtual blades in 4.1, the need for read-only disconnected mode has all but vanished given that a domain controller can be installed on a virtual blade (VB) in the branch office (discussed in Chapter 10, "Branch Office Virtualization"). Print services are still available whether legacy CIFS or CIFS AO is used, but the need is diminished due to the ability—again—to use print services on a Windows operating system in a VB.

The first edition of this book dedicates an entire chapter to configuration of CIFS acceleration in what we now call *legacy CIFS*. This edition does not cover legacy CIFS in any detail but rather covers the CIFS AO. Should you need to configure legacy CIFS, it is recommended that you first reconsider, and then if you determine that you need to configure legacy CIFS, consult the first edition of this book along with the documentation found either in the CM GUI (online help) or at Cisco.com:

- **WAAS v4.1.3 Configuration Guide:** http://tinyurl.com/dl8qq5

- **WAAS v4.1.3 Configuration Guide—Configuring File Services:** http://tinyurl.com/yfhm9qa

For reference, the legacy CIFS configuration items in WAAS v4.1.3 include:

- Creation of a Wide Area File Services (WAFS) core cluster (a type of device group)

- Enabling WAFS Core services on devices that are deployed near file servers (**Device > Configure > Acceleration > Legacy Services > WAFS Core Configuration**)

- Assignment of WAFS Core devices into a Legacy WAFS Core Cluster device group (**My WAN > Manage Device Groups**)

- Enabling WAFS edge services on devices in the branch (**Device > Configure > Acceleration > Legacy Services > WAFS Edge Configuration**)

- Configuration of connectivity directives between edge-side devices and core clusters (found at **My WAN > Configure > Connectivity**)

Use of the CIFS AO eliminates the need to perform these steps. As mentioned previously, legacy CIFS should only be used when compatibility with WAAS v4.0 is required, and when the entire network has migrated to WAAS v4.1, it is recommended that legacy CIFS be removed in favor of the CIFS AO.

Note   A thorough overview of CIFS is available from the Storage Networking Industry Association (SNIA) website at http://www.snia.org/tech_activities/CIFS/.

Additionally, Microsoft provides an overview of CIFS on the MSDN website at http://msdn.microsoft.com/en-us/library/aa302188.aspx.

For those that are interested in the actual data structures used over the network (and source code for developing client and server components), the authors recommend Implementing CIFS by Christopher Hertel, which is available on Amazon at http://www.amazon.com/Implementing-CIFS-Common-Internet-System/dp/013047116X.

Windows Print Acceleration

Similar to CIFS file server acceleration capabilities that are provided by WAAS, Windows print acceleration is also provided. Printing to printers that are shared by servers in Microsoft Windows environments involves a multi-step process whereby the Windows client uses the CIFS protocol and MS-RPC (remote procedure calls) to open, write, and close a file on the printer share on the print server. The print server then spools the job, and sends it over the network to the physical printer using the protocol required by the printer. Generally, the interaction between the print server and the printer is done using raw sockets, Line Printer Daemon (LPD) protocol, or the Internet Printing Protocol (IPP).

Note   An overview of LPD and IPP can be found at the following URLs:

http://en.wikipedia.org/wiki/Line_Printer_Daemon_protocol

http://en.wikipedia.org/wiki/Internet_Printing_Protocol

When performing these operations in the branch office, that is, the user, print server, and printer are all co-located, the amount of time necessary to print a document or other file is negligible as the latency of the network is low and the bandwidth on the network is high. Given that CIFS and MS-RPC are used for the client to print server interaction, any latency that might exist between the client and that print server can have devastating consequences on the performance of the print operation due to the chattiness of the protocol, and any bandwidth constraints that might exist also have a negative impact due to the large amount of data that needs to be transferred. As a result, organizations have found it difficult to centralize print servers from branch offices into the data center because of the performance problems of having print jobs traverse the WAN from the client to the print server and back to the printer. Windows print acceleration solves this issue using similar techniques to those listed previously for CIFS, including:

- **Local response handling:** Certain messages are handled locally to minimize the impact of latency by reducing the amount of *chatter* that must traverse the WAN, thereby increasing throughput of print operations.

- **Connection reuse:** Connection state to print servers is retained temporarily after user disconnection to minimize setup time when the next user connects.

- **Metadata caching:** Information about the printers is temporarily cached in WAAS and reused when safe to do so. This again minimizes the chatter that must traverse the network, thereby improving throughput.

Figure 9-4 provides an overview of the techniques used by WAAS acceleration for Windows print.

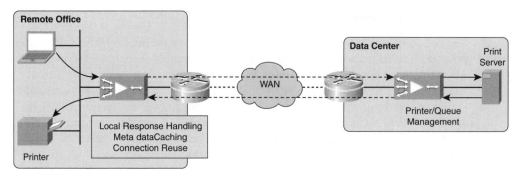

Figure 9-4 *Windows Print Acceleration Techniques*

Many organizations see value in centralizing print servers from remote offices into managed data center locations. By centralizing print servers, higher levels of utilization can be achieved on a smaller number of servers, resulting in lower costs both from a capital perspective as well as from an operational perspective. Centralizing print servers does introduce availability as a concern for the branch office users that need to print should the WAN be down. Most organizations choose to either live with the concern (the WAN is not down frequently), deploy a high-availability WAN configuration in the branch (might be cost-prohibitive), or deploy a Windows server in a WAAS virtual blade (discussed in Chapter 10) with print servers to provide a local print server. In any case, options do exist, each with their own positive and negative attributes.

NFS Acceleration

Cisco WAAS provides robust protocol acceleration for UNIX environments where the Network File System (NFS) protocol is being used for file exchange. This is common in environments where Computer Aided Design/Computer Aided Manufacturing (CAD/CAM) is used, as well as software development environments. Like CIFS and other application protocols, performance in NFS environments is constrained by latency due to the chattiness of the protocol and bandwidth due to the potentially large amount of data that can be transferred. Employing acceleration within WAAS helps improve performance of accessing remotely exported mount points, which fosters productivity. Coupled with the powerful WAN optimization capabilities provided by WAAS, NFS acceleration helps to improve file access performance—both interactive access and during transfer—by mitigating the negative effects of latency and bandwidth constraints. The capabilities for NFS acceleration provided by WAAS include:

■ **Metadata optimization:** Interactive operations such as directory traversal are pipelined by WAAS to minimize the amount of time necessary to traverse directories and view file and directory meta information. Additionally, metadata information is cached temporarily when safe by WAAS to minimize future performance-limiting operations that traverse the WAN.

■ **Read-ahead optimization:** WAAS performs read-ahead operations on behalf of the requesting node to pre-fetch data from within the file being accessed. This enables the data to be readily available at the client-side device for faster read throughput.

■ **File write optimization:** Asynchronous write operations are used to batch write messages and eliminate the *send-and-wait* nature of NFS file write operations while working in conjunction with existing NFS protocol semantics to guarantee file data integrity.

Figure 9-5 provides an overview of the techniques used by WAAS acceleration for NFS.

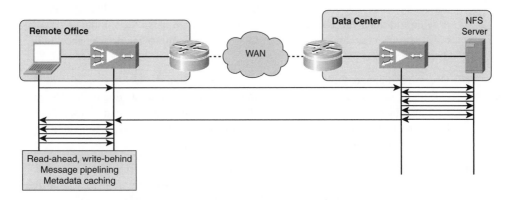

Figure 9-5 *NFS Acceleration Techniques*

> **Note**   An overview of NFS can be found at the following URLs:
>
> http://en.wikipedia.org/wiki/Network_File_System_(protocol)
> http://tools.ietf.org/html/rfc3530
> http://tools.ietf.org/html/rfc1813
> http://tools.ietf.org/html/rfc1094

MAPI Acceleration

One of the interfaces Microsoft Exchange Server relies upon is the Messaging Application Programming Interface (MAPI), which uses Remote Procedure Calls (RPC) as a transport between client and server to deliver e-mail, calendaring, contacts, and more to Outlook users for collaboration and productivity. Like many applications, Exchange is performance-limited by bandwidth limitations and latency found in the WAN. Many organizations have deployed Exchange servers throughout the network (some have deployed to every site) and a compelling ROI exists if these servers can be centralized into the data center locations. WAAS provides a number of acceleration services for Exchange to help improve performance for remote users, providing similar levels of performance as they would receive if the Exchange server were local. WAAS acceleration for

Exchange was developed in conjunction with Microsoft to ensure correctness and compatibility with all major versions of Exchange, without relying on reverse engineering of protocols. The following acceleration capabilities are provided by WAAS for Exchange:

■ **Full application support:** WAAS acceleration for Exchange is developed in conjunction with Microsoft to ensure full compatibility with all major versions, including Outlook 2000, 2003, and 2007, and the same versions for Exchange.

■ **Advanced e-mail compression:** WAAS can automatically defer native compression provided by the Exchange server and Outlook in favor of WAAS Data Redundancy Elimination (DRE) and Persistent Lempel-Ziv (PLZ). Additionally, WAAS can natively decode messages encoded by Exchange or Outlook, which enables DRE and PLZ to provide additional levels of compression, thereby minimizing the amount of data that must be transferred and reducing transfer times, thus improving performance. Full data coherency is preserved end-to-end.

■ **Object read-ahead:** Objects that are being fetched from the server, such as e-mail, calendar items, or address books, are done at an accelerated rate due to WAAS prefetching objects on behalf of the user. This helps minimize the "send-and-wait" behavior of Exchange and Outlook and improves throughput and performance, which provides user-perceivable improvements in responsiveness.

■ **Object delivery acceleration:** Objects that are sent to the server, such as an e-mail, folder update, calendar entry, and more, are optimized using message pipelining and message batching to ensure higher efficiency of transfer while minimizing send-and-wait.

■ **Payload aggregation:** WAAS recognizes many Exchange messages that are small in nature and can either batch them together for optimized delivery or dynamically adjust DRE and PLZ to improve compression ratios on these messages.

■ **Transparent integration:** WAAS acceleration for Exchange does not keep user sessions open like other solutions, which can lead to security vulnerabilities and limit the overall scalability of the Exchange server itself.

Figure 9-6 provides an overview of the techniques used by WAAS acceleration for Microsoft Exchange (MAPI).

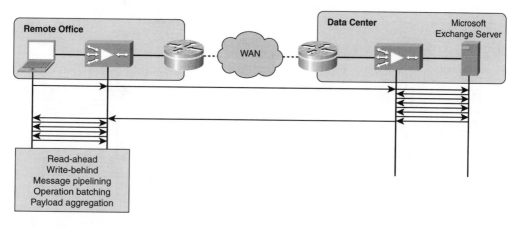

Figure 9-6   *MAPI Acceleration Techniques*

HTTP Acceleration

Applications, such as Oracle, SAP, Sharepoint, and others, are the backbone of today's enterprise organizations. WAAS provides acceleration capabilities for enterprise applications that use HTTP to not only minimize bandwidth consumption and improve WAN efficiency (through WAN optimization), but also mitigate the negative impact caused by latency found in the WAN for these applications. By employing latency-mitigation capabilities along with WAN optimization, organizations realize a substantial increase in application responsiveness when accessed over the WAN, which translates directly into branch user productivity. WAAS provides fast connection reuse to decrease the load time of complex pages or pages with numerous embedded objects when the client or server cannot use persistent connections. Optimized connections on the WAN remain active for a short period of time to be reused should additional data between the client-server pair need to be exchanged. As connections established between clients and servers are reused rather than re-established, latency caused by establishing multiple connections between clients and servers can be minimized. Figure 9-7 provides an overview of the acceleration capabilities provided by WAAS for applications that use HTTP.

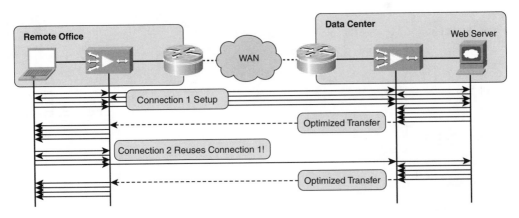

Figure 9-7   *HTTP Acceleration Techniques*

Note   You can find an overview of HTTP at the following URLs:

http://tools.ietf.org/html/rfc2616

http://tools.ietf.org/html/rfc1945

http://en.wikipedia.org/wiki/Http

SSL Acceleration

Many organizations find themselves moving to use encryption for data in motion and data at rest to ensure compliance with regulatory requirements and minimize threats to corporate data. Encryption techniques such as Secure Sockets Layer (SSL) and Transport Layer Security (TLS) are fundamentally at odds with WAN optimization and application acceleration, because they obfuscate the packet contents and prevent techniques that rely on visibility into the payload from being able to function (as the payload can no longer be seen). To effectively optimize SSL traffic using a symmetric system such as WAAS, each device in the path that is applying some optimization technique to the flow must have an understanding of the key material used to encrypt the flow. With this understanding, the stream can be decrypted, and then optimized. After optimization, the stream can be re-encrypted to ensure that data—even if obfuscated through optimization—remains secure.

WAAS provides SSL optimization capabilities that integrate seamlessly with existing data center key management and trust models. Encryption key-pairs (public and private) are stored securely in a password-protected secure vault on the CM and distributed securely to the WAAS devices in the data center. To enable the remote office WAAS devices to participate in acceleration of the encrypted traffic, the derived session key is distributed to the remote office WAAS device. Additionally, disk encryption can be configured on accelerator devices to ensure that any chunks of data that are stored as part of the compression history are protected should the hard disks of a WAAS device be physically compromised.

Figure 9-8 shows how WAAS SSL optimization integrates transparently with existing application key exchanges and preserves trust boundaries of server private keys.

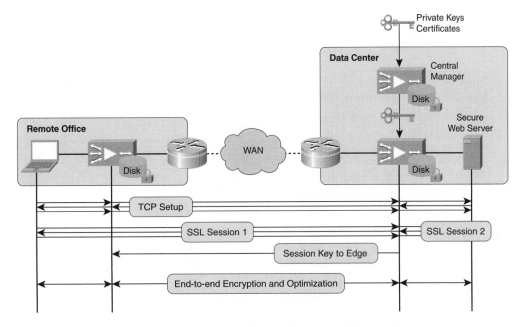

Figure 9-8   *SSL Acceleration Techniques*

WAAS SSL acceleration is considered one of the most complete implementations of SSL acceleration as of this writing due to providing a number of capabilities that are not found in alternative solutions. These include:

- **Preservation of trust boundary:** WAAS does not distribute private keys beyond the data center WAAS devices. Only the data center devices have a copy of private keys (stored in the SSL secure store, which is encrypted), and the client-side devices only see temporary session keys.

- **Secure storage of keys:** All certificates and private keys are stored securely on the WAAS Central Manager, which prevents new attack vectors from being established.

- **Interoperability with proxy devices:** WAAS provides full support for automatic identification, interception, optimization, and acceleration of SSL traffic even in environments where web proxies have already been deployed or clients are configured to use explicit proxies.

- **Client authentication support:** Full support for client certificate-based authentication during initial session establishment.

- **Online Certificate Status Protocol (OCSP) support:** By providing support for OSCP, WAAS can provide a real-time security check of certificates to improve security by validating that certificates have not been revoked by the issuer.

- **Disk encryption:** Disk encryption can be enabled selectively or globally. When enabled, disk encryption keys are managed by the CM and fetched interactively by WAAS devices as they boot and stored in memory. This helps ensure compliance with Payment Card Industry (PCI) regulation along with other federal and industry-related compliance initiatives, and ensures that SSL-encrypted data that is optimized by WAAS is stored on internal drives in an encrypted manner.

Note WAAS provides support for both SSLv3 and TLSv1. An overview of SSL and TLS can be found at the following URLs:

> http://en.wikipedia.org/wiki/Ssl
>
> http://en.wikipedia.org/wiki/TLS
>
> http://www.ietf.org/rfc/rfc2246.txt
>
> http://tools.ietf.org/html/rfc4346

Video Acceleration

One of the most challenging applications to deploy in an enterprise-wide manner is business video, including video streaming (live video) and video-on-demand (VoD). WAAS provides a series of optimizations that help improve video delivery—and minimize the challenges that are normally presented when deploying video enterprise-wide. WAAS video delivery services minimize the burden video places on the network while providing an architecture that ensures quality broadcast performance and playback for remote users. Figure 9-9 highlights the acceleration features of WAAS video delivery on user performance, WAN bandwidth, and server scalability.

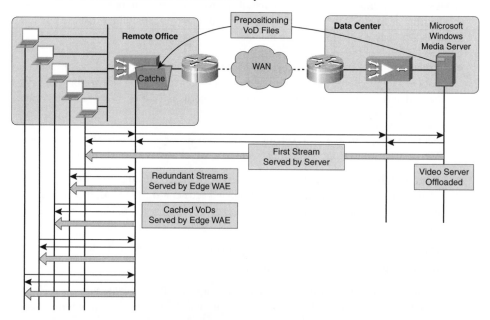

Figure 9-9 *Video Acceleration Techniques*

WAAS provides the following optimizations for video delivery:

- **Windows media stream splitting:** WAAS interoperates with Windows Media Technologies (WMT) over RTSP to enable one video stream over the WAN to be served to numerous users in the remote branch office, thereby minimizing bandwidth consumption of video traffic without any administrative or program configuration.

- **Data-reduction and optimization for video that is not WMT/RTSP:** WAAS provides bandwidth reduction for other video formats including video over HTTP, Flash, QuickTime, RealVideo, and any other video protocol that uses TCP as a transport.

- **Video-on-demand caching:** WAAS CIFS acceleration can be used in conjunction with prepositioning to provide a VoD delivery architecture for enterprise e-Learning, training, and video message archival and playback, providing similar benefits to VoD playback that are provided for live streaming.

- **Intelligent video server offload:** WAAS video delivery services minimize the burden placed on the origin video server by intelligently distributing streams to simultaneous remote users over a single stream per location or locally serving VoD files that have been cached. Thus, video servers see fewer connections and are required to transfer less data, thereby minimizing server workload and enabling video server scalability.

- **Digital signage:** WAAS provides integration with Cisco Digital Media System (DMS) in the data center and Digital Media Player (DMP) in the branch. DMP can stream video from the WAAS CIFS cache at the edge to display video on digital signage units in retail locations and others.

Note   You can find an overview of Windows Media and RTSP at the following URLs:

http://en.wikipedia.org/wiki/Windows_Media

http://en.wikipedia.org/wiki/Real_Time_Streaming_Protocol

http://msdn.microsoft.com/en-us/library/cc245238(PROT.10).aspx

Now that you have an introduction to the acceleration capabilities provided by WAAS, the next sections focus on configuration, verification, and monitoring of these features. Most acceleration features provided by WAAS require that only a single box be checked in order to become operational. However, certain acceleration features such as prepositioning and SSL require additional configuration. The next sections cover these topics in detail.

Enabling Acceleration Features

WAAS devices in their default configuration—from the factory, or after a fresh installation of software—automatically have every AO enabled by default. Before an AO can be used as part of an action against a TCP connection, the AO must be enabled and usable.

If an AO is disabled, it is not used, even if the policy definition specifies that the AO should be used. The desire to use the AO is not included in automatic discovery if the AO is not enabled, thus, the peer device does not think it is even an option to be applied to the particular flow in question.

Enabling and disabling AOs is simple and can be performed from either the device CLI or from the WAAS CM. Figure 9-10 shows how to enable or disable features (including AOs) from the WAAS CM. It is recommended that these features be configured from within the context of a device group, although they can be configured within the context of an individual device. From either context, visit **Configure > Acceleration > Enabled Features.**

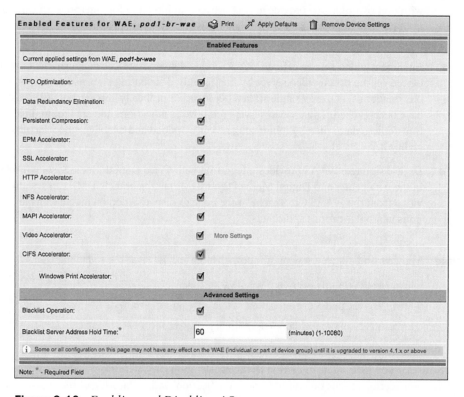

Figure 9-10 *Enabling and Disabling AOs*

Note   The Windows print accelerator AO requires the CIFS accelerator AO. This is why Windows print accelerator is indented and explains why Windows print accelerator disappears when CIFS accelerator is unchecked.

It is similarly easy to enable or disable AOs from the device CLI. Example 9-1 shows the commands necessary to enable or disable an AO, along with those necessary to verify the operational status of an AO.

Example 9-1   *Enabling/Disabling and Verifying AOs from CLI*

```
pod1-br-wae# show accelerator ?
  cifs    Display CIFS accelerator status
  detail  Display accelerator status and configuration in detail
  epm     Display EPM accelerator status
  http    Display HTTP accelerator status
  mapi    Display MAPI accelerator status
  nfs     Display NFS accelerator status
  ssl     Display SSL accelerator status
  video   Display Video accelerator status
  |       Output Modifiers
  <cr>
pod1-br-wae# show accelerator


Accelerator      Licensed        Config State     Operational State
— — — —·         — — —           — — — — —        — — — — — — —·
cifs             Yes             Enabled          Running
epm              Yes             Enabled          Running
http             Yes             Enabled          Running
mapi             Yes             Enabled          Running
nfs              Yes             Enabled          Running
ssl              Yes             Enabled          Running
video            Yes             Enabled          Running
wafs-core        Yes             Disabled         Shutdown
wafs-edge        Yes             Disabled         Shutdown
pod1-br-wae# show accelerator cifs ?
  |       Output Modifiers
  <cr>
pod1-br-wae# show accelerator cifs


Accelerator      Licensed        Config State     Operational State
— — — —·         — — —           — — — — —        — — — — — — —·
cifs             Yes             Enabled          Running


CIFS:
    Policy Engine Config Item          Value
    — — — — — — — — — — — —·            — —·
    State                              Registered
    Default Action                     Use Policy
    Connection Limit                   750
    Effective Limit                    740
    Keepalive timeout                  5.0 seconds


pod1-br-wae# show accelerator nfs
```

```
Accelerator     Licensed       Config State     Operational State
— — — — —·      — — —          — — — — —        — — — — — — —·
nfs             Yes            Enabled          Running

NFS:
    Policy Engine Config Item          Value
    — — — — — — — — — — — —·            — —·
    State                              Registered
    Default Action                     Use Policy
    Connection Limit                   750
    Effective Limit                    740
    Keepalive timeout                  5.0 seconds

pod1-br-wae# config term
pod1-br-wae(config)# no accelerator nfs enable
Disabled nfs accelerator.
pod1-br-wae(config)# end
pod1-br-wae# show accelerator

Accelerator     Licensed       Config State     Operational State
— — — — —·      — — —          — — — — —        — — — — — — —·
cifs            Yes            Enabled          Running
epm             Yes            Enabled          Running
http            Yes            Enabled          Running
mapi            Yes            Enabled          Running
nfs             Yes            Disabled         Shutdown
ssl             Yes            Enabled          Running
video           Yes            Enabled          Running
wafs-core       Yes            Disabled         Shutdown
wafs-edge       Yes            Disabled         Shutdown
!
! "Config State" refers to whether or not the accelerator has been
! enabled or disabled through administrative configuration.
! "Operational State" refers to whether or not the accelerator is
! active (running) or inactive (shutdown).  "Licensed" indicates
! whether or not the appropriate license has been installed on the
! device to support use of the accelerator.
!
pod1-br-wae# show accelerator nfs

Accelerator     Licensed       Config State     Operational State
— — — — —·      — — —          — — — — —        — — — — — — —·
nfs             Yes            Disabled         Shutdown
```

```
NFS:
   Policy Engine Config Item          Value
   ------------.                      --.
   State                              Not Registered
   Default Action                     Use Policy
   Connection Limit                   750
   Effective Limit                    750
   Keepalive timeout                  5.0 seconds
!
! "State" is controlled by the license, config, and operational
! states mentioned earlier in the example.  The "Connection Limit"
! and "Effective Limit" determine the maximum number of connections
! that can be handled concurrently by this accelerator.  The
! "Keepalive timeout" is how long connection information should be
! retained without being in receipt of a keepalive for that connection
! before the connection data is removed from the accelerator, thus
! freeing up connection resources within the accelerator to be used
! on other connections.
!
pod1-br-wae# config term
pod1-br-wae(config)# accelerator nfs enable
Enabled nfs accelerator
pod1-br-wae(config)# end
pod1-br-wae#
```

Notice that the CLI provides additional information that is not provided in the CM GUI. Within the CLI, you can see the operational state of the AO (registered, not registered), the default action, connection limits, and keepalive limits. If you want to see the full details for each AO in the system, simply append **detail** to the **show accelerator** command as shown in Example 9-1. Additionally you can see whether or not AOs are allowed based on the license applied to the system. As a reminder, the Enterprise license is required to use any AO. Video is required to use the Video AO.

Enabling the AOs is the first step to being able to use them. AOs must also be listed as policy actions before a device attempts to use an AO against a TCP connection that matches the classifier conditions. WAAS policies, by default, already include AOs as actions where appropriate. However, for reference, we cover both CM and CLI configuration for reference. To configure an AO as a policy action in the CM, visit either the device or device group context, followed by **Configure > Acceleration > Policy Definitions**. To ensure consistency, it is recommended that policy configuration be done within the device group context as discussed in Chapter 8. Click the **Edit** icon next to a policy definition, and notice the **Accelerate** selection box. Simply select the relevant accelerator and submit the policy to save it, as shown in Figure 9-11.

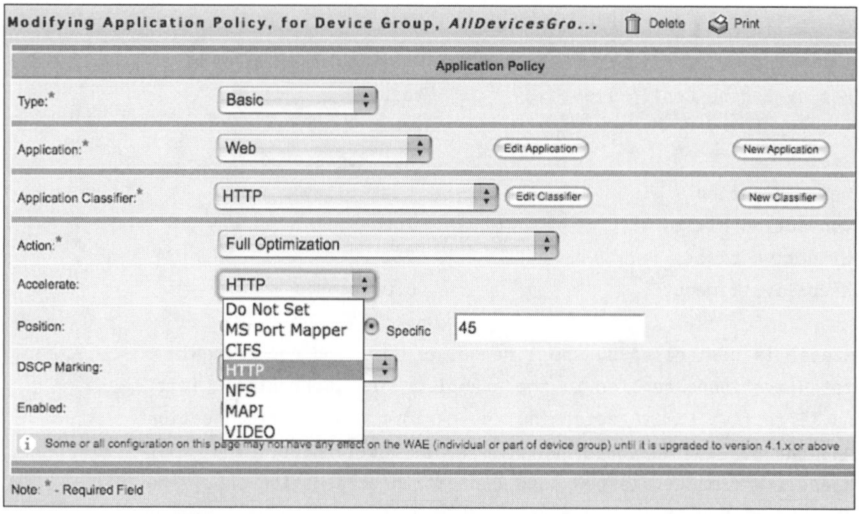

Figure 9-11 *Adding an AO to a Policy in the CM*

Note If you want to use an accelerator for certain clients or certain servers but not for others, it is recommended that you have two separate policies that overlap. The first would include both IP and TCP match conditions with the appropriate policy actions and would need to be configured as the higher priority policy. The second would include only the TCP match conditions with the appropriate policy actions. This policy would catch all traffic that matched the TCP match conditions defined in either policy but also would catch all traffic that did not match the IP address match conditions listed in the higher priority policy. This topic is also discussed in Chapter 8 and should be reviewed if appropriate to your deployment or network.

Configuring a policy to use an AO as an action is covered in Chapter 8, but is reviewed here as well. In this example, we configure a policy for HTTP traffic to a specific server using a new classifier and specify that it should be accelerated using the HTTP AO, and optimizing using both DRE and PLZ. It should be noted that by default all preconfigured policies have the appropriate AO listed as an *accelerate* action, and the configuration example presented in Example 9-2 should only be used should an AO need to be added or removed from an existing policy, or should a new policy need to be created.

Example 9-2 *Enabling/Disabling AOs in Policy and Verifying from CLI*

```
pod1-br-wae# config term
pod1-br-wae(config)# policy-engine application
pod1-br-wae(config-pol-eng-app)# ?
  classifier  Define an Application classifier
  exit        Exit from this submode
```

```
   map         Policy map list
   name        Define Application name
   no          Negate a command or set its defaults
   set-dscp    Define default DSCP marking
pod1-br-wae(config-pol-eng-app)# classifier ?
  WORD  Classifier name (30 characters max)
pod1-br-wae(config-pol-eng-app)# classifier HTTP-Internal ?
  list   List classifier's conditions
  match  Add/Modify match condition of the classifier
  <cr>
pod1-br-wae(config-pol-eng-app)# classifier HTTP-Internal
pod1-br-wae(config-app-cls)# match ?
  all  All traffic will be matched
  dst  Condition on the destination side
  src  Condition on the source side
pod1-br-wae(config-app-cls)# match dst ?
  host  Specific host name
  ip    IP address and wildcard mask
  port  Condition on the port
pod1-br-wae(config-app-cls)# match dst ip ?
  A.B.C.D  IP address
pod1-br-wae(config-app-cls)# match dst ip 10.10.10.100 ?
  A.B.C.D  wildcard mask
pod1-br-wae(config-app-cls)# match dst ip 10.10.10.100 0.0.0.0 ?
  port  Condition on the port
  src   Condition on the source side
  <cr>
pod1-br-wae(config-app-cls)# match dst ip 10.10.10.100 0.0.0.0 port ?
  eq     Port Equal
  range  Port Range
pod1-br-wae(config-app-cls)# match dst ip 10.10.10.100 0.0.0.0 port eq ?
  <1-65535>  Port number
pod1-br-wae(config-app-cls)# match dst ip 10.10.10.100 0.0.0.0 port eq 80 ?
  src   Condition on the source side
  <cr>
pod1-br-wae(config-app-cls)# match dst ip 10.10.10.100 0.0.0.0 port eq 80
pod1-br-wae(config-app-cls)# exit
pod1-br-wae(config-pol-eng-app)# ?
  classifier  Define an Application classifier
  exit        Exit from this submode
  map         Policy map list
  name        Define Application name
  no          Negate a command or set its defaults
  set-dscp    Define default DSCP marking
```

```
pod1-br-wae(config-pol-eng-app)# map ?
  adaptor   Advanced policy map lists - separate for every adaptor
  basic     Basic policy map list - based on L3/L4 parameters only
  other     Define the action on non-classified traffic
pod1-br-wae(config-pol-eng-app)# map basic ?
  delete    Delete specific Application Policy Map from the list
  disable   Disable specific Application Policy Map from the list
  insert    Add new Application Policy Map into specific position
  list      List Application Policy Map
  move      Move specific Application Policy Map from one position to a new one
            in the list
  name      Application Name
  <cr>
pod1-br-wae(config-pol-eng-app)# map basic name ?
  WORD   the Application Name - has to be already defined
pod1-br-wae(config-pol-eng-app)# map basic name Web ?
  classifier  Application traffic classifier
pod1-br-wae(config-pol-eng-app)# map basic name Web classifier ?
  WORD   the Application Traffic Classifier Name - has to be already defined
pod1-br-wae(config-pol-eng-app)# map basic name Web classifier HTTP-Internal ?
  action   the Action that should be taken
  disable  Add this policy disabled
pod1-br-wae(config-pol-eng-app)# map basic name Web classifier HTTP-Internal
action ?
  optimize      Apply Generic Optimization
  pass-through  Don't touch the traffic, pass-through without any modification
pod1-br-wae(config-pol-eng-app)# map basic name Web classifier HTTP-Internal
action optimize ?
  DRE   To Apply Generic Redundancy Optimization or not?
  full  Apply Full Generic Optimization
pod1-br-wae(config-pol-eng-app)# map basic name Web classifier HTTP-Internal
action optimize full ?
  accelerate  Accelerate Traffic using special adapter
  set-dscp    Define mapping's DSCP marking
  <cr>
pod1-br-wae(config-pol-eng-app)# map basic name Web classifier HTTP-Internal
action optimize full accelerate ?
  cifs            CIFS Accelerator
  http            HTTP Accelerator
  mapi            MAPI Accelerator
  MS-port-mapper  Microsoft Endpoint Port Mapper
  nfs             NFS Accelerator
  video           VIDEO Accelerator
pod1-br-wae(config-pol-eng-app)#$imize full accelerate http ?
  set-dscp  Define mapping's DSCP marking
```

```
    <cr>
pod1-br-wae(config-pol-eng-app)# map basic name Web classifier HTTP-Internal
accelerate http
pod1-br-wae(Config-pol-eng-app)# end
pod1-br-wae# sh run
!
! ... portions removed for clarity ...
!
policy-engine application
   name Web
   classifier HTTP-Internal
      match dst host 10.10.10.100 port eq 80
   exit
   name Web classifier HTTP-Internal action optimize full accelerate http
   exit
pod1-br-wae# show policy-engine application name
Number of Applications: 32
 #   Application Name                  Handle   DSCP
—— ————————————————    ———   —————
! ... portions removed ...
 28) Web                              ( 23)     inherit
 * ) Other                           (  0)     inherit
pod1-br-wae# show policy-engine application classifier
Number of Application Classifiers: 161
! ... portions removed ...
 43) HTTP-Internal
        match  dst host 10.10.10.100 port eq 80
pod1-br-wae# show policy-engine application classifier name HTTP-Internal
HTTP-Internal
        match  dst host 10.10.10.100 port eq 80
```

With the AOs enabled and included in policies as shown in the preceding example, WAAS devices automatically begin to leverage them when a peer can be identified that supports the same AO. The only AO and AO-related items that require additional configuration are video, SSL acceleration, and CIFS prepositioning, which are discussed in the next three sections.

Additional Video Settings

Video has a (small) handful of configurable parameters that are managed outside of the policy definition. These configurable parameters specify the way that the video AO should handle traffic that is not accelerated and configuration settings related to Windows Media. Given that video places a heavy burden on the network, it might be beneficial to drop video traffic that is not accelerated to ensure that the network is not flooded. Granted, DRE can be used to minimize the bandwidth consumption over the WAN for redundant TCP video streams; however, for Internet video, the likelihood of identifying any measurable levels of redundancy is low, given that the number of users accessing that video in a given location is also likely to be low.

Video configuration parameters are available in both the device or device group context. Like many other configurable parameters, it is recommended that configuration be applied to device groups to ensure consistency across devices in the network. To configure video parameters, visit **Configure > Acceleration > Video Settings**, where you can configure the following parameters:

- **Client First Message Reception Timeout:** Specifies the number of seconds the WAAS device waits between initial client message and server response before considering the operation to have timed out. This value can be between 10 and 180 seconds, with the default being 60. A lower value results in faster timeout, but system resources are recycled for reuse more aggressively. A higher value results in slower timeout, which is better for degraded network conditions, but system resources are recycled for reuse less frequently.

- **Drop:** Defines the behavior the WAAS device employs when video streams that cannot be accelerated are identified. Valid options are:

  - **All:** Drop under any condition, including overload (too many video streams being handled) and unsupported transport or format.

  - **Overload only:** Drop video streams only when the video AO is overloaded.

  - **None:** Apply optimization to the video stream according to the policy definition. The video AO does not drop video streams in this case.

- **Enable Transaction Logs:** Specifies whether video transaction logs, which are similar to TFO transaction logs (but video focused) are enabled or not. Additional settings can be configured by clicking the **More Settings** link.

- **Enable Log Forwarding:** Specifies whether or not the WAAS device forwards Windows Media logs to the upstream Windows Media server.

- **Client Idle Connection Timeout:** Specifies the maximum idle period the WAAS device allows between client requests before tearing down the connection. This value can be anywhere between 30 and 300 seconds, with 60 seconds being the default.

Note   Video settings can also be configured from the device CLI as follows:

```
pod1-br-wae(config)# accelerator video ?
  enable                   Enable accelerator
  exception                Exception handling for AO
  max-initial-setup-delay  Maximum delay between connection accept and first message
from client(in secs)
  unaccelerated-traffic    Video unaccelerated traffic configuration
  windows-media            Windows Media configuration
```

```
pod1-br-wae(config)# accelerator video max-initial-setup-delay ?
  <10-180>  Maximum initial setup delay. Default: 60
pod1-br-wae(config)# accelerator video unaccelerated-traffic ?
  type  Traffic type
pod1-br-wae(config)# accelerator video unaccelerated-traffic type ?
  all       All traffic
  overload  Overload condition traffic
pod1-br-wae(config)# accelerator video unaccelerated-traffic type all ?
  action  Action type
pod1-br-wae(config)# accelerator video unaccelerated-traffic type all action ?
  drop  drop unaccelerated traffic (default: pipethrough)
pod1-br-wae(config)# accelerator video unaccelerated-traffic type all action drop ?
  <cr>
pod1-br-wae(config)# accelerator video unaccelerated-traffic type overload ?
  action  Action type
pod1-br-wae(config)# accelerator video unaccelerated-traffic type overload action ?
  drop  drop unaccelerated traffic (default: pipethrough)
pod1-br-wae(config)# accelerator video unaccelerated-traffic type overload action drop
?
  <cr>
pod1-br-wae(config)# accelerator video windows-media ?

  client          Client side configuration
  log-forwarding  Upstream device logs forwarding configuration
pod1-br-wae(config)# accelerator video windows-media client ?
  idle-timeout  Client idle timeout (in secs) configuration
pod1-br-wae(config)# accelerator video windows-media client idle-timeout ?
  <30-300>  Client idle timeout. Default: 60
pod1-br-wae(config)# accelerator video windows-media client idle-timeout 60 ?
  <cr>
pod1-br-wae(config)# accelerator video windows-media log-forwarding ?
  enable  Enable upstream device logs forwarding
pod1-br-wae(config)# accelerator video windows-media log-forwarding enable ?
  <cr>
```

Configuring SSL Acceleration

SSL is the only AO in WAAS that is not configured as an *accelerate* action in the policy definition. Unlike other AOs, the SSL AO actually runs as a service and requires additional configuration elements. To employ SSL acceleration against a certain type of traffic, an *accelerated service* must be configured and activated on the data center WAAS devices that are deployed in front of the web servers that use SSL for encryption (the terminology used is to *place in service*). Additionally, a *secure store* must be configured on the CM to store private keys and certificates associated with the configured SSL accelerated services. It is generally considered a best practice to first configure disk encryption on any WAAS device participating in acceleration of SSL-encrypted traffic to ensure that sensitive data at rest on the WAAS device disk (DRE cache data) is stored in a secure manner. The SSL secure store, which is on the CM and any data center WAAS device that stores key material, is already secure. We first examine configuration and verification of disk encryption before moving on to the remainder of SSL acceleration.

It should be noted that SSL and TLS are topics that many brilliant people have devoted a substantial amount of time discussing and documenting. This book assumes that the reader has a fundamental understanding of how SSL, TLS, and cryptography in general work, and does not provide an overview of the inner workings of these protocols. The following books are recommended to help develop and increase a level of understanding around this important topic:

- *Applied Cryptography* (Schneier)

- *Network Security: Private Communication in a Public World* (Kaufman, Perlman, Speciner)

- *SSL and TLS: Designing and Building Secure Systems* (Rescorla)

- *Network Security with OpenSSL* (Viega, Messier, Chandra)

Configuring Disk Encryption

WAAS accelerator devices support disk encryption using AES-256 (one of the strongest commercially available symmetric encryption algorithms) with centralized and secure key management. When enabled, disk encryption keys are generated and stored on the CM. When a WAAS accelerator boots, it connects to the CM to fetch its disk encryption key using the secure channel (SSL-encrypted) between itself and the CM. After the key is fetched, it is stored in memory only as shown in Figure 9-12, to prevent an ill-intentioned person from being able to compromise the disk (the key is lost when power is lost). With the key stored in memory, the device can then unlock the local file systems that contain DRE and other data. If the CM is not reachable, the device continues to boot, but DRE and other acceleration functions that rely on encrypted file systems are not usable. In such a case, connections are handled as pass-through.

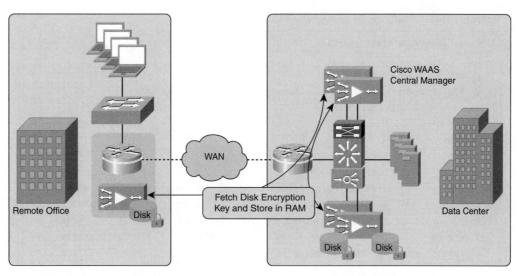

Figure 9-12 *Disk Encryption Overview*

Disk encryption can be configured from the device or device group context within the CM by going to **Configure > Storage > Disk Encryption**. It is generally recommended that, for simplicity, disk encryption be configured on a device group as opposed to discretely on individual devices. Figure 9-13 shows the configuration page for disk encryption. Enabling or disabling disk encryption requires only checking or unchecking a single box in the CM. It should be noted that when you enable disk encryption or disable disk encryption, cached data (including DRE and CIFS) is completely erased. Thus, disk encryption should be one of the items configured prior to enabling the device to begin optimization, and should only be disabled when absolutely necessary.

Figure 9-13 *Disk Encryption Configuration in CM*

Disk encryption can also be configured from the CLI. Additionally, the CLI provides insight into the status of disk encryption, which is helpful in determining whether or not the WAAS device has finished encrypting its disk for the first time. Disk encryption is configured using the global **disk encrypt enable** command. Example 9-3 shows the use of this command with disk status before and after, as well as the disk status through the course of encryption to completion.

Example 9-3   *Enabling/Disabling Disk Encryption from CLI*

```
pod1-br-wae# show disks details

Physical disk information:
  disk00: Present     Y66E58PE    (h02 c00 i00 l00 - Int DAS-SATA)
          238472MB(232.9GB)

Mounted file systems:
  MOUNT POINT       TYPE       DEVICE          SIZE       INUSE       FREE   USE%
  /sw               internal   /dev/sdb1       991MB      912MB       79MB    92%
  /swstore          internal   /dev/sdb2       991MB      879MB      112MB    88%
  /state            internal   /dev/sdb3      3967MB      135MB     3832MB     3%
  /local/local1     SYSFS      /dev/sdb7     11903MB     1186MB    10717MB     9%
  /disk00-04        CONTENT    /dev/sdb6    211161MB     7969MB   203192MB     3%
  .../local1/spool  PRINTSPOOL /dev/sdb8       991MB       16MB      975MB     1%

No RAID devices present.

Disk encryption feature is disabled.
pod1-br-wae# config
pod1-br-wae(config)# disk ?
  disk-name       Disk name
  encrypt         Encrypt CONTENTFS, SPOOL & swap partitions
  error-handling  Configure disk error handling
pod1-br-wae(config)# disk encrypt ?
  enable   Enable disk encryption feature
pod1-br-wae(config)# disk encrypt enable ?
  <cr>
pod1-br-wae(config)# disk encrypt enable
Contacting Central Manager... Succeed.
This change will take effect after reload.
Warning!!! All cached data will be deleted after reload.
pod1-br-wae(config)# end
pod1-br-wae# show disks details

Physical disk information:
  disk00: Present     Y66E58PE    (h02 c00 i00 l00 - Int DAS-SATA)
          238472MB(232.9GB)

Mounted file systems:
  MOUNT POINT       TYPE       DEVICE          SIZE       INUSE       FREE   USE%
  /sw               internal   /dev/sdb1       991MB      912MB       79MB    92%
  /swstore          internal   /dev/sdb2       991MB      879MB      112MB    88%
  /state            internal   /dev/sdb3      3967MB      135MB     3832MB     3%
  /local/local1     SYSFS      /dev/sdb7     11903MB     1186MB    10717MB     9%
```

```
 /disk00-04        CONTENT     /dev/sdb6        211161MB    6899MB   204262MB   3%
 .../local1/spool  PRINTSPOOL  /dev/sdb8          991MB     16MB      975MB    1%


No RAID devices present.


Disk encryption is currently disabled, but will be enabled after reload.
pod1-br-wae# reload
Proceed with reload?[confirm] yes
Shutting down all services, will timeout in 15 minutes.
reload in progress ..
!
! ... portions removed, device rebooted ...
!


pod1-br-wae login: admin
Password:
System is initializing. Please wait...
Please use 'show disks details' to monitor system status.
pod1-br-wae# show disks details


Physical disk information:
   disk00: Present    Y66E58PE   (h02 c00 i00 l00 - Int DAS-SATA)
            238472MB(232.9GB)


Mounted file systems:
 MOUNT POINT       TYPE       DEVICE           SIZE      INUSE      FREE  USE%
 /sw               internal   /dev/sdb1        991MB     912MB      79MB   92%
 /swstore          internal   /dev/sdb2        991MB     879MB     112MB   88%
 /state            internal   /dev/sdb3       3967MB     135MB    3832MB    3%
 /local/local1     SYSFS      /dev/sdb7      11903MB    1183MB   10720MB    9%


No RAID devices present.


System is initializing. Please wait...
Disk encryption feature is enabled.
!
! Notice above that the disk encryption feature is enabled, but the system
! remains in an 'initializing' state while the CONTENT, PRINTSPOOL, and other
! internal file systems are being encrypted.
!
pod1-br-wae# show disks details


Physical disk information:
   disk00: Present    Y66E58PE   (h02 c00 i00 l00 - Int DAS-SATA)
```

```
          238472MB(232.9GB)

Mounted file systems:
  MOUNT POINT     TYPE       DEVICE           SIZE     INUSE       FREE  USE%
  /sw             internal   /dev/sdb1        991MB     912MB      79MB   92%
  /swstore        internal   /dev/sdb2        991MB     879MB     112MB   88%
  /state          internal   /dev/sdb3       3967MB     135MB    3832MB    3%
  /local/local1   SYSFS      /dev/sdb7      11903MB    1183MB   10720MB    9%

Encrypted file systems:
  /obj1           CONTENT    /dev/mapper/obj1   172596MB    128MB  172468MB    0%
  /dre1           CONTENT    /dev/mapper/dre1    29757MB    128MB   29629MB    0%
  /ackq1          internal   /dev/mapper/ackq1    1189MB     32MB    1157MB    2%
  /plz1           internal   /dev/mapper/plz1     2379MB     65MB    2314MB    2%
  .../local1/spool PRINTSPOOL /dev/mapper/sdb8     991MB     16MB     975MB    1%

No RAID devices present.

Disk encryption feature is enabled.
pod1-br-wae#
```

Disk encryption is not required for SSL acceleration but it is highly recommended. The next step, configuration of the *secure store*, is required and discussed in the next section.

Managing the Secure Store

Disk encryption on WAAS devices relies on connectivity to the CM to initially fetch the key used for encrypting and decrypting data stored on the device file system. With the CM acting as the key management system for disk encryption keys, it is not feasible to assume that the CM could use itself for key management of disk encryption keys, as you would encounter a "chicken-and-egg" problem: How can the CM securely store keys to encrypt and decrypt its own disk, when it would need a key to decrypt the disk to fetch the disk encryption key? The answer to that problem is that you simply can't. Nonetheless, secure storage of SSL private keys and certificates is required. Thus, the secure store is a passphrase-protected file system on the CM device, which is used for this purpose.

The secure store can be configured from the device CLI using the **cms secure-store init** command. However, it is recommended that configuration of the secure store be done from the CM GUI. The secure store is configured in the CM from the **My WAN** context under **Admin > Secure Store** as shown in Figure 9-14. After the passphrase has been configured and accepted by the system, the **Admin > Secure Store** page changes to one that allows you to change the passphrase if necessary.

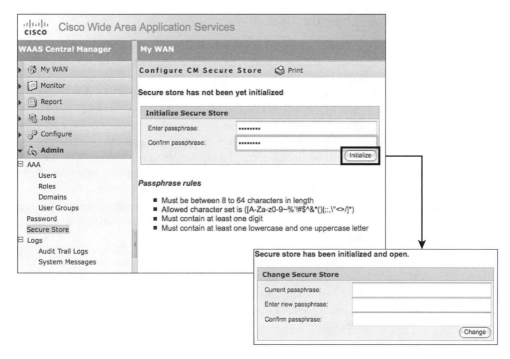

Figure 9-14 *Enabling Secure Store in CM*

Note Should you happen to forget the passphrase for the secure store, use the **cms secure-store reset** command from the CM device CLI. This command reinitializes the CM secure store, and all contents contained in the CM secure store are lost.

The secure store can *not* be opened automatically when the CM boots. Therefore, it is necessary that you open the secure store after rebooting the CM using the page shown in Figure 9-14, or using the CM device CLI command **cms secure-store open**.

```
pod1-cm1-wae# cms secure-store ?
  change  Change secure store passphrase
  clear   Clear secure store
  init    Initialize secure store
  open    Open secure store
  reset   Reset secure store
```

With the secure store configured and open, the next step is to configure SSL accelerated services.

Configuring SSL Accelerated Services

An SSL accelerated service is a series of configuration elements that enable data center WAAS devices to understand the encryption key material necessary to be able to convert ciphertext to cleartext, perform some function, and convert the resultant cleartext back to ciphertext. The first use of this service is to enable a data center WAAS device to act as an SSL proxy on behalf of the server. This enables the data center WAAS device to learn the session key that is derived. This session key—which is transient in nature—can be transmitted securely to the peer client-side WAAS device, to enable it and the data center WAAS device to both be able to decrypt and encrypt traffic for the TCP connection in question and in a coordinated manner. In this way, there are essentially three TCP connections (as discussed in Chapter 8, two original connections and one optimized connection) and two SSL sessions (one between client and data center WAAS device, and the other between data center WAAS device and server). Figure 9-8 demonstrated an example of this earlier in the chapter.

Configuration of an SSL accelerated service involves handling of server private keys and certificates. Thus it is recommended that configuration of SSL accelerated services be controlled through RBAC to minimize the number of users that can access this part of the system. Further, it is recommended that such configuration be done from a secured system, and that practices surrounding handling of server private keys be upheld on each system used throughout the process. To configure an SSL accelerated service, the following items are needed:

- **Server hostname(s) or IP address(es):** One or many servers can be configured in an SSL accelerated service. This is common when many servers are used to handle load for an application.

- **Server port number(s):** One port number can be configured for each server defined; however, multiple entries (each with a different port number) can be configured.

- **Existing server certificate and private key:** A certificate and private key is necessary to enable the data center WAAS device to proxy the SSL session between the client and the server to enable optimization. If the server certificate and private key cannot be obtained, you can substitute another certificate and private key. Self-signed certificates and keys can be generated, which can also be used; however, this is recommended only for simplicity and speed in proof-of-concept environments and not for production environments.

- **Passphrase for decrypting the private key:** Private keys are encrypted using passphrases, and this passphrase is needed to enable the data center WAAS devices to be able to read the private key contents.

The next two sections examine configuration of SSL accelerated services and related parameters from the CM GUI and from the CLI. It is recommended that the CM GUI be used, as it simplifies the workflow and—through the use of device groups—ensures consistency in configuration across devices. As such, the next section focuses on the CM GUI first, and the section following focuses on the device CLI.

Using the CM GUI to Configure SSL

SSL accelerated services can be configured from either the device or device group context. It is recommended that SSL accelerated services are configured only on data center devices—which implies that either configuration should be applied discretely, or, device groups containing only data center WAAS devices should be created. SSL accelerated services are configurable in both the CM GUI and the device CLI.

To configure an SSL accelerated service in the CM GUI from either the device or device group context, visit **Configure > Acceleration > SSL Accelerated Services**, as shown in Figure 9-15.

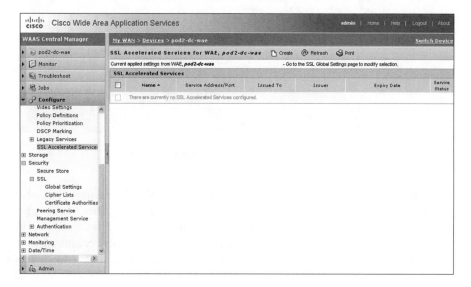

Figure 9-15   *Configuring SSL Accelerated Service in CM*

From this page, all the SSL accelerated services that have been configured are displayed. To create a new SSL accelerated service, simply click the **Create** button. Alternatively, if you want to edit an existing SSL accelerated service (for instance, to add a new server, change a port number, and upload a new certificate and private key), simply click the **Edit** icon next to the name of the accelerated service. In either case, the SSL accelerated service properties become visible, as shown in Figure 9-16.

From this page, supply the IP address or hostname of each server, along with the TCP port number. Click the **Add** button after each to add the entry to the table at the bottom of the page. The **In service** checkbox should be checked to enable this SSL accelerated service to be used. Should you need to disable the SSL accelerated service, the **In service** checkbox can be unchecked. With the servers and ports defined, use the links lower on the page to generate a self-signed certificate and private key (useful for lab environments), import existing certificate and private key, export existing certificates and private keys, or generate a certificate signing request (CSR).

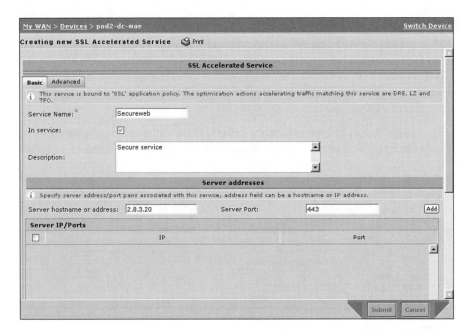

Figure 9-16   *SSL Accelerated Service Configuration Page in CM*

Generating a self-signed certificate and private key is helpful in lab environments where you have full control of the server but do not have a certificate or private key already. Clicking this link expands the window as shown in Figure 9-17. On this screen, you must provide the key size, common name of the server (such as the FQDN), organization, organizational unit, location, state, country, e-mail address of the administrator, and the number of days before the certificate expires. When added, the self-signed certificate is then added to the accelerated service and can be exported using the Export Certificate and Key link to be imported into the server for encrypting and decrypting client traffic. In cases where you do not have the certificate and private key, or cannot import a self-signed certificate and private key, SSL traffic can still be accelerated because the data center WAAS device is acting as the SSL server to the client and acting as the SSL client to the server.

In a production deployment, it is assumed that the administrators have access to the certificates and private keys of the server. These need to be imported into the CM using the **Import existing certificate and optionally private key** link, as shown in Figure 9-18.

After the certificate and private key have been either generated or imported, the window changes to show the certificate information in text format as well as the PEM-encoded format, as shown in Figure 9-19. After you have verified that the information is correct, click the **Submit** button to save certificate and private key information into the SSL accelerated service. This returns you to the SSL accelerated services listing, which is shown previously in Figure 9-15.

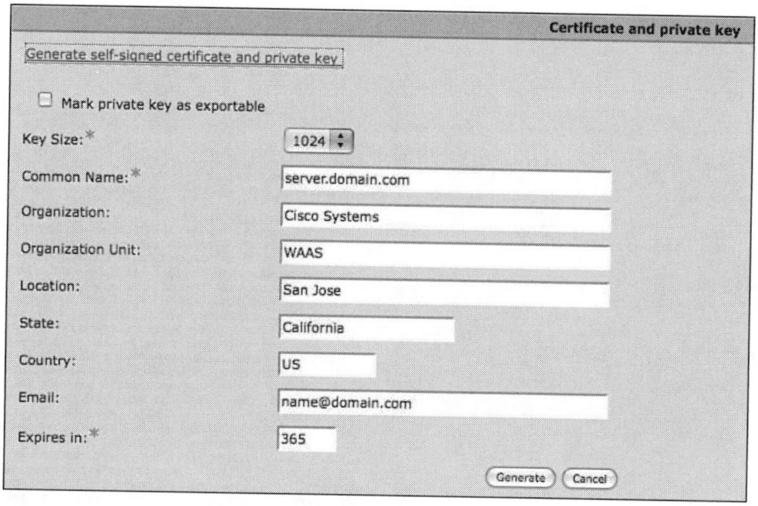

Figure 9-17 *Generating Self-Signed Certificate in CM*

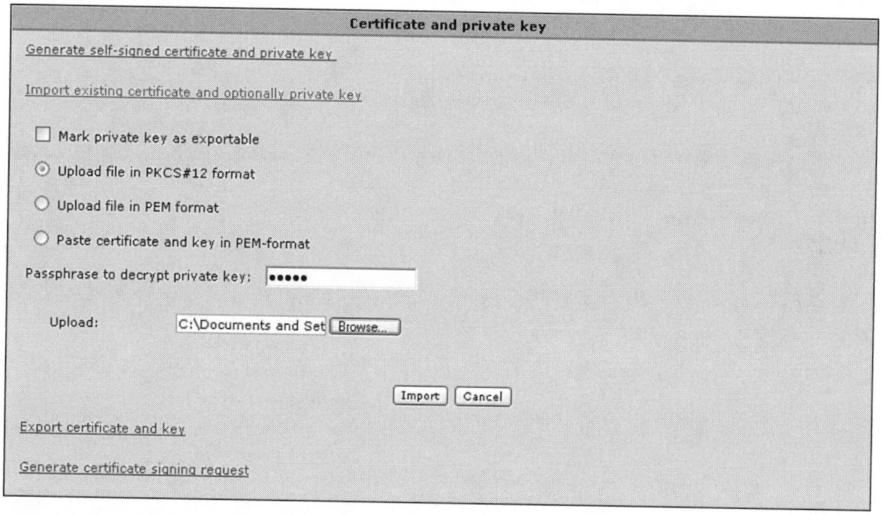

Figure 9-18 *Importing Certificate and Private Key in CM*

On the **Advanced** tab of the SSL accelerated service, the SSL version, cipher list, and certificate verification settings are displayed as shown in Figure 9-20. From this page, you can configure the following parameters:

■   **SSL version:** Specify the SSL version that is allowed with this accelerated service. This can be set to SSLv3, TLSv1, All (both SSLv3 and TLSv1), or Inherited, which uses the global settings found at **Configure > Security > SSL > Global Settings** to determine which version(s) to allow.

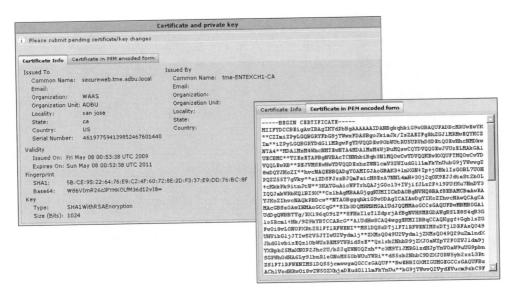

Figure 9-19   *Viewing Certificate Information in CM*

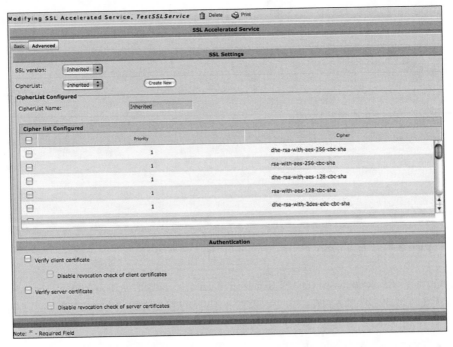

Figure 9-20   *Advanced SSL Accelerated Service Parameters in CM*

■   **Cipher List:** Specifies a cipher list to use, which defines the ciphers that can be used for traffic that is encrypted using the certificate and private key. This is set to

Inherited by default, which uses the cipher list found in the global settings, which are available at **Configure > Security > SSL > Cipher Lists**.

- **Verify client certificate:** Verifies the validity of the client certificate both by examining its contents and validating the certificate all the way up to a trusted root CA certificate in its CA store. If the WAAS device fails to verify the certificate in the hierarchy, it reports that the certificate verification process failed. The certificate verification process can also perform a real-time revocation check using the Online Certificate Status Protocol (OCSP) to the certificate responder listed in the certificate. The OCSP check can be optionally disabled by checking the box next to **Disable revocation check of client certificates**. Certificate validation and verification occurs for both client certificates and server certificates.

- **Verify server certificate:** Similar to **Verify client certificate**, but for server certificates.

When finished, click the **Submit** button, which saves the settings for the SSL accelerated service and returns you to the tabular listing, which shows all of the configured SSL accelerated services, as shown in Figure 9-21.

SSL Accelerated Services for WAE, *pod2-dc-wae* ⬜ Create ⟳ Refresh 🖨 Print					
Current applied settings from WAE, ***pod2-dc-wae***			- Go to the SSL Global Settings page to modify selection.		
SSL Accelerated Services				*Items 1-1 of 1* | Rows per page: 25 ⏷ Go	
☐ **Name ▲**	**Service Address/Port**	**Issued To**	**Issuer**	**Expiry Date**	**Service Status**
☐ 📝 Secureweb	2.8.3.20:443	secureweb.tme.adbu.local	tme-ENTEXCH1-CA	May 08 2011	Enabled
Delete				Page 1 of 1 ⏮ ◀ ▶ ⏭	

Figure 9-21   *SSL Accelerated Services List in CM*

With the SSL accelerated service configured for each server where SSL acceleration is required, WAAS devices can begin employing optimization against traffic to and from those server ports. The server-side WAAS device—which has been configured with the SSL accelerated service—acts as a proxy for the SSL session, effectively breaking the session into two (one between user and server-side WAAS device, and the second between the server-side WAAS device and the server). The server-side WAAS device employs a *peering service* to securely transfer the session key that was created between the client and the server-side WAAS device to the client-side WAAS device, thereby enabling it to participate in optimization of that particular SSL connection. If SSL traffic is received that does not match a configured SSL accelerated service, it is handled according to the policy action assigned to the classifier that matches the flow's tuple.

These settings can also be configured from the device CLI; however, it is recommended that the CM GUI be used for these purposes. To ensure a consistent configuration, it is generally recommended that a device group be created encompassing all data center WAAS devices that participate in SSL acceleration, and that the configuration is applied to that device group. The next section examines the CLI configuration of an SSL accelerated service and related parameters.

Using the CLI to Configure SSL

Additionally, the CLI can be used to configure SSL accelerated services on WAAS devices. This is, however, not recommended, because the configuration is more complex and cumbersome than found in the CM GUI. The first step is to configure the global settings (which are found at **Configure > Security > SSL > Global Settings** in the CM GUI) using the **crypto** command in global configuration mode. This command enables you to specify the SSL versions that are supported by the device, configure the machine certificate key (a .p12 file must be uploaded to the WAAS device filesystem prior to configuring the machine certificate key), and the cipher list that can be used (along with the priority order of the ciphers). Example 9-4 shows an annotated example.

Example 9-4   *Configuring SSL Global Parameters from CLI*

```
pod1-dc-wae# config term
pod1-dc-wae(config)# crypto ?
  pki  Configure PKI
  ssl  Configure SSL
pod1-dc-wae(config)# crypto ssl ?
  cipher-list         Configure Cipher list
  management-service  Configure Management service
  services            Configure SSL services
pod1-dc-wae(config)# crypto ssl services ?
  accelerated-service  Configure accelerated service
  global-settings      Configure SSL service global settings
  host-service         Configure host-services
pod1-dc-wae(config)# crypto ssl services global-settings ?
  cipher-list       Configure cipher list
  machine-cert-key  Configure the Machine Certificate Key
  version           Configure the SSL version
  <cr>
pod1-dc-wae(config)# crypto ssl services global-settings version ?
  all   All supported versions
  ssl3  SSL Version 3.0
  tls1  TLS Version 1.0
pod1-dc-wae(config)# crypto ssl services global-settings version all
!
! 'all' indicates that either SSLv3 or TLSv1 can be used
!
pod1-dc-wae(config)# crypto ssl services global-settings cipher-list ?
  WORD  Cipher list name
pod1-dc-wae(config)# crypto ssl services global-settings cipher-list MasterList ?
  <cr>
pod1-dc-wae(config)# crypto ssl services global-settings cipher-list MasterList
pod1-dc-wae(config)# crypto ssl cipher-list ?
  WORD  Cipher list name (Max 64 chars)
```

```
pod1-dc-wae(config)# crypto ssl cipher-list MasterList ?
  cipher   Change a cipher suite in the cipher-list
  <cr>
pod1-dc-wae(config)# crypto ssl cipher-list MasterList cipher ?
  dhe-rsa-export-with-des40-cbc-sha
  dhe-rsa-with-3des-ede-cbc-sha
  dhe-rsa-with-aes-128-cbc-sha
  dhe-rsa-with-aes-256-cbc-sha
  dhe-rsa-with-des-cbc-sha
  rsa-export-with-des40-cbc-sha
  rsa-export-with-rc4-40-md5
  rsa-export1024-with-des-cbc-sha
  rsa-export1024-with-rc4-56-sha
  rsa-with-3des-ede-cbc-sha
  rsa-with-aes-128-cbc-sha
  rsa-with-aes-256-cbc-sha
  rsa-with-des-cbc-sha
  rsa-with-rc4-128-md5
  rsa-with-rc4-128-sha
pod1-dc-wae(config)# crypto ssl cipher-list MasterList cipher rsa-with-3des-ede-
cbc-sha ?
  priority   Priority of cipher suite (Default priority: 1)
  <cr>
pod1-dc-wae(config)# crypto ssl cipher-list MasterList cipher rsa-with-3des-ede-
cbc-sha priority ?
  <1-15>   Priority Number (1: Lowest priority ,15: Highest priority)
pod1-dc-wae(config)# crypto ssl cipher-list MasterList cipher rsa-with-3des-ede-
cbc-sha priority 1 ?
  <cr>
pod1-dc-wae(config)# crypto ssl cipher-list MasterList cipher rsa-with-3des-ede-
cbc-sha priority 1
!
! multiple ciphers can be configured, and will be used
! according to the priority order specified in the
! commands that are applied
!
pod1-dc-wae(config)# crypto ssl services global-settings machine-cert-key ?
  WORD   Machine certificate and key PKCS12 filename, must have .p12 extension
pod1-dc-wae(config)# crypto ssl services global-settings machine-cert-key
device_cert_key.p12
!
! the certificate file must have an extension of .p12 and
! be present on the WAAS device file system prior to
! executing this command
!
```

```
pod1-dc-wae(config)# end
pod1-dc-wae# show run
!
! ... portions removed ...
!
!
crypto ssl cipher-list MasterList
   cipher rsa-with-3des-ede-cbc-sha priority 1
   exit
!
crypto ssl services global-settings
   version all
   machine-cert-key device_cert_key.p12
   cipher-list MasterList
   exit
!
```

Global settings for certificate revocation verification can also be performed from the device CLI, as shown in Example 9-5.

Example 9-5 *Configuring Certificate Revocation from CLI*

```
pod1-dc-wae# config term
pod1-dc-wae(config)# crypto pki ?
  ca               Specify the Certificate Authority
  global-settings  Modify the global settings
pod1-dc-wae(config)# crypto pki global-settings ?
  ocsp             Configure OCSP
  revocation-check Configure certificate revocation methods
  <cr>
pod1-dc-wae(config)# crypto pki global-settings ocsp ?
  url  Configure the OCSP url starting with 'http://'
pod1-dc-wae(config)# crypto pki global-settings ocsp url ?
  WORD  URL starting with 'http://'
pod1-dc-wae(config)# crypto pki global-settings ocsp url
http://www.company.com/ocspresponder
 !
 ! use this command if you have an explicit URL that you
 ! wish to use to check certificate status, use in conjunction
 ! with 'crypto pki global-settings revocation-check ocsp-url'
 !
pod1-dc-wae(config)# crypto pki global-settings ?
  ocsp             Configure OCSP
  revocation-check Configure certificate revocation methods
```

```
  <cr>
pod1-dc-wae(config)# crypto pki global-settings revocation-check ?

  ocsp-cert-url  Use the url from the Certificate
  ocsp-url       Use the url from the global OCSP setting
pod1-dc-wae(config)# crypto pki global-settings revocation-check ocsp-cert-url ?
  none  A null method that returns revocation success
  <cr>
!
! use 'revocation-check none' if you want the system to act
! as though it is performing verification, but the result will
! always be a success, i.e. the certificate is still valid
!
pod1-dc-wae(config)# crypto pki global-settings revocation-check ocsp-cert-url
!
! use this command to perform revocation checks on all
! certificates using the OCSP certificate URL supplied
! in the certificate
!
pod1-dc-wae(config)# crypto pki global-settings ?
  ocsp             Configure OCSP
  revocation-check  Configure certificate revocation methods
  <cr>
pod1-dc-wae(config)# crypto pki global-settings revocation-check ?
  ocsp-cert-url  Use the url from the Certificate
  ocsp-url       Use the url from the global OCSP setting
pod1-dc-wae(config)# crypto pki global-settings revocation-check ocsp-url ?
  none  A null method that returns revocation success
  <cr>
!
! use 'revocation-check none' if you want the system to act
! as though it is performing verification, but the result will
! always be a success, i.e. the certificate is still valid
!
pod1-dc-wae(config)# crypto pki global-settings revocation-check ocsp-url
!
! use this command to perform revocation checks on all
! certificates using the OCSP URL supplied above in the
! 'crypto pki global-settings ocsp url' command
!
pod1-dc-wae(config)# end
pod1-dc-wae#sh run
!
! ... portions removed ...
```

```
!
crypto pki global-settings
   ocsp url http://www.company.com/ocspresponder
   revocation-check ocsp-url
   exit
!
```

By default, Cisco WAAS devices include a list of many well-known CA certificates that can be used on the WAAS device. In the CM GUI, the well-known CAs can be imported using the **Import Well-Known CAs** button, and this must be done before certificate verification or OCSP revocation checking can be enabled. Additional certificate authorities (CAs), such as those specific to your organization, can also be configured in the device CLI, which are also configurable in the CM GUI at **Configure > Security > SSL > Certificate Authorities.** In the device CLI, the CAs must be defined manually as shown in Example 9-6, so it is recommended that the import of well-known CA certificates be performed from the CM.

Example 9-6   *Configuring Certificate Authorities from CLI*

```
pod1-dc-wae# conf t
pod1-dc-wae(config)# crypto ?
  pki   Configure PKI
  ssl   Configure SSL
pod1-dc-wae(config)# crypto pki ?
  ca                Specify the Certificate Authority
  global-settings  Modify the global settings
pod1-dc-wae(config)# crypto pki ca ?
  WORD   Certificate Authority Name (Max 64 chars)
pod1-dc-wae(config)# crypto pki ca sampleca
!
! defines the CA, and enters CA configuration mode
!
pod1-dc-wae(config-ca)# ?
  ca-certificate    Specify Certificate Authority certificate
  description       Certificate Authority Description
  exit              Exit from this submode
  no                Negate a command or set its defaults
  revocation-check  Configure certificate revocation methods
pod1-dc-wae(config-ca)# ca-certificate ?
  WORD   Certificate filename with '.ca' extension (Max 32 chars)
pod1-dc-wae(config-ca)# ca-certificate sampleca.ca ?
  <cr>
pod1-dc-wae(config-ca)# ca-certificate sampleca.ca
!
```

```
! the CA certificate must have a file name that ends in
! .ca, and must be uploaded to the WAAS device file system
! prior to executing this command
!
pod1-dc-wae(config-ca)# description ?
  WORD   Text describing this CA (Max 256 chars)
pod1-dc-wae(config-ca)# description "Sample certificate authority"
pod1-dc-wae(config-ca)# revocation-check ?
  none             A null method that returns revocation success
  ocsp-cert-url    Use the url from the Certificate
  ocsp-url         Use the url from the global OCSP setting
!
! 'ocsp-cert-url' uses the URL found in the certificate itself
! for any revocation checks. 'ocsp-url' uses the URL defined in
! the global settings for revocation checks. 'none' disables
! revocation checks for any certificates that are issued by this
! particular CA
!
pod1-dc-wae(config-ca)# revocation-check ocsp-url ?
  none  A null method that returns revocation success
  <cr>
!
! use 'revocation-check none' if you want the system to act
! as though it is performing verification, but the result will
! always be a success, i.e. the certificate is still valid
!
pod1-dc-wae(config-ca)# revocation-check ocsp-cert-url ?
  none  A null method that returns revocation success
  <cr>
!
! use 'revocation-check none' if you want the system to act
! as though it is performing verification, but the result will
! always be a success, i.e. the certificate is still valid
!
pod1-dc-wae(config-ca)# revocation-check ocsp-cert-url
pod1-dc-wae(config-ca)# end
pod1-dc-wae# show run
!
! ... portions removed ...
!
!
crypto pki ca sampleca
   description Sample certificate authority
   revocation-check ocsp-cert-url
```

```
    exit
!
```

With the global settings and CA settings configured, the SSL accelerated service can now be configured. Similar to what is shown in Example 9-6, the SSL accelerated service includes the server IP addresses and port numbers, the server certificate and optional private key, and an **inservice** flag that specifies that the service is operational and ready for use. Example 9-7 shows the configuration of the SSL accelerated service.

Example 9-7 *Configuring SSL Accelerated Service from CLI*

```
pod1-dc-wae#config term
pod1-dc-wae(config)# crypto ssl ?
  cipher-list          Configure Cipher list
  management-service   Configure Management service
  services             Configure SSL services
pod1-dc-wae(config)# crypto ssl services ?
  accelerated-service  Configure accelerated service
  global-settings      Configure SSL service global settings
  host-service         Configure host-services
pod1-dc-wae(config)# crypto ssl services accelerated-service ?
  WORD   Service name (Max 128 chars)
pod1-dc-wae(config)# crypto ssl services accelerated-service Secureweb ?
  cipher-list          Configure cipher list
  client-cert-verify   Turn on front-end client certificate verification
  description          Configure description string
  inservice            Activate service
  server-cert-key      Configure certificate and private key
  server-cert-verify   Turn on backend server certificate verification
  server-ip            Configure IP address and TCP port (Max 32 entries)
  version              Configure SSL version
  <cr>
pod1-dc-wae(config)# crypto ssl services accelerated-service Secureweb
!
! by hitting 'enter' after specifying the accelerated-service
! name, the CLI places you in accelerated service config mode.
! Similar to policy-engine, all of the parameters can be nested
! on a single-line command. However, for clarity, the commands
! are separated out using accelerated service config mode.
!
pod1-dc-wae(config-ssl-accelerated)# description "Secure service"
pod1-dc-wae(config-ssl-accelerated)# server-cert-key ?
  WORD   File name (PKCS#12 format, must have .p12 extension)
pod1-dc-wae(config-ssl-accelerated)# server-cert-key Secureweb.p12
```

```
!
! the server certificate and (optional) private key must
! be uploaded to the WAAS device file system prior to
! execution of this command. The file must have a .p12
! extension.
!
pod1-dc-wae(config-ssl-accelerated)# server-ip 10.10.10.100 ?
  port  Configure the TCP port
pod1-dc-wae(config-ssl-accelerated)# server-ip 10.10.10.100 port ?
  <1-65535>  Port Number
pod1-dc-wae(config-ssl-accelerated)# server-ip 10.10.10.100 port 443 ?
  <cr>
pod1-dc-wae(config-ssl-accelerated)# server-ip 10.10.10.100 port 443
!
! specify the IP address and port number of the server. The
! CM allows you to specify the hostname/FQDN, however, this is
! resolved to an IP address prior to being added to the tabular
! listing (see bottom of Figure 9-16) and only the IP address
! is stored in the running-config.
!
pod1-dc-wae(config-ssl-accelerated)# client-cert-verify ?
  revocation-check  Configure certificate revocation methods
  <cr>
pod1-dc-wae(config-ssl-accelerated)# client-cert-verify revocation-check ?
  none  A null method that returns revocation success
!
! use 'revocation-check none' if you want the system to act
! as though it is performing verification, but the result will
! always be a success, i.e. the certificate is still valid
!
pod1-dc-wae(config-ssl-accelerated)# client-cert-verify
pod1-dc-wae(config-ssl-accelerated)# server-cert-verify ?
  revocation-check  Configure certificate revocation methods
  <cr>
!
pod1-dc-wae(config-ssl-accelerated)# server-cert-verify revocation-check ?
  none  A null method that returns revocation success
!
! use 'revocation-check none' if you want the system to act
! as though it is performing verification, but the result will
! always be a success, i.e. the certificate is still valid
!
pod1-dc-wae(config-ssl-accelerated)# server-cert-verify
pod1-dc-wae(config-ssl-accelerated)# version ?
```

```
   all    All supported versions
   ssl3   SSL Version 3.0
   tls1   TLS Version 1.0
!
! specify the versions that are supported in this accelerated
! service. If versions are not specified, the versions defined
! in the global settings are used as seen in example 9-5.
!
pod1-dc-wae(config-ssl-accelerated)# version all ?
  <cr>
pod1-dc-wae(config-ssl-accelerated)# version all
pod1-dc-wae(config-ssl-accelerated)# end
pod1-dc-wae# show run
!
! ... portions removed ...
!
crypto ssl services accelerated-service Secureweb
   description Secure service
   version all
   server-ip 10.10.10.100 port 443
   server-cert-verify
   client-cert-verify
   exit
!
```

When an SSL accelerated service is created and placed "inservice" on the server-side WAAS device, a number of steps occur internally to prepare the system to accelerate SSL-encrypted traffic:

Step 1. The server IP address and TCP port number are used to generate a dynamic classifier containing the IP address and TCP port number as match conditions.

Step 2. The dynamic classifier is automatically attached to the SSL application policy.

Step 3. The optimization action for this dynamic classifier and application is configured to use DRE, PLZ, and TFO (full optimization, as discussed in Chapter 8).

You can verify the SSL accelerated service using the commands as shown in Example 9-8.

Example 9-8 *Verifying SSL Accelerated Service from CLI*

```
pod1-dc-wae# show policy-engine application dynaminc
Dynamic Match Freelist Information:
  Allocated: 32768  In Use: 1  Max In Use: 4  Allocations: 366
```

```
Dynamic Match Type/Count Information:
  None                   0
  Clean-Up               0
  Host->Host             0
  Host->Local            0
  Local->Host            0
  Local->Any             0
  Any->Host              1
  Any->Local             0
  Any->Any               0

Individual Dynamic Match Information:
  Number:    1   Type: Any->Host (6)  User Id: SSL (4)
    Src: ANY:ANY  Dst: 10.10.10.100:443
    Map Name: basic
    Flags: SSL
    Seconds: 0  Remaining: - NA -  DM Index: 32766
    Hits: 1  Flows: - NA -  Cookie: 0x00000000
```

At this point, the device is ready to begin optimizing SSL-encrypted traffic. More detailed monitoring for SSL-accelerated traffic is discussed in the "Acceleration Monitoring and Reporting" section of this chapter.

Configuring Preposition

The compression history provided by DRE and the object cache provided for CIFS traffic are of tremendous value in terms of improving application throughput and improving response times when accessing information. Many organizations find it useful to have these repositories of optimization data preloaded with useful information to maximize performance for the first user accessing this information or to minimize ongoing work-load from the perspective of the server (in the case of CIFS). WAAS provides a facility called *prepositioning*, which does exactly that. With prepositioning, a job is created and scheduled that defines a set of content (stored on CIFS file servers) to distribute to target WAAS devices at scheduled intervals. Prepositioning is useful, as discussed earlier, in environments where large objects or collections of objects are used frequently by remote users, including software distribution files, video-on-demand (VoD) for electronic learning (eLearning) applications, CAD/CAM, and software development environments.

Preposition jobs utilize two or more WAAS devices:

- A set of *edge* target devices or device groups are defined to specify where the files should be prepositioned.

- A *core* location (with the WAAS devices defined as being members in that location) specifies a pool of devices that are available to stage the files.

Based on the configuration of the preposition job (called a *directive*), a selected core device fetches the files specified in the preposition directive from the server specified, and store them in a revolving staging area. A listing of these files is sent then to the edge target devices, and each device begins an iterative process of comparing the listing to the contents of their CIFS object cache. Each device then requests files based on whether the files have changed, only new files, or all files, depending on the configuration of the preposition directive. Figure 9-22 depicts a high-level overview of this process.

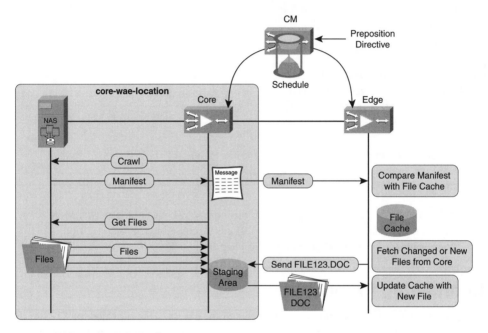

Figure 9-22   *Overview of Preposition*

Preposition is a global service configured in the My WAN context under **Configure > File Services > Preposition**. Each preposition job is called a *directive* and associates a number of parameters:

■   **Directive name:** A unique name that identifies the directive.

■   **Transport mode:** Specifies whether or not legacy CIFS transport mode is used.

■   **Status:** Enables or disables the directive. An enabled directive executes on the configured schedule, whereas a disabled directive does not execute until enabled.

■   **File server parameters:** Specifies the name of the file server, access credentials (username and password), and location where the file server resides in the network.

Note   The credentials specified must have read access to the directories that the files you want to preposition are stored in, as well as read access to the files themselves.

The location definition enables the CM to determine which WAAS devices can be used for fetching files into the staging area. Edge devices, configured later, then fetch the files directly from the staging area, and update their CIFS cache and DRE compression history accordingly.

- **DSCP value for preposition packets:** Specifies the DSCP value to be applied to packets used for transferring prepositioned files.

- **Cache parameters:** Specify the maximum percentage of the CIFS cache to occupy (0–100%), maximum file size filter, minimum file size filter, and maximum time duration of the preposition directive for each iteration.

Note The core device only fetches files that are between the minimum and maximum file sizes defined. Files that extend beyond these size boundaries are not included in the manifest that is sent to the edge device, thus, the edge device does not request them. The edge device does stop requesting files after it determines that any additional file requests exceed the cache capacity allocation.

- **Type of job:** Specifies whether **All Files** (self-explanatory), **Files Changed Since Last Preposition** (compare timestamps of the files on the server against the timestamp from the termination of the last preposition iteration), or **Files Changed Since** (specify a time frame in minutes, days, or weeks; files changed within this time frame is collected) should be fetched.

- **Contents to preposition:** Specifies whether hidden directories and files are transferred, whether to use recursive operation (traverse child directories), and what files should be prepositioned. A helpful directory browser is present, which enables you to view the contents of the server and interactively choose shares, files, and directories.

Figure 9-23 shows an example preposition directive.

After the parameters have been defined on the preposition directive configuration page, devices or groups of devices must be assigned by moving to the **Assign Edge Devices** or **Assign Edge Groups** tabs, each of which is shown in Figure 9-24. To select a device or device group, simply click the blue "X" next to the device, which changes to a green arrow, and then click the **Submit** button at the bottom of the page. To unselect a device, simply click the icon again.

After the target devices and groups have been selected and the changes submitted, click the **Schedule** tab. On this page, you can define the schedule for the preposition directive, which includes the following parameters, as shown in Figure 9-25:

- **Start time:** The time of day that the directive should begin execution.

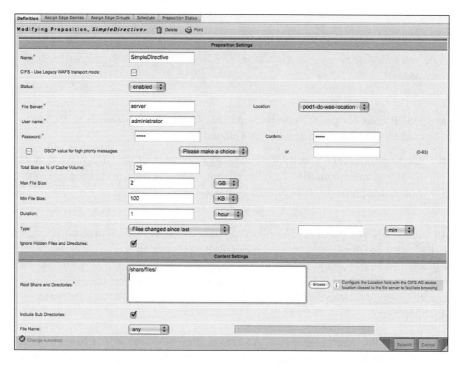

Figure 9-23   *Configuration of a Preposition Directive*

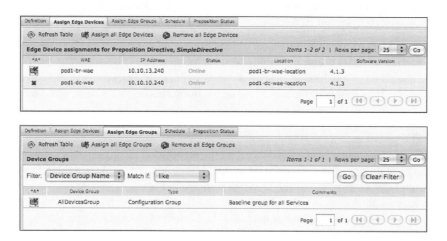

Figure 9-24   *Assigning Devices and Groups to a Preposition Directive*

- **Schedule type:** The type of schedule that should be used with the preposition directive, including:

   - **Not scheduled:** The preposition directive does not operate on a schedule and does not execute until scheduled.

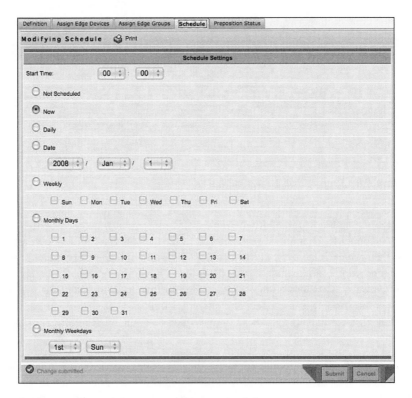

Figure 9-25 *Preposition Directive Schedule*

■ **Now:** Schedules the preposition directive to run immediately and only one time.

■ **Daily:** Schedules the preposition directive to run every day at the start time specified previously.

■ **Date:** Schedules the preposition directive to run at a specific date and at the start time specified previously. The directive runs only once.

■ **Weekly:** Schedules the preposition directive to run weekly on specific days of the week at the start time specified.

■ **Monthly Days:** Schedules the preposition directive to run monthly on the days of the month specified, starting at the start time specified.

■ **Monthly Weekdays:** Schedules the preposition directive to run monthly on a specific occurrence of a specific day of the week, for instance, the third Sunday of each month. The directive executes at the start time specified in the Start Time parameter.

After the schedule is configured, click **Submit.**

With the content, targets, and schedule configured, the preposition directive executes accordingly. The progress of the preposition directive can be monitored by using the **Preposition Status** tab, as shown in Figure 9-26.

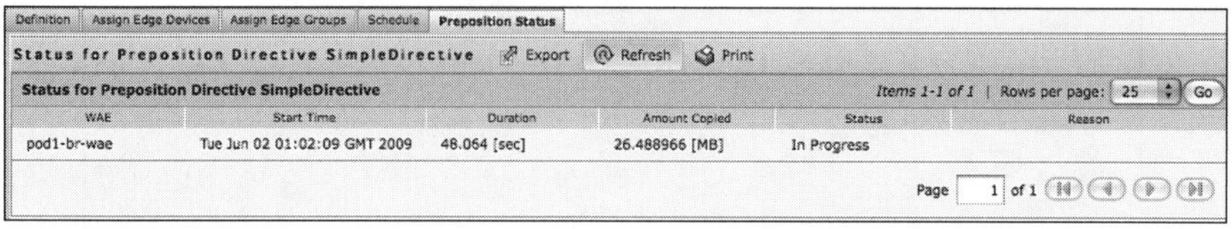

Figure 9-26 *Preposition Directive Status*

Note Preposition is a feature that requires the CM for system-wide coordination. Preposition cannot be configured or monitored from the CLI. The **Preposition Status** tab provides the primary interface for monitoring the progress of a preposition directive, and as such, preposition is not included in the "Acceleration Monitoring and Reporting" section to follow. However, CIFS-related monitoring and reporting commands and charts that are related to prepositioning is discussed. Similarly, the commands discussed in Chapter 8 surrounding DRE are equally applicable to determine how much DRE cache is utilized.

Prepositioning content not only populates the CIFS object cache in the target edge devices, but also populates the DRE compression history. By populating the compression history in addition to the object cache, users receive tremendous performance improvements for the first access of the file *and* for any changes that are applied to the file when saved back to the origin server. As such, many customers choose to run preposition directives on a daily basis for project-related files that are accessed in an interactive read-write manner. For files that are accessed in a read-only manner (such as software distribution files or VoDs), many customers choose to schedule preposition directives for immediate (Now) execution, and when complete, change the execution to a weekly, monthly, or monthly day schedule.

Note Preposition can also be configured from the device CLI in global configuration mode using the command **accelerator cifs preposition** as demonstrated in the following:

```
pod1-br-wae(config)# accelerator cifs preposition ?
  <0-2147883647>  Preposition ID
  remove          Remove preposition task
pod1-br-wae(config)# accelerator cifs preposition 1 ?
  credentials         Sets user and password credentials. Use password 0 to use
and show a password as a
                      plaintext, and password 1 to store and show a DES-encrypted
password
  dscp                Defines dscp for the task data
  duration            Sets the maximum duration limit minutes that the task can
run
```

```
    enable              Enables the directive (use no enable to disable)
   ignore-hidden-dir   Ignore hidden directories
   max-cache           Sets the maximum percentage of the cache that the task can
occupy
   max-file-size       Sets maximum file size (KB) limit
   min-file-size       Sets minimum file size (KB) limit
   modified            Update directive modified time
   name                Sets the name of the directive
   pattern             Sets a string filter on the file names
   recursive           Defines if the preposition is recursive
   root                Adds a preposition root. Multiple roots are supported
   scan-type           Sets the type of the scan in the preposition directive
   schedule            Sets the schedule to start the task
   server              Sets server name for the directive. Only one server is
allowed
   <cr>
```

Acceleration Monitoring and Reporting

The previous sections provided an overview on the application acceleration facilities provided by WAAS, along with configuration and verification. This section focuses on the monitoring and reporting capabilities provided by the CM as well as the device CLI for purposes of verification, statistics, and troubleshooting. As described in Chapter 7 and Chapter 8, powerful reporting facilities exist in the CM for scheduling regular reports, and an XML-API is present, which provides a foundation for integration with third-party visibility products. The section closes with an examination of the APIs that are focused on application acceleration components.

Acceleration Monitoring Using Device CLI

The device CLI provides complete visibility into the monitoring statistics that are available for each of the AOs in the WAAS device. These statistics are the foundation by which the CM charts are populated with data and help provide understanding into how the AOs are operating, what levels of acceleration are being provided, and the health of each service. The first command we examine was introduced in Chapter 8, which is **show statistics connection**. The command output includes overall optimized connection statistics, and each individual connection listed has one or more **accel** flags, which indicate the type of optimization or acceleration capabilities that have been applied, as demonstrated in Example 9-9.

Example 9-9 *Examining Accelerated Connections from CLI*

```
pod1-br-wae# show statistics connection

Current Active Optimized Flows:                     6
```

```
          Current Active Optimized TCP Plus Flows:          6
          Current Active Optimized TCP Only Flows:          0
          Current Active Optimized TCP Preposition Flows:   0
Current Active Auto-Discovery Flows:                        0
Current Active Pass-Through Flows:                          2
Historical Flows:                                        100


D:DRE,L:LZ,T:TCP Optimization,
A:AOIM,C:CIFS,E:EPM,G:GENERIC,H:HTTP,M:MAPI,N:NFS,S:SSL,V:VIDEO
!
! notice in the legend above that each of the AOs are listed and
! can be found in the 'Accel' column below. 'A:AOIM' refers to the
! AO infrastructure manager, which is used to manage AO
! incompatibilities across versions while permitting/denying use
! of the configured AO through automatic discovery filtering. It
! should rarely (if ever) be seen. 'G:GENERIC' refers to a generic
! AO which serves as a pipe-through when the original AO as defined
! in the policy could not be used due to load, configuration, or
! other reasons.
!

ConnID  Source IP:Port        Dest IP:Port          PeerID             Accel
31432   10.10.13.100:4676     10.10.10.100:135      00:14:5e:41:eb:78  TE
31433   10.10.13.100:4678     10.10.10.100:1026     00:14:5e:41:eb:78  TDL
31438   10.10.13.100:4705     10.10.10.100:80       00:14:5e:41:eb:78  THDL
31443   10.10.13.100:4701     10.10.10.100:445      00:14:5e:41:eb:78  TCDL
31446   10.10.13.100:4710     10.10.10.100:21       00:14:5e:41:eb:78  TDL
31447   10.10.13.100:4711     10.10.10.100:10001    00:14:5e:41:eb:78  TDL
!
! notice in the table above, one connection is using the EPM AO
! (which is discussed in chapter 8), another is using the HTTP AO,
! and another is using the CIFS AO.
!
```

For an additional level of detail about the AO, you can issue the **show statistics connection** command and filter by the connection identifier (shown as ConnID in the tabular listing in Example 9-9). As discussed in Chapter 8, this command provides detailed output about the connection itself, including each of the optimization and acceleration components. Example 9-10 is annotated and shows this command output.

Example 9-10 *Examining HTTP AO-Accelerated Connection Details from CLI*

```
pod1-br-wae# show statistics connection conn-id 32220

Connection Id:                32220
    Peer Id:                  00:14:5e:41:eb:78
    Connection Type:          EXTERNAL CLIENT
    Start Time:               Mon Jun  1 19:32:57 2009
    Source IP Address:        10.10.13.100
    Source Port Number:       2820
    Destination IP Address:   10.10.10.100
    Destination Port Number:  80
    Application Name:         Web
    Classifier Name:          HTTP
    Map Name:                 basic
    Directed Mode:            FALSE
    Preposition Flow:         FALSE
    Policy Details:
            Configured:       TCP_OPTIMIZE + DRE + LZ
              Derived:        TCP_OPTIMIZE + DRE + LZ
                 Peer:        TCP_OPTIMIZE + DRE + LZ
           Negotiated:        TCP_OPTIMIZE + DRE + LZ
             Applied:         TCP_OPTIMIZE + DRE + LZ
    Accelerator Details:
              Configured:     HTTP
                Derived:      HTTP
                Applied:      HTTP
!
! the 'Configured', 'Derived', and 'Applied' specify the
! accelerator configured locally on the device (Configured),
! the accelerator negotiated through automatic discovery
! (Derived), and the accelerator applied to the connection
! (Applied). Derived may be different from Configured if the
! peer device is overloaded, does not have the same policy
! configuration, or does not have the AO enabled. Applied
! may be different than Configured and Derived if the local
! device is in an overload condition.
!
                                  Original         Optimized
                                  ----------       ----------
    Bytes Read:                   0                9243
    Bytes Written:                0                1037

HTTP : 32220

   Time Statistics were Last Reset/Cleared:       Mon Jun  1 19:32:57 2009
   Total Bytes Read:                              565        20324298
```

```
    Total Bytes Written:                        565        20324298
    Total Bytes Buffered:                         0               0
    Fast connections:                             4
!
! notice above how the AO-specific statistics are presented, including
! the number of bytes read and written by the AO, total bytes buffered
! by the AO (at time of executing the command), and the number of 'fast'
! connections. In the case of HTTP, a 'fast' connection one that
! re-used an existing connection over the WAN, to mitigate the connection
! setup time.
!
! ... portions removed ...
!
```

Example 9-11 shows similar output, but in this example, a CIFS-accelerated connection is examined.

Example 9-11   *Examining CIFS AO-Accelerated Connection Details from CLI*

```
pod1-br-wae#show statistics connection conn-id 32895
!
! ... portions removed ...
!
Connection Id:              32895
    Peer Id:                00:14:5e:41:eb:78
    Connection Type:        EXTERNAL CLIENT
    Start Time:             Mon Jun  1 19:42:47 2009
    Source IP Address:      10.10.13.100
    Source Port Number:     4501
    Destination IP Address: 10.10.10.100
    Destination Port Number: 445
    Application Name:       WAFS
    Classifier Name:        CIFS
    Map Name:               basic
    Directed Mode:          FALSE
    Preposition Flow:       FALSE
    Policy Details:
            Configured:     TCP_OPTIMIZE + DRE + LZ
             Derived:       TCP_OPTIMIZE + DRE + LZ
                Peer:       TCP_OPTIMIZE + DRE + LZ
           Negotiated:      TCP_OPTIMIZE + DRE + LZ
             Applied:       TCP_OPTIMIZE + DRE + LZ
    Accelerator Details:
                Configured: CIFS
```

```
                       Derived:   CIFS
                       Applied:   CIFS
                          Hist:   None


                                              Original          Optimized

                                          ----------        ----------

      Bytes Read:                              41456             718207
      Bytes Written:                        15397723              15045

CIFS : 32895


    Time Statistics were Last Reset/Cleared:        Mon Jun  1 19:42:47 2009
    Total Bytes Read:                            41393      16983828
    Total Bytes Written:                      15332059         28321
!
! you'll notice that the statistics are similar across the AOs. This
! is in large part due to a component of the internal software
! architecture that abstracts application-specific acceleration
! components from the I/O that occurs internally, which provides a
! uniform representation of data from AO to AO.
!
! ... portions removed ...
!
```

Statistics that are global to the AO can also be gathered from the CLI using the command **show statistics accelerator** *accelerator* **detail**, as demonstrated in Example 9-12, which is annotated for both CIFS and HTTP.

Example 9-12 *Accelerator Global Statistics in CLI*

```
pod1-br-wae# show statistics accelerator cifs detail

CIFS:
   Global Statistics

   ---------·

   Time Accelerator was started:                   Mon Jun  1 11:53:24 2009
   Time Statistics were Last Reset/Cleared:        Mon Jun  1 11:53:24 2009
   Total Handled Connections:                                    76
   Total Optimized Connections:                                  51
!
! notice above the timestamp from when the accelerator was last
! started and the timestamp from when the statistics were last
! reset or cleared. In this case, they are the same, as statistics
! are automatically reset upon reboot. Statistics shown in this
```

```
! output are cumulative since the last reset. The number of handled
! connections since reset is displayed above, along with the number
! of connections that were optimized.
!
  Total Connections Handed-off with Compression Policies Unchanged:    0
  Total Dropped Connections:                                           0
  Current Active Connections:                                          1
  Current Pending Connections:                                         0
  Maximum Active Connections:                                          3
!
! 'Active' connections refers to connections that are established
! and are not in a tear-down state. 'Pending' connections refers
! to those that are in the process of being established. 'Maximum
! Active' connections refers to the peak value seen by the
! accelerator since the last reset.
!
  Number of local reply generating requests:                      20888
  Number of remote reply generating requests:                       687
  The Average time to generate a local reply (msec):                  5
  Average time to receive remote reply (ms):                        296
!
! The CIFS AO provides local message responses for certain message
! types. The statistics above show how many messages were handled
! with a local response, the number of messages that were generated
! toward the server to request a remote response (i.e. message from
! client that must be handled by the server), the average time taken
! to generate a local response, and the average amount of time taken
! to receive a response from the server.
!
! ... portions removed for readability ...
!
pod1-br-wae# show statistics accelerator http detail


HTTP:
  Global Statistics
  — — — — — — —·
  Time Accelerator was started:              Mon Jun  1 11:53:01 2009
  Time Statistics were Last Reset/Cleared:   Mon Jun  1 11:53:01 2009
  Total Handled Connections:                                     14818
  Total Optimized Connections:                                   14818
  Total Connections Handed-off with Compression Policies Unchanged:    0
  Total Dropped Connections:                                         0
  Current Active Connections:                                        1
```

```
   Current Pending Connections:                                    0
   Maximum Active Connections:                                     3
   Total Time Saved (ms):                                     995893
!
! 'Total Time Saved' is a statistic that is common across many of the AOs
! which is calculated based on the number of round-trips mitigated by use
! of the AO. This is also used to populate the charts that will be
! discussed in the next section. This number is an estimate only.
!
   Current Active Connections Free For Fast Connection Use:        1
!
! this line displays the number of connections that are available to be
! 're-used' by HTTP.
!
! ... portions removed ...
!
   Total Fast Connection Successes:                            13330
   Total Fast Connection Failures:                                 0
!
! these lines show the number of successes and failures by the HTTP AO
! to re-use an existing connection.
!
   Maximum Fast Connections on a Single Connection:               13
!
! this line shows the maximum number of connections that took advantage
! of a single re-used connection since the last statistics reset.
!
   Percentage of Connection Time Saved:                           89
   Total Round Trip Time For All Connections (ms):            115393
!
! the lines above help quantify the improvement provided by the AO. In
! this case, almost 90% of connection setup time was saved by having the
! AO enabled and applied, and the amount of time saved is shown to be
! over 115 seconds across all accelerated connections since the last
! reset of the statistics.
!
! ... portions removed for readability ...
!
```

Each AO has its own unique output for these CLI commands, but many of the data points displayed are common across AOs. While this section examined the CLI statistics available for AO-accelerated connections, the next section focuses on the statistics and charts found in the CM GUI.

Acceleration Monitoring Using CM GUI

The statistics found in the CLI provide visibility into virtually any data element necessary. Many of the CLIs use cumulative values, that is, they don't clear until the statistics are reset or the system is rebooted. The CM provides visualization capabilities for the most commonly used data elements that are found in the CLI, but unlike the CLI, values are normalized over time and not cumulative. Many of the charts are consistent across AOs (with some exceptions), and the primary motivation behind the charts is to answer questions such as the following:

■ How well are my accelerators working?

■ How much productivity improvement have my employees realized?

■ How many connections are my accelerators handling?

■ What conditions exist that are causing my accelerators to not accelerate traffic?

All the charts that are available for display in the CM—like the traffic and optimization charts—can be displayed either in the My WAN context or a device context. These charts can be found and visualized on the dashboard page, and they are also found in the **Monitor** drawer under **Acceleration**. Along with the charts, the supporting data tables used to create the charts is presented on the same page. Table 9-1 lists all of the charts that are available as of WAAS version 4.1.3, the data that is plotted, and the use case for each.

Note   CIFS acceleration charts are displayed only in the device context and are not displayed in the My WAN context. Certain aspects of CIFS acceleration statistics cannot be usefully summarized across devices.

Table 9-1   *Accelerator Charts in CM GUI*

Accelerator(s)	Chart Name	Plotted Elements	Use Case
HTTP, MAPI, NFS	Estimated Time Savings	Response time savings (percentage) over time	Helps identify the estimated percentage of application time saved through use of the AO
HTTP, MAPI, NFS, Video, SSL, CIFS	Connection Details (Connection Statistics)	Connections handled versus bypassed over time	Helps identify the AO workload and number of optimized connections compared to unoptimized connections
HTTP, MAPI, NFS, Video, SSL	Bandwidth Optimization	Effective capacity (X-Factor) over time for "All Traffic" and AO traffic	Helps identify whether the AO-accelerated traffic is contributing to or detracting from overall effective capacity

Table 9-1 *Accelerator Charts in CM GUI*

Accelerator(s)	Chart Name	Plotted Elements	Use Case
MAPI, CIFS, NFS	Request Optimization	Percentage local responses versus percentage remote responses over time	Helps identify what portion of AO-accelerated requests were able to be handled locally by the AO as compared to those that required handling by the server (remote)
MAPI, NFS	Versions Detected	Distribution of protocol versions over sample period	Helps identify what version of applications and protocols are in use
MAPI, NFS, Video, SSL	Acceleration Bypass Reason	Distribution of bypass reasons over sample period	Helps identify why application traffic was not accelerated by the AO
MAPI, NFS	Response Time Optimization	Average response time for local response messages compared to remote response messages over time	Helps identify ongoing network conditions, particularly latency, as traffic is optimized
Video	Stream Optimization	Incoming bytes compared to outgoing bytes over time	Helps visualize the amount of throughput improvement and bandwidth savings provided by the video AO
CIFS	Request Optimization	Request hit rate over time	Shows the effectiveness of the CIFS AO in mitigating request workload from the origin server
CIFS	Cached Objects	Number of cached objects over time	Quantifies the number of files that are stored in the CIFS object cache
CIFS	Cache Utilization	Disk space utilization and cache resources utilization over time	Helps understand trends in cache capacity utilization both in terms of available disk space as well as maximum number of resources
CIFS	File Optimization	Open and accelerated files over time	Shows the number of files that users have opened that have been accelerated by the device over time
CIFS	Client Average Throughput	Throughput in KB/s over time	Shows the amount of throughput perceived by the client over the sample period of time

Figure 9-27 provides an example of the charts that are provided in the CM for accelerators. In this example, HTTP AO statistics are viewed from the **HTTP Acceleration Report** link, found in the device or My WAN context at **Monitor > Acceleration > HTTP Acceleration Report**. As described in Chapters 7 and 8, any monitoring chart can be added into an existing (or new) report, which can be scheduled for automatic delivery via e-mail or printed to PDF.

Similar to the connection statistics table that is shown in Example 9-9, the CM connection statistics table (also discussed in Chapter 8) provides a visual indication of the optimization and acceleration components applied to the connections that are being handled by the device. Notice in Figure 9-28 that the first and fourth connection are handled by the CIFS and HTTP accelerators respectively. Similarly, when you open the connection monitor for an AO-accelerated connection, the icon and the AO name are shown.

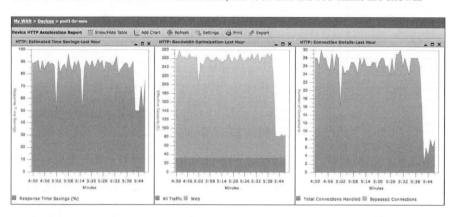

Figure 9-27   *Central Manager Accelerator Charts*

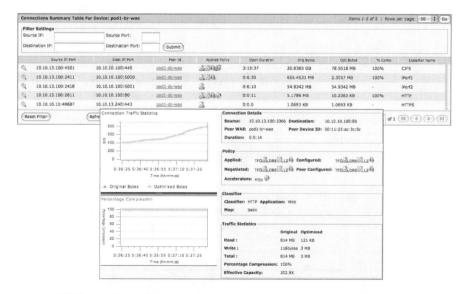

Figure 9-28   *AO Icon in Connection Table and Connection Monitor*

Acceleration Monitoring with XML-API

Chapter 7 introduced the XML-API that is provided by the WAAS CM, and Chapter 8 highlighted the WAN optimization-related statistics that are made accessible via the API. Having an XML-API enables integration of monitoring statistics with third-party visibility systems that monitor multiple data sources, mediate and correlate data, and provide unified views of application performance end-to-end. The XML-API provides a service for each of the AOs that are available in the system. Each of these services is available at the following WSDL URLs:

- **CIFSStats:** https://*<ip-or-hostname-of-cm>*:8443/ws/CIFSStats?wsdl

- **SSLStats:** https://*<ip-or-hostname-of-cm>*:8443/ws/SSLStats?wsdl

- **VideoStats:** https://*<ip-or-hostname-of-cm>*:8443/ws/VideoStats?wsdl

- **HttpStats:** https://*<ip-or-hostname-of-cm>*:8443/ws/HttpStats?wsdl

- **MapiStats:** https://*<ip-or-hostname-of-cm>*:8443/ws/MapiStats?wsdl

- **NfsStats:** https://*<ip-or-hostname-of-cm>*:8443/ws/NfsStats?wsdl

The following sections examine each of these services, their interfaces, and the supporting use cases. It should be noted that the XML-API is primarily used by independent software vendors (ISVs) that have chosen to integrate Cisco WAAS into their end-to-end performance visibility solutions. However, that should not discourage enterprise customers from using their own tools and taking advantage of this interface to integrate WAAS programmatically into their existing management infrastructure.

CIFSStats

The CIFSStats service provides interfaces that enable extraction of CIFS acceleration statistics from WAAS devices in the network through the CM. The CIFSStats service includes the interfaces that follow Figure 9-29, which provides a soapui screen capture of the available CIFSStats interfaces. Note that all the CIFSStats interfaces have an identical set of parameters including:

- Device or device group name.

- Type (wae or waegroup).

- Type of traffic (optimized or passthrough).

- Traffic direction (inbound, outbound, bidirectional).

- Timeframe filter including start time, end time, interval, time zone. Please see Chapter 7 for more details on these elements.

- **getCIFSClientAvgThroughput:** Returns the average client throughput for each sample over the time frames specified.

- **getCIFSCoreCount:** Useful only for legacy CIFS deployments and not applicable to CIFS AO deployments. Returns the number of connected WAFS Core devices at each interval over the time frame specified.

- **getCIFSCoreEdgeTraffic:** Useful only for legacy CIFS deployments and not applicable to CIFS AO deployments. Returns the amount of traffic to remote WAFS Edge devices from this device at each interval over the time frame specified.

- **getCIFSEdgeCoreTraffic:** Useful only for legacy CIFS deployments and not applicable to CIFS AO deployments. Returns the amount of traffic to remote WAFS Core devices from this device at each interval over the time frame specified.

- **getCIFSEdgeCount:** Useful only for legacy CIFS deployments and not applicable to CIFS AO deployments. Returns the number of connected WAFS Edge devices at each interval over the time frame specified.

- **getDiskCapacity:** Returns the disk capacity at each interval over the time frame specified.

- **getOpenFileCount:** Returns the number of open files at each interval over the time frame specified.

- **getOptCIFSSessionCount:** Returns the number of optimized CIFS sessions at each interval over the time frame specified.

- **getRequestCount:** Returns the number of CIFS requests received at each interval over the time frame specified.

- **retrieveCacheObjectCount:** Returns the number of objects stored in the CIFS object cache at each interval over the time frame specified.

- **retrieveCacheUtilization:** Returns the percentage of cache utilized along with the percentage of resources utilized (total number of cached objects compared to the maximum number of cached objects) at each interval over the time frame specified.

- **retrieveRequestHitRate:** Returns the request hit rate (requests handled locally by the WAAS device) at each interval over the time frame specified.

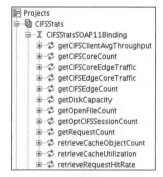

Figure 9-29 *CIFSStats Service Interfaces*

Note   All the CIFSStats interfaces take the same input. Therefore, it is helpful (when using soapui) to open Notepad (or a similar text editing program) and simply copy and paste the interface parameters there for later use with other CIFSStats interfaces. For example, this set of parameters works with all CIFSStats interfaces and specifies a branch WAAS device, optimized traffic, bidirectional statistics, and a last hour time frame. This is also shown in Figure 9-30.

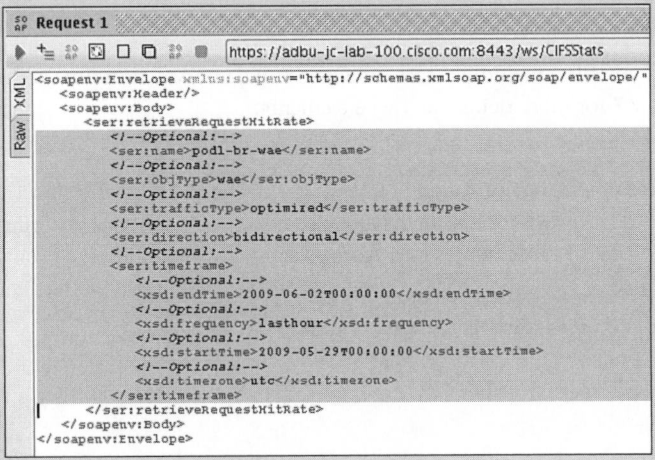

Figure 9-30   *Common Elements in CIFSStats*

```
<!—Optional:—>
<ser:name>pod1-br-wae</ser:name>
<!—Optional:—>
<ser:objType>wae</ser:objType>
<!—Optional:—>
<ser:trafficType>optimized</ser:trafficType>
<!—Optional:—>
<ser:direction>bidirectional</ser:direction>
<!—Optional:—>
<ser:timeframe>
    <!—Optional:—>
    <xsd:endTime>2009-06-02T00:00:00</xsd:endTime>
    <!—Optional:—>
    <xsd:frequency>lasthour</xsd:frequency>
    <!—Optional:—>
    <xsd:startTime>2009-05-29T00:00:00</xsd:startTime>
    <!—Optional:—>
    <xsd:timezone>utc</xsd:timezone>
</ser:timeframe>
```

SSLStats

The SSLStats service provides interfaces that enable extraction of SSL acceleration statistics from WAAS devices in the network through the CM. The CIFSStats service includes the interfaces that follow. Note that all the SSLStats interfaces that an identical set of parameters including:

- Device or device group name.

- Type (wae or waegroup).

- Timeframe filter including start time, end time, interval, and time zone. Please see Chapter 7 for more details on these elements.

> **Note**   Similar to the behavior found in CIFSStats, all the SSLStats interfaces take the same input. As mentioned previously, it might be helpful to keep a copy of the query parameters stored in a text file for reuse across interfaces as shown in the following example.
>
> ```
> <!—Optional:—>
> <ser:name>pod1-br-wae</ser:name>
> <!—Optional:—>
> <ser:objType>wae</ser:objType>
> <!—Optional:—>
> <ser:timeframe>
>     <!—Optional:—>
>     <xsd:endTime>2009-06-02T00:00:00</xsd:endTime>
>     <!—Optional:—>
>     <xsd:frequency>lasthour</xsd:frequency>
>     <!—Optional:—>
>     <xsd:startTime>2009-05-29T00:00:00</xsd:startTime>
>     <!—Optional:—>
>     <xsd:timezone>utc</xsd:timezone>
> </ser:timeframe>
> ```

- **getBytesCount:** Returns the byte counts handled by the SSL AO for each sample period in the interval specified, including bytes read in (LAN and WAN) and bytes written out (LAN and WAN).

- **getErrorConnCount:** Returns the quantity of connections by error condition for each sample period in the interval specified, including dropped due to revocation, dropped due to inability to verify, dropped due to other reasons, and total dropped connections.

- **getOptConnCount:** Returns the number of connections that were optimized by the SSL AO for each sample period in the interval specified.

- **getTotalConnCount:** Returns the number of connections that were handled by the SSL AO for each sample period in the interval specified.

- **getUnAccelConnCount:** Returns the quantity of nonaccelerated connections by cipher mismatch, non-SSL flows, version mismatch, and pipe-through for each sample period in the interval specified.

VideoStats

The VideoStats service provides interfaces that enable extraction of Video (stream-splitting; caching is covered in CIFSStats) acceleration statistics from WAAS devices in the network through the CM. The VideoStats service includes the interfaces that follow.

- **retrieveHistoricalStats:** Takes a device or device group name, type (wae or waegroup), and timeframe filter as input, and returns values for each sample period in the time frame specified for number of accelerated connections, number of error connections, total incoming versus outgoing bytes, bandwidth savings (percentage), and number of accelerated connections.

- **retrieveCurrentStats:** Takes a device or device group name, type (wae or waegroup), and URL, and returns per-URL video stream statistics for each sample period in the time frame specified, including incoming bandwidth, client count, list of clients, and bytes received.

HttpStats

The HttpStats service provides interfaces that enable extraction of HTTP acceleration statistics from WAAS devices in the network through the CM. The HttpStats service includes the interfaces that follow. Note that all of the HttpStats interfaces that an identical set of parameters including:

- Device or device group name.

- Type (wae or waegroup).

- Timeframe filter including start time, end time, interval, and time zone. Please see Chapter 7 for more details on these elements.

Note   Similar to the behavior found in CIFSStats, all the HttpStats interfaces take the same input. As mentioned previously, it might be helpful to keep a copy of the query parameters stored in a text file for reuse across interfaces as shown in the following example:

```
<!—Optional:—>
<ser:name>pod1-br-wae</ser:name>
<!—Optional:—>
<ser:objType>wae</ser:objType>
<!—Optional:—>
<ser:timeframe>
    <!—Optional:—>
    <xsd:endTime>2009-06-02T00:00:00</xsd:endTime>
    <!—Optional:—>
    <xsd:frequency>lasthour</xsd:frequency>
    <!—Optional:—>
    <xsd:startTime>2009-05-29T00:00:00</xsd:startTime>
    <!—Optional:—>
    <xsd:timezone>utc</xsd:timezone>
</ser:timeframe>
```

■ **getConnOptRate:** Returns the percentage of connection time saved over each interval of the sample period defined by the timeframe filter.

■ **getMaxConnReuseCount:** Returns the maximum number of times that a connection has been reused over each interval of the sample period defined by the timeframe filter.

■ **getOptConnCount:** Returns the number of connections that were optimized by the HTTP AO (reused an existing connection) for each sample period in the interval specified.

■ **getTotalConnCount:** Returns the number of connections that were handled by the HTTP AO for each sample period in the interval specified.

■ **getUnAccelConnCount:** Returns statistics from each period based on the timeframe filter defined for number of idle connections, percentage of round-trip time saved, number of reused connections, and number of reused peers.

MapiStats

The MapiStats service provides interfaces that enable extraction of MAPI acceleration statistics from WAAS devices in the network through the CM. The MapiStats service includes the interfaces that follow. Note that all of the MapiStats interfaces that an identical set of parameters including:

- Device or device group name.

- Type (wae or waegroup).

- Timeframe filter including start time, end time, interval, and time zone. Please see Chapter 7 for more details on these elements.

> **Note**   Similar to the behavior found in CIFSStats, all the MapiStats interfaces take the same input. As mentioned previously, it might be helpful to keep a copy of the query parameters stored in a text file for reuse across interfaces as shown in the following example:
>
> ```
> <!—Optional:—>
> <ser:name>pod1-br-wae</ser:name>
> <!—Optional:—>
> <ser:objType>wae</ser:objType>
> <!—Optional:—>
> <ser:timeframe>
>     <!—Optional:—>
>     <xsd:endTime>2009-06-02T00:00:00</xsd:endTime>
>     <!—Optional:—>
>     <xsd:frequency>lasthour</xsd:frequency>
>     <!—Optional:—>
>     <xsd:startTime>2009-05-29T00:00:00</xsd:startTime>
>     <!—Optional:—>
>     <xsd:timezone>utc</xsd:timezone>
> </ser:timeframe>
> ```

- **getSessionCount:** Returns the number of sessions handled by the MAPI AO over each interval of the sample period defined by the timeframe filter.

- **retrieveClientConnCount:** Returns the number of client connections by client software version (Outlook 2000, Outlook 2003, and Outlook 2007) over each interval of the sample period defined by the timeframe filter.

- **retrieveDataReadStats:** Returns a number MAPI AO-specific values for each sample period in the interval specified by the timeframe filter, including read-ahead sizes and stream sizes.

- **retrieveRequestTypeStats:** Returns the number of connections that were either using an Outlook version newer than 2007 or older than 2000. Also, the number of secured connections is shown. These data points are shown for each sample period in the interval specified.

- **retrieveResponseStats:** Returns statistics from each period based on the timeframe filter defined for average local response time, average remote response time, number of locally handled messages, and number of remotely handled messages.

NfsStats

The NfsStats service provides interfaces that enable extraction of NFS acceleration statistics from WAAS devices in the network through the CM. The NfsStats service includes the interfaces that follow. Note that all of the NfsStats interfaces that an identical set of parameters including:

- Device or device group name.

- Type (wae or waegroup).

- Timeframe filter including start time, end time, interval, and time zone. Please see Chapter 7 for more details on these elements.

Note   Similar to the behavior found in CIFSStats, all the NfsStats interfaces take the same input. As mentioned previously, it might be helpful to keep a copy of the query parameters stored in a text file for reuse across interfaces as shown in the following example:

```
<!—Optional:—>
<ser:name>pod1-br-wae</ser:name>
<!—Optional:—>
<ser:objType>wae</ser:objType>
<!—Optional:—>
<ser:timeframe>
    <!—Optional:—>
    <xsd:endTime>2009-06-02T00:00:00</xsd:endTime>
    <!—Optional:—>
    <xsd:frequency>lasthour</xsd:frequency>
    <!—Optional:—>
    <xsd:startTime>2009-05-29T00:00:00</xsd:startTime>
    <!—Optional:—>
    <xsd:timezone>utc</xsd:timezone>
</ser:timeframe>
```

- **getSessionCount:** Returns the number of sessions handled by the NFS AO over each interval of the sample period defined by the timeframe filter.

- **retrieveNFSTypeStats:** Returns the number of connections by NFS version over each interval of the sample period defined by the timeframe filter.

- **retrieveRequestTypeStats:** Returns the number of connections for each sample period in the interval specified based on the authentication flavor utilized.

- **retrieveResponseStats:** Returns statistics from each period based on the timeframe filter defined for average local response time, average remote response time, number of locally handled messages, and number of remotely handled messages.

Summary

This chapter provided an overview of the application acceleration capabilities present in Cisco WAAS, which operate at the application layer to mitigate performance-limiting factors caused by the WAN (and poor application design). This chapter also examined configuration and verification both from the device CLI and also CM GUI. The CLI command outputs, which are generally cumulative, provide the same information that is used to populate charts in the CM GUI, which are normalized to a timescale. SSL acceleration was discussed in detail, including configuration global settings and SSL accelerated services, which map servers and ports to certificates and corresponding private keys. The server-side accelerator proxies SSL sessions on behalf of the server, effectively splitting the SSL sessions into two. Traffic optimized by way of the SSL AO is first decrypted, then optimized, and then re-encrypted by the SSL AO to ensure that data is transmitted securely. Further, file systems on the WAAS devices can be encrypted using AES-256, and a passphrase-protected secure store is available for certificate and key storage on the CM. Preposition is a useful feature for pre-populating the CIFS and DRE cache of devices throughout the network to improve the first-access performance. Similarly, by populating both the CIFS and DRE cache, any changes to the content that is written back might possibly be compressed substantially, assuming a significant portion of the object had not changed. The XML-API provided by the CM enables integration of AO monitoring statistics into third-party ISV products that enable users visibility into end-to-end application performance by spanning multiple data sources to effectively triangulate and correlate performance and events.

Chapter 10

Branch Office Virtualization

The previous chapters provided you with the knowledge of how to design and integrate a Wide Area Application Services (WAAS) solution to enable application acceleration and server consolidation, along with an introduction to the management facilities provided by the WAAS Central Manager (CM).

This chapter focuses on the branch office virtualization capabilities of the Cisco Wide Area Virtualization Engine (WAVE) appliance family. It should be noted that the WAE-674, although not a *WAVE* by name, provides the same virtualization capabilities as the WAVE devices and is treated as such in this chapter. This chapter provides an overview of the use cases and motivation for branch office virtualization technologies, and how it can be achieved through WAAS Virtual Blades (VB). This chapter then focuses on the configuration and management aspects of VBs and concludes with an examination of VB monitoring and troubleshooting guidelines.

It should be noted that the focus of this chapter is on the operations of the VBs and doesn't cover the installation, configuration, and management of the guest operating system or applications. For more information on the specifics of installation for the operating systems or applications that run on top of those operating systems, the procedures for a physical server are identical to that of a VB, with the exception being how the system is accessed (physical console for a physical server as opposed to a virtual console for a virtual server).

Branch Office Virtualization Overview

Cisco WAAS offers a comprehensive WAN optimization and application acceleration solution that improves the performance of applications over the WAN and delivers video to the branch office in a scalable manner. This enables IT organizations to centralize applications, servers, and storage from the branch offices into the data center, while maintaining LAN-like application performance. A centralized architecture provides IT organizations better control over their infrastructure; they can improve the security and protection of critical business data at rest and in-flight, therefore maintaining compliance with the ever-increasing pressure from industry and government regulation. Furthermore, organizations can achieve significant cost savings on capital and operational expenditure through management of fewer pools of data and higher utilization of shared components.

Although most of the applications and infrastructure deployed in the branch office can be centralized successfully with the WAN optimization and application acceleration techniques provided by Cisco WAAS, many IT organizations find it desirable to keep certain applications local to the branch. These applications are generally foundational to enabling a user to access the network or handle localized workloads that require availability even when the WAN is disconnected. For instance, a print server is a good example of a localized workload where availability is critical in some businesses. When a user prints a document, the print job is first sent from the client machine to the print server. The job is then spooled, and the result contains formatting data that becomes often several times larger than the original document size. The job is then sent from the print server to the printer over the network. If the print server is in the data center, the print job traffic traverses the WAN twice, which consumes network bandwidth and can make the process very slow. Similarly, if the WAN is down, users cannot print. Although WAAS print acceleration helps overcome the bandwidth consumption and poor performance caused by printing over the WAN (where the printer is local but the print server is remote), it does nothing to address the issue of printing while the WAN is down.

User authentication and IP address allocation are examples of services that are foundational to enabling a user to access the network. These services are critical considering the user productivity impact should this process be delayed due to WAN conditions—or unavailable due to WAN outage. Keeping these services locally eliminates the impact of WAN latency. Due to the transient nature of the traffic, these services cannot always be effectively optimized over the WAN, and optimization certainly does nothing to address the availability challenges present if the WAN is down.

There are also services or business applications that are specific to certain branch offices or certain types of employees. Consolidation of these services or business applications to data center locations does not offer much value in these scenarios, potentially due to availability requirements that would be compromised in the event of a WAN outage.

VBs enable IT organizations to keep these services local in the branch office, without incurring the additional operational expenditure (such as rack space, power, and cooling) associated with having one or more additional servers. VBs enable IT organizations to migrate branch-office critical services to the extensible Cisco WAVE appliance platform while preserving existing management models for these operating systems, applications, and services.

The business benefits of branch office virtualization through Cisco WAAS VBs are as follows:

■   **Lower total cost of ownership (TCO):** The result is reduced capital and operational costs for devices at branch offices. The reduction of physical server count in the branch office results in less power and less cooling.

- **Platform and service isolation:** Resources (such as CPU, memory, and disk) allocated to the VBs are dedicated to virtualization services. Therefore, there is no competition of resources between the guest system and the underlying WAAS optimization and acceleration services. The load condition of WAAS services does not impact the performance of the guest operating systems and applications, and vice versa.

- **Transparency and flexibility:** Customers can use existing tools to manage and monitor the guest operating systems and applications. In the case of Microsoft Windows, integration into existing management tools and network services is transparent. Management access to the operating systems hosted on the VB can be fully optimized and accelerated by Cisco WAAS.

Overview of Virtual Blades

Cisco WAAS enables data center server consolidation through WAN optimization and application acceleration technologies, it also provides a virtualization platform to enable branch office server virtualization. VBs enable the hosting of other services and applications on virtualization-capable WAAS devices. This feature enables customers to retain certain critical services in the branch office, such as Microsoft Active Directory, Domain Name System (DNS), Dynamic Host Configuration Protocol (DHCP), and print services without deploying extra hardware.

As of WAAS software release 4.1.3, Cisco provides full support for Microsoft Windows Server Core 2008 and other versions when running the services mentioned previously, and a broader set of Cisco and partner applications are planned to be added in the future. Cisco provides full support on these services through the Technical Assistance Center (TAC). Other operating systems—including Linux, UNIX, or other versions of Windows—can also run on VBs. In those cases, WAAS and the VBs are supported by Cisco TAC, but support for the operating system and applications must be acquired from the operating system and application vendors.

Microsoft Windows Server on Cisco WAAS (Windows Server on WAAS [WoW]) is a jointly developed and supported program from Microsoft and Cisco to optimize branch-office IT infrastructure services delivery. With WoW, system administrators can provide branch-office Windows server infrastructure services, including Read-Only Active Directory Services (ROADS), DNS, DHCP, and print services. Cisco TAC supports the deployment of these key branch office services on Windows Server 2008 Server Core. Other Windows services running on VBs are supported by the customer's Windows support agreement. Because WAAS as a platform is validated under the Microsoft Server Virtualization Validation Program (SVVP) for Windows, customers are not required to reproduce issues directly on standalone hardware. Therefore, customers can deploy services on VBs with confidence. More information is available at the Cisco and Microsoft joint website of Windows Server on WAAS (http://www.windowsserveronwaas.com/).

Versions of Microsoft Windows Server can be managed by using commonly deployed Windows management tools, including the Microsoft System Center Operations Manager and Microsoft Management Console, just as they would be managed in the case of physical server, which provides operational transparency for the IT organization.

Management of Virtual Blades

Resources for the VBs hosted on WAAS appliances can be provisioned on the CM in a unified and centralized manner. Alternatively, VB resource allocation can be done on individual devices through the command-line interface (CLI) directly. A VB boot image can be transferred to the Cisco WAAS device using an FTP utility provided by the WAAS software. The boot image can also be in the form of an installation media such as CD/DVD. This image can then be used to boot the VB and install the operating system. If the boot image is transferred through WAN, the transmission of this traffic can be optimized by WAAS.

The responsibility of managing the operating system, applications, and services running on the VB might fall under different groups in an organization. The WAAS administrator can leverage the role-based access control (RBAC) capabilities provided in the CM as described in Chapter 7, "System and Device Management," to delegate the administration, ownership, and ongoing management of the VB infrastructure to the appropriate IT team (or teams) to ensure transparent integration into the existing business processes.

Virtual Blade Hardware Emulation

A VB is the equivalent of a generic computer running inside of Cisco WAAS. Each VB has its own virtualized CPUs, memory, firmware, disk drives, CD drives, network interface cards (NIC), and so on. A process embedded in the Linux-based WAAS operating system provides an emulated hardware environment within the WAVE device. Emulated devices, such as video and network adapters, are provisioned as part of the VB configuration process. An administrator can create VBs on virtualization-capable WAAS platforms, allocate memory and hard disk to each of the VBs created, host other operating systems, and provide additional services to users.

CPU resources on WAAS are partitioned to two halves when virtualization is enabled. The WAAS processes and VBs each have their own dedicated CPU(s). On a system with two CPUs, such as the WAVE-274 and WAVE-474, the WAAS acceleration utilizes CPU 1, and VB(s) utilizes CPU 2. On a system with four CPUs, including the WAVE-574 and WAE-674, VBs number 1, 3, and 5 use CPU 3; VBs number 2, 4, and 6 use CPU 4. WAAS processes use CPU 1 and 2.

Disk capacity for VBs is hard partitioned. VB disk space and image files use a special partition of the file system on the appliance. Physical memory is allocated to a VB and is considered dedicated. A virtual bridge interface controls the communications between the VB and the outside network. Network services are provided through configuration of a bridge interface that acts as a Layer 2 network interface. An IP address can be assigned to the emulated NIC manually, or via DHCP within the guest operating system, but not via the VB configuration or Cisco WAAS.

Figure 10-1 shows the hardware emulation of VBs within a Cisco WAAS appliance.

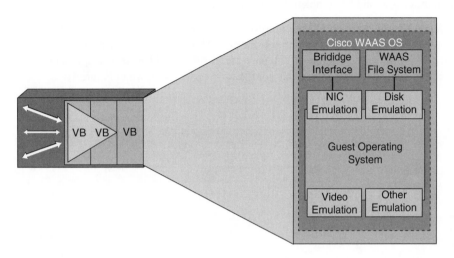

Figure 10-1   *VB Hardware Emulation*

Virtualization Capable WAAS Platforms

VBs are supported on selected hardware platforms, including the entire WAVE family and the Wide-area Acceleration Engine (WAE) model 674 (WAE-674). A special VB partition is pre-allocated on the file system for these devices. Available disk capacity varies by platform. Table 10-1 summarizes the total disk space, memory allocation, and the maximum number of VBs that can be installed on each of the supported WAAS Appliances running version 4.1.3.

Table 10-1   *VB Platforms and Capacity*

Appliance	VB Disk Capacity	VB Memory Capacity	Maximum Number of VBs (512 MB RAM each)
WAVE-274	30 GB	1 GB	2
WAVE-474	30 GB	1 GB	2
WAVE-574-3GB	60 GB	1 GB	2
WAVE-574-6GB	175 GB	3 GB	6
WAE-674-4GB	120 GB	1 GB	2
WAE-674-8GB	200 GB	3 GB	6

Creating Virtual Blades

Before configuring a VB, the basic WAAS device network configuration and CM registration process should be completed as outlined in Chapter 7.

A VB license, in addition to the Enterprise license, is needed to run virtualization service. You can verify license configuration from the CM, or with the **show license** command. From the CM, select the device, and navigate to **Admin > License Management**. Licenses can be activated from this configuration page as shown in Figure 10-2.

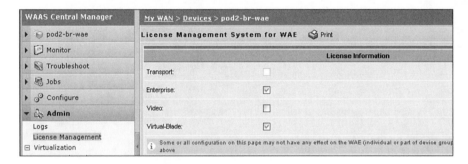

Figure 10-2   *Verify License from CM*

Example 10-1 shows the output of the **show license** command. Active licenses are displayed, along with the activation date of the license, and the source of the activation. Central manager system (CMS) indicates that the VB license was activated from the CMS.

Example 10-1   *Verify License from CLI*

```
pod1-br-wae#show license
License Name    Status      Activation Date Activated By
————————————    ——————.     ————————.  ————————

Transport       not active
Enterprise      active      05/01/2009      admin
Video           not active
Virtual-Blade   active      05/05/2009      CMS
```

To activate a license, use the **license add** command. Example 10-2 illustrates the process to activate the Video license using this command. After the license is added, the **show license** command displays the status of the license as **active**.

Example 10-2   *Add License from CLI*

```
pod1-br-wae#license add ?
  LINE  Enter a license name ('show license' displays the list of valid names)
```

```
pod1-br-wae#license add Video ?
LINE  <cr>
pod1-br-wae#license add Video
WARNING: There is an enabled accelerator in the system, but accelerator
doesn't optimize the traffic yet. It takes about 2 minutes to start
the traffic optimization after the license is activated.
pod1-br-wae#show license ?
  |     Output Modifiers
  <cr>
pod1-br-wae#show license
License Name    Status       Activation Date Activated By
———————   ——————.  ————————.  ——————

Transport       not active
Enterprise      active       05/05/2009       CMS
Video           active       05/06/2009       admin
Virtual-Blade   active       05/05/2009       CMS
```

After the license has been verified, you can enable virtualization on the device (if it is not
enabled by default). To enable the VB from the CM, select the WAAS device from the
My WAN > Managed Devices page. Then, navigate to **Admin > Virtualization >
General Settings**, select the **Enable Virtualization** checkbox, and click **Submit**. An
example of this is shown in Figure 10-3.

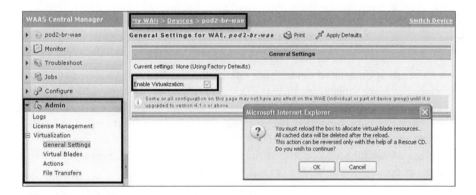

Figure 10-3 *Enable Virtualization from CM*

Similarly, you can enable VB support through the CLI and verify its status as demonstrated in Example 10-3.

Example 10-3 *Enabling Virtualization*

```
pod1-br-wae# config term
pod1-br-wae(config)# virtual-blade enable
```

```
pod1-br-wae(config)# exit
pod1-br-wae# write memory
pod1-br-wae# reload
! ... portions removed for readability ...
pod1-br-wae# show virtual-blade
Virtual-blade resources:
  VB Memory: 0MiB configured, 1024MiB available.
  VB Disk space: 0GiB configured, 242GiB available.
  VB Image space /local1/vbs: 2528MiB used, 251246MiB available
  CPU(s) assigned: 3 4
Virtual-blade(s) state:
  No virtual-blades have been configured
```

Note   Virtualization on Cisco WAVE devices is enabled by default. On WAE-674 appliances purchased without Windows on WAAS, the device is shipped without resources allocated to VBs. Virtualization on such devices can be enabled after adding the Virtual-Blade license. Enabling the virtualization services on such devices requires a reload in order to repartition the disk space and allocation of resources for VB usage. As a result of the changes to the disk partition on the device, any cached data (Data Redundancy Elimination [DRE], Common Internet File System [CIFS]) is lost. It is best to perform this step prior to having the device optimize traffic.

After the VB resources are allocated, you are not able to restore the disk partition to the original state (where resources are not allocated to virtualization) unless you use the rescue CD.

Each virtualization-enabled device has a disk partition called */vbspace* created for VB storage. The user visible items, such as CD images, reside in */local/local1/vbs*, which is a symbolic link to *vbspace/vbs*. This is the staging area for image files used for installing guest operation systems in the VB. The capacity of this directory is limited to 5 GB, which is ample storage to support today's ISO files. This partition is not present on systems that do not support VBs such as the WAE-512 and WAE-612. Similarly, this partition is not present on the WAE-674 until virtualization is enabled.

You can verify the */vbspace* disk partition with the **show disk details** CLI command. You can display the vbs directory, which is the VB staging area visible to the user, by using **dir** command to list the WAAS file system directory.

As shown in Example 10-4, the */vbspace* partition is present in the command output, and 254926MB has been allocated to this partition. This example also shows that there is an ISO image *WoW66.iso* in the vbs directory.

Example 10-4 *Verifying Disk Partition*

```
pod1-br-wae#show disk details


!
! ... portions removed for readability ...
!Mounted file systems:
 MOUNT POINT      TYPE        DEVICE         SIZE       INUSE    FREE       USE%
 /local/local1    SYSFS       /dev/sda6      22318MB    184MB    22134MB    0%
 /vbspace         GUEST       /dev/data1/vbsp 254926MB   2656MB   252270MB   1%


pod1-br-wae#dir
     size           time of last change             name
——————— ——————————————-.            —————.
!
! ... portions removed for readability ...
!
        4096  Sun May  3 12:25:51 2009  <DIR>     vbs


pod1-br-wae#dir /local1/vbs
     size           time of last change             name
——————— ——————————————-.            —————.
   2648248320  Sun May  3 12:27:49 2009             WoW66.iso
```

As discussed in the previous section, CPU resources are also partitioned and dedicated to VBs, similar to disk capacity. You can examine the resources allocated to the VBs from the CM by navigating to the WAAS device context and selecting **Admin > Virtualization > Actions.** When the drop-down box next to the Virtual Blade () is **All**, the Virtual Blade Actions window displays resources available for all VBs as shown in Figure 10-4.

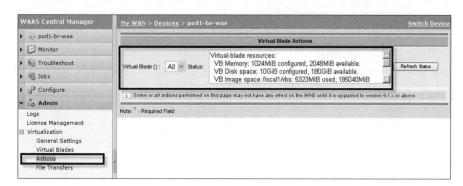

Figure 10-4 *Examine Virtual-Blade Hardware Resources*

This information is also available from the WAAS device directly by issuing the **show virtual-blade** command as demonstrated in Example 10-5. According to the command output, 1024 MB of memory, 242 GB of disk space, and both CPU3 and CPU4 are assigned for use by VBs. No VBs have been configured yet.

Example 10-5 *Examine Available VB Resources*

```
pod1-br-wae# show virtual-blade
Virtual-blade resources:
  VB Memory: 0MiB configured, 1024MiB available.
  VB Disk space: 0GiB configured, 242GiB available.
  VB Image space /local1/vbs: 0MiB used, 253774MiB available
  CPU(s) assigned: 3 4
Virtual-blade(s) state:
  No virtual-blades have been configured
```

Guest OS Boot Image

There are two options for an administrator to install software onto the VB:

■ Install from a physical installation CD/DVD using the CD/DVD drive on the WAAS appliance.

■ Install from an ISO image that has been copied to the */local1/vbs* partition on the appliance.

When using the physical CD/DVD drive, an administrator needs to have physical access to the device to insert the installation media to the CD/DVD drive and eject the CD from the drive after installation is completed.

Using an ISO image copied to the WAAS appliance, the installation can be done over the network and no physical access to the device is necessary. The first step is to copy the guest OS ISO image onto the virtual-blade staging area, in the */local1/vbs* directory. This can be accomplished using either the copy utility provided on the CM, or from the CLI on the WAAS device. Figure 10-5 shows an example of copying an ISO image to the device using the file transfer utility in the CM.

Similarly, this operation can be performed from the device CLI using the **copy ftp disk** *ftp server ip directory image.iso* **/local1/vbs/***image.iso* command. Example 10-6 also shows the verification commands necessary to validate that the image copied successfully.

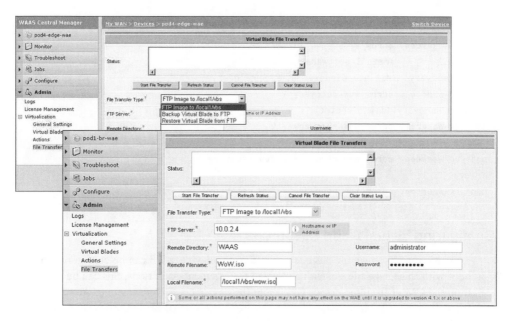

Figure 10-5 *Copying an ISO Image to the VB Staging Area*

Example 10-6 *Copy Guest OS Image to Virtual Blade Staging Area*

```
pod1-br-wae# copy ftp disk 10.0.2.4 WAAS WoW_1.0.1.iso /local1/vbs/WoW_1.0.1.iso
!
! ... portions removed for readability ...
!
pod1-br-wae# dir /local1/vbs
Size          Time of last change        Name
2648248320 Tue Jul 29 17:19:44 2008 WoW_1.0.1.iso
```

On WAVE devices purchased with Windows Server on WAAS (WoW), the Windows
Server 2008 installer ISO image is pre-staged on the WAVE device hard disk, under
/local1/vbs file system. To install WoW on a previously purchased WAVE device, the
Microsoft Windows Server 2008 for Cisco WAAS recovery DVD is used. Insert the
Recovery DVD into the WAVE CD/DVD drive and copy Windows Server on WAAS files
to the WAVE device with the **copy cdrom wow-recovery** command as demonstrated in
Example 10-7. This command copies the Windows Server on WAAS files to the
/local1/vbs directory on the WAVE device.

Example 10-7   *Copy WoW Image from a Recovery DVD Using CLI*

```
pod1-br-wae#copy cdrom ?
  install       Install software release file
  wow-recovery  Initiate Windows on WAAS recovery
pod1-br-wae#copy cdrom wow-recovery ?
  WORD  Recovery file directory
pod1-br-wae#copy cdrom wow-recovery / ?
  WORD  Recovery file name
pod1-br-wae#copy cdrom wow-recovery / WOW_recovery ?
  <cr>
pod1-br-wae#copy cdrom wow-recovery / WOW_recovery
```

Configuring Virtual Blade Resources

Now that the OS image file has been copied to the device, a VB can be configured to boot with this image file. As with almost all management operations, this can be done from the CM or from the device CLI. From the device context, navigate to **Admin > Virtualization > Virtual Blades**. Select **Create** in the Virtual Blade Entries window, and the Virtual Blade configuration pane is displayed as shown in Figure 10-6.

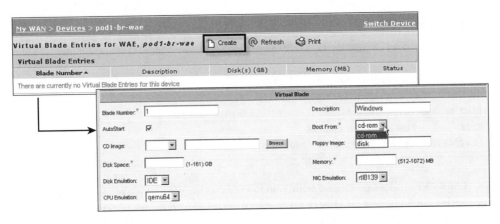

Figure 10-6   *Create Virtual Blade and Configure Resources*

On the Virtual Blade configuration page, the administrator can define all of the system parameters. Examine the parameters in the Virtual Blade configuration window, because this is a critical step of VB configuration and resource assignment.

Note   Before configuring the VB system parameters, please consult the manufacturer of the operating system and applications you plan to install and follow its recommendations. You need to configure adequate resources, including disk and memory, required for the guest system to run properly. As an example, Windows Server 2008 System Requirements are available at the following location on Microsoft's Internet website:

http://www.microsoft.com/windowsserver2008/en/us/system-requirements.aspx

- **Blade Number:** This is a required field. Enter a numeric value as the identifier for the VB. On WAVE-574 and WAE-674 platforms, two CPUs are available for virtualization services. CPU resource is distributed in a round-robin fashion. The VBs with odd numbers use one CPU, and VBs with even numbers use another CPU. The number of VBs supported per platform with WAAS software 4.1.3 release is listed previously in the section, "Virtualization Capable WAAS Platforms." More information and number of VBs supported on other software releases (other than 4.1.3) is published on the data sheet for that release version.

- **Description:** This is an optional field. Provide a name for the VB.

- **AutoStart:** If checked, the VB starts automatically when the WAAS appliance starts.

- **Boot from and CD-Image fields:** These two fields specify the source from which the VB boots.

As discussed previously in the section, "Guest OS Boot Image," there are two methods used to install software into the VB: from physical installation media (using the CD/DVD drive) or an ISO file. During the initial software installation, select **cd-rom** to boot the VB from either a CD image (ISO file) hosted on the VB staging area or on a physical CD-ROM. When using the physical CD/DVD drive, configure the **Boot From** and the **CD-Image** to **cd-rom**, and leave the **CD-Image** field blank, as shown in Figure 10-7. This causes the system to use the physical drive.

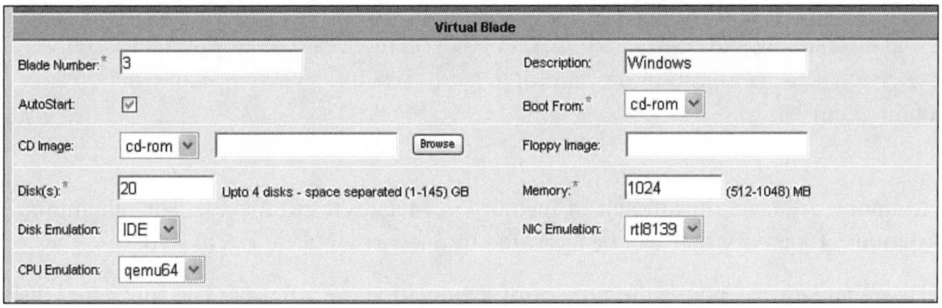

Figure 10-7 *Configure Virtual Blade to Boot from Physical CD/DVD*

When using an ISO image, configure **Boot From** as **cd-rom** and **CD-Image** as **disk**. Then, browse to select the ISO image located on the **/local1/vbs/** staging area, as shown in Figure 10-8. This causes the system to use the ISO file to boot the VB.

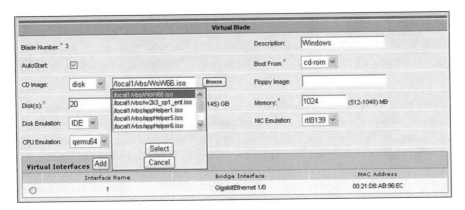

Figure 10-8 *Configure Virtual Blade to Boot from CD Image Copied to Disk*

After the underlying operating system is installed onto the VB, change the **Boot from** field to **disk** to ensure that the VB boots from the installed operating system, rather than re-attempting to boot from either the installation media (CD/DVD) drive or ISO file.

- **Floppy Image:** This field enables the administrator to reserve resources for a virtual floppy disk on a VB. Enter the pathname and filename of the floppy image in this field. The path must be **/local1/vbs/**.

- **Disk(s):** This field enables the administrator to allocate hard disk capacity to the VB. Up to four virtual hard disks can be configured on one VB by specifying the disk size separated by spaces.

Note If IDE disk emulation is used, the size of the third disk must be 0, because this IDE bus position is reserved for a CD-ROM.

The configuration of multiple hard disks for a VB is available only from the CM for WAAS devices that are running WAAS version 4.1.3. For WAAS devices that are running WAAS software version 4.1.1, configuration of multiple hard disks for a VB is available only from the CLI on the device.

- **Memory:** Allocate the amount of memory in Megabytes to the VB. The minimum amount of memory that can be allocated to one virtual blade is 512 MB.

- **Disk Emulation:** Choose the type of disk emulation the VB uses. The supported disk emulation methods are Integrated Drive Electronics (IDE) and VirtIO. This is an optional field—the default emulation is IDE.

IDE specifies an IDE or Advanced Technology Attachment (ATA) type disk emulator, which is a common type of hard disk drive. VirtIO is a Linux standard for network and disk drivers that enable high performance in virtualization environments. To use the VirtIO emulator, you must have the para-virtualization (PV) drivers installed in the guest operating system. Please check with your operating system manufacturer to verify whether the operating system includes para-virtualization drivers.

- **NIC Emulation:** Defines the NIC emulation for the VB. Supported emulation methods are rtl8139, e1000, or VirtIO. This is an optional field—the default emulation is rtl8139.

RTL8139 specifies a Realtek network card emulator for 10/100M Fast Ethernet. E1000 specifies emulation of Intel e1000 network driver, which provides Gigabit Ethernet connection speed.

VirtIO is a para-virtualization driver that provides even greater performance than other emulated drivers. By presenting a block interface to the guest operation system that is closer to the actual hardware, performance closer to the non virtualized hardware might be achieved. To use the VirtIO emulator, you must have the para-virtualization drivers installed in the guest operating system. Please check with your operating system manufacturer to verify whether the operating system includes para-virtualization drivers.

- **CPU Emulation:** Depending on the operating systems installed on the VB, select qemu64 for a 64-bit processor emulator or qemu32 for a 32-bit processor emulator. This is an optional field—the default emulation is qemu64.

Network interface is a part of VB configuration. The next section, "Virtual Blade Interface Bridging Considerations," reviews different scenarios when deploying VBs in a network with WAAS optimization. To configure VB network interfaces, on the Virtual Blade configuration page, click the **Add** button next to the Virtual Interfaces menu. The **Add/Edit Interface** window is displayed as shown in Figure 10-9.

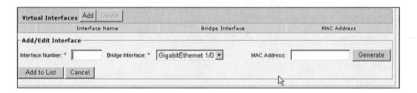

Figure 10-9 *Configure VB Network Interfaces*

You can configure multiple interfaces for one VB; each of the interfaces is identified by a numeric value defined in the **Interface Number** field. The **Bridge Interface** field associates the new virtual interface with a network interface on the appliance itself. The Bridge Interface can be either one of the Gigabit Ethernet interfaces or a port channel interface. A MAC address can be automatically generated by the system or manually assigned by the administrator. Click the **Add to List** button to add the virtual interface to the virtual-blade interface list, and then submit the configuration. Figure 10-10 shows the review of the completed configuration of a VB.

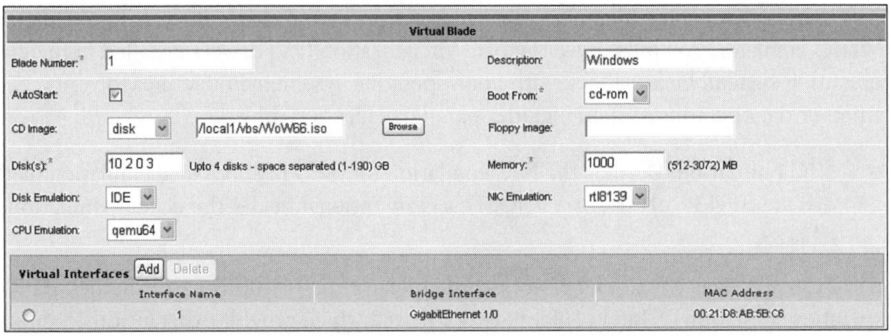

Figure 10-10   *Reviewing a Configured Virtual Blade Configuration*

You can perform the VB configuration and resource allocation from the device CLI as well, as shown in Example 10-8. This example also shows the output of the **show** commands used to verify the VB configuration. Notice that the device emulation methods for CPU, disk, keyboard, and NIC are optional configurations; the system applies default values for these parameters if they are not configured by the administrator. With this configuration and state, the VB is ready to boot.

Example 10-8   *Configure VB Using CLI*

```
pod1-br-wae# config term
pod1-br-wae(config)# virtual-blade 1
pod1-br-wae(config-vb)# description Windows
pod1-br-wae(config-vb)# autostart
pod1-br-wae(config-vb)# boot from cd-rom
pod1-br-wae(config-vb)# boot cd-image disk /local1/vbs/WoW_1.0.1.iso
pod1-br-wae(config-vb)# memory 1000
pod1-br-wae(config-vb)# disk 10 2 0 3
pod1-br-wae(config-vb)# interface 1 bridge gigabitEthernet 1/0
pod1-br-wae(config-vb)# end
pod1-br-wae# show virtual-blade 1
virtual-blade 1
config:
 description Windows
 device cpu qemu64
 device nic rtl8139
 device disk IDE
 device keyboard en-us
 memory 1000
 disk 10 2 0 3
 interface 1 bridge GigabitEthernet 1/0 mac-address 00:21:D8:AB:5B:C6
no boot fd-image
 boot cd-image disk /local1/vbs/WoW66.iso
 boot from cd-rom
 autostart
```

```
state:
 stopped
```

Virtual Blade Interface Bridging Considerations

Just as with any physical PC, a VB needs to have network interfaces to communicate with the rest of the network. Because the VB resides on a WAAS appliance that uses network interfaces for traffic interception, the administrator needs to consider the WAAS appliance usage of interfaces when associating a physical interface on the WAAS appliance to the VB.

The virtual interface used to support a VB is created by using a Layer 2 bridging interface, which can be assigned to either a Gigabit Ethernet interface or a port channel interface (encompassing multiple Gigabit Ethernet interfaces). If the bridge interface is configured to be used by the underlying WAAS optimization components, either for interception or for management, the IP address assigned to the VB needs to reside on the same IP subnet.

Note   VB interface bridging is not supported when the standby interface feature is configured (discussed in detail in Chapter 4, "Network Integration and Interception").

Because the main purpose of the VB is to host services that are critical to the branch office, the system on the VB should be deployed in the same subnet as the users. By being deployed with an interface on the user subnet in the branch office, any traffic between local users and the VB does not traverse multiple network segments. Additionally, any traffic between the VB and remote users or nodes, either for the management of the guest system or serving remote client requests, can be optimized by the underlying WAAS optimization components.

Inline Interception

When an inline group is used on a WAAS device for interception, the management of the WAAS devices can be done either over a logical inline group interface, or over an onboard Gigabit Ethernet (GigE) interface.

In the case of an inline group interface used for management, an IP address is assigned to that logical inline group interface. WAAS optimized traffic traverses the LAN and WAN ports of inline group, and WAAS management traffic binds to the logical interface of the inline group. In this case, the VB can bind to any of the physical (non inline) GigE interfaces. Connect the onboard Gigabit Ethernet interface to the LAN switch, and ensure that the switch port is in the same VLAN as the branch clients. As shown in Figure 10-11, the VB is bound to the GigE 1/0 interface, which connects into the same subnet as the client workstations. Traffic traversing the WAN is optimized as it crosses the inline group of the WAAS device, and traffic to or from the VB uses the dedicated Gigabit Ethernet interface.

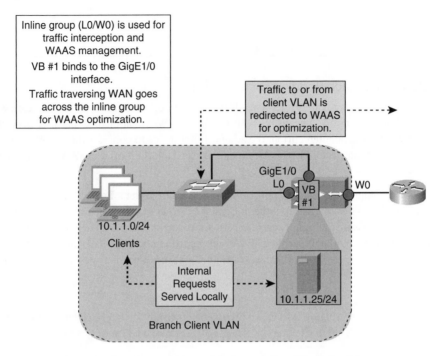

Inline group (L0/W0) is used for traffic interception and WAAS management.

VB #1 binds to the GigE1/0 interface.

Traffic traversing WAN goes across the inline group for WAAS optimization.

Traffic to or from client VLAN is redirected to WAAS for optimization.

GigE1/0
L0   VB   W0
     #1

10.1.1.0/24

Clients

Internal Requests Served Locally

10.1.1.25/24

Branch Client VLAN

Figure 10-11   *Inline Interception with IP on Inline Group for Management*

In the case of an onboard Gigabit Ethernet port used for Cisco WAAS appliance management with inline interception, the WAAS management network might not be in the same subnet as the client workstations. If that is the case, bind the VB to a different Gigabit Ethernet interface. Connect that interface to a switch port in the same VLAN as the branch clients.

As shown in Figure 10-12, GigE 1/0 is used for management of WAAS and resides on a different subnet from the clients. The VB uses the GigE 2/0 interface and connects to a switchport in the client VLAN. Internal traffic between the guest system on the VB and the clients stays within the VLAN, without additional router hop.

Note   The IP address configuration of the VB is done from the guest operating system and cannot be done from the WAAS appliance CLI or CM. The figures shown in this section give examples of the IP address that could be configured on the VB (from within the guest operating system) for the purpose of illustrating that the VB is on the client subnet.

WCCP Interception

If the Web Cache Communication Protocol version 2 (WCCPv2) is used for interception without Generic Routing Encapsulation (GRE) return, the WAAS appliance needs to be on its own subnet, so that the intercepting router can exclude this subnet from interception and avoid WCCP loops. If GRE return is not configured, the VB should be configured to use a separate GigE interface on the Cisco WAAS device, so that it can stay on the same subnet as client workstations, and VB traffic traversing the WAN can be optimized. As illustrated in Figure 10-13, the interface GigE 2/0 is used as a primary interface for WAAS device management and for WCCPv2 traffic diversion for optimization. The VB uses interface GigE 1/0, an interface separate from WCCPv2 diversion for optimization. This interface (GigE 1/0) connects to the switch and resides on the client subnet. Traffic between the local clients and the VB stays local to the VLAN and within the user subnet. Outbound traffic is intercepted by the WCCPv2 router and redirected to the WAAS appliance for optimization. Outbound traffic flow is illustrated in detail in Figure 10-13 to provide an example. Inbound traffic is redirected by the router and follow the same flow.

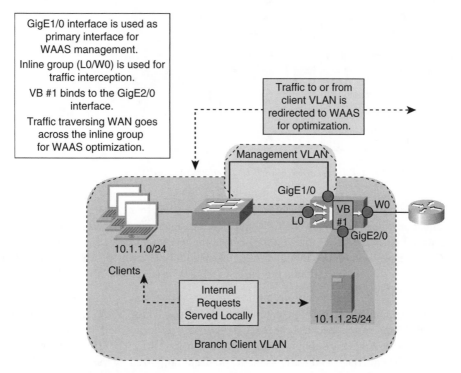

Figure 10-12 *Inline Interception with Gigabit Ethernet Interface for Management*

When WCCP negotiated return is used, WAAS optimized traffic is encapsulated in a GRE tunnel when returning to the router, thus can be differentiated from the original traffic seen by the intercepting WCCPv2 router. When GRE return is negotiated, this is functionally equivalent to having GRE return manually configured. In this case, the WAAS appliance can be on the same subnet as clients. Similarly, the VB can bind to the same interface WAAS device uses for optimization and management and be on the same client VLAN.

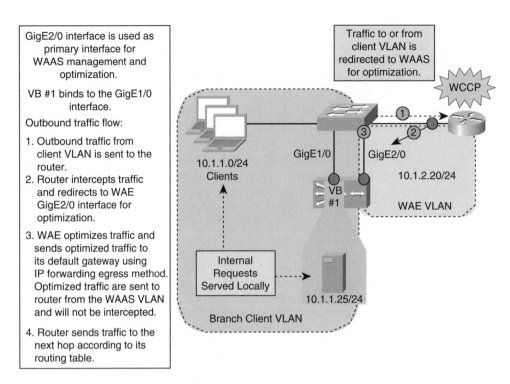

Figure 10-13   *WCCP Interception with IP Forwarding and VBs*

Outbound traffic either from client workstations or from systems on VB, which meets the redirection criteria set on the WCCPv2 intercepting router, is redirected to the WAAS device for optimization. Optimized traffic from the WAAS device is sent to the router in a GRE encapsulated tunnel. Inbound traffic destined for the client VLAN is redirected to WAAS device for optimization in the same way. Traffic between the VB and the local clients stay inside the VLAN.

As illustrated in Figure 10-14, the interface GigE 1/0 is used for WAAS management and WCCPv2 interception. Because the WCCP negotiated return method is used, this interface can be on the client subnet (traffic is returned using GRE). The VB can bridge to the same GigE1/0 interface, and traffic is intercepted and optimized by the Cisco WAAS device. This configuration is the simplest VB configuration that enables acceleration.

Another alteration of this configuration is to use port channel, instead of a single interface. In that case, the VB is bridged to the port channel interface, which is also used for the WAAS management and traffic interception. The port channel configuration not only increases the bandwidth, but also provides higher availability of the VB.

Note   After a VB is configured, any change of resources, such as memory and the bridged interface, requires the VB to be in *stopped* state first. Then, start the VB after the changes are made.

Please note any changes to the disk allocation, or disk emulation, result in loss of data, because it is functionally equivalent to replacing storage in a physical server. Similarly, if the emulation method of a NIC is changed, previous configuration of that interface card might not be recognized by the new interface card.

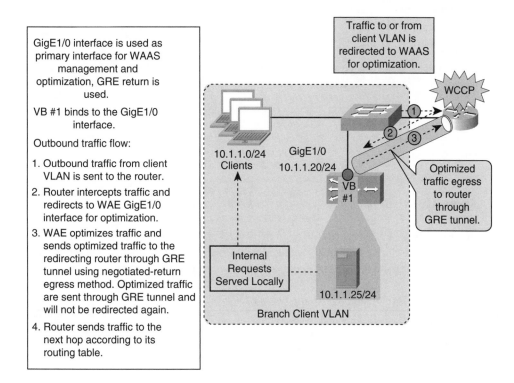

Figure 10-14   *WCCP Interception with GRE Return and VBs*

Starting Virtual Blades

After the initial configuration, the VB is in a *stopped* state. The VB can then be started, which is equivalent to powering on a physical machine. When the VB starts initially, it boots from the installation image and starts the guest OS installation process. To start a selected VB, simply click the **Start Virtual Blade** button. A startup delay timer can be specified to enable some time to connect through the Virtual Network Computing (VNC) console. The VB should be in *running* state after it is started.

The state of the VB is updated in the CM in the device context under **Admin > Virtualization > Actions**. From this page, select the VB number from the drop-down menu, and click the **Refresh** button to view the current state of the selected VB. The state of a VB can also be viewed from the Virtual Blade window, as shown in Figure 10-15.

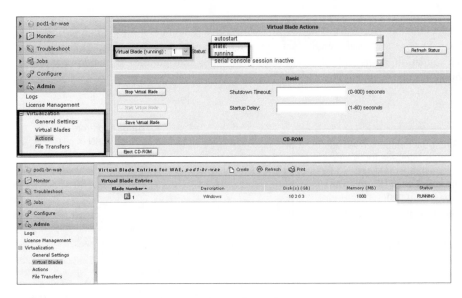

Figure 10-15 *Examine the State of a VB from the CM*

Additionally, you can start the VB from the WAAS appliance CLI as demonstrated in Example 10-9. Notice the state of virtual-blade 1 was initially **stopped**, and after execution of the **virtual-blade n start** command, the state changes to **running**.

Example 10-9 *Starting a VB with the Device CLI*

```
pod1-br-wae# show virtual-blade 1
virtual-blade 1
!
! ... portions removed for readability ...
!
 boot cd-image disk /local1/vbs/WoW66.iso
 boot from cd-rom
 autostart
state:
 stopped
pod1-br-wae# virtual-blade 1 start ?
  <1-60>  Startup delay in seconds
  <cr>
pod1-br-wae# virtual-blade 1 start
pod1-br-wae# show virtual-blade 1
virtual-blade 1
!
! ... portions removed for readability ...
!
 boot cd-image disk /local1/vbs/WoW66.iso
```

```
boot from cd-rom
autostart
state:
 running
```

Virtual Blade Console Access

Several options exist to access the VB console. An administrator can enable remote access such as Telnet, SSH, or RDP services after the guest system is configured. WAAS also provide console access to the VB, which is essential during the guest OS installation process. An administrator can access the guest system by either opening a reverse telnet session provided the guest system supports it, or using a VNC viewing application (such as VNC Viewer, www.realnc.com) to connect to the VB console. The VNC console capability to the guest OS is enabled by default. It can be disabled after the initial system installation and configuration, if required to conform to existing security policy. To disable VNC, use the **no vnc** CLI command under the VB in configuration mode as demonstrated in Example 10-10.

Example 10-10   *Disable VNC Server on VB from CLI*

```
pod1-br-wae# show virtual-blade 1
virtual-blade 1
config:
! ... portions removed for readability ...
state:
 running
 serial console session inactive
 vnc server active
 no vnc client connected
 current cd [not inserted]
 current floppy [not inserted]

pod1-br-wae# configure term
pod1-br-wae(config)# virtual-blade 1
pod1-br-wae(config-vb)# no vnc
pod1-br-wae(config-vb)# end

pod1-br-wae# show virtual-blade 1
virtual-blade 1
config:
! ... portions removed for readability ...

no vnc
 autostart
```

```
state:
 running
 serial console session inactive
 vnc server disabled
 current cd [not inserted]
 current floppy [not inserted]
```

The command in Example 10-11 shows how a reverse Telnet session can be established to access the VB console.

Example 10-11   *Reverse Telnet to Access VB Console*

```
pod1-br-wae# virtual-blade 1 session ?
  clear   Terminate telnet connection to remote host/port
  <cr>
pod1-br-wae# virtual-blade 1 session
Trying 127.0.0.1...
Connected to localhost.
Escape character is '^]'.
```

Using a VNC viewer application, the administrator can connect to the guest operating system console by using the Cisco WAAS appliance management IP address and the VB number in the format of *Management IP address: VB number*. The VNC application traffic uses port 5900 by default. By using this format, VNC traffic for VBs uses port number 5900+N, where N equals the VB number. For example, VB number 1 uses port 5901, VB number 2 uses port 5902, and so on. In Figure 10-16, the VNC console is connecting to VB 1, and the VNC traffic uses port 5901.

Figure 10-16   *VNC Connection to Access VB Console*

Stopping Virtual Blades

To stop a VB, navigate to the device context, go to **Admin > Virtualization > Actions** page, select the VB number from the display panel on the right side, and click the **Stop Virtual Blade** button. On this page, there is an option to give the operating system some time before forcing the shutdown by using the **Shutdown Timeout** field. When the time-out value is not defined, WAAS forces the shutdown of the VB immediately. The action of stopping a VB is equivalent to pulling the power plug on a physical machine. To safely power down the virtual machine, recommended practice dictates performing the shut-down from the operating system hosted in the virtual machine. The facilities to shut down a VB in the WAAS appliance CLI or CM should be used only if the operating system hosted in the VB is unable to shut down. Figure 10-17 shows the location of the **Stop Virtual Blade** button on the CM.

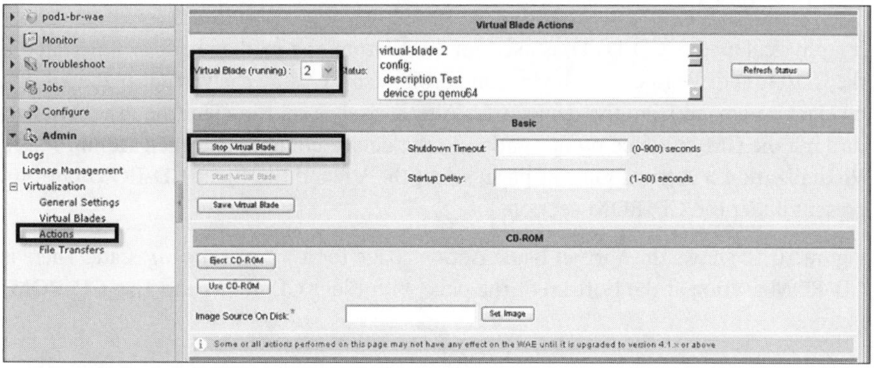

Figure 10-17 *Stop a VB Using CM*

Example 10-12 shows the CLI command to stop a VB.

Example 10-12 *Shutting Down a VB Using the Device CLI*

```
pod1-br-wae# virtual-blade 2 stop ?
  <0-900>   Shutdown timeout in seconds
  <cr>
pod1-br-wae# virtual-blade 2 stop 15
Sent powerdown request to virtual-blade 2
^[[A^H^H^H

Shutdown did not happen, forcing virtual blade quit
pod1-br-wae# show virtual-blade 2
virtual-blade 2
config:

! ... portions removed for readability ...
state:
 stopped
```

Changing Virtual Blade Boot Sequence

Upon successful installation of the operating system image from the installation media or ISO file (stored on disk), the administrator should change the **Boot From** configuration to disk, so that the next time the system boots up, it boots up from the installed operating system. Newer Windows operating systems check for the presence of a bootable CD and ask for a key invocation to boot from the CD/DVD. If no keystroke is detected, the operating system continues to boot from the image on the hard drive; however, other operating systems might not behave this way and forcefully boot from a bootable CD/DVD if one is detected. In either case of physical CD-ROM or virtual ISO image, after installation is completed, the boot sequence configuration of the VB should be configured to **boot from disk**.

If a physical media (CD/DVD) is used for installation, the media needs to be ejected from the CD/DVD drive first, which you can accomplish by using the **virtual-blade** *number* **cd eject** command from the device CLI. Alternatively, you can eject the installation media through the CM interface by navigating to the device context, and then **Admin > Virtualization > Action**. On this page, select the VB and the **Eject CD-ROM** button is present under the CD-ROM section.

Figure 10-18 shows the Virtual Blade Actions page for a VB in *running* state. There is a CD-ROM section at the bottom of the page with **Eject CD-ROM** and **Use CD-ROM** buttons.

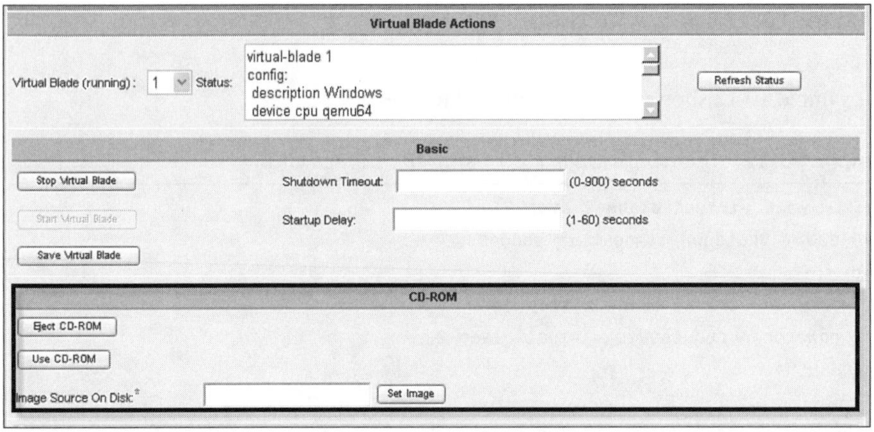

Figure 10-18 *Eject or Use CD-ROM from CM*

Example 10-13 illustrates the CLI command to eject a CD-ROM for a VB.

Example 10-13 *Eject CD-ROM from VB Using the CLI*

```
pod1-br-wae#virtual-blade 1 cd ?
  cd-rom  Use the local CD-ROM drive
  disk    Set the image source to an ISO file on disk
  eject   Eject the CD
pod1-br-wae#virtual-blade 1 cd eject ?
  <cr>
```

An administrator can also use this CD-ROM facility provided in the CM and CLI to exchange CD/DVD(s) during guest system installation process when multiple CD/DVDs are involved.

To change the VB boot source, shut down the guest system first. After the VB is in *stopped* state, navigate to the **Virtual Blade** configuration page to change the **Boot From** field to **disk** (refer back to Figure 10-6). Submit the change, and then start the VB from the **Actions** page.

Example 10-14 shows the CLI commands to change **Boot From** to **disk**. The VB was shut down from the guest operating system and is in **stopped** state after the shutdown process completes. The VB boot sequence is then changed to **boot from disk**.

Example 10-14 *Change Boot Source to Disk Using the CLI*

```
pod1-br-wae# show virtual-blade 3
virtual-blade 3
config:
 description Windows
 device cpu qemu64
 device nic rtl8139
 device disk IDE
 device keyboard en-us
 memory 1024
 disk 20
 interface 1 bridge GigabitEthernet 1/0 mac-address 00:21:D8:AB:96:EC
 no boot fd-image
 boot cd-image cd-rom
 boot from cd-rom
 autostart
state:
 stopped
pod1-br-wae# configure term
pod1-br-wae(config)# virtual-blade 3 boot from disk
pod1-br-wae(config)# exit
pod1-br-wae# write memory
pod1-br-wae# virtual-blade 3 start
pod1-br-wae# show virtual-blade 3
virtual-blade 3
config:
 ! ... portions removed for readability ...

 boot from disk
 autostart
state:
 running
! ... portions removed for readability ...
```

The next time the VB boots, it boots with the installed software image hosted on the disk. An administrator can console into the guest operating system and begin the initial setup of the guest system.

Managing Virtual Blades

After the VB is running on the WAAS appliance, the operating system and the installed applications can be managed just as if they were running on any other physical or virtual platforms in the network using the native management and monitoring tools. The underlying hardware resources are managed from the Cisco WAAS CM or the CLI on the WAAS device that is hosting the VBs. Recommended practice dicates using the CM, because it is a highly scalable tool capable of managing multiple devices (and thus the hardware resources for multiple VBs) from a single console. The CM's roles-based access control (RBAC) capability can be used to provide granular control, enabling federated management of the system. The responsibility of managing the operating system and applications that are installed on a VB can be delegated to the server team, whereas the networking aspects of WAAS devices can be isolated to the network management team.

Using RBAC, an administrator can create users or a user group for the team responsible for managing the operating systems and applications running on the VBs, define a role to access only the virtualization services, and associate the role with that specific user or user group. Figure 10-19 demonstrates an example where a *sysadmin* role is defined, with access only to the virtualization pages of the WAAS services through CM. For more details on configuring RBAC, please visit Chapter 7 of this book.

From the CM or device CLI, an administrator can create VBs, assign resources to the VBs, control (start and stop) VBs, and reassign or reconfigure other hardware resources such as memory and interfaces. In order to make configuration changes, the VB must be in a *stopped* state.

When migrating from a physical device to a VB, any existing management systems or tools used to manage the physical device can be used to manage the virtual system installed on the VB. When installing a new system on the VB, any industry standard management systems or vendor-compliant tools can be used for that system. For Microsoft Windows Server on the VB, standard Microsoft management tools are available including Microsoft Management Console (MMC), or System Center Operations Manager (SCOM) and System Center Configuration manager (SCCM).

> **Note**   More information on SCOM 2007 and SCCM is available from the following Microsoft websites:
>
> ■   http://www.microsoft.com/systemcenter/operationsmanager/en/us/default.aspx
>
> ■   http://www.microsoft.com/systemcenter/configurationmanager/en/us/default.aspx

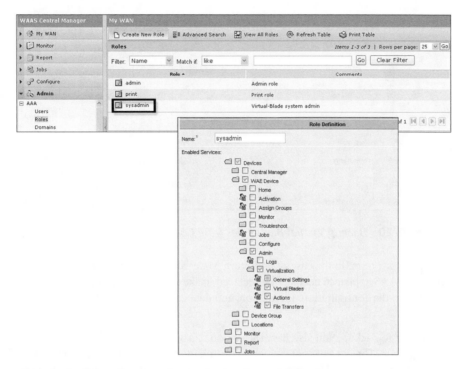

Figure 10-19   *Defining Roles on the CM for Virtualization Management*

Backup and Restore of Virtual Blades

The virtualized guest system can be backed up using any vendor compliant tools just as with any physical server. WAAS software provides a utility to enable a low-level full system backup and restoration.

As shown in Figure 10-20, an administrator can back up and restore the VB image to or from an external FTP server. To use the backup utility on the CM, from Device context, navigate to **Admin > Virtualization > File Transfers** page. Select **Backup virtual Blade to FTP** from the **File Transfer Type** drop-down menu, configure the FTP destination information, select the VB number and disk number to be backed up. The VB needs to be in *stopped* status when the image is being copied. The backup process takes a snapshot of the VB, including the guest operating system configuration, and any data stored in the disk space is backed up.

You should save a backup copy of the system image after completing configuration of the guest system, so that the initial system configuration information is preserved. Backup of the VB should be performed on a regular basis after the guest system is in service. It is best to also make a backup copy of VBs before powering down the WAAS

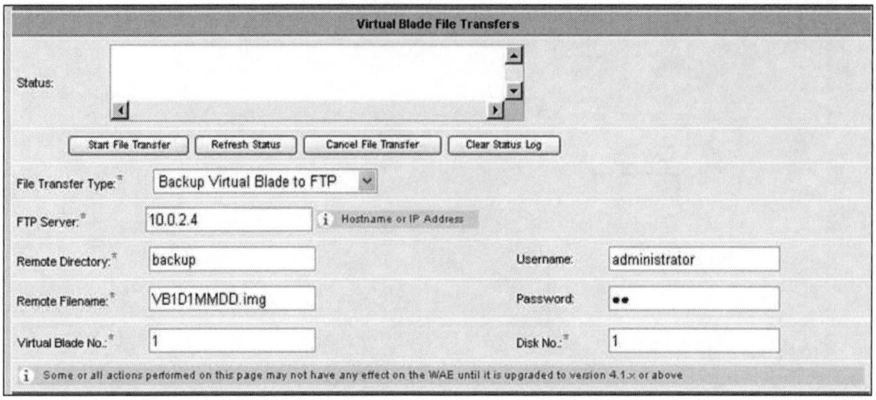

Figure 10-20 *Backup Virtual Blade Files from CM*

appliance long term. In the case of an Return Material Authorization (RMA) situation where a WAAS appliance needs to be replaced, make sure a backup copy of the VB(s) is available so the configuration, installation, and data can be restored onto the replacement appliance.

In addition to backup, you also have the option to save a snapshot of the VB in its *running* state. The current running processes and memory state are saved to the WAAS disk under */local1/vbs*. This option is available via the **virtual-blade** *number* **save** command. If maintenance work needs to be performed on the guest system, you can use this command to manually save a snapshot and later restart the system from the saved state.

When a WAAS device is rebooting, the WAAS software performs a save automatically and attempts to restore the state after the WAAS device reload is complete.

To restore a backup copy of one VB to a new VB, ensure the new VB has the same configuration as the original VB, with the same version of guest operating system installed.

Example 10-15 shows how to back up the virtual blade 1 image to an FTP server using the filename *vb1.img*, and Example 10-16 shows how to restore this file.

Example 10-15 *Backup VB Image Files to an FTP Server*

```
pod1-br-wae# copy virtual-blade ?
  <1-6>  Virtual blade number
pod1-br-wae# copy virtual-blade 1 ?
  disk  Virtual blade disk number
pod1-br-wae# copy virtual-blade 1 disk ?
  <1-4>  Virtual blade disk number
pod1-br-wae# copy virtual-blade 1 disk 1 ?
  ftp  Write to FTP server
pod1-br-wae# copy virtual-blade 1 disk 1 ftp ?
  Hostname or A.B.C.D  FTP server's IP address
```

```
pod1-br-wae# copy virtual-blade 1 disk 1 ftp 10.0.2.4 ?
  WORD   Remote file directory
pod1-br-wae# copy virtual-blade 1 disk 1 ftp 10.0.2.4 /backup ?
  WORD   Remote filename
pod1-br-wae# copy virtual-blade 1 disk 1 ftp 10.0.2.4 /backup vb1.img
```

Example 10-16   *Restore VB Image Files from an FTP Server*

```
pod1-br-wae# copy ftp virtual-blade 1 disk 1 10.0.2.4 /backup vb1.img
```

Monitoring and Troubleshooting Virtual Blades

Although the previous sections have focused on providing an overview and basic management of VBs, this section focuses on monitoring and troubleshooting VBs.

Monitoring Virtual Blades

The health of the guest operating system running on the VBs should be monitored using the tools available with that guest system and any applications that are installed. This section discusses the monitoring and troubleshooting from the perspective of the VB, and not from the perspective of the guest operating system or applications.

An administrator can monitor the VB through either the WAAS CM or the device CLI. Using the CM, you can display the configuration and the state of a VB by going to the device context and visiting **Admin > Virtualization > Virtual Blades**, or the **Admin > Virtualization > Actions** page. When **All** VBs are selected, the status window displays memory and disk resources utilized by configured VBs and the remaining resources. At the end of the display, the status of an individual VB is presented. Figure 10-15 previously displayed a screen from the CM that highlights this. The equivalent CLI command for this is **show virtual-blade**, as discussed in previous sections, and as shown in Example 10-5.

To display the configuration and state of an individual VB, select the VB number from the drop-down window. You find the hardware configuration, including CPU, disk emulation, disk allocation, memory allocation, NIC emulation, interface assignment, boot source, and VBstate. The **Refresh Status** button instructs the CM to poll the device for an immediate update instead of waiting for the regular polling interval as defined in the system properties page (as discussed in Chapter 7, the default polling interval is 5 minutes). Figure 10-15 previously displayed the CM showing this information.

Executing the CLI command **show virtual-blade** *number* from the WAAS appliance provides an instantaneous update of the VBstate. In addition to reviewing configuration and monitoring the state of the VB, there are additional CLI commands to monitor the VB disk I/O and interface usage. These commands are helpful in the process of troubleshooting or verifying that the VB is functioning correctly.

Example 10-17 provides the CLI output of the **show virtual-blade** *number* **blockio** and the **show virtual-blade** *number* **interface** commands.

The output of **show virtual-blade** *number* **blockio** indicates the disk I/O activity, with cumulative read/write bytes and read/write operations. When this command is executed on a VB with a running system in multiple successive iterations, a high number of changes indicate the system is busy reading or writing to a particular disk.

The **show virtual-blade** *number* **interface** *number* command output shows the input and output packet counts and interface status. On an active system, the **Packet Received** and **Packet Sent** counts should increment, and any of the error or dropped counts on interface should remain at 0.

Example 10-17 *Disk Block I/O and Interface Statistics*

```
pod1-br-wae# show virtual-blade 1 ?
  blockio    Display virtual-blade block I/O statistics
  interface  Display virtual-blade interface statistics
  |          Output Modifiers
  <cr>
pod1-br-wae# show virtual-blade 1 blockio ?
  |      Output Modifiers
  <cr>
pod1-br-wae# show virtual-blade 1 blockio
device         read_bytes      read_ops       write_bytes      write_ops
   cd              69632            31                 0              0
disk 1         202041856         58800           3035136            601
disk 2             8192            16                 0              0
disk 4             8192            16                 0              0
   fd                 0             0                 0              0
pod1-br-wae# show virtual-blade  1 interface ?
  <1-2>  Select an interface name
pod1-br-wae# show virtual-blade  1 interface 1 ?
  |      Output Modifiers
  <cr>
pod1-br-wae# show virtual-blade  1 interface 1
Type:Ethernet Maximum Transfer Unit Size:1500
Metric:1
Packets Received: 161
Input Errors: 0
Input Packets Dropped: 0
Input Packets Overruns: 0
Input Packets Frames: 0
Packet Sent: 1011
Output Errors: 0
Output Packets Dropped: 0
```

```
Output Packets Overruns: 0
Output Packets Carrier: 0
Output Queue Length:500
Collisions: 0
Flags:UP BROADCAST RUNNING MULTICAST
```

Alarms and Error Messages

If a VB stops running without the user issuing the VB **stop** command from the CLI or CM, or the user initiating shutdown from the guest operating system, then a critical alarm (alarm number 445012) is raised and an error (#445017) is logged.

This error condition generates a syslog message, and a critical alarm is seen from the CM. The critical alarm also triggers a Simple Network Management Protocol (SNMP) trap to the configured SNMP management station. Example 10-18 shows the syslog messages for this error.

Example 10-18   *Syslog Message for VB Faulty Shutdown*

```
2009 Feb 18 01:07:48 pod1-br-wae Sysmon: %WAAS-SYSMON-3-445017: Report an alarm
for Virtual blade 1 (State 0 Enabled 1)
2009 Feb 18 01:07:48 pod1-br-wae Sysmon: %WAAS-SYSMON-3-445012: Fault detected:
Virtual Blade #1 has stopped without cli command.
```

A critical alarm is also raised under this condition, as shown in Example 10-19. This alarm can also be seen on the CM GUI, as shown in Figure 10-21.

Example 10-19   *Critical Alarm Raised on VB Faulty Shutdown*

```
VM-674-BR1-06#show alarms detail
Critical Alarms:
    Alarm ID              Module/Submodule      Instance
    ----------            ------------          ----------

  1 VB1_stopped           sysmon                Virtual Blade
     Feb 18 01:07:48.306 UTC, Processing Error Alarm, #000005, 1000:445012
     Virtual Blade #1 has stopped without cli command.
```

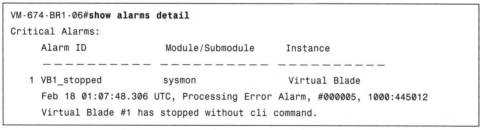

Figure 10-21   *VB Alarm on CM*

The VB error log is stored in the *local1/errorlog/* directory, under the *virtual-blade* log file. This file contains the commands executed on the VBs and the results of these commands. This file can be viewed by using the **type-tail /local1/errorlog/virtual-blade** command and is mainly used by Cisco engineers to troubleshoot VB related issues.

Troubleshooting Common Issues with Virtual Blades

When encountering issues with a VB that is hosted on a WAAS device, it is best to first examine the VB's configuration and state. It is important to gather a full understanding of the problem and its symptoms, and to identify whether the issue is related to the VB infrastructure or from the guest operating system or its applications. This section examines a few common issues that occur with VBs and their possible causes. It is not intended to be an exhaustive troubleshooting guide.

Failure to Boot

Should the guest operating system fail to boot beyond the BIOS startup screen, it is best to check for a corrupted image or a misconfiguration. The image that the VB boots from might be corrupted due to several reasons. An image could potentially be corrupted during or after the installation process, or it could have become corrupted or truncated during the file transfer process. An unclean shutdown or system crash might also cause disk corruption, which can also lead to a corrupted image. When disk corruption occurs, reinstallation of the guest operating system might be required. If there is a repair CD/DVD, you can boot from the repair CD/DVD and try to repair the disk. The moral of the story is that it is a best practice to keep a known working copy of the VB to handle such scenarios.

Failure to boot can also be indicative of a configuration issue. For example, if the disk or CPU emulation configured is not supported by the guest operating system, or if the resource allocation is insufficient based on the manufacturer's requirements, the guest operating system might not boot up or function properly. If a saved copy is available from one VB and is used to boot a new VB, make sure the configuration of the new VB matches the configuration of the original VB.

Remember to change the boot parameters of the VB to disk after the initial installation of the operating system. When the VB is configured to boot from CD-ROM or from an ISO image, upon restart of the VB, the system might try to go through the installation process again if the installation media is still in the drive or if the ISO is still on the WAAS device file system. If the **boot-from** field points to a CD-ROM, but there is no CD, or the CD is non-bootable, the system on the VB fails to start.

Verify the configuration of the VB, make sure the resource allocation is sufficient, and the hardware emulation configured is supported by the guest operating system.

Failure to start a VB from a saved image can be caused by a mismatch in the configuration, or a difference in the WAAS software version. Use the **virtual-blade** *number* **kill-save-state** command as shown in Example 10-20 to remove any saved memory state; this commonly helps issues with inability to restart VBs when software versions might have changed.

Example 10-20   *Remove VB Saved Memory State*

```
VM-674-BR1-06#virtual-blade 1 ?
  cd                    Change virtual blade cd
  kill-save-state       Delete the virtual-blade saved state
  save                  Save memory state of virtual blade
  session               Open telnet connection to remote host/port
  start                 Start the virtual blade
  stop                  Stop the virtual blade
VM-674-BR1-06#virtual-blade 1 kill-save-state
VM-674-BR1-06#
```

Blue Screen of Death

The infamous and eponymous Blue Screen of Death (BSOD) is indicative of a fatal error that occurred within a Microsoft Windows operating system. The BSOD is a blue screen that is displayed after the operating system encounters a critical system error and contains pertinent information about the error. BSODs can be caused by poorly written device drivers, hardware issues such as faulty memory, or even overheating of hardware components. It can also be caused by incompatible dynamic link library (DLL) files or defects in the operating system. BSODs are most frequently caused by issues within the guest operating system, and not issues related to the VB infrastructure. However, it can be caused by hardware resources and compatibility issues between those resources and the guest operating system. Error codes and memory dump files can be helpful in understanding the root cause of these errors.

If a BSOD occurs while you are connected via VNC, you can capture the screen, which generally contains the error codes and possible cause, and use available support resources such as Microsoft Technet to identify the root case. Memory dump files are helpful to determine the root cause of the error as well. On a Windows system, memory dump files are typically found in the *C:\Windows\Memory.dmp* directory. Figure 10-22 demonstrates the steps to locate the memory dump file in the Windows operating system.

On Linux systems, when a kernel encounters an unrecoverable error, it calls the *panic* function. The system locks up and appears to be unresponsive. There are open source utilities available to perform postmortem system analysis of kernel panic. The Linux Kernal Crash Dump (LKCD) and Kdump are examples of such tools. Kdump is a kernel crash dumping utility. When a system crashes, it can boot into a second kernel with little memory and capture the dump image.

LKCD enables the Linux system to write the kernel memory image when the system crash occurs; this memory image can be recovered after the system boots back and can be analyzed to determine the root cause of the failure.

Note   You can find more information on Kdump at http://lse.sourceforge.net/kdump/. You can find more information on LKCD package at http://lkcd.sourceforge.net/.

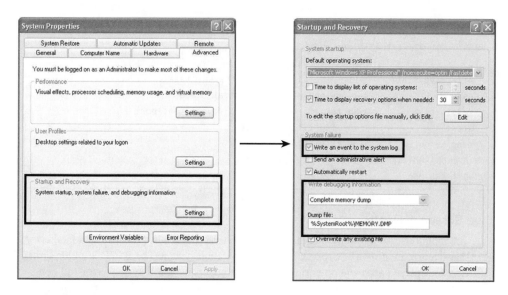

Figure 10-22 *Locate Memory Dump File in Windows*

Hang Conditions

A hang or freeze is when the guest operating system becomes unresponsive to keyboard and mouse input and the computer screen becomes static. There are several causes to this condition, and most often it is not related to hardware or virtualization services. When such conditions occur, it is important to determine what causes the unresponsiveness. Is the guest operating system experiencing a high load, or is it in a hanging condition? Or is there an emulation compatibility issue with the guest operating system that could be causing problems? Is the VB itself not responding?

If the guest operating system is unresponsive to mouse clicks or keyboard entry through VNC, but the system is accessible from Telnet or RDP, then the system is not in a hang condition. The unresponsiveness of VNC itself could be caused by the virtual emulation process. If the guest OS doesn't respond to any service requests, for example, if it is a DHCP server and no IP addresses are being assigned to new clients, then it could be a guest operating system hang, or the operating system is under load. From the guest system itself, check the running processes and resource utilization. To determine whether the VB is in a hung condition, execute the command **show virtual-blade** *number* **blockio** command followed by **show virtual-blade** *number* **interface** command in multiple successive iterations. Examine the output of these commands, and note whether or not the counters are incrementing. Example 10-17 earlier in the chapter gives an example of the command output. It might also be helpful to try and generate disk or network activity on the VB while running these tests.

In a guest operating system hang situation, you can save and restart the VB. If stopping the VB causes the guest operating system to go through its shutdown logic, then this condition is not caused by or related to the VB infrastructure.

If possible, you might want to examine the VB memory statistics within the guest operating system to determine what process is consuming a high amount of resources (such as CPU, memory, and network). In some cases, a misbehaving process might be consuming a substantial amount of resources or have inherent memory leaks. If you are unable to determine the source of a hang condition on a VB, or would prefer assistance in identifying the root cause, it might be in your best interest to involve the Cisco Technical Assistance Center (TAC). In such cases, it is helpful to have the guest operating system version (including service pack-related data), manifest of installed applications and services, system report, and WAAS configuration files ready.

Summary

The virtualization capabilities provided by the Cisco WAAS appliance family enables IT organizations to consolidate costly branch office infrastructure into the extensible WAAS appliance to minimize cost while preserving service availability and performance for applications that require localized deployment. Through the CM and CLI, Cisco WAAS offers a comprehensive and flexible solution to configure, monitor, manage, and troubleshoot VBs. VBs can be installed either via installation media (CD/DVD) or by copying ISO image files over the network to the WAAS appliance in the branch. Full control of the VBs is available in the CM or in the device CLI. Operational transparency is maintained with VBs in that the guest operating system and applications continue to be manageable using the same tools that were used previously, with the added benefit that customers enjoy reduced hardware footprint in the branch offices.

Chapter 11

Case Studies

The previous chapters provided you with the knowledge to successfully design, integrate, and deploy Cisco Wide Area Application Services (WAAS). This chapter applies that knowledge to different deployment scenarios in a multisite WAAS design. Each site in the example design is treated like a mini case study, where a set of site-specific requirements are presented, potential design/configuration options are discussed, and the final solution is described. The full device configurations are presented for each location in the design.

Common Requirements

For this design, a set of common requirements exist that apply to every location or the solution as a whole. The common requirements for this case study are defined as follows:

- No significant changes should be made to the existing network topology or routing policy.

- All TCP traffic (excluding VoIP) destined for the WAN should be intercepted and redirected to WAAS.

- Voice-over-IP (VoIP) control traffic should not be intercepted.

- Traffic on TCP ports 3250–3255 should not be optimized by WAAS.

- No WAE redundancy is required in the remote office deployments.

Existing WAN Topology

The existing WAN is built on an MPLS-based service from a national service provider. The WAN service provides any-to-any connectivity for remote-to-remote and remote-to-Data Center connectivity. WAN bandwidth ranges from 1.5 Mbps at the smallest remote sites up to 180 M bps (aggregate) at the Data Center. There is a single Data Center included in this design, supporting 250 domestic remote offices. Figure 11-1 shows a high-level overview of the existing WAN topology.

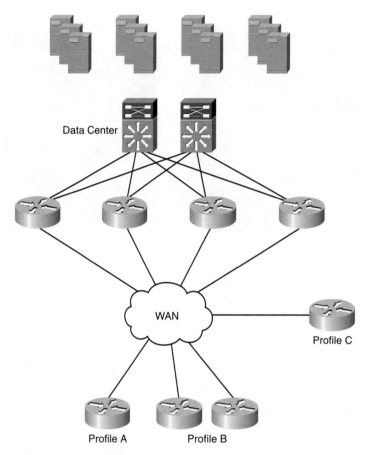

Figure 11-1   *High-Level WAN Topology*

The following key aspects of the WAN topology need to be considered for the design:

- Remote offices should be grouped based on common characteristics, such as business function, topology, networking equipment used, user community characteristics, and so on.

- The MPLS-based WAN service provides any-to-any connectivity. The location of client/server resources and the traffic flow impact on connection resources and fan out should be taken into consideration for WAE sizing.

- Some remote sites and the Data Center have multiple connections to the WAN. The routing policy and path preference needs to be understood and accounted for in the design.

Remote Site Profile A

To simplify the design and provide a consistent deployment across the Enterprise, the remote sites in this design have been grouped into three "profiles." A remote site "Profile A" is the first remote office deployment we review.

Profile A Site Requirements

The following site-specific requirements exist for remote offices grouped in Profile A:

- Field sales offices with between 25 and 40 users.

- Single 1.5 Mpbs connection to the WAN.

- WAN transport terminates on Cisco 3600 Series router.

- All L3 services (routing and so on) are provided by the WAN router.

- The link between the router and primary LAN switch is an 802.1q trunk.

- VoIP traffic is isolated to a separate VLAN.

Site Network Topology

Figure 11-2 shows the topology for remote offices in Profile A.

WAE Placement and Interception

One of the first design decisions is to determine the options for WAE placement and the interception method that will be used. Recall from Chapter 5, "Branch Office Network Integration," that the two most common interception methods for branch office deployments are WCCP and Inline. In this case, we use the inline interception method to avoid any potential performance issues on the 3600 series router caused by the increased throughput from the WAE. Based on the number of users at the site, the WAE-512 is the WAE model that is deployed. The WAE is placed physically inline between the WAN routers and the LAN switch. A single InlineGroup is used because no redundant connections exist between the WAN router and LAN switch. No configuration changes are required on the WAN router or LAN switches.

To meet the common requirement that VoIP control traffic is not intercepted, the dedicated VoIP VLAN (VLAN 101) is explicitly excluded as part of the InlineGroup configuration. To simplify the deployment, the management IP address of the WAE is configured on InlineGroup 1/0. This prevents the need for a separate physical connection for management. The IP address assigned to the WAE is allocated from one of the existing IP address ranges assigned to the site.

Figure 11-3 shows the Profile A site topology with the WAE deployed.

WAE Configuration Details

Example 11-1 shows the WAE configuration for Profile A sites.

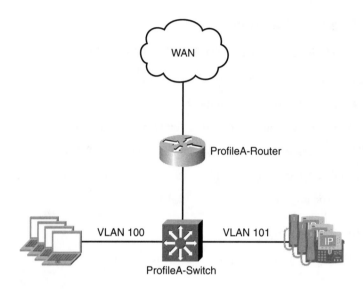

Figure 11-2   *Profile A Remote Office Topology*

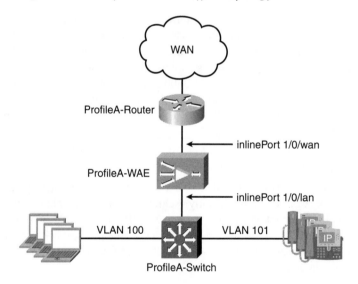

Figure 11-3   *Profile A Final Topology*

Example 11-1   *Profile A Site WAE Configuration*

```
ProfileA-WAE# show running-config no-policy
! WAAS version 4.1.3b (build b9 Jul 30 2009)
!
device mode application-accelerator
!
hostname ProfileA-WAE
```

```
                !
                primary-interface InlineGroup 1/0
                !
                interface GigabitEthernet 1/0
                 shutdown
                 exit
                interface GigabitEthernet 2/0
                 shutdown
                 exit
                interface InlineGroup 1/0
                 ip address 10.88.81.5 255.255.255.240
                 inline vlan all
                 no inline vlan 101
                 exit
                interface InlineGroup 1/1
                 inline vlan all
                 shutdown
                 exit
                !
           ip default-gateway 10.88.81.1
           !
           no auto-register enable
           !
           ! ip path-mtu-discovery is disabled in WAAS by default
           !
           ntp server 10.88.80.142
           !
           username admin password 1 $1$gfYExN4R$WlJ9i/.C34QsNRpuPgpz.1
           username admin privilege 15
           username admin print-admin-password 1
CEC32C13191F9B56AAD3B435B51404EE 6E73ED22ADDAFAA4FACD2513341E6B7C
           !
           authentication login local enable primary
           authentication configuration local enable primary
           !
           central-manager address 10.88.80.142
           cms enable
           !
      ! End of WAAS configuration
      ProfileA-WAE#
```

WAN Router Configuration Details

Example 11-2 shows the WAN router configuration for Profile A sites.

Example 11-2 *Profile A Site WAN Router Configuration*

```
ProfileA-Router# show running-config
Building configuration...

Current configuration : 979 bytes
!
version 12.3
service timestamps debug datetime msec
service timestamps log datetime msec
no service password-encryption
!
hostname ProfileA-Router
!
boot-start-marker
boot-end-marker
!
logging buffered 163843 debugging
no logging console
enable secret 5 $1$jq0n$Cr5PxpMX8IJ/eJan1hmQS/
!
no aaa new-model
ip subnet-zero
!
ip cef
no ip domain lookup
!
interface FastEthernet0/0
 no ip address
 duplex auto
 speed auto
 !
interface FastEthernet0/0.100
  description ** User Data VLAN **
  encapsulation dot1Q 100
ip address 10.10.10.1 255.255.255.0
!
interface FastEthernet0/0.101
 description ** Dedicated VoIP VLAN **
 encapsulation dot1Q 34
 ip address 10.10.11.1 255.255.255.0
```

```
    !
    interface Serial0/0
     description ** MPLS WAN Service **
     ip address 10.88.80.253 255.255.255.252
     !
    router ospf 100
     log-adjacency-changes
     passive-interface default
     no passive-interface Serial0/0
     network 10.88.80.252 0.0.0.3 area 10
     network 10.10.10.0 0.0.0.255 area 10
     network 10.10.11.0 0.0.0.255 area 10
     !
    no ip http server
    ip classless
    !
    line con 0
     password cisco
    line aux 0
    line vty 0 4
 password cisco
 login
!
end
ProfileA-Router#
```

LAN Switch Configuration Details

Example 11-3 shows the LAN switch configuration for Profile A sites.

Example 11-3   *Profile A Site LAN Switch Configuration*

```
ProfileA-Switch# show running-config
Building configuration...

Current configuration : 7537 bytes
!
upgrade fpd auto
version 12.2
service timestamps debug uptime
service timestamps log datetime msec localtime show-timezone
service password-encryption
service internal
service counters max age 5
```

```
!
hostname ProfileA-Switch
!
boot-start-marker
boot-end-marker
!
logging buffered 16384 debugging
no logging console
enable secret 5 $1$Yw6R$/H/1bMJdjEkKhjh8wkbZE0
!
                    no aaa new-model
                    !
                    no ip domain-lookup
                    vtp mode transparent
                    !
                    vlan internal allocation policy ascending
                    vlan access-log ratelimit 2000
                    !
                    vlan 100
                     name USER-DATA
                    !
                    vlan 101
                     name DEDICATED-VOICE
                    !
                    interface GigabitEthernet1/16
                     description ** ProfileA-WAE, interface LAN0 **
                     switchport
                     switchport trunk encapsulation dot1q
                     switchport trunk allowed vlan 100,101
                     switchport mode trunk
                    !
                    interface Vlan100
                     ip address 10.10.10.2 255.255.255.0
                    !
                    ip default-gateway 10.10.10.1
                    !
                no ip http server
                no ip http secure-server
                !
                control-plane
                !
                dial-peer cor custom
                !
                line con 0
```

```
     password 7 140005
line vty 0 4
 password 7 140005
 login
 transport input lat pad udptn telnet rlogin ssh
line vty 5 15
 password 7 120E12
 login
 transport input lat pad udptn telnet rlogin ssh
!
scheduler runtime netinput 300
!
end
ProfileA-Switch#
```

Remote Site Profile B

Now we look at the second type of remote sites, which we call "Profile B." Sites in this profile are unique in that they are small kiosk locations within other business. In addition to being space constrained, kiosks are frequently shutting down and reopening in different locations based on business demands. Let's see how these types of sites are addressed from a design perspective.

Profile B Site Requirements

The following site-specific requirements exist for remote offices grouped in Profile B:

- Kiosk structures within rented space on other business property.

- Each kiosk is staffed with one or two users.

- Single 1.5Mpbs connection to the WAN.

- WAN transport terminates on Cisco 2800 Series router.

- All L3 services (routing and so on) are provided by the WAN router.

- Physical space consumption for IT hardware should be kept to a minimum.

Site Network Topology

Figure 11-4 shows the topology for remote offices in Profile B.

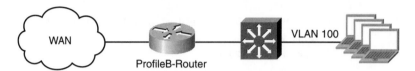

Figure 11-4   *Profile B Remote Office Topology*

WAE Placement and Interception

Given the physical space challenges at Profile B locations and a desire to minimize the amount of infrastructure that has to be moved when kiosks close and relocate, the NME-WAE-522 is the WAE model that is deployed. The NME-WAE is physically installed in the existing 2800 series router, preventing the need for any additional rack space. WCCP is used as the interception method, transparently redirecting all TCP traffic across the internal interface to the NME-WAE.

To meet the common requirement that VoIP control traffic is not intercepted, traffic to/from the dedicated VoIP VLAN (VLAN 101) is excluded from interception using a WCCP redirect-list. Because the internal connection between the WAN router and NME-WAE functions like a point-to-point link, a /30 network is allocated to each Profile B site. The two usable IP addresses in this network is used for the router IntergratedServicesEngine interface IP address and WAE IP address.

Figure 11-5 shows the final topology for remote offices in Profile B.

Figure 11-5   *Profile B Final Topology*

WAE Configuration Details

Example 11-4 shows the WAE configuration for Profile B sites.

Example 11-4   *Profile B Site WAE Configuration*

```
ProfileB-WAE# show running-config
! WAAS version 4.0.15 (build b6 Dec 13 2007)
!
device mode application-accelerator
```

```
                       !
               hostname ProfileB-WAE
               !
               clock timezone CST6CDT -6 0
               !
               ip domain-name asdcnp-waas.cisco.com
               !
               exec-timeout 5
               !
               primary-interface GigabitEthernet 1/0
               !
               interface GigabitEthernet 1/0
                ip address 10.88.80.222 255.255.255.252
                no autosense
                bandwidth 1000
                full-duplex
                exit
               interface GigabitEthernet 2/0
                shutdown
                exit
               !
               ip default-gateway 10.88.80.221
               !
               no auto-register enable
               !
               ! ip path-mtu-discovery is disabled in WAAS by default
               !
           ip name-server 10.88.80.53
           !
           ntp server 10.88.80.132
           !
           wccp router-list 1 10.88.80.221
           wccp tcp-promiscuous router-list-num 1
           wccp version 2
           !
           username admin password 1 1Kat1k753Qknw
           username admin privilege 15
           username admin print-admin-password 1
CEC32C13191F9B56AAD3B435B51404EE 6E73ED22ADDAFAA4FACD2513341E6B7C
           !
           windows-domain netbios-name "PROFILEB-WAE"
           !
           authentication login local enable primary
           authentication configuration local enable primary
```

```
!
no telnet enable
!
no sshd version 1
sshd enable
!
central-manager address 10.88.80.132
cms enable
!
! End of WAAS configuration
ProfileB-WAE#
```

WAN Router Configuration Details

Example 11-5 shows the WAN router configuration for Profile B sites.

Example 11-5 *Profile B Site WAN Router Configuration*

```
ProfileB-Router# show running-config
Building configuration...

Current configuration : 1935 bytes
!
version 12.4
service timestamps debug datetime msec
service timestamps log datetime msec
no service password-encryption
!
hostname ProfileB-Router
!
boot-start-marker
boot-end-marker
!
no logging console
enable secret 5 $1$Ox0L$yBovhDx4AYaumzLBVVNOT0
!
no aaa new-model
ip wccp 61
ip wccp 62 redirect-list PT-VOICE-CONTROL
!
ip cef
!
no ip domain lookup
!
```

```
    multilink bundle-name authenticated
    !
    voice-card 0
    no dspfarm
   !
   interface FastEthernet0/0
     no ip address
     duplex auto
     speed auto
     !
   interface FastEthernet0/0.100
     description ** User Data VLAN **
     encapsulation dot1Q 100
     ip address 10.10.20.1 255.255.255.0
     ip wccp 61 redirect in
     !
   interface FastEthernet0/0.101
     description ** Dedicated VoIP VLAN **
     encapsulation dot1Q 101
     ip address 10.10.21.1 255.255.255.0
     !
   interface Serial0/0
     description ** MPLS WAN Service **
     ip address 10.88.80.249 255.255.255.252
     ip wccp 62 redirect in
     !
 interface Integrated-Service-Engine1/0
  ip address 10.88.80.221 255.255.255.252
  service-module ip address 10.88.80.222 255.255.255.252
  service-module ip default-gateway 10.88.80.221
  no keepalive
 !
 router ospf 100
  log-adjacency-changes
  passive-interface default
  no passive-interface Serial0/0
  network 10.10.20.0 0.0.0.255 area 0
 network 10.10.21.0 0.0.0.255 area 0
 network 10.88.80.220 0.0.0.3 area 0
 !
 no ip http server
no ip http secure-server
 !
 ip access-list extended PT-VOICE-CONTROL
```

```
   deny    ip any 10.10.21.0 0.0.0.255
   deny    ip 10.10.21.0 0.0.0.255 any
   permit ip any any
  !
 control-plane
!
 line con 0
  password cisco
                       line aux 0
                       line vty 0 4
                         password cisco
                        login
                        !
                        scheduler allocate 20000 1000
                        !
                        end
                        ProfileB-Router#
```

Remote Site Profile C

The final remote office profile is "Profile C." Profile C sites are some of the largest remote offices in the Enterprise and have redundant network infrastructure for increased availability. Recall that preservation of the existing topology and routing policy was an important common requirement. Let's see how these requirements and the site-specific requirements are addressed.

Profile C Site Requirements

The following site-specific requirements exist for remote offices grouped in Profile C:

- Large Admin and Engineering offices with between 125 and 500 users.

- Multiple multi-Mbps connections to the WAN.

- WAN transport terminates on Cisco 3800 or 7200 Series routers.

- All L3 services (routing and so on) are provided by the WAN routers.

- The links between the routers and LAN switches are 802.1q trunks.

- VoIP traffic is isolated to a separate VLAN.

- Gateway Load Balancing Protocol (GLBP) is used for default-gateway redundancy and outbound distribution of client load across both WAN routers.

Site Network Topology

Figure 11-6 shows the topology for remote offices in Profile C.

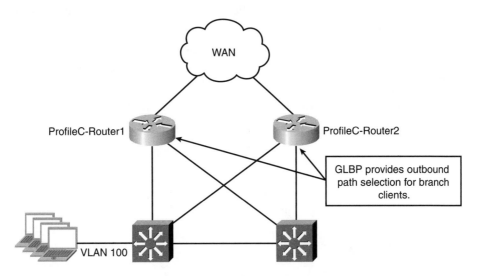

Figure 11-6 *Profile C Remote Office Topology*

WAE Placement and Interception

Both WAN routers at Profile C locations are connected to both LAN switches; therefore, there are too many connections for inline interception to be an option. WCCP is used as the interception method at Profile C locations. Based on the sizing requirement for the site, the WAE-7341 is the WAE model that is deployed. A separate VLAN is created for the WAE, which allows for HSRP to be used as the default-gateway redundancy mechanism. In addition, during a review of the WAN router configurations, it was discovered that the customer had Unicast Reverse Path Forwarding (uRPF) configured on the client LAN interfaces.

Note uRPF is defined in RFC3704. More information is available at the following location: http://tools.ietf.org/html/rfc3704

Because WAAS is functioning as a transparent proxy, traffic from the WAE can appear to uRPF as entering the router on the incorrect interface. By placing the WAEs in a separate, dedicated segment, the uRPF feature can be left off of that router interface.

To preserve the default-gateway selection (via GLBP) made by the client, the egress-method for Profile C sites is set to **negotiated-return**. This causes the WAE to send traffic back to the intercepting router that redirected the traffic to it, as opposed to using the configured default-gateway. As an additional optimization, the WAE is configured with a static route for each intercepting router's WCCP router-id. The next-hop of each static route is the directly connected IP address of the intercepting router that router-id belongs to. This allows the WAE to return the traffic directly back to the intercepting router, as opposed to forwarding the traffic to its configured default-gateway when the router-id is not directly connected.

To meet the common requirement that VoIP control traffic is not intercepted, traffic to/from the dedicated VoIP VLAN (VLAN 101) is excluded from interception using a WCCP redirect-list.

Figure 11-7 shows the final topology for remote offices in Profile C.

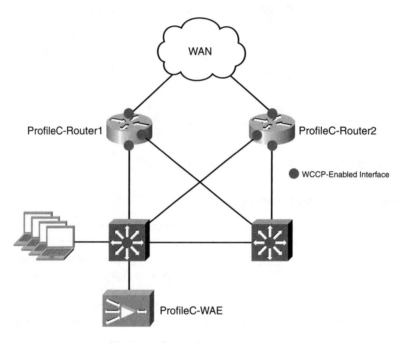

Figure 11-7 *Profile C Final Topology*

WAE Configuration Details

Example 11-7 shows the WAE configuration for Profile C sites.

Example 11-7 *Profile C Site WAE Configuration*

```
ProfileC-WAE# show running-config
! WAAS version 4.0.13 (build b23 Dec 20 2007)
!
device mode application-accelerator
!
hostname ProfileC-WAE
```

```
          !
          clock timezone CST6CDT -6 0
          !
          ip domain-name asdcnp-waas.cisco.com
          !
          exec-timeout 5
          !
          primary-interface GigabitEthernet 1/0
          !
          interface GigabitEthernet 1/0
            ip address 10.10.32.5 255.255.255.0
            exit
      interface GigabitEthernet 2/0
        shutdown
        exit
      !
      ip default-gateway 10.10.32.1
      !
      no auto-register enable
      !
      ! ip path-mtu-discovery is disabled in WAAS by default
      !
      ip name-server 10.88.80.53
      !
      ip route 10.99.99.1 255.255.255.255 10.10.32.2
      ip route 10.99.99.2 255.255.255.255 10.10.32.3
      !
      ntp server 10.88.80.132
      !
      wccp router-list 1 10.10.32.2 10.10.32.3
      wccp tcp-promiscuous router-list-num 1
      wccp version 2
      !
      egress-method negotiated-return intercept-method wccp
      !
      username admin password 1 1Kat1k753Qknw
      username admin privilege 15
      !
windows-domain netbios-name "PROFILEC-WAE"
!
authentication login local enable primary
authentication configuration local enable primary
!
no telnet enable
```

```
!
no sshd version 1
sshd enable
!
central-manager address 10.88.80.132
cms enable
!
no adapter epm enable
!
! End of WAAS configuration
ProfileC-WAE#
```

WAN Router 1 Configuration Details

Example 11-8 shows the WAN router configuration for Profile C sites.

Example 11-8   *Profile C Site WAN Router Configuration*

```
ProfileC-Router1# show running-config
Building configuration...

Current configuration : 979 bytes
!
version 12.4
service timestamps debug datetime msec
service timestamps log datetime msec
no service password-encryption
!
hostname ProfileC-Router1
!
boot-start-marker
boot-end-marker
!
logging buffered 163843 debugging
no logging console
enable secret 5 $1$jq0n$Cr5PxpMX8IJ/eJan1hmQS/
!
no aaa new-model
ip wccp 61
ip wccp 62 redirect-list PT-VOICE-CONTROL
ip subnet-zero
```

```
        !
        ip cef
        no ip domain lookup
        !
        interface Loopback0
         ip address 10.99.99.1 255.255.255.255
         !
        interface FastEthernet0/0
         no ip address
         duplex auto
         speed auto
         !
        interface FastEthernet0/0.100
    description ** User Data VLAN **
    encapsulation dot1Q 100
    ip address 10.10.30.2 255.255.255.0
    ip verify unicast reverse-path
    ip wccp 61 redirect in
    glbp 1 ip 10.10.30.1
    glbp 1 priority 110
    glbp load-balancing host-dependent
    !
    interface FastEthernet0/0.101
     description ** Dedicated VoIP VLAN **
     encapsulation dot1Q 101
     ip address 10.10.31.2 255.255.255.0
     ip verify unicast reverse-path
     glbp 2 ip 10.10.31.1
     glbp 2 priority 110
     glbp load-balancing host-dependent
     !
    interface FastEthernet0/0.300
     description ** WAE Service VLAN **
     encapsulation dot1q 300
     ip address 10.10.32.2 255.255.255.0
     standby 1 ip 10.10.33.1
     standby 1 priority 105
     !
    interface Serial0/0
 description ** MPLS WAN Service **
 ip address 10.88.80.241 255.255.255.252
 ip wccp 62 redirect in
 !
router ospf 100
```

```
        log-adjacency-changes
        passive-interface default
        no passive-interface Serial0/0
        no passive-interface FastEthernet0/0.300
        network 10.10.30.0 0.0.0.255 area 10
        network 10.10.31.0 0.0.0.255 area 10
        network 10.10.32.0 0.0.0.255 area 10
        !
        no ip http server
        !
        ip access-list extended PT-VOICE-CONTROL
         deny    ip any 10.10.31.0 0.0.0.255
         deny    ip 10.10.31.0 0.0.0.255 any
         permit ip any any
        !
        ip classless
        !
        line con 0
        password cisco
        line aux 0
        line vty 0 4
   password cisco
   login
 !
end
ProfileC-Router1#
```

WAN Router 2 Configuration Details

Example 11-9 shows the WAN router configuration for Profile C sites.

Example 11-9 *Profile C Site WAN Router Configuration*

```
ProfileC-Router2# show running-config
Building configuration...

Current configuration : 979 bytes
!
version 12.4
service timestamps debug datetime msec
service timestamps log datetime msec
no service password-encryption
!
hostname ProfileC-Router2
```

```
!
boot-start-marker
boot-end-marker
!
logging buffered 163843 debugging
no logging console
enable secret 5 $1$jq0n$Cr5PxpMX8IJ/eJan1hmQS/
!
no aaa new-model
ip wccp 61
ip wccp 62 redirect-list PT-VOICE-CONTROL
ip subnet-zero
!
ip cef
no ip domain lookup
!
interface Loopback0
 ip address 10.99.99.2 255.255.255.255
!
interface FastEthernet0/0
 no ip address
 duplex auto
 speed auto
!
interface FastEthernet0/0.100
 description ** User Data VLAN **
 encapsulation dot1Q 100
 ip address 10.10.30.3 255.255.255.0
 ip verify unicast reverse-path
 ip wccp 61 redirect in
 glbp 1 ip 10.10.30.1
 glbp load-balancing host-dependent
!
interface FastEthernet0/0.101
 description ** Dedicated VoIP VLAN **
 encapsulation dot1Q 101
 ip address 10.10.31.3 255.255.255.0
ip verify unicast reverse-path
glbp 2 ip 10.10.31.1
glbp load-balancing host-dependent
!
interface FastEthernet0/0.300
 description ** WAE Service VLAN **
 encapsulation dot1q 300
```

```
             ip address 10.10.32.3 255.255.255.0
             standby 1 ip 10.10.33.1
             !
            interface Serial0/0
             description ** MPLS WAN Service **
             ip address 10.88.80.245 255.255.255.252
             ip wccp 62 redirect in
             !
            router ospf 100
             log-adjacency-changes
             passive-interface default
             no passive-interface Serial0/0
             no passive-interface FastEthernet0/0.300
             network 10.10.30.0 0.0.0.255 area 10
             network 10.10.31.0 0.0.0.255 area 10
             network 10.10.32.0 0.0.0.255 area 10
             !
            no ip http server
             !
        ip access-list extended PT-VOICE-CONTROL
         deny    ip any 10.10.31.0 0.0.0.255
         deny    ip 10.10.31.0 0.0.0.255 any
         permit ip any any
        !
        ip classless
        !
        line con 0
         password cisco
        line aux 0
        line vty 0 4
         password cisco
         login
        !
        end
        ProfileC-Router2#
```

Data Center Profile

Now that all of the remote office profiles have been addressed, we take a closer look at the WAAS deployment in the Data Center. It is usually recommended to evaluate each Data Center on its own, as opposed to trying to group them into common profiles.

Data Center Site Requirements

The following site-specific requirements exist for the Data Center:

- Hosts resources accessed by all remote offices with WAAS deployed.

- Multiple 45Mpbs connections to the WAN.

- WAN transport terminates on multiple Cisco 7200 Series routers.

- Traffic to/from remote offices is divided between the available WAN routers based on route metrics advertised to the MPLS cloud.

- All WAN routers aggregate into a single pair of Cisco Catalyst 6500 Series switches.

- Access to other Data Centers is also provided through the same MPLS cloud used by remote offices.

- Data Center-to-Data Center traffic should be excluded from interception.

Site Network Topology

Figure 11-8 shows the topology for the Data Center.

WAE Placement and Interception

The first preference for the interception method in the Data Center is WCCP. The Cisco 7200 Series routers terminating the WAN transport are a potential location to enable WCCP, but the customer is concerned about the potential performance impact due to the high volume of traffic flowing between the Data Center and WAN. The pair of Catalyst 6500 switches where all the WAN routers aggregate is another possibility. The benefit of configuring WCCP on the 6500 is that all the interception can be handled in hardware. Another benefit is that the 6500s have a full view of the routing table from the WAN access routers, allowing them to make the optimum forward decision for optimized traffic from the WAEs destined to the WAN. Based on the sizing requirements of the deployment, two WAE-7371s are required. To provide N+1 redundancy for the WAEs in the Data Center, a third WAE is deployed. Each WAE-7371 is connected to both 6500 switches using the Standby Interface feature. This provides an additional level of redundancy in the event of a switch or interface failure. A separate VLAN is created and trunked between the Catalyst 6500 switches. HSRP is used on the WAE VLAN to provide default-gateway redundancy.

To meet the requirement that Data Center-to-Data Center traffic is not intercepted, a WCCP redirect-list is used. The egress-method configured on the WAEs will be IP forwarding. The 'l2-redirect' and 'mask-assign' options are used to ensure complete WCCP redirection in hardware on the Catalyst 6500 switches, as opposed to the hash assignment method, which might cause an increase in MSFC CPU utilization.

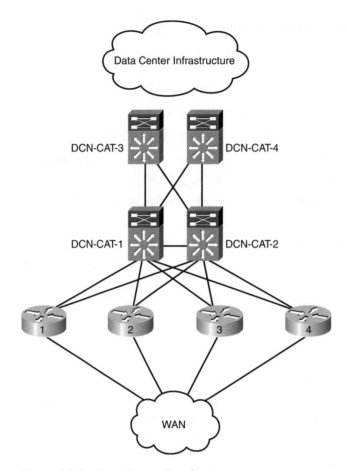

Figure 11-8 *Data Center Topology*

Figure 11-9 shows the final topology for the Data Center.

WAE Configuration Details

Example 11-10 shows the WAE configuration for the Data Center.

Example 11-10 *Data Center WAE Configuration*

```
DataCenter-WAE# show running-config
! WAAS version 4.0.13 (build b23 Dec 20 2007)
!
device mode application-accelerator
!
hostname DataCenter-WAE
!
```

```
                     clock timezone CST6CDT -6 0
                     !
                     ip domain-name asdcnp-waas.cisco.com
                     !
            exec-timeout 5
            !
            primary-interface Standby 1
            !
            interface Standby 1
             ip address 20.20.20.5 255.255.255.0
             exit
            !
            interface GigabitEthernet 1/0
             standby 1 priority 110
             exit
            interface GigabitEthernet 2/0
             standby 1
             exit
            !
            ip default-gateway 20.20.20.1
            !
            no auto-register enable
            !
            ! ip path-mtu-discovery is disabled in WAAS by default
            !
            ip name-server 10.88.80.53
            !
            ntp server 10.88.80.132
            !
            wccp router-list 1 20.20.20.2 20.20.20.3
wccp tcp-promiscuous mask src-ip-mask 0x2e8200 dst-ip-mask 0x0
wccp tcp-promiscuous router-list-num 1 l2-redirect mask-assign
wccp version 2
!
username admin password 1 1Kat1k753Qknw
username admin privilege 15
!
windows-domain netbios-name "PROFILEC-WAE"
!
authentication login local enable primary
authentication configuration local enable primary
!
no telnet enable
!
no sshd version 1
```

```
sshd enable
!
central-manager address 10.88.80.132
cms enable
!
no adapter epm enable
!
<default ATP removed>
!
! End of WAAS configuration
DataCenter-WAE#
```

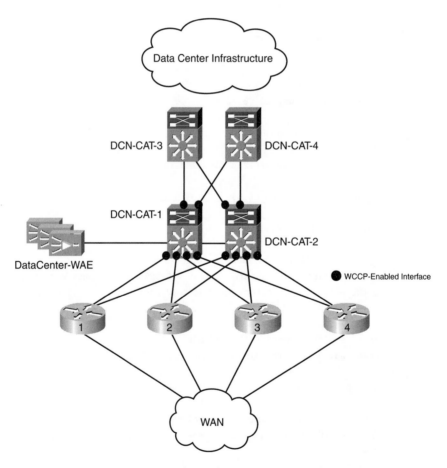

Figure 11-9 *Data Center Final Topology*

Data Center Switch 1 Configuration Details

Example 11-11 shows the WAN router configuration for the Data Center.

Example 11-11   *Data Center Switch 1 Configuration*

```
      DCN-CAT-1# show running-config
   Building configuration...

   Current configuration : 7537 bytes
   !
   upgrade fpd auto
   version 12.2
   service timestamps debug uptime
   service timestamps log datetime msec localtime show-timezone
   service password-encryption
   service internal
   service counters max age 5
   !
   hostname DCN-CAT-1
   !
   boot-start-marker
   boot-end-marker
   !
   logging buffered 16384 debugging
   no logging console
   enable secret 5 $1$Yw6R$/H/1bMJdjEkKhjh8wkbZE0
   !
   no aaa new-model
   ip subnet-zero
   ip wccp 61 redirect-list PT-DC-TO-DC
   ip wccp 62 redirect-list PT-DC-TO-DC
   !
no ip domain-lookup
vtp mode transparent
mls netflow interface
no mls flow ip
mls cef error action reset
!
redundancy
 keepalive-enable
 mode sso
 main-cpu
```

```
   auto-sync running-config
spanning-tree mode pvst
diagnostic cns publish cisco.cns.device.diag_results
diagnostic cns subscribe cisco.cns.device.diag_commands
!
vlan internal allocation policy ascending
         vlan access-log ratelimit 2000
      !
      vlan 300
 name WAE-SERVICE-VLAN
!
interface Port-channel1
 description ** Trunk to DCN-CAT-2 **
 switchport
 switchport trunk encapsulation dot1q
 switchport mode trunk
                     !
                     interface GigabitEthernet1/1
                      description ** Link to DCN-WAN-RTR-1 **
                      ip address 10.88.80.225 255.255.255.252
                      ip wccp 61 redirect in
                      !
                     interface GigabitEthernet1/2
                      description ** Link to DCN-WAN-RTR-2 **
                      ip address 10.88.80.229 255.255.255.252
                      ip wccp 61 redirect in
                      !
                     interface GigabitEthernet1/3
                      description ** Link to DCN-WAN-RTR-3 **
                      ip address 10.88.80.233 255.255.255.252
                      ip wccp 61 redirect in
                      !
                     interface GigabitEthernet1/4
                      description ** Link to DCN-WAN-RTR-4 **
                      ip address 10.88.80.237 255.255.255.252
                      ip wccp 61 redirect in
                      !
                     interface GigabitEthernet1/5
                      switchport
                      switchport mode trunk
                      channel-group 1 mode desirable
                      !
                  interface GigabitEthernet1/6
                    switchport
```

```
      switchport mode trunk
      channel-group 1 mode desirable
      !
     interface GigabitEthernet1/7
      switchport
      switchport mode trunk
      channel-group 1 mode desirable
      !
     interface GigabitEthernet1/8
      switchport
      switchport mode trunk
      channel-group 1 mode desirable
      !
     interface GigabitEthernet1/9
      description ** Link to DCN-CAT-3 **
      ip address 10.88.80.209 255.255.255.252
      ip wccp 62 redirect in
      !
     interface GigabitEthernet1/10
      description ** Link to DCN-CAT-4 **
      ip address 10.88.80.213 255.255.255.252
      ip wccp 62 redirect in
      !
     interface Vlan300
 description ** WAE Service VLAN **
 ip address 20.20.30.2 255.255.255.0
 standby 1 ip 20.20.20.1
 standby 1 priority 105
!
router ospf 100
 log-adjacency-changes
 passive-interface default
 no passive-interface Vlan300
 network 10.88.80.0 0.0.1.255 area 0
 network 20.20.30.0 0.0.0.255 area 0
 default-information originate always
!
ip classless
ip route 0.0.0.0 0.0.0.0 Null0
!
no ip http server
no ip http secure-server
!
ip access-list extended PT-DC-TO-DC
```

```
          deny    ip 10.10.10.0 0.0.0.255 10.10.20.0 0.0.0.255
          deny    ip 10.10.20.0 0.0.0.255 10.10.10.0 0.0.0.255
          permit ip any any
          !
          control-plane
          !
 dial-peer cor custom
 !
 line con 0
  password 7 140005
 line vty 0 4
  password 7 140005
  login
  transport input lat pad udptn telnet rlogin ssh
 line vty 5 15
  password 7 120E12
  login
  transport input lat pad udptn telnet rlogin ssh
 !
 scheduler runtime netinput 300
 !
 end
 DCN-CAT-1#
```

Data Center Switch 2 Configuration Details

Example 11-12 shows the LAN switch configuration for the Data Center.

Example 11-12 *Data Center Switch 2 Configuration*

```
          DCN-CAT-2# show running-config
          Building configuration...

          Current configuration : 7537 bytes
          !
          upgrade fpd auto
          version 12.2
          service timestamps debug uptime
          service timestamps log datetime msec localtime show-timezone
          service password-encryption
              service internal
              service counters max age 5
              !
              hostname DCN-CAT-2
```

```
!
boot-start-marker
boot-end-marker
!
logging buffered 16384 debugging
no logging console
enable secret 5 $1$Yw6R$/H/1bMJdjEkKhjh8wkbZE0
!
no aaa new-model
ip subnet-zero
ip wccp 61 redirect-list PT-DC-TO-DC
ip wccp 62 redirect-list PT-DC-TO-DC
!
no ip domain-lookup
vtp mode transparent
mls netflow interface
no mls flow ip
mls cef error action reset
!
redundancy
 keepalive-enable
 mode sso
main-cpu
 auto-sync running-config
spanning-tree mode pvst
diagnostic cns publish cisco.cns.device.diag_results
diagnostic cns subscribe cisco.cns.device.diag_commands
!
vlan internal allocation policy ascending
 vlan access-log ratelimit 2000
 !
 vlan 300
 name WAE-SERVICE-VLAN
!
interface Port-channel1
 description ** Trunk to DCN-CAT-1 **
 switchport
 switchport trunk encapsulation dot1q
 switchport mode trunk
!
interface GigabitEthernet1/1
 description ** Link to DCN-WAN-RTR-1 **
 ip address 10.88.80.193 255.255.255.252
 ip wccp 61 redirect in
```

```
                    !
                    interface GigabitEthernet1/2
                     description ** Link to DCN-WAN-RTR-2 **
                     ip address 10.88.80.197 255.255.255.252
              ip wccp 61 redirect in
            !
           interface GigabitEthernet1/3
            description ** Link to DCN-WAN-RTR-3 **
            ip address 10.88.80.201 255.255.255.252
            ip wccp 61 redirect in
            !
           interface GigabitEthernet1/4
            description ** Link to DCN-WAN-RTR-4 **
            ip address 10.88.80.205 255.255.255.252
            ip wccp 61 redirect in
            !
           interface GigabitEthernet1/5
            switchport
            switchport mode trunk
            channel-group 1 mode desirable
            !
           interface GigabitEthernet1/6
            switchport
            switchport mode trunk
            channel-group 1 mode desirable
            !
           interface GigabitEthernet1/7
            switchport
            switchport mode trunk
            channel-group 1 mode desirable
            !
           interface GigabitEthernet1/8
            switchport
            switchport mode trunk
            channel-group 1 mode desirable
            !
           interface GigabitEthernet1/9
            description ** Link to DCN-CAT-3 **
            ip address 10.88.80.217 255.255.255.252
            ip wccp 62 redirect in
            !
           interface GigabitEthernet1/10
            description ** Link to DCN-CAT-4 **
            ip address 10.88.80.221 255.255.255.252
            ip wccp 62 redirect in
```

```
    !
    interface Vlan300
     description ** WAE Service VLAN **
     ip address 20.20.30.3 255.255.255.0
     standby 1 ip 20.20.20.1
     !
    router ospf 100
     log-adjacency-changes
     passive-interface default
     no passive-interface Vlan300
     network 10.88.80.0 0.0.1.255 area 0
 network 20.20.30.0 0.0.0.255 area 0
 default-information originate always
!
ip classless
ip route 0.0.0.0 0.0.0.0 Null0
!
no ip http server
no ip http secure-server
!
ip access-list extended PT-DC-TO-DC
 deny    ip 10.10.10.0 0.0.0.255 10.10.20.0 0.0.0.255
 deny    ip 10.10.20.0 0.0.0.255 10.10.10.0 0.0.0.255
 permit ip any any
!
control-plane
!
dial-peer cor custom
!
line con 0
 password 7 140005
line vty 0 4
 password 7 140005
 login
 transport input lat pad udptn telnet rlogin ssh
line vty 5 15
 password 7 120E12
                       login
                       transport input lat pad udptn telnet rlogin ssh
                       !
                       scheduler runtime netinput 300
                       !
                       end
                       DCN-CAT-2#
```

Application Traffic Policy

To handle the requirement that traffic on TCP ports 3250–3255 should not be optimized by WAAS, we need to create a custom policy-map entry. The best place to do this is in the Central Manager *AllDevicesGroup*, which ensures that the policy is applied consistently to all WAEs in the deployment.

Figures 11-10 and 11-11 show the Central Manager configuration screens for the custom policy.

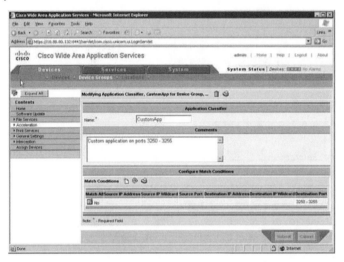

Figure 11-10   *Custom Application Traffic Classifier*

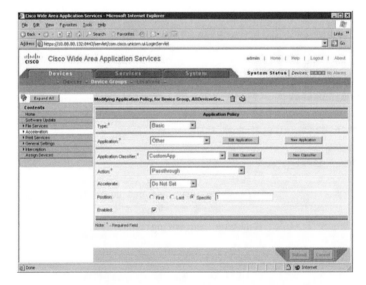

Figure 11-11   *Custom Application Traffic Policy-Map*

The resulting ATP CLI configuration is shown in Example 11-13.

Example 11-13 *Custom Application Traffic Policy CLI*

```
!
policy-engine application
classifier CustomApp
      match dst port range 3250 3255
   exit
   map basic
      name Other classifier CustomApp action pass-through
exit
!
```

Summary

This chapter showed the practical application of the knowledge gained throughout this book. Several different types of site deployment were analyzed, with slightly varying implementation solutions chosen at each site. The example design in this chapter highlights the use of various different interception methods in the same overall deployment. Detailed example configurations were provided for all the key components in the design.

Appendix A

WAAS Quickstart Guide

The Cisco Wide Area Application Services (WAAS) software provides a command-line interface (CLI) setup wizard to assist in the initial configuration of a WAAS device. This appendix offers a step-by-step guide to enable and validate Cisco WAAS optimization using the setup wizard in a simulated network environment. This appendix also covers the procedure to test and measure application performance before and after WAAS installation. The same process can be followed to set up a WAAS test lab for a proof-of-concept and demonstrate the benefits of WAAS optimization. At the end of the appendix, some useful tools are listed for more extensive performance testing.

Test Lab Setup

The following resources are required to use this guide:

- Three WAAS devices—one configured as a Central Manager (CM), two application accelerators (one of them deployed using an inline card, and the other deployed using Web Cache Coordination Protocol version 2 [WCCPv2])

- One WAN simulation device (a PC with two network cards and a CD/DVD drive that can be used for booting the system)

- Two Cisco 2800 Integrated Services Routers (ISR) or similar, and two Cisco Layer 2 switches (or a switch that supports VLANs)

- One Microsoft Windows workstation with Microsoft Office applications

- Application server(s) with Microsoft Windows file shares (using the Common Internet File System [CIFS] protocol) and Microsoft Internet Information Services (IIS) for web services and FTP services

This quickstart guide assumes that all devices are physically installed and properly connected with correct cabling. This guide also assumes that end-to-end network connectivity has been verified and that the appropriate router and switch configurations have been applied. Figure A-1 shows the network layout of the sample WAAS lab used in this guide with IP address assignment on each of the devices and interfaces.

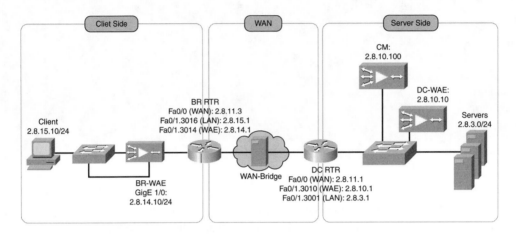

Figure A-1   *Sample Test Lab Topology*

For this guide, the Cisco wide-area network (WAN)-Bridge WAN emulation software is used for WAN simulation and is set to simulate a T1 link with 80 ms round trip latency and 0.5% packet loss. WAN-Bridge is a WAN emulation tool developed by Cisco and is based on Linux netem function. The ISO image of WAN-Bridge can be downloaded free from Cisco.com (a login is required) and run on any system that has two NICs and can boot from CD (http://www.cisco.com/cgi-bin/tablebuild.pl/fe_util). To use WAN-Bridge, burn the ISO file to a CD as a boot image and boot the system from this CD.

Test files of various sizes need to be staged on the Microsoft Windows file server and made accessible via IIS. A *5MB.ppt* test file (with 5 MB file size) is used in this quickstart guide as an example to demonstrate the testing process. This file is staged on the file server in the shared directory on a file share on the Microsoft Windows file server and hosted on the web server running on Microsoft IIS.

Inline is the preferred interception method for WAAS demonstration or lab tests due to its simplicity and is recommended on both client and server sides. To demonstrate the usage of the device setup wizard with inline and WCCPv2 interception methods, this quickstart guide leads you through configuration of inline on the client side and WCCP on the server side.

Baseline Performance Tests

Before turning on WAAS optimization, you should establish baseline application performance for key applications and application protocols driving the WAN optimization decision. This quickstart guide illustrates the process of performance test before and after WAAS installation using CIFS and FTP. Other applications or protocols can be added to the testing and the selection of applications should reflect an organization's business goals and priorities.

Table A-1 shows a sample worksheet, which can be used and modified to track the before and after performance measurements. In this table, *native* refers to *no optimization; cold* refers to the performance achieved during the first pass with WAAS optimization; and *hot* refers to the performance achieved on subsequent tests using the same data.

It is worth noting that a variety of testing tools are available and can be used to test and measure application performance. Although the quickstart guide doesn't cover the usage of these tools, the "Application Testing Tools" section found later in this appendix provides a list of available tools.

Table A-1 *Application Test Sample Worksheet*

Application or Application Protocols	Operations Tested	File Name and Size	Native Time	WAAS Cold Time	WAAS Hot Time
CIFS	Copy and Paste	5MB.ppt			
CIFS	Drag and Drop	5MB.ppt			
CIFS	Edit and Save	5MB.ppt			
FTP	Put	5MB.ppt			
FTP	Get	5MB.ppt			

Baseline Measurements of Windows File Services

To measure baseline performance of Windows file services, follow these steps:

Step 1.   Connect to the Branch Office MS Windows XP workstation and log in using either the physical console or using Remote Desktop Protocol (RDP) or similar remote desktop access tool.

Step 2.   Verify network connectivity and determine WAN latency. You can accomplish this by clicking **Start > Run** and entering the command **cmd** to access a command window. Issue the command **ping** *server IP address*. Note the latency of the WAN as shown in Figure A-2. In this example, the average round trip time (RTT) is 80 ms.

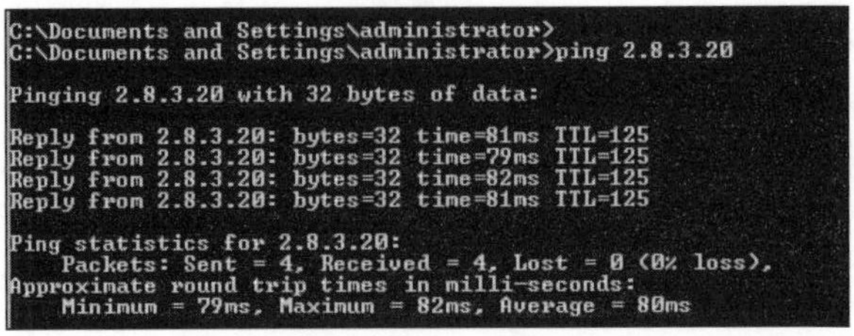

Figure A-2   *Verify WAN Emulation Settings*

Step 3.   Map a network drive using the **net use** command as demonstrated in the example in Figure A-3. Supply the login credentials necessary to access the share if required. Confirm the network mapping by issuing the **net use** command as shown in Figure A-3.

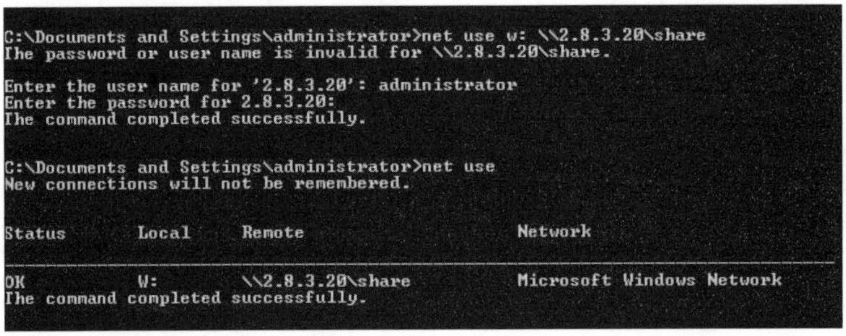

Figure A-3   *Map Network Drive*

Step 4.   Open the file share and locate the test file **5MB.ppt** in the file share. Copy the file from the file share by right-clicking on the file name and selecting **copy**.

Step 5.   From the client desktop, right-click and select **Paste** to start the file transfer using CIFS. Measure the time taken for this operation using a stopwatch, and record it under the **Native Time** column in the worksheet presented in Table A-1.

Note   Other operations, such as opening a file on the remote file share or saving a file to the remote file share, can also be performed during baseline testing. The entries in Table A-1 have been created for you.

Step 6.   Delete the copied file on the desktop. Close the file share on the client desktop.

Step 7.   Connect to the file server by either using RDP from the client desktop or via physical console access. Log in to the server.

Step 8. On the server, click **Start > Programs > Administrative Tools > Computer Management**. In the Computer Management window, under **System Tools > Shared Folders**, select **Sessions**. Connected sessions are displayed in the right panel. The connected client workstations are identified by either the computer names or IP addresses. Select the established session from your client workstation and right-click it. Choose **Close Session** to disconnect the CIFS session. See Figure A-4.

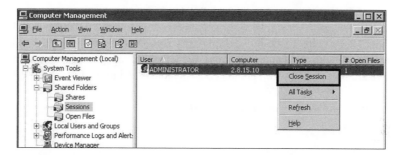

Figure A-4 *Disconnect Persistent CIFS Session*

Note CIFS connections are persistent. Enabling WAAS optimization after CIF connection establishment causes the CIFS connection to be put in pass-through (PT) mode by WAAS. To ensure that client sessions are disconnected from the server, close the session from the server or reboot the client workstation. This can also be accomplished by simply logging out of the client workstation and then logging back in.

Baseline Measurements of FTP

To measure baseline performance of the FTP application, perform the steps in the list that follows. Ensure that the test files are accessible via FTP. The FTP server properties can be examined in the IIS MMC window, which shows the directory on the server into which the files should be placed.

Step 1. From the client workstation, open a command window by selecting **Start > Run** and entering the command **cmd**, and then click **Ok**.

Step 2. From the command line, enter **ftp** *server IP address*. Log in to the FTP server. List the files in the FTP root directory using either the **ls** or **dir** command, and locate the test file 5MB.ppt.

Step 3. Download the test file by typing **get** *file name*. The file transfer using FTP starts.

Step 4. Upon completion of the file transfer, the amount of time taken for this file transfer is reported by the FTP utility. Record the time under the **Native Time** column in the worksheet in Table A-1.

Configure WAAS Using Setup Wizard

After you capture the baseline performance measurements, use the setup wizard to enable basic WAAS optimization. The WAAS CM should be configured before any of the application accelerators.

Configure WAAS Central Manager Using Setup Wizard

Connect to the serial console port of the WAAS device with terminal emulation software such as HyperTerminal or similar. Set the connection properties to use your serial port, 9600 baud, 8 data bits, 1 stop bit, and no parity bits. Disable hardware flow control. Log in to the device with the default username and password (admin, default), and start the setup wizard by entering **setup** command as demonstrated in the following:

```
Cisco Wide Area Application Engine Console
Username: admin
Password:
System Initialization Finished.
NO-HOSTNAME# setup


Press the ESC key at any time to quit this session.
WARNING: Changing any of the network settings from a
telnet session may render the device inaccessible on
the network. Therefore it is suggested that you have
access to the console before modifying the network settings.
```

The setup wizard begins with a set of default configuration parameters based on common best practices and the result of hardware and software discovery. The device mode is set to application-accelerator by default. Enter **n** when prompted to reject the default parameters and start to configure each element from beginning.

Step 1.   The following defaults can be configured:

```
Device mode: Application-accelerator
Interception Method: WCCP
Management Interface: GigabitEthernet 1/0
Autosense: yes
DHCP: yes
Timezone: UTC 0 0
To keep above defaults and continue configuration, press 'y'
To change above defaults and continue configuration, press 'n' [y]: n
```

Step 2.   The device mode needs to be configured first. WAAS devices are set to be application-accelerator by default. Select **2** to change the device mode to central-manager. Changing the device mode from application-accelerator to central-manager requires a reboot of the device. Press **Enter** to enable the device to automatically enable CMS after reboot:

```
Configure WAAS Settings
— — — — — — — — — — —
Select device mode :
1.application-accelerator
2.central-manager
Enter your choice [1]: 2


This configuration will take effect after a reload.
Enable CMS automatically after reload(y/n) [y]:
```

Step 3. Select the management interface to be used for WAAS CM communication with the WAAS devices that it manages. A list of available interfaces along with the status of each interface is presented. In this lab setup, the GigabitEthernet 1/0 interface is connected and is used for management. Press 1 to select the GigabitEthernet 1/0 interface:

```
Configure network settings
— — — — — — — — — — — —.
Select interface to configure as management interface:

NO    INTERFACE NAME        STATUS    IP ADDRESS    NETMASK
1: GigabitEthernet 1/0     UP        unassigned    unassigned
2: GigabitEthernet 2/0     DOWN      unassigned    unassigned
Enter choice [1]:
```

Step 4. Next, configure the appropriate network setting for the management interface (speed and duplex or auto-negotiation), network layer configuration (Dynamic Host Configuration Protocol [DHCP] configuration, a static IP address, subnet mask, default gateway, DNS server, NTP server, and domain name), hostname, and time zone. Refer to the lab topology in Figure A-1 for the IP addresses used in this example:

```
Configure autosense for duplex and speed on this interface(y/n)[y]:
Enable DHCP on this interface (y/n) [n]:
IP address of interface: 2.8.10.100
Netmask of this interface: 255.255.255.0
Default gateway: 2.8.10.1
Domain name server IP: 2.8.3.2
Domain name: csbu.local
Enter hostname[none]: CM
Configure NTP [none]:
Enter timezone [UTC 0 0] :PST -8 0
```

Step 5.   Finally, the setup process prompts for license configuration based on the device mode configured and the hardware platform. On devices configured with the CM device mode, only the Enterprise license is presented, because the CM requires the Enterprise license:

```
The product supports the following licenses:
1. Enterprise
Enter the license(s) you purchased [1]:
```

Step 6.   Based on the parameters entered, the configuration is presented for review. Review the configuration, and press **Enter** to accept the configuration. Press **Enter** again to apply the configuration:

```
Based on the input, the following configurations will be done:
Press the ESC key at any time to quit this session.

device mode central-manager
no central-manager address
no wccp version 2
interface GigabitEthernet 1/0
ip address 2.8.10.100 255.255.255.0
autosense
exit
ip default-gateway 2.8.10.1
ip name-server 2.8.3.2
ip domain-name  csbu.local
primary-interface GigabitEthernet 1/0
hostname CM
clock timezone PST -8 0

Do you accept these configurations (y/n) [y]:

Would you like to apply the configurations (y/n) [y]:

This may take few moments. Please wait..
All CLI configurations were applied successfully.
Press the ESC key at any time to quit this session

For your reference, configuration generated
during this setup session is available at
/local1/setup_gen_config.txt.
You can view this file with the command, "type /local1/setup_gen_con-
fig.txt".

Press any key to continue..
```

Step 7.   At this point, configuration changes have been applied successfully. Because the device mode has been changed to CM, a reload is required on the device. Save the configuration and reload the device:

```
CM# write memory
CM# reload

Proceed with reload?[confirm] yes
Shutting down all services, will timeout in 15 minutes.
reload in progress ..
```

Step 8.   After the device has reloaded, log in to the CLI and verify that the Central Management Service (CMS) is running using the command **show cms info**:

```
CM# show cms info
Device registration information :
Device Id                             = 164
Device registered as                  = WAAS Central Manager
Current WAAS Central Manager role     = Primary

CMS services information :
Service cms_httpd is running
Service cms_cdm is running
```

Step 9.   After verifying the status of the CMS service, disconnect from the console port. The CM configuration is complete.

Configure Server-Side WAAS Device Using Setup Wizard

The steps in this section configure the server-side WAAS device with WCCPv2 interception.

Connect to the server-side WAAS device console port with terminal emulation software. Set the connection to use your serial port, 9600 baud, 8 data bits, 1 stop bit, and no parity bits. Disable any flow control. Log in to the device with the default username and password (admin/default), and start the setup process by entering **setup** command at the NO_HOSTNAME# prompt:

```
Cisco Wide Area Application Engine Console

Username: admin
Password:

System Initialization Finished.
NO-HOSTNAME# setup
WARNING: Changing any of the network settings from a
```

```
telnet session may render the device inaccessible on
the network. Therefore it is suggested that you have
access to the console before modifying the network settings.
```

The setup wizard begins with a set of default configuration parameters based on common best practices and the result of hardware and software discovery. The default configuration can be accepted if applicable. In this lab setup, IP addresses are assigned statically. Type **n** to reject the default and start configuration of each parameter from the beginning.

Step 1.   The following defaults can be configured:

```
Device mode: Application-accelerator
Interception Method: WCCP
Management Interface: GigabitEthernet 1/0
Autosense: yes
DHCP: yes
Timezone: UTC 0 0
To keep above defaults and continue configuration, press 'y'

To change above defaults and continue configuration, press 'n' [y]: n
```

Step 2.   Configure the device mode of the server-side WAAS device to be an application-accelerator:

```
Configure WAAS Settings
— — — — — — — — — — —
Select device mode :
1.application-accelerator
2.central-manager
Enter your choice [1]:
```

Step 3.   Provide the IP address of the CM:

```
Enter Central Manager address [none] : 2.8.10.100
```

Step 4.   Select the interception method for the server-side WAAS device. When an inline card is not detected in the hardware configuration, **wccp** is presented by the setup wizard as the default interception method. Select WCCP if it is not presented as the default interception method, because WCCP is what is used in this guide.

```
Select interception method (inline¦wccp¦other) [wccp]:
```

Step 5.   Select the management interface to be used for communicating with the CM. In the case of WCCP interception, the setup wizard also uses the management interface for traffic interception and optimization. A list of available interfaces, along with the status of each interface, is presented. In this lab setup, the GigabitEthernet 1/0 interface is connected and used:

```
Configure network settings
```

```
— — — — — — — — — — — — — —.
Select interface to configure as management interface:

NO     INTERFACE NAME        STATUS   IP ADDRESS    NETMASK
  1:   GigabitEthernet 1/0   UP       unassigned    unassigned
  2:   GigabitEthernet 2/0   DOWN     unassigned    unassigned
Enter choice [1]:
```

Step 6.   Configure the network settings for the management interface (speed and duplex or auto-negotiation), network layer configuration (DHCP or static IP address, subnet mask, default gateway, DNS server, NTP server, and domain name), hostname, and time zone. In this lab setup, no DHCP server is deployed and IP addresses are assigned statically. Refer to the lab topology in Figure A-1 for IP address assignment.

```
Configure autosense for duplex and speed on this interface(y/n)[y]:
Enable DHCP on this interface (y/n) [n]:
IP address of interface: 2.8.10.10
Netmask of this interface: 255.255.255.0
Default gateway: 2.8.10.1
Domain name server IP:    2.8.3.2
Domain name: csbu.local
Enter hostname[none]: DC-WAE
Configure NTP [none]:
Enter timezone [UTC 0 0] :PST -8 0
```

Step 7.   Next, configure the WCCPv2 router list, which contains a list of devices that can redirect traffic to this WAAS device. Up to four devices can be defined in one router list. The default redirect device is prompted by the setup wizard using the default gateway IP address configured on the WAAS device. In this lab setup, the default gateway is the WCCPv2 router. Accept the default by simply pressing **Enter**.

```
Enter the space separated list of routers(maximum 4) for WCCPv2
[2.8.10.1]:
```

Step 8.   The setup process then prompts for license configuration based on the device mode configured and the hardware platform. On devices configured as application accelerators, available licenses include Transport, Enterprise, Video, and Virtual-Blade. The setup wizard presents a list of possible combinations. On virtualization capable devices (including all WAVE platforms and the WAE-674), the additional option of Virtual-Blade license is presented:

```
The product supports the following licenses:
1. Transport
2. Enterprise
3. Enterprise & Video
Enter the license(s) you purchased [2]:
```

Step 9.   Finally, the setup process offers a configuration template that can be used to configure the WCCPv2 redirection device. This quickstart guide does not cover the configuration steps of the redirection device and assumes the redirection router is fully configured. More information on configuration of WCCP redirection and configuration examples can be found in Chapter 5, "Branch Office Network Integration," and Chapter 6, "Data Center Network Integration."

```
Please copy, paste the following in the router config mode:
ip wccp version 2
ip wccp 61
ip wccp 62
interface <Router LAN sub-interface 1>
ip wccp 61 redirect in
interface <Router WAN interface>
ip wccp 62 redirect in
interface <Router LAN sub-interface 2>
ip wccp redirect exclude in

Please type 'ENTER' to continue...
```

Step 10.   Based on the parameters entered, the final configuration is presented for review. Review the configuration, and press **Enter** to accept the configuration. Press **Enter** again to apply the configuration:

```
Based on the input, the following configurations will be done:
central-manager address 2.8.10.100
interface GigabitEthernet 1/0
ip address 2.8.10.10 255.255.255.0
autosense
exit
ip default-gateway 2.8.10.1
ip name-server 2.8.3.2
ip domain-name  csbu.local
primary-interface GigabitEthernet 1/0
hostname DC-WAE
clock timezone PST -8 0
wccp version 2
wccp router-list 8 2.8.10.1
wccp tcp-promiscuous router-list 8
cms enable
```

```
Do you accept these configurations (y/n) [y]:

Would you like to apply the configurations (y/n) [y]:
This may take few moments. Please wait..
Please wait. Running 'cms enable'..


All CLI configurations were applied successfully.

For your reference, configuration generated
during this setup session is available at
/local1/setup_gen_config.txt.
You can view this file with the command, "type /local1/setup_gen_con-
fig.txt".


Press any key to continue..
```

Step 11. The server-side WAAS device configuration is complete. Verify the network connectivity to the CM by pinging the CM IP address. If the default gateway or CM is unreachable, check your network configuration and make corrections where appropriate. Verify that the device is registered to the CM by using the **show cms info** command:

```
DC-WAE#show cms info

Device registration information :
Device Id                             = 233
Device registered as                  = WAAS Application Engine
Current WAAS Central Manager          = 2.8.10.100
Registered with WAAS Central Manager  = 2.8.10.100
Status                                = Online
Time of last config-sync              = Thu May 14 03:14:05 2009
```

Note   If the device status shows **Pending (CM is Busy) retry later**, wait a moment, and try the **show cms info** command again.

Configure Client-Side WAE Using Setup Wizard

The steps in this section configure the client-side WAAS device with inline interception. Connect to the client-side WAAS device console port with terminal emulation software such as HyperTerminal. Set the connection to use your serial port, 9600 baud, 8 data bits, 1 stop bit, and no parity bits. Disable any flow control. Log in to the device with the default username and password (admin, default), and start the setup process by entering the **setup** command at the NO_HOSTNAME# prompt:

```
Cisco Wide Area Application Engine Console

Username: admin
Password:

System Initialization Finished.
NO-HOSTNAME# setup
WARNING: Changing any of the network settings from a
telnet session may render the device inaccessible on
the network. Therefore it is suggested that you have
access to the console before modifying the network settings.
```

The setup wizard has detected the presence of an inline card and suggested using inline for interception and using the inline group interface for management. This default configuration can be accepted as shown if applicable. In this lab setup, inline group interfaces are used for interception and the GigabitEthernet 1/0 interface is used for management. Type **n** to reject the default, and start the configuration of each parameter from the beginning:

Step 1.   The following defaults can be configured:

```
Device mode: Application-accelerator
Interception Method: Inline
Management Interface: InlineGroup 1/1
Autosense: yes
Timezone: UTC 0 0


To keep above defaults and continue configuration, press 'y'
To change above defaults and continue configuration, press 'n' [y]: n
```

Step 2.   Configure the device mode of the client-side WAAS device to be an application-accelerator, and provide the IP address of the CM:

```
Configure WAAS Settings
_ _ _ _ _ _ _ _ _ _ _ _
Select device mode :
1.application-accelerator
2.central-manager
Enter your choice [1]:
Enter Central Manager address [none] : 2.8.10.100
```

Step 3.   As inline interfaces are detected, the inline interception method is provided by the setup wizard as the recommended default. Accept the default to select inline interception:

```
Select interception method (inline¦wccp¦other) [inline]:
```

Step 4.   Select the management interface. In the case of inline interception, any of the inline group interfaces or Gigabit Ethernet interfaces can be used for communicating with the CM. A list of available interfaces and the status of each interface is presented. In this lab setup, the GigabitEthernet 1/0 interface is connected and is used for management traffic. Type **3** to select this interface as the management interface:

```
Configure network settings
— — — — — — — — — — — — .

Select interface to configure as management interface:

    NO        INTERFACE NAME    STATUS    IP ADDRESS    NETMASK
    1:        InlineGroup 1/0   UP        unassigned    unassigned
    2:        InlineGroup 1/1   UP        unassigned    unassigned
    3: GigabitEthernet 1/0      UP        unassigned    unassigned
    4: GigabitEthernet 2/0      DOWN      unassigned    unassigned
Enter choice [1]: 3
```

Step 5.   Configure the network settings for the management interface (speed and duplex or auto-negotiation), network layer configuration (DHCP or static IP address, subnet mask, default gateway, DNS server, NTP server, and domain name), hostname, and time zone. In this lab, no DHCP server is deployed and IP addresses are assigned statically. Refer to the lab topology figure for IP address assignment:

```
Configure autosense for duplex and speed on this interface(y/n)[y]:
Enable DHCP on this interface (y/n) [n]:
IP address of interface: 2.8.14.10
Netmask of this interface: 255.255.255.0
Default gateway: 2.8.14.1
Domain name server IP: 2.8.3.2
Domain name: csbu.local
Enter hostname[none]: BR-WAE
Configure NTP [none]:
Enter timezone [UTC 0 0] :PST -8 0
```

Step 6.   When the four-port inline card is present, two inline groups are available. Select the inline group for interception. In this lab setup, the inline group 1/0 is connected and is used for interception. The group you select should be the group that is deployed inline between your switch and router:

```
Select interface for inline interception:
1) InlineGroup 1/0
2) InlineGroup 1/1
Enter choice : 1
Configure autosense for duplex and speed on this interface(y/n)[y]:
```

Step 7.   As seen in the previous section, license configuration options are provided based on the device mode configured and the hardware platform. In this case, a virtualization capable device is used, thus the available license options are Enterprise, Enterprise & Video, Enterprise & Virtual-Blade, and Enterprise, Video & Virtual-Blade:

```
The product supports the following licenses:
1. Enterprise
2. Enterprise & Video
3. Enterprise & Virtual-Blade
4. Enterprise, Video & Virtual-Blade
Enter the license(s) you purchased [1]: 4
```

Step 8.   Based on the parameters entered, the configuration is presented for review. Review the configuration, and press **Enter** to accept the configuration. Press **Enter** again to apply the configuration:

```
Based on the input, the following configurations will be done:
central-manager address 2.8.10.100
interface GigabitEthernet 1/0
ip address 2.8.14.10 255.255.255.0
autosense
exit
ip default-gateway 2.8.14.1
ip name-server 2.8.3.2
ip domain-name  csbu.local
primary-interface GigabitEthernet 1/0
hostname BR-WAE
clock timezone PST -8 0
interface InlineGroup 1/0
no shutdown
autosense
exit
cms enable

Do you accept these configurations (y/n) [y]:

Would you like to apply the configurations (y/n) [y]:
This may take few moments. Please wait..
Please wait. Running 'cms enable'..All CLI configurations were
applied successfully.

For your reference, configuration generated
during this setup session is available at
/local1/setup_gen_config.txt.
You can view this file with the command, "type /local1/setup_gen_con-
fig.txt".

Press any key to continue..
```

Step 9.   The client-side WAE configuration is completed. Verify the network connectivity to the CM by pinging the CM IP address. If the default gateway or CM is unreachable, check your network configuration and make corrections where appropriate. Verify that the device is registered to the CM by using the **show cms info** command:

```
BR-WAE# show cms info
Device registration information :
Device Id                            = 219
Device registered as                 = WAAS Application Engine
Current WAAS Central Manager          = 2.8.10.100
Registered with WAAS Central Manager  = 2.8.10.100
Status                               = Online
Time of last config-sync             = Thu May 14 03:15:01 2009
```

Note   If the device status shows **Pending (CM is Busy) retry later,** wait a moment and try the **show cms info** command again.

WAAS Setup Verification

Device configuration and CM registration are completed on all WAAS devices in the previous sections. The WAAS devices automatically start to optimize traffic, and the CM begins to manage registered WAAS devices and collect statistics. Follow the steps in this section to access the CM GUI:

Step 1.   Open your web browser from either the client workstation or the server, and connect to the CM using the URL of **https://<CM IP address>:8443**

Step 2.   Log in using the default credentials (admin/default). You see the CM home page. Click on the **Manage Devices** entry under the **My WAN** drawer, and verify that all three devices are online and that no major alarms are present, as shown in Figure A-5.

Figure A-5   *Verify CM Registration and Device Status from CM GUI*

Measure Application Performance with WAAS Enabled

WAAS devices are now ready to accelerate traffic. In this section, application optimization tests are run using CIFS and FTP (identical to the native/baseline tests performed previously). A *cold* transfer is when the data is requested by the user for the first time. A *cold* transfer populates the Data Redundancy Elimination (DRE) compression history and CIFS object cache (when CIFS is used).

The subsequent transfers of the same file are considered *hot*, as the compression history and any object caches are populated with the data. A *warm* transfer is transmitting a modified file when the data cache is populated with the original file.

Performance Measurements of Windows File Transfer with WAAS Enabled

Perform the steps in the list that follows to measure performance of Windows File Transfer application.

Step 1.   Connect to the client workstation and verify there is no existing CIFS session by using the **net use** command. If there is any existing session, forcefully disconnect the session from the server by following Step 8 in the "Baseline Measurement of Windows File Transfer" section.

Step 2.   Follow Steps 3 through 6 in the "Baseline Measure of Windows File Services" section. Measure the time taken for this operation using a stopwatch, and record it under the **WAAS Cold Time** column in the worksheet presented in Table A-1.

Note   Other operations, such as opening a file on the remote file share or saving a file to the remote file share, can also be performed during baseline testing and cold testing. The worksheet provided in Table A-1 can be used to record the time taken for each operation.

Step 3.   Delete the copied file from the desktop.

Step 4.   Repeat Steps 3 to 6 in the "Baseline Measure of Windows File Services" section to perform a hot transfer.

Step 5.   Record the time taken for the hot transfer under the **WAAS Optimized (Hot)** in the worksheet provided in Table A-1.

Note   The DRE compression history and CIFS cache can be reset to force a *cold* transfer during lab tests. To reset either of these, you can use the CLI command **clear cache {dre | cifs}**. This command is disruptive because it restarts the TCP proxy or CIFS processes (based on the selection used in the command). As a result, all existing optimized connections are reset. In addition, some application or application protocols (CIFS and NFS, as examples) with persistent connections are passed through by WAAS after the cache has been cleared. The impact of this command needs to be carefully considered before execution. Recommended practice dictates limiting usage of the **clear cache** command to lab testing only or when directed by Cisco TAC.

Hot Transfer Measurements of FTP

Because the DRE cache is protocol agnostic, data transferred by one protocol populates the DRE compression history and can be used by other protocols. Another protocol accessing the same data set benefits from the DRE contents generated by traffic that used a different protocol. The following steps demonstrate using the FTP application to access the same file transferred by CIFS protocol earlier. This is a *hot* transfer as the DRE compression history is already populated. If the *cold* transfer performance needs to be measured for each application or protocol in the testing process, use the **clear cache dre** command to clear the DRE cache. Be aware of the impact of this command as stated in the previous section:

Step 1.   From the client workstation, open a command window by select **Start > Run**, enter **cmd** and click **Ok**.

Step 2.   From the command line, enter **ftp** *server IP address* and log in to the ftp server. List the files in the ftp root directory and locate the test file 5MB.ppt.

Step 3.   Download the test file by typing **get** *file name*. The file transfer starts.

Step 4.   Upon completion of the file transfer, the amount of time taken for this file transfer is reported by the ftp utility. Record the time under the **WAAS Hot Time** column in the worksheet in Table A-1.

Examine WAAS Optimization Results from CM

Application response time improvements achieved are measured in the applications used for testing and can be documented in a worksheet as illustrated in Table A-1 in previous sections. More detailed application response time reporting can be accomplished through use of the Cisco Network Analysis Module (NAM) or a third-party product such as NetQoS Performance Center. The WAAS CM collects traffic statistics and offers a rich set of reports on application traffic and optimization results. This section samples a few charts available in the CM. A detailed review of available charts and reports can be obtained from Chapters 7, "System and Device Management," Chapter 8, "Configuring WAN Optimization," and Chapter 9, "Configuring Application Acceleration," or from online documentation.

Figure A-6 shows the system-wide traffic summary. On the upper half of the screen, **Traffic Summary** charts display top volume applications in a pie chart format, along with original and optimized traffic over time. You can customize the screen through the **Settings** button and selecting different charts and reporting timeframes. The **System**

Traffic Summary table displayed at the bottom of the page contains the traffic summary of each device. The Original (LAN side), optimized (WAN side) and pass-through (un-optimized) traffic volumes are displayed, along with calculated results of bandwidth reduction and effective capacity. You can use this page to summarize overall application traffic distribution and compression benefit of WAAS devices.

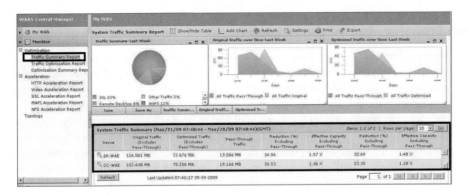

Figure A-6 *System Traffic Summary Charts*

Traffic-optimization and application-acceleration statistics are generally more relevant on the client-side WAAS devices, where acceleration is most needed and where additional optimization technologies such as object caching, local response handling, and stream-splitting are applied. Therefore, application-acceleration and traffic-optimization reports should be examined from the context of the client-side WAAS device. Figure A-7 shows an example of Application Traffic Mix report from the client side device. The original (LAN side), optimized (WAN side), and pass-through (un-optimized) traffic statistics for each monitored application and calculated results of bandwidth reduction and effective capacity are presented in this table.

Acceleration charts and reports are specific to application accelerators. These charts can be used for reporting application-specific bandwidth and response-time improvements. Connection statistics and bypass-reasons charts are also available and can be used for troubleshooting purposes. Figure A-8 shows an example of available SSL acceleration charts, containing information on connection statistics, bandwidth optimization, and acceleration bypass reasons pertinent to the SSL sessions going through the WAAS device.

Application Testing Tools

This appendix has provided a basic step-by-step guide to configuring WAAS devices for the purpose of simple application-acceleration testing using the setup wizard and CM GUI for validation. The effect of WAAS optimization was demonstrated with CIFS and FTP with a manual traffic generation process and stop-watch measurement approach. Although the manual approach is sufficient for user-level demonstration, automation is desirable to simulate multi-user environments, generate more data points for analysis, and eliminate the ever-present human error factor. Table A-2 lists some examples of useful tools to generate application traffic, which can be employed in WAN optimization tests.

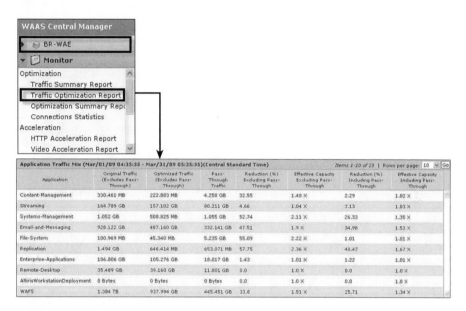

Figure A-7   *Device Level Application Traffic Mix Report*

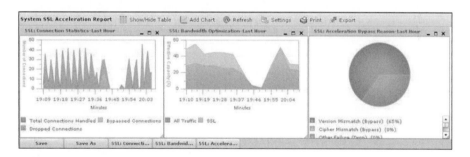

Figure A-8   *SSL Acceleration Charts*

Summary

This appendix provided a simple step-by-step guide to configure WAAS devices, including the CM and two application accelerator devices, using the setup wizard available from the WAAS 4.1.3 software. Baseline (native) application performance is established before enabling WAAS and is compared with measurements taken after WAAS deployment to demonstrate the improvements. Through the WAAS CM, a rich set of charts and tables are available to monitor the effectiveness of WAAS optimization and acceleration.

Appendix B

Troubleshooting Guide

A successful Wide Area Application Services (WAAS) deployment begins with good design and planning. The content of this book equips you with the knowledge to design, integrate, and deploy WAAS in an enterprise network. As all applications and networks are not created equal, even with a well-planned and carefully designed WAAS network, there can be occasional and unexpected performance challenges. Although the symptoms of the performance challenges might be similar—slow application response time, for example—the causes of the issue could come from different sources. Having a solid understanding of the application data flow is important to troubleshooting the source of performance degradation.

The first step in isolating whether performance or other challenges are WAAS-related is to examine the traffic interception and the health of the WAAS devices in the optimization path. Is application traffic simply being passed through by the WAAS devices? In the situation where the application traffic is being processed by WAAS, what optimization techniques are applied to the traffic and how effective are each of the techniques? Sometimes performance issues are not WAAS-related. For example, they might be due to an overloaded server or high amount of traffic on the network. Tools such as NetQoS SuperAgent and the Cisco Network Analysis Module (NAM) track and measure end-to-end application response time (ART) and provide metrics such as network, server, and application latency. These tools are valuable in establishing a baseline and identifying the bottleneck of application performance, especially when the performance-limiting factors are not related to WAAS.

In addition to application-performance improvements, customers deploying WAAS also expect the benefits of higher bandwidth efficiency from data reduction and compression and other techniques such as TCP optimization and application acceleration. When the overall compression ratio is low, it is helpful to understand the percentage of the data being optimized as compared to being passed through, the reasons of passthrough, and whether the data sets are good candidates for optimization.

This appendix focuses on the most common optimization challenges encountered in WAAS implementations, their possible causes, and steps to rectify these issues. The validation process for the most common issues, such as interception, duplex, and policy configuration are examined in detail. This appendix also reviews the troubleshooting capabilities provided by the WAAS Central Manager (CM), including the CM diagnostic tool and platform monitoring functions. Finally, the appendix discusses generation of a system report, which is useful for further troubleshooting activities.

Note   This appendix provides high-level guidelines to the most common issues found in WAAS deployments and does not cover all possible application performance issues.

Common Issues with WAAS Deployment

Table B-1 provides a summary of the most common symptoms seen in WAAS deployment, their possible causes, and the suggested actions to resolve these issues.

The following sections focus on the key areas that cause most of the common issues. These areas include duplex, auto-discovery, interception and WCCP configuration, firewall integration, low compression ratios, and application policy configuration.

Table B-1   *Possible Causes and Resolutions for Common WAAS Deployment Issues*

Common Issues	Possible Causes	Verification and Resolution
Performance Degradation on All Applications	Half-duplex interface operation.	Check duplex settings end to end, including WAAS devices, routers, switches, clients, servers, and any other intermediary devices. Half-duplex can bring performance to a crawl if found anywhere in the path between client and server.
	WCCP running on nonsupported IOS version and/or platform.	Upgrade the WCCP redirecting device to supported hardware platform and/or IOS version. Legacy hardware and older IOS versions might not provide the optimal operating environment for traffic diversion.
Performance Degradation on Certain Applications	Policy configuration.	Review and modify policy configured on WAAS devices. Incorrect policies could lead to less than optimal optimization.
Low Compression Ratio	Application data is pre-compressed or encrypted.	Turn off application-native compression and encryption.
		For SSL traffic, configure SSL accelerated service on the WAAS devices to accelerated SSL traffic.
		Alternatively, if encryption cannot be changed, change the application policy to TFO-only optimization. Pre-compressed or pre-encrypted traffic makes it difficult for additional levels of compression or redundancy elimination to be applied.

Table B-1   *Possible Causes and Resolutions for Common WAAS Deployment Issues*

Common Issues	Possible Causes	Verification and Resolution
No Performance Improvements Observed on Any Application (Auto-Discovery Failures)	No peer.	Verify interception for both client and server side WAAS devices. Verify that devices exist on both ends of the network.
	Asymmetric routing.	Verify interception for both inbound and out-bound directions, and ensure that all ingress and egress points within a location are covered by network interception.
	Overload.	Verify connection statistics on both WAAS devices. Connections beyond the rated device capacity are handled as pass-through. If necessary, trim back certain policies to limit the scope of applications that WAAS provides optimization for.
	Firewall in the acceleration path.	On Cisco firewall devices, enable WAAS inspection. On non-Cisco firewall devices, change the policy to allow WAAS auto-discovery. Alternatively, if these firewall devices cannot be changed, use WAAS directed mode. If the device is scrubbing TCP options, disable this behavior, or consider deploying the device on the LAN-side of WAAS.
Performance Improvement Seen for Only Some Users	Redirect list, VLAN not included for inline interception.	Verify WCCP redirect list configuration, and inline port VLAN configuration.
	Persistent sessions that existed prior to enabling optimization.	Reset persistent sessions to ensure the initial setup is intercepted by WAAS devices.

Table B-1   *Possible Causes and Resolutions for Common WAAS Deployment Issues*

Common Issues	Possible Causes	Verification and Resolution
Applications Not Working after WAAS Installation	Traffic blackhole caused by WCCP redirection loop.	Use **redirect exclude** configuration if **redirect out** is used, or ensure that WCCP negotiated return egress method is assigned when the WAE is on the host subnet.
	Firewall in the path between WAAS devices dropping traffic.	On Cisco firewall devices, enable WAAS inspection. On non-Cisco firewall devices, use directed mode, or permit TCP options and TCP traffic that has shifted sequence numbers.

Half-Duplex

Duplex mismatches are one of the most common issues that lead to performance problems. In a network with 10/100 Ethernet, when one side is configured with full-duplex, and the other side is configured to auto-negotiate the duplex setting, it can result in a half-duplex condition between the two devices. Half-duplex causes poor performance on all applications traversing the link. The application traffic appears to be intercepted and optimized by WAAS; however, the application performance is poor and the LAN throughput is low.

When half-duplex conditions are detected on the WAAS interfaces, an alarm is generated on the Command Line Interface (CLI), Syslog, and in the CM Graphical User Interface (GUI). The diagnostic tool discussed in later sections of this appendix can also check for half-duplex on WAAS interfaces. In addition, issuing the **show interface** command on a WAAS device also provides the negotiated speed and duplex information on the interface. As Example B-1 shows, collision and interrupt counts increment when an interface is in half-duplex mode.

Example B-1   *Detecting Half-Duplex*

```
WAE# show interface gigabitEthernet 1/0
Type:Ethernet
Ethernet address:00:14:5E:AC:2D:79
Internet address:10.88.80.135
Broadcast address:10.88.80.255
Netmask:255.255.255.128
Maximum Transfer Unit Size:1500
Metric:1
Packets Received: 14298
Input Errors: 0
```

```
Input Packets Dropped: 0
Input Packets Overruns: 0
Input Packets Frames: 0
Packet Sent: 12946
Output Errors: 0
Output Packets Dropped: 0
Output Packets Overruns: 0
Output Packets Carrier: 0
Output Queue Length:1000
Collisions: 64
Interrupts:16
Flags:UP BROADCAST RUNNING MULTICAST
Mode: autoselect, half-duplex, 100baseTX
```

Half-duplex conditions can exist anywhere in the network, not necessarily on a link connected to a WAAS interface. A half-duplex condition might even exist before the WAAS implementation resulting in a negative impact on the application performance before WAAS installation. The negative performance impact of half-duplex is amplified by WAAS optimization, as more data packets are placed on the LAN at any given time, more collisions are generated on a half-duplex network. Therefore, the duplex condition needs to be examined end-to-end, segment-by-segment, and from client to server. This includes all intermediary devices in the path between client and server, including switches, routers, firewalls, WAAS devices, and others that might exist.

Pass-Through Traffic

After the completion of WAAS installation and initial setup, WAAS optimization starts immediately on a network with traffic flows. Use the **show statistics connection** command to verify that connections are intercepted and optimized by the WAAS devices. If this command returns no connections, then the interception method and its configuration and statistics should be examined carefully. More details on common issues with interception are discussed in the next section.

The output of the **show statistics connection** command also provides visibility into whether an intercepted connection is being optimized, the type of optimization applied for optimized connections, and the reasons for pass-through on pass-through connections. Example B-2 shows sample output from this command.

Example B-2   *Review Connection Statistics*

```
WAE# show statistics connection

Current Active Optimized Flows:                         4
   Current Active Optimized TCP Plus Flows:             3
   Current Active Optimized TCP Only Flows:             1
   Current Active Optimized TCP Preposition Flows:      0
Current Active Auto-Discovery Flows:                    0
Current Active Pass-Through Flows:                       0
Historical Flows:                                       100



D:DRE,L:LZ,T:TCP Optimization,
A:AOIM,C:CIFS,E:EPM,G:GENERIC,H:HTTP,M:MAPI,N:NFS,S:SSL,V:VIDEO


ConnID   Source IP:Port         Dest IP:Port         PeerID              Accel

36       2.8.15.10:3261         10.0.2.4:445         00:14:5e:cd:0d:85   TCDL
916      2.8.15.10:2572         2.8.3.20:80          00:14:5e:cd:0d:85   THDL
917      2.8.15.10:2573         2.8.3.20:80          00:14:5e:cd:0d:85   THDL
919      2.8.15.10:2575         2.8.3.20:3389        00:14:5e:cd:0d:85   T
```

The decision to optimize or pass-through each connection is made during the WAAS *automatic discovery* stage. A detailed review of WAAS auto-discovery is available in Chapter 8, "Configuring WAN Optimization," of this book. As discussed in Chapter 8, WAAS relies on the interception of the initial TCP setup flow to discover its optimization peer and negotiate optimization policy. During the TCP three-way handshake, the initiating WAAS device uses the option field in the synchronize (SYN) packets to indicate its own device ID and optimization capabilities. The initiating WAAS device determines the type of optimization for each connection based on its own *configured policy* and the current load condition of the device. This is also known as a *derived policy*. As the receiving WAAS device gets the SYN packet with option field, it obtains the knowledge of its peer's device ID and the policy set by the peer. The receiving WAAS device also generates its own derived policy based on configured policy and load condition. Comparing the *peer's policy* with its own derived policy, the lowest common denominator becomes the final *negotiated policy* and is applied to the connection. Unless an unexpected load condition is encountered, the *applied policy* is the same as the negotiated policy.

Should a WAAS device receive both Transmission Control Protocol (TCP) SYN and synchronize/acknowledge (SYN/ACK) packets without the option field set, this device has no peer in the communication path of this flow, thus it puts the connection to pass-through. This connection is seen in the **show statistics connection pass-through** command output as a pass-through connection with the ConnType of PT No Peer, as shown in Example B-3.

Example B-3 *Review Pass-Through Connection Statistics*

```
WAE# show statistics connection pass-through

Current Active Optimized Flows:                         1
    Current Active Optimized TCP Plus Flows:            0
    Current Active Optimized TCP Only Flows:            0
    Current Active Optimized TCP Preposition Flows:     0
Current Active Auto-Discovery Flows:                    22
Current Active Pass-Through Flows:                       2
Historical Flows:                                       100


Local IP:Port          Remote IP:Port        Peer ID         ConnType
171.68.96.12:19140     171.68.65.252:8080    N/A             PT No Peer
171.68.96.12:22390     171.68.65.252:8080    N/A             PT No Peer
171.68.65.252:8080     171.68.96.12:22390    N/A             PT No Peer
171.68.65.252:8080     171.68.96.12:19140    N/A             PT No Peer
```

On the other hand, if both SYN and SYN/ACK are received with option fields set, then the receiving device knows that it is an intermediate device and it puts the connection to pass-through. The ConnType is displayed as PT intermediate.

Asymmetric routing is another reason for auto-discovery failure that results in pass-through connections. It occurs when only one direction of traffic is intercepted by a WAAS device.

When encountering any of these auto-discovery failure scenarios, verify WAAS interception on both the local and remote sites. A firewall placed in between peering WAAS devices that scrubs the TCP option field causes the auto-discovery process to fail. Verify the application traffic flow and the network topology to ensure that both inbound and outbound traffic flow are intercepted by the same WAAS device.

When an established TCP flow is intercepted by a WAAS device without any knowledge of the initial TCP setup, this connection is passed through as an in-progress connection. Connections can also be in pass-through due to policy configuration or overload condition of either WAAS device.

You can use the **show statistics pass-through** command to troubleshoot pass-through connections. The command output lists the number of active and completed pass-through connections and the reasons for pass-through as demonstrated in Example B-4.

Example B-4   *Statistics on Pass-Through Connections*

```
WAE# show statistics pass-through

                        Outbound
                        — — — — — — — — — —
PT Client:
      Bytes                          4179
      Packets                          58
PT Server:
      Bytes                       1711871
      Packets                       18470
PT In Progress:
      Bytes                       5265916
      Packets                       30008


                        Active                  Completed
                        — — — — — — — — — —      — — — — — — — — — —
Overall                      1                    35933
No Peer                      0                    13706
Rjct Capabilities            0                        0
Rjct Resources               0                        1
App Config                   0                      367
Global Config                0                        0
Asymmetric                   0                      346
In Progress                  1                    19713
Intermediate                 0                        0
Overload                     0                        0
Internal Error               0                     1800
App Override                 0                        0
Server Black List            0                        0
AD Version Mismatch          0                        0
AD AO Incompatible           0                        0
AD AOIM Progress             0                        0
DM Version Mismatch          0                        0
```

Interception Issues

As discussed in the previous section, interception misconfiguration can cause connection pass-through or even performance degradation. As reviewed in Chapter 4, "Network Integration and Interception," of this book, WAAS supports multiple interception methods, including inline, Web Cache Coordination Protocol version 2 (WCCPv2), Policy-Based Routing (PBR), and the Application Control Engine (ACE) appliance and module for the Cisco Catalyst 6500 series switch. Among these, the most predominant interception methods are inline and WCCPv2. The next two subsections focus on the key areas of concern with the inline and WCCPv2 interception methods.

Common Issues with Inline Interception

Due to its simplicity and ease of use, inline interception is the preferred method of deployment in a Proof of Concept (POC) or small branch production environment. An administrator can verify the presence of the inline group interface by issuing the **show hardware** or **show running-config** command. If the hardware is physically installed but not recognized by the WAAS device, the inline card might be defective or not installed properly. Example B-5 shows the sample output of the **show hardware** and **show running-config** commands.

Example B-5   *Inline Card Verification*

```
WAE# show hardware
Cisco Wide Area Application Services Software (WAAS)
Copyright (c) 1999-2009 by Cisco Systems, Inc.
Cisco Wide Area Application Services Software Release 4.1.3 (build b55 Apr 18 20
09)
Version: oe574-4.1.3.55
!
! ... portions removed for readability ...
!


2 GigabitEthernet interfaces
1 InlineGroup interface.
1 Console interface
!
! ... portions removed for readability ...
!


WAE#show running-config
! WAAS version 4.1.3 (build b55 Apr 18 2009)
!
device mode application-accelerator
!
! ... portions removed for readability ...
!
```

```
interface InlineGroup 1/1
 inline vlan all
 exit
!
! ... portions removed for readability ...
!
```

To verify whether the inline group interface is in intercepting or bypass mode, you can use the **show interface inlinegroup** *slot/number* command. Example B-6 illustrates the output of this command and shows the inline interface is in **intercept operating** mode.

Example B-6 *Inline Interception Verification*

```
WAE#show interface inlinegroup 1/1
Interface is in intercept operating mode.
!
! ... portions removed for readability ...!
!
```

Note To switch between intercept and bypass operating mode, it is recommended to use the **no inline vlan all** command because it is less intrusive to the network, instead of administratively shutting down the interface.

The WAAS inline card fails to wire as a crossover cable when the device is powered down or fails. Correct cabling is essential to ensure proper operation of bypass (that is, fail to wire) mode. The inline module cabling guidelines supplied in Chapter 4 should be followed. When the incorrect cables are used, network connectivity might not be an issue when the inline group is in intercept operating mode; however, connectivity is lost when the WAAS inline group is in bypass operating mode and the automatic medium-dependent interface crossover (Auto-MDIX) feature is not supported on the connected devices. When the WAAS inline group is in bypass operating mode, it performs a cross-connect between the LAN and WAN ports, creating a cross-over cable between the network elements the inline group connects to, which might cause loss of network connectivity.

In a production network, it is recommended that you connect the WAAS device in power-down mode first during the installation maintenance window to verify the correct cabling and test connectivity during a failed-to-wire scenario (when the device is off, it is inherently in a failed-to-wire configuration).

In addition to cabling, duplex configuration should be verified end-to-end to avoid performance issues caused by half-duplex conditions, as discussed previously.

Another consideration with inline interception is VLAN configuration. By default, all VLANs traverse the WAAS inline group interface, and all TCP traffic is intercepted and inspected by WAAS software to determine the optimization policy. To avoid the unnecessarily added latency, traffic that is not intended for WAAS optimization, such as Voice over IP (VoIP) traffic, should be excluded from interception. The VLANs to be inter-cepted are configured by **inline vlan** *number* command.

Common Issues with WCCP Interception

WCCPv2 is the most frequently used off path redirection and interception mechanism as it provides configuration flexibility, higher scalability, and high availability. Chapter 4 of this book covers WCCPv2 features, configuration options, and best integration practices. This section reviews the key aspects in WCCP troubleshooting, including verification of the operational status, connectivity, and configuration of WCCP.

It is imperative that you run a recommended IOS version for WCCP on the redirecting device. Minimum recommended IOS versions are listed in the "Network Integration Best Practices" section of Chapter 4. Running WCCPv2 on an unsupported platform or with an unsupported IOS version causes performance issues on the network.

Verification should also be done on the configuration and connectivity between the redi-rection device (router or switch) and the WAAS device. On the redirection device, con-firm that the service group 61 and 62 are configured properly so that both inbound and outbound application traffic is redirected to the same device. Ensure that there is no WCCP redirection loop by using **redirect exclude** on the interface connecting to the WAAS device (when **redirect out** is used), or use the WCCP negotiated Generic Routing Encapsulation (GRE) return, or use the generic GRE return as egress method on the WAAE device. Make sure that the redirect list is configured properly.

Useful commands on routers include **show ip wccp**, as shown in Example B-7, and **show ip wccp** *service group* **detail**.

Example B-7 *Verify WCCPv2 Service Group on Software-Based Redirection Platforms*

```
Pod1-DC-RTR# sh ip wccp
Global WCCP information:
    Router information:
        Router Identifier:              2.8.11.1
        Protocol Version:               2.0

    Service Identifier: 61
        Number of Cache Engines:        1
        Number of routers:              1
        Total Packets Redirected:       5979289
        Process:                        2
        Fast:                           0
        CEF:                            5979287
        Redirect access-list:           -none-
        Total Packets Denied Redirect:  0
        Total Packets Unassigned:       0
        Group access-list:              -none-
```

```
        Total Messages Denied to Group:        0
        Total Authentication failures:         0
        Total Bypassed Packets Received:        0


Service Identifier: 62
        Number of Cache Engines:               1
        Number of routers:                     1
        Total Packets Redirected:              5255742
        Process:                               0
        Fast:                                  0
        CEF:                                   5255743
        Redirect access-list:                  -none-
        Total Packets Denied Redirect:         0
        Total Packets Unassigned:              0
        Group access-list:                     -none-
        Total Messages Denied to Group:        0
        Total Authentication failures:         0
        Total Bypassed Packets Received:        1
```

Examine the output from the **show ip wccp** command on a software-based WCCP redirection device (ISR or Cisco 7200). Verify that the WCCP Protocol Version is 2.0, and the Service Identifiers 61 and 62 are configured properly. Each of the service groups should have the expected number of routers and clients listed. On a software-based WCCP redirection device, Cisco Express Forwarding (CEF) should be used when WCCP is configured. The counter of **Total Packets s/w Redirected** increments as traffic is redirected to WAAS device(s).

Note   On hardware-based platforms, such as Catalyst 4500/4900, Catalyst3560/3750, Catalyst 6500, Nexus 7000 Series, and ASR 1000 Series, packet redirection counters do not increment as packets are being processed in hardware. Each platform has different CLI commands that can be used to obtain packet redirection counts.

The **Total Packets Denied Redirect** counter increments for packets being denied by a WCCP redirect-list. When WCCP authentication is used, the **Total Authentication failures** counters increment when the password is not set correctly.

Some platforms, such as the Catalyst 4500/4900, Catalyst3560/3750, Catalyst 6500 with Sup2/Sup32, support hardware-based WCCP redirection. On these platforms, L2 redirection with mask assignment should always be used to take advantage of the hardware switching and avoid high CPU load.

Other hardware-based platforms, such as Catalyst 6500 with Sup720, Nexus 7000 Series, and ASR 1000 Series are capable of processing WCCP GRE redirect in hardware; however, mask assignment is still required for hardware processing.

Furthermore, on the hardware-based platforms such as Catalyst 6500, WCCP GRE return traffic is still processed in software, causing high CPU load. Thus, Generic GRE (GGRE) return should be used instead of WCCP GRE return on these platforms to leverage hardware assistance for return traffic.

On the Catalyst 6500, the **ip wccp** *service group* **accelerated** command can be used to enable hardware acceleration for WCCP and enforce that the WCCP client registration only be accepted if L2 redirection and mask assignment are configured on the WAE.

Avoid the use of outbound redirection, redirect exclude, and hash assignment on hardware platforms, because these configurations involve Layer 3 processing and result in high CPU utilization. To ensure hardware redirection is achieved, check the switch's WCCP service group. Example B-8 illustrates the output of the service group 61 on a Catalyst 6500 platform and highlights that redirection is performed using L2, and mask assignment is used for load distribution across WAAS devices.

Example B-8 *Verify WCCPv2 Service Group on Hardware-Based Redirection Platforms*

```
Cat6k# show ip wccp 61 detail
WCCP Client information:
    WCCP Client ID:         10.88.80.135
    Protocol Version:       2.0
    State:                  Usable
    Redirection:            L2
    Packet Return:          GRE
    Packets Redirected:     0
    Connect Time:           1d18h
    Assignment:             MASK
!
! ... portions removed for readability
!
```

Example B-9 shows the output from the **show tcam interface** command on a Cat6K to verify that WCCP is handled in hardware. The **policy-route** entries indicate full hardware redirection on **Cat6K/7600** platform. The match count in **Punt** entry indicates software redirection and causes CPU load. Check the WCCP configuration and avoid the use of outbound redirection, redirect exclude, hash assignment, or any unknown WAE MAC.

Example B-9 *Verify Hardware Redirection on Catalyst 6000/7600 Platforms*

```
Cat6k# show tcam interface Vlan900 acl in ip
* Global Defaults not shared
Entries from Bank 0
Entries from Bank 1
permit       tcp host 10.88.80.135 any
policy-route tcp any 0.0.0.0 255.255.232.190 (60 matches)
```

```
policy-route tcp any 0.0.0.1 255.255.232.190 (8 matches
     punt           ip any any (8 matches)
!
! ... portions removed for readability
!
```

On the WAAS device, inspect the health of interception and correlate this with desired forwarding and return path mechanism between the redirection device (router/switch) and the WAAS device.

The following **show wccp status** and **show wccp services** commands are useful to check the status of WCCP interception and verify whether WCCPv2 is configured and enabled on the WAAS device. Example B-10 shows the output from these commands.

Example B-10 *Confirm the Status of WCCP on WAE*

```
WAE# show wccp status
WCCP version 2 is enabled and currently active

WAE# show wccp services
Services configured on this File Engine
        TCP Promiscuous 61
        TCP Promiscuous 62
```

Use the **show wccp routers** command to verify successful negotiation of the WCCP protocol between the redirecting device and WAAS device as demonstrated in Example B-11. The **Router ID** is elected by IOS, usually the highest IP address or loopback address on the router. The **Sent To** is the IP address configured in the WAAS device router-list. When doing WCCP GRE return, make sure the WAE can reach the IOS WCCP router ID.

Example B-11 *Confirm WCCP Router Configuration on WAE*

```
WAE# show wccp routers

Router Information for Service: TCP Promiscuous 61
        Routers Seeing this Wide Area Engine(1)
Router Id       Sent To       Recv ID       AssKeyIP      AssKeyCN      MemberCN
2.8.11.1        2.8.10.1      0004B2E6      2.8.10.10     1             2
        Routers not Seeing this Wide Area Engine
                -NONE-
        Routers Notified of from other WAE's
                -NONE-
        Multicast Addresses Configured
```

```
              -NONE-

Router Information for Service: TCP Promiscuous 62
        Routers Seeing this Wide Area Engine(1)
Router Id         Sent To        Recv ID       AssKeyIP      AssKeyCN      MemberCN
2.8.11.1          2.8.10.1       0004B2E4      2.8.10.10     1             2
        Routers not Seeing this Wide Area Engine
              -NONE-
        Routers Notified of from other WAE's
              -NONE-
        Multicast Addresses Configured
              -NONE-
```

Example B-12 shows the output from the **show wccp gre** command on the WAAS device. The top three lines indicate the number of packets received by the device from any interception mechanism:

■ The **Transparent GRE packets received** counter indicates packets received from redirection via WCCP GRE.

■ The **Transparent non-GRE packets received** counter indicates the number of packets received from WCCP L2-redirect forwarding method used by the WCCP-enabled switch.

■ The **Transparent non-GRE non-WCCP packets received** counter shows the amount of packets received from non-WCCP interception, for example, inline, PBR, or from a Content switching device such as ACE.

Example B-12 *Confirm Traffic Interception in WAAS Device CLI*

```
WAE# show wccp gre
Transparent GRE packets received:               5531561
Transparent non-GRE packets received:           0
Transparent non-GRE non-WCCP packets received:  0
Total packets accepted:                         5051
!
! ... portions removed for readability ...
!
```

Examine the counters in this output and correlate with the redirection method implemented, and confirm that packets are received via the intended interception mechanism.

Firewall Integration

During the auto-discovery process, WAAS devices add an option field to the TCP connection setup (SYN and SYN/ACK) packets. Upon successful completion of the auto-discovery process, WAAS devices shift the TCP sequence number of an optimized TCP flow to differentiate it from the original flow. Firewalls in general prohibit unrecognized TCP options (used by automatic discovery) and sequence number shifts (caused by WAAS to enable differentiation between original and optimized connections). Therefore, when there are firewalls in the acceleration path (in between the WAAS devices) that scrub the options field, WAAS auto-discovery fails. Some firewalls allow the options field to pass but terminate connections with any sequence numbers outside of the original range. In such cases, the accelerated traffic is blocked. Cisco WAAS has unique integration capabilities with Cisco Firewalls such as IOS Firewall, Firewall Services Module (FWSM), and ASA/PIX, as discussed in Chapter 5, "Branch Office Network Integration," and Chapter 6, "Data Center Network Integration." On these Cisco Firewalls with WAAS interoperability, the **ip inspect WAAS enable** command on IOS-FW or the **inspect waas** command on FWSM and ASA/PIX enable WAAS optimization and preserve full stateful firewall functions for optimized traffic. On non-Cisco firewalls in the acceleration path, the WAAS directed mode can be configured to enable acceleration through UDP tunnels, but still requires that the firewall be configured to permit TCP options. For more details on WAAS directed mode, please refer to the "Directed Mode" section in Chapter 4 and Chapter 8. With directed mode, WAAS still relies on the option field for auto-discovery. The firewalls should be configured to permit TCP options to pass. Please consult the firewall vendor's documentation on commands to permit options to pass.

Low Compression Ratio

Low compression ratios on certain application traffic are usually caused by the lack of redundant patterns and incompressibility in the data set, as seen in pre-compressed or encrypted data or in transient data. A Transport Flow Optimization (TFO)-only policy should be used on WAAS for this type of data, unless native compression and encryption can be turned off from the application.

WAAS software comes with a set of default classifiers that identify common ports associated with those applications with pre-compressed, encrypted, or transient data and apply TFO-only to these applications. WAAS can fully optimize SSL/TLS traffic when the SSL AO is enabled and SSL acceleration service is configured. SSL traffic without SSL accelerated service configured is processed by WAAS with TFO-only policy. Any application traffic without a matching classifier falls into the *other* classifier with the default policy of *Full* optimization.

For any application with encrypted, compressed, or transient data utilizing custom ports, custom policies should be created to apply TFO-only. Such data cannot benefit from Data Redundancy Elimination (DRE) or Persistent Lempel-Ziv (PLZ) compression; sending them through DRE/LZ negatively impacts performance because it introduces latency and pollutes the DRE cache with content that might not be helpful when optimizing more common applications.

Another option is to turn off native application encryption and implement SSL, which can be securely accelerated by WAAS. Likewise, check with the application vendor to see if data compression can be turned off, and use WAAS compression instead. Because DRE leverages redundancy across different clients and different protocols, it is typically more effective than the application's native compression. Take Remote Desktop Protocol (RDP) for example, the WAAS default policy for this application is TFO-only, as RDP by default compresses and encrypts data. RDP is the underlying protocol for the VMware View applications and for Microsoft Remote Desktop and Terminal Services. Used in branch office virtual desktop environments, the RDP sessions across branch office users are highly redundant, and the encryption is implemented over SSL (in the case of VMWare View 3). In this case, WAAS full optimization can be achieved by turning off the native compression and encryption on RDP (and using the SSL AO to keep encryption), changing WAAS optimization policy for RDP to Full Optimization, and configuring SSL AO to securely optimize the virtual desktop application. As a result, WAAS can effectively optimize the virtual desktop delivery traffic and increase the scalability of the solution.

The **show statistics connection conn-id** *id* command, as demonstrated in Example B-13, provides details on a particular connection including the application and classifier matched, the policy applied, the compression statistics, and WAAS processing latency. Verify the policy and application accelerator applied on the connection are as expected, and determine if further tuning is needed.

Example B-13 *Examine Policy and Compression Statistics on Specific Connection*

```
BR-Box#sh statistics connection conn-id 2618

Connection Id:                2618
    Peer Id:                  00:14:5e:cd:0d:85
    Connection Type:          EXTERNAL CLIENT
    Start Time:               Wed May 20 12:22:41 2009
    Source IP Address:        2.8.15.10
    Source Port Number:       2640
    Destination IP Address:   10.0.2.4
    Destination Port Number:  445
    Application Name:         WAFS
    Classifier Name:          CIFS
    Map Name:                 basic
    Directed Mode:            FALSE
    Preposition Flow:         FALSE
    Policy Details:
            Configured:       TCP_OPTIMIZE + DRE + LZ
              Derived:        TCP_OPTIMIZE + DRE + LZ
                 Peer:        TCP_OPTIMIZE + DRE + LZ
            Negotiated:       TCP_OPTIMIZE + DRE + LZ
              Applied:        TCP_OPTIMIZE + DRE + LZ
```

```
        Accelerator Details:
                  Configured:   CIFS
                    Derived:    CIFS
                    Applied:    CIFS
                       Hist:    None


  !
  ! ... portions removed for readability ...
  !


  — — — — — — — · Flow 2618 dre stats — — — — — — — ·


  Conn-ID: 2618 2.8.15.10:2640 — 10.0.2.4:445  Peer No:  0 Status: Active
  — — — — — — — — — — — — — — — — — — — — — — — — — — — — — — — — — —
  Open at 05/20/2009 12:22:41, Still active
  Encode:
      Overall: msg:        140, in:   2224 KB, out:  15787 B, ratio:  99.31%
          DRE: msg:         77, in:   2204 KB, out:  15017 B, ratio:  99.33%
  DRE Bypass: msg:         103, in:  19612 B
           LZ: msg:        140, in:  35374 B, out:  15787 B, ratio:  55.37%
   LZ Bypass: msg:           0, in:      0 B
      Avg latency:      0.469 ms    Delayed msg:         37
    Encode th-put:  33884 KB/s
    Message size distribution:
      0-1K=10%  1K-5K=8%  5K-15K=20%  15K-25K=10%  25K-40K=6%  >40K=44%
  Decode:
      Overall: msg:        101, in:   4028 B, out:  19272 B, ratio:  79.10%
          DRE: msg:          4, in:   1510 B, out:   1468 B, ratio:   0.00%
  DRE Bypass: msg:         201, in:  17804 B
           LZ: msg:        101, in:   4028 B, out:  20092 B, ratio:  79.95%
   LZ Bypass: msg:           0, in:      0 B
      Avg latency:      0.037 ms
    Decode th-put:   5101 KB/s
    Message size distribution:
      0-1K=0%  1K-5K=0%  5K-15K=0%  15K-25K=0%  25K-40K=0%  >40K=0%


  !
  ! ... portions removed for readability ...
  !
  — — — — — — — · Flow 2618 tfo stats — — — — — — — ·


  !
  ! ... portions removed for readability ...
  !
```

```
                              Encode-Flow              Decode-Flow

!
! ... portions removed for readability ...
!
  Encode/Decode:
     Number of calls:            140                       101
     Latency(ms):                0.47                      0.04
     Send data/ack frames:       140                         1

!
! ... portions removed for readability ...
!
```

Application Acceleration

Application accelerators provide application level awareness and employ a variety of acceleration techniques, including (but not limited to) object caching, metadata caching, local response handling, asynchronous data processing, prepositioning, multiplexing, and stream splitting. Used with WAN optimization techniques, Application Optimizers (AO) can further reduce application response time by overcoming latency and bandwidth constraints within the application. To take advantage of application accelerators, the proper license (Enterprise) should be activated and the accelerator should be enabled on all WAAS devices involved. The recognition of application traffic and the application acceleration are done automatically by WAAS as long as the acceleration feature is enabled. The only accelerator that requires additional configuration beyond enabling the feature is SSL AO, due to the nature of secured optimization and involvement of security certificates.

If an accelerator is not applied to application traffic as expected, check the operational state of the accelerator and verify the traffic policy is properly configured. Example B-14 shows the output of the **show accelerator** command, which is used to verify the **Config State** and **Operational State** of each AO.

Example B-14 *Verify Accelerator State Using CLI*

```
WAE#show accelerator

Accelerator      Licensed       Config State      Operational State
— — — — .        — — — —        — — — — —         — — — — — — — — .
cifs             Yes            Enabled           Running
epm              Yes            Enabled           Running
http             Yes            Enabled           Running
mapi             Yes            Enabled           Running
nfs              Yes            Enabled           Running
```

```
ssl            Yes        Enabled        Running
video          Yes        Enabled        Running
wafs-core      Yes        Disabled       Shutdown
wafs-edge      Yes        Disabled       Shutdown
```

The **show statistics connection optimized** command output displays the type of optimization techniques applied to each flow. Inspect the output of this command to determine whether desired level of acceleration, such as generic WAN optimization (TFO/DRE/LZ) and application specific acceleration, is achieved. Example B-15 shows that the connection with ConnID 2618 is CIFS traffic going over port 445, the acceleration techniques applied are TFO/DRE/LZ and CIFS Accelerator, listed as **TCDL** under the **Accel** column.

Example B-15 *Examine Acceleration on Optimized Connections*

```
WAE#show statistics connection optimized
!
! ... portions removed for readability ...
!
D:DRE,L:LZ,T:TCP Optimization,
A:AOIM,C:CIFS,E:EPM,G:GENERIC,H:HTTP,M:MAPI,N:NFS,S:SSL,V:VIDEO


ConnID   Source IP:Port        Dest IP:Port          PeerID             Accel

2618     2.8.15.10:2640        10.0.2.4:445          00:14:5e:cd:0d:85  TCDL
```

One possible cause for CIFS AO not able to accelerate Windows file sharing traffic is when Server Message Block (SMB) signing, or digital signatures, are enabled and required on such traffic. As of the 4.1.3 release, the CIFS AO *pushes down* the optimization to *generic* Layer 4 optimization (TFO/DRE/LZ) when digital signatures are required. In this case, the **show statistics connection** command displays optimization applied as **GTDL**. In the **show statistics accelerator CIFS details** command output, the **Total connections Handed-off with Compression Policies Unchanged** counter increments. Disabling SMB signing (or setting it to optional instead of required) enables full CIFS acceleration. More information on SMB signing, configuration, and verification is available on Microsoft's Technet website (http://support.microsoft.com/?kbid=887429).

When the clients access a secured server that is accelerated by the WAAS SSL AO through a web proxy, HTTP AO can intelligently detect the SSL connection request and hand off to the SSL AO for full optimization. The connection is shown as **Handed-off to SSL** from the HTTP AO, as demonstrated in Example B-16.

Example B-16   *Inspect HTTP Accelerator Statistics*

```
pod1-br-wae# show statistics accelerator http

HTTP:
   Global Statistics
   — — — — — — — — ·
   Time Accelerator was started:                                  Sun May
17 06:11:35 2009
   Time Statistics were Last Reset/Cleared:                       Wed May
20 18:02:48 2009
   Total Handled Connections:                                     2
   Total Optimized Connections:                                   1
   Total Connections Handed-off with Compression Policies Unchanged:   0
   Total Dropped Connections:                                     0
   Current Active Connections:                                    1
   Current Pending Connections:                                   0
   Maximum Active Connections:                                    2
   Total Time Saved (ms):                                         0
   Current Active Connections Free For Fast Connection Use:       0
   Total Connections Handed-off:                                  1
   Total Connections Handed-off with Compression Policies Disabled:    0
   Total Connections Handed-off to SSL:                           1
   Total Connection Hand-off Failures:                            0
   Total Fast Connection Successes:                               0
   Total Fast Connection Failures:                                0
   Maximum Fast Connections on a Single Connection:               0
   Total CONNECT Requests with Incomplete Message:                0
   Percentage of Connection Time Saved:                           0
   Total Round Trip Time For All Connections (ms):                80
   Total Fast Connections Initiated by Peer:                      0
```

The connection hand-off requires the HTTP AO to handle the initial client connection to the proxy server. If the proxy port is not configured for HTTP acceleration, a custom policy needs to be created for the proxy.

In addition to these CLI commands, the CM GUI provides Acceleration Bypass Reasons charts along with the total optimized verses bypass connection counts, for most of the AOs including Message Application Programming Interface (MAPI), Network File System (NFS), Video, and SSL. These charts are helpful in troubleshooting bypass connections.

Platform Health and Diagnostic Tool

The location and liveliness of WAAS devices are essential to effective use of their optimization capabilities. The WAAS devices should be online and have proper network connectivity. The device hardware and software components, such as interfaces, disk, and optimization components should be functional and error free. The WAAS CM provides a unified management interface for WAAS deployment. Alarms are displayed on the CM GUI dashboard and on the Device page, as shown in Figure B-1.

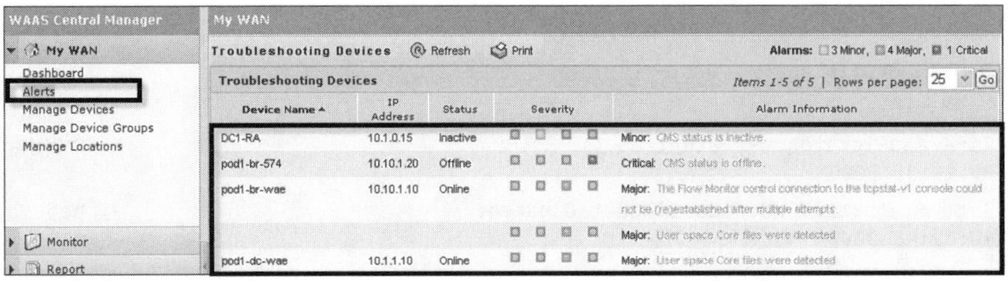

Figure B-1   *View Alarms on CM GUI*

The CM comes with built-in tools for monitoring platform health and executing diagnostic tests to assist with troubleshooting. Diagnostic tests are available under the device or device group context, under the **Troubleshoot** drawer. From there, an administrator can select to run a variety of tests including basic device configuration, connectivity, interface, inline and WCCP interception, system health, and configuration. Figure B-2 shows an example of the diagnostic tests available and the reports of running such tests on the CM.

Alternatively, the diagnostic tests can be run from CLI, using the command **test self-diagnostic** *test* to run all or selected tests as demonstrated in Example B-17.

Example B-17   *Run Diagnostic Test from CLI*

```
pod1-br-wae# test self-diagnostic ?
  all            Run all self-diagnostic tests
  basic          Basic device configuration
  connectivity   Basic device connectivity
  inline         Inline groups and ports
  interfaces     Physical interfaces
  system         Device operation
  tfo            TFO/DRE configuration
  wafs           WAFS connectivity
  wccp           WCCP configuration and operation
```

In addition to the diagnostic tests, CPU utilization and disk information are available in the CM for each WAAS device. From the device context, navigate to **Monitor > Platform** and select **CPU Statistics** to see the CPU utilization of the device, or select **Disk** to view the health of the disks. Depending on platforms, WAAS devices are built with RAID-1 or RAID-5 for high availability. Failure of one disk does not impact the performance of WAAS device. If more than one disk is in defunct, rebuilding status, or not present, then there is a performance impact. Figure B-3 illustrates the GUI report on physical disks of the **pod1-br-wae** device.

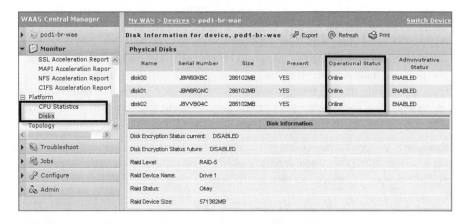

Select diagnostic tests to run

☑	Test	Description
☑	Device Operation	Check device status, presence of coredump files or alarms of major or critical severity
☑	Basic Configuration	Check device basic network configuration
☑	Basic Connectivity	Check device connectivity to configured external devices(dns, authentication, ntp servers, etc)
☑	Physical Interface	Check configuration and operation of device physical interfaces
☑	Traffic Optimization	Checks TFO configuration and operation
☑	WCCP configuration and operation	Checks configuration and operation of WCCP traffic interception
☑	Inline configuration and operation	Check configuration and operation of inline group interfaces
☑	WAFS configuration and operation	Check configuration and operation of WAFS services

[Run]

Diagnostic Report for Device **pod1-br-wae** performed on **5/20/2009 22:36:10**

Basic Configuration	PASS
Network Connectivity	PASS
Physical Interfaces	PASS
Traffic Optimization	PASS
WCCP configuration and operation	NONE
	NONE - Skipping test because WCCP is not enabled
Inline configuration and operation	WARN
	WARN INLINE_SHUTDOWN Inline group 2/1 interface is in bypass mode(shutdown)
	Recommendation: Use 'interface inlineGroup slot/group' cli command followed by 'no shutdown' to enable the interface.
Device Operation	PASS
WAFS configuration and operation	NONE
	NONE - Skipping test because Wafs is not enabled

Figure B-2   *Running Diagnostic Tests on CM GUI*

WAAS Central Manager	My WAN > Devices > pod1-br-wae					Switch Device
▸ 🖥 pod1-br-wae	**Disk Information for device, pod1-br-wae** 📄 Export ⟳ Refresh 🖨 Print					
▾ 🖵 Monitor	**Physical Disks**					
SSL Acceleration Report	Name	Serial Number	Size	Present	Operational Status	Administrative Status
MAPI Acceleration Repor	disk00	J8W60KBC	286102MB	YES	Online	ENABLED
NFS Acceleration Report	disk01	J8W6RGNC	286102MB	YES	Online	ENABLED
CIFS Acceleration Report	disk02	J8VVBG4C	286102MB	YES	Online	ENABLED
⊟ Platform						
CPU Statistics			**Disk Information**			
Disks	Disk Encryption Status current: DISABLED					
Topology	Disk Encryption Status future: DISABLED					
▸ 🔧 Troubleshoot	Raid Level: RAID-5					
▸ 📋 Jobs	Raid Device Name: Drive 1					
▸ ⚙ Configure	Raid Status: Okay					
▸ 🔧 Admin	Raid Device Size: 571382MB					

Figure B-3   *Check WAE Disk Details Using CM GUI*

The CLI command **show disks details** provides the same level of information on device level as demonstrated in Example B-18.

Example B-18   *Check Disk Details Using CLI*

```
WAE# show disks details

Physical disk information:
  disk00: Present     WD-WCANK8112995   (h02 c00 i00 l00 - Int DAS-SATA)
          238472MB(232.9GB)

  disk01: Present     WD-WCANK8403543   (h02 c00 i01 l00 - Int DAS-SATA)
          238472MB(232.9GB)

! "Portions removed for Readability"

Software RAID devices:
  DEVICE NAME  TYPE    STATUS              PHYSICAL DEVICES AND STATUS
  /dev/md0     RAID-1  NORMAL OPERATION    disk00/00[GOOD]  disk01/00[GOOD]
  /dev/md1     RAID-1  NORMAL OPERATION    disk00/01[GOOD]  disk01/01[GOOD]
  /dev/md2     RAID-1  NORMAL OPERATION    disk00/02[GOOD]  disk01/02[GOOD]
  /dev/md3     RAID-1  NORMAL OPERATION    disk00/03[GOOD]  disk01/03[GOOD]
  /dev/md4     RAID-1  NORMAL OPERATION    disk00/04[GOOD]  disk01/04[GOOD]
  /dev/md5     RAID-1  NORMAL OPERATION    disk00/05[GOOD]  disk01/05[GOOD]

Disk encryption feature is disabled.
```

Generate System Report

The WAAS system report, also known as *sysreport*, contains a compressed archive of all relevant support and system health information. When requesting assistance for further troubleshooting from the Cisco Technical Assistance Center (TAC), it is helpful to have the system report along with network topology diagram ready. The system report provides information including CLI command output, platform configuration with logs, platform state information, print services configuration with logs, authentication configuration with logs, internal services and acceleration logs, CMS configuration with logs, and system logs. The system report can be generated and sent to external FTP or TFTP servers from the device CLI with the **copy sysreport** {**disk**| **ftp** | **tftp**} command.

Example B-19 demonstrates using this command to generate a system report with a starting date/time filter; the system report is saved on the local disk with the filename of *pod1-br-wae.tar.gz*, which can then be transferred to an external FTP server.

Example B-19   *Generate System Reports on WAE*

```
pod1-br-wae# copy sysreport disk pod1-br-wae.tar.gz start-date 20 may 2009
Generating sysreport ...
Successfully generated sysreport as pod1-br-wae.tar.gz
pod1-br-wae# dir
```

```
      size              time of last change              name
—————— ———————————————.              —————.
      5295122   Wed May 20 22:51:28 2009              pod1-br-wae.tar.gz
!
! ... portions removed for readability ...
!
```

In addition to the WAAS system report, the **show tech-support** CLI output contains essential system information such as software version, hardware and software configuration, CPU, memory, alarm, and statistics, which are necessary for Cisco TAC to assist you with troubleshooting a WAAS device. Note that the **show tech-support** command output can be long, and it is included in the system report.

Summary

This appendix reviewed the most frequently encountered challenges in WAAS deployment, analyzed common causes leading to the challenges, and offered suggestions and best practices to prevent or resolve these issues. Cisco WAAS comes with a set of self-diagnostic tests which help isolate issues and proactively identify them. The CM also provides a rich set of tools to assist with troubleshooting and monitoring.

Appendix C

4.0/4.1 CLI Mapping

This appendix provides the command-line interface (CLI) mapping between the WAAS software 4.0 release and 4.1 release for the most commonly used commands. For a complete listing of CLI commands, please refer to the Cisco WAAS Software Command Reference documentation on Cisco.com.

Mode	4.0 CLI	4.1 CLI	Usage
EXEC	clear statistics tfo auto-discovery	clear statistics auto-discovery	Clears the auto-discovery statistics.
	show tfo auto-discovery	show statistics auto-discovery	Displays auto-discovery statistics, including success, failure counts, and reasons.
	show tfo auto-discovery blacklist entries	show auto-discovery blacklist	Displays all entries in the Auto-Discovery blacklist server table.
	show tfo auto-discovery list	show auto-discovery list	Lists the connections in auto-discovery state.
	show statistics tfo pass-through	show statistics pass-through	Displays pass-through statistics, including byte and packet counts of pass-through traffic, and a list of pass-through connection counts and their reasons.

Mode	4.0 CLI	4.1 CLI	Usage
EXEC	show tfo connection	show statistics connection optimized tfo	Displays connection statistics of active and optimized flows, including connection ID, source and destination IP:Port, PeerID, and Acceleration applied.
	show tfo connection summary	show statistics connection	Displays connection statistics of active and historical optimized flows, auto-discovery flows, and pass-through flows.
	show statistics tfo peer	show statistics peer	Displays the performance statistics for application of the peering WAAS devices.
	show statistics tfo [*app_name* | savings *app_name*]	show statistics application [*app_name* | savings *app_name*]	Displays the performance statistics for application and savings for applications on the WAE device.
	show tfo accelerators	show accelerator *acceleratorName*	Displays accelerator status.
	show tfo egress-methods	show statistics connections egress-methods	Displays detailed egress method-related information about the connection segments for a WAE.
	show statistics dre peer	show statistics peer dre	Displays the peering WAE device DRE statistics.
	show statistics dre connection	show statistics connection optimized dre [detail]	Displays connection statistics of active and flows that are optimized by Data Redundancy Elimination (DRE). Includes detailed DRE statistics.
	show statistics dre connection id *ID*	show statistics connection conn-id *ID*	Displays connection statistics of a specific connection, including detailed DRE statistics.
	show standby	Removed (Use **show interface standby 1**)	Displays standby interface group information.
	show tfo status	Removed	

Mode	4.0 CLI	4.1 CLI	Usage
Global configuration	tfo auto-discovery	auto-discovery	Configures auto-discover black-list operation, specifies origin servers (such as those servers behind firewalls) that cannot receive TCP packets with WAAS setup options, and adds these server IP addresses to a blacklist for a specified number of minutes.
Global configuration	interface standby	interface standby 1	This command has changed from v4.0 to v4.1. The "errors" option has been removed, and only one standby interface can be specified. The interface standby group number is always 1.
Interface configuration	standby	standby 1	Removed the capability to specify more than one standby group number, removed the description, errors, ip, priority, and shutdown options. The interface standby group number is always 1.

Added the "primary" option. |
| | show tfo auto-discovery list | show auto-discovery list | Lists the connections in auto-discovery state. |

Index

A

B

M

N

O

S

U

W

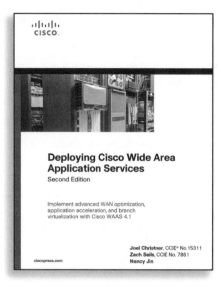

FREE Online Edition

Your purchase of **Deploying Cisco Wide Area Application Services** includes access to a free online edition for 45 days through the Safari Books Online subscription service. Nearly every Cisco Press book is available online through Safari Books Online, along with more than 5,000 other technical books and videos from publishers such as Addison-Wesley Professional, Exam Cram, IBM Press, O'Reilly, Prentice Hall, Que, and Sams.

SAFARI BOOKS ONLINE allows you to search for a specific answer, cut and paste code, download chapters, and stay current with emerging technologies.

Activate your FREE Online Edition at
www.informit.com/safarifree

> **STEP 1:** Enter the coupon code: KSCQFDB.

> **STEP 2:** New Safari users, complete the brief registration form.
> Safari subscribers, just log in.

If you have difficulty registering on Safari or accessing the online edition, please e-mail customer-service@safaribooksonline.com